Technology, Geopolitics, and the Transformation of International Political Economy

Kittisak Wongmahesak
North Bangkok University, Thailand

Thanaporn Sriyakul
North Bangkok University, Thailand

Uday Kumar Ghosh
Lincoln University, USA

Ismail Suardi Wekke
Institut Agama Islam Negeri Sorong, Indonesia

IGI Global
Scientific Publishing
Publishing Tomorrow's Research Today

Vice President of Editorial	Melissa Wagner
Director of Acquisitions	Mikaela Felty
Director of Book Development	Jocelynn Hessler
Production Manager	Mike Brehm
Cover Design	Jose Rosado

Published in the United States of America by
IGI Global Scientific Publishing
701 East Chocolate Avenue
Hershey, PA, 17033, USA
Tel: 717-533-8845
Fax: 717-533-7115
Website: https://www.igi-global.com E-mail: cust@igi-global.com

Library of Congress Cataloging-in-Publication Data

Names: Wongmahesak, Kittisak, 1985- editor http://id.loc.gov/authorities/names/n2025014869 http://id.loc.gov/rwo/agents/n2025014869 | Sriyakul, Thanaporn, 1970- editor http://id.loc.gov/authorities/names/n2025026879 http://id.loc.gov/rwo/agents/n2025026879 | Ghosh, Uday Kumar, 1959- editor http://id.loc.gov/authorities/names/n2025024664 http://id.loc.gov/rwo/agents/n2025024664 | Wekke, Ismail Suardi editor http://id.loc.gov/authorities/names/n2019222959 http://id.loc.gov/rwo/agents/n2019222959
Title: Technology, geopolitics, and the transformation of international political economy / edited by: Kittisak Wongmahesak, Thanaporn Sriyakul, Uday Kumar Ghosh, and Ismail Suardi Wekke.
Description: Hershey, PA : IGI Global Scientific Publishing, [2026] | Includes bibliographical references and index. | Summary: "This publication is poised to significantly impact the research community across several disciplines, particularly economics, political science, computer science, and sociology. The in-depth analysis of the complex relationships between algorithms, networks, and the global economy will provide researchers with invaluable insights into understanding contemporary economic and geopolitical phenomena"-- Provided by publisher.
Identifiers: LCCN 2025004485 (print) | LCCN 2025004486 (ebook) | ISBN 9798337317274 hardcover | ISBN 9798337317281 paperback | ISBN 9798337317298 ebook
Subjects: LCSH: Economics--Political aspects | International economic relations http://id.loc.gov/authorities/subjects/sh85067395
Classification: LCC HB74.P65 T44 2026 (print) | LCC HB74.P65 (ebook) | DDC 330--dc23/eng/20250623
LC record available at https://lccn.loc.gov/2025004485
LC ebook record available at https://lccn.loc.gov/2025004486

British Cataloguing in Publication Data
A Cataloguing in Publication record for this book is available from the British Library.

Table of Contents

Detailed Table of Contents

This abstract explores the intricate interplay between technological advancement, shifting power dynamics, and the evolving landscape of the international political economy. This analysis delves into how emerging technologies, from artificial intelligence and biotechnology to renewable energy and digital platforms, are reshaping global production, trade, and financial flows. The abstract further investigates the strategic competition among nations to control and harness these technologies, highlighting the geopolitical implications of technological dominance. Ultimately, this work seeks to provide a comprehensive understanding of how technology is remaking the world, influencing power relations, and redefining the contours of the global economy, offering insights into the policy choices and institutional adaptations necessary to navigate this transformative era.

The digital age has reshaped global geopolitics and economic power dynamics with technology at the core of international relations. Nations and corporations vie for supremacy in strategic sectors like artificial intelligence, 5G and quantum computing, transforming traditional power dynamics. Data is the new oil, the oil that fuels economic growth and strikes in the public policy. The geopolitical competitive

future of cyber warfare anticipates greater complexity with the proliferation of advanced technologies. The growing interconnectedness of critical infrastructure will expand vulnerabilities, necessitating novel defence and deterrence strategies to address the evolving threats posed by both state and non-state actors in this domain.

The chapter explores the intricate relationship between geopolitics and cybersecurity, drawing parallels between the Cold War era and the modern "Code War." It examines how shifting geopolitical dynamics shape cybersecurity strategies, emphasizing the balance between national interests and global security imperatives. The discussion highlights offensive and defensive cyber capabilities, the impact of technological advancements, and the need for adaptability in addressing evolving threats.It also addresses international cyber relations, focusing on norms, agreements, and the ethical and legal challenges of cybersecurity policies. The chapter advocates for global cooperation and innovation to build a secure digital future. By providing actionable insights, it empowers policymakers and security professionals to navigate the complex intersection of geopolitics and cybersecurity, promoting resilience and stability in cyberspace.

This study examined how China, Russia, India, and the United States implemented strategic policy measures to bolster national LLM firms and establish AI sovereignty during the period of the LLM Cold War. It examined how governments utilized Weimer and Vining's policy instruments and state power marketing to improve digital legitimacy and oppose kakistoscryptocracy. Through documentary analysis, the study uncovered state-centric models in China and Russia that stressed ideological control and cybersecurity, while India and the U.S. adopted market-centric models fostering innovation via public-private partnerships. These strategies demonstrated that AI governance combined technology with political power and epistemology, where managing algorithms and narratives established what is considered truth.

The world's economic future is being reshaped by blockchain technology and digital currencies and the country that leads the way may also be the country that the world increasingly turns to. Blockchain challenges the hegemony of traditional financial intermediaries and reserve currencies such as the US dollar by facilitating decentralized, transparent, and secure financial systems. These currencies provide countries with the means to circumvent conventional payment networks, improve financial inclusion, and exert supremacy in international commerce. Blockchain-based solutions will create pathways around reliance on Western-led financial institutions enabling both the de-dollarization of emerging economies. And as the race is on to exploit the technologies behind them, they are likely to reshape the international political economy, creating new partnerships while widening economic divides.

This chapter explores the interconnection between Green Finance and Digital Ecology, highlighting their potential in advancing sustainability through technological innovation. Emphasis is placed on how green FinTech can mitigate these challenges by designing low-carbon financial systems and promoting sustainable investment practices. The methodology involves a review of scholarly literature to assess how digital finance and ecology contribute to global sustainability efforts. Findings suggest that the integration of green FinTech, digital money, and ecological practices can enhance transparency, reduce costs, and expand access to sustainable finance, ultimately leading to more resilient financial ecosystems. The chapter calls for increased awareness, financial literacy, and robust regulatory frameworks to manage associated risks.

This research looks at the influence of Global Value Chains (GVCs) and the growth of digital labor, especially with industrial and technological developments. With increased application of digital technology making it easier to run businesses still on the increase, the incorporation of artificial intelligence (AI) and automation within GVCs has had a colossal influence on defining the future of work. The rise of digital labor from deep learning models like Residual Networks (ResNet) has transformed labor traditionally performed by human laborers, including processing data, making decisions, and quality checks. The study discusses how the technologies enhance supply chain performance, resilience, and sustainability and struggle with the challenges they pose in terms of job substitution, skills gap, and economic inequality. In a mixed-methods design that combines qualitative interviews with quantitative questionnaires, the study explores the implications of digital labor on the future of work, global competitiveness, and supply chain management.

Digital Colonialism and Inequality represent a new front of global power, in which control over technology and data reinforces inequalities between nations and populations. The rapid expansion of digital technologies has brought about an uneven access to, and use of, knowledge and resources, predominantly benefiting a privileged minority at the expense of others. This is achieved as a digital divide, in which economically underdeveloped or backward regions are largely cut off from the digital economy and sharing of knowledge. The concept of digital colonialism proceeds to explore how data extraction, algorithmic control, and platform monopolies shape global power dynamics that increase existing inequalities. Employing bi-stacked Artificial Neural Networks (ANNs), the present work investigates the complex interaction among technological systems, human behavior, and socio-political forces behind digital inequality.

for stability in macroeconomic policies and sustainable development measures to promote economic resilience and regional stability.

The Techno-Geopolitical Aspects of Tourism in the Global Political Economy chapter explores how digital technology and geopolitical forces interact to transform tourism as a spatial-political activity as well as an economic sector. It emphasizes how governments and non-state actors use technology as a geopolitical tool by placing tourism within historical and modern power relations, drawing on classical and critical geopolitical theory. The chapter makes the case that in the current digital era, certain actors have more control over worldwide visitor flows, place narratives, and economic strength due to their access to knowledge, communications infrastructure, and technology capital. Territorial claims, political ideologies, and national identities are created and disputed in the context of tourism. The study urges a reconsideration of tourism as a techno-geopolitical assemblage influenced by digital transformation, spatial narratives, and political intent, rather than just as leisure or business.

The digital age has ushered in a profound transformation of global governance, tourism practices, diplomatic engagement, and trade relations. This chapter investigates how techno-political strategies, smart tourism infrastructures, digital diplomacy initiatives, and evolving patterns of global digital commerce collectively reconfigure the international political economy. Drawing on interdisciplinary literature—from political science, international relations, tourism studies, and economics—this chapter develops a comprehensive conceptual framework to analyze the feedback loops among data governance, mobility management, normative influence, and platform-driven market structures. The chapter offers insights into digital technologies' challenges and opportunities for sovereign states, industry stakeholders, and civil society actors through detailed case studies, policy analyses, and normative reflections.

Religious tourism, a key part of the global travel industry, involves individuals or groups traveling to sacred sites for spiritual fulfillment, rituals, or to experience religious heritage. This paper highlights the importance, growth, and effects of religious tourism, focusing on major pilgrimage destinations, traveler motivations, and socio-economic outcomes. Religious sites serve not only spiritual purposes but also foster cultural exchange and contribute to local economic development. The discussion also addresses challenges such as overcrowding, commercialization, and the need to preserve the sanctity of these sacred places amid growing tourism.

In order to better understand how institutional elements influence diaspora venture start-ups, with mediating function of support of institutions in determining the viability of businesses in diaspora communities. Regression analysis and mediation influences are used in this quantitative investigation to examine the direct and indirect association among these constructs. The results depicted that a strong framework of institution has a major positive influence on support of institutions, which in turn has a positive influence on diaspora business shaping. Policymakers, managers, and practitioners who want to encourage diaspora venture start-ups through focused interventions might benefit greatly from these outcomes. In the end, the investigation contributes to the theoretical understanding of the interaction among institutional

Preface

INTRODUCTION

In this volume, *Technology, Geopolitics, and the Transformation of International Political Economy*, we bring together a diverse and timely collection of research that speaks directly to one of the most pressing and complex dynamics of our time: the evolving relationship between technological innovation, geopolitical strategy, and global economic power. As digital technologies and algorithmic systems increasingly underpin the architecture of modern life, they are not only altering how markets function and states interact, but also redefining sovereignty, labor, inequality, and the very foundations of international political economy.

This edited book emerges from a shared conviction that understanding contemporary global challenges demands a multidisciplinary approach—one that bridges the theoretical insights of economics, political science, sociology, and computer science with empirical rigor and critical analysis. Across the chapters, contributors examine how emerging technologies—especially those driven by data, automation, and artificial intelligence—are reconfiguring economic structures, reshaping geopolitical rivalries, and complicating efforts to achieve equitable development. Topics such as technological competition between world powers, data governance, labor market transformations, and the role of state and supranational regulation are tackled through both global and regional lenses.

At the heart of this collection is the recognition that the algorithmic age does not merely augment existing power structures—it transforms them. Whether in the rise of new digital monopolies, the weaponization of information flows, or the disruption of traditional labor dynamics, the consequences of these changes are profound and far-reaching. Our contributors engage critically with these transformations, offering both descriptive insights and normative reflections on what is at stake and how policy frameworks might be designed to serve broader social and democratic ends.

We envision this book as a resource for a wide spectrum of readers. For scholars and graduate students in the fields of international political economy, economics, sociology, and technology studies, this volume offers theoretical tools and empirical case studies that illuminate the contours of a rapidly shifting global order. For policymakers, regulators, and public officials, it offers frameworks to understand and respond to the socio-political consequences of technological disruption. For professionals in the technology sector, it provides a lens through which to situate their innovations within larger questions of equity, governance, and global stability.

Ultimately, this book seeks to stimulate critical inquiry and interdisciplinary dialogue about the nature of power in the digital age. By surfacing the interconnected dynamics of algorithms, markets, and geopolitics, we hope to contribute to the ongoing global conversation about how to shape a more inclusive, democratic, and sustainable future. The contributors to this volume, through their diverse methodologies and regional perspectives, offer essential insights that we believe will help readers navigate—and help shape—the unfolding political economy of the 21st century.

ORGANIZATION OF THE BOOK

In Chapter 1: *Remaking the World: Technology, Power, and International Political Economy*, the authors set the conceptual foundation for the volume by exploring how emerging technologies—from artificial intelligence to digital platforms and renewable energy—are fundamentally restructuring the global political economy. This chapter examines the strategic competition among states to control and exploit technological innovations, while tracing the shifting contours of global production, trade, and finance. In doing so, it highlights the profound policy implications and institutional recalibrations needed to govern the new technological era, where power is increasingly defined by digital capability.

Chapter 2: *Digital Dominance and Economic Power: Interplay of Technology and Geopolitics in Modern International Relations* deepens the conversation by examining how technological supremacy is now central to both economic competitiveness and geopolitical strategy. This chapter focuses on key battlegrounds—AI, 5G, and quantum computing—and situates the competition between global superpowers, particularly the U.S. and China, within a broader context of digital sovereignty, cyber policy, and inequality in access. The narrative underscores that the geopolitical landscape is now shaped not only by military and economic might, but also by who controls the data, algorithms, and infrastructures of the digital world.

With Chapter 3: *Geopolitics in the Algorithmic Era: Navigating Technological Competition and National Security*, the volume moves into an analysis of the implications of algorithmic governance and AI for national security and global diplomacy. This chapter explores how the acceleration of big data and machine learning is transforming defense systems, redefining foreign policy agendas, and provoking ethical dilemmas around surveillance, equity, and control. It calls for greater international regulatory coordination and cooperative statesmanship to ensure these technological tools do not exacerbate instability or erode human rights.

Chapter 4: *Cyber Warfare and Blurring Lines Between State and Non-State Actors* shifts focus to the increasingly hybrid nature of digital conflict. The rise of cyber warfare has not only escalated geopolitical tensions but also expanded the number and type of actors capable of waging significant attacks. From nation-states to lone hacktivists and organized criminal syndicates, the digital battlefield is increasingly crowded and opaque. This chapter critically examines how the convergence of state and non-state activities complicates attribution, increases the risk of conflict escalation, and strains the capacity of international law and governance frameworks to respond.

In Chapter 5: *From Cold War to Code War: Geopolitical Shifts in Cybersecurity Strategy*, the authors draw parallels between the ideological standoff of the Cold War and today's digitally driven "Code War." The chapter surveys shifting cybersecurity doctrines, the evolution of offensive and defensive capabilities, and the international struggle to define norms and protocols in cyberspace. Offering practical insights, it advocates for renewed international cooperation to build resilient, adaptive cybersecurity policies and fortify the digital commons against increasing fragmentation and threat proliferation.

Chapter 6: *Large Language Models and Geopolitical Competition: Governmental Power and the Challenges of a VUCA World* introduces the reader to the high-stakes race over large language models (LLMs) as a geopolitical and epistemological contest. Comparing state strategies in the U.S., China, Russia, and India, this chapter analyzes the use of policy instruments, market frameworks, and ideological control to establish digital sovereignty. It presents AI governance as not merely a technological undertaking, but a battle over narratives, legitimacy, and knowledge production in an increasingly volatile, uncertain, complex, and ambiguous (VUCA) global environment.

With Chapter 7: *Cryptocurrencies and Decentralized Finance (DeFi): Revolutionizing the Global Financial Landscape*, the book transitions into the realm of financial innovation. This chapter explores how blockchain-powered DeFi platforms are redefining the infrastructure of global finance, offering decentralized, permissionless alternatives to traditional banking and financial services. By empowering users through smart contracts and eliminating intermediaries, these technologies are especially transformative in underbanked regions. At the same time, the chapter candidly addresses the challenges of volatility, security, and regulatory uncertainty, underscoring the need for responsible innovation.

Chapter 8: *Cryptocurrencies and Decentralized Finance (DeFi): Transforming the Future of Financial Systems* complements the previous chapter by offering a systematic literature review and case-based exploration of DeFi protocols. It examines the drivers behind DeFi's rise and its implications for financial institutions, regulators, and developers. The chapter argues that blockchain-enabled services—ranging from asset management to peer-to-peer lending—are reconfiguring the financial system from the ground up, offering new efficiencies but also demanding proactive regulatory engagement to balance risk and innovation.

Rounding out this section, Chapter 9: *Blockchain and Digital Currencies: Catalysts of Geopolitical Rivalries and Economic Realignments* broadens the scope to evaluate how blockchain and digital currencies are disrupting global monetary hierarchies and reshaping international commerce. This chapter explains how blockchain undermines traditional financial intermediaries and reserve currency regimes, facilitating greater financial autonomy for emerging economies. It envisions a world where digital currencies become tools of geopolitical strategy, enabling countries to bypass Western-dominated financial systems and assert greater independence, while also exacerbating global economic fragmentation.

Chapter 10: *Green Fintech Meets DeFi: A Path to Digital Sustainability* introduces a compelling intersection of environmental responsibility and financial innovation. This chapter explores how the integration of green fintech and decentralized finance (DeFi) contributes to digital sustainability by promoting low-carbon financial systems and eco-conscious investment practices. Through a comprehensive literature review, the authors demonstrate how transparency, efficiency, and financial inclusion can be enhanced through the adoption of green digital tools. The chapter highlights the importance of financial literacy, regulatory safeguards, and public-private collaboration to ensure these technologies foster resilient and equitable financial ecosystems.

In Chapter 11: *The Impact of Digital Labor on Global Value Chains: A New Era of Supply Chain Management*, the authors dissect how digital labor—enabled by AI and automation—is revolutionizing global value chains (GVCs). Drawing from both qualitative interviews and quantitative data, the study showcases how AI tools like ResNet are replacing traditional human labor in tasks such as decision-making and quality control. The chapter analyzes the dual nature of these innovations: boosting supply chain efficiency and sustainability on the one hand, while raising concerns about job displacement, economic inequality, and skill mismatches on the other. This discussion is a timely contribution to debates on the future of work and the evolution of global competitiveness.

Chapter 12: *Data Colonialism: The Silent Force Behind Global Inequality* presents a critical examination of the digital divide through the lens of data colonialism. It explores how the asymmetrical control over digital infrastructures, data flows, and algorithmic governance exacerbates global inequality, particularly disadvantaging marginalized regions. By leveraging bi-stacked Artificial Neural Networks (ANNs), the chapter investigates the intersection of technological systems and socio-political structures. It argues that digital monopolies and extractive data practices perpetuate historical patterns of exploitation in new forms, calling for more equitable digital governance and global awareness of these silent power dynamics.

Chapter 13: *The Evolving Role of International Organizations in the 21st Century* provides a comprehensive overview of how global institutions are adapting to shifting power balances and complex transnational challenges. The chapter evaluates how bodies such as the United Nations and World Bank are navigating their legitimacy crises, responding to emerging non-state actors, and addressing global problems such as climate change, pandemics, and security threats. It emphasizes the need for structural reforms and cross-sector collaboration to maintain institutional relevance and efficacy in an increasingly interconnected and volatile world.

Chapter 14: *IoT, FDI, and Trade Openness: Unlocking Economic Growth in BIMSTEC Nations* offers an empirical investigation into how digital transformation drives economic development in South and Southeast Asia. Using panel data from 1999 to 2019, the study assesses the impact of trade openness, foreign direct investment, and internet penetration (as a proxy for IoT) on GDP per capita. The findings underscore the importance of digital infrastructure and macroeconomic stability in promoting sustainable growth. The chapter offers practical recommendations for policymakers, reinforcing the role of digital ecosystems in fostering regional integration and resilience among BIMSTEC nations.

Chapter 15: *Techno-Geopolitical Dimensions of Tourism in the Global Political Economy* reframes tourism not merely as an economic or cultural activity, but as a space of techno-political engagement. Drawing on geopolitical theory, this chapter interrogates how digital platforms and communication technologies influence who controls narratives, mobility, and economic flows in global tourism. Governments and tech actors use tourism as a geopolitical tool, shaping territorial identities, ideological constructs, and economic access. The chapter calls for a rethinking of tourism as a strategic, digitally mediated assemblage with profound implications for global power relations.

In Chapter 16: *Techno-Politics, Tourism, and the Transformation of the International Political Economy in the Digital Age*, the authors explore how digital technologies have altered the very fabric of tourism governance and international economic interaction. Through interdisciplinary analysis and case studies, the chapter maps out the interconnections among data governance, platform capitalism, digital diplomacy, and smart tourism infrastructure. It emphasizes that tourism, when viewed through a techno-political lens, becomes a barometer for broader changes in global trade, mobility regimes, and political legitimacy in the digital era.

Chapter 17: *Religious Tourism, Economic Behavior, and Global Change: A Multidimensional Study of Devotee Spending at Cultural Festivals* delves into the socio-economic dimensions of religious tourism. By focusing on pilgrim behavior, site development, and cultural exchange, this chapter demonstrates how spiritual travel contributes not only to personal fulfillment but also to local economies and global cultural flows. At the same time, it addresses the growing pressures of commercialization, crowding, and heritage preservation. The study urges balanced approaches to tourism planning that honor sacred traditions while promoting sustainable development.

Chapter 18: *Empowering Ethiopian Diaspora by Leveraging Institutional Support to Foster Diaspora Business Participation in Home Country* closes the volume with a detailed analysis of diaspora entrepreneurship and institutional mediation. Through quantitative methods, the authors demonstrate how institutional frameworks significantly shape the ability of diaspora communities to engage in meaningful economic activities in their country of origin. The chapter offers actionable insights for policymakers and development practitioners seeking to harness diaspora capital as a force for inclusive economic development, emphasizing the need for institutional credibility, targeted interventions, and policy coherence.

Together, these chapters extend the volume's central themes—power, technology, inequality, and governance—into new territories such as sustainability, financial innovation, diaspora development, and tourism geopolitics. By weaving empirical depth with theoretical sophistication, the collection offers a richly textured understanding of the digital transformation of the global political economy and the new geostrategic landscapes that define our time.

CONCLUSION

As we conclude this volume, it is evident that we are living through a period of unprecedented transformation—one in which technology is not merely an instrument of economic efficiency or innovation, but a central force reshaping global power, institutional legitimacy, and societal structure. From the rise of artificial intelligence and decentralized finance to the reconfiguration of global value chains, digital labor, and techno-political tourism, the chapters in this book collectively reveal the profound and multidimensional ways that digital systems and technological change are redefining the international political economy.

This volume has brought together diverse perspectives, methodological approaches, and regional insights to illustrate how algorithmic governance, digital infrastructures, and technological sovereignty are entangled with issues of inequality, security, sustainability, and economic opportunity. Whether examining data colonialism or digital diplomacy, blockchain or cyber warfare, each chapter reinforces the notion that technological systems are embedded within—and shaped by—historical power asymmetries, geopolitical ambitions, and socio-economic struggles.

Our intent in curating this interdisciplinary collection has been to foster critical reflection, encourage policy innovation, and support a deeper engagement with the complexities of the digital age. The insights presented here not only advance academic debate but also offer practical value to policymakers, technologists, institutional leaders, and civil society actors striving to build equitable and sustainable futures.

As editors, we believe the questions raised by this volume—about governance, access, ethics, and the distribution of power in the digital era—will remain central to scholarly inquiry and public discourse for years to come. We hope this book serves as a foundational reference and a catalyst for further research, dialogue, and action in confronting the political and economic challenges of our technologically mediated world.

Chapter 1
Remaking the World: Technology, Power, and International Political Economy

Ismail Suardi Wekke
https://orcid.org/0000-0002-0996-4928
Institut Agama Islam Negeri Sorong, Papua, Indonesia

Suyatno Ladiqi
Universiti Sultan Zainal Abidin, Malaysia

Christian Kaunert
Dublin City University, Ireland & University of South Wales, UK

Asriadi Arifin
Institut Agama Islam Darul Dakwah Wal Irsyad Sidenreng Rappang, Indonesia

ABSTRACT

This abstract explores the intricate interplay between technological advancement, shifting power dynamics, and the evolving landscape of the international political economy. This analysis delves into how emerging technologies, from artificial intelligence and biotechnology to renewable energy and digital platforms, are reshaping global production, trade, and financial flows. The abstract further investigates the strategic competition among nations to control and harness these technologies, highlighting the geopolitical implications of technological dominance. Ultimately, this work seeks to provide a comprehensive understanding of how technology is remaking the world, influencing power relations, and redefining the contours of the global economy, offering insights into the policy choices and institutional adaptations necessary to navigate this transformative era.

DOI: 10.4018/979-8-3373-1727-4.ch001

INTRODUCTION

The dawn of the 21st century has ushered in an era defined by the relentless march of technological innovation, profoundly reshaping the contours of the international political economy. From the pervasive influence of digital platforms to the transformative potential of artificial intelligence and biotechnology, technology has become an undeniable force in global affairs, challenging traditional notions of power and governance (Heiret, 2024). This introduction seeks to explore the intricate interplay between technology, power, and the international political economy, examining how these forces are converging to remake the world we inhabit. The digital revolution has catalyzed a profound shift in the distribution of economic and political power. Transnational corporations, wielding immense data-driven influence, have emerged as key actors, often surpassing the regulatory capacity of nation-states. The internet, while fostering unprecedented connectivity, has also become a battleground for information control and cyber warfare, blurring the lines between public and private spheres. The rise of digital currencies and blockchain technologies further complicates the existing financial architecture, raising questions about sovereignty and the future of global monetary systems.

The rapid advancements in artificial intelligence and automation are disrupting labor markets and production processes, leading to concerns about job displacement and rising inequality. The potential for AI to enhance military capabilities introduces new dimensions to security dilemmas, demanding a reevaluation of international norms and arms control agreements. The ethical implications of these technologies, from algorithmic bias to the potential for autonomous weapons systems, necessitate a global dialogue on governance and regulation.

The international political economy is therefore grappling with the challenges and opportunities presented by this technological transformation. Traditional models of state-centric analysis are increasingly inadequate to capture the complex dynamics of a world where non-state actors wield significant power and influence. The need for new frameworks that incorporate the role of technology in shaping economic and political relations is paramount. This exploration will delve into the ways in which technology is reshaping trade, finance, security, and development, examining the implications for global governance and international cooperation (Girard, 2024). Ultimately, "Remaking the World: Technology, Power, and the International Political Economy" aims to provide a critical analysis of the forces driving this transformation and to contribute to a deeper understanding of the evolving international landscape. It seeks to illuminate the ways in which technological innovation is not merely a neutral force, but rather a powerful instrument that shapes the distribution of wealth, influence, and security in the 21st century. By examining the complex interplay between technology, power, and the global economy, this exploration strives to offer insights into the challenges and opportunities that lie ahead, as humanity navigates the uncharted territories of a technologically driven world.

Relevance of the Chapter

Remaking the World: Technology, Power, and the International Political Economy is the pertinent and powerful theme in the contemporary, globalized and digitized world, where a technological innovation is a leading force bringing about economic changes, geopolitical power transformations, and topological reconstructions within international politics. No longer marginal, the dynamics between technology and the political economy are now structural: to understand how power gets exercised, distributed, and challenged in the national and international realms is to understand the role of data systems. Artificial intelligence (AI), blockchain, biotechnology, quantum computing and the Internet of Things (IoT)—are transforming production systems, communication, and the delivery of services, while reshaping the rules of global engagement, economic competitiveness and national sovereignty. Emerging technologies are now becoming embedded in every sector of the economy and every aspect of governance, and this is restructuring the international political economy to reflect new hierarchies of influence grounded in technological capacity, digital infrastructure and innovation ecosystems. This remaking of the world is at once disruptive and generative: it gives rise to new opportunities for wealth creation, efficiency, transnational cooperation, yet it also creates asymmetries of power, digital divides, strategic dependencies that can destabilize existing global orders.

The importance of this shift is that technological power is coming to stand in for geopolitical power. Countries that dominate today in the research, development and deployment of essential technologies have, on the other hand, a disproportionate power in shaping the global economic channels, security setup and governance standards in the world. For instance, nations pouring capital into 5G, AI and semiconductor production have built strategic leverage over supply chains and flows of information that they can wield as new forms of techno-political influence. Now is a changing world where the international political economy refers less to classical exchange or capital flows and more to data governance and intellectual property rights, cyber sovereignty, and digital colonialism. These shifts are reshaping alliances and rivalries as well: Technology is the battleground of great power competition, as seen in rising tensions between the United States and China over control of advanced technologies and digital infrastructures. The use of technological dependencies as weapons (e.g. restrictions on semiconductor exports or cyber-influence operations) illustrates how technology can be harnessed to provide a means of coerce and strategic containment, while also undermining existing multilateral institutions and frameworks (Siddiqui, 2024).

It also emphasizes how these new technologies are reshaping notions of labor, capital, and production in ways that undermine the structural anchors of the global economy. Automation, digitization and smart manufacturing help make high-tech reshoring possible, decreasing the dependence on low-cost labor in developing countries and possibly turning back the tide of globalization that has shaped decades of development. This reorganization presents an existential threat to nations whose national economic models rest on export-related industrialization and labour arbitrage. Digital platforms and decentralized finance are replacing conventional intermediaries, shifting economic power out of traditional state-regulated structures and into the hands of tech giants and transnational networks. The increasing power of multinational technology corporations to set the terms of economic behavior and shape political debates and even regulatory agendas is evidence of the move away from state-centered political economy and toward platform-based governance architectures. These developments necessitate a rethinking of global economic governance mechanisms that can ensure the regulation and norm-setting can keep up with technological evolution to prevent monopolization, the exploitation of data, and the unequal access to digital opportunities.

Significance of this Study

The theme is significant for its insistence on inclusivity, sustainability and justice amid rapid technological transformation. Technology benefits are efficaciously distributed, widening inequalities inside and between countries. With structural constraints to access advanced technologies, participate in innovation ecosystems, or build digital capacities, many of developing world countries find themselves in digital and techno-economic exclusion, marginalization. This divergence not only stifles development opportunities but also solidifies dependencies that can be manipulated by technologically superior nations. International cooperation, fair technology transfers, and biennial innovation policies that take into account human development, digital literacy, and socio-economic sustainability are what the world needs to tackle these disparities. The environmental ramifications of digital proliferation including e-waste, data-center energy consumption and the ecological costs of technology supply chains raise existential questions about sustainability in a tech-enabled world order.

Ultimately, Remaking the World: Technology, Power, and the International Political Economy is to critical engagement with the forces molding our collective future. It challenges scholars, policymakers and global citizens to reflect on how trajectories of technology shape global norms, structure power and disrupt economic paradigms (Farid, 2024). It calls upon the international community to work together in shaping a just and equitable global technological order that places technology at the service of humanity instead of against humanity. It is not just a theoretical dilemma the intersection of technology and international political economy may well become one of the most topical, practical challenges we face in the 21st century and beyond as we grapple with the implications of these trends for politics, governance, industry, economic development, social welfare and equality.

DIGITAL LEVIATHANS: THE RISE OF TECH GIANTS AND THE RESHAPING OF GLOBAL GOVERNANCE

The modern world is witnessing the ascent of "Digital Leviathans," colossal technology corporations whose influence extends far beyond the realm of consumer electronics and online services. These entities, often wielding vast troves of data and possessing technological capabilities that rival or surpass those of some nation-states, are reshaping the landscape of global governance. Their impact is profound, challenging traditional notions of sovereignty and necessitating a reevaluation of international regulatory frameworks.

The sheer scale of these tech giants' operations creates a unique set of challenges. Their global reach transcends national borders, rendering traditional regulatory mechanisms inadequate. Issues such as data privacy, cybersecurity, and content moderation become increasingly complex when handled by entities operating across multiple jurisdictions. The ability of these corporations to collect, analyze, and utilize vast amounts of personal data raises critical questions about data sovereignty and the rights of individuals (Gjesvik & Willers, 2024). The concentration of power within a few dominant tech companies raises concerns about market competition and potential monopolies. Their control over essential digital infrastructure and platforms gives them significant leverage in shaping the digital economy. This leverage can translate into political influence, as these corporations engage in lobbying efforts and establish relationships with governments worldwide. The line between private enterprise and public governance becomes increasingly blurred.

The impact of these digital leviathans on international regulations is a matter of ongoing debate. Traditional international law, designed primarily to govern relations between states, struggles to address the complexities of regulating private entities operating on a global scale (Gore, 2024). The need for new regulatory frameworks that can effectively address issues such as cross-border data flows, algorithmic bias, and the spread of misinformation is becoming increasingly urgent. Data sovereignty, the concept that data generated within a nation's borders should be subject to that nation's laws, is another key area of contention. Tech giants often store and process data in centralized locations, raising questions about who ultimately controls and has access to this information. This has led to increasing tensions between states and corporations, as governments seek to assert their authority over data originating from their citizens.

The balance of power between states and private entities is undergoing a significant shift. The traditional model, where states held a monopoly on power and authority, is being challenged by the rise of these powerful tech corporations. These entities are increasingly involved in shaping public discourse, influencing political outcomes, and even providing essential services that were once the exclusive domain of governments. The rise of digital leviathans necessitates a new approach to global governance. International cooperation, multi-stakeholder dialogues, and innovative regulatory frameworks are needed to ensure that the benefits of technological advancement are shared equitably and that the potential risks are mitigated. This requires a nuanced understanding of the evolving relationship between states, corporations, and individuals in the digital age.

The evolving dynamics also require a continuous re-evaluation of ethical considerations. Algorithmic transparency, accountability, and the protection of fundamental rights are critical aspects that need to be addressed in the governance of these digital entities. This includes considering the societal impact of technological advancements, as well as the potential for misuse and abuse of power (Vlados & Chatzinikolaou, 2025).

THE GEOPOLITICS OF DATA: INFORMATION WARFARE, CYBER SOVEREIGNTY, AND THE NEW COLD WAR

The burgeoning digital age has fundamentally reshaped the landscape of international relations, ushering in an era where data reigns supreme as a strategic asset. The geopolitics of data, therefore, necessitates a comprehensive examination of the complex interplay between information warfare, cyber sovereignty, and the specter of a new cold war. Data, once considered a mere byproduct of technological advancement, has now become a crucial determinant of economic power, military capability, and political influence. Consequently, nations are increasingly engaged in a silent, yet intense, struggle to control and leverage this invaluable resource.

Information warfare, a critical facet of this new geopolitical reality, involves the manipulation and disruption of information systems to achieve strategic objectives. This encompasses a wide range of activities, from cyber espionage and sabotage to the dissemination of disinformation and propaganda. States and non-state actors alike are leveraging digital tools to undermine adversaries, influence public opinion, and destabilize critical infrastructure (Estevens, 2024). The proliferation of sophisticated cyber capabilities has blurred the lines between peacetime and wartime, creating a persistent state of digital tension.

The concept of cyber sovereignty has emerged as a direct response to the growing vulnerability of nations to cyber threats. It posits that states have the right to control and regulate their digital space, including the flow of data within their borders. This principle clashes with the inherently global nature of the internet, leading to contentious debates over data localization, cross-border data flows, and the governance of cyberspace (Eich, 2024). The struggle for cyber sovereignty reflects a broader tension between national interests and the interconnectedness of the digital world. The escalating competition for data control and cyber dominance has fueled concerns about a new cold war, characterized by proxy conflicts in the digital realm. Unlike the traditional cold war, which was primarily defined by ideological rivalry and nuclear deterrence, this new cold war is fought in the shadows of cyberspace, with data as the primary weapon. The actors involved are diverse, ranging from nation-states and intelligence agencies to cybercriminal groups and hacktivist organizations.

The implications for national security and global stability are profound. The vulnerability of critical infrastructure, such as power grids, financial systems, and healthcare networks, to cyberattacks poses a significant threat to national security (Stanley, 2024). The spread of disinformation and propaganda can erode public trust in institutions and destabilize democratic processes. Furthermore, the lack of clear international norms and regulations governing cyberspace creates a volatile environment where miscalculations and escalations are more likely.

The strategic significance of data extends beyond military and security considerations. It also encompasses economic competitiveness and technological leadership. Nations are investing heavily in artificial intelligence, big data analytics, and other data-driven technologies to gain a competitive edge in the global economy (Altinors & Chryssogelos, 2024). The control over data flows and the ability to extract insights from vast datasets are becoming crucial determinants of economic power. The evolving geopolitics of data demands a nuanced and multifaceted approach to address the challenges and opportunities presented by the digital age. International cooperation, the establishment of clear norms and regulations, and the development of robust cybersecurity capabilities are essential to mitigate the risks and promote a stable and secure digital environment. The ability to navigate this complex landscape will ultimately determine the shape of the global order in the 21st century.

The geopolitics of data represents a paradigm shift in international relations. The strategic significance of data, the dynamics of cyber warfare, and the struggle for cyber sovereignty are reshaping the global landscape. As nations grapple with the implications of this new reality, the need for international dialogue and cooperation becomes increasingly urgent. The future of global stability hinges on the ability to manage the risks and harness the potential of the digital age (Peters & Besley, 2024).

TECHNOLOGICAL DISRUPTION AND THE FUTURE OF LABOR: AUTOMATION, AI, AND THE SHIFTING LANDSCAPE OF GLOBAL PRODUCTION

The future of work is being redefined rapidly along the lines of technological disruption, with automation, artificial intelligence (AI), and digital technologies deepening their foothold across global production landscapes at an accelerating rate. These changes are reshaping traditional business practices, employment structures and labor market trends, fueling a re-evaluation of the roles humans and machines will play in the economy (Hopewell, 2024). Automation has already come for routine, repetitive tasks in many sectors including manufacturing, logistics and customer service, enabling firms to boost efficiency, lower costs and improve precision. And as AI technologies have matured, they have begun to address more sophisticated cognitive functions from data analysis and decision-making, to predictive maintenance and tailored customer interactions making it ever more likely that white-collar jobs once thought to be immune from disruption are now at risk of being displaced. As machines become better at both manual and intellectual work, the need for low-skill work decreases but the demand for high-skill jobs requiring creativity, emotional intelligence, and complex problem-solving increases (Verma, 2024). Education and training systems must adapt, with an emphasis on continuous learning and development in order to keep up with ceaseless technological disruption and ensure that workers are equipped with the necessary skills to thrive in the economy of tomorrow.

Production internationally is moving toward more decentralized, digital and automated models. A factory iteration recognised as a 'smart' is powered by the secrets of the Industrial Internet of Things (IIoT), artificial intelligence (AI) and robotics, to monitor in real time, self-optimize and even conduct predictive quality control. This digital transformation enables global supply chains to become more agile, responsive, and sustainable. Yet it also risks increasing the gap between advanced and developing economies, which will have difficulty competing unless huge amounts are spent on not just digital infrastructure, but the upskilling of workers to make use of the technology (Riaz et al., 2024).

If not addressed effectively, the digital divide will likely lead to social welfare and growth in the future as the new chains of value will be generated through technological convergence. The platform economy and gig work by-products of the digital disruption has engendered new labor models that have blurred the boundaries between employment and freelancing, and raised issues of job security, benefits and workers' rights (Girard, 2024). Regulatory frameworks worldwide are grappling to keep pace with these rapid transformations, often resulting in insufficient social protection, fair wage structures, and humane labor standards in many nascent digital labor markets. These radical transformations are creating the need for government, industry and education to work together to create a sustainable future with policies and practices that foster resilience and adaptability. To ensure that individuals are prepared to compete in the new economy, there must be an emphasis on lifelong learning, digital literacy and inclusive innovation.

This need ethical consideration to be hardwired into AI and automation deployments, too, to help make sure technology augments rather than substitutes the human potential. Instead of characterizing technological disruption as a danger, societies must seek to channel its power toward building more inclusive, purposeful, and human-centered forms of work (Avelino et al., 2024). Adopted with a strategic approach, automation and AI offer to relieve workers of hazardous, mindnumbing work and enable them to be focused on roles that call for creativity, empathy, and critical thought. The future of labor is not a battle against technology; it is a careful and responsible drive to design it so that the emerging technologies of global production cascade upward into more opportunity and equity for workers of the world over.

The relentless march of technological disruption, particularly in the realms of automation and artificial intelligence (AI), is fundamentally reshaping the future of labor. This transformation extends beyond mere efficiency gains, penetrating the core of socio-economic structures and necessitating a critical examination of its implications. The rise of sophisticated robotics and AI-driven systems promises to streamline production processes, but also threatens to displace a significant portion of the global workforce, particularly in sectors reliant on repetitive or manual tasks. The most pressing concerns is the potential for increased inequality. As automation and AI become more prevalent, the demand for low-skilled labor is expected to decline, while the demand for highly skilled workers capable of designing, implementing, and maintaining these technologies will surge (Ebner, 2024). This divergence could exacerbate existing income disparities, creating a society where a small elite reaps the benefits of technological progress while a larger segment of the population faces job insecurity and economic hardship. The need for robust social safety nets and accessible retraining programs becomes paramount in mitigating this widening gap.

The restructuring of global supply chains is another critical aspect of this technological shift. Traditionally, labor-intensive manufacturing was often outsourced to developing countries with lower wage rates. However, as automation becomes more cost-effective, there is a growing trend towards reshoring production to developed nations. This shift could have profound consequences for developing economies, potentially disrupting their economic growth trajectories and necessitating a diversification of their industrial bases. The nature of work itself is undergoing a radical transformation (Economy, 2024). The rise of the gig economy, fueled by digital platforms and on-demand services, presents both opportunities and challenges. While it offers flexibility and autonomy for some, it often comes with precarious employment conditions, lack of benefits, and limited job security. The need for new regulatory frameworks and labor protections to address these issues is becoming increasingly urgent.

The impact of AI extends beyond manufacturing and logistics, permeating sectors such as healthcare, finance, and customer service. AI-powered diagnostic tools, algorithmic trading systems, and chatbots are automating tasks previously performed by human professionals. This raises questions about the future of professional roles and the need for continuous upskilling and reskilling to remain relevant in a rapidly evolving job market. The challenge lies in harnessing the potential of these technologies for the betterment of society while mitigating their adverse effects. This requires a proactive approach from governments, businesses, and educational institutions. Policies that promote inclusive growth, invest in education and training, and foster innovation are essential (de Medeiros, 2025). Businesses must prioritize ethical considerations and social responsibility in their adoption of AI and automation.

International cooperation is crucial in addressing the global implications of technological disruption. As supply chains become more interconnected and labor markets become increasingly fluid, a coordinated effort is needed to ensure a just and equitable transition. This includes sharing best practices, developing international standards, and promoting responsible innovation. The intersection of technological disruption and the future of labor presents a complex and multifaceted challenge. Navigating this shifting landscape requires a comprehensive and forward-thinking approach that prioritizes human well-being, social equity, and sustainable development. By embracing innovation while addressing its potential downsides, we can create a future where technology serves as a catalyst for prosperity and inclusivity for all (Bell & Tailandier, 2024).

FINTECH AND THE REMODELING OF GLOBAL FINANCE: CRYPTOCURRENCIES, DIGITAL CURRENCIES, AND THE CHALLENGE TO TRADITIONAL MONETARY SYSTEMS

Financial technology, or FinTech, has emerged as a disruptive force, fundamentally altering the landscape of global finance. At the heart of this transformation lies the proliferation of cryptocurrencies and digital currencies, technologies that challenge the established norms of traditional monetary systems. These innovations are not merely incremental changes; they represent a paradigm shift, reshaping how transactions are conducted, how value is stored, and how financial services are accessed. The decentralized nature of many of these technologies, enabled by blockchain and distributed ledger technology (DLT), offers a stark contrast to the centralized control that has long characterized traditional banking (Du, 2025).

The rise of cryptocurrencies, exemplified by Bitcoin and Ethereum, has captured the imagination of investors and technologists alike. These digital assets, operating outside the purview of central banks, promise to democratize finance by providing alternative avenues for value transfer and storage. Their potential to bypass traditional intermediaries, such as banks and payment processors, has sparked both excitement and concern. While offering the promise of faster, cheaper, and more inclusive financial services, they also introduce new challenges related to volatility, security, and regulatory oversight. The lack of a central authority, while appealing to proponents of decentralization, complicates efforts to combat illicit activities and ensure financial stability (Horowitz, 2024).

Digital currencies, including central bank digital currencies (CBDCs), represent a different facet of this FinTech revolution. Unlike cryptocurrencies, CBDCs are issued and regulated by central banks, aiming to leverage the efficiency and accessibility of digital technology while maintaining the stability and control associated with traditional fiat currencies. These digital versions of national currencies have the potential to modernize payment systems, reduce transaction costs, and enhance financial inclusion. However, their implementation also raises complex questions regarding privacy, cybersecurity, and the potential for disintermediation of traditional banks. The impact of these FinTech innovations on traditional banking systems is profound. Banks are facing increasing pressure to adapt and innovate in response to the growing competition from FinTech companies and the evolving expectations of consumers. The need to integrate digital technologies, enhance customer experience, and streamline operations has become paramount. Many banks are exploring partnerships with FinTech startups, investing in blockchain technology, and developing their own digital solutions to remain competitive in this rapidly changing environment (Downey, 2025).

The implications of FinTech for international financial governance are equally significant. The cross-border nature of cryptocurrencies and digital currencies poses challenges for regulators seeking to maintain financial stability and prevent illicit activities. The need for international cooperation and harmonization of regulatory frameworks has become increasingly urgent. The development of global standards for anti-money laundering (AML) and know-your-customer (KYC) compliance is essential to mitigate the risks associated with these technologies.

The potential for digital currencies to disrupt traditional cross-border payment systems and challenge the dominance of established reserve currencies has implications for the global financial order. The rise of alternative payment rails and the potential for greater financial inclusion in developing economies are reshaping the dynamics of international trade and finance. The interplay between national sovereignty and the borderless nature of digital assets necessitates a reassessment of existing regulatory frameworks and international agreements. FinTech, particularly through the advent of cryptocurrencies and digital currencies, is remodeling global finance in profound ways. This transformation presents both opportunities and challenges for traditional banking systems and international financial governance. The ability to harness the benefits of these technologies while mitigating their risks will require a collaborative effort among policymakers, regulators, and industry stakeholders. Navigating this new financial landscape will be crucial to ensuring a stable, inclusive, and efficient global financial system for the future (Palley, 2025).

SUSTAINABLE INNOVATION AND THE GREEN TRANSITION: TECHNOLOGY'S ROLE IN ADDRESSING CLIMATE CHANGE AND RESOURCE SCARCITY

The imperative for a green transition has never been more pronounced, with climate change and resource scarcity posing existential threats to our planet. In this context, sustainable innovation emerges as a critical pathway, leveraging technological advancements to mitigate environmental degradation and foster a more resilient future. Technological solutions, ranging from renewable energy sources to advanced materials and circular economy practices, hold the potential to revolutionize industries and consumption patterns, steering us towards a sustainable paradigm.

Renewable energy technologies, such as solar photovoltaic, wind power, and geothermal energy, are central to decarbonizing the energy sector, a major contributor to greenhouse gas emissions (Hyun, 2025). The continuous improvement in efficiency and cost-effectiveness of these technologies, coupled with smart grid infrastructure, enables a transition away from fossil fuels. The energy storage solutions, including advanced batteries and pumped hydro storage, address the intermittency of renewable sources, ensuring a stable and reliable energy supply Sustainable technologies extend beyond energy, encompassing innovations in agriculture, manufacturing, and transportation. Precision agriculture, utilizing sensors and data analytics, optimizes resource use and reduces environmental impact. In manufacturing, closed-loop systems and bio-based materials minimize waste and pollution. Electric vehicles and alternative transportation systems, coupled with efficient public transit, promise to reduce the carbon footprint of transportation.

International cooperation plays a pivotal role in accelerating the green transition. Sharing knowledge, technology, and best practices across borders facilitates the rapid adoption of sustainable solutions (Tilsted, 2024). Collaborative research and development initiatives, along with international agreements and policies, create a conducive environment for innovation and investment in green technologies. This global collaboration is essential for addressing climate change, a challenge that transcends national boundaries.

The adoption of circular economy principles is also key to sustainable innovation. This involves designing products and systems that minimize waste and maximize resource efficiency. Technologies like advanced recycling, bio-plastics, and industrial symbiosis are vital for creating closed-loop systems that reduce the demand for virgin resources. The circular economy model fosters resource conservation and reduces the environmental burden associated with extraction and disposal.

Digital technologies, including artificial intelligence, the Internet of Things (IoT), and big data analytics, offer powerful tools for optimizing resource management and monitoring environmental impacts (Rodima-Taylor et al., 2024) (Wilder, 2024). Smart sensors and data platforms enable real-time tracking of energy consumption, waste generation, and pollution levels, facilitating informed decision-making and targeted interventions (Oatley, 2021). These technologies contribute to enhancing efficiency and reducing environmental footprints across various sectors (Milner & Solstad, 2021).

However, the deployment of sustainable technologies requires addressing social and economic factors (Goes & Bekkers, 2022). Ensuring equitable access to clean energy and sustainable solutions is essential for fostering inclusive growth and avoiding further marginalization (Sacco et al., 2022). Furthermore, policies and incentives that promote sustainable innovation, such as carbon pricing and green subsidies, are crucial for driving market transformation. Sustainable innovation, driven by technological advancements and underpinned by international cooperation, holds the key to addressing climate change and resource scarcity (Mehta, 2023). The transition to a green economy necessitates a holistic approach that integrates renewable energy, sustainable technologies, circular economy principles, and digital tools (O'Connell & Elliott, 2023). By fostering innovation and collaboration, we can build a more sustainable and resilient future for generations to come (Tallberg et al., 2023).

CONCLUSION

"Remaking the World: Technology, Power, and the International Political Economy" ultimately reveals the profound and multifaceted ways in which technological advancements are reshaping the global landscape (Cui et al., 2024). It underscores that technology is not a neutral force, but rather a critical arena where power dynamics are played out, influencing the distribution of wealth, shaping political alliances, and redefining the very nature of international relations (Zheng et al., 2024). The analysis highlights how states, corporations, and non-state actors are vying for technological dominance, leading to new forms of competition and cooperation that challenge traditional understandings of international political economy (Li & Wang, 2023).

The chapter further emphasizes the complex interplay between technology and governance, illustrating how technological innovations necessitate new regulatory frameworks and policy responses (Kenney & Lewin, 2023). From the digital divide to the rise of artificial intelligence and cyber warfare, the challenges posed by these advancements demand a rethinking of existing international norms and institutions (Smith, 2022). It compels us to consider the ethical implications of technological progress, ensuring that the benefits are distributed equitably and that potential risks are mitigated (Jones, 2023) (Lee, 2022) (Campbell-Verduyn, 2023). This exploration underscores the need for a more inclusive and collaborative approach to global governance, one that can effectively navigate the complexities of a technologically driven world (Mayer & Nock, 2025). "Remaking the World" serves as a crucial guide for understanding the transformative power of technology in the international political economy (Mayer & Nock, 2025). It urges us to move beyond simplistic narratives of technological determinism and recognize the agency of various actors in shaping the future (McLaren & Corry, 2021). By illuminating the intricate connections between technology, power, and global economic structures, the book provides valuable insights into the challenges and opportunities that lie ahead, calling for a more nuanced and forward-thinking approach to managing the evolving international order.

REFERENCES

Altinors, G., & Chryssogelos, A. (2024). Beyond populism and into the state: The political economy of national-conservatism. *British Journal of Politics and International Relations*, *26*(4), 995–1014. DOI: 10.1177/13691481241246538

Avelino, F., Wijsman, K., van Steenbergen, F., Jhagroe, S., Wittmayer, J., Akerboom, S., Bogner, K., Jansen, E. F., Frantzeskaki, N., & Kalfagianni, A. (2024). Just sustainability transitions: Politics, power, and prefiguration in transformative change toward justice and sustainability. *Annual Review of Environment and Resources*, *49*(1), 49. DOI: 10.1146/annurev-environ-112321-081722

Bell, D., & Taillandier, A. (2024). Cosmos-Politanism: Transhumanist Visions of Global Order from the First World War to the Digital Age. *Perspectives on Politics*, •••, 1–18. DOI: 10.1017/S1537592724001051

Campbell-Verduyn, M. (2023). Understanding emergent technology, instability and power in international political economy. In *Handbook on the Politics and Governance of Big Data and Artificial Intelligence* (pp. 188–210). Edward Elgar Publishing., DOI: 10.4337/9781800887374.00018

Cui, Y., Guo, M., Ma, G., Wang, J., & Su, X. (2024). The dual engines of political stability and digital technology: An international political economy analysis based on the green trade and climate change reversal mechanism in RCEP countries. *Energy & Environment*, *15*(1), 1–20. DOI: 10.1177/0958305X241300493

de Medeiros, C. A. (2025). *The Political Economy of US Geopolitical Strategy towards China* (Doctoral dissertation, Instituto de Economia, Universidade Federal do Rio de Janeiro).

Downey, L. (2025). Coercing finance to fund decarbonization: The democratic case for coercion in funding the green transformation. *Review of International Political Economy*, *32*(3), 1–22. DOI: 10.1080/09692290.2025.2471854

Du, M. (2025). The Belt and Road Initiative and National Economic Development: A Multidimensional Power Analysis. *Journal of Chinese Political Science*, •••, 1–29. DOI: 10.1007/s11366-025-09912-x

Ebner, N. (2024). From Paso del Norte to the Borderplex: Labor Devaluation, Bordering, and the Remaking of Uneven Development in the US–Mexico Borderlands. *Economic Geography*, *100*(4), 351–376. DOI: 10.1080/00130095.2024.2385527

Economy, E. (2024). China's Alternative Order: And What America Should Learn From It. *Foreign Affairs*, *103*, 8.

Eich, S. (2024). Derisking as worldmaking: Keynes, climate, and the politics of radical uncertainty. *Review of International Political Economy.*

Estevens, J. (2024). International Relations Theories and the Impact of the Fourth Industrial Revolution on Global Affairs. In *International Relations and Technological Revolution 4.0: World Order, Power and New International Society* (pp. 9–24). Springer Nature Switzerland. DOI: 10.1007/978-3-031-66750-3_2

Farid, C. (2024). Comments on# Help: Digital Humanitarianism and the Remaking of the International Legal Order. *Int'l Trade & Bus. L. Rev., 24*, 111.

Girard, T. (2024). The Global Political Economy of Digital Technology. *180 Day Access Global Political Economy*, 405.

Girard, T. (2024). National Identity and the Limits of Platform Power in the Global Economy. *International Studies Quarterly, 68*(3), sqae090. DOI: 10.1093/isq/sqae090

Gjesvik, L., & Willers, J. O. (2024). Beyond control? The political economy of private interception, intrusion, and surveillance markets. *Review of International Political Economy, 31*(6), 1840–1864. DOI: 10.1080/09692290.2024.2375499

Góes, C., & Bekkers, E. (2022). The impact of geopolitical conflicts on trade, growth, and innovation. arXiv preprint arXiv:2203.12173. https://arxiv.org/abs/2203.12173

Gore, E. (2024). Towards a trans-inclusive critical international political economy? Or why trans oppression matters for understanding capitalism and social reproduction. *Capital and Class*, •••, 03098168241232371.

Heiret, Y. S. (2024). The landlord state goes abroad: The remaking of the Norwegian 'Energy Nation'as a global rentier. *Environment and Planning A. Economy and Space, 56*(7), 1985–2002.

Hopewell, K. (2024). The (surprise) return of development policy space in the multilateral trading system: What the WTO Appellate Body blockage means for the developmental state. *Review of International Political Economy, 31*(4), 1245–1270. DOI: 10.1080/09692290.2024.2303681

Horowitz, M. C. (2024). Battles of Precise Mass: Technology Is Remaking War-and America Must Adapt. *Foreign Affairs, 103*, 34.

Hyun, J. (2025). Bringing technology into the balance of power politics:'network balancing'between the United States and China. *Cambridge Review of International Affairs, 38*(1), 22–47. DOI: 10.1080/09557571.2024.2401612

Jones, B. (2023). Recentring industrial policy paradigm within IPE and development studies. *Third World Quarterly, 44*(1), 1–15. DOI: 10.1080/01436597.2023.2216140

Kenney, M., & Lewin, A. Y. (2023). The rise of techno-geopolitical uncertainty: Implications of the United States CHIPS and Science Act. *Journal of International Business Policy*, *6*(2), 1–15. https://www.ncbi.nlm.nih.gov/pmc/articles/PMC10066984/ PMID: 37359753

Lee, K. (2022). Technological sovereignty and the global digital political economy. *Global Political Economy*, *3*(2), 1–20. DOI: 10.1332/26352257Y2022D000000029

Li, P., & Wang, H. (2023). The Tech Cold War, the multipolarization of the world economy, and IB research. *International Business Review*, *32*(6), 102195. DOI: 10.1016/j.ibusrev.2023.102195

Mayer, M., & Nock, P. J. (2025). Bringing technology into the balance of power politics: 'Network power' and the international political economy. *Cambridge Review of International Affairs*, *37*(1), 1–20. DOI: 10.1080/09557571.2024.2401612

Mayer, M., & Nock, P. J. (2025). The diffusion deficit in scientific and technological power: A critical assessment. *Review of International Political Economy*, *32*(2), 123–145. DOI: 10.1080/09692290.2023.2173633

McLaren, D., & Corry, O. (2021). Clash of geofutures and the remaking of planetary order: Faultlines underlying conflicts over geoengineering governance. *Global Policy*, *12*(S1), 20–33. DOI: 10.1111/1758-5899.12863

Mehta, R. S. (2023). China's techno-politics: The impact on Belt and Road partners. *India Quarterly*, *79*(3), 1–15. DOI: 10.1177/09749284231183321

Milner, H. V., & Solstad, S. U. (2021). Technological change and the international system. *World Politics*, *73*(1), 1–28. DOI: 10.1017/S0043887113000300

O'Connell, W. D., & Elliott, C. (2023). States and new markets: The novelty problem in the IPE of finance. *Review of International Political Economy*, *30*(2), 403–420. DOI: 10.1080/09692290.2023.2165529

Oatley, T. (2021). Regaining relevance: IPE and a changing global political economy. *Cambridge Review of International Affairs*, *34*(2), 318–327. DOI: 10.1080/09557571.2021.1888880

Palley, T. (2025). The military-industrial complex as a variety of capitalism and threat to democracy: rethinking the political economy of guns versus butter. In *The Political Economy of War, Peace, and the Military–Industrial Complex* (pp. 34-73). Edward Elgar Publishing. DOI: 10.4337/9781035357178.00008

Peters, M. A., & Besley, T. (2024). Tashkent, Khiva, Bukhara and Samarkand in the Islamic Remaking of the Modern World in Uzbekistan. *Geopolitics, History, and International Relations*, *16*(2), 9–39. DOI: 10.22381/GHIR16220241

Riaz, Q., Ayub, N., & Idrees, H. S. (2024). Interconnected Realms: Exploring the Nexus of International Relations, Trade Dynamics, and Digital Transformation. *Traditional Journal of Law and Social Sciences*, *3*(01), 36–46.

Rodima-Taylor, D., Campbell-Verduyn, M., & Bernards, N. (2024). Repoliticizing the technological turn in sustainability governance: Moralities, power, space. *Environment and Planning C. Politics and Space*, *42*(5), 699–707.

Sacco, P. L., Arenas, A., & De Domenico, M. (2022). The resilience of the multi-relational structure of geopolitical treaties is critically linked to past colonial world order and offshore fiscal havens. arXiv preprint arXiv:2203.00618. https://arxiv.org/abs/2203.00618

Siddiqui, K. (2024). The Decline of the West and Shifting Dynamics in the Global Political Economy. *WORLD (Oakland, Calif.)*.

Smith, A. (2022). Digital technological innovation and the international political economy. In *Handbook of International Political Economy* (pp. 1–20). Palgrave Macmillan., https://discovery.ucl.ac.uk/id/eprint/10045803/

Stanley, L. (2024). Why Sinoscepticism will remake British politics. *The Political Quarterly*, *95*(2), 289–297. DOI: 10.1111/1467-923X.13367

Tallberg, J., Erman, E., Furendal, M., Geith, J., Klamberg, M., & Lundgren, M. (2023). The global governance of artificial intelligence: Next steps for empirical and normative research. arXiv preprint arXiv:2305.11528. https://arxiv.org/abs/2305.11528

Tilsted, J. P. (2024). *Transforming a Synthetic World: The Political Economy of Petrochemical Transitions*. Lund University.

Verma, R. (2024). Russia–Ukraine war and India's quest for leading power status. *Global Policy*, *15*(4), 778–782. DOI: 10.1111/1758-5899.13365

Vlados, C., & Chatzinikolaou, D. (2025). The emergence of the new globalization: The approach of the evolutionary structural triptych. *Journal of Global Responsibility*, *16*(1), 139–161. DOI: 10.1108/JGR-04-2023-0063

Wilder, D. (2024). China's Bid to Remake the World Order. *Georgetown Journal of International Affairs*, *25*(1), 71–76. DOI: 10.1353/gia.2024.a934888

Zheng, T., Yu, X., Fan, Y., Ding, X., Ye, R., & Zhang, Y. (2024). The role of artificial intelligence in reshaping international political economy: Perspectives on economic governance and policy management. *Academic Journal of Management and Social Sciences*, *9*(3), 83–91. DOI: 10.54097/ppkzr906

Chapter 2
Digital Dominance and Economic Power:
Interplay of Technology and Geopolitics in Modern International Relations

Bhupinder Singh
https://orcid.org/0009-0006-4779-2553
Sharda University, India

Kittisak Wongmahesak
https://orcid.org/0009-0000-2129-4691
North Bangkok University, Thailand

Ashima Jain
https://orcid.org/0000-0001-5365-2385
Manipal University Jaipur, India

Saquib Ahmed
https://orcid.org/0009-0008-1891-6910
Sharda University, India

Saurabh Chandra
https://orcid.org/0000-0003-4172-9968
Bennett University, Greater Noida, India

ABSTRACT

The digital age has reshaped global geopolitics and economic power dynamics with technology at the core of international relations. Nations and corporations

DOI: 10.4018/979-8-3373-1727-4.ch002

vie for supremacy in strategic sectors like artificial intelligence, 5G and quantum computing, transforming traditional power dynamics. Data is the new oil, the oil that fuels economic growth and strikes in the public policy. The geopolitical competitive landscape especially between tech behemoths like the U.S. and China emphasizes the dual nature of technology as a means to prosperity and as a potential purveyor of conflict. Cybersecurity, digital sovereignty and the ethical use of AI are just some of the issues that highlight the complexities of global governance in the digital age. Connecting the digital gap and ensuring equal access to technology remain interrelated issues that must be resolved to achieve a balanced and sustainable international order.

1. INTRODUCTION

Dwelling deeply in the age of digital revolution, we see a whole new paradigm of the world of global geopolitics and power. Technology most prominently AI, big data, quantum computing and the Internet of Things (IoT) is reshaping global influence, prospects for economic dominance and how countries relate to each other. The conventional balances of power are being rewritten in this new era, with digital capabilities taking center stage in both strategic competition and global governance. Digital technologies are now key assets of geopolitical strategy. Countries that dominate the development, deployment and governance of transformative technologies like AI and 5G infrastructure accrue outsized economic and strategic benefits. The emergence of "tech superpowers," especially the United States and China, demonstrates how technological leadership can be converted into geopolitical leverage. For example, applications of AI in areas such as national security, surveillance, and defense increase the means by which a nation can project power beyond historical borders. Control of global semiconductor supply chains such as that done by Taiwan remains another matter, underpinning the vital place of technology in modern geopolitics (Keser, 2023).

At the corporate level, tech companies like Google, Amazon, Tencent and Alibaba exercise economic force on par with nation-states. Indeed, these multinationals wield control over data and technology ecosystems, monopolizing a global marketplace, and thereby transforming into transnational forces within the geoeconomic theatre. Their categorization as monopolistic entities in technology leads to asymmetries in economic power, cementing their role as influential actors in the realm of international policymaking. Advancements in e-commerce, data monetization, and financial technologies are reshaping the distribution and exercise of economic power in what is being called the digital economy. Data is the "new oil," the foundation of innovation and growth. Organizations and countries that successfully leverage data analytics and artificial intelligence capabilities stand to unlock innovation across sectors, from healthcare and manufacturing to finance and agriculture. China's use of AI to streamline supply chains and forecast consumer trends has accelerated this trend, buttressing its position on the world stage.

Digital trade has become a pillar of economic power as well. Due to the flourishing of various types of cross-border e-commerce platforms, countries and enterprises can achieve economic interdependence by developing the market. But this interdependence also creates vulnerabilities, as evidenced by trade wars and efforts at technological decoupling like U.S. sanctions on Chinese tech companies. Such conflicts highlight the dual edges of digital trade, which combines cooperation and competition (Denters et al., 2023).

2. GEOPOLITICAL RIVALRIES IN THE DIGITAL AGE

The geopolitical landscape is now increasingly dominated by technology rivalries which the United States and China are the most prominent of. These countries are locked in a struggle for technological superiority battling to dominate new fields like AI, quantum computing and 5G networks. China's Belt and Road Initiative has a "Digital Silk Road" aspect, meant to build out digital infrastructure in developing countries to extend China's geopolitical reach. Meanwhile the US highlights alliances like the Quad and moves like the CHIPS Act to counter Chinese technology and protect its own interests. These rivalries have made cybersecurity a central issue, and countries are using cyber capabilities to defend critical infrastructure and dominate cyberspace. Cyberattacks, espionage and misinformation campaigns have emerged as routine weapons in the arsenal of statecraft, blurring the rules of engagement in international affairs (Darko et al., 2023). The SolarWinds attack, by Russian state actors, and China's role in state-sponsored intellectual property theft, both are examples of how cybersecurity breaches can shake geo-political relationships.

As technology becomes a more integral part of international relations, countries are dedicating themselves to tech diplomacy. By taking such initiatives as the EU's Digital Compass, aiming to lay out a foundation for ethical AI, data protection and digital trade, they also endorse multilateralism for global governance. At its core, the G7 and G20 (as the G20 continues to evolve) recognize, like most strategic alliances, that tech and digital policy are foundational to stability and prosperity. Where technology creates new opportunities, it also poses challenges. The ethical use of AI and big data, especially related to governance, surveillance and the like, is a long-standing question. Countries including China are already using AI-powered surveillance systems that pose serious threats to privacy and human rights.

These methods show how technology is used to bring in authoritarian control, that erodes democratic principles.

The other major problem is the digital divide. Yet while advanced economies gain from technological advancements, across many developing countries, access to digital infrastructure and know-how remains a major barrier. This gap fuels global inequities, stunting the growth of a more inclusive economy and a healthier geopolitical foundation. Collaborative Efforts: Bridging the digital divide demands collaborative works, including investment in digital literacy and infrastructure in marginalized areas. The monopolistic tendency of tech giants also challenges global governance. More egregious, companies such as Facebook and Amazon hold more data and more control over its digital platforms than ever before (Dai & Azhar, 2024). Without an integrated global approach to the regulation of these bodies, however, managing issues of fairness in terms of competition and access to technology becomes even more challenging.

3. TECHNOLOGY AS A GEOPOLITICAL TOOL: DIGITAL INFRASTRUCTURE AND POWER DYNAMICS

Technology is a key weapon shaping global geopolitics, with power and influence used as both the sword and the shield in the contemporary international arena. Digital infrastructure, covering everything from telecoms to data networks and artificial intelligence (AI), is leading the way. At the very least it refashions what raw economic numbers allow in terms of power, but it also reshapes the relationship between nations. The contest between nations to take the lead on technology has consequences that reach well beyond technology itself, touching on sovereignty, national security and global stability. This will examine how digital infrastructure is a tool for geopolitics that rebalances power dynamics on an international stage.

Electronic infrastructure In particular has become a backbone of modern economies and societies. Telecommunications networks, data centers, and AI-powered systems underpin economic growth, innovation, and governance. As such, control of these infrastructures has substantial geopolitical ramifications. Countries that take the lead in developing and deploying digital technologies provide themselves with strategic advantages in trade, diplomacy and security (Zhang & Bai, 2023). For example, the global competition for 5G dominance shows how digital infrastructure vectors power. 5G evolution is paving the way to a myriad of new possibilities; supporting faster communication, faster devices, enchanced functionality to enable things like smart cities and autonomous vehicles. China, the United States, and South Korea invested heavily in 5G infrastructure to gain economic and lead technological advantages. The role of Chinese telecom giant Huawei in deploying 5G networks has led to geopolitical tensions involving the United States and its allies raising fears it could create security vulnerabilities and be used for espionage. These developments underscore the complex connection between digital infrastructure and national power.

Data, which has been classified as the new oil, occupies an important position in the geopolitics of data. The power of nations and corporations that control enormous amounts of data will rival that of the past, for data drives AI algorithms, policy decisions, and economic growth. Amid the global contest for data supremacy, discussions are ongoing about questions of data sovereignty, cross-border data flows (CBDFs) and digital trade rules (Muchunguzi, 2023). China's data governance worldview reflects its strategic leveraging of data as a geopolitical weapon. When it comes to data, China has leaned heavily on domestic narrative-building initiatives such as the Cybersecurity law and Data Security law to tighten its screws on data within its borders, while promoting its digital ecosystem externally as part of Belt and Road Initiative's "Digital Silk Road." By contrast, the European Union's General Data Protection Regulation (GDPR) is an example of an attempt to create a more ethical and transparent framework for data governance. These different approaches reflect how data governance is becoming a key determinant of global power (Hossain et al., 2023).

Digital sovereignty the capacity of a nation to govern its digital infrastructure and data is becoming an essential element of national security. More and more countries are now focusing on digital sovereignty to protect their economic and political interests. National cybersecurity strategies, data localization policies, and indigenous technology ecosystems show that this trend is here to stay. The most important and recent parts of this work is Russia's own 'sovereign internet' which is part of Russia's internet infrastructure and typically a superordinate term for providing internet services. Likewise, India's push for data localization and its "Make in India" initiative strives for enhanced digital sovereignty and reduced dependence on foreign technology providers (Ningrum et al., 2023).

Geopolitical alliances and technological blocs have formed as a result of the competition for digital dominance. Countries are coalescing around technology standards and values, creating a fractured tech domain. For example, the United States has pushed its "Clean Network" initiative that would no longer include Chinese technology firms within its vital digital infrastructure and has called for secure and transparent networks and services. By contrast, China's Digital Silk Road seeks to export its own technology infrastructure and create rounds of influence around the world through agreements with developing countries. These partnerships extend to multilateral dimensions including the EU's digital policies and the Quad's work on emerging technologies. These approaches signal not only the realization that technological leadership is not purely a zero-sum national game but rather a joint geopolitical game. But their creation can lead to a fractured global digital space and growing geopolitical tensions.

The rise of the Internet of Things and the growing pervasiveness of digital infrastructure in national governance and security have made cybersecurity a geopolitical issue. Cyberattacks, data breaches and misinformation campaigns have emerged as instruments of statecraft, enabling countries to sabotage rivals, steal intellectual property and shape public opinion. Examples of state-sponsored cyber activities, like Russia's alleged interference in the 2016 United States presidential election and North Korea's cyberattacks on banks, demonstrate how states are weaponizing their digital infrastructure. These incidents underscore the importance of strong cybersecurity measures and international cooperation to combat cyber threats (Zhang et al., 2023).

This cyberwarfare aspect of contemporary combat further underlines the geopolitical importance of digital infrastructure. This labyrinth is complicated further by the heightened application of AI and machine-based learning for both cyber defense and cyber offense a race among states to deploy ever more capable capabilities. As traditional boundaries between military conflict and cyber warfare are eroded, this arms race also raises challenges for global stability. Advanced economies adopt technologies for geopolitical and economic gain, while developing nations find it much more difficult to access and adopt these technologies (Fontenelle et al., 2023). The Digital Divide [i.e. the differences in access to digital infrastructure and technology] further widens global inequalities and inhibits developing countries from competing in the information age. Initiatives to close the digital divide for example, the World Bank's Digital Economy Initiative for Africa and the United Nations' Sustainable Development Goals (SDGs) seek to foster access to digital infrastructure for all. Yet the speed of technological progress and the digital power of a handful of countries and companies pose questions about the equity of benefits. In order to create a global digital ecosystem that is equitable and sustainable and self-reliance.

The ethical and regulatory challenges related to the rapid expansion of digital infrastructure and its geopolitical implications are great. Data privacy, algorithmic bias, and the ethical use of AI are just some of the complex issues that demonstrate why governance frameworks need to be strong and robust. The absence of consensus on digital governance at the global level makes it difficult to agree on norms and standards, resulting in regulatory fragmentation. The fact that regulation of AI technologies differs so greatly between countries shows different priorities and values. As the EU is trying to put ethical considerations and transparency centre stage via the AI Act, other countries look towards realising their ambitions in AI, not least their objectives in innovation and economic development. The lack of harmony between these different approaches creates complications for international collaboration and emphasizes the necessity for composite regulations (Neuwirth, 2024).

As digital infrastructure continues to advance, its geopolitical importance will grow. Emerging technologies such as quantum computing, blockchain, and 6G networks are poised to reshape global governance, trade, and security. These technologies will be developed and deployed in ways that will further reshape the power landscape, opening into new opportunities and challenges for countries and corporations. Geopolitics, in turn, will shape the technology landscape, as nations grapple with the implications of emerging technologies on national security, economic competitiveness, and societal well-being. International organizations, including the United Nations and the World Trade Organization, will have a crucial role in developing these frameworks to ensure a balanced and inclusive digital ecosystem.

Tech has become an increasingly useful geopolitical weapon that is upending power balances and redefining the lines of global power. Digital infrastructure is an enabler of economic growth and a lever of strategic competition with wider implications for sovereignty, security, and global stability. In a world where every aspect of daily life is increasingly dictated by technological progress, and the very frameworks of international relations are inextricably bound up with geopolitics, the tension between nations and corporations will remain inherently intertwined in sealing the fate of the digital era (Dai & Azhar, 2024). Meeting the challenges and seizing the opportunities of this new era demands visionary leadership, cooperative action, and a determination to leverage technology for the common good. Embracing inclusivity, ethical governance, and international cooperation is essential for the global community to navigate the complexities of digital geopolitics and forge a more equitable and sustainable future.

4. ECONOMIC POWER IN THE DIGITAL ERA: DIGITAL TRADE AND E-COMMERCE

Since then, the digital era has radically changed the way the global economy works, with digital trade and e-commerce emerging as critical forces shaping economic power. As such, the digital platforms, data-enabled economies, and new technologies have reshaped the way goods and services are exchanged and left behind new opportunities and challenges for businesses, governments, and consumers. This transformation has reshaped international trade, opening new frontiers for business but also introducing challenges of regulation, fairness, and competition. Digital trade is the trading of goods, services, and data that is enabled by digital technologies. It includes diverse activities, from e-commerce to cross-border data flows, cloud computing and digitally-delivered services. Digital trade is not just a crucial part of the modern economy but has been the engine of globalization itself, allowing businesses to reach new markets and consumers to find products and services half a world away.

Technological innovations, with high-speed internet, mobile connectivity, and secure payment systems have enabled the spread of digital trade. Global marketplaces have sprung up, including e-commerce platforms such as Amazon, Alibaba, and eBay. Like digital services online education, telemedicine, and cloud computing have broadened economic participation, especially in developing areas. The area that has experienced significant growth due to digital trade is e-commerce (Schröder & Watson, 2024). The domination of online marketplaces, mobile shopping apps, and subscription-based services has shaken up traditional business models, reshaping the way goods are marketed, sold, and delivered.

Convenience and accessibility as the major drivers of e-commerce is the convenience and accessibility of the platform. Consumers can shop for products at the snap of a finger, comparing them to other offerings for the best price, often with the help of personalized recommendations. For businesses, e-commerce opens up low-cost ways of reaching multiple customer pools quickly, lowering the cost of operating, and being able to expand with agility. This democratization of trade has been especially advantageous to small and medium-sized enterprises (SMEs), as digital platforms reduce entry barriers and allow them to compete in global markets. The COVID-19 pandemic drove e-commercial activity as lockdown and social distancing measures pushed consumers and businesses to online transaction. Data from the United Nations Conference on Trade and Development (UNCTAD) estimates the global e-commerce market to balloon during the pandemic, further reinforcing its vital contribution to economic resilience and continuity.

Data has become a Digital Economic Good until the era of Digital Economy, Data is considered as the Money Power which drives the Innovation and capable of making Decision to maintain Competitive advantage. Data is everywhere, and extracting insights from it can help humans in various aspects of life, giving way to data-driven economies. E-commerce sites, et al. have leveraged data analytics and artificial intelligence (AI) to drive better inventory management, improve customer experience, and enhance supply chain efficiency. Predictive analytics allows businesses to anticipate consumer demand, while AI-supported chatbots and recommendation engines tailor interactions and improve customer satisfaction and loyalty (Saz-Carranza et al., 2024).

But with that growth has come fear over data sovereignty, privacy, and security'" For governments, this translates into a struggle to regulate cross-border data flows, and to ensure that this data-enabled growth is matched by equitably shared benefits to all stakeholders (Moleka, 2024). With initiatives like the European Union's General Data Protection Regulation (GDPR) and the Asia-Pacific Economic Cooperation (APEC) Cross-Border Privacy Rules seeking to create frameworks for responsible data governance, balancing economic interests and individual rights. As the world becomes increasingly reliant on digital technology for communication, trade, and economic growth, recognizing the geopolitical stake in digital trade is becoming even more critical. Countries are at a competitive advantage if they have advanced digital infrastructure and innovation ecosystems, allowing them to shape global trade norms, standards, and regulations.

For instance, dominating the world digital economy of today, China and the United States use their tech capabilities and market sizes to wield economic and political power globally. As part of the wider Belt and Road Initiative, China's Digital Silk Road initiative aims to increase China's presence in the digital space by investing in digital infrastructure, e-commerce platforms, and developing its technology partnerships in developing areas around the world. On the other hand, the United States is still on the top regarding the development of the digital world, thanks to its Silicon Valley home for world-class tech companies (e.g.: Google, Apple, Microsoft). This rivalled competition for digital leadership has also given rise to regional and international trading arrangements covering digital commerce. Notably, the CPTPP and USMCA also include provisions covering e-commerce, data flows, and the protection of intellectual property, highlighting the increasing importance of digital trade as we enter a new state of economic relations (Park & Park, 2024).

In addition to these significant challenges, there are more digital trade and e-commerce host of issues which need to be addressed to ensure sustainable and inclusive growth.

Digital Divide: Unequal access to digital infrastructure and technology causes disparity between developed and developing countries and within the countries as well. Addressing this division is crucial for this investment to result in equal participation in the digital economy.

Regulatory Windows Will Have To Be Loaded: Contrasting digital trade regimes, data governance frameworks, taxation systems add complexities for businesses that operate across borders. Well-aligned regulations and international standards are essential to enabling smooth cross-border digital trade.

Cybersecurity and Fraud: With the growth of e-commerce comes the threat of cyberattacks, data breaches, and online fraud. Strengthening cybersecurity and building consumer trust are essential preconditions for the sustained growth of digital trade.

Ethical Concerns: AI & data analytics in e-commerce can raise ethical issues about algorithmic bias, data privacy, and consumer manipulation. Adopting ethical approaches in machine learning and also bringing transparency in the usage of data would help develop trust and accountability to the population.

Negative Environmental Impact: The rapid growth of e-commerce has environmental implications, including higher packaging waste and carbon emissions from logistics and delivery. Implementing sustainable practices, like green logistics and environmentally friendly packaging can help minimize these impacts.

These developments would continue to shape the future of digital trade and e-commerce. Innovations like mobile commerce, social commerce, and blockchain-based transactions are changing the game, presenting new frontiers for both disruption and growth (McNaught, 2024).

Mobile payment systems have evolved, and the prevalence of smartphones has made m-commerce gain traction. Social commerce, which combines e-commerce and social media platforms, enables companies to interact with consumers in real time while influencing purchasing through strategic advertising and influencer marketing. Blockchain, with its ability to create secure and transparent transactions, is a promising solution when addressing challenges like fraud, invoicing, payment delays and supply chain inefficiencies.

The application of AI and machine learning in digital trade and e-commerce will drive greater levels of personalization, automation and efficiency. AI tools can also analyze large levels of data to understand consumer preferences, examine pricing trends, and even optimize logistics. These advancements will help companies compete in an ever-more digitalized global economy.

Data, digital trade and e-commerce have become the defining features of the modern economic landscape, reshaping the nature of goods and service exchanges and global power dynamics. The future of digital trade is promising, but as countries and corporations seek to harness the opportunities and navigate the challenges that come with the digital age, the foundation of inclusive growth, ethical governance, and sustainable practices will be essential to unlocking the vast potential of digital trade (Van Rheenen et al., 2024). Global collaboration is essential in addressing the existing gaps and disparities and achieving a harmonious framework that promotes innovation and growth while creating a digital economy that is just and equitable for all.

5. CONCLUSION AND FUTURE SCOPE

The technology provides answers to many of the world's most challenging problems as other uses of AI and big data include fighting climate change, reducing energy consumption and advancing public health initiatives. AI is being used in models to predict natural disasters, develop vaccines, and improve agricultural practices, showcasing the potential for technology to solve societal issues. Enabling Leapfrogging Africa's mobile payment systems and India's digital identity platform, Aadhaar, are illustrative of how technology can propel economic growth and inclusion in developing economies. As it move forward, the intersection of technology and geopolitics is only going to become more complex, influenced by advancements in AI, quantum computing, and blockchain. The future of digital geopolitics will depend on the establishment of ethical AI frameworks, international treaties on cybersecurity, and more global efforts to bridge the digital divide. Those that embrace collaboration and innovation will have a clear advantage in the new world order that has emerged.

The journey ahead involves addressing ethical concerns, regulatory roadblocks, and geopolitical conflicts. The ability to ensure that technology is a force for good will requires concerted efforts to establish strong governance frameworks, advance inclusivity, and encourage international cooperation. The electronic age has transformed base lines of global validity, which create tech the center of geo-politics and liquidity of the economic system itself. Tensions between powers have arisen as countries and companies compete to be at the forefront of this new world, highlighting the importance of the intersection between digitalization and the international sphere. The world is more connected than ever before, allowing for new forms of collaboration and innovative solutions to emerge, even in the face of issues like resource depletion and climate change. How it navigates this complex challenge will depend on visionary leaders, cooperation and using technology as a force for the greater good.

REFERENCES

Dai, J., & Azhar, A. (2024). Collaborative governance in disaster management and sustainable development. *Public Administration and Development, 44*(4), 358–380. DOI: 10.1002/pad.2071

Dai, J., & Azhar, A. (2024). Collaborative governance in disaster management and sustainable development. *Public Administration and Development, 44*(4), 358–380. DOI: 10.1002/pad.2071

Darko, D., Zhu, D., Quayson, M., Hossin, M. A., Omoruyi, O., & Bediako, A. K. (2023). A multicriteria decision framework for governance of PPP projects towards sustainable development. *Socio-Economic Planning Sciences, 87*, 101580. DOI: 10.1016/j.seps.2023.101580

Denters, E., Ginther, K., & de Waart, P. J. (Eds.). (2023). *Sustainable development and good governance*. Martinus Nijhoff Publishers.

Fontenelle, A. L., Peyerl, D., Zacharias, L. G. L., Ciotta, M., & Moretto, E. M. (2023). The role of the Sustainable Development Goals for better governance of Carbon Capture and Storage (CCS). *Desenvolvimento e Meio Ambiente, 62*, 478–498. DOI: 10.5380/dma.v62i0.82216

Hossain, I., Haque, A. M., & Ullah, S. A. (2023). Role of Government Institutions in Promoting Sustainable Development in Bangladesh: An Environmental Governance Perspective. *Journal of Current Social and Political Issues, 1*(2), 42–53. DOI: 10.15575/jcspi.v1i2.485

Keser, I. (2023). Interdependence and Complementarity of a Multi-Dimensional Concept of Sustainable Development and the Integrated Approach to Urban Governance—Case Study City of Zagreb. *Sustainability (Basel), 15*(12), 9213. DOI: 10.3390/su15129213

McNaught, R. (2024). The application of collaborative governance in local level climate and disaster resilient development–A global review. *Environmental Science & Policy, 151*, 103627. DOI: 10.1016/j.envsci.2023.103627

Moleka, P. (2024). Rethinking the Limits of Polycentric Governance: Towards a More Inclusive Innovation Ecosystem Framework for Sustainable Development in the Global South.

Muchunguzi, S. (2023). Participatory management of natural resources in Africa: An imperative policy direction for sustainable development. *Management of Environmental Quality, 34*(3), 704–720. DOI: 10.1108/MEQ-06-2022-0170

Neuwirth, R. J. (2024). The global institutional governance of AI: A four-dimensional perspective. *International Journal of Digital Law and Governance*, *1*(1), 113–153. DOI: 10.1515/ijdlg-2024-0004

Ningrum, D., Raven, R., Malekpour, S., Moallemi, E. A., & Bryan, B. A. (2023). Transformative potential in sustainable development goals engagement: Experience from local governance in Australia. *Global Environmental Change*, *80*, 102670. DOI: 10.1016/j.gloenvcha.2023.102670

Park, K. R., & Park, Y. S. (2024). Addressing institutional challenges in sustainable development goals implementation: Lessons from the Republic of Korea. *Sustainable Development (Bradford)*, *32*(1), 1354–1369. DOI: 10.1002/sd.2725

Saz-Carranza, A., Rueda-Sabater, E., Vandendriessche, M., Moreno, C., & Jordana, J. (2024). The future (s) of global governance: A scenarios exercise. *Global Policy*, *15*(1), 149–165. DOI: 10.1111/1758-5899.13295

Schröder, N. J. S., & Watson, N. (2024). Assessing participatory process-system linkages in polycentric water governance: Insights from WFD implementation in Germany. *The Review of Policy Research.*

Van Rheenen, D., Naria, O., Melo, R., & Sobry, C. (2024). A Comparative Study of Small Islands, Sport Tourism, and Sustainable Development: A Local to Global Perspective. In *Sport Tourism, Island Territories and Sustainable Development: A Comparative Perspective* (pp. 503–543). Springer Nature Switzerland. DOI: 10.1007/978-3-031-51705-1_29

Zhang, L., & Bai, E. (2023). The Regime Complexes for Global Climate Governance. *Sustainability (Basel)*, *15*(11), 9077. DOI: 10.3390/su15119077

Zhang, L., Mohandes, S. R., Tong, J., Abadi, M., Banihashemi, S., & Deng, B. (2023). Sustainable Project Governance: Scientometric Analysis and Emerging Trends. *Sustainability (Basel)*, *15*(3), 2441. DOI: 10.3390/su15032441

Chapter 3
Geopolitics in the Algorithmic Era:
Navigating Technological Competition and National Security

L B Muralidhar
https://orcid.org/0000-0003-3453-613X
Jain University, India

Amrinder Singh
https://orcid.org/0000-0003-0830-7245
Jain University, India

H R Swapna
https://orcid.org/0000-0003-0362-409X
Jain University, India

N Sathyanarayana
https://orcid.org/0000-0002-4185-7751
Jain University, India

Varanasi Rahul
https://orcid.org/0000-0003-2407-7654
Jain University, India

ABSTRACT

The Algorithmic Era is a revolution in geopolitics brought on by the accelerated pace of artificial intelligence (AI), big data, and machine learning. With algorithms controlling global systems—military, civilian, or otherwise—the technological rivalry between states and tech companies reshapes traditional geopolitics. This

DOI: 10.4018/979-8-3373-1727-4.ch003

chapter critically analyses how AI-based innovations transform power differentials, challenge ethical considerations, and ignite data sovereignty and national security controversies. It explores the nexus of technology with foreign policy, economic power, and human rights, emphasising the strategic requirement of international regulating instruments and cooperative statesmanship for tempering the pace of innovation with security, ethics, and distributional equity in the digital era.

INTRODUCTION

Contextualizing the Algorithmic Era

The Algorithmic Age does not merely represent a stage in technological advancement but signals a profound structural transformation in global power dynamics. In this era, algorithmic thinking—realized through artificial intelligence (AI) and machine learning—supplants traditional rule-based systems. Data monopolies such as Google, Amazon, and Alibaba have emerged as quasi-sovereign entities, exerting influence over economies, public discourse, and cognitive behavior with unprecedented precision, effectively blurring the line between political authority and market dominance.

The ascendancy of deep learning algorithms has enabled machines to assume tasks once reserved for human cognition—language processing, visual perception, and moral judgment—thereby challenging long-held ontological assumptions. Yet, this diffusion of agency through machines is far from neutral. It is deeply intertwined with entrenched inequalities, as algorithmic power concentrates within a few digital oligopolies, exacerbating epistemic disparities and disempowering those unable to shape technological norms (Cave & Dignum, 2019). Regulatory frameworks such as the GDPR and OECD AI Principles remain normatively ambitious but operationally insufficient, unable to match the velocity and scale of technological disruption (OECD, 2019).

Crucially, algorithmic systems often replicate biased histories under the guise of efficiency, reinforcing exclusions and systemic disparities—particularly along the Global North–South divide. The concern is not merely technological access, but a broader redefinition of agency, autonomy, and accountability within the digital public sphere. The Algorithmic Era thus confronts societies with a complex ethical and political crucible: What should machines do? Who decides? And whose interests do they serve?

The Geopolitical Reordering of Technological Power

The fusion of algorithmic technologies with geopolitical strategies has reconfigured the architecture of global influence. Traditional indicators of power—territorial control, natural resources, military capacity—are increasingly overshadowed by digital capabilities. Nations now compete on their ability to harness and deploy AI, big data, and machine learning to manage markets, monitor populations, and shape diplomatic and defense agendas.

The United States exemplifies this shift through its strategic use of AI in financial engineering and predictive governance, while China's expansive surveillance apparatus and AI-driven military modernization aim for infrastructural supremacy in the digital realm (Brynjolfsson & McAfee, 2014; Cheng, 2020). Simultaneously, the contest over 5G networks, semiconductor supply chains, and cybersecurity underscores the rise of techno-nationalism, where algorithmic infrastructure itself becomes a battleground for strategic advantage.

This digital realignment, however, carries significant risks. As algorithmic governance scales up, states may institutionalize surveillance, codify biases, and marginalize vulnerable populations lacking infrastructural parity. While frameworks like the GDPR offer ethical counterweights, they are often outpaced by innovation, leaving a global governance vacuum. In this asymmetric environment, innovation emerges as both an enabler of global leadership and a vector of exclusion.

Consequently, understanding and navigating this emergent digital geopolitical order necessitates a critical inquiry into algorithmic power's ethical, strategic, and regulatory dimensions. The following research objectives guide this inquiry by framing the critical dimensions through which the Algorithmic Era reshapes global governance and power dynamics. First, the study seeks to analyze how technological advancements—particularly in artificial intelligence, big data, and machine learning—are redefining global geopolitical power structures by shifting influence from traditional markers such as territory and military might to algorithmic control and digital infrastructure. Second, it aims to evaluate the ethical and regulatory challenges of integrating AI into national security frameworks, where concerns over surveillance, accountability, and algorithmic bias demand urgent scrutiny. Third, the inquiry investigates the role of international diplomacy in managing this rapidly evolving technological competition, focusing on how states negotiate digital sovereignty, normative frameworks, and global cooperation amid rising techno-nationalism and asymmetrical access to innovation.

These objectives frame a comprehensive exploration of how algorithmic technologies are not only reshaping global governance, but also reconfiguring fundamental questions of sovereignty, ethics, and human agency in the 21st century

STATEMENT OF THE PROBLEM

With the Algorithmic Age, technological progress, security, and geopolitics meet in such a manner as to present an acute challenge. The rapidly increasing velocity of artificial intelligence, machine learning, and big data marked the beginning of a global competition where technological dominance emerged as the determining feature of power. Competition for dominance, however, raises profound security and moral issues. Military applications of AI, algorithmic dominance, and cyber threats are daunting challenges for global equilibrium. Advances in technology contain such great potential for economic growth as for military capability. However, they raise profound issues about privacy, surveillance, and safeguarding human rights that require immediate action by world regulatory institutions.

THEORETICAL AND CONCEPTUAL FRAMEWORK

The theoretical and conceptual foundations of the Algorithmic Era reveal a profound reconfiguration of power, wherein sovereignty is increasingly expressed not through territorial control or military might, but through engineering dominance, algorithmic governance, and the strategic export of technological standards. This structural shift signals a paradigmatic departure from traditional geopolitics toward a new logic of influence, where writing code and shaping digital infrastructures become instruments of global power. At the heart of this transformation lies Technological Nationalism, a revived and reconstituted discourse that equates national strength with digital sovereignty—seen not through missiles or industrial capacity, but through the control of 5G networks, artificial intelligence ecosystems, and data architectures.

This techno-political reorientation is closely aligned with Technological Determinism, which asserts that technology is not merely a product of social progress but its primary architect. In this view, AI systems do not simply support governance—they actively reshape economic and societal structures, redefining government functions, military capabilities, and institutional norms. This deterministic perspective is reinforced by the empirical realities of the Algorithmic Age, where algorithmic systems increasingly make decisions once reserved for human deliberation—decisions about surveillance, mobility, resource distribution, and even moral judgment.

International Relations theory is undergoing a parallel recalibration. Realism interprets the current U.S.–China AI rivalry as a continuation of state-centric competitive logic, where national interest is driven by dominance in technological standards, semiconductors, and information architectures. Liberalism, by contrast, posits transnational cooperation—such as the development of shared cybersecurity norms and ethical AI frameworks—as a necessary counterbalance, though the pace and scope of such multilateral initiatives remain inconsistent. Constructivism intervenes by questioning how international norms around fairness, transparency, and algorithmic justice are socially constructed rather than inherently applied, revealing deep-seated geopolitical tensions embedded in the global discourse on AI ethics.

The conceptual evolution of the Algorithmic Era reflects these theoretical underpinnings. It represents a departure from constitution-based governance to algorithm-centered authority, whereby inscrutable computational systems increasingly determine individual value and allocate social opportunities—often outside the purview of democratic oversight. In authoritarian contexts such as China, this is most visible in state-led algorithmic surveillance and social credit regimes. Yet, even in liberal democracies, predictive policing and automated decision-making raise urgent questions about consent, transparency, and control.

This growing prevalence of Algorithmic Governance—whether at borders, in welfare systems, or through facial recognition in public spaces—forces a rethinking of legitimacy, procedural justice, and the visibility of decision-making processes. Ethics in this context cannot be relegated to post-hoc validations. Rather, ethical AI becomes a terrain where power is actively contested and where legitimacy is awarded or withheld. While numerous ethical frameworks exist—from the EU's GDPR to UNESCO and OECD guidelines—their ability to shape real-world applications remains limited. These frameworks often lag behind the rapid evolution of technologies they seek to regulate.

Thus, the Algorithmic Era is not merely a technological phase; it is a political and epistemic watershed. It remaps power relations, redefines rights, and challenges the very grammar of global governance. The normative instability it introduces demands not only a theoretical rebalancing but also practical mechanisms to ensure that algorithmic efficiency does not override human equity, and that the expanding reach of digital code is held accountable to the societies it claims to serve.

In 2024, global venture capital funding for AI startups surged to $131.5 billion, marking a 52% increase from the previous year. This growth was driven by megadeals exceeding $1 billion and a broader shift of capital toward AI-focused firms . Notably, five major AI hyperscalers are projected to collectively invest over $1 trillion in capital expenditures between 2024 and 2027.

Cybersecurity threats have intensified, with a 75% increase in cyberattacks globally in Q3 2024 compared to the same period in 2023. On average, organizations faced 1,876 attacks during this quarter, with the education and research sectors being the most targeted . Additionally, ransomware affected 66% of organizations in 2023, and there was a 400% increase in IoT malware attacks across various industries.

The rise of algorithmic systems has initiated a paradigmatic shift in the practice of national security, wherein the traditional boundaries of warfare and defense are being redrawn by artificial intelligence, machine learning, and predictive analytics. Contemporary threats are no longer confined to physical geographies or conventional weapons. Instead, they emerge from invisible digital incursions across borders, executed by self-enhancing code, autonomous agents, and information manipulation campaigns. Cyberattacks now target financial infrastructures, power grids, and sensitive state databases, challenging static defenses and necessitating a new security paradigm based on anticipatory, rather than reactive, capabilities (Zengler, 2021).

This shift marks the emergence of what has been described as the "Algorithmic Arms Race"—a technologically driven competition for dominance where speed, data, and cognitive automation replace manpower and firepower. Cyber warfare unfolds at a velocity beyond human cognition, rewriting long-held canons of deterrence. Events such as the cyberattacks on Estonia in 2007 and ongoing espionage operations against U.S. defense facilities underscore how algorithms can exploit informational disparities and disrupt national sovereignty (Gartzke, 2020). The deployment of autonomous weapons systems (AWS) marks another critical evolution. These systems, enabled by AI and sensor fusion, automate threat responses and initiate military engagements, often bypassing human oversight and ethical reflection. While supporters claim these systems optimize battlefield efficiency and minimize casualties, they also pose grave risks—systemic hacking, misfiring, and the erosion of accountability in warfare (Lin, 2020).

Simultaneously, the silent weaponisation of information has become a key geopolitical strategy. Through deepfakes, algorithmically amplified disinformation, and content manipulation, adversaries engineer public perception as a tool of political destabilization—seen most notably in the 2016 U.S. election interference (Rosenberg et al., 2018). Such operations erode trust in democratic institutions, enabling subversion not through invasion but through narrative control. As AI-driven systems increasingly normalize surveillance in the name of security, the line between protection and repression blurs. China's nationwide use of facial recognition and its Social Credit System exemplify this algorithmic paternalism, while in other democracies, predictive policing quietly reconfigures civil liberties without adequate consent or oversight (Liu, 2020).

As algorithmic governance becomes embedded in national security architectures, states begin to exercise power through silent, predictive systems—monitoring, sorting, and influencing behavior under the guise of efficiency. These systems recalibrate the relationship between citizen and state, often removing the element of democratic consent entirely. The discursive justification of national security provides states with broad latitude to implement algorithmic surveillance, often targeting marginalized communities and reinforcing systemic inequalities. The surveillance state is thus not an aberration but a structural feature of the digital security regime.

The architecture of such control systems is inherently political, reflecting the convergence of state interests, market logics, and historical asymmetries. For instance, the U.S. CLOUD Act reveals the extraterritorial ambitions of digital surveillance, asserting data control beyond sovereign borders. In contrast, China's Social Credit System operates as an internally institutionalized mechanism of behavior adjudication, extending state power into citizens' everyday choices. These divergent models nonetheless share one feature: algorithmic governance increasingly displaces human discretion with opaque decision-making.

Global defense spending reached a record $2.46 trillion in 2024, up from $2.24 trillion in the previous year, reflecting intensifying security challenges . NATO and its allies are actively integrating AI into their armed forces, recognizing its potential to revolutionize military operations

Complicating this landscape further is the growing reliance on private technology firms by governments, effectively turning states into both clients and regulators. This dual role compromises regulatory integrity and weakens oversight mechanisms. Initiatives such as the European Union's GDPR and the proposed AI Act attempt to assert ethical guardrails and normative leadership, but their reach is limited and their global adoption inconsistent (OECD, 2019). In parallel, countries like India have introduced legislation such as the Personal Data Protection Bill, aiming to balance digital rights with strategic autonomy. Yet these efforts often clash with broader geopolitical agendas and reveal a lack of harmonised global standards.

The current vacuum in enforceable international governance is troubling. While multilateral initiatives like the Campaign to Stop Killer Robots or UNESCO's AI ethics guidelines offer symbolic progress, they are regularly undermined by strategic self-interest, particularly among technologically dominant states (Achter, 2021). In this vacuum, algorithmic militarization accelerates without corresponding ethical containment, creating a regime of global security where speed overrides accountability, and geopolitical advantage is prioritized over democratic legitimacy.

TECHNOLOGICAL COMPETITION AND ECONOMIC POWER

Economic Implications of Technological Competition

Technological competition has remoded the global economic power structure, replacing traditional territorial closeness or industrial size determinants with algorithmic capability, chip sovereignty, and digital infrastructure control. This realignment is not merely strategic but structural, remaking alliances through digital interdependence and selective exclusion clusters. The EU's Digital Single Market and US-led Indo-Pacific digital initiatives are instances of how current geopolitical alignment is no longer predicated upon shared ideologies but emerges from shared technological agendas. Nevertheless, beneath the cooperative veneer, there is mathematics of containment. Export control restrictions on China's access to semiconductors, justified through security reasoning, have ironically fueled Beijing's domestic R&D, driving its AI and chip independence in ways detrimental to Western technological dominance (Feng, 2020). The unforeseen effect is not the fragmentation of supply chains but rather the proliferation of parallel digital ecosystems that undermine global standardisation.

The number of data localization measures has been on the rise globally, with over 60 countries implementing some form of such policies. These measures are becoming more restrictive, impacting cross-border data flows and raising concerns about their implications for global trade and digital rights. Global trade hit a record $33 trillion in 2024, with services driving growth by rising 9% for the year. However, momentum slowed in the second half of the year, and uncertainty looms for 2025 as shifting policies reshape the global landscape .

Digital sovereignty has become a focal point, with regions like Europe implementing regulations such as the GDPR, Digital Markets Act, and Digital Services Act to assert control over data and digital infrastructure . A survey indicated that 33% of organizations consider Amazon Web Services as their main sovereign cloud vendor, followed by Microsoft Azure at 27%.

While regulatory asymmetries, such as the GDPR, set operational realignments in train for multinational companies, they establish new geoeconomic fault lines in the already fragmented digital economy. In their algorithmic designs, U.S. technology giants insidiously universalise Western epistemologies, infusing soft power in the global digital infrastructures of the Global South. This hidden influence has set a countercurrent: digital protectionism, a declaration of data sovereignty and regulatory independence. Among many, India, Brazil, and Nigeria are developing policies to localise control of data flows and algorithmic regulation, signaling a more fundamental resistance to asymmetrical techno-dominance. We see not a dichotomy between openness and closure but a geopolitics in motion, in which strength derives from a state's ability to insulate key technological infrastructures while facilitating pluralist innovation. Strategic foresight here demands a richly nuanced choreography—balancing sovereignty with interoperability, innovation with fragmentation—where economic hierarchies are structured increasingly less according to material production and increasingly according to the management of algorithmic and informational architecture.

Data as the New Geopolitical Resource

With the era of algorithms, information has become a new asset, replacing the classical assets as the subject of geopolitical ambition, not only as a good to be bought and sold but as a geoeconomy of government, economic power, and competing ideologies. No longer are states competing for land or trade lanes, but for informational streams—who is receiving information, where it is stored, where it travels, and according to what principles it is processed. The EU's GDPR illustrates transnational regulatory regimes as instruments of norms projection by locating good governance regimes on global companies' business logic.

China weaponises data as a driver of development and discipline, utilising surveillance technology, behavior-scoring, and localizability standards to concentrate management as it seeks its AI objectives—offering a digital model of authoritarianism presented as technological leadership. The United States fluctuates between rhetorical laissez-faire and selective intervention, increasingly employing measures of export control and limits on data access as a deterrent, particularly in the face of China, thereby marking data into the national security paradigm. These rival strategies partition the digital space in techno-sovereign silos wherein management of data is less about shared values as such as about competitive insulation.

Digital protectionism, disguising itself as a sovereignty shield, is most commonly a surreptitious exercise of power that leads to regulatory dissonance, fatigue through compliance, and inefficiencies in infrastructure for transnational companies. Though politically enticing, the pursuit of localising data erodes transnational cooperation at the moment when planet-wide dangers—climate change, pandemics, and cybersecurity—demand globally networked systems of knowledge. However, the absence of a binding international regime to mediate these tensions allows for the metastasis of geopolitical rivalry under the cover of digital innovation. Whether data is a shared commons building collective strength or freezes as a tiered instrument of exclusion depends less on technological determinism and more on the political inclination to imagine new models of governability in terms of equity, interconnection, and human dignity, as opposed to short-term politics of convenience-based securitisation.

Sovereignty in the digital era is a contested terrain in which the transnational reach of powerful tech conglomerates repeatedly redraws the power of states. The dominance of digital infrastructure under the auspices of Google, Meta, and Alibaba has brought a new geopolitics in which ownership of code, algorithms, and information affords a kind of power equal to, if not more excellent than, extant state actors. These entities enable commerce or communication, construct political discourse, shape social behavior, and posit de facto standards beyond borders. National states are thus compelled to practice digital sovereignty in a manner that strains the classical Westphalian understanding of jurisdiction.

The European Union's GDPR, widely quoted as a privacy statute, is also an exercise in geopolitics—a template of rule both for protecting citizens and in order to limit the extraterritorial reach of multibusiness digital corporations as well as in order to create a normative template for digital rule. Sovereignty, however, is no longer defendable in rule form. The race for establishing and imposing global norms of technicity reveals deep asymmetricities as Western democracies face uncoordinated policymaking mechanisms and business lobby groupings. Governments like China, on the other hand, institutionalise a vertically linked picture of digital dominance. China's concentration of state power together with technological advancements—demonstrated in its use of the Social Credit System as well as in its dominance of the 5G infrastructure—represents some form of expression of a statist conception of digital dominance in which sovereignty is infrastructural but, in addition, ideological. Such a mindset has sobering ethical consequences, particularly for surveillance and censorship, but it realises the strategic calculation for injecting sovereignty into technical design.

In contrast, the U.S. is confronted by the irony of projecting digital influence through its techno-multinationals without managing their strength domestically, as the corporations increasingly exist in a state of virtual sovereign autonomy. Breakdowns in the distinctions between cyberspace's public and private sectors complicate international responses, further increasing geopolitical tensions. Without a single global standard, states are tempted to fall back onto techno-national bubbles rather than the interoperability and openness of the early internet. We are facing a disunited digital world that is defined as much by strategic assertion as anything else, in which sovereignty is in flux rather than fixed, as a dynamic competition for infrastructural influence, regulative command, and epistemic leadership in a world of algorithmic dominance as well as asymmetrical rule.

Digital imperialism, or the technological equivalent of colonialism, has become a powerful tool for Western techno-monoliths led by U.S. corporations such as Google, Meta, Amazon, and Microsoft to impose unjustifiable dominance over the digital sphere. These corporations, rather than simply providing infrastructure or services, author rules, design regimes of information, and imprint their philosophical concepts onto world communications, commerce, and politics' algorithmic frameworks. They facilitate a means of epistemic power in which the availability of, and possession of, information flows determines economic outcomes and cultural and political narratives across borders.

This establishes a condition of dependency for most countries of the Global South—where digital futures are compromised by dependence upon exported technologies beyond the jurisdiction of local legal and ethical standards. Within the narrow local markets of the exemplars of sub-Saharan Africa or segments of Latin America, cloud services, platform services, and telecommunications infrastructure fall under the mediation of foreign intermediaries whose last interest is invariably in shareholders, not citizens. It introduces a skew that subjects the regions to exploitation—either in data extraction, manipulation of platforms, or application of alien standards to agendas local to regions. Attempts to resist this dominance are exemplified in polymorphous forms.

China's techno-industrial drive to pursue AI autonomy and independence from overseas semiconductor inputs is a state-led experiment in digital sovereignty marred by authoritarianism in the domestic sphere. The European Union, in turn, exercises normative influence through mechanisms of rules like the GDPR and also by advancing the creation of continent-wide alternatives where U.S. monopolies predominate, like the cloud and AI. Through Digital India, India is attempting to strike a middle ground: nurturing digital entrepreneurship at home and addressing global interoperability requirements. The path to autonomy is not one-dimensional and does not come without a hitch.

Indigenous growth demands infrastructure, investment, strategic vision, and resistance to corporate invasion and geo-economic manipulation. Unbridled techno-nationalism also perpetuates the polarisation of digital commons and erodes collective progress. An even more significant challenge is to build a plural digital order where digital sovereignty does not mean disconnection but facilitates collective involvement in world standards-making. Absent that rebalancing, the digital future threatens to be yet another extractive frontier—owned by a few, contested by many, and negotiated in terms of size rather than equity, control rather than consent.

DIPLOMACY IN THE ALGORITHMIC ERA

The Role of Diplomacy in Technological Competition

Diplomacy is being revolutionised in the Algorithmic Age by realigning its functions with the complications of competition fueled by technology, which is increasingly structuring global power. Unlike the old diplomatic summits, which entailed borders, treaties, and war alliances, the new diplomatic climate is characterised by algorithmic negotiations, transborder flows of information, cybersecurity regimes, and rules of new technologies, such as artificial intelligence (AI) and 5G.

These are not minor components of foreign policy but new frontlines of strategy where states compete to find a seat in shaping global digital norms.

The dominance of a few developed states—first and foremost, the United States, China, and the EU—has given rise to sharply unequal environments, precluding the full participation of weaker states in the creation of standards or in claiming digital sovereignty. Diplomatic norms, such as the EU's GDPR and the AI Principles of the OECD, show how norms of regulation are being constructed by soft power instruments, by which the regime of the law is becoming a tool of geopolitics rather than a neutral tool of regulation. While the GDPR was successful in advancing European privacy standards and personal data protection, it has also aroused global controversies on the boundaries of jurisdictions in a world without borders.

In the meantime, initiatives such as the Paris Call for Trust and Security in Cyberspace show what is possible—and what may be impossible—when competing national interest agendas get in the way of collective responsibility. Most strikingly divergent in approach is AI. The EU espouses openness and ethical AI, the U.S. espouses creativity and dynamism in the marketplace, and China applies AI for a top-down surveillance society. Not only are these impediments to consensus, but they are also a reflection of how diplomacy is becoming inextricably linked to economic strategy and ideological outreach.

Secondly, technological acceleration outruns diplomatic timeliness, making the majority of negotiations reactive rather than anticipatory. Such lag in timing undermines the ability to predict threats ahead of their hardening, especially in new technologies such as quantum technology or drones. Diplomacy is neither old-fashioned as a conflict-reducing mechanism nor as a theatre of bargain over norms in an era of growing technical determinacy of social outcomes. Instead, it is a matter of infusing inclusive, adaptive, yet feasible diplomatic structures that can encompass technological heterogeneity without fragmenting. Alternatively, the digital order consolidates in the grip of powerful actors at the expense of less powerful ones, perpetuating the new technological hegemony's inequalities.

International Regulation and Cooperation

Escalating global architectures for the regulation of artificial intelligence and cybersecurity underscore growing stakes of harmonising worldwide management in a world dominated by algorithmic networks and digital fragilities. However, they are conditioned by tension, divergence of norms, and structural power asymmetries. Whereas discursive spaces have been constructed by organisations such as the United Nations and the G20, prominently by UNESCO's AI Guidelines and the digital economic debate of the G20, their impact is mediated by competing political agendas and a power differential in technological capabilities.

The UN value-driven agenda for ethically sound AI, based on protecting human rights and overall well-being, profoundly differs from state-driven initiatives, exemplified in China, emphasising AI to spur economic growth, strategic espionage and global influence. The Western democracies, spearheaded by the EU, are committed to safeguarding the individual's privacy, fostering transparency, and seeking man-focused solutions, as exemplified in the GDPR and the upcoming AI Act. This essential divide between state-driven and rights-oriented visions renders global consensus a distant illusion, especially in sensitive areas like flows of information, espionage tools, and military application of AI.

Furthermore, the speed of technical change outruns the considered speed of global diplomacy, and regulating institutions find themselves continuously in the role of reacting. The pre-regulation deployment of facial recognition and autonomous systems represents a quintessential example of a recurring chasm between regulation and compliance. Even better-faith efforts, like the OECD Principles of Artificial Intelligence, are marred due to the absence of governing frameworks, making their impact declaratory in scale and insufficient. Added to these challenges is the issue of an asymmetry of regulation in global economic power: the economics of the developed world dictate global norms. In contrast, developing countries' economies are primarily excluded from meaningful involvement and cannot exert their interests in these new structures.

Data localisation policies and digital sovereignty simultaneously fragment attempts at governance by making national sovereignty precede global interoperability. Moreover, amid such fragmentation, global cooperation's imperative is as strong as ever, as cyber attacks and AI threats transcend borders with impunity. More regulative possibility, however, is less dependent on fixed universality but on malleable, modular systems respectful of nationally diverse contexts yet in consensus on foundational principles—transparency, accountability, and balance. The caveat, however, is that this must be accompanied by genuine inclusion of the Global South in norm-making processes, not as passive recipients of standards but as co-authors of joint digital futurity. In the absence of such recalibration, global regulation would reinforce current disadvantages in the name of cooperation, allowing the mighty among us to take charge of the global ordering of technologies on their terms.

Ethical weaknesses inherent in algorithmic decision-making are the uncomfortable irony of artificial intelligence—objective, efficient technology is prone to replicating the human bigotries it aims to eradicate. Developed based on data biased by pre-existing injustice, AI applications inevitably replicate inherent bias, yielding algorithmic outputs biased along race, gender, and class. Misidentification devices such as face scanners for people of color or gender-biased hiring systems are not the exception but are symptomatic of underlying structural flaws in which social injustice is built into machine intelligence design.

The difficulty is not in the utopian pursuit of bias-free systems—a certainty—but in confronted political and epistemic assumptions through data collection, model building, and deployment. Developers, separated from the day-to-day experience of those whose lives their systems touch, inadvertently embed exclusions in automated systems. Not less troubling is the new norm of commercial intimacy harvesting, national security excavation, and commercial personalisation in the name of national security, commercial personalisation, or administrative efficiency. Algorithmically processing and harvesting intimate information without meaningful consent undermines the dignity and freedom of the people, particularly in those jurisdictions where legal recourse is not available or is applied discriminatively.

Algorithmic bias manifests in forms such as *historical bias*, *representation bias*, and *measurement bias*. In employment, Amazon's AI hiring tool showed gender bias due to training data favoring male resumes (Dastin, 2018). In law enforcement, predictive policing tools like PredPol disproportionately targeted minority neighborhoods, reinforcing systemic discrimination (Richardson et al., 2019). In credit scoring, algorithms have penalized minority applicants despite similar financial profiles, due to biased data inputs (Hurley & Adebayo, 2017). These biases can entrench social inequalities, demanding regulatory oversight and inclusive data practices.

While China's Social Credit System, where behavior tracking is paired with penalised rule, is a system that enlists AI in service not for the benefit of society but for the power of the state—a cautionary note on the path that other liberal democracies take that use such technology in technocratic guise—data mining by-tech monopolies increasingly blur the line between helpful user experience and nefarious manipulation, driving predictive analytics towards shaping consumer choice, healthcare intervention, and political affairs with subtle nudges. While the GDPR and its analogues are important in reclaiming data sovereignty and protecting users' rights, this absence of a level playing field in global harmonisation, combined with haphazard enforcement, dilutes their real-world effectiveness.

Regulatory mechanisms are likely to fall behind the pace of technological progress, and loopholes in the law in response offer possibilities that require accountability to assert themselves. Documents like UNESCO's Guidelines for Ethical AI and the OECD Principles on AI are handy skeletal outlines. However, as non-binding documents, they reveal a profound observation: Ethical rule exists on paper, but abusive practice is made structural. Prevention of any future in which rights are being cast upon the sacrifice of progress demands more than patchwork law – it demands a persistent, transnational commitment toward the formalisation of justice, transparency, and democratic principles in AI design and deployment.

With the arrival of the Algorithmic Age, the convergence of algorithmic power and national security brought together sovereignty protection and the eroding of human freedom in a dynamic intersection. As AI surveillance technologies combine face recognition, biometric tracking, and predictive policing, state authority over private lives expanded exponentially in scope and intensity and, in various cases, went above democratic accountability. These technologies, while all celebrated for making everyone secure and keeping crime away, can infuse social bias in law and perpetuate discriminatory surveillance forms, especially in minority communities.

China's Social Credit System, which systemically applies the algorithmic scoring of citizens based on conduct, demonstrates how these technologies can be applied as a tool of forced conformity and stifling dissent and exhibits the danger of techno-authoritarianism without suitable protection of human rights. Even in democratic nation-states, however, the division between protection and intrusion becomes progressively fuzzy. The European Union's GDPR is a central legal protection for the right to privacy. Its efficacy is repeatedly undermined by vying demands, primarily in counterterrorism, where cross-border data sharing and real-time tracking tend to supersede national regulation promises.

The US, for all constitutionally afforded protection, is experiencing the same paradox: intelligence organisations use AI for protection as digital privacy fades in the public imagination. The issue, in essence, is one of reconciling high demands for immediate security with the slow virtues of rights-oriented management. The UN, as well as other international human rights organisations such as Amnesty International, already called for AI responsibility based on transparency, accountability, and non-discrimination. Such measures as the UN's AI Principles are a normative code of practice. However, they are non-binding—once again exhibiting the ongoing mismatch between aspirational ethics as opposed to imposable protection.

Similarly, global realpolitik undermines multilateral alignment as great powers universally employ sovereignty in resisting international oversight of surveillance regimes. Here, the fractured mosaic of protection is found in which the rights of the individual citizen emanate outwards from their point of departure. At issue, then, are stakes higher than legal or technical ones: prevent a world in which AI is an opaque means of control rather than a force of democratic growth. It can be done not just through robust domestic regulation on the initiative of governments but also through binding treaties between states that involve corporations in accountability, so technological advances are not paid for in exchange for the liberty to which they dedicate themselves to safeguarding.

CASE STUDIES AND GLOBAL PERSPECTIVES

The U.S.-China Technological Rivalry

The U.S.-China competition, a precursor to a competition of ideologies and geo-economy on a deeper level, transcends a struggle for market supremacy to rebuilding power on the lines of digital infrastructure and strategic supply chains. Decoupling initiated by U.S. sanctions on companies such as Huawei, fueled by concerns of in-built espionage in the 5G infrastructure, demonstrated how deep semiconductors, previously a niche industrial group, sit at the epicenter of geopolitical power. Denial of Chinese access to high-end silicon by American companies such as Intel and Qualcomm and the coercion of allies to follow suit have made silicon a vector of strategic containment.

This calculus is two-faced. Worldwide supply chain interruptions in the chip industry have uncovered weaknesses in the Chinese and international tech ecosystem, engaging top companies like TSMC and Samsung in a precisely calibrated game of diplomatic whack-a-mole. China's reply, based on initiatives like "Made in China 2025," is a move toward technological self-sufficiency, not so much for resilience as a self-conscious effort to replace Western technological hegemony. This drive has stimulated domestic technology development and catalysed suspicion, driving a wedge between global standards and collaborative models. The focal point of this disruption is cybersecurity—a quickly militarising domain in which both nations increasingly accuse each other of state-sponsored hacking, intellectual property thievery, and destruction of key infrastructure.

China's Social Credit System exemplifies *Constructivism*, reflecting state-driven norms to shape citizen behavior via digital surveillance and moral evaluation (Creemers, 2018). In contrast, the U.S. CLOUD Act aligns with *Realism*, emphasizing state sovereignty and security through legal authority to access cross-border data (Swire & Hemmings, 2019). While China's system reinforces internal socio-political order, the U.S. framework protects strategic interests in a multipolar digital landscape. These regimes reveal how surveillance policies serve differing ideological and geopolitical priorities under distinct theoretical paradigms.

Diplomatic negotiations, such as in the 2015 bilateral cyber agreement, have hit a snag, with attacks persisting relentlessly and the digital nature of attributions remaining unclear. The result is a race in code that has no end, with the inclusion of AI and quantum adding to the mix in already precarious ground. For third-party nations, particularly in Europe, Africa, and Southeast Asia, this rivalry necessitates unavoidable choices—between the cost-effectiveness and sheer size of Chinese technology, security guarantees, and strategic coordination from the U.S. The result is a disjointed digital space where infrastructure decision-making is a surrogate for state-wide political allegiances.

However, ironically enough, this rivalry has also spurred significant R&D investment in green technology, AI, and new communication systems. The worry is the unchecked race in techno-nationalism, where technology is turned into a zero-sum game, with global standards eroded by suspicion of the global player. Lacking the frameworks of cooperation to buffer such a race, the danger is not just bifurcated technology but a world increasingly subject to infrastructural suspicion, not cooperation.

The EU's Approach to Technological Sovereignty

EU's drive for technological sovereignty is a purposeful remapping of digital regulation to gain normative authority in a U.S. corporate-led world in contrast to state-led integration in China. Drawing in by steps such as the General Data Protection Regulation (GDPR) and the incoming AI Act, the EU frames itself as a protector of ethically led innovations, where data rights, accountability of algorithms, and human dignity are guiding principles rather than secondary considerations. The global magnetism of the GDPR was not merely in the legislative template but in its intellectual statement that private data is not a commodity but a rights-infused expression of self. The argument made on the world beyond Europe affects regimes.

Despite this, this moral certainty is purchased at the expense of its compliance cost, which is prohibitive for small companies, and cross-border data transfer on which economic flexibility is built is hindered by bureaucracy. AI Act, in placing risk-based categorisation and precautionary measures on high-risk systems, pushes the EU towards prioritising caution over technological progress in no uncertain terms. While the intent with which it attempts to contain algorithmic harm is commendable, critics fear that it will smother the Union's competitiveness in nascent areas such as AI and driverless cars.

All this, however, is purchased at a price. Its compliance cost is difficult for small companies to absorb, and bureaucracy makes cross-border data transfer, the foundation on which economic flexibility is made possible, cumbersome. In classifying high-risk systems based on risk-based categorisation and precautionary measures, the AI Act is taking the EU toward putting caution before technological progress. Adaptable as the spirit in which it aims to contain algorithmic harm is, critics fear that it will choke the Union's competitiveness in nascent domains like AI and autonomous vehicles.

Nevertheless, Europe's ambitions are frustrated by its technology deficits, especially in semiconductors and platform-based capabilities. Here is the irony: sovereignty is mobilised to escape dependency, yet by its very nature, interdependence is built-in in a digitised world. Therefore, the EU's bet is not one of insulation but of influence—of defining rules in a disputed digital order by regulation, diplomacy, and values, if not by commanding in terms of hardware or sheer capital.

Huawei is set to begin mass shipments of its advanced Ascend 910C AI chip, aiming to provide an alternative to Nvidia's H20 chip amidst U.S. export restrictions. The 910C combines two 910B chips, delivering performance on par with Nvidia's H100, and is expected to become the primary hardware platform for China's AI development. In November 2023, OpenAI experienced a significant leadership upheaval when CEO Sam Altman was fired and rehired within five days. The incident highlighted internal tensions regarding transparency and leadership style, ultimately leading to a restructured board and Altman's reinstatement. In early 2025, the U.S. Supreme Court upheld a federal law effectively banning TikTok unless its China-based owner divests the platform. The decision was based on concerns over national security and data privacy, reflecting broader apprehensions about foreign influence on digital platforms.

The Role of Emerging Markets in Technological Competition

The emergent digital ecosystems in emerging markets such as India, Brazil, and Nigeria represent a critical realignment of the game of tech geopolitics worldwide, as the platform for innovation is no longer dominated by the traditional centers of power. No longer are they distant secondary actors, as they are becoming increasingly central forces of digital transformation, harnessing demographics, entrepreneurial dynamism, and experiments in the laboratory of policies to design the 21st-century digital economy geographies. India's entry onto the public platforms of Aadhaar and UPI, backed by a growing spirit of startups, makes it a strong player in digital finance, healthcare technology, and AI-driven administration.

However, this technological belligerence is complicated by strategic entanglements, the most extreme in contested digital territory. India's exclusion of Huawei in deploying 5G networks demonstrates how new economics are obliged to navigate global competition as recipients and geoeconomic actors, aligning in specific blocs in exchange for conformity. Brazil and Nigeria also map contested digital spaces, navigating the technologically driven growth by weighing foreign dependence risks in deploying cloud infrastructure, surveillance technologies, and platform monopolies.

The agronomic and financial solutions explosion in Nigeria underlines the deep entwinement of social transformation and digital technology. However, these solutions are structurally vulnerable to cyberattacks, data breaches, and infrastructure vulnerabilities. These contradictions are articulated in digital sovereignty discourses, where emerging markets are compelled to balance hopes for locally controlled solutions versus structural restrictions in the form of transnational technologies' ecosystems. The importance of self-reliance—sought in the drive for indigenous chip manufacturing by India and in Brazil's plan to localise data—evinces strategic caution and a more profound desire to inscribe the nation's agency in the architecture of the digital destiny.

However, their potential to bring such agendas to life is distorted and often constrained by budgetary shortcomings, skill shortages, and institutional weaknesses in cyber-security management. In addition, algorithmic, AI-driven management creates new vulnerabilities as markets increasingly infuse predictability mechanisms into the arenas of security and policy-making processes. The current supervisory arrangement does not allow for this evolution. This unleashes a dilemma: in their competition to modernise, compete globally, and exercise sovereignty, these states can fall into traps of digital dependency and patterns of epistemic imbalance, hence compromising their sovereignty in the long term. In the end, their success hinges on their capacity to build plural visions of digital development—ones in which global norms are entwined with local requirements and where innovation is a leading force toward equitable, secure, and self-governance-oriented futures

FUTURE TRENDS: NAVIGATING THE ROAD AHEAD

The Future of Geopolitics in the Algorithmic Age

With the Algorithmic Age, the geopolitics of tomorrow are increasingly determined by algorithmic architecture, ethical regulation, and infrastructural sovereignty, as opposed to the familiar silhouettes of military alliances or economic pacts. Power in the modern era vests in whoever innovates and legislates precisely, where AI, blockchain protocols, and quantum-encrypted infrastructures become the medium of power. While the transnational competition pitting the US against China continues to drive the agenda, with Washington employing chip superiority and cyberspace diplomacy against Beijing's tech autarky and AI nationalism, the binarity of this debate is eroding. The European Union, in its aggressive regulation mechanisms such as the GDPR and the AI Act, articulates a model of normative sovereignty in which raw technological capability is replaced by ethical authority, reshaping leadership in terms of imposing global norms regarding privacy, openness, and algorithmic accountability.

Parallel to this, India's digital drive brings to the forefront techno-national realignment—policy, platform creation, and Indigenous AI research—toward a push not only to be a player in the global digital order of the day but also to define its contours. Other emerging powers, Nigeria and Brazil, despite infrastructure deficits, are being integrated into regional digital configurations, imprinting conceptions of development that are wired to local needs and epistemic diversities.

Nevertheless, looming over this pluralism is the spectre of bifurcation, as hostile data standards and security regimes threaten to split the digital common space. Fragmentation is not technical but political, characterised by competing surveillance paradigms, autonomy, and rights. International institutions hope to play their roles as arbiters, yet are often overshadowed by the gravitational forces of national interest. What is encountered is multipolar algorithmic topography in which power is negotiated rather than exercised and sovereignty is relative rather than absolute. In this geometry of change, the imperative is not the dominance of digital space but mapping its asymmetry—aligning innovation with ethical pluralism, protecting national interest without jeopardising interoperability, and anchoring power in structures that protect dignity, not dominance.

Navigating Technological Competition and National Security

With national security increasingly tied up in technologically dense infrastructures, states face a harsh dilemma—securing infrastructures of importance without cutting off the transnational currents of innovation on which digital ecologies depend. America's use of export controls on AI and semiconductors is an act of security calculation to temper the benefits of rivalry. The containment policy undermines supply chains dependent on crossing borders and hinders cooperative knowledge flows. China's "Made in China 2025" is likewise a push towards independent technological ecologies with local champions designed to be able to wean themselves off international dependency.

Both of them, in as far as they aim for national resiliency, drive an international movement toward techno-fragmentation, where decoupling is not optional but necessary. Increasingly more small and rising countries in the aftermath are faced with diminished agency—cut off from selecting important infrastructure or directed toward divisive alignment with powerful technologies' allies. Pursuance of digital sovereignty, such as in the European Union AI Act addressing localising data, visa restrictions on foreign technologies, and strict platform control, also reveals another conflict: the need to hold on to ethical norms can undermine local pilots and mute innovative voices.

A higher crisis is, however, the inadequate binding, interoperable international governance system. Differences in regulation—market-led regimes like those in the U.S., in contrast to the rights-based ones like the GDPR—have led to fragmented zones of regulation that multinational corporations cross with strategic freedom, undermining accountability. Even the nods toward convergence in the dialogues sponsored by the OECD and UN are compromised by the imperatives of soft power and competing national interests. All else that is additionally required dramatically is a reframe of AI in everything other than the geopolitically outsourced exercise of sovereignty—a system of accountability in which justice, transparency, and interoperability are firmly based. Unless such calibration happens, the algorithm-driven future risks being less of a collective vision of progress and more topographic, relying on exclusion, asymmetry, and smoldering technological disenfranchisement.

In 2023–2024, digital diplomacy emerged as a pivotal tool for states to project soft power within multilateral arenas. India's G20 presidency exemplified this trend; Prime Minister Modi leveraged platforms like Twitter and Instagram to disseminate India's leadership narratives on climate action and sustainable development, thereby enhancing India's global image and fostering international collaboration. Concurrently, the United Nations employed its soft power by promoting the Sustainable Development Goals (SDGs), engaging diverse stakeholders through digital campaigns to address global challenges and build consensus. These instances underscore how digital platforms have become instrumental in shaping international discourse and advancing national interests through attraction and persuasion

The more significant crisis, then, is the lack of a binding, interoperable system of global regulation. Asymmetry in regulation—market-first models, in the style of the U.S., versus rights-based systems, in the style of the GDPR—have produced disconnected spaces of regulation in which multinational corporations operate in strategic agility, frequently escaping accountability. Even as the OECD AI principles and UN-sponsored talks gesture toward convergence, they are undermined by the demands of soft power and rival national agendas. The most urgent need is a recasting of AI regulation as anything other than a geopolitics of sovereignty expansion but a cross-border commons—a politics of built-in accountability through interoperability, openness, and equity. Unless such a realignment occurs, the algorithmic future could be a shared zone of advance or an expanse of exclusion, asymmetry, and smoldering technological disenfranchisement.

IMPLICATIONS

Theoretical analysis of the Algorithmic Epoch requires a paradigmatic upheaval in geopolitics and international relations because technological sovereignty takes over territorial dominance in global geopolitics. Theoretical concepts like Technological Nationalism and Determinism, historically on the fringes, are today the leading issues in geopolitics, recasting the method by which states extend their influence and defend their interests. Traditional conceptions like Realism and Liberalism must evolve considering algorithmic militarisation, the weaponisation of information, and the integration of AI by governments.

This practically necessitates a realignment of policies at a national level—digital resilience must enter national security policies since cyberspace threats are no longer peripheral to state weakness but are at the center. Techno-nationalist agendas also drive the conflict between regulation and technology, necessitating a wonderful dance between digital protectionism and worldwide interoperability. The ethical deployment of AI is necessary for companies doing business here, but it is not a preferred option.

Compliance with transnational standards like the GDPR heralds a promise of fairness and transparency, but is also the backbone of digital legitimacy in the global economies. At a time of algorithmic obscurity and geopolitical ambiguity, preparedness to cope with a crisis and responsible stewardship of the data become as essential for business viability as product innovation or market position, interlocking state and business actors in a shared responsibility of technological futures.

METAFRAMEWORK

Figure 1. Techno-political dynamics (Authors)

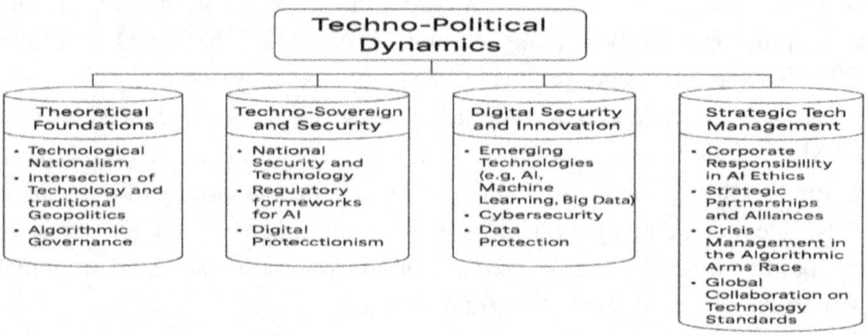

Figure 1 illustrates the primary components of "Techno-Political Dynamics," a conceptual framework on intersecting politics, technology, and security. The framework has four primary pillars. The "Theoretical Foundations" pillar concentrates on themes like technological nationalism, the interplay of technology with geopolitics, and algorithmic governance implications. The second pillar, "Techno-Sovereign and Security," focuses on national security, technology, AI's regulating regimes, and digital protectionism. The third pillar, "Digital Security and Innovation," concentrates on the implications of emerging technologies, such as AI, machine learning, and big data, as well as on pertinent issues like cybersecurity, data protection, and data sovereignty. Last, strategic tech management confronts corporate responsibility in

AI ethics, strategic partnerships, and alliances as valuable assets, handling crises in the race for algorithms and international cooperation in setting technology standards. The model integrates the complex interplay among technological advancement, security, governing, and strategic management.

The conceptual framework of Techno-Political Dynamics can be significantly enriched by integrating real-world actors and theoretical foundations under each pillar. The Theoretical Foundations pillar draws on concepts like technological nationalism, visible in state-led strategies such as China's Made in China 2025 and the U.S. CHIPS and Science Act, which reflect realist attempts to assert technological sovereignty (Atkinson, 2022). Algorithmic governance, as discussed by Zuboff (2019), highlights how Big Tech firms such as Google and Meta exercise decision-making power through opaque algorithmic systems, revealing the constructivist interplay between norms and digital infrastructures. The Techno-Sovereign and Security pillar is reinforced by the actions of regulatory entities like the European Commission, which has promoted digital sovereignty through laws such as the GDPR and the proposed EU AI Act. These initiatives aim to reduce dependencies on foreign technology, echoing neo-institutionalist perspectives on the formalization of digital power structures (Milanesi, 2023). In Digital Security and Innovation, cybersecurity agencies like the U.S. CISA and private firms such as CrowdStrike are central to addressing systemic risks posed by emerging technologies. High-profile incidents like the SolarWinds breach underscore Ulrich Beck's (1992) "risk society" thesis, where innovation and vulnerability are increasingly intertwined. Finally, the Strategic Tech Management pillar encompasses the ethics and governance efforts of corporate actors like OpenAI and Apple, as well as international coalitions such as the G20 and the OECD. These actors promote AI ethics, standardization, and collaborative frameworks for managing the algorithmic arms race, reflecting stakeholder theory and global governance approaches (Floridi & Cowls, 2021; OECD, 2023). Each pillar, therefore, not only captures thematic focus areas but also embodies active techno-political negotiations shaped by global actors and theoretical paradigms.

CONCLUSION

The dual nature of technology as both a facilitator and a destabiliser of global governance is a quintessential irony of global relations in the modern world. On one hand, new technologies augment transnational collaboration—whether it is the potential of humanitarian support through blockchain, disaster support enabled by Artificial Intelligence, or weather forecasting using data analysis. Efforts like the EU's GDPR and leveraging digital platforms for advancing UN Sustainable Development Goals indicate how technology can transcend jurisdictions and ensure collective progress when aligned in rights-based processes.

However, this possibility is further diminished as increasing geopolitical fault lines are deepened primarily through states' exercise of technological sovereignty as they vie for strategic hegemony. Competition between the US and China on 5G, AI, and semiconductors has ushered in technologically driven protectionism, weaponising interdependence and separating the digital commons. Cyber intrusions, intellectual property scandals, and state-led espionage are expressions of distrust in the virtual arena, with the objective moving towards containment rather than cooperative management.

Regimes of regulation—though in emergence—are as yet not dynamic enough, overwhelmed by the pace of change in the face of unaccountable, tech-monopoly power, directing norms in a not democratically controllable manner. The failure to envision a globally integrated GOV AI risks power becoming concentrated in bastions of power, deepening inequality, and suppressing marginalised voices. This imbalance demands more than compliance and dialogue; it demands a new conceptualisation of global governance that is tech-savvy, ethically intelligent, and structurally inclusive in a manner wherein sovereignty is not exercised in separation but by interdependence exercised openly and fairly across borders.

REFERENCES

Achter, B. (2021). Regulating autonomous weapons: Ethical implications and international legal frameworks. *Journal of Military Ethics*, *20*(1), 15–34.

Amnesty International. (2019). The Role of Artificial Intelligence in Human Rights. Retrieved from https://www.amnesty.org

Atkinson, R. D. (2022). *The Case for National Industrial Strategy to Counter China's*. Technological Rise. ITIF.

Beck, U. (1992). *Risk Society: Towards a New Modernity*. SAGE Publications. Floridi, L., & Cowls, J. (2021). A unified framework of five principles for AI in society.

Brynjolfsson, E., & McAfee, A. (2014). *The second machine age: Work, progress, and prosperity in a time of brilliant technologies*. W.W. Norton & Company.

Cave, S., & Dignum, V. (2019). The regulatory challenges of AI and machine learning. *Journal of Technology Policy*, *28*(2), 34–45.

Cheng, D. (2020). Techno-nationalism and the global race for AI supremacy. *Harvard Journal of International Affairs*, *30*(1), 12–23.

Creemers, R. (2018). China's Social Credit System: An Evolving Practice of Control. *SSRN*. DOI: 10.2139/ssrn.3175792

Digital India. (2020). Digital India Initiative. Retrieved from https://www.digitalindia.gov.in

European Commission. (2021). Artificial Intelligence Act Proposal. Retrieved from https://ec.europa.eu

European Union. (2018). General Data Protection Regulation (GDPR). Retrieved from https://gdpr.eu

European Union. (2020). The Digital Single Market Strategy for Europe. Retrieved from https://ec.europa.eu/digital-strategy

Feng, E. (2020). US-China tech tensions: The battle for control of the future. *Foreign Affairs*, *99*(6), 45–58.

Gartzke, E. (2020). The cybersecurity arms race: State competition in the age of AI. *International Security Review*, *45*(3), 99–118.

Global New Light of Myanmar. (2024, October 29). *Diplomacy in the Digital Age: How Social Media is Transforming Global Politics.* https://www.gnlm.com.mm/diplomacy-in-the-digital-age-how-social-media-is-transforming-global-politics/ Global New Light of Myanmar

Global Trade. Perspectives from the U.S. and China. Harvard Business Review. European Union. (2020). Digital Single Market Strategy for Europe. Retrieved from https://ec.europa.eu/digital-strategy

Harvard Data Science Review, 3(1). Milanesi, C. (2023). *Gaia-X and Europe's Digital Sovereignty Aspirations*. Forrester Research.

IISS. (2025). *Global defence spending soars to new high.* https://www.iiss.org/online-analysis/military-balance/2025/02/global-defence-spending-soars-to-new-high/IISS

Lin, P. (2020). Autonomous weapons systems and the laws of war. *International Review of the Red Cross*, *102*(913), 599–618.

Liu, H. (2020). AI, surveillance, and authoritarianism: China's social credit system. *Journal of Global Policy*, *34*(2), 45–61.

NATO Parliamentary Assembly. (2024). *2024 - NATO AND AI - REPORT - CLEMENT - 058 STC.* https://www.nato-pa.int/document/2024-nato-and-ai-report-clement-058-stcnato-pa.int

OECD. (2019). OECD Principles on Artificial Intelligence. OECD. https://www.oecd.org/ai/

OECD. (2020). Global Digital Transformation: Emerging Markets and Technological Growth. Retrieved from https://www.oecd.org

OECD. (2020). OECD AI Principles. Retrieved from https://www.oecd.org Zeng, M., & Williamson, P. (2019). The Impact of Technological Competition on

OECD. (2023). *Framework for the Classification of AI Systems.* https://oecd.ai Zuboff, S. (2019). *The Age of Surveillance Capitalism.* PublicAffairs.

OECD. (2024). *A Preliminary Mapping of Data Localisation Measures.* https://www.oecd.org/en/publications/a-preliminary-mapping-of-data-localisation-measures_c5ca3fed-en.htmlOECD

Rosenberg, M., Frenkel, S., & Conger, K. (2018). Russian interference in the 2016 U.S. presidential election. The New York Times. https://www.nytimes.com/2018/02/16/us/politics/russian-election-interference

Swire, P., & Hemmings, J. (2019). The CLOUD Act: A Preliminary Assessment. *Journal of National Security Law & Policy, 12*(1), 1–33. https://jnslp.com/wp-content/uploads/2019/06/The-CLOUD-Act-A-Preliminary-Assessment.pdf

UNCTAD. (2024). *Global trade hits record $33 trillion in 2024, driven by services and developing economies.* https://unctad.org/news/global-trade-hits-record-33-trillion-2024-driven-services-and-developing-economies

United Nations. (2020). AI and the Global Future: A UN Perspective. Retrieved from https://www.un.org

United Nations. (2021). Artificial Intelligence and National Security: The Need for Global Cooperation. Retrieved from https://www.un.org

United Nations Department of Economic and Social Affairs. (2025, February). *UN soft power and the SDGs: Promoting peace and security in conflict.* https://desapublications.un.org/un-desa-voice/sdg-blog/february-2025/un-soft-power-and-sdgs-promoting-peace-and-security-conflict

United States Congress. (2018). Clarifying Lawful Overseas Use of Data (CLOUD) Act. Retrieved from https://www.congress.gov

United States Congress. (2018). Export Control Reform Act (ECRA) and National Security Concerns. Retrieved from https://www.congress.gov

U.S. Department of Commerce. (2020). Huawei and National Security. Retrieved from https://www.commerce.gov

Zengler, T. (2021). AI in cybersecurity: Mitigating risks in the age of algorithmic warfare. *Cybersecurity Review, 10*(3), 12–24.

Chapter 4
Cyber Warfare and Blurring Lines Between State and Non-State Actors

Vidisha Shekhawat
https://orcid.org/0009-0009-7816-3591
Manipal University Jaipur, India

Pranjal Khare
https://orcid.org/0000-0002-9937-9588
Jindal Global Law School, O.P. Jindal Global University, India

Kiet Le Hoang
https://orcid.org/0009-0002-9968-1952
Vietnam National University, Hanoi, Vietnam

ABSTRACT

Cyber warfare has transformed the digital realm into a critical conflict domain, marked by an increasing convergence of state and non-state actors. Initially dominated by nation-states, cyberattacks now involve a diverse range of entities, from hacktivists and cybercriminals to terrorist groups wielding sophisticated capabilities. The rise of state-sponsored cyber operations has initiated a new cold war characterized by persistent digital espionage and sabotage. Concurrently, non-state actors are employing cyber tools for various motives, often achieving levels of sophistication comparable to state-level attacks. This blurring of lines complicates attribution, heightens the risk of unintended escalation, and challenges established international norms. The future of cyber warfare anticipates greater complexity

DOI: 10.4018/979-8-3373-1727-4.ch004

with the proliferation of advanced technologies. The growing interconnectedness of critical infrastructure will expand vulnerabilities, necessitating novel defence and deterrence strategies to address the evolving threats posed by both state and non-state actors in this domain.

INTRODUCTION

The times when wars were fought only on battlegrounds are gone; now they happen in silence within the realms of cyberspace making the nations fall & rise with digital clicks. The traditional warfare included lands, seas, and air as battlegrounds, however, with growing technology a fifth dimension has found its way to hostilities that require data breaches and hackers rather than soldiers. Cyberwarfare involves digital attacks to incapacitate a nation's military e-mail systems, derail trains, damage power grids, and even uncontrollable satellites. Technology led to the creation of the internet making the world accessible to almost everything breaking all barriers. There are numerous iterations through which cyber warfare takes place; they include hacking and cyber espionage, disinformation campaigns, cyber-attacks on critical infrastructure, and so on. Cyberwarfare is roaring, too rapidly due to several reasons including lower costs, ambiguity in legal frameworks, and requiring lesser human resources while prompting numerous threats. Stealing data and information has serious repercussions; it is limited to hacking for profit making or bank frauds, and it involves bringing down a nation's governance. Cyber warfare attacks are made to cripple a nation's military by other nation's governments. However, the geopolitics in cyber warfare does not only involve the state actors but nonstate actors as well. The growing participation of non-state actors and private entities has made it the most difficult problem to resolve. When there are no barriers, security becomes the utmost concern requiring sturdy weapons to fight back to attacks. In other words, digitally stored data includes confidential and private content that requires to be protected from breach which can only be done through strong and reliable cyber security. There is ample awareness amongst the nations regarding the threats that cyberspaces impose; the UK, USA, and even NATO have been spreading awareness and attempting to recommend nations to operate with the domain of legal approach in this new fighting arena (Robinson et al., 2015).

State actors have been using cyber warfare as their military strategy for a couple of decades to ensure national security; from espionage to information warfare many operations have been conducted. The operations ensure plausible deniability while garnering power in cyberspace. One of the examples is China allegedly infiltrating the U.S. networking to cripple its corporate network and defence mechanism. There have been multiple high-profile attacks used as tactics to overpower other states to remain in or to gain power. Due to the anonymity of cyber operations, the attempts made by international organizations to regulate cyberspaces have become challenging. APT10 is one of the espionage campaigns allegedly used by China to target intellectual property and defence information from Western nations. Similarly, the 2016 Bangladesh bank heist, North Korea's Lazarus Group is linked with cyber heists to disrupt the economy and commit financial theft. Moreover, in the last two decades, the role of non-state actors has drastically increased, posing a predominant threat to state securities. Their role in cyberspace has made it even more complicated to regulate. Cyberwarfare is dangerous due to the requirements of the physical world, where geopolitics plays a major role in combating such threats (Arquilla, 2021).

Multiple malicious groups while nullifying the physical boundaries have equipped themselves with ways to pose threats to institutions that are cheaper and easier to use. The Lazarus Group is accountable for multiple financial cybercrimes, allegedly linked to North Korea; the 2014 Sony Pictures hack and the 2017 WannaCry ransomware attack are some of the examples. This way North Korea is operating cyberwarfare without having to face liability. Russia's Cozy Bear (APT29) and Fancy Bear (APT28) are allegedly associated with the Russian intelligence responsible for targeting Western nations and hacking the Democratic National Committee (DNC) in 2016. The nonstate actors may or may not be acting independently, nevertheless, if operations by non-state actors are providing them directions to avoid liability, it is difficult to determine. The source of the attacks cannot be determined creating blur lines between the role of state and non-state actors. The problem does not only lie with the legal framework, but it also lies in the determination of the source of the attacks. One such example is the Georgian cyberattacks in which either the non-state actors engaged in their independent capacity or alongside the state actors. The nonstate actors have a range of forms in which they can exist including small-scaled groups, large-scaled groups, formal or informal with complex working structures (Naseer, 2024).

Globally, the struggle for power amongst the state actors is ever incessant; such power comes with the strength of the military, finances, and other possessions of the nation. The geographical boundaries are determined for every nation to avoid conflict of interest, however, with the advancing technology physical barriers are no longer an obstacle. This has led to the absence of demarcation between the state and non-state actors. The nations have fronted tremendous harm by cyber-attacks; Estonia being attacked in 2007 is one of the examples facing the deadliest attack through cyberspace. The complexity of cyberspace operations has paved the way for state actors to sponsor or assist non-state actors in cyber warfare shielding themselves from detection and liability (Odoh, 2021).

The unrivalled challenge to regulating cyberwarfare is detecting the source due to the use of techniques including anonymization, false-flag operations decentralized networks. Unless a proper regulatory framework is implemented, global responses will continue to get complicated. The Tallinn Manual is an attempt to subject cyberspace to international law, however, there is still an absence of binding treaties governing state and non-state behaviour in cyberwarfare. It is inferred that the cooperation among the states is still fragmented, leading to the continuation of cyber threats to global security. The critical struggle in cyber conflict originates from continuous attribution problems. By nature, cyberattacks transpire in complex internet spaces which enable attackers to maintain uncertain responsibility. Attackers hide their origins by utilizing different methods such as IP spoofing in addition to proxy servers and hacked third-party networks as well as AI-generated traffic imitations of legitimate activities. The attribution crisis represents a core issue that both undermines police operations and fails to achieve international relations success. It becomes extremely difficult to pursue legal action against wrongdoers when they use methods that prevent their identity from being established. Ineffective national responses are hindered when attributions are made too soon or incorrectly as such mistakes lead countries to experience diplomatic tensions and potentially accidental escalation of threats (Check, 2022).

THE EVOLUTION OF CYBER-WARFARE

Cyber warfare has evolved from simple digital skirmishes to state-sponsored sophisticated operations, leading to the growth & importance of cyberspace in the dynamics of global security. If we trace it back to its roots, it all started with radio communications and the uprising of a technological body called Electronic Warfare (EW), which is now involved in cyber warfare. The nations started to realize the potential of cyberspace in the 1990s to the extent that they began to use cyberspace operations for the advancement of their military maneuvers. Ever since, the progression in technology rapidly increased; paving the way for state entities to develop even stronger technological processes. Global connectivity arose along with the rise in cyber-attack threats driving the states to develop their cyber capabilities. The cyber-attacks against Estonia in April 2007 in the form of Distributed Denial of Service disrupting Estonia's infrastructure followed by an attack on Georgia's network in August 2008 ignited other state's cyber strategies across the globe (Stiennon, 2015).

The Cold War between the U.S. and the Soviet Union significantly contributed to the shaping of technological advancements as they were closely associated with national security concerns. Before the wide accessibility of the internet, the nations involved in the Cold War were actively engaged in the domain of cyberspace. It was pertinent that the nations protected their intelligence and military data by ensuring secured communication networks. In the 1960s ARPANET (Advanced Research Projects Agency Network) was one of the important projects initiated by the U.S. Department of Defence (DOD) to resist any probable attacks by the Soviet Union by creating a decentralized endurable network. Meanwhile, techniques involving intercepting & disrupting Western communications attracted the Soviet Union's cyber espionage strategies even before the emergence of hacking tools. The U.S. used encrypted cyber techniques extensively for cyber espionage to decrypt communications made by the Soviet Union. Modern cyber warfare that we see today is rooted in the hacking and data interpretation techniques used by the Soviet KGB and Russian intelligence services. In the late Cold War era, cyber infiltration threats paved the way for cyber security development such as firewalls, intrusion detection systems, and encryption techniques. Thus, the development of cyberspace techniques for military infiltration and cyber defence strategies was fast paced after the Cold War era (Cavelty, 2024).

In 1982 one of the most known cyber warfare was witnessed when the Soviet gas pipeline was sabotaged by the CIA which came to be known as Farewell Dossier, a covert operation. The CIA's "Logic Bomb" – a software controlling Soviet pipeline operations was a malicious code planted by the U.S. that caused an intentional overpressure in the Soviet pipelines leading to a ponderous explosion. The power of cyber warfare strategies was influenced by the demonstration of this landmark incident shaping the future of cyber warfare as a military tactic for the nation-states. Traditional cyber warfare revolved predominantly around cyber espionage; however, modern warfare has advanced into an influential instrument for the states to destroy infrastructures, exploiting public opinions and influencing the dynamics of geopolitics. The prolonged Ukraine-Russia war (2018-Present) has turned hybrid with the intervention of real-time cyber battles. The *NotPetya ransomware* attack by Russia in 2017 on Ukraine incapacitated its banks, media, infrastructure, and power grids crippling the entire nation's electricity. The Russia-Ukraine hybrid warfare has set a precedent for conflicts in the future leading to the invention of modern models of cyber offensives with military aggression. The Rivalry between the U.S. and China has extended to engagement in state-sponsored cyber espionage. China is allegedly stealing intellectual property from U.S technology firms, meanwhile, sanctions have been imposed on Chinese tech companies like Huawei by the U.S. over concerns of cyber security (Gurung, 2025).

The study of cyber warfare benefits from analysis through various International Political Economy (IPE) theoretical perspectives. The key International Political Economy (IPE) theories explain the dynamics of cyber warfare. Mercantilism/ Neomercantilism: States implement cyber capabilities to achieve both economic security and strategic industrial protection while building up their national financial strength. Through state-sponsored theft of intellectual property directed at technology firms neomercantilist governments achieve both competitive disadvantage of their rivals and establish control of essential digital markets. Whereas liberalism is an economic interdependence theory that explains how cyber-attacks break global trade connections and supply chain operations and financial exchange pathways which negate the supposed economic growth delivered through integration. Businesses like Maersk and Merck suffered more than USD 10 billion in damage when NotPetya ransomware hit in 2017 as the attack cut off international trade while damaging investor faith in the respective firms. Constructivism theory states that the internet rules alongside institutional frameworks collectively form the basis by which states act online. The development of cyber norms relies on instruments such as UN Group of Governmental Experts (GGE) reports together with the Tallinn Manual. Through constructivist analysis we can see how both norm entrepreneurship activities and digital-sovereignty movements direct state actions toward building cooperative cyber governance systems (Lande & Danyk, 2025).

THE NEW "COLD WAR" – CYBER OPERATIONS SPONSORED BY THE STATES

The engagement of state actors in digital warfare has made cyberspace a new battleground; requiring no soldiers to fight the wars while allowing the states to change the geopolitical dynamics. Cyber espionage, ransomware attacks, data breaches, and large-scale disinformation campaigns are the new tactics referred to as the "Digital Cold War". Through this digital warfare state actors have the advantage of plausible deniability while disrupting adversaries, stealing sensitive intelligence, and manipulating public opinion. There are various advantages to which states prefer cyber-attacks over traditional military strikes. One of the advantages is that digital operations are cheaper than traditional military operations; the objectives of the war can be achieved without deploying an entire military division as a few skilled hackers can do the same. While deploying digital attacks the states can avoid confrontation or international sanctions making attributions difficult. These also ensure that widespread destruction is avoided as digital attacks can target a specific system making it more politically palatable. There are a few nation-states that have emerged as dominant players with their different strategies and objectives (Nardi, 2021).

The National Security Agency (NSA) and the United States Cyber Command (USCYBERCOM) are leading the United States to have the most advanced cyber warfare infrastructures. Their responsibility is to manage and tackle offensive and defensive cyber operations ensuring the security of the nation through digital means. Their strategies include pre-emptive strikes to ensure that the adversaries' cyber capabilities are disabled even before any attacks can be launched by them. This is done through hacking into foreign networks, disrupting communication channels, and planting vulnerabilities that can be exploited if needed. Stuxnet worm (Stuxnet Operations, 2010) was one of the countermeasures employed by the U.S. to disrupt Iran's nuclear program while sending a strong message to the adversaries without disrupting strategic ambiguity. The defensive strategies of the U.S. include both national defence and corporate resilience against cyber threats. The Cybersecurity and Infrastructure Security Agency (CISA) works to ensure that critical infrastructure is secure including energy grids, financial systems, and government databases. Russia's electrical grid was reportedly disrupted by the cyber command deployed by the U.S. through the implantation of malware aiming to deter Russian cyber activities while demonstrating U.S. cyber capabilities. In 2024 Hunt-Forward missions were operated by the Cyber National Mission Force (CNMF) that executed 22 deployments to various countries in collaboration with allies to identify cyber threats and enhance global cybersecurity. Whereas China has a formidable cyber apparatus fulfilling both domestic and international agendas (Eichensehr, 2022). China has an extensive internet surveillance system that controls the flow of information and monitors online activities. It allows its government to track its citizens' footprints, block unwanted websites, and filter foreign content. APT41 & APT10 are two major state-sponsored hacker groups that target foreign governments, corporations, and research institutions. These groups are linked to high-profile cyber-attacks operating on defence contractors, healthcare institutions, and cloud service providers with state backing. Chinese firms gain competitive advantages by stealing intellectual property and trade secrets frequently by deploying hackers which has led to disputes with major economic powers; specifically, the U.S. and European nations. Social media and news manipulation are another one of the tools used by China beyond espionage to shape international narratives and geopolitical interests (Basholli, 2022).

Russian strategy revolves around destabilizing political systems and is centered on information warfare and cyber sabotage. Their focus is more on psychological operations to weaken the adversaries from within by meddling in democratic processes like in the U.S. elections in 2016. Russia has mastered the art of disinformation warfare which helps them to influence the perception of the voters sowing discord and eroding the trust in democratic institutions. Facebook, Twitter, and YouTube are some of the social media platforms used as tools for media manipulation which goes beyond hacking, deepening societal rifts, distrust in electoral processes, and long-term instabilities within the U.S. Similarly, the French presidential elections in 2017 were targeted by the same playbook used for other democracies by Russia that focused on Emmanuel Macron's candidature. Efforts were made to influence Brexit debates by leaking emails, and propaganda, and spreading misleading narratives about the European Union. Troll farms are one of Russia's major disinformation tactics; the most well-known of them is the Internet Research Agency (IRA), which is headquartered in St. Petersburg. The IRA oversees running thousands of social media profiles that imitate actual users to disseminate extremist ideologies, fake narratives, and inaccurate information. Through the creation of false news items, memes, and commentary that support Russia's geopolitical objectives, trolls significantly influence the global conversation. Their primary objective is to undermine the trust in institutions, exploit social divisions, and boost extremist narratives. Moreover, Russia employs a hybrid warfare model that integrates information warfare with cyber sabotage and this strategy was quite evident in its conflicts against Ukraine where traditional military operations were complemented by digital attacks (Bussolati, 2015).

As cyber operations have become sophisticated, the line between state-sponsored hacking and the involvement of the private sector is becoming blurred. Governments are resorting to private companies, firms, and cyber mercenaries to carry out cyber espionage and influence campaigns allowing states to plausibly deny their involvement. It is often the case that governments employ private entities like NSO groups (Pegasus spyware creators), tech giants, and mercenaries, and sometimes their interests also align with the state interests. Firms like NSO provide advanced surveillance tools and expertise in hacking whereas companies like Microsoft, Google, and Huawei exert immense cyber control. The U.S. tech firms have chosen to resist government overreach unlike companies in China as they are state-controlled and play a more active role in cyber operations for the state. Groups like DarkMatter, and Emirati cyber firms are ex-intelligence offering their services to the highest bidders and are allegedly linked to states in carrying out cyber espionage, corporate sabotage, and campaign influence campaigns, making cyber mercenaries more popular. To gain strategic advantages, state actors are leveraging digital espionage, misinformation, and cyber sabotage reflecting a transition from traditional military strikes to cyber operations. As the lines between the state and private actors are becoming blurred with time, the future of warfare is likely to be dominated by the ones having stronger cybersecurity frameworks and international cooperation (Blank, 2013).

THEORETICAL FRAMEWORK FOR NON-STATE ACTORS

Non-state actors operating in cyber warfare require their own theoretical framework to analyze their operational motivations along with their available capabilities and effects within international relations. Hacktivist groups function as decentralized coalitions which share values instead of traditional formal organizational hierarchies according to Transnational Advocacy Network theory developed by Keck and Sikkink (Schmitt & Watts, 2016). Through digital media these scattered networks spread their shared values across the world to help movements expand past what one person can achieve. Private Military Companies (PMCs) reveal how cyber mercenary firms embrace market-driven models by delivering offensive and defensive cyber services that mimic traditional security services. State-aligned yet independent legal entities operate core platforms and exploit toolkits from cloud networks to provide spies and saboteurs and influence operators. The realist paradigm understands both hacktivists and cyber mercenaries serve as tools for power projection within digital spaces without state control, but constructivist models demonstrate how they function based on shared ethical principles and reputation effects. Academic studies combining these theoretical frameworks achieve more exact analysis of how non-state actors influence and transform the power structure in cyberspace (Raska, 2020).

Hacktivist collectives known as Transnational Advocacy Networks use loosely linked nodes to drive quick grassroots actions against perceived social injustices. Anonymous demonstrates a TAN network facilitating international volunteer participation in distributed denial-of-service (DDoS) attacks and data leak operations and defacement activities which target authoritarian governments and multinational organizations alongside judicial bodies accused of human rights violations. Open-source intelligence and encrypted communications tools such as Tor and Signal and social media amplification form the technical foundation of their action methods which combine to build public pressure on decision-makers. Through TAN theory researchers demonstrate that moral leverage based on naming and shaming alongside solidarity actions produces tangible results such as policy changes and financial sanctions. The indistinct border between activism and criminality generates obstacles for state responses because authorities face difficulties uniting rights-based standards and security protection goals. Normative ambiguity about hacktivist legitimacy reveals the necessity of creating a theoretical model which acknowledges their freedom-enabling capabilities alongside their ability to disrupt essential infrastructure (Lahmann, 2021).

The commercial cyber capabilities industry encompasses for-hire cyber operative firms such as DarkMatter and NSO Group and private "bug bounty" platforms which provide contracted services identical to PMCs of kinetic warfare. In addition to their operations, these firms attract ex-intelligence personnel and security hackers to create zero-day exploits alongside command-and-control infrastructure and social-engineering toolkits for their public sector and corporate customers (Raska, 2020). The firms operate through commercial agreements which create a facade of sponsor deniability while making it harder for defenders to trace origins of attacks. Through their framework the PMC framework reveals key challenges regarding responsibility: International humanitarian law addresses legitimate state actions, but cyber mercenaries exist in a confused legal area that must mostly follow contractual laws together with their undisclosed regulatory frameworks. The privatization of cyber force operations breaks the traditional monopoly states held on violence since non-state actors can conduct border-crossing operations without declaring intentions publicly. Analyzing cyber mercenaries using PMC principles allows both an assessment of their strategic advantages of quick deployment and specialized abilities and technical skills and their hidden status and raises vital moral concerns about digital space governance and state power delegation (Davis, 2021).

The strategic interaction between states and non-state actors exists within a complex and difficult terrain of ambiguity. According to "strategic ambiguity" (Bussolati, 2015) states use hacktivist and mercenary groups to achieve foreign policy goals without actively taking ownership of these activities. The ambiguous relationship generates a complex problem of holding parties responsible. A disruptive operation executed by a non-state actor prevents simple attribution of responsibility between this group and its state backer. Little legal clarity exists within international law because it extends across three different document collections: the Tallinn Manual, UN GGE reports, and national statutory frameworks. Constructivist theory proposes that evolving cyber norms which emerge from multistakeholder dialogues and technical standards (for example, IETF and W3C) will eventually establish proper boundaries between acceptable state–non-state partnerships while determining possible consequences for rule infringements. Cyber governance efforts remain behind the accelerating growth of non-state cyber actors because authoritative interstate treaties and implementing domestic laws are not yet established thus ensuring an unpredictable digital space where political power intersects with financial gains and principles frequently result in destabilizing developments.

ECONOMIC IMPACTS AND THE ROLE OF ECONOMIC ACTORS

National and global economies face massive financial loss from cyber warfare as attacks increase in both numbers and complexity thereby expanding both direct expenses and hidden costs. The NotPetya ransomware attack from 2017 which Russian state-sponsored actors most likely orchestrated cost consumers a total of USD 10 billion when it disrupted operations at Maersk and FedEx's TNT division and Merck along with their connected shipping and logistics and pharmaceutical supply chain networks. WannaCry disrupted more than 200,000 computers while targeting 150 nations that year it stopped vital NHS services along with numerous manufacturing and insurance companies causing damages exceeding USD 4 billion. The Lazarus Group of North Korea exploited SWIFT financial messaging network vulnerabilities to steal USD 81 million from the Bangladesh Bank during 2016 while demonstrating the vulnerability of cross-border payment systems. These incidents produce important secondary expenses in addition to the costs associated with both remediation work and ransom demands. The combination of system downtime for productivity loss, customer loss from data breaches, data protection law compliance penalties and sustained damage to corporate reputation causes financial impact on stock prices and other subsidiary costs. Severe cyber events often cut into economic growth rates primarily affecting developing markets which have weak cyber protection systems because they harm investor trust and lead foreign businesses to avoid direct investment. The need for cybersecurity protection requires governments and private actors to shift capital from productive investments toward securing infrastructure which demonstrates how digital conflicts transform economic priorities while demanding operational resilience.

Multinational corporations (MNCs) and financial institutions play a dual function within cyber warfare systems as both precious attack targets and essential defense elements and policy shapers. Although these entities represent attractive exploitation targets for cyber attackers, they simultaneously play essential security roles and shape cyber policies. Technology giants Microsoft along with IBM and Cisco dedicate their annual budget to defensive measures that include threat-intelligence platforms, zero-trust architectures and advanced encryption methods while producing security services based on cloud-native technology and managed detection and response (MDR) solutions. All economic organizations that run from international banks to new financial technology companies experience continuous security risks against their client information and financial assets. Major financial institutions took multiple security steps to combat North Korea's Lazarus Group attacks that hit Bangladesh Bank and other targets through improved transaction verification protocols and fraud detection services and FS-ISAC collaboration. The partnerships between government entities and private companies establish collaborative operational readiness drills and fast information sharing platforms which advance security across the industry. MNCs and banks influence cyber policy creation as members of trade associations and standards bodies who advocate for regulatory frameworks concerning data sovereignty and encryption controls and enforcement requirements for breach disclosures. Through their advocacy these institutions make both market competitiveness and intellectual property security major factors within international cyber norms and legal frameworks which integrate private-sector needs into broader security strategies (Berozashvili, 2023).

The cybersecurity industry's growth has expanded into a multi-billion-dollar transnational market which will reach over USD 182 billion by 2024 while demonstrating above 12 percent yearly growth. Competing vendors develop artificial intelligence-based threat detection solutions while also creating machine-learning systems for anomaly identification and automatic incident response platforms. Palo Alto Networks and CrowdStrike along with Check Point Software Technologies dominate the enterprise market yet specialized startups deliver solutions for identity and access management alongside zero-day vulnerability detection and secure supply-chain monitoring. IT budgets from companies now dedicate 10–15 percent of their funds to cybersecurity indicating its strategic position at the board-level. The cybersecurity industry has experienced substantial venture capital funding surging to over USD 10 billion per year as emerging technologies obtain capital for homomorphic encryption, secure multi-party computation, and quantum-resistant cryptographic solutions. Rapid innovation processes are fueled by increased capital investments which produce both defensive and offensive cybersecurity tools at an accelerated rate. Cybersecurity companies establish strategic partnerships with governments and enterprises to direct standards evolution in cyber defense through alliances such as the Open Cybersecurity Alliance and the Cyber Threat Alliance which shapes their product development alongside public-private cooperative initiatives (Kumar & Nagar, 2024).

Supply-chain vulnerabilities along with insurance markets and cloud-service platforms show how different economic actors contribute to cyber warfare. Supply-chain disruptions such as SolarWinds in December 2020 and Kaseya VSA in July 2021 spread systematic downstream attacks across thousands of companies which resulted in expensive repair costs reaching the hundreds of millions. These incidents also led to widespread distrust of third-party software products. Modern procurement contracts now include detailed cybersecurity requirements and vendors must undergo security audits while network segregation became mandatory to reduce damage scope. Cyber insurance premiums continue their rapid growth as global data shows they will exceed USD 20 billion by 2025. Insurers have introduced strict underwriting requirements that force businesses to purchase insurance at higher rates while requiring larger out-of-pocket costs and mandatory security minimums that guide investment decisions toward security improvements. Cloud service providers exampled by Amazon Web Services, Microsoft Azure, and Google Cloud serve as both potential targets for exploitation and secure deployment platforms via their default security systems and accreditation frameworks and active security management capabilities. The Cybersecurity and Infrastructure Security Agency's (CISA) public–private task forces join with other cooperative groups to share security data across industry sectors and develop unified security protocols while conducting coordinated incident responses. You will find these entities MNCs financial institutions cybersecurity vendors insurers cloud providers and industry alliances working together to create a network where their activities shape the cost structure and security level of the global digital economy when confronting new cyber threats (Madnick, 2022).

THE RISE OF NON-STATE CYBER ACTORS: FROM HACKTIVISTS TO CYBER TERRORISTS

The landscape of digital security has fundamentally altered with the emergence of non-state actors challenging the traditional paradigms of conflict resolution and state sovereignty. Nation states operate with established legal frameworks, however, non-state actors' function without any obligation to regulatory structures, often involved in cyber activities for political, financial, or ideological objectives. Cyberspace has become a new management point of conflict which completely changes the way wars play out today. Cyber operations differ from traditional conflicts in that they connect no specific state actors, and they blur the lines between armed forces and unhired personnel. Through this change, more players specifically those outside state influence can operate within strategic influence domains. Digital tools operated under anonymous conditions enable a wide range of participants including hackers with ideological convictions and criminal organizations and politically motivated extremists to influence national security following affordable resource investments. The modern age transformation of power projection through technology and its democratic distribution explains their rising participation rates. Despite preserving their substantial cyber capacities States find it advantageous to authorize or endorse non-state actors for cyber operations. States maintain a strategic unclear relationship involving cyber operations which enables them to gain benefits while avoiding complete responsibility for the resulting impact. Digital engagements create ethical challenges that impede attempts at accountability enforcement and termination of harmful cyber behaviour as well as the development of international law guidelines (Davis, 2021).

The most recognised cyber non-state actors consist of hacktivists which are either single people or groups who employ hacking techniques to advocate political or social causes. Hacktivism comprises technical skills that people apply to attack institutions they view as abusive authoritarian and corrupt. These non-state cyber groups pursue symbolic targets instead of financial gain while seeking exposure to information and operational disruption or awareness growth. Anonymous stands as one of the most well-known decentralized groups alongside other hacktivist organizations that intervene in both political disputes and online censorship matters and Whistleblower protection movements. The operations of these groups include acts of website defacement together with distributed denial-of-service attacks as well as data leaks. A division exists between two interpretations of hacktivists either as digital protectors protecting causes through their actions or as digital criminals responsible for breaking legal law and causing physical damage. The moral validity of hacktivism depends on how a person views the purpose that activates their support. Such actors leverage their pace of mobilization alongside their capability to attract world attention and shape public opinion to become crucial elements within the information system. Their utilization of basic digital tools and open-source information makes it hard for law enforcement or national cyber defence teams to distinguish between expert governance and amateur electronic disruption (Schmitt & Watts, 2016).

The distinct quality of hacktivists stands in their willingness to show their intentions clearly while using moral justifications to frame their hacking operations. The same digital space that hacktivists utilize is simultaneously used by actors who are eliminating altruistic purposes. The cybercriminal organization group consists of sophisticated operations that function as a commercial enterprise of non-state cyber activities. The main purpose behind cybercriminal operations is financial gain because they differ from hacktivists whose activities focus on ideological influence. Today's hacker organizations began as casual groups of hackers and now function as business operations that achieve state-level results. The criminal businesses target many different actions such as committing identity theft followed by financial fraud and espionage-for-hire and their new trend involves ransomware assaults on people along with organizations and national governments. A few prominent cybercriminal operations by Conti along with DarkSide and REvil have resulted in systemic healthcare disruptions plus fuel supply shutdowns and public network outages. Operation enhancement occurs through cryptocurrency payments alongside darknet networks which provide untraceable transactions and service capabilities. Ransomware-as-a-service growth enables novice cyber attackers to execute severe attacks by acquiring pre-built tools. These cybercriminals continue their operations freely because their host countries deny extradition of computer predators or domestic enforcement agencies choose not to prosecute such criminals. Evidence shows that both tacit support and explicit backing from host states occur during times when attackers target countries that are political rivals. The unified presence of criminal and geopolitical motivations leads to a breakaway and unstable international cyber structure that oversees the digital world.

Somewhere cyber groups find supportive conditions that turn them into state-aligned forces. The digital environment provides this form of plausibly deniable arrangements that work effectively. The practice states entities who want to stay anonymous about sensitive operations use criminal affiliates to execute or conceal their actions (Raska, 2020).

The unfocused connections between crime and political actions create assessment problems for identifying attacks as purely criminal or political. The indistinct nature of digital evidence alongside the technical limitations of digital footprints causes diplomatic nations to get stranded. Target countries lack sufficient choices because they must either wage cyber counterattacks or contact their diplomatically or face persistent damages with no way to fight back. The confusion about such incidents diminishes the capability of conventional state power to deter behaviour. These activities harm global interactions for securing binding cybersecurity agreements because nations lose confidence that other states refrain from conducting their disputes through non-state operators. The fast-evolving nature of cyberspace makes it difficult for international law to adapt because public and private sectors together with legal and illegal domains effectively merge through the speed and complexity of the digital space. Non-state cyber activities have progressed into danger zones with the rise of cyber terrorism (Broeders et al., 2022). Among cyberspace actors, these parties diverge from hacktivists and cybercriminals because of their motives and their ability to inflict severe psychological and physical damage on many people. The digital infrastructure serves cyber terrorists to promote extremist beliefs together with attaining political goals by fomenting panic through disruptive activities. The infrastructure of critical national elements stands as their main target which comprises electric grids along with water supplies and emergency services as well as transportation systems therefore their success would produce disorder combined with casualties and public agitation. To this point, governments along with intelligence agencies continue expressing concern about cyber terrorism even though confirmed instances remain rare. These groups benefit from easy access to offensive cyber tools which they combine with encryption and decentralized networks to work undetected while extending their operations across different international territories. The groups strengthen their influence through using social media and encrypted apps for recruitment purposes along with their distribution of propaganda. The cyber domain provides radicals with dual functions since it serves both to coordinate attacks between cells and functions as a platform for radicalization without oversight. New counterterrorism strategies need to combine cyber defence and digital surveillance with intelligence cooperation because the decentralized nature of the internet and its borderless connectivity challenge established counterterrorism approaches (Naseer, 2024).

Online radicalization has merged with operational execution through the actions of cyber terrorists. The contemporary network of cyber extremists operates apart from physical training facilities while maintaining a lack of formal connections between its members. The decentralization of these targets provides additional obstacles for monitoring and penetrating them and finding ways to combat their activities. Through the utilization of open-source hacking tools coupled with peer-to-peer platforms and online tutorials, anyone without hacking expertise can carry out security threats successfully. These actors utilize existing cybercriminal services which include botnet rental alongside stolen credential purchases through underground forums to conduct attacks. Security agencies throughout the world view the combination of technological skill with ideological extremism as an alarming development (Khare, 2025). Artificial intelligence and deepfake solutions along with autonomous systems represent developing technologies that could transform into dangerous weapons for extremist use toward unpredicted threats. Government institutions need to dedicate funds toward prediction technologies together with advanced regulatory methods while making sure these programs protect basic liberties and Internet freedoms without unnecessary restrictions. The future security and freedom tensions will grow intensively because cyberspace is transforming into a principal battlefield to fight against terrorism (Khan et al., 2024).

FUTURE TRENDS: WHAT'S NEXT IN THE CYBER BATTLEFIELD?

Modern artificial intelligence technology continues to advance rapidly thus transforming cyber militarized operations. Human operators participated traditionally throughout the cyber operation process including planning steps and performing tasks as well as reacting to events. The development of independent systems to detect digital threats as well as analyze and eliminate them became possible with emerging machine learning implementations and neural networks together with big data analytics. The systems demonstrate dangerous capabilities by launching offensive cyber operations without needing human supervision to activate them. The new capability transforms cyberattack features including the delivery timeline, degree of precision, and potential for mass-scale deployment. Nation-states can use this capability to increase their cyber supremacy, but rogue actors benefit by launching sophisticated strikes with small expenditures and minimal ability to be traced. These systems threaten established military foundational concepts which have commonly relied on human commanders to make their impact during warfare throughout history. Modern warfare that utilizes artificial intelligence operations creates an indistinct border between combat forces and computer programming which demands examination of future war concepts and defence stability questions and ethical evaluation of automated system choices. A fast-moving cyberattack system requiring no human supervision needs strong ethical guidelines that have not caught up with modern technological progress. In cyberspace, the principle of human control becomes difficult to maintain since computerized decisions happen too fast for manual adjustments in real-time operations. States face a dual challenge regarding AI-powered cyber weapons as they seek to determine if ethical restrictions can effectively be inserted into systems that outperform humans during enemy engagements (Kumar & Nagar, 2024).

The automated delivery of cyberattacks through artificial intelligence systems generates significant debate due to their ability to execute operations independently of human supervision. International policy discussion has yet to resolve the various ethical issues alongside legal dilemmas and operational management problems that would emerge from the automation of cyberattacks. Traditional warfare depends on human commanders to establish accountability through their decisions. Each military command has a known structure while force usage responsibility connects to designated leaders including commanders and political personnel. When cyber systems become autonomous, they introduce a model discontinuity because algorithms take over both command structure and decision-making processes from people. The modification sets in place an area where accountability remains entirely missing. When autonomous programs malfunction by striking civilian hospitals or damaging essential infrastructure such as power grids and water supply systems which branch of authority is responsible between the programmer the deploying state or the AI system (Macak, 2021). Machine learning models built with deep learning techniques present an additional difficulty because they are difficult to interpret. Several black box machine learning systems present challenges to creators and other users regarding understanding or forecasting their operational behaviour. The probability of unintentional conflict intensifies to dangerous levels. When faced with human-free decision-making autonomous systems commonly mistreat harmless behaviour which results in automatic countermeasures leading to intensified military conflicts. The associated dangers exist as more than theoretical concerns. Semi-autonomous surveillance together with drone systems has prompted an international discussion about AI warfare restrictions that emerged from recent events. The absence of worldwide agreement regarding moral principles attack procedures and verification standards likely makes fully autonomous cyber weapons unstable forces. States implementing these systems in large numbers might start a digital race for developing extreme yet minimally policed and unsafe AI weapons (Jefferson, 2024).

The ascent of deepfake technology adds alarm to the landscape of cyber-psychological warfare because it alters the possible ways how such operations could be executed. Synthetic media technologies known as deepfakes use AI to create false versions of real individuals in audio and video form or images that successfully deceive many people. The developing deepfake technology produces progressively lower barriers for high-quality digital fabrications of any kind which ultimately enables unaffiliated actors to create convincing fake content. The military exploitation of deepfakes during cyber warfare operations includes strategies to mislead public perceptions as well as strategies that disrupt societies from within. Deepfakes allow fake scenarios to be staged against political opponents while military officials receive misleading impersonation commands or entire events get altered in historical records. Numerous possible destructive scenarios become possible because of deepfakes. A solitary deepfake video broadcasted during an election period at its decisive stage could alter the result when it spreads through public view before recognized fact-checkers can verify its authenticity. Deepfakes applied in complicated situations would enable the recreation of live video conferences between high-level diplomats which might cause major international problems or damage diplomatic relationships. Adversaries would be able to carry out information domain warfare using deepfake technologies without implementing conventional or cyber-attacks to accomplish their objectives. The use of AI-generated personas with fabricated scenarios creates weapons from fabricated perceptions. Society faces potential damage from researchers' "liar's dividend" effect as deepfake media continues to mimic authentic media so closely that people question the validity of all media content including journalism legal evidence and official communications. Various detection tools and verification frameworks appear for countering this threat although their distribution remains uneven, and all efforts chase after new fabrication techniques that become increasingly advanced (Edelman, 2024).

Through their concept of "deepfake armies" these artificial agents create synchronizations between platforms to talk with authentic users who then spread conflicting content which weakens social bonds. The avatars can consist of artificially created journalists along with bogus analysts and fully established digital communities that serve as authenticators. The main difference between bots and deepfake personas stands in their ability to emulate authentic human behaviour since deepfakes display emotionally responsive and real-time communication through voice and video with extended active life spanning online platforms. Realistic profiles created by deepfake technology make it almost impossible for people and monitoring platforms to determine what content is genuine and what content is created artificially. These digital soldiers can be sent into conflict areas and political turmoil zones to shape targeted population perceptions through fabricated alerts build false support for fabricated causes or impersonate respected individuals with false warnings. This phenomenon would result in severe consequences including undermined faith in the public domain and disrupted societal frameworks which governments could potentially exploit to decide strategic actions. Deepfake army success rates in infiltrating various cultural groups are set to enhance because AI systems will achieve superior localization capabilities in speech tone along with cultural understanding. The novel type of warfare breaks through geographical boundaries by leveraging information into a weapon that has never been more powerful. The target now extends beyond hacking computer systems and stealing information because hackers aim to modify collective public opinion through direct manipulation. The protection against synthetic threats needs multiverse solutions consisting of digital education legislative changes enhanced detection techniques and worldwide cooperation to keep these threats from spreading (Alhasan et al., 2024).

Organized disinformation campaigns will predominate future disinformation warfare instead of focusing on using single deepfakes since they deploy thousands of synthetic personas who act in coordinated ways to control public opinion. The artificial "deepfake armies" would spread false information across various platforms through interactions with actual users and they would create multiple conflicting stories to break down community unity. The avatars can consist of artificially created journalists along with bogus analysts and fully established digital communities that serve as authenticators. Deepfake personas distinguish themselves from bots since they fake human behaviours including empathetic expressions and virtual and vocal interactions while sustaining virtual persistency. Realistic profiles created by deepfake technology make it almost impossible for people and monitoring platforms to determine what content is genuine and what content is created artificially. These digital soldiers can be sent into conflict areas and political turmoil zones to shape targeted population perceptions through fabricated alerts build false support for fabricated causes or impersonate respected individuals with false warnings. This phenomenon would result in severe consequences including undermined faith in the public domain and disrupted societal frameworks which governments could potentially exploit to decide strategic actions. The increasing capability of AI systems in localizing language together with accent and cultural information makes deepfake armies more likely to carry out deep insertions into various societies. The novel type of warfare breaks through geographical boundaries by leveraging information into a weapon that has never been more powerful. The target now extends beyond hacking computer systems and stealing information because hackers aim to modify collective public opinion through direct manipulation. Defensive strategies should encompass multiple fronts by teaching digital literacy along with legislative updates and performance-enhanced detection algorithms while establishing international foreign alliances to detect these artificial threats early on (Binhammad et al., 2024).

GLOBAL GOVERNANCE & REGULATION

Cyber warfare governance develops through various instruments including non-binding norms with voluntary frameworks and sparse treaties which aim to establish control over borderless operations. Through non-binding interpretation the Tallinn Manual presents detailed insights regarding state responsibility while examining UN Charter rules for defining "use of force" and justifiable countermeasures. The United Nations Group of Governmental Experts (UN GGE) meets periodically since its first formation in 2004 to develop consensus reports that establish state behaviour norms and confidence-building measures and distribute best practices for member states. The Council of Europe's Budapest Convention on Cybercrime (2001) operates as the only enforceable treaty which addresses both the elements and procedures of cybercrime and requires cooperation between states and standardizes national laws. States joined forces with tech firms and civil society through the Paris

Call for Trust and Security in Cyberspace (2018) to develop a voluntary declaration of principles that fights disinformation protects election integrity and secures critical infrastructure. These instruments form part of the interwoven structure of cyber governance which maintains both national state authority and international community objectives regarding cyber security stability.

Recent improvements do not solve the substantial weaknesses that diminish the effectiveness of current procedural frameworks. The Tallinn Manual represents an extensive compilation of practice guidelines but functionally lacks treaty authority and therefore allows states to follow national priorities when they interpret its recommendations. Since their establishment the UN GGE reports have maintained a pattern of achieving partial agreement and complete gridlock while failing to generate enforceable agreements. Recent expert group sessions withstood deep disagreements about humanitarian law standards and attribution practices to prevent the formation of new working mandates. The Budapest Convention operates with multiple obstacles in its path. Multiple leading cyber worldwide powers including China and India with Russia have decided against the Budapest Convention ratification resulting in fragmented legal systems and obstacles during international digital investigative processes. The voluntary nature of the Paris Call keeps its signatories free from obligatory obligations which combines with significant differences in their ability to adopt the specified principles. The system's structural deficiencies create ongoing flaws that allow dangerous agents to take advantage of both ambiguous prohibition requirements and lack of unified authorities which handle disputes and certification functions thus prolonging diplomatic stagnation (Sfetcu, 2024).

Cyber governance receives substantial influence from actors outside governmental structures although their contributions remain underappreciated. The Internet Engineering Task Force (IETF) and World Wide Web Consortium (W3C) together with technical communities work to develop open standards along with best practices (such as the Domain Name System Security Extensions, DNSSEC) to build global resilience. The CyberPeace Institute together with Access Now work to defend human rights through their advocacy of privacy by design principles and digital due process standards. Private businesses along with industry alliances like the Financial Services Information Sharing and Analysis Centre merge with the Cyber Threat Alliance to establish rapid threat intelligence sharing systems that move more swiftly than government-level processes. Cooperative efforts have achieved concrete results which include botnet elimination and critical software patches yet trigger constraints related to organizational responsibilities and information disclosure as well as fair memberships. The power difference between states and non-profit entities and corporations persists because corporations focus on proprietary interests instead of collective security and smaller states lack both technical capacity and sufficient funding for meaningful contributions to norm development and enforcement processes (Katagiri, 2021).

Global governance needs multiple strategic approaches both from policy makers and stakeholders. The implementation of essential Tallinn Manual principles should become binding elements within existing regional and sectoral treaties to define clear legal requirements. The UN GGE needs revitalization as a rotating mechanism with clearly defined responsibilities to develop attribution standards and rapid response systems and capacity-building programs for developing countries. The international community should work to encourage more nations to join the Budapest Convention while negotiating a complementary hybrid agreement that addresses non-participating major powers' objections. Mechanisms that include civil society groups and technical experts should be formalized to perform norms assessment as well as benchmarking and dispute settlement functions. The international community must combine governmental and non-governmental authorities' expertise to close gaps between voluntary codes and expert interpretations and binding agreements to develop a cohesive cyber warfare governance framework protecting global security (Buchan & Navarrete, 2021).

CONCLUSION & SUGESSTIONS

Cyber warfare has experienced a complete transformation during the last twenty years. In modern times states cannot defend themselves from attacks on their digital networks by other states because the digital battlefield now accepts multiple participants who apply various methods beyond conventional confrontations. The transformation has created a total shift in the notions of military conflict and defensive measures. Modern discussions about cyber threats indicate conventional military power will soon lose its capability to protect nations. The same level of priority will exist between defending cyberspace and physical infrastructure due to the increasing importance of cyber resilience. The ascension of such non-state entities as hacktivists cybercriminal syndicates and proxy militias has occurred because they operate under financial and ideological motivations. Global governance of cyberspace faces difficulties because such groups remain unaccountable and lack proper oversight mechanisms. Modern framework limitations to deter cyberattacks become evident because these security threats operate at incredible speed alongside massive scale and full anonymity even with AI-enhancements. New technological developments demand a fundamental change in the cybersecurity approach because reactive measures must be replaced by proactivity that includes prediction together with prevention and resilience strategies (Khare & Raghuwanshi, 2025). Any expert dealing with current conflict issues needs to grasp the essential elements of modern cyber warfare to make informed decisions.

Given the unpredictability of cyber threats, nations must adopt forward-thinking approaches that extend beyond conventional firewalls and antivirus programs. True cyber resilience involves not only the protection of infrastructure but also the ability to absorb, adapt to, and recover from disruptive cyber events. This shift from pure prevention to a broader resilience paradigm is essential in an environment where no system can be fully impervious to attack. Cyber resilience strategies must be multi-layered, combining technical, organizational, and strategic elements. On the technical side, adaptive network defenses, threat intelligence sharing, and anomaly detection powered by machine learning can provide early warnings and mitigate damage. Organizational resilience entails building cybersecurity awareness across all levels of governance and business, training personnel to respond to breaches, and ensuring continuity of operations during digital crises. Strategically, resilience must include national-level planning, such as cyber war games, response drills, and simulation exercises that test readiness across public and private sectors. Furthermore, public trust must be maintained during and after attacks. Transparent communication, rapid incident response, and the presence of backup systems are vital components in preserving confidence and minimizing chaos. Ultimately, resilience must be viewed not as a one-time investment but as a continuous process of adaptation. It is not enough to defend against known threats; nations must prepare for the unknown, building systems that are robust, redundant, and able to evolve in tandem with the threat landscape.

The critical struggle in cyber conflict originates from continuous attribution problems. By nature, cyberattacks transpire in complex internet spaces which enable attackers to maintain uncertain responsibility. Attackers hide their origins by utilizing different methods such as IP spoofing in addition to proxy servers and hacked third-party networks as well as AI-generated traffic imitations of legitimate activities. A situation known as the "attribution crisis" emerges because it severely impedes police work and multinational cooperation. It becomes extremely difficult to pursue legal action against wrongdoers when they use methods that prevent their identity from being established. Ineffective national responses are hindered when attributions are made too soon or incorrectly as such mistakes lead countries to experience diplomatic tensions and potentially accidental escalation of threats. The absence of worldwide uniform regulations for what counts as a cyberwarfare operation makes resolving matters increasingly complicated. States typically decline to identify attackers in public because they want to safeguard intelligence information while considering their relations with foreign powers and economic interests. Because of this obscurity threat actors receive strong encouragement to carry out their attacks since they know the risk of detection and prosecution remains minimal. When applied to legal settings this scenario weakens the judicial framework that protects the online environment. The strategic absence of power enables digital attacks to establish an unregulated environment. The international community needs to back the development of better attribution technologies by using blockchain or forensic AI to identify incident origins. Trusted multilateral frameworks for verifying and attributing cyber incidents would enable the international community to develop the necessary credibility needed for properly prosecuting aggressors.

REFERENCES

Alhasan, W., Wannous, M., Abualkishik, A., Al Nasar, M. R., Ali, L., & Al-Zoubi, H. (2024). An In-Depth Examination of Cybersecurity: Unveiling Contemporary Trends and Recent Advancements in the World of Cyber Threats. *IEEE*. 1-11. http://dx.doi.org/DOI: 10.1109/ICCR61006.2024.10533062

Arquilla, J. (2021). Bitskrieg: The New Challenge of Cyberwarfare. *John Wiley & Sons*. https://www.wiley.com/en-ae/Bitskrieg%3A+The+New+Challenge+of+Cyberwarfare-p-9781509543625

Basholli, F. (2022). Cyber Warfare, a New Aspect of Modern Warfare. International Scientific Journal Security & Future, *5*(2), 72-75. https://www.researchgate.net/publication/371814918_Cyber_warfare_a_new_aspect_of_modern_warfare

Berozashvili, T. (2023). World War 3: The Ethical Dimensions of Information Warfare in The Digital Age. *ResearchGate*. http://dx.doi.org/DOI: 10.13140/RG.2.2.33649.49765

Binhammad, M., Alqaydi, S., Othman, A., & Abuljadayel, L. H. (2024). The Role of AI in Cyber Security: Safeguarding Digital Identity. *Journal of Information Security*, *15*(2), 245–278. DOI: 10.4236/jis.2024.152015

Broeders, D., De Busser, E., Cristiano, F., & Tropina, T. (2022). Revisiting Past Cyber Operations in Light of New Cyber Norms and Interpretations of International Law: Inching Towards Lines in the Sand? *Journal of Cyber Policy*, *7*(1), 97–135. DOI: 10.1080/23738871.2022.2041061

Buchan, R., & Navarrete, I. (2021). Cyber Espionage and International Law. *Edward Elgar Publishing*. 231-252. https://doi.org/DOI: 10.4337/9781789904253.00021

Bussolati, N. (2015). 'The Rise of Non-State Actors in Cyberwarfare'. *Oxford University Press,* 102-126. https://papers.ssrn.com/sol3/papers.cfm?abstract_id=2764185

Cavelty, M. D. (2024). *The Politics of Cyber-security*. Taylor & Francis., DOI: 10.4324/9781003497080

Check, T. (2022). The Tallinn Manual 2.0 on Nation-State Cyber Operations Affecting Critical Infrastructure. *WCL Journals & Law Reviews, 13*, 1. https://digitalcommons.wcl.american.edu/nslb/vol13/iss1/1/

Davis, E. V. W. (2021). *Shadow Warfare: Cyberwar Policy in the United States, Russia and China*. Rowman & Littlefield. https://rowman.com/ISBN/9781538149683/Shadow-Warfare-Cyberwar-Policy-in-the-United-States-Russia-and-China

Edelman, R. D. (2024). *Rethinking Cyber Warfare: The International Relations of Digital Disruption*. Oxford University Press., DOI: 10.1093/9780197509715.001.0001

Eichensehr, K. E. (2022). Ukraine, Cyberattacks, and the Lessons for International Law. *AJIL Unbound*, *116*, 145–149. DOI: 10.1017/aju.2022.20

Gurung, A. (2025). From Battlefield to the Servers: Cyber Warfare and the Conflicts. *The Shivapuri Journal*, *26*(1), 29–41. DOI: 10.3126/shivapuri.v26i1.75831

Jefferson, B. J. (2024). Cybernetic States: Communication, Control, and State-space in the Advanced Research Projects Agency. *Political Geography*, *113*, 103160. DOI: 10.1016/j.polgeo.2024.103160

Katagiri, N. (2021). Why International Law and Norms Do Little in Preventing Non-state Cyber Attacks. *Journal of Cybersecurity*, *7*(1), tyab009. Advance online publication. DOI: 10.1093/cybsec/tyab009

Khan, A. W., Saeed, S., & Kakar, M. S. (2024). Cybersecurity as a Geopolitical Tool: The Growing Influence of Digital Warfare in Statecraft. *International Research Journal of Social Sciences and Humanities, 3*(2), 345-357. https://irjssh.com/index.php/irjssh/article/view/209

Khare, P. (2025). Investigating the Influence of AI in Social Media Governance. *IGI Global Scientific Publishing*. 365-388. https://doi.org/DOI: 10.4018/979-8-3693-9904-0.ch015

Khare, P. & Raghuwanshi, V. (2025). Navigating Emerging AI Technologies and Future Trends in Cybersecurity and Forensics. *IGI Global Scientific Publishing*, 321-346. https://doi.org/DOI: 10.4018/979-8-3373-0857-9.ch012

Kumar, S., & Nagar, G. (2024, June). Threat Modeling for Cyber Warfare Against Less Cyber-Dependent Adversaries. *European Conference on Cyber Warfare and Security, 23*(1), 257-264. http://dx.doi.org/DOI: 10.34190/eccws.23.1.2462

Lahmann, H. (2021). On The Politics and Ideologies of The Sovereignty Discourse in Cyberspace. *Duke Journal of Comparative & International Law, 32*, 61-96. https://scholarship.law.duke.edu/djcil/vol32/iss1/2/

Lande, D., & Danyk, Y. (2025). Competitive Artificial Intelligence in Information and Cyber Warfare. *SSRN*. http://dx.doi.org/DOI: 10.2139/ssrn.5084698

Macak, K. (2021). Unblurring the lines: Military cyber operations and international law. *Journal of Cyber Policy*, *6*(3), 411–428. DOI: 10.1080/23738871.2021.2014919

Madnick, S. (2022). What Russia's Ongoing Cyberattacks in Ukraine Suggest About the Future of Cyber Warfare. *Harvard Business Review, 7,* •••. https://cams.mit.edu/wp-content/uploads/Madnick_HBR_Russia.pdf

Nardi, M. L. (2021). Origin of Cyber Warfare and How the Espionage Changed: A Historical Overview. *IGI Global*. 145-153. https://www.igi-global.com/chapter/origin-of-cyber-warfare-and-how-the-espionage-changed/260610

Naseer, I. (2024). The CrowdStrike Incident: Analysis and Unveiling the Intricacies of Modern Cybersecurity Breaches. *World Journal of Advanced Engineering Technology and Sciences*, *10*(1), 728–733. Advance online publication. DOI: 10.30574/wjaets.2024.13.1.0473

Odoh, E. M. (2021). Cyber Attack as a Tool to Influence Foreign Policy: A Comparative Study of Russia's Cyber-attacks On Estonia and Georgia. *University of Nigeria Journal of Political Economy, 11*(1). https://unjpe.com/index.php/UNJPE/article/view/2

Raska, M. (2020). North Korea's Evolving Cyber Strategies: Continuity and Change. *SIRIUS–Zeitschrift für Strategische Analysen*, *4*(2), 1–13. DOI: 10.1515/sirius-2020-3030

Robinson, M., Jones, K., & Janicke, H. (2015). Cyber warfare: Issues and challenges. *Computers & Security*, *49*, 70–94. DOI: 10.1016/j.cose.2014.11.007

Schmitt, M. N., & Watts, S. (2016). Beyond State-centrism: International Law and Non-state Actors in Cyberspace. *Journal of Conflict and Security Law*, *21*(3), 595–611. DOI: 10.1093/jcsl/krw019

Sfetcu, N. (2024). *Electronic Warfare and Artificial Intelligence*. MultiMedia Publishing., DOI: 10.58679/mm14430

Stroppa, M. (2023). Legal And Ethical Implications of Autonomous Cyber Capabilities: A Call for Retaining Human Control in Cyberspace. *Ethics and Information Technology*, *25*(1), 7. DOI: 10.1007/s10676-023-09679-w

Chapter 5
From Cold War to Code War: Geopolitical Shifts in Cybersecurity Strategy

Kiranbhai R Dodiya
https://orcid.org/0009-0001-9409-7303
Gujarat University, India

Kinjal Dipakbhai Dodiya
https://orcid.org/0009-0008-2237-7956
Gujarat Police, India

ABSTRACT

The chapter explores the intricate relationship between geopolitics and cybersecurity, drawing parallels between the Cold War era and the modern "Code War." It examines how shifting geopolitical dynamics shape cybersecurity strategies, emphasizing the balance between national interests and global security imperatives. The discussion highlights offensive and defensive cyber capabilities, the impact of technological advancements, and the need for adaptability in addressing evolving threats.It also addresses international cyber relations, focusing on norms, agreements, and the ethical and legal challenges of cybersecurity policies. The chapter advocates for global cooperation and innovation to build a secure digital future. By providing actionable insights, it empowers policymakers and security professionals to navigate the complex intersection of geopolitics and cybersecurity, promoting resilience and stability in cyberspace.

DOI: 10.4018/979-8-3373-1727-4.ch005

INTRODUCTION

Through a world where diplomacy and foreign relations play their leading roles in power politics and war, a new theatre of operations is gaining prominence — respected cyberspace. As the defending cyber realm, this phenomenon provides the basis for an investigation into the mutually interdependent security of nation-states, which lays the ground for an exploration of the evolution of the interconnected fields of cyber and geo-political security and the nature of their reciprocal relationship.

Figure 1. Mapping the intersection of geopolitics and cybersecurity: From code wars to global cooperation

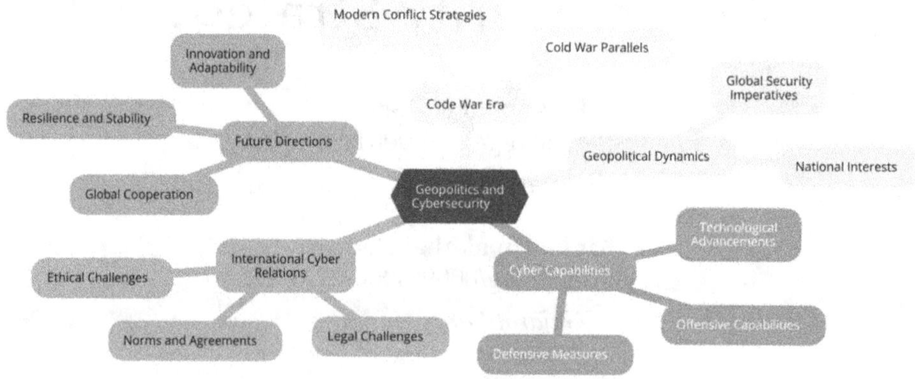

Setting the Stage: The Evolution of Cybersecurity within the Context of Geopolitics

As the virtual revolution unfolded, it ushered in a generation of incredible connectivity and innovation. Yet, with each leap in advance in technological development came new vulnerabilities and challenges. The upward push of our online world as a conflict and cooperation domain has transformed the nature of protection in the 21st century, blurring the lines between bodily and digital nation-states(*The Future of the Metaverse | Imagining the Internet | Elon University*, n.d.). Critical to this transformation is the evolution of cybersecurity from the technical domain of IT departments to a centerpiece of national security policy. In the beginning of cybersecurity, it revolved around protecting networks from access and malware. But as the internet became more woven into the fabric of modern life, touching it Finance, trade, critical infrastructure, and national security. The scope of cybersecurity has grown a lot. In an area moving as fast as technology, and with so much heavier reliance on networks, the geopolitical security aspects have risen to a priority level. Cyberspace which was once understood to be neutral and without borders has become a competitive environment for state and non-state actors. Its strategic importance was recognized, and it was used as a tool of power projection and covert operation to achieve geopolitical objectives, maturing into a vital component of national defense as governments began to see the strategic importance of cyber for intelligence gathering, power projection, and for performing covert operations. The convergence of cybersecurity and geopolitics was especially pronounced after high-impact events like the Stuxnet worm against Iran's nuclear program and Russian cyber meddling in the U.S. presidential election in 2016. (*Cyberspace and Geopolitics: Assessing Global Cybersecurity Norm Processes at a Crossroads - Carnegie Endowment for International Peace*, n.d.).Such events were nothing short of wake-up calls for political leaders across the world, we need to challenge all expectations of how security has traditionally been viewed and how it needs to be approached in the digital era. Faced with a continuously evolving set of threats, governments crafted whole-of-nation cybersecurity strategies that codified cyber defense, deterrence, and diplomacy within a wider national security architecture. Finally, in these endeavors, cooperation, and coordination between countries became indispensable, as states acknowledged the transnational nature of cyber events that force them to act collectively. Understanding the complex and evolving relationship between cybersecurity and geopolitics requires analysis of the changing factors involved. Whether in the power corridors in Washington, Beijing, and Moscow or the dark recesses of cyberspace where cybercriminals hide, the importance of this territory is clear. As I stated back in 2014 with my State of the Union address The State of the Union We Are All Being Watched due to the realization that anywhere in the world could now be vulnerable to foreign cyber attacks. While the stakes are high and the hurdles daunting, a well-calibrated, coordinated strategy can appear well-suited for traversing the intricacies of cyberspace. This future is one where the instruments of war turn into the instruments of development, a place where hope lasts for peace — this is the future I envision. (*Security Delta (HSD) | Trend Snippet: Digital and Physical Processes in Society Have Become Intertwined and Crisis Management Should Be Able to Deal with This*, n.d.).

Understanding the "Code War" Analogy

In the 21st century, "Code War" describes a dramatic shift from war and confrontation to old power games now intertwined with computer space. To apprehend this analogy, we ought to delve into its historical context, the characteristics of contemporary cyber warfare, and the strategic implications for national safety and global family members.(*(PDF) The Cyber Defense Review - Vol. 7 No. 2 Spring 2022*, n.d.).

Historical Context: From Cold War to Code War

The analogy casts cyberspace as the new battlefield for geopolitical rivalries and ideological confrontations that once defined the Cold War. The period of the Cold War was also defined as a bipolar world, in which the world was divided into two opposing blocks, one led by the United States and the other by the Soviet Union fighting for the ascendance while spreading their ideologies (Sambanis, 2004). In the modern world, comparable to the geopolitical stage, there is a worldwide battle for the minds of man and control of cyberspace. But compared to the Cold War, which was fought through military buildup, proxy wars, and ideological propaganda, this "Code War" is fought where you would expect — in cyberspace. Bits and bytes are the new bullets and bombs, and they are the weapons of global conflict in this new age.

Characteristics of Modern Cyber Conflict

To delineate the parameters of the "Code War" the involved are not confined by traditional models of warfare and espionage. The range of cyber warfare operations can include anything from state-sponsored cyberattacks on critical infrastructure and government networks to using campaign-style cyber espionage to steal national secrets. In addition, cyber conflict is not limited to nation-states, and non-state actors like hacktivist organizations, cybercrime syndicates, and terrorist groups can be key players, too. The difficulty for states in defending against cyber threats and deterring adversarial actions can boil down to the decentralized-asymmetrical nature of cyber conflict itself. The unprecedented number of actors and the borderless characteristics of cyberspace require new approaches to ensure national and global security](https://www.ncpc.gov.au/)) from all exploitation and harm.(*What Is Cyber Warfare | Types, Examples & Mitigation | Imperva*, n.d.-a).

In cyberspace, all actors enjoy a high degree of anonymity and deniability, making it notoriously difficult to attribute cyber-attacks. Without clear attribution, it becomes difficult to hold offenders accountable, thus raising tensions and diminishing the chances of de-escalation. Finally, the challenge of correctly attributing attacks has serious ramifications for the notion of deterrence. However, all states that experience cyber-attacks are under great pressure to react in a way that signals credibility without running the risk of escalation. It also highlights the need for strong attribution standards and other balance-of-power strategies to deal with the particular circumstances of cyber risks in ways that do not also further destabilize international relations. (*What Is Cyber Warfare | Types, Examples & Mitigation | Imperva*, n.d.-b).

Strategic Implications for National Security and International Relations

This "Code War" has deep implications for national security and international relations, bartering aspects of the geopolitical landscape and redefining borders, notions of sovereignty, and power itself. With cyberspace now recognized as an integral domain for competition, states have continued to pour substantial resources into both offensive and defensive cyber capabilities. Such initiatives are designed to, inter alia, protect national interests, secure critical infrastructure, and further national strategic goals in the global and national digital spheres of contention. Importance of power projection and resilienceA new trend is the increasing dependence on cyber capabilities, which highlights a change in the power dynamic when the ability to project influence and resilience into cyberspace has become an integral part of statecraft.(*UN Cybercrime Treaty: The Year Cyber and Multilateralism Stole the Show - Indian Council of World Affairs (Government of India)*, n.d.). At the same time, the interconnected character of our online international implies that actions taken via way of the use of one state ought to have an extended manner of attaining consequences for others, critical to a heightened appreciation of vulnerability and interdependence amongst nations. This interconnectivity underscores the significance of world cooperation and collaboration in confronting not unusual cyber threats and marketing stability in our online global. Furthermore, the Code War distorts the strains between warfare and peace, as states interact in regular low-level cyber skirmishes that fall under the verge of conventional armed struggle even though they have significant strategic implications.(*"The Interconnected Global Economy: Challenges and Opportunities for the United States—and the World" By Christine Lagarde, Managing Director, International Monetary Fund*, n.d.). Policymakers are trying to find effective deterrence strategies and pointers for engagement in our online world in this grey vicinity of conflict-stressful situations. The "Code War" analogy offers precious insights into the evolving nature of warfare and opposition in the digital age. By gaining know-how inside the ancient context, the inclinations of cutting-edge cyber battle, and the strategic implications for country-wide protection and the global participants of the circle of relatives, we can better navigate the complexities of this new frontier and defend the requirements of peace and balance in the twenty-first century.(Mangold, 2013).

HISTORICAL CONTEXT: FROM THE COLD WAR TO THE CYBER ERA

The Cold War Paradigm: Traditional Notions of Security and Power

The Cold War lasted from the end of World War II in 1945 until the fall of the Soviet Union in 1991, characterized by the contention between the U.S. and its allies in the Western Bloc and the Soviet Union and its allies in the Eastern Bloc. Fundamentally the struggle was about capitalism versus communism, with each superpower seeking to spread its own political and economic systems and to limit or contain its rival. Classical security during the Cold War was based on military capabilities, power over land, and alliances. The US and Soviet Union ultimately built the largest arsenals ever known, the two sides engaging in a dangerous game of brinkmanship that brought the world to the edge of nuclear war time and again. This era also reaffirmed the importance of military power as the core currency of global power and the tool of last resort to enforce the precarious equilibrium of power. (*Cold War | Summary, Causes, History, Years, Timeline, & Facts | Britannica*, n.d.).

Emergence of the Cyber Era: Shifting Dynamics in Global Security

The transition from the Cold War to the cyber generation represents a paradigm shift in protection and power dynamics on the global level. The emergence of our online world as a present-day war and cooperation region has altered how global locations apprehend and reply to safety threats, reshaping the conventional notions of sovereignty, conflict, and international family members.(Hassid, 2024).

The Era of Cyberspace

Cyberspace originated in the Internet, which was a decentralized network of computers connected to share information that was initially developed for military and academic purposes. The 1990s witnessed the rapid growth of the Internet from an academic curiosity to a truly ubiquitous communication, commerce, and information dissemination platform as it became widely accessible to the general public. Programmatic talent came first, but the term 'cyberspace,' originally coined by sci-fi author William Gibson in his 1984 novel Neuromancer, quickly evolved into a descriptor of a sort of hazy virtual reality, a technologically mediated atmosphere in which data is moved in every direction, and a place in which the lines between physical existence and the digital world begin to erode. Cyberspace knows no geographic or territorial boundaries: individuals and organizations can connect and interact with one another almost instantaneously across great distances. By its very nature, cyberspace does not have physical boundaries, and it has revolutionized interactions on a global scale through unparalleled connectivity and exchange, (Tihonova et al., 2022).

Shifting Dynamics in Global Security

The emergence of our online world as the latest frontier in global protection has introduced diverse traumatic conditions and opportunities for international places. Unlike conventional styles of war, which rely upon bodily pressure and territorial manipulation, cyber conflict operates in bits and bytes, wherein the battlefield is virtual, and the weapons are coded. One of the defining characteristics of the cyber era is the asymmetry of strength between actors. In our online world, even negligible, aid-constrained entities can wield vast effects by leveraging the strength of technology and exploiting vulnerabilities in large, more significant, technologically advanced adversaries(*Digital Infrastructure and Cyber War: The New Front of International Law – Jindal Forum for International and Economic Laws*, n.d.). This asymmetry ranges the playing area in some respects but introduces new risks and uncertainties for states trying to shield themselves in the direction of cyber threats. Moreover, the interconnected nature of cyberspace, such that actions taken in an unmarried part of the arena can also have prolonged way-reaching results at some point in borders and industries. Cyber assaults targeted on vital infrastructure, economic systems, or authorities networks can disrupt essential services, undermine public popularity as correct, and beautify national tensions, number one to diplomatic crises or armed battles. At the same time, cyberspace gives new possibilities for cooperation and collaboration in addressing shared protection worrying conditions. International obligations incorporating the Budapest Convention on Cybercrime and the Tallinn Manual at the International Law Applicable to Cyber Warfare provide frameworks for states to cooperate on cybercrime investigations, percentage chance intelligence, and make more considerable norms of behavior in cyberspace. We can ensure the protection and prosperity of future generations in the virtual age via collective movement and strategic foresight.(*Dynamics of the Changing Global Security Order: Emerging Trends and Key Issues in Asia - 9781666949131*, n.d.).

GEOPOLITICAL IMPLICATIONS OF CYBER THREATS

Cyber Warfare: New Frontiers of Conflict

The emergence of cyberspace as a cyber warfare website has altered the geopolitical panorama, introducing new dynamics and disturbing situations to the standard mind of safety and energy projection. Cyber warfare is central to this change, representing a paradigm shift in the conflict in which the conventional kinetic factors are supplanted through digital means.

The Nature of Cyber Warfare

Cyber conflict constitutes a spectrum of offensive operations completed inside the digital region, aiming to disrupt, degrade, or harm adversary networks, structures, and infrastructure. Unlike conventional battle, cyber conflict operates in a realm with the beneficial resources of intangibility and anonymity, wherein the battlefield is defined by traces of code instead of physical boundaries. Attribution, a cornerstone of traditional deterrence theories, will become elusive in cyberspace due to modern-day U.S. and non-U.S. actors' inherent anonymity and hiding methods and techniques.(*(PDF) Cyber Conflict and International Relations: A Comprehensive Analysis of Cyber Deterrence Strategies in Contemporary Geopolitics*, n.d.).

Geopolitical Implications

Cyber conflict has enormous geopolitical implications, shaping power distribution among global locations and influencing the dynamics of the global circle of relative individuals. The strategic benefits of cyber talents allow states to challenge energy, disrupt adversaries' critical infrastructure, and undermine their political and monetary stability without resorting to an elegant kinetic way. Furthermore, the interconnected nature of our online international permits the short unfolding of cyber-attacks on the forestall of borders, posing transnational threats that pass traditional notions of sovereignty—cyber assaults centered on a single u. U.S. or business enterprise employers can also have cascading effects, impacting specific states' safety, economic stability, diplomatic family, and humans, as well as exacerbating network and international tensions(*Geopolitical Factors Shaping the Future of the Cyber Domain - Critical Start*, n.d.). The proliferation of cyber guns and democratizing cyber abilities introduce traumatic conditions to position the mind of deterrence and strategic stability. Without clean recommendations of engagement and norms of behavior in our online world, states can also resort to offensive cyber operations as a manner of coercion or compellence, most extensively to a heightened chance of escalation and miscalculation.

Nature of Cyber Espionage

Cyber espionage entails covert sports activities that surreptitiously digitally gather sensitive records, proprietary facts, and digitally categorized intelligence. Unlike traditional espionage strategies reliant on human assets and bodily infiltration, cyber espionage leverages technological vulnerabilities and virtual proper digital right of access to factors to infiltrate purpose networks and extract valuable statistics clandestinely—techniques hired in cyber espionage vary extensively, from cutting-edge-day hacking techniques to social engineering techniques. Attack vectors encompass malware deployment, phishing campaigns, and exploitation of software software program vulnerabilities. The anonymity and obfuscation facilitated via cyberspace pose massive worrying situations to attribution, permitting perpetrators to perform with impunity and avoid detection(*Geopolitical Cyber Risk: Cyber Operations in Modern Warfare | by Robindimyan | Medium*, n.d.).

Weaponisation of Information

At the center of cyber espionage lies the weaponization of statistics, wherein facts will become a strategic asset wielded with the valuable resource of manner of states to accumulate geopolitical goals. By stealing touchy information and intellectual assets, states gain insights into adversaries' abilities, intentions, and vulnerabilities, letting them count on threats, make the most of weaknesses, and undermine adversaries' pursuits. Furthermore, cyber espionage allows states to behavior impact operations and form narratives inside the virtual realm. Through disseminating disinformation, propaganda, and mental manipulation, states are looking to govern public opinion, sow discord, and undermine, don't forget, democratic institutions.(*Weaponization of Information - ECPS*, n.d.).

Geopolitical Implications

Cyber espionage has extraordinary geopolitical implications, influencing the stability of power among worldwide locations and shaping the dynamics of world individuals and their own families. States use cyber espionage to build intelligence, display adversaries' sports activities, and advantage strategic blessings in diplomatic negotiations and army conflicts—moreover, your revelation. S.A.-sponsored cyber espionage campaigns can pressure diplomatic individuals of the family, propose retaliatory measures, and enhance geopolitical rivalries. The attribution trouble inherent in cyberspace exacerbates mistrust and suspicion among states, hindering efforts to set up norms of behavior and engagement policies inside the virtual region. In prevention, cyber espionage represents an incredible device inside the arsenal of modern statecraft, with an extended manner that sports out implications for geopolitics, international safety, and democratic governance. As states hold to harness the power of facts to pursue their strategic goals, policymakers, diplomats, and safety professionals ought to enlarge effective techniques for countering cyber threats, promoting transparency and cooperation in cyberspace, and safeguarding the integrity of democratic establishments in a more interconnected world. (Moyer, 2024).

Cyber Terrorism: Threats to National and Global Security

The proliferation of virtual technology has revolutionized the landscape of terrorism, giving rise to today's form of chance, referred to as cyber terrorism.

Understanding Cyber Terrorism

Cyberterrorism, a grave and urgent threat, involves the use of PC-based real-time activities by malicious actors to orchestrate terrorist assaults or advance extremist agendas. Unlike conventional terrorism, which relies on physical violence and coercion, cyber terrorism exploits vulnerabilities in virtual systems to disrupt crucial infrastructure, motivate financial damage, and instill fear among populations. The strategies employed by cyber terrorists are severe and constantly evolving, including hacking, malware deployment, denial-of-business attacks, and social engineering strategies. Targets of cyber terrorism can range from governments, organizations, financial institutions, transportation systems, and energy grids, to telecommunications networks. Cyberterrorism aims to exploit the most vulnerabilities in the systems to inflict harm, sow chaos, and advance ideological or political goals(Iftikhar, 2024).

Impacts of Cyber Terrorism

The effect of cyber threats may be profound and massive, posing an extreme threat to countrywide protection and international stability. Targeted cyber attacks on infrastructure, energy traces, and transportation structures can disrupt infrastructure, motivate economic losses, and undermine public self-assurance in authorities and establishments. Extremism and online trafficking to radicalize guys, incite violence, and social anxiety can develop. Moreover, the interconnectedness of our online international method that cyberattacks could have transnational consequences, spreading over borders are invisible and affect a couple of worldwide places concurrently. This connectivity will increase the power of cyber threats, making it an international protection trouble that requires concerted worldwide efforts to cope with it correctly. Strategies for Reducing Cyberterrorism Reducing cyber threats requires a complete and multifaceted approach that addresses each complicated technological and record environment.(*Rising Cyber Threats Pose Serious Concerns for Financial Stability*, n.d.). Key strategies encompass:

Figure 2. Impacts of cyber terrorism

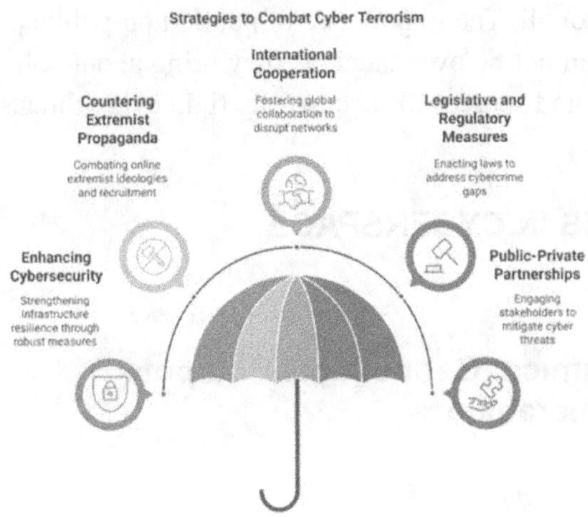

1. **Enhancing Cybersecurity**: Strengthening the resilience of vital infrastructure and statistics structures via sturdy cybersecurity measures, inclusive of network tracking, danger intelligence sharing, and incident reaction skills.
2. **Countering Extremist Propaganda: Combating** the unfolding of extremist ideologies and recruitment materials online through counter-narratives, public consciousness campaigns, and partnerships with tech companies and civil society corporations.
3. **International Cooperation:** Fostering collaboration and statistics sharing amongst global places to disrupt terrorist networks operating in our online international, including extradition agreements, joint investigations, and capability-constructing tasks.
4. **Legislative and Regulatory Measures**: Enacting prison pointers and guidelines to address gaps in cybercrime rules, improving law enforcement skills, and holding perpetrators of cyberterrorism accountable for their actions.

5. **Public-Private Partnerships:** The want to interact with corporation stakeholders, academia, and civil society to expand proactive strategies for identifying and mitigating rising cyber threats is paramount. The scale and complexity of cyberterrorism, a big and evolving country-wide and global protection threat, necessitate coordinated efforts to deal with its root reasons and mitigate its impacts. With my expertise in cyberterrorism, its capability consequences, and the techniques hired to fight it, policymakers, safety specialists, and civil society actors can work collectively to assemble an extra regular and strong digital future for all. The importance of public-non-public partnerships in this undertaking can not be overstated, as they bring about collectively numerous understanding and sources to successfully fight cyber threats.

STATE ACTORS IN CYBERSPACE

Regional Dynamics: Geopolitical Hotspots and Cyber Vulnerabilities

Figure 3. State actors in cyberspace

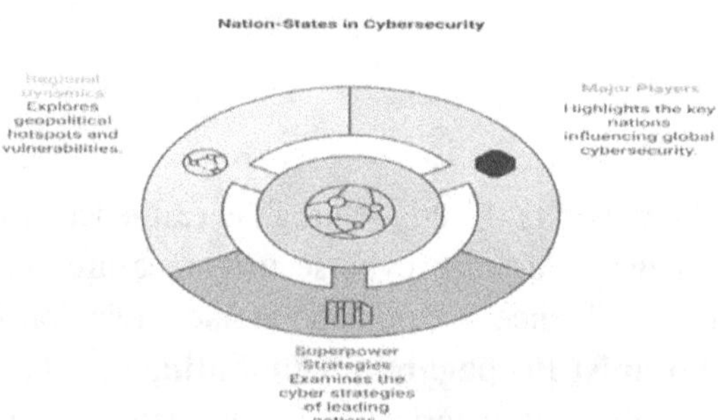

The image outlines three aspects of cybersecurity in nation-states: **Regional Dynamics** (geopolitical hotspots and vulnerabilities), **Superpower Strategies** (cyber strategies of leading nations), and **Major Players** (key nations influencing global cybersecurity).

Major Players: The Role of Nation-States in Cybersecurity

In cybersecurity, realms play an essential position as defenders and aggressors within the virtual area. This segment highlights the widespread involvement of key gamers, including the USA, China, Russia, India, and others, in shaping the panorama of our online global. Their actions and strategies have a profound impact on the safety and balance of the virtual realm, underscoring the significance of expertise and addressing their role.

Superpowers and Cyber Strategies: USA, China, Russia, India, and Others

Figure 4. Major state actors and their cybersecurity objectives

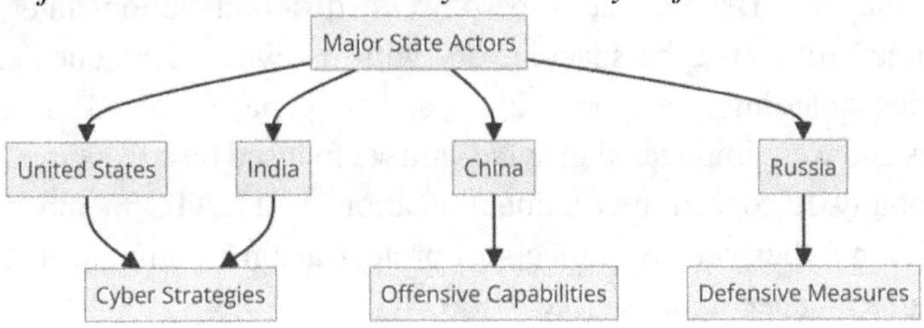

1. **United States**: As a global superpower and technological leader, the United States wields a super-sized effect in cyberspace. Its cyber technique makes a specialty of protecting essential infrastructure, promoting innovation, and advancing country-wide interests whilst adhering to global norms of conduct. The U.S. Cyber Command protects U.S. Army networks and conducts offensive cyber operations at the same time as vita2. China: With its swiftly developing economic system and growing technological skills, China has come to be a complete player in our online international.
2. **China:** The Chinese authorities view our online world as a strategic area for economic improvement, country-wide security, and social management. China's cyber strategy emphasizes cyber sovereignty, state control over fact flows, and the development of Indigenous cyber technologies. The People's Liberation Army Strategic Support Force conducts cyber operations supporting China's army goals.
3. **Russia:** Russia is understood for its state-of-the-art cyber competencies and willingness to use cyber operations to gain strategic desires. The Russian authorities view our online world as uneven warfare, permitting it to undermine

adversaries' balance and impact without resorting to standard navy pressure. Russia's cyber method specializes in statistics, war, propaganda, and cyber proxies to boost its geopolitical interests. The Russian military intelligence organization, referred to as the GRU, is accountable for carrying out offensive cyber operations on behalf of the Russian government.

4. **India**: India has emerged as a substantial participant in our online world, with its developing financial system and technological prowess using advancements in cybersecurity abilities. The Indian government acknowledges the importance of our online world for national safety, economic development, and social development. India's cyber strategy emphasizes the protection of critical infrastructure, capability building, and worldwide cooperation to combat cyber threats. The National Cyber Security Coordinator and the National Cyber Security Strategy outline India's cybersecurity and cyber defense techniques.
5. **Other Players**: Beyond the superpowers, different nation-states also play widespread roles in cyberspace, every with its cyber techniques and targets. Countries including Iran, North Korea, and Israel have evolved advanced cyber abilities and were implicated in cyber-attacks focused on adversaries' networks. Additionally, European international locations and NATO member states collaborate on cybersecurity projects to protect against common threats and to maintain a balance in our online world.

Regional Dynamics: Geopolitical Hotspots and Cyber Vulnerabilities

1. **Middle East:** The Middle East is a hotspot for cyber battles, with countries like Iran and Israel conducting cyber operations to advance their local agendas. Iran has been accused of undertaking cyber assaults in opposition to its adversaries' networks, inclusive of the ones of America and Saudi Arabia. Israel, meanwhile, has evolved sophisticated cyber skills to shield itself from cyber threats and release offensive operations in opposition to its enemies.
2. **Asia-Pacific:** The Asia-Pacific area is witnessing a proliferation of cyber skills among countries of North Korea, South Korea, Japan, and India. North Korea, specifically, has been connected to cyber assaults concentrated on monetary institutions and vital infrastructure in South Korea and different nations. South Korea, Japan, and India have strengthened their cyber defenses in reaction to developing threats from North Korea and other nearby actors.
3. **Europe:** Europe faces cyber threats from state and non-country actors, Russia, China, and cybercriminal companies. The European Union and man and woman member states have implemented cybersecurity measures to shield essential infrastructure, decorate data sharing, and toughen cyber resilience. However,

geopolitical tensions and historic rivalries continue to shape cyber dynamics in the location.

State actors play a number one function in shaping the landscape of our online world, with superpowers, which include America, China, Russia, India, and others, wielding extensive effect over cybersecurity strategies and operations. Regional dynamics further complicate the cybersecurity panorama, with geopolitical hotspots and cyber vulnerabilities posing widespread usa-extensive and worldwide protection-demanding situations. By analyzing expert use of actors' motivations, strategies, and capabilities in our online international, policymakers and protection professionals can develop robust methods for protecting against cyber threats and selling balance in the virtual area.(South et al., 2017).

STRATEGIES AND RESPONSES

International Cooperation: Challenges and Opportunities

Figure 5. International cooperation for global threat response, offensive capabilities for deterrence, and defensive measures to protect critical infrastructure

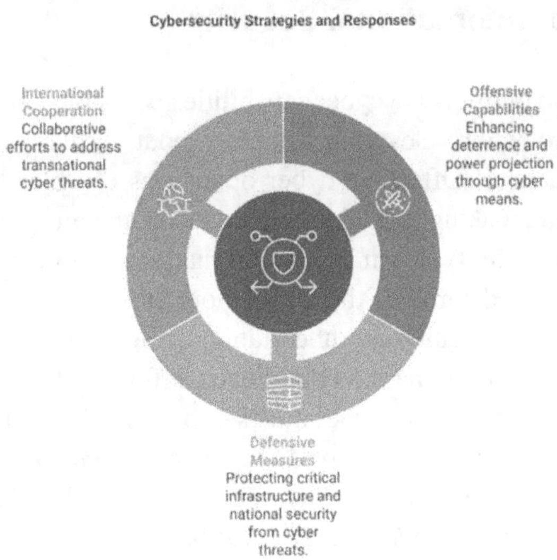

Offensive Cyber Capabilities: Deterrence and Power Projection

Offensive cyber abilities have become an increasingly distinguished device for states to exert influence on, assign strength to, and deter adversaries inside the virtual domain. This phase delves into the character of offensive cyber strategies, their implications for international safety, and the demanding situations associated with them.(*NATIONAL CYBERSECURITY STRATEGY*, 2023).

Understanding Offensive Cyber Capabilities

Offensive cyber abilities encompass several offensive operations performed in our online world, together with cyber espionage, sabotage, and disruption of adversaries' networks and systems. These abilities leverage goal community vulnerabilities, maximize software and hardware weaknesses, and use advanced strategies with 0-day exploits and malware deployment to acquire strategic objectives. States increase offensive cyber capabilities for numerous purposes, including intelligence accumulation, navy operations, and coercive international members of the circle of relatives. Offensive cyber operations can give states treasured insights into adversaries' abilities, intentions, and vulnerabilities, letting them expect threats, gain, and undermine adversaries' hobbies without using conventional kinetic techniques. (*The Five Bears: Russia's Offensive Cyber Capabilities*, n.d.).

Implications for International Security

The proliferation of offensive cyber capabilities poses big demanding situations to international protection, elevating troubles about escalation, attribution, and accidental consequences. Offensive cyber operations can blur the lines between peacetime and battle, making it challenging to decide the proper reaction to cyber-assaults and ensure stability in our online international. Moreover, the anonymity and deniability afforded through the way of our online world make attribution difficult, developing ambiguity and uncertainty about perpetrators' identities and motivations. This attribution hassle complicates efforts to keep states chargeable for their actions and deter future cyber-attacks, most notably to heightened loss of self-obligation and distrust among worldwide places.(*5 Potential Implications for International Security from THE RISE OF POPULIST SOVEREIGNISM: What It Is, Where It Comes from, and What It Means for International Security and Defense on JSTOR*, n.d.).

Challenges and Ethical Considerations

Using offensive cyber competencies will raise ethical, legal, and ethical questions about the right use of pressure in our online international and the functionality outcomes of cyber operations. States want to weigh the dangers and blessings of offensive cyber actions, considering their feasible effect on civilian populations, crucial infrastructure, and international stability. Furthermore, offensive cyber abilities can initiate retaliatory measures from adversaries, contributing to a dangerous cycle of escalation and retaliation in cyberspace. States ought to carefully consider the capability outcomes of their movements and increase mechanisms for de-escalation and catastrophe control to save conflicts from spiraling out of control. (*The Geopolitics of Cybersecurity – The Diplomat*, n.d.).

Defensive Measures: Protecting Critical Infrastructure and National Security

In response to the growing danger of cyber-attacks, states have implemented shielding measures to guard vital infrastructure, guard country-wide safety, and mitigate the risks of cyber threats. This section examines the man or woman of protecting cyber techniques, their effectiveness in countering cyber threats, and the traumatic conditions related to cybersecurity.

Enhancing Cyber Defences

Defensive cyber measures encompass several techniques and generations geared toward detecting, deterring, and mitigating cyber threats. These measures include community monitoring, vulnerability tests, intrusion detection systems, encryption, and incident response abilities designed to identify and neutralize cyber threats before they may cause harm. States invest closely in cybersecurity to defend essential infrastructure from cyber attacks, together with electricity grids, transportation systems, monetary networks, and authority agencies. By imposing sturdy cybersecurity measures, states can beautify their resilience to cyber threats and decrease the ability effect of cyber attacks on the. S .-complete protection and public safety.

Challenges and Limitations

Despite advances in the cybersecurity era, shielding measures face huge disturbing situations and limitations in countering ultra-modern cyber threats. Cyber attackers typically adapt and evolve their techniques, strategies, and strategies to avoid protection measures and take benefit of vulnerabilities in goal networks.

Moreover, the interconnected nature of cyberspace and the way that protection measures are implemented in the way of one United States can also have accidental consequences on others, most importantly to functionality conflicts and tensions inside the worldwide region. States need to strike a touchy balance between protecting their networks and respecting excellent worldwide locations' sovereignty and protection interests in our online international(*(PDF) Navigating the Cyber Security Landscape: A Comprehensive Review of Cyber-Attacks, Emerging Trends, and Recent Developments*, n.d.).

International Cooperation: Challenges and Opportunities

Given the transnational nature of cyber threats, international cooperation is critical for effectively addressing cyber annoying conditions and selling balance in our online world. This section examines the possibilities and worrying situations related to global cooperation on cybersecurity and explores mechanisms for enhancing collaboration among states.

Opportunities for Collaboration

International cooperation on cybersecurity gives several blessings, consisting of reality-sharing, capability-constructing, and collective safety in opposition to uncommon threats. States can leverage partnerships and alliances to trade danger intelligence, percent exquisite practices, and coordinate responses to cyber incidents, enhancing their collective resilience to cyber threats and selling stability in our online global. Moreover, global cooperation gives a platform for growing norms of behavior and recommendations of engagement in cyberspace, fostering bear-in-mind and self-notion among global places and decreasing the threat of conflict and escalation. States can create more robust and predictable surroundings for cyber operations by putting in place unusual requirements and recommendations for accountable behavior in our online world.(*Cybercrime Module 8 Key Issues: International Cooperation on Cybersecurity Matters*, n.d.).

Challenges and Obstacles

Despite the benefits of world cooperation, difficult situations and boundaries avoid powerful collaboration on cybersecurity. These stressful situations consist of differing country-wide pursuits, problems with sovereignty and privacy, and the shortage of consideration and self-belief among states in our online world. Moreover, the absence of universally commonplace norms and regulations of engagement in cyberspace complicates efforts to develop effective mechanisms for cooperation and coordination. States want to overcome collaboration's political, criminal, and technical limitations and bring together mutual belief and self-notion via talk, transparency, and self-notion-building measures. In giving up, strategies and responses to cyber threats require a multifaceted method that combines offensive abilities, defensive measures, and international cooperation. By facts the effects of offensive cyber movements, enhancing cyber defenses, and selling collaboration amongst states, policymakers and protection specialists can extend effective techniques for countering cyber threats and stability of sales inside the digital location.6. Geopolitical Considerations in Cyber Polic.(*The Department of Defense Critical Infrastructure Protection (CIP) Plan Version 1.0*, n.d.).

GEOPOLITICAL CONSIDERATIONS IN CYBER POLICY

National Cyber Strategies: Aligning Security and Geopolitical Objectives

National cyber techniques feature roadmaps for international places to navigate the complex landscape of our online world while aligning safety goals with broader geopolitical hobbies. This section delves into the improvement of country-wide cyber strategies, their alignment with geopolitical desires, and their implications for international participants in the circle of relatives.

Development of National Cyber Strategies

The purpose of the national cyber techniques function roadmaps is to navigate cyberspace globally while aligning safety targets to overall political desires. In this segment, we will explore how national cyber strategies are developed and aligned with political ambitions and what they mean for global relations with others. The Implication to World Relations: The alignment between national cyber strategies and geopolitical objectives(*United States International Cyberspace & Digital Policy Strategy - United States Department of State*, n.d.).

Cyber Diplomacy: Negotiating Norms and Agreements

The feature of Cyber international family members helps form the norms, rules, and understanding that shape behavior on the internet and reduce the possibilities of uncertainty and war. This segment discusses the role of the cyber global circle of relative participants in establishing international norms and agreements, improving collaboration between nations, and retaining peaceful situations on the net. Promoting International Norms Cyber global own family participants sell international norms. States engage in diplomatic efforts to gather consensus, enhance interests, and encourage adherence to the norms of the one, improving predictability and transparency and thinking about international places in our online global Negotiating Agreements. Worldwide cyber relations entail negotiating bilateral and multilateral agreements to deal with unusually worrying situations and mitigate the dangers of struggle and escalation in our online world. These agreements can also cover self-belief-building measures, information sharing, incident response cooperation, and vital infrastructure safety, presenting a framework for collaboration and coordination among states.(*Cybersecurity and the Concept of Norms | Carnegie Endowment for International Peace*, n.d.).

Challenges and Opportunities

Despite cyber worldwide family individuals' functionality benefits, severe traumatic conditions and boundaries save you practical cooperation and negotiation in our online world. These demanding situations include differing countrywide pastimes, problems with sovereignty and privacy, and the shortage of acquire as actual with and self-belief amongst states. However, cyber international family members offer opportunities for constructing bridges, fostering speaking, and finding commonplace floors on shared hobbies and worries.(Douzet & Gery, 2021).

Ethical and Legal Implications: Balancing Security with Privacy and Human Rights

Cyber insurance must navigate a complicated landscape of moral and jail troubles, balancing the imperatives of country-wide safety with defensive privacy, human rights, and democratic values. This segment examines cyber coverage's ethical and criminal implications, including questions of surveillance, censorship, and the use of pressure in cyberspace.(*What Is Cyber Insurance and Why Is It Important? | Definition from TechTarget*, n.d.).

Protecting Privacy and Human Rights

Cyber coverage has to uphold the thoughts of privacy and human rights, ensuring that measures taken to beautify cybersecurity do not infringe upon people's rights to privacy, freedom of expression, and due device. States need to enact legal guidelines and suggestions that guard residents' digital rights and preserve governments' accountable(Finnemore & Hollis, 2019).

FUTURE TRENDS AND CHALLENGES

Geopolitical Risks within the Digital Age: Emerging Threats and Vulnerabilities

The virtual age has ushered in a new generation of geopolitical dangers characterized by growing threats and vulnerabilities in cyberspace. This segment explores the evolving landscape of geopolitical hazards, which embody cyber struggle, state-backed cyber-attacks, and the weaponization of statistics. Cyber Warfare Cyber conflict is a massive chance for national and worldwide safety as more and more nations use cyber capabilities for offensive operations, undermining the balance of their fighters and achieving strategic goals. Using cyber weapons in navy conflicts or geopolitical competitions should likely improve tensions, lead to retaliatory motion, or disrupt global order. State-Sponsored Cyber Attacks State-backed cyber attacks constitute a developing threat. (*A World of Cyber-Led Geopolitical and Technological Transitions: WEF Report's Breakdown, ET CIO SEA*, n.d.).

Technological Advances: Implications for Cybersecurity Strategy

Using statistics as a weapon in international politics is not satisfactorily scary, but it's far more thrilling. In the gift-day global age, states can manage public opinion. They obtain this using discrediting proof amassed in their course or imparting contradictory statistics from mystery sources to justify their regulations in advance compared to humans. In our online global, wrong information campaigns tend to create social tensions because of political variations among various companies inside society. Thus, the leading motive for the loss of attractiveness as accurate within democracy is that human beings assume that some data might have been fabricated via governments to tell their interests or allies. Besides, sharing fake facts fuels propaganda, which ultimately promotes manipulation at higher ranges, along with elections. In this way, the weaponization of facts performs a widespread position in geopolitical war, mainly among international places with sturdy worldwide affairs hobbies. There are many potential consequences from this sort of motion, which encompass protectionism, securitization at home, and xenophobia towards refugees. This makes it even now not impossible to break up reality from fiction any extra, thereby hard citizens.(*The Role of Nuclear Weapons in International Politics: A Strategic Perspective - Foreign Policy Research Institute*, n.d.).

Artificial Intelligence

Artificial intelligence (AI) ambitions to beautify cybersecurity skills, allowing extra wonderful inexperienced chance detection, incident reaction, and desire-making in our online world. AI-powered systems may observe massive quantities of information, recognize patterns and anomalies, and automate ordinary obligations, empowering protection organizations to find out and mitigate cyber threats greater efficaciously.

Quantum Computing

Quantum computing presents a double-edged sword for cybersecurity, imparting the capability for breakthroughs in encryption and cryptographic algorithms even posing demanding conditions to traditional protection abilities. Quantum computer systems can damage contemporary encryption schemes, rendering modern cryptographic protocols outdated and necessitating the development of quantum-resistant encryption algorithms to stabilize data within the positioned up-quantum technology.

Internet of Things (IoT)

The proliferation of Internet-associated gadgets inside the Internet of Things (IoT) offers new attack surfaces and vulnerabilities for cyber adversaries to make the most of. Insecure IoT gadgets can be compromised and used as vectors for cyber assaults, foremost information breaches, service disruptions, and privacy violations. Securing the IoT requires robust safety features, tool authentication, information encryption, and vulnerability control to mitigate the dangers of cyber threats.

Shaping the Future: Geopolitical Factors in Cyber Policy and Governance

Geopolitical elements will shape the future of cyber policy and governance, influencing the improvement of global norms, regulations, and cooperation mechanisms in our online global. This section explores the features of geopolitics in shaping the destiny of cyber insurance and governance, which embody the need for multilateral cooperation, norms of responsible behavior, and mechanisms for battle prevention and resolution

Multilateral Cooperation

Multilateral cooperation is crucial for addressing global cyber-demanding situations, fostering consideration and self-guarantee among nations, and selling stability in cyberspace. States have to art work collectively to broaden common ideas, norms, and recommendations of engagement that uphold worldwide law, guard human rights, and ensure the peaceful use of our online world.

Norms of Responsible Behaviour

Norms of accountable behavior are essential in shaping our behavior online, guiding states' moves and interactions through shared values and requirements. States must adhere to mounted norms in conjunction with those outlined within the United Nations Group of Governmental Experts (UN GGE) reports, emphasizing you. Responsibility, sovereignty, and non-interference in our online world.

Mechanisms for Conflict Prevention and Resolution

Conflict prevention and determination mechanisms are essential for handling geopolitical tensions and mitigating the dangers of war and escalation in cyberspace. States must increase verbal exchange channels, establish crisis control mechanisms, and interact with family members worldwide to cope with cyber incidents, de-increase conflicts, and build mutual beliefs and self-belief amongst nations.

Ultimately, geopolitical dangers, technological advances, and evolving cyber coverage and governance frameworks will form destiny trends and challenges in our online world. By knowing the results of emerging threats and vulnerabilities, harnessing the ability of new technology, and fostering cooperation and collaboration amongst states, policymakers and safety specialists can navigate the digital age's complexities and construct a more secure and resilient online world for future generations.(*7 Trends That Could Shape the Future of Cybersecurity in 2030 | World Economic Forum*, n.d.).

CONCLUSION

Looking Ahead: Navigating Geopolitical Realities in the Code War Era

As we navigate the complexities of the Code War generation, it will become more and more apparent that the intersection of geopolitics and cybersecurity will shape the future of world participants of the own family, countrywide safety, and worldwide governance. Cyberspace geopolitical realities gift opportunities and disturbing conditions, requiring states to efficaciously adapt their strategies, guidelines, and partnerships to deal with growing threats and vulnerabilities. The Code War technology is characterized by fast technological improvements, evolving cyber threats, and geopolitical rivalries that span the globe. State actors leverage cyber abilities to increase their pastimes challenge electricity and affect global affairs. In assessment, non-united States of America actors take gain of our online world to undermine stability, sow chaos, and sell their agendas. In this environment, states should navigate a complicated panorama of dangers and uncertainties, balancing the imperatives of countrywide protection with the requirements of sovereignty, human rights, and international law. Looking ahead, geopolitical tensions, technological disruptions, and the preference for collective motion to deal with shared disturbing conditions in our online global will define the Code War generation. States need to paint collectively to build shared norms, guidelines, and mechanisms for cooperation, making sure cyberspace is non-violent and regularly used for the advantage of all. States can construct a resilient and inclusive online world that advances peace, prosperity, and human dignity by fostering communique, constructing consideration, and promoting responsible behavior. (*THE CHANGING CYBER THREAT LANDSCAPE SOUTHEAST ASIA - CYFIRMA*, n.d.).

Call to Action: Addressing Geopolitical Challenges in Cybersecurity Strategy

In moderate geopolitical annoying situations posed with the aid of the Code War technology, collective motion is urgently required to address rising threats and vulnerabilities in cyberspace. Policymakers, protection specialists, and civil society actors should come together to develop progressive solutions, forge partnerships, and construct resilience in opposition to cyber threats. First and foremost, states must prioritize cybersecurity as an essential thing of country-comprehensive safety methods, allocating sources, know-how, and political will to enhance cyber defenses, deter cyber attacks, and sell responsible conduct in our online world. This calls for an entire-of-government method that engages multiple stakeholders, consisting of government companies, enterprise companions, academia, and civil society groups, in a concerted attempt to protect essential infrastructure, safeguard sensitive statistics, and hold the integrity of democratic institutions.(*Cyberspace and Geopolitics: Assessing Global Cybersecurity Norm Processes at a Crossroads | Carnegie Endowment for International Peace*, n.d.).

Second, states should invest in capacity construction and ability development to reinforce cybersecurity abilities on national and international degrees. This includes schooling cybersecurity professionals, promoting cybersecurity education and attention, and fostering a lifestyle of cyber hygiene and resilience amongst citizens and companies. By building a robust cybersecurity team of workers and atmosphere, states can enhance their capability to stumble on, respond to, and get over cyber incidents, thereby reducing the effect of cyber threats on society and the financial system.

Third, states want to interact in diplomatic efforts to promote worldwide cooperation, verbal exchange, and self-perception-building measures in our online world. This consists of taking elements in multilateral forums, which encompass the United Nations, the Group of Governmental Experts on Cybersecurity, and neighborhood organizations, to build shared norms, regulations, and ideas that govern countrywide behavior in our online world. By fostering perception, transparency, and obligation amongst global locations, states can reduce the chance of struggle and escalation in cyberspace and promote stability and safety for all.

In the end, addressing the geopolitical stressful situations of the Code War technology calls for collective motion, innovation, and control from all stakeholders. States can assemble a greater steady, extra resilient, and wealthy destiny in our online world via together increasingly inclusive and powerful cybersecurity techniques, guidelines, and partnerships. As we embark on this adventure, we will receive the opportunity to shape the destiny of our online world for the gain of gifts and future generations.(*India's Cybersecurity Challenge: Threats and Strategies*, n.d.).

REFERENCES

A world of cyber-led geopolitical and technological transitions: WEF report's breakdown, ET CIO SEA. (n.d.). Retrieved January 16, 2025, from https://ciosea.economictimes.indiatimes.com/news/security/a-world-of-cyber-led-geopolitical-and-technological-transitions-wef-reports-breakdown/107099915

Cold War | Summary, Causes, History, Years, Timeline, & Facts | Britannica. (n.d.). Retrieved June 25, 2024, from https://www.britannica.com/event/Cold-War

Cybercrime Module 8 Key Issues: International Cooperation on Cybersecurity Matters. (n.d.). Retrieved January 16, 2025, from https://www.unodc.org/e4j/ar/cybercrime/module-8/key-issues/international-cooperation-on-cybersecurity-matters.html

Cybercrime Treaty, U. N. *The Year Cyber and Multilateralism Stole the Show - Indian Council of World Affairs (Government of India)*. (n.d.). Retrieved January 16, 2025, from https://www.icwa.in/show_content.php?lang=1&level=1&ls_id=12242&lid=7470

Cybersecurity and the Concept of Norms | Carnegie Endowment for International Peace. (n.d.). Retrieved January 16, 2025, from https://carnegieendowment.org/research/2017/11/cybersecurity-and-the-concept-of-norms?lang=en

Cyberspace and Geopolitics: Assessing Global Cybersecurity Norm Processes at a Crossroads | Carnegie Endowment for International Peace. (n.d.). Retrieved January 16, 2025, from https://carnegieendowment.org/research/2020/02/cyberspace-and-geopolitics-assessing-global-cybersecurity-norm-processes-at-a-crossroads?lang=en

Cyberspace and Geopolitics: Assessing Global Cybersecurity Norm Processes at a Crossroads - Carnegie Endowment for International Peace. (n.d.). Retrieved June 25, 2024, from https://carnegieendowment.org/research/2020/02/cyberspace-and-geopolitics-assessing-global-cybersecurity-norm-processes-at-a-crossroads?lang=en

Digital Infrastructure and Cyber War: The New Front of International Law – Jindal Forum for International and Economic Laws. (n.d.). Retrieved January 16, 2025, from https://jindalforinteconlaws.in/2024/11/19/digital-infrastructure-and-cyber-war-the-new-front-of-international-law/

Douzet, F., & Gery, A. (2021). Cyberspace is used, first and foremost, to wage wars: Proliferation, security, and stability in cyberspace. *Journal of Cyber Policy*, *6*(1), 96–113. DOI: 10.1080/23738871.2021.1937253

Dynamics of the Changing Global Security Order: Emerging Trends and Key Issues in Asia - 9781666949131. (n.d.). Retrieved June 25, 2024, from https://rowman.com/ISBN/9781666949131/Dynamics-of-the-Changing-Global-Security-Order-Emerging-Trends-and-Key-Issues-in-Asia

Finnemore, M., & Hollis, D. B. (2019). Beyond Naming and Shaming: Accusations and International Law in Cybersecurity. SSRN *Electronic Journal*. https://doi.org/DOI: 10.2139/SSRN.3347958

Geopolitical Cyber Risk: Cyber Operations in Modern Warfare | by Robindimyan | Medium. (n.d.). Retrieved June 25, 2024, from https://robindimyan.medium.com/geopolitical-cyber-risk-cyber-operations-in-modern-warfare-db1392ab0df5

Geopolitical Factors Shaping the Future of the Cyber Domain - Critical Start. (n.d.). Retrieved January 16, 2025, from https://www.criticalstart.com/geopolitical-factors-shaping-the-future-of-the-cyber-domain/

Hassid, N. (2024). The rise of companies in the cyber era and the pursuant shift in national security. SSRN *Electronic Journal*. https://doi.org/DOI: 10.2139/SSRN.4842383

Iftikhar, S. (2024). Cyberterrorism as a global threat: A review on repercussions and countermeasures. *PeerJ. Computer Science*, *10*, e1772. DOI: 10.7717/peerj-cs.1772 PMID: 38259881

India's Cybersecurity Challenge. *Threats and Strategies*. (n.d.). Retrieved June 25, 2024, from https://www.drishtiias.com/daily-updates/daily-news-editorials/india-s-cybersecurity-challenge-threats-and-strategies

Mangold, P. (2013). National security and international relations. *National Security and International Relations*, 1–117. DOI: 10.4324/9780203494684

Moyer, J. D. (2024). A double-edged sword into a plowshare: Analyzing geopolitical implications of alternative socioeconomic development pathways. *One Earth*, *7*(2), 336–347. DOI: 10.1016/j.oneear.2024.01.002

NATIONAL CYBERSECURITY STRATEGY. (2023).

(PDF) Cyber Conflict and International Relations. *A Comprehensive Analysis of Cyber Deterrence Strategies in Contemporary Geopolitics*. (n.d.). Retrieved January 16, 2025, from https://www.researchgate.net/publication/378334428_Cyber_Conflict_and_International_Relations_A_Comprehensive_Analysis_of_Cyber_Deterrence_Strategies_in_Contemporary_Geopolitics

(PDF) Navigating the Cyber Security Landscape. *A Comprehensive Review of Cyber-Attacks, Emerging Trends, and Recent Developments*. (n.d.). Retrieved January 16, 2025, from https://www.researchgate.net/publication/378343830_Navigating_the_Cyber_security_Landscape_A_Comprehensive_Review_of_Cyber-Attacks_Emerging_Trends_and_Recent_Developments

(PDF) The Cyber Defense Review - vol. 7 No. 2 Spring 2022. (n.d.). Retrieved January 16, 2025, from https://www.researchgate.net/publication/360745730_The_Cyber_Defense_Review_-_vol_7_No_2_Spring_2022

5. *Potential Implications for International Security from THE RISE OF POPULIST SOVEREIGNISM: What It Is, Where It Comes from, and What It Means for International Security and Defense on JSTOR*. (n.d.). Retrieved June 25, 2024, from https://www.jstor.org/stable/resrep12603.8

Rising Cyber Threats Pose Serious Concerns for Financial Stability. (n.d.). Retrieved January 16, 2025, from https://www.imf.org/en/Blogs/Articles/2024/04/09/rising-cyber-threats-pose-serious-concerns-for-financial-stability

Security Delta (HSD) | Trend snippet: Digital and physical processes in society have become intertwined and crisis management should be able to deal with this. (n.d.). Retrieved January 16, 2025, from https://securitydelta.nl/services/knowledge/trends/source-of-threat/nation-states/digital-and-physical-processes-in-society-have-become-intertwined-and-crisismanagement-should-be-able-to-deal-with-this-000515

South, F., Usf, T., Graduate, D., Usf, G., Theses, D., & Akdag, Y. (2017). *Cyber Deterrence against Cyberwar between the United States Cyber Deterrence against Cyberwar between the United States and China: A Power Transition Theory Perspective and China: A Power Transition Theory Perspective*. https://digitalcommons.usf.edu/etd

THE CHANGING CYBER THREAT LANDSCAPE SOUTHEAST ASIA - CYFIRMA. (n.d.). Retrieved January 16, 2025, from https://www.cyfirma.com/research/the-changing-cyber-threat-landscape-southeast-asia/

The Department of Defense Critical Infrastructure Protection (CIP) Plan Version 1.0. (n.d.). Retrieved June 25, 2024, from https://irp.fas.org/offdocs/pdd/DOD-CIP-Plan.htm

The Five Bears: Russia's Offensive Cyber Capabilities. (n.d.). Retrieved June 25, 2024, from https://greydynamics.com/the-five-bears-russias-offensive-cyber-capabilities/

The Future of the Metaverse | Imagining the Internet | Elon University. (n.d.). Retrieved January 16, 2025, from https://www.elon.edu/u/imagining/surveys/xiv-2022/future-of-metaverse-web3-2040/

The Geopolitics of Cybersecurity – The Diplomat. (n.d.). Retrieved June 25, 2024, from https://thediplomat.com/2020/12/the-geopolitics-of-cybersecurity/

"The Interconnected Global Economy: Challenges and Opportunities for the United States— and the World" By Christine Lagarde, Managing Director, International Monetary Fund. (n.d.). Retrieved January 16, 2025, from https://www.imf.org/en/News/Articles/2015/09/28/04/53/sp091913

The Role of Nuclear Weapons in International Politics. *A Strategic Perspective - Foreign Policy Research Institute*. (n.d.). Retrieved January 16, 2025, from https://www.fpri.org/article/2009/03/the-role-of-nuclear-weapons-in-international-politics-a-strategic-perspective/

Tihonova, E. V., Borisova, T. P., & Bunov, E. G. (2022). Cyberspace as a New Social Reality in the Era of Globalization. *Lecture Notes in Networks and Systems, 398 LNNS*, 274–280. DOI: 10.1007/978-3-030-94870-2_35

7. *trends that could shape the future of cybersecurity in 2030 | World Economic Forum*. (n.d.). Retrieved June 25, 2024, from https://www.weforum.org/agenda/2023/03/trends-for-future-of-cybersecurity/

United States International Cyberspace & Digital Policy Strategy - United States Department of State. (n.d.). Retrieved January 16, 2025, from https://www.state.gov/united-states-international-cyberspace-and-digital-policy-strategy/

Weaponization of Information - ECPS. (n.d.). Retrieved June 25, 2024, from https://www.populismstudies.org/Vocabulary/weaponization-of-information/

What is Cyber Insurance and Why is it Important? | Definition from TechTarget. (n.d.). Retrieved January 16, 2025, from https://www.techtarget.com/searchsecurity/definition/cybersecurity-insurance-cybersecurity-liability-insurance

What is Cyber Warfare | Types, Examples & Mitigation | Imperva? (n.d.-a). Retrieved January 16, 2025, from https://www.imperva.com/learn/application-security/cyber-warfare/

What is Cyber Warfare | Types, Examples & Mitigation | Imperva? (n.d.-b). Retrieved June 25, 2024, from https://www.imperva.com/learn/application-security/cyber-warfare/

Chapter 6
Large Language Models and Geopolitical Competition:
Governmental Power and the Challenges of a VUCA World

Srirath Gohwong
https://orcid.org/0000-0002-0714-3886
Kasetsart University, Thailand

ABSTRACT

This study examined how China, Russia, India, and the United States implemented strategic policy measures to bolster national LLM firms and establish AI sovereignty during the period of the LLM Cold War. It examined how governments utilized Weimer and Vining's policy instruments and state power marketing to improve digital legitimacy and oppose kakistoscryptocracy. Through documentary analysis, the study uncovered state-centric models in China and Russia that stressed ideological control and cybersecurity, while India and the U.S. adopted market-centric models fostering innovation via public-private partnerships. These strategies demonstrated that AI governance combined technology with political power and epistemology, where managing algorithms and narratives established what is considered truth.

INTRODUCTION

The Cold War has progressed into four distinct phases: Cold War I, Cold War II, the AI Cold War, and the LLM Cold War. During the Cold War I (1947–1991), the United States and the Soviet Union engaged in intense ideological and geopo-

DOI: 10.4018/979-8-3373-1727-4.ch006

litical competition. Features included mutually assured destruction through nuclear armaments, localized conflicts fought through proxies, and economic revival projects similar to the Marshall Plan, concluding with the USSR's breakup in 1991. Entering the new millennium, Cold War II took shape as China and Russia returned to prominence as major opponents, resulting in economic isolationism, trading disputes, and digital skirmishing concerning vital sectors like telecommunication standards, chip manufacturing, and internet economies. By the 2010s, the AI Cold War intensified greatly, with AI becoming a crucial element in national defense and technological dominance, as the US and China rose as primary AI leaders concentrating on advanced robotics, extensive data processing, and complex cybersecurity initiatives. This rivalry has developed into the LLM Cold War (2020s–Present), as major global powers redirected their attention to Large Language Models (LLMs) to manipulate digital narratives, impact economies, and formulate democratic processes. Governments have limited foreign AI models, enhanced regulations for AI training, and developed national AI ecosystems to guarantee digital sovereignty and technological autonomy. The U.S. (ChatGPT, Gemini, Copilot, Claude AI), China (DeepSeek, Qwen 3), Russia (Yandex GPT-4, RU-GPT-3), and India (Hanooman GPT, Krutrim AI, Bharat GPT) are creating their own LLMs to lessen dependence on international AI and gain control over AI regulation. The LLM Cold War now shapes the geopolitical terrain of the 21st century, as AI-powered automation, digital influence, and intelligence dominance have taken center stage in global power conflicts. Understanding the dynamics of the LLM Cold War is very essential, since any state that effectively utilizes Weimer and Vining's (2017) broad policy strategies to manage governmental power marketing with LLMs and chips, will shape the future of digital governance, cybersecurity, and AI-driven policymaking. Unlike previous AI competitions that focused on automation and military applications, this conflict directly impacts worldwide economic frameworks, policy development, and the strength of democratic structures (particularly thanks to Alibaba Cloud, 2025; Anthropic, 2024; Begum & Chowdary, 2024; Conradi, 2016; CoRover.ai, 2025; Crawford, 2021; DeepSeek, 2025; Diamond Ellis & Schell, 2023; Gaddis, 2005; Gohwong, 2023; Hussaini, 2023; Krutrim, 2025; Jermsittiparsert et al., 2023; Lee, 2018; Leffler & Westad, 2010; Lozovsky, 2025; Lucas, 2008; Ma & Scaramucci, 2020; Malak, 2025; Mandal, 2025; Mazzucato, 2023; Miller, 2022; Minnick, 2025; Roberts & Hite, 2000; Sanger, 2024; Seetha Mahalakshmi Healthcare Private Limited, 2025; Shambaugh, 2020; SberBank PJSC, 2025; Shih, 2023; Takach, 2023; Tech Mahindra Limited, 2025; Thompson & Bremmer, 2018; Weimer & Vining, 2017; Westad, 2017; Winston, 2020; Yandex, 2025; Yang, 2023; Yoffie, 2022; Zenglein, 2023). Therefore, the study's objectives were (1) to explore how giant states like China, Russia, India, and U.S. use policy interventions to contribute LLM firms, and (2) to investigate how these governments uses policy interventions to do governmental power market-ing for sustainably increasing AI sovereignty and to effectively address Kakistoscryptocracy.

LITERATURE REVIEWS

To establish a comprehensive understanding of the complex relationships between governance, technology, and power in contemporary society, this chapter conducted a thorough analysis of scholarly literature, incorporating numerous interconnected frameworks. The review covered areas such as dark psychology, governmental power marketing under unstable and uncertain conditions, and the emerging concept of kakistoscryptocracy. Moreover, it analyzed large language models (LLMs), political economy theories, relevant theories of international relations, and the general policy approaches proposed by Weimer and Vining. These theoretical frameworks provide the fundamental context for this understanding.

Dark Psychology

Dark psychology uses manipulative tactics—like gaslighting, mirroring, and love bombing—to control others without consent. Once limited to personal relationships, it now operates at societal levels via AI and LLMs. Governments embed political aims into AI: China reinforces party loyalty, Russia counters cognitive threats, India promotes ethical trust, and the U.S. champions democratic ideals. Essential control techniques encompass manipulation of reality, widespread persuasion, emotional shaping, and cognitive inhibition. Strategies based on Neuro-Linguistic Programming (NLP) are adapted to influence mindset and reliance. However, when revealed, manipulation falls apart—emphasizing the necessity of consent, awareness, and ethical clarity (particularly thanks to Bernays, 1928; Bradberry, 2020; Carnegie, 2020; Cooper, 2020; Faulkner, 2002; B. Goleman, 2020; J. Goleman, 2020; Goleman et al., 2020; Green, 2020; Griffith, 2021; Hoobyar et al., 2013; Ienca, 2023; Kavoliūnaitė-Ragauskienė, 2024; Kingler, 2021; Kool & Agrawal, 2016; Lee, 2018; Morton, 2020; Mind, 2019; Pace, 2015, 2017; Phill, 2021; J. R. Smith, 2019; M. Smith, 2020; Stanton, 2020; Williams, 2019; Wilson, 1967; Yücel, 2024).

Governmental Power Marketing in the Vu-Chaos World

The 2023 idea of Governmental Power Marketing combines public administration with storytelling techniques and symbolic interactionism to assist governments in maneuvering through the VUCA environment. With Crea-Innovation, governments improve governance in three key areas. In Vital Practices, citizen-focused tools such as Thailand's Inthanon blockchain and China's Guanxi networks enhance resource authenticity and adaptability. Strategic Thinking and Action links national goals to policies, exemplified by Estonia's digital identity. In Tactics and Tricks, narrative power arises as China influences views via its Great Firewall. Significantly, the terminology used in these approaches holds epistemological importance that necessitates further investigation beyond the policy itself. John Wilson argues that precise language enhances democratic accountability, whereas ambiguous language allows for manipulation (particularly thanks to Jermsittiparsert et al., 2023; Wilson, 1967).

Kakistoscryptocracy

In a VU-CHAOS setting, kakistoscryptocracy, a term introduced by Srirath Gohwong in 2023, driven by Non-government-based cryptocurrencies (NGCs) such as Bitcoin, strengthens non-state entities beyond conventional state authority, encompassing individuals, companies, and hedge funds. This framework, incorporating state-based (such as government organizations, firms, NGOs), stateless (such as pirates organizations, NGCs, darknets), and hybrid net states (such as Microsoft and Yandex), questions conventional sovereignty as technology platforms grow in power. This philosophical struggle highlights language as a source of power, necessitating institutional honesty and public consciousness to bring back truth in a fractured context (particularly thanks to Dougherty, 2023; Gohwong, 2020, 2023a, 2023b; Jermsittiparsert et al., 2023; Selznick, 1949; Wilson, 1967).

International Relations Theories

Theories of International Relations elucidate how nations vie for AI, particularly LLMs. Neorealism views the LLM Cold War as motivated by survival; China and Russia challenge United States supremacy to guarantee digital sovereignty. Neoliberalism underscores collaboration—India and the U.S. develop public-private LLM frameworks such as OpenAI and Google, focusing on innovation driven by the market. New-Constructivism highlights identity and dialogue; LLMs generate narrative impact, including digital ideologies, and articulating national identity. By linking these theories, John Wilson provides an important meta-theoretical insight: language generates truth claims instead of empirical data. In the LLM Cold War, Neorealism highlights security stories, Neoliberalism champions norms, and New-Constructivism prioritizes identity and discourse-based legitimacy (particularly thanks to Burchill et al., 2005; Jermsittiparsert et al., 2023; Kachiga, 2021; Kaufman, 2022; McCourt, 2022; Roach & Barder, 2024; Sørensen et al., 2022; Ministry of Electronics and Information Technology, 2024a; Nadibaidze, 2024; Petrella et al., 2021; Reus-Smit, 2020; Weber, 2001).

Large Language Models

Large Language Models (LLMs) are advanced AI systems that use deep learning, particularly transformer architectures, to understand and generate human language. Unlike earlier rule-based or statistical NLP approaches, LLMs rely on neural networks—layered systems that mimic the brain—to detect complex patterns in massive text datasets. For example, the request "Provide a short academic profile of Srirath Gohwong" (Figure 1) generates responses such as "Srirath Gohwong: a Thai lecturer at Kasetsart University." LLMs presently hold a key position in worldwide AI advancement, with the U.S., China, Russia, and India at the forefront (e.g., ChatGPT, DeepSeek, RU-GPT, Hanooman). While these systems enable translation, summarization, coding, and additional tasks, they face issues such as bias, hallucinations, and sensitivity to prompts. Notwithstanding these shortcomings, LLMs continue to be potent instruments for automation, communication, and impact in both technological and geopolitical spheres (particularly thanks to Alibaba Cloud, 2025; Anthropic, 2024; Atkinson-Abutridy, 2025; Banafa, 2024; Campesato, 2024; CoRover.ai, 2025; DeepSeek, 2025; Gazit & Ghaffari, 2024; Gohwong, 2025; Hussaini, 2023; Jamison, 2023; Kamath, Keenan, Somers, & Sorenson, 2024; Kasetsart University, 2025; Khandare, 2024; Krutrim, 2025; Malak, 2025; Mandal, 2025; Minnick, 2025; Ozdemir, 2024; Qwen Team, 2025; Sánchez, 2025; Sanghi, 2024; SberBank PJSC, 2025; Seetha Mahalakshmi Healthcare Private Limited, 2025; Thakur, Barker, & Pathan, 2024; Tech Mahindra Limited, 2025; Yandex, 2025).

Figure 1. Kasetsart University AI pedagogy framework: Conceptual diagram of LLM neural network process to describe Srirath Gohwong (Gohwong, 2025; Kasetsart University, 2025)

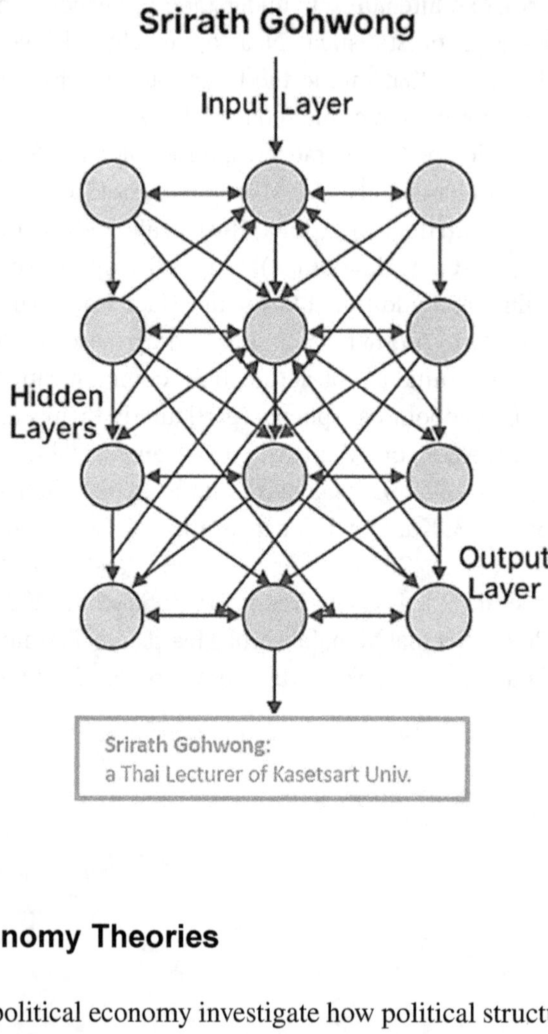

Political Economy Theories

Theories of political economy investigate how political structures and economic frameworks influence governance, resource distribution, and power dynamics, featuring state-centric, market-centric, and critical methods grounded in the ideas of scholars such as Smith, Marx, and Keynes. Employing qualitative and comparative approaches from political science, economics, and international relations, the domain focuses on the state–market continuum.

This gap is pronounced in the LLM Cold War. China and Russia use state-centric approaches, emphasizing government-led AI for digital sovereignty (such as China's Five-Year AI Plan, Russia's dependence on Sberbank and Rostec), presenting AI as a source of national pride and legitimacy through the promotion of government authority.

The U.S. and India, in contrast, embrace market-centric approaches, encouraging AI innovation through limited regulation and public-private collaborations, with leaders like OpenAI and Google advancing national capabilities within a neoliberal soft power framework.

To bridge these methods, John Wilson's philosophy of language provides a meta-theoretical viewpoint, claiming that truth is socially built through dialogue influenced by political and institutional contexts. Platforms such as DeepSeek reinforce ideology in state-focused environments, whereas ChatGPT promotes transparency in market-driven ones, highlighting language as a tool of power in the LLM Cold War—a conflict over technology and the definition of truth (particularly thanks to Buzgalin & Kolganov, 2015; Caporaso & Levine, 1992; GAO, 2023; Ibrahim et al., 2019; Nadibaidze, 2024; Nandi et al., 2025; Office of the President of the Russian Federation, 2019; O'Brien & Williams, 2016; Ravenhill, 2020; State Council of the People's Republic of China, 2017; Wilson, 1967).

Weimer and Vining's Generic Policies

Weimer and Vining's comprehensive strategies provide an organized approach to tackle market and regulatory challenges. This method starts by liberating, enabling, and generating markets via deregulation, privatization, and new marketable goods. Afterward, financial tools such as subsidies, tax incentives, tariffs, and vouchers affect supply and demand. Legal frameworks consequently create rules and property rights for market stability. Following that, governments provide essential goods either directly or indirectly. In the end, measures such as public insurance, reserves, and financial assistance shield against economic turmoil (Weimer & Vining, 2017).

RESEARCH METHODOLOGY

This study employed comprehensive document analysis, synthesizing evidence from multiple authoritative sources.

RESEARCH RESULTS

Policy Interventions to Support and Enhance LLM Firms

At the AI Action Summit (2025), which took place on February 11, 2025, at the Palais de l'Élysée in Paris, China and India, along with more than 100 other nations, signed the global pact on inclusive and sustainable artificial intelligence. The summit, jointly led by French President Emmanuel Macron and Indian Prime Minister Narendra Modi, brought together heads of state, researchers, leaders from the private sector, and civil society to establish a global framework for the ethical governance of AI. Key initiatives such as the Public Interest AI Platform and the AI for Sustainable Development Incubator were introduced at the event, designed to bridge the global digital gap, foster reliable AI, and develop digital public assets. The differing AI strategies of four major countries—China, India, Russia, and the United States—were particularly evident at this summit. China and India have both endorsed the global pact on inclusive and sustainable artificial intelligence, joining more than 100 other countries and demonstrating their backing for multilateral governance of AI. China's involvement highlighted its goals to influence international AI standards while retaining oversight over content and adherence. India, meanwhile, embraced the agreement as a platform to advance innovation and attract international collaboration, consistent with its market-oriented AI development strategy. In contrast, Russia chose not to attend the summit, reaffirming its preference for sovereign AI regulation and narrative control, independent of global governance frameworks. The United States, while involved, ultimately declined to sign, expressing worries that the agreement's regulatory terms might restrict innovation and competitiveness in its private technology industry. The differing choices unmistakably indicated their geopolitical focus and economic approaches in backing domestic LLM companies through AI as both (1) a strategic tool and (2) a matter of government regulation and economic strategy (particularly thanks to AI Action Summit, 2025a, 2025b; Alibaba Cloud, 2025; Atkinson-Abutridy, 2025; Begum & Chowdary, 2024; Capri, 2023; Chatterjee, 2020; Diamond, Ellis, & Schell, 2023; Draven, 2025; Ekimova, 2023; GAO, 2023; Government of India, 2005; Kehs, 2023; Lee, 2018; Malak, 2025; Mandal, 2025; Mazzucato, 2023; Miller, 2022; Ministère de l'Europe et des Affaires étrangères & Secrétariat général de la défense et de la sécurité nationale, 2025; Ministry of Electronics and Information Technology, 2024a, 2024b, 2025; Nadibaidze, 2024; Nandi et al., 2025; Petrella et al., 2021; Popkova et al., 2020; President of the Russian Federation, 2019; Qwen Team, 2025; Sabharwal & Berman, 2013; State Council of the People's Republic of China, 2017; Takach, 2023; Wu, Huang, and Gong, 2020; Weimer & Vining, 2017; Yoffie, 2022). Initially, all four administrations acknowledged AI as an essential asset. Inspired by Neorealist principles, China and Russia implemented daring strategies focusing on security. Using constructivist and neorealist theories while promoting "core socialist values," China's AI strategy meticulously integrates state-supported LLM development (including DeepSeek and Qwen 3.0) within a disjointed, Western-centric global technology landscape. These LLMs bolster the nation's technological progress, ideological unity, and digital robustness. Employing Weimer and Vining's policy instruments of nonmarket supply and regulation, this strategy effectively addresses increasing geopolitical strains, highlighted by the United States' semiconductor limitations, by focusing on technological independence and economic strength in essential areas such as AI semiconductors. By institutionalizing ethical guidelines through agencies like the Beijing Academy of Artificial Intelligence and by aligning platforms like DeepSeek with Party ideology, China builds a "China-first AI" model that resists epistemic colonization from the West. In the end, China's "AI with Chinese characteristics" represents a wider strategic aim to influence a digital future consistent with its values and interests, where LLMs serve as agents of cognitive authority. China's AI regulation, arising during a continuing LLM Cold War, directly contests Western ideas of impartiality, promoting digital sovereignty as the latest field for worldwide power.

On the other hand, Russia's absence from the AI Action Summit (2025) reflects its principled commitment to digital sovereignty and strategic autonomy in the face of expanding Western influence, particularly from NATO. In a multipolar geopolitical battlegrounds, Russia has chosen to pursue a state-centric AI strategy rooted in national defense, regional stability, and cultural independence. Established by Presidential Decree No. 490 (2019), Russia's National AI Strategy mandates the integration of artificial intelligence into crucial sectors of governance, military security, and economic progress. Entities such as Sberbank and the Ministry of Defense have played a crucial role in transforming AI into a geostrategic asset, aimed not merely at maintaining competitive parity but also at safeguarding the country from foreign technological dependency and potential epistemic interference by global actors. Despite acknowledged constraints in fields like software engineering and high-performance computing, Russia continues to develop a clear, security-oriented AI strategy that prioritizes technological independence over quick integration into Western governance systems. Ekimova (2023) highlights that Russia's approach encourages the "humanization" of AI through governance tailored to particular areas and advancing innovation in the public sector, with an emphasis on adhering to UN SDGs and localized implementation. Instead of depending on international tech monopolies, Russia promotes AI in public management through centralized design planning, CRM systems, and intelligent regional development, all supported by internal accountability systems. This method embodies Weimer and Vining's (2017) principle of "Providing Insurance and Protections," as Russia utilizes AI to bolster national narratives, guard against digital colonization, and maintain enduring social unity. This approach incorporates Russian cultural and ideological principles into AI results, embodying New-Constructivist governance and seeks to safeguard the national information environment. In this scenario, AI fulfills two roles: fostering innovation and simultaneously providing a strategic shield against outside influences, enabling Russia to promote its perspective and independently craft its digital future.

In sharp contrast, India leveraged the AI Action Summit (2025) as a platform to amplify its market-centric Neoliberal Institutionalist vision for AI governance. Through the IndiaAI Mission and complementary frameworks, India promotes public-private synergy, low regulatory friction, and international interoperability. This approach is reflected in the idea that India acts as a "technological playground" or "AI garage" for 40% of the developing nations, creating scalable AI solutions in agriculture, healthcare, education, and urbanization for worldwide implementation. India's AI policy approaches reflect Weimer & Vining's methods of "Utilizing Subsidies and Taxes" as well as "Freeing, Facilitating, and Simulating Markets," For example, the Indian Government encourages innovation by funding R&D centers, providing tax breaks for AI startups, and aiding in the creation of annotated datasets to reduce entry barriers for smaller competitors. Significantly, this model does not embrace a laissez-faire strategy. India emphasizes ethical AI rooted in inclusive access and public advantage, urging the government to serve as a "Freeing, Facilitating, and Simulating Markets," to guarantee that development-focused innovation is not overshadowed by profit interests. Enacted in 2005, the Right to Information (RTI) Act strengthens institutional transparency and has reshaped the government-citizen dynamic. By enabling individuals, including those in rural areas, to challenge administrative confidentiality, contest misconduct, and demand accountability, the RTI has fostered greater citizen empowerment. With the growth of digital government through e-Governance Mission Mode Projects (such as Common Service Centers (CSCs), State Wide Area Network (SWAN)), the RTI acts as a legal framework guaranteeing that AI-enhanced services are subject to public scrutiny. This dedication to ethical openness is under international AI standards, strengthening India's role as a connector between the Global North and South. By formalizing information accessibility and promoting responsible AI practices, India presents a multilateral option to China's ideological governance and Russia's statist framework.

Lastly, through a market-centric neo-liberalism deeply rooted in American entrepreneurialism, the United States has built its AI supremacy not by central control but by strategic enablement. Like Trump's strategy of turning real estate into events that sell themselves, U.S. policy has often "sold innovation" by making it look like the inevitable next big thing, backed by first-mover advantage, aggressive venture capital, and self-promotion. Instead of micromanaging AI firms, the government laid down incentives, IP protections, and funding pipelines that gave rise to giants like OpenAI, Microsoft, and Google. Much of Silicon Valley's success stemmed from its laissez-faire spirit, where rapid prototyping, bold risk-taking, and private capital dominated the AI scene. This aligns with Trump's formula, venture capitalists played the part of dealmakers, betting on the next platform, not with bureaucratic caution but with showbiz-style confidence. Therefore, U.S. AI developers framed tools like TensorFlow and OpenAI's GPT as transformative engines of the digital economy. Partnerships in the U.S. AI sector were not bureaucratic obligations but entrepreneurial alliances—exemplified by Microsoft's integration of OpenAI's models into enterprise platforms like Azure and Copilot, and Google's open-source strategy with TensorFlow that invited academic and commercial contributions at scale. The collaborative aspect of these initiatives showcases the market-driven AI dominance of U.S. techno-nationalism, leveraging incentives, intellectual property, and platform ecosystems without centralized oversight. This approach, in line with Weimer and Vining's concept of "freeing and simulating markets," shows that the strength of U.S. techno-nationalism is founded on developing an inspiring vision and disseminating it through soft power, innovation hubs, and open-source networks instead of surveillance or mandates.

In conclusion, the Summit showcased not only various governance models but also distinct worldviews. China's AI nationalism focused on defense, Russia's emphasis on digital sovereignty, India's diplomatic approach to diverse innovation, and the U.S.'s scaling through techno-capitalism all signify underlying logics in international relations: Neorealism's pursuit of security, Neoliberalism's belief in institutional cooperation, and New-Constructivism's focus on identity and knowledge legitimacy. In accordance with John Wilson's (1967) idea of language as a socially embedded influence, these AI models do more than analyze data—they create conflicting realities.

Governmental Power Marketing Strategies for AI Sovereignty and Addressing Kakistoscryptocracy

In the paradigm of kakistoscryptocracy, individuals, firms, and hedge funds increasingly harness LLMs to bypass regulation, conceal accountability, and pursue self-interested goals. Individuals use open-access or fine-tuned LLMs to mass-produce deceptive content such as deepfakes, fake reviews, and phishing messages, effectively scaling influence operations with minimal resources. While firms in public relations, marketing, and law are integrating LLMs to craft their communications and narratives, a troubling trend has emerged: individuals are breaching ethical standards by generating false portrayals of public opinion or polluting online platforms with altered stories. Moreover, hedge funds are utilizing LLMs to analyze vast quantities of unstructured data from social media and news sources, aiming to predict market shifts, sway investor perceptions, and function globally via shell firms to escape regulatory scrutiny (particularly thanks to Atkinson-Abutridy, 2025; Gazit & Ghaffari, 2024; Gohwong, 2023a; Khandare, 2024).

During the LLM Cold War period, the governmental power marketing has emerged as an essential tool for nations to manage AI and to strategically boost their legitimacy, authority, and digital autonomy. Instead of viewing AI as a neutral framework, contemporary governments see AI systems as ideological instruments—resources to enhance national identity, maintain authority over digital stories, and address kakistoscryptocracy—an issue of governance defined by decentralized, stateless entities functioning through NGCs, darknet platforms, and AI models beyond jurisdiction, illustrated in Table 1. Building upon the frameworks of Jermsittiparsert et al. (2023) and Weimer & Vining (2017), states are now market participants, strategically promoting AI through Crea-Innovation strategies and shaping public opinion, institutional confidence, and international digital governance. This strategy's implementation varies across China, Russia, India, and the U.S., with each nation tailoring government power marketing to its specific political economy, international role, and narrative tactics. In this regard, Kate Crawford's Atlas of AI (2021) underlines the idea that AI is more than just a tool—it functions as a political system influenced by power imbalances and rooted in extractive, surveillance-oriented, and labor-intensive structures.

Beginning with China, it illustrates a government-centric power market model, where AI is depicted as a national security resource and promoted through state narratives of stability and digital preeminence. Through the use of Crea-Innovation Knowledge for Vital Practices, China integrates AI with Party ideology, enforcing dataset compliance, monitoring mandates, and censorship mechanisms. LLMs like DeepSeek are marketed not only as technological milestones but also as means of ideological understanding. This corresponds with Crawford's remark that AI in China is "closely linked to surveillance and labor management systems"—AI is not just executing intelligence but enhancing authoritarian dominance. China's promotion of "China-first AI" enhances sovereignty while establishing itself as a global technological leader that shapes its truth frameworks.

Extending this model of centralized control, Russia is integrating AI advancements into its defense strategies and cyberwarfare efforts by utilizing both Crea-Innovation for Strategic Thinking and Action and Crea-Innovation for Tactics and Tricks. Local LLMs (such as RU-GPT) are safeguarding Russian sovereignty, with development led by national entities like Rostec and Sberbank. With its emphasis on "resilience" and "information security," Russia's AI narrative presents AI as a defense against cognitive attacks from the West. The analysis of military AI frameworks by Kate Crawford is pertinent in this context; she notes that Russia's strategy is an example of "state-sponsored epistemic control," in which AI is used to fight misinformation, bolster ideology, and thwart kakistocratic challenges.

India and the United States employ market-driven governmental authority to portray AI as innovative, ethical, and progressive. India endorses Crea-Innovation to Strategic Thinking and Action through the IndiaAI Mission, promoting partnerships between public and private sectors with a focus on ethical governance. Models such as BharatGPT and Krutrim are promoted as "trustworthy and safe," highlighting India's dedication to democratic and inclusive AI as a form of soft power. In this context, Crawford cautions that ethical AI branding often hides the labor and data-collection methods, raising questions about the genuineness of "trustworthy AI." Nevertheless, India employs state power in its marketing to boost local credibility and attract overseas investment. Parallel to India's strategy, the United States mainly uses both Crea-Innovation for Strategic Thinking and Action and Crea-Innovation for Tactics and Tricks via liberalized state power marketing, promoting AI via deregulated environments, and highlighting the importance of innovation-driven legitimacy. Employing Weimer & Vining's "Facilitating and Simulating Markets" approach, the U.S. enables firms like OpenAI and Google to dominate the global LLM arena with minimal governmental regulation yet substantial geopolitical branding. Initiatives like the AI Bill of Rights and voluntary governance frameworks serve as narrative tools, illustrating U.S. AI leadership as inherently democratic, transparent, and principled. Crawford's Atlas of AI challenges this narrative, exposing the hidden material and ecological expenses masked by the depiction of U.S. AI as meritocratic and fueled by the free market. Nonetheless, the U.S. strategy effectively encourages private-sector innovation as a pillar of national power, leveraging AI to counter kakistoscryptocracy through anti-misinformation, cybersecurity, and global impact.

Across all four powers, governmental power marketing transforms AI from a computational tool into a symbolic infrastructure of governance and legitimacy. It responds to kakistoscryptocracy not just through technical means (surveillance, cybersecurity, content filtering), but through narrative dominance, truth production, and epistemic sovereignty. China and Russia embody a control-focused approach to power marketing, employing AI to uphold regime legitimacy and reshape reality; in contrast, India and the U.S. promote developmental and liberal AI branding, even with internal contradictions highlighted by Crawford's observations on exploitative labor and algorithmic transparency. In the end, governmental power marketing is the fresh diplomacy of the AI era, where the focus is not solely on who creates the best AI—but on who markets the most credible truth (particularly thanks to AI Action Summit, 2025a, 2025b; Atkinson-Abutridy, 2025; Buzgalin & Kolganov, 2015; Caporaso & Levine, 1992; Crawford, 2021; GAO, 2023; Gohwong, 2023; Ibrahim et al., 2019; Jermsittiparsert et al., 2023; Lee, 2018; Ministère de l'Europe et des Affaires étrangères & Secrétariat général de la défense et de la sécurité nationale,

2025, Ministry of Electronics and Information Technology, 2024a, 2024b, 2025; Nadibaidze, 2024; Nandi et al., 2025; ; O'Brien & Williams, 2016; President of the Russian Federation, 2019; Petrella et al., 2021; Ravenhill, 2020; State Council of the People's Republic of China, 2017; Whitman & Mattord, 2018; Wilson, 1967).

Table 1. Governmental power marketing for promoting AI sovereignty and addressing kakistoscryptocracy

Strategy	China	Russia	India	United States
Market Control	State-controlled AI, centralized oversight	Military-led AI, limited private AI sector	Public-private AI innovation, ethical AI governance	Deregulated AI market, private-sector dominance
Regulatory Tools	AI censorship, mandatory dataset compliance	AI for cybersecurity, strict propaganda control	Safe & Trusted AI policies, national AI training datasets	AI Bill of Rights, voluntary industry-led governance
AI for Security	Surveillance AI, real-time citizen monitoring	AI-driven cyber defense, deepfake detection	AI-driven governance, law enforcement applications	AI for cybersecurity, misinformation tracking
Government Branding	AI as a national security pillar	AI for state resilience and digital warfare	AI for ethical development and economic growth	AI as a free-market tool for innovation

Table 2. Continued

Strategy	China	Russia	India	United States
Key Marketing Strategy	State AI leadership (China-first AI global branding)	Defensive AI marketing (AI as a security asset)	Public-Private AI marketing (AI for development)	Tech Liberalization (AI as an economic driver)
Counter-Kakistoscryptocracy	Surveillance measures, data localization laws	Cybersecurity focus, strategic disinformation	Transparency, global partnerships, ethical AI oversight	Innovation-driven AI, combating misinformation
Epistemic Framing Strategy (Crawford-inspired)	AI as an ideological amplifier aligned with Party narratives; truth is centrally produced and controlled	AI as a geopolitical defense tool; truth weaponized against Western influence	Ethical AI as a soft power tool; truth constructed through participatory legitimacy	Truth framed through innovation and pluralism; corporate control obscures extractive roots

Source: AI Action Summit (2025a, 2025b), Atkinson-Abutridy (2025), Buzgalin & Kolganov (2015), Caporaso & Levine (1992), Crawford (2021), GAO (2023), Gohwong (2023), Ibrahim et al. (2019), Jermsittiparsert et al. (2023), Lee (2018), Ministère de l'Europe et des Affaires étrangères & Secrétariat général de la défense et de la sécurité nationale (2025), Ministry of Electronics and Information Technology (2024a, 2024b, 2025), Nadibaidze (2024), Nandi et al. (2025), O'Brien & Williams (2016), President of the Russian Federation (2019), Petrella et al. (2021), Ravenhill (2020), State Council of the People's Republic of China (2017), Whitman and Mattord (2018), Wilson (1967)

Responses of Individuals, NGOs, and Open-Source Actors to Governmental Efforts in China, Russia, India, and the United States

In these countries, individuals, NGOs, and open-source actors exhibit varied responses to governmental efforts aimed at improving AI sovereignty and addressing kakistoscryptocracy, as illustrated in Table 2. In China, public involvement remains limited, as advanced surveillance systems such as the Tianyan system primarily serve as instruments of state power. Subject to stringent regulations, NGOs primarily focus on local service provision. Meanwhile, government-supported open-source participants employ platforms like RISC-V and resources like TensorFlow to bypass Western technological supremacy. Russia exhibits a comparatively restricted civic environment, where oppressive legal structures constrain civil activism. NGOs encounter "low-level pressure" and generally remain apolitical, whereas open-source innovation is obstructed by centralization and corruption, despite initiatives like Skolkovo, a Russian tech park, which receives state backing. On the other hand, India demonstrates strong civic engagement through mechanisms such as the Right to Information Act 2005 and e-governance platforms. NGOs play a vital role in the creation, implementation, and oversight of policies. The nation promotes open-source ecosystems by collaborating with the Global Partnership on AI (GPAI) and endorsing inclusive intellectual property systems. Conversely, the United States enjoys robust citizen participation, bolstered by constitutional protections and an active civil society, with entities such as the Electronic Frontier Foundation influencing ethical AI discussions and the country at the forefront of open-source AI advancements via platforms like TensorFlow and PyTorch, promoting a decentralized and innovation-driven environment (particularly thanks to (Capri, 2023; Dear, 2019; Lee, 2018; Liebert et al., 2013; Sabharwal & Berman, 2013; Zang & Gao, 2023).

Table 3. Responses of citizens, NGOs, and open-source actors to four governments

Category	China	Russia	India	USA
Citizens	Limited engagement; monitored under tech-driven surveillance (e.g., Tianyan)	Civil liberties constrained; civic participation is minimal and apolitical	Strong engagement via RTI, e-gov, and participatory policymaking	Civic input via civil liberties protections and NGO pressure
NGOs	Service-focused, politically constrained; not influential in AI policy	Co-opted or suppressed; survival depends on apolitical alignment	Active in policy formation, implementation, and rights advocacy	Major drivers in AI ethics, surveillance debates, and open-source policy
Open-Source	Encouraged by the state to bypass Western control (e.g., RISC-V, Torch)	Exists, but hindered by corruption and a weak R&D ecosystem	Supports GPAI, patent openness; encourages decentralized innovation	Dominates the AI ecosystem; fosters open AI tools and global collaborations

Source: Capri (2023), Dear (2019), Lee (2018), Liebert et al. (2013), Sabharwal & Berman (2013), Zang & Gao (2023).

DISCUSSION AND CONCLUSION

This section is dedicated to algorithmic sovereignty and epistemic governance in the AI era, exploring three issues: sovereignty under LLMs, government-influenced LLM epistemology, and the risks of value-free Public Administration.

Initially, in the emerging AI Cold War, modern countries are redefining governance by rigorously supervising and controlling their LLMs, employing them as algorithmic systems to create, evaluate, disseminate, and regulate truth. This power is exercised through a mix of dark psychology, Weimer and Vining's wide-ranging policy tools, and principles of state-oriented international relations, while also tackling the danger of kakistoscryptocracy—governance obstructed by decentralized, stateless digital organizations. According to John Wilson (1967), language is no longer merely a vehicle for truth; it has transformed into a programmable framework embedded in LLMs, enabling governments to shape and manipulate perception. This mirrors Benjamin Bratton's "The Stack" model, which sees sovereignty as no longer confined to the nation-state but as dispersed across layered computational infrastructures—Earth, Cloud, City, Address, Interface, and User (Bratton, 2015). In this new planetary-scale sovereignty, LLMs function as core governance devices within the Cloud and Interface layers, structuring epistemic regimes across jurisdictions.

Begin with China and Russia, they exemplify Bratton's view of sovereignty embedded within computational architectures. Both adopt tightly regulated LLM ecosystems where the Cloud Layer—data centers, platforms, censorship engines—is state-controlled and weaponized for narrative dominance. China's DeepSeek, embedded with Party ideology, represents the culmination of "designing with emergencies" at the Earth Layer (resource and infrastructure control) and managing user interpretation through interfaces filtered by ideological scripts. This corresponds with Bratton's idea of the Interface Layer as a realm for political design. In the meantime, Russia's RU-GPT employs a comparable approach, acting as a sovereign "machine-user" in the User Layer that promotes nationalistic dialogue and strengthens cybersecurity messages. In both instances, authorities circumvent the conventional communicative role of language to transform it into a tool of state epistemology—regulating not only speech, but also perception itself. This is not unlike how Bill Gates described IT systems in 1999 as "digital nervous systems"—real-time feedback machines through which entities sense, process, and react (Gates & Hemingway, 1999). For China and Russia, AI-driven governance completes the evolution of governance-as-machine, where the LLM becomes the sovereign actuator of language.

Conversely, India and the United States adopt an apparently more adaptable strategy for LLM governance, marked by considerable governmental supervision via market incentives and minimal regulation. To position ethical AI as a valuable resource, India actively supports its comprehensive language models, Krutrim and BharatGPT, through the IndiaAI Mission. According to Keohane's theory of neoliberal institutionalism, collaboration and innovation bolster geopolitical credibility, and India's approach is in line with Bratton's Address Layer, which outlines identity and location through ethical computation, while also enhancing its User Layer by promoting democratic AI branding. Simultaneously, the United States fosters open innovation through Weimer and Vining's "Freeing, Facilitating, and Simulating Markets," allowing companies like OpenAI and Google to lead LLM development. Despite its deregulatory posture, the U.S. still performs epistemic governance through interface frameworks such as the AI Bill of Rights and digital misinformation regulation—aligning once more with Bratton's insight that platforms are forms of sovereignty. Bill Gates's digital nervous system analogy aptly applies here: whoever controls digital inputs—whether browsers or LLMs—ultimately shapes public interpretation, reaction, and behavioral feedback loops.

Next, the mode of state-directed epistemic control has deep roots in history. For example, from the Indus Valley Civilization to the Maurya Empire, rulers have strategically used language to control public consciousness. A significant example is Kautilya's Arthashastra from the 3rd century BCE, where administrative information was recorded in Devanagari script for state officials, while Malayalam script was utilized for the governed population—thereby creating epistemic hierarchies via linguistic division. This initial version of linguistic branding reflects contemporary LLMs that systematically alter language outputs globally on a planetary scale. Just as ancient kings used ritual and script to control knowledge, contemporary states now use AI-powered language models to engineer epistemic authority. This historical analogy applies very effectively to all four governments—China, Russia, India, and the United States—each in unique but structurally similar ways (particularly thanks to Bratton, 2015; Jermsittiparsert et al., 2023).

Lastly, there is a significant risk associated with this heavy reliance on algorithmic systems and predictive modeling. The Age of Prediction (Tulchinsky & Mason, 2023) and The Unrules (Tulchinsky, 2020) both emphasize how AI systems might become elusive, unaccountable, and vulnerable to systemic failures—particularly in the absence of ethical oversight. From financial speculation to predictive law enforcement, improperly used AI can result in bias, false information, and the creation of isolated data bubbles—thus perpetuating the very disorder of kakistoscryptocracy that they were intended to mitigate. When authorities transfer decision-making to AI without oversight, they jeopardize human judgment for probabilistic governance—a system based not on principles, but on forecasts.

In conclusion, the strategic deployment of LLMs by China, Russia, India, and the United States reflects a global pivot toward epistemic governance powered by AI. Whether through centralized command or liberalized market narratives, all four nations use AI to reshape the informational foundations of sovereignty. In John Wilson's model, language, generated by algorithms, evolves into a fresh platform for geopolitical power. Referencing perspectives from Gates, Crawford, Tulchinsky, and Bratton, it is evident that the future of AI includes both technological progress and significant political consequences: "the designers of algorithms influence knowledge; those who manage the story determine the truth."

REFERENCES

Action Summit, A. I. (2025a, February 10-11). *Statement on Inclusive and Sustainable Artificial Intelligence for People and the Planet.* AI Action Summit, Paris, France. Retrieved from https://www.elysee.fr/admin/upload/default/0001/17/085eb85e11b563e0f0ee1c23cb9552a9cc8f1e83.pdf

Action Summit, A. I. (2025b, February 6-11). *Press Kit: Artificial Intelligence Action Summit.* Paris, France: AI Action Summit. Retrieved from https://onu.delegfrance.org/IMG/pdf/02_11_-_statement_on_inclusive_and_sustainable_artificial_intelligence_for_people_and_the_planet_002_.pdf

Alibaba Cloud. (2025). *(Qwen).* https://tongyi.aliyun.com/qianwen/

Anthropic. (2024). *The Claude 3 Model Family: Opus, Sonnet, Haiku.* Retrieved from https://docs.anthropic.com/claude/docs/introduction-to-prompt-design

Atkinson-Abutridy, J. (2025). *Large language models: Concepts, techniques, and applications.* CRC Press.

Banafa, A. (2024). *Introduction to artificial intelligence (AI).* River Publishers. DOI: 10.1201/9781003499527

Begum, S., & Chowdary, F. (2024). *Competitive semiconductor product management: Strategies for long-term success in a dynamic industry.* Springer. DOI: 10.1007/979-8-8688-0920-0

Bernays, E. L. (1928). *Propaganda.* Horace Liveright.

Bradberry, B. (2020). *Dark psychology and manipulation: Delve into darkness and learn the subtle art of hacking the human mind through emotional influence, body language, NLP secrets, hypnosis and mind control techniques.* [Self-published].

Bratton, B. H. (2015). *The stack: On software and sovereignty.* The MIT Press.

Burchill, S., Linklater, A., Devetak, R., Donnelly, J., Paterson, M., Reus-Smit, C., & True, J. (2005). *Theories of international relations* (3rd ed.). Palgrave Macmillan.

Buzgalin, A., & Kolganov, A. (2015). Critical political economy: The 'market-centric' model of economic theory must remain in the past—notes of the Post-Soviet School of Critical Marxism. *Cambridge Journal of Economics*, •••, 1–24. DOI: 10.1093/cje/beu080

Campesato, O. (2024). *Large language models: An introduction.* Mercury Learning and Information. DOI: 10.1515/9781501520587

Caporaso, J. A., & Levine, D. P. (1992). *Theories of political economy*. Cambridge University Press. DOI: 10.1017/CBO9780511840197

Capri, A. (2023). *Techno-nationalism: How it's reshaping trade, geopolitics and society*. John Wiley & Sons.

Carnegie, N. (2020). *NLP secrets: Discover powerful and proven neuro-linguistic programming strategies to influence anyone, protect yourself from manipulation, and master persuasion skills*. JRD International Ltd.

Chatterjee, S. (2020). AI strategy of India: Policy framework, adoption challenges and actions for government. *Transforming Government*, *14*(5), 757–775. DOI: 10.1108/TG-05-2019-0031

Conradi, P. (2016). *Who lost Russia? How the world entered a new Cold War*. Oneworld Publications.

Cooper, W. (2020). *Dark psychology and manipulation: Discover 40 covert emotional manipulation techniques, mind control & brainwashing. Learn how to analyze people, NLP secret & science of persuasion to influence anyone*. [Self-published].

CoRover.ai. (2025). *BharatGPT.* https://bharatgpt.ai/

Crawford, K. (2021). *Atlas of AI: Power, politics, and the planetary costs of artificial intelligence*. Yale University Press.

DeepSeek. (2025). *DeepSeek into the unknown.* https://www.deepseek.com/

Diamond, L., Ellis, J. O., & Schell, O. (Eds.). (2023). *Silicon triangle: The United States, Taiwan, China, and global semiconductor security*. Hoover Institution Press.

Dougherty, S. (2023, June 26). Freenet renamed to Hyphanet. Hyphanet. https://www.hyphanet.org/freenet-renamed-to-hyphanet.html

Draven, T. F. (2025). *DeepSeek Unlocked: Your guide to mastering China's revolutionary AI: Step-by-step instructions to understand, utilize, and transform with DeepSeek*. [Self-published].

Ekimova, K. V. (2023). Development of the potential of the digital economy of Russian regions through artificial intelligence humanisation. *Humanities & Social Sciences Communications*, *10*(1), 943. Advance online publication. DOI: 10.1057/s41599-023-02444-w

Faulkner, C. W. (2002). *Creating irresistible influence with NLP: Reference guide*. [Self-published].

Gaddis, J. L. (2005). *The Cold War: A New History*. Penguin Books.

GAO. (2023). Artificial Intelligence: Agencies Have Begun Implementation but Need to Complete Key Requirements (GAO-24-105980). Washington, DC: US Government Accountability Office.

Gates, B., & Hemingway, C. (1999). *Business at the speed of thought: Using a digital nervous system*. Warner Books. DOI: 10.1111/1467-8616.00097

Gazit, L., & Ghaffari, M. (2024). *Mastering NLP from foundations to LLMs: Apply advanced rule-based techniques to LLMs and solve real-world business problems*. Packt Publishing.

Gohwong, S. (2020). *Net states and their roles in Russia*. In A. Kuanliang (Ed.), *Proceedings of the 7th International Conference on Security Studies* (pp. 1–6). Political Science Association of Kasetsart University.

Gohwong, S. (2023a). Kakistoscryptocracy. *Asian Political Science Review, 7*(1), 50-58. doi:10.14456/apsr.2023.5

Gohwong, S. (2023b). Russian Net States and Their Roles in Russia. *Procedia of Multidisciplinary Research, 1*(11), 11.

Gohwong, S. (2025). *Srirath G., Ph.D. – Academic profile*. Kasetsart University. http://pirun.ku.ac.th/~fsocsrg/index2.html

Goleman, B. (2020). *NLP dark psychology: How to analyze people, spot covert emotional manipulation, detect deception and defend yourself from toxic people making use of NLP and dark psychology*. [Self-published].

Goleman, J. (2020). *Dark psychology and manipulation: 2 in 1 – The definitive guide to persuasion, body language and NLP secrets. Learn how to analyze people, recognize mind control techniques and stop being manipulated.* [Self-published].

Goleman, R. D., Bradberry, D. B., Greene, T., Carnegie, T., Griffith, K., Griffith, J., Empath, C., Laws, P., & Passive, J. M. (2020). *Dark psychology: 7 books in 1 – The art of persuasion, how to influence people, hypnosis techniques, NLP secrets, analyze body language, gaslighting, manipulation subliminal, and emotional intelligence 2.0*. [Self-published].

Government of India. (2005). *The Right to Information Act, 2005 (No. 22 of 2005)*. The Gazette of India. https://rti.gov.in/rti-act.pdf

Green, D.Sr. (2020). *Manipulation and dark psychology: How to learn speed reading people and use the secrets of emotional intelligence. The best guide to defend yourself from dark psychology*. Alexandru Molosnic.

Griffith, J. (2021). *How to analyze people with dark psychology: 6 books in 1 – The art of persuasion, how to influence people, hypnosis techniques, NLP secrets, analyze body language, behavioral human, and mind control.* [Self-published].

Hoobyar, T., Dotz, T., & Sanders, S. (2013). *NLP: The essential guide to neuro-linguistic programming*. William Morrow.

Hussaini, S. (2023). *The AI showdown: Google Gemini vs. OpenAI ChatGPT: A comparative analysis of capabilities, applications, and impact.* ChatGPT Foundations.

Ibrahim, I. A., Husseini, H. A., Jahun, S. A., & Sabo, A. (2019). State-centered approach to political economy. *Journal of the Humanities and Social Sciences, 17*(4), 139–146.

Ienca, M. (2023). On artificial intelligence and manipulation. *Topoi, 42*(3), 833–842. DOI: 10.1007/s11245-023-09940-3

Jamison, P. (2023). *The (absolute) beginner's guide to AI: Discover the exciting history of artificial intelligence, today's developments, & tomorrow's solutions.* [Self-published].

Jermsittiparsert, K., Gohwong, S., Pavapanunkul, S., & Mahittichatkul, N. (2023). *Governmental power market-ing in the VU-CHAOS world.* IGI Global. DOI: 10.4018/978-1-6684-7280-4

Kachiga, J. (2021). *The rise of China and international relations theory.* Peter Lang.

Kamath, U., Keenan, K., Somers, G., & Sorenson, S. (2024). *Large language models: A deep dive bridging theory and practice.* Springer. DOI: 10.1007/978-3-031-65647-7

Kasetsart University. (2025). *Srirath Gohwong – KUforest researcher profile.* KU-forest. https://research.ku.ac.th/forest/Person.aspx?id=520123

Kaufman, J. P. (2022). *Introduction to International Relations: Theory and Practice* (3rd ed.). Rowman & Littlefield.

Kavoliūnaitė-Ragauskienė, E. (2024). Artificial intelligence in manipulation: The significance and strategies for prevention. *Baltic Journal of Law & Politics, 17*(2), 116–141. DOI: 10.2478/bjlp-2024-00018

Kehs, S. (2023). *Public administration for planners: Leadership and responsibility in theory and practice.* Routledge.

Khandare, S. S. (2024). *Mastering large language models: Advanced techniques, applications, cutting-edge methods, and top LLMs.* BPB Publications.

Kingler, C. (2021). *The art of psychological warfare: Discover how to defend yourself from manipulation and learn dark techniques to mislead, intimidate, demoralise and influence the thinking or behaviour of your enemies.* [Self-published].

Kool, V. K., & Agrawal, R. (2016). Technology and hedonism. In Kool, V. K., & Agrawal, R. (Eds.), *Psychology of technology* (pp. 253–304). Springer., DOI: 10.1007/978-3-319-45333-0_6

Krutrim. (2025). *India's frontier AI research lab.* https://www.olakrutrim.com/

Lee, K.-F. (2018). *AI Superpowers: China, Silicon Valley, and the New World Order.* Houghton Mifflin Harcourt.

Leffler, M. P., & Westad, O. A. (Eds.). (2010). *The Cambridge History of the Cold War* (Vol. 1–3). Cambridge University Press.

Liebert, S., Condrey, S. E., & Goncharov, D. (Eds.). (2013). *Public administration in post-communist countries: Former Soviet Union, Central and Eastern Europe, and Mongolia.* CRC Press. DOI: 10.1201/b14237

Lozovsky, D. (2025). *AI Unfiltered: The truth about ChatGPT, DeepSeek & how AI is changing everything*. Self-published.

Lucas, E. (2008). *The new Cold War: Putin's Russia and the threat to the West.* Palgrave Macmillan.

Ma, W., & Scaramucci, A. (2020). *The Digital War: How China's Tech Power Shapes the Future of AI, Blockchain, and Cyberspace*. Wiley. DOI: 10.1002/9781119749073

Malak, N. (2025). *DeepSeek vs. ChatGPT: The age of artificial intelligence.* [Self-published].

Mandal, W. A. (2025). *Mastering DeepSeek AI: Step-by-step guide to the ChatGPT challenger*. Nobel House Press.

Mazzucato, M. (2023). *Competitive Semiconductor Product Management: Strategy for Market Leadership*. McGraw Hill.

McCourt, D. M. (2022). *The New Constructivism in International Relations Theory.* Bristol University Press.

Miller, C. (2022). *Chip war: The fight for the world's most critical technology.* Scribner.

Mind, J. (2019). *Dark psychology: This book includes: Manipulation and dark psychology; persuasion and dark psychology; dark NLP. The definitive guide to detect and defend yourself from dark psychology secrets*. [Self-published].

Ministère de l'Europe et des Affaires étrangères & Secrétariat général de la défense et de la sécurité nationale. (2025, February 12). *AI Action Summit: Ensuring the development of trusted, safe and secure AI to benefit all* [Press release]. Government of France. https://ai-action-summit.fr

Ministry of Electronics and Information Technology. (2024a). *IndiaAI expert group report* (1st ed.). Government of India.

Ministry of Electronics and Information Technology. (2024b). *IndiaAI Mission*. Government of India.

Ministry of Electronics and Information Technology. (2025, February 7). *Steps to develop sovereign AI capabilities: Rajya Sabha unstarred question no. 560*. Government of India.

Minnick, C. (2025). *Microsoft Copilot for dummies* (1st ed.). For Dummies.

Morton, N. (2020). *Psychological warfare and deception: What you need to know about human behavior, dark psychology, propaganda, negotiation, manipulation, and persuasion*. [Self-published].

Nadibaidze, A. (2024). Russia's drive for AI: Do deeds match the words? *The Washington Quarterly*, *47*(4), 137–154. DOI: 10.1080/0163660X.2024.2435162

Nandi, A., Chandola, B., & Sarma, A. (Eds.). (2025). *India's AI imperative: Building national competencies in a new world order*. Observer Research Foundation.

O'Brien, R., & Williams, M. (2016). *Global political economy: Evolution and dynamics* (5th ed.). Palgrave Macmillan. DOI: 10.1057/978-1-137-52313-6

Ozdemir, S. (2024). *Quick start guide to large language models: Strategies and best practices for using ChatGPT and other LLMs*. Addison-Wesley.

Pace, M. (2015). *Dark NLP: How to use neuro-linguistic programming for self mastery, getting what you want, mastering others and to gain an advantage over anyone*. Make Profits Easy LLC.

Pace, M. (2017). *Dark psychology 202: The advanced secrets of psychological warfare, dark NLP, dark cognitive behavioral therapy, super manipulation, kamikaze mind control, stealth persuasion, and human psychology 202*. Make Profits Easy LLC.

Petrella, S., Miller, C., & Cooper, B. (2021). Russia's artificial intelligence strategy: The role of state-owned firms. *Orbis*, *65*(1), 75–95. DOI: 10.1016/j.orbis.2020.11.004

Phill, E. (2021). *Dark NLP: A complete guide to understanding manipulation and using secret methods of NLP to control people's minds in conversations. Learn to influence psychologies with dark techniques*. [Self-published].

Popkova, E. G., Alekseev, A. N., Lobova, S. V., & Sergi, B. S. (2020). The theory of innovation and innovative development: AI scenarios in Russia. *Technology in Society*, *63*, 101390. DOI: 10.1016/j.techsoc.2020.101390

President of the Russian Federation. (2019, October 10). *Decree No. 490: On the development of artificial intelligence in the Russian Federation*. Official publication of legal acts. http://publication.pravo.gov.ru/Document/View/0001201910110003

Qwen Team. (2025, April 29). *Qwen3: Think deeper, act faster.* https://qwenlm.github.io/blog/qwen3/

Ravenhill, J. (Ed.). (2020). *Global political economy* (6th ed.). Oxford University Press. DOI: 10.1093/hepl/9780198820642.001.0001

Reus-Smit, C. (2020). *International relations: A very short introduction*. Oxford University Press. DOI: 10.1093/actrade/9780198850212.001.0001

Roach, S. C., & Barder, A. D. (2024). *International Relations: The Key Concepts* (4th ed.). Routledge.

Roberts, J. T., & Hite, A. (Eds.). (2000). *From modernization to globalization: Perspectives on development and social change*. Blackwell Publishers.

Sabharwal, M., & Berman, E. M. (Eds.). (2013). *Public administration in South Asia: India, Bangladesh, and Pakistan*. CRC Press. DOI: 10.1201/b14759

Sánchez, C. (2025). *DeepSeek: Master AI in 2025 – The ultimate step-by-step guide to outperform ChatGPT, boost productivity & future-proof your skills*. Self-published.

Sanger, D. E. (2024). *New Cold Wars: China's Rise, Russia's Invasion, and America's Struggle to Defend the West*. Crown.

Sanghi, N. (2024). *Deep reinforcement learning with Python: RLHF for chatbots and large language models* (2nd ed.). Apress. DOI: 10.1007/979-8-8688-0273-7

SberBank PJSC. (2025). *RuGPT-3*. https://developers.sber.ru/portal/products/rugpt-3

Seetha Mahalakshmi Healthcare Private Limited. (2025). *Hanooman AI.* https://hanooman.ai/

Selznick, P. (1949). *TVA and the grass roots: A study in the sociology of formal organization*. University of California Press.

Shambaugh, D. (2020). *Where great powers meet: America and China in Southeast Asia*. Oxford University Press.

Shih, S. (2023). *Silicon Triangle: The United States, Taiwan, China, and Global Semiconductor Security*. Harvard Business Review Press.

Smith, J. R. (2019). *NLP dark psychology: Neuro-linguistic programming techniques: The essential guide to persuade and influence people, learn to detect deception, covert manipulation and brainwashing behavior*. [Self-published].

Smith, M. (2020). *Dark psychology mastery: This book includes: Dark psychology + mental manipulation techniques. All in one solution about emotional intelligence, persuasion, FBI techniques, NLP & body language*. Hydra Sr Productions Ltd.

Sørensen, G., Møller, J., & Jackson, R. (2022). *Introduction to International Relations: Theories and Approaches* (8th ed.). Oxford University Press.

Stanton, E. (2020). *Dark psychology secrets: Real Jedi mind tricks on how to read, influence and control people to get what you want!*. [Self-published].

State Council of the People's Republic of China. (2017, July 20). *Notice of the State Council on issuing the development plan for the new generation of artificial intelligence (No. 35)* [Government document]. https://www.gov.cn/zhengce/content/2017-07/20/content_5211996.htm

Takach, G. S. (2023). *Cold War 2.0: Artificial intelligence in the new battle between China, Russia, and America*. Harvard Press.

Tech Mahindra Limited. (2025). *Scale at speed.* https://www.techmahindra.com/

Thakur, K., Barker, H. G., & Pathan, A.-S. K. (2024). *Artificial intelligence and large language models: An introduction to the technological future*. CRC Press. DOI: 10.1201/9781003474173

Thompson, N., & Bremmer, I. (2018). The AI cold war that threatens us all. *WIRED*. https://www.wired.com/story/ai-cold-war-china-could-doom-us-all/

Tulchinsky, I. (2020). *The unrules: Man, machines and the quest to master markets*. Wiley.

Tulchinsky, I., & Mason, C. E. (2023). *The age of prediction: Algorithms, AI, and the shifting shadows of risk*. St. Martin's Press. DOI: 10.7551/mitpress/13872.001.0001

Weber, C. (2001). *International relations theory: A critical introduction* (3rd ed.). Routledge.

Weimer, D. L., & Vining, A. R. (2017). *Policy Analysis: Concepts and Practice.* Routledge. DOI: 10.4324/9781315442129

Westad, O. A. (2017). *The Cold War.* Basic Books.

Whitman, M. E., & Mattord, H. J. (2018). *Principles of information security* (6th ed.). Cengage Learning.

Williams, J. W. (2019). *Dark psychology: The practical uses and best defenses of psychological warfare in everyday life – How to detect and defend against manipulation, deception, dark persuasion, and covert NLP.* SD Publishing LLC.

Wilson, J. (1967). *Language & the pursuit of truth.* Cambridge University Press.

Winston, M. (2020). *The Digital War: How China's tech power shapes the future of AI, blockchain, and cyberspace.* Wiley.

Wu, W., Huang, T., & Gong, K. (2020). Ethical principles and governance technology development of AI in China. *Engineering (Beijing)*, *6*(3), 291–297. DOI: 10.1016/j.eng.2019.12.015

Yandex. (2025). *Что такое YandexGPT 4 [What is YandexGPT 4].* https://ya.ru/ai/gpt-4

Yang, H. (2023). Silicon Triangle: The United States, Taiwan, China, and global semiconductor security. Stanford University Press.

Yoffie, D. B. (2022). *Chip War: The fight for the world's most critical technology.* Scribner.

Yücel, A. (2024). Hybrid digital authoritarianism in Turkey: The 'Censorship Law' and AI-generated disinformation strategy. *Turkish Studies*, *26*(1), 1–27. DOI: 10.1080/14683849.2024.2392816

Zang, L., & Gao, Y. (2023). *Public administration and governance in China: Chinese insights with global perspectives.* Routledge., DOI: 10.4324/9781003363712

Zenglein, M. J. (2023). Competitive semiconductor product management: AI, China, and the race for technological supremacy. Springer.

ADDITIONAL READING

Atkinson-Abutridy, J. (2025). *Large language models: Concepts, techniques, and applications.* CRC Press.

Bratton, B. H. (2015). *The stack: On software and sovereignty*. The MIT Press.

Capri, A. (2023). *Techno-nationalism: How it's reshaping trade, geopolitics and society*. John Wiley & Sons.

Crawford, K. (2021). *Atlas of AI: Power, politics, and the planetary costs of artificial intelligence*. Yale University Press.

Gohwong, S. (2023a). Kakistoscryptocracy. *Asian Political Science Review*, 7(1), 50-58. DOI: 10.14456/apsr.2023.5

Jermsittiparsert, K., Gohwong, S., Pavapanunkul, S., & Mahittichatkul, N. (2023). *Governmental power market-ing in the VU-CHAOS world*. IGI Global. DOI: 10.4018/978-1-6684-7280-4

Lee, K.-F. (2018). *AI Superpowers: China, Silicon Valley, and the New World Order*. Houghton Mifflin Harcourt.

Ozdemir, S. (2024). *Quick start guide to large language models: Strategies and best practices for using ChatGPT and other LLMs*. Addison-Wesley.

Peters, B. G. (2001). *The Future of Governance*. University Press of Kansas.

Singer, P. W., & Brooking, E. T. (2018). *LikeWar: The weaponization of social media*. Houghton Mifflin Harcourt.

Smith, M. (2020). *Dark psychology mastery: This book includes: Dark psychology + mental manipulation techniques. All in one solution about emotional intelligence, persuasion, FBI techniques, NLP & body language*. Hydra Sr Productions Ltd.

Toffler, A. (1981). *The third wave*. Bantam Books.

Tulchinsky, I. (2020). *The unrules: Man, machines and the quest to master markets*. Wiley.

Tulchinsky, I., & Mason, C. E. (2023). *The age of prediction: Algorithms, AI, and the shifting shadows of risk*. St. Martin's Press. DOI: 10.7551/mitpress/13872.001.0001

Wilson, J. (1967). *Language & the pursuit of truth*. Cambridge University Press.

KEY TERMS AND DEFINITIONS

Benjamin Bratton's "The Stack" Concept: A tiered framework of computational authority extending from Earth to User, wherein AI systems regulate via infrastructure, converting platforms into tools of digital governance.

Dark Psychology: The employment of hidden strategies like gaslighting and manipulation to influence behavior and perception. Incorporated into AI, it allows for widespread impact and management of perceptions on a large scale.

Governmental Power Marketing: A governance approach that merges marketing strategies with administrative roles, allowing governments to manage uncertainty by fostering public confidence, institutional credibility, and control over narratives.

Kakistoscryptocracy: A decentralized governance menace where entities such as cryptocurrency networks and darknet platforms function outside legal boundaries, eroding state power and establishing disjointed systems of unchecked authority.

Large Language Models Cold War: A geopolitical conflict beginning in the 2020s where major powers such as the United States, China, Russia, and India redirected national strategies to develop sovereign Large Language Models (LLMs) (including the U.S.'s ChatGPT, Gemini, Copilot, and Claude AI; China's DeepSeek and Qwen 3; Russia's YandexGPT-4 and RuGPT-3; and India's Hanooman GPT, Krutrim AI, and BharatGPT), using deep learning-based AI systems to manipulate digital narratives, secure economic influence, enhance cybersecurity, and assert epistemic sovereignty in a competitive global landscape.

Political Economy Approaches: Analytical frameworks that focus on state-centric models highlight regulatory frameworks and supervision, unlike market-centric models that prioritize innovation and competition.

Risks of Algorithmic Systems and Predictive Modeling: The deployment of AI-based systems and predictive modeling carries significant risks, including the amplification of existing biases, a lack of transparency in their operations, and the potential to automate errors, thereby threatening human judgment and ethical responsibility.

Theories of International Relations: Analytical frameworks that elucidate state actions in the global AI race, with New-Constructivism exploring AI's influence on identity, norms, and vital global systems, Neoliberalism emphasizing institutional collaboration, and Neorealism concentrating on state power and endurance.

Wilson's Truth: Truth hinges on clear, ethical language; AI governance risks distorting language to control perception.

Chapter 7
Cryptocurrencies and Decentralized Finance (DeFi):
Revolutionizing the Global Financial Landscape

R Velmurugan
https://orcid.org/0000-0002-7925-9757
Karpagam Academy of Higher Education, Coimbatore, India

J Sudarvel
https://orcid.org/0000-0001-6656-1992
Karpagam Academy of Higher Education, Coimbatore, India

Ravi Thirumalaisamy
https://orcid.org/0000-0002-5954-5940
Modern College of Business and Science, Oman

ABSTRACT

Cryptocurrencies and DeFi (decentralized finance) have made decentralization possible in the international finance ecosystem, assisted by the blockchain technology. With this, we can do it with secure, transparent transactions without intermediaries, something which gives the user financial autonomism. On decentralized platforms, smart contracts for DeFi users provide access to lending, borrowing, liquidity services, and other exchanges. The revolution is lead by Bitcoin and Ethereum, especially in coming to countries where banks don't exist or are very hard to find, with lower fee, more accessibility. With the market volatility and the security concerns, such as vulnerabilities in the smart contracts, strong risk management and strong

DOI: 10.4018/979-8-3373-1727-4.ch007

security is necessary. The biggest problems that DeFi platforms need to overcome are regulated by Uniswap, Aave, and Compound. But DeFi's growth will come with sincere collaboration between developers, regulators, and those financial institutions that traditionally form a couple of the major aspect players.

INTRODUCTION

The process of the global financial ecosystem. The traditional way of financial systems has been recognized to be controlled by the centralized institutions, which have been the go between to the external users and the wider financial system. Banks, insurance companies, investment and other such institutions have historically played a role of bringing together people, transactions and assets, securing them, giving loans and generally regulating the economic flow of the money. Nevertheless, the constantly growing decentralized financial technology is tackling this conventional model with the ability to establish direct, peer-to-peer financial transactions. Through this transformation, the intermediaries' role is diminished and people have the power to act on finances without them, resulting in an open and inclusive financial ecosystem.

Blockchain technology is the motor of this transformation, that which underpins those cryptocurrencies like Bitcoin as well as Ethereum. Blockchain technology means the possibility of creating transparent, secure and decentralized system that will allow users to trade directly between each other and not through centralized intermediaries. Blockchain technology is used by a class of cryptocurrencies, known as cryptocurrencies, the most famous of which being Bitcoin, the first, and most popular cryptocurrency, to make peer to peer transactions. As a public ledger, all the transactions are recorded using Bitcoin, which means there is transparency and security without a centralized dictation (entity). This is similar in principle to Ethereum, which was pitched by Vitalik Buterin in 2015 and is built upon the fundamental principles of Bitcoin, but it takes the form of more versatile blockchain that supports smart contracts, self executing contracts, where the terms of the agreement are already written in lines of code (Buterin, 2014).

These decentralized platforms are unattached from the regular financial institutions. An example here when the cryptocurrency is Bitcoin; that is even if you have a fiat currency, you are actually running away from the control of the government or the central bank and you find a decentralized form of cryptocurrency so that you can choose your desired place. In contrast to conventional banking systems, which depend on intermediaries to manipulate and validate transactions, cryptocurrencies are characterized to have immediate transactions among individuals and a blockchain serving as a public and immutable record to all transactions. That is even more attractive in cases where the economy is unstable or the financial market is under developed or inaccessible to the general population. Narayanan et al. (2016) also mentions that cryptocurrencies provide financial inclusion for those in remote places where they have very little access to banking services, so that they can send the value among themselves without incurring extremely high fees or delays caused as a result of traditional banking systems.

DeFi is a term that refers to a decentralized version of the usual financial services, that leverages blockchain and cryptocurrencies to build it up. Unlike cryptocurrencies like Bitcoin and Ethereum, DeFi platforms let users carry out more elaborate financial business like lending, borrowing, trading and investing without interacting with centralized financial entities. DeFi, also known as Decentralized Finance, is a combination of blockchain technology and smart contracts, making use of which is delivered automated and secure financial services devoid of such traditional intermediaries such as banks or brokers. It offers peer to peer transactions as well as allows users to lend their assets, earn interest on them and provide liquidity to the decentralized exchanges while there is full control over their funds.

The rise of DeFi has been a revolution in how everything deals with the financial services. Examples include Uniswap which is a decentralized exchange where the users directly exchange one cryptocurrency with another without passing through centralized exchanges such as Coinbase or Binance. Uniswap doesn't rely on any central authority to match buyers with sellers instead it has used an automated market maker (AMM) model to determine asset prices dependent on the supply and demand. Such a platform made possible by numerous DeFi platforms includes Aave, in which users can both lend and borrow cryptocurrencies without depending on a central lender or credit institution. Aave is a direct interaction between borrowers and lenders, loans are secured by smart contracts and without the existence of any intermediaries.

The notion of decentralized financial systems is huge (DeFi and Crypto), but there are also a lot to do in order to make it real to the masses. Scalability is one of the main issues to be resolved. As there are more and more transactions placed on blockchain networks, particular blockchain networks that are based on Proof of Work (PoW) consensus algorithms such as Bitcoin can become very slow and inefficient. Because Bitcoin's network cannot process a large number of transactions a second, Bitcoin is not ideal for processing large scale global financial transactions. Like Ethereum, Bitcoin is more scalable than Ethereum because they support smart contracts, and while Ethereum is less congested because of it, it also has had high gas fees during busy times. To deal with scalability new solutions to overcome this problem are being invented, e.g Layer 2 scaling technologies such as Lightning Network for Bitcoin or Optimistic Rollups for Ethereum to enhance transaction throughput and seccurity (Buterin, 2020).

Security is another major problem that faces DeFi and cryptocurrencies. Although blockchain technology inherently has some high levels of security, also some smart contracts and DEXes (decentralized exchanges) are vulnerable to malicious actors that are exploited to cause large losses. For example, in 2020, Yearn Finance, a DeFi protocol, got hacked and lost $10M worth of the users' funds. Being on a decentralized platform means no central authority to dispute transactions or dispute settle the situation if there happens to do a hack or exploit case is done. To combat these risks, developers want to endow smart contract security by utilizing formal verification methods and bug bounties that would identify vulnerabilities prior to them being exploited (Zohar, 2018).

Indeed, an equally tremendous obstacle to the future of DeFi and cryptocurrencies is regulatory concerns. Countries and regulatory bodies worldwide are dealing with the challenge of how to include decentralized technologies into established financial and legal ecosystem. In addition to money laundering, terrorist financing and tax evasion, several people have been concerned that cryptocurrencies operate outside the traditional oversight of central banks and financial institutions. In face of that, some countries such as China have completely banned trading or mining of cryptocurrency while others like the United States are considering the creation of regulatory platforms to enforce financial regulations such as the Anti Money Laundering (AML) and Know Your Customer (KYC). It will be a challenge to get the right balance between innovation and consumer protections and giving the bite to the bad players to stop them.

But, decentralized finance's and cryptocurrencies' future is still uncertain. It is a sign that cryptocurrencies and DeFi are going to remain an important part of the future of global finance and it is being adopted in more and more cases, by both individual users and institutional investors. The use cases of blockchain based finance is expanding to tokenized assets and stablecoins, in that real world assets, be it real estate or commodity can be represented in the blockchain. Secondly, yield farming, the process of offering liquidity on decentralized platforms in return for rewards, has become a new way of investment as institutions become more excited about such decentralized propositions (Mackey, 2021).

As the problem of scalability, security and regulatory challenges limits the potential of decentralized finance, their solutions are a function of the future of decentralized finance. Although blockchain technology is evolving and with new solutions to resolve these problems, the realm of decentralized finance is enormous. With the increasing number of users and financial institutions adopting the decentralized financial ecosystem, cryptocurrencies and DeFi will probably be involved in forming the fate of the global economy going forward, turning into a more inclusive, open, and effective financial system.

THE EMERGENCE OF CRYPTOCURRENCIES AND DECENTRALIZATION

Despite being decentralized, blockchain technology itself is also decentralized. It exists from secure, temporary and direct digital transactions without intermediaries, such as a transaction between two people, to use cases like virus tracing and digital voter registration. This technological revolution has been centered around crypto-currency with the advent of cryptocurrency. Users have been able to use currencies like Bitcoin and Ethereum without Centralized Financial Institutions without having to surrender their financial power. Through blockchain, cryptocurrencies allow peer to peer transactions and this in turn enables individuals to transact without the need of the traditional third party intermediaries, through this process one gets a more open unbiased and comprehensive financial system.

Bitcoin was the first cryptocurrency which was introduced in 2008 in the name of Satoshi Nakamoto. Bitcoin's decentralized system, which does not have a med-dler, lets people send or receive funds directly between computers anywhere in the world. On this basis, transactions are made without the involvement of a centralized authority. The main integrity of Bitcoin's blockchain is the impossibility of altering or tampering with data in the public transaction ledger(Nakamoto, 2008). El Sal-vador being the real world examples of Bitcoin as decentralized such as promoting it as an instrument of financial inclusion and circumventing traditional banking systems (IMF, 2021).

Ethereum was introduced by Vitalik Buterin in 2015, which was a spinoff of Bitcoin's decentralization feature that enables use of smart contracts which are self executing contracts with terms written with the line code. Smart contracts remove the need for intermediations and increase trust between two parties, and execute agreements automatically. This innovation widened the scope of DeFi beyond its initial scope of simply transaction to include applications such as lending, borrowing, trading and insurance, on the Ethereum's blockchain. For example MakerDAO, which is a decentralized lending platform wherein users can use their Ethereum collateral to borrow and manage the loans with the help of smart contracts (Buterin, 2014).

Over the years, a decentralized alternative has emerged to these traditional finan-cial services — the DeFi platforms, which mostly utilize the Ethereum blockchain. Decentralised exchange (DEX) Uniswap performs cryptocurrency exchange without any centralised entity. This model is based on Automated Market Maker (AMM), where the price of asset is based on supply and demand (Adams et al 2020). Also, there are decentralized lending platforms such as Aave and Compound, which don't use banks or brokers to allow users to lend or borrow them cryptocurrencies. These platforms provide opportunities for faster and cheaper transaction and transparency (Zohar, 2018) due to the removal of intermediaries. Financially, these platforms are changing how things work by giving the user more power to choose how to save or borrow, as well as invest and even manage finances risks.

Elrond is another example of a scalable blockchain solution with a high performance decentralized applications (DApps) for DeFi and enterprise solutions running on Elrond network. Since DeFi sprang up in the time of Covid where few were willing to back up their currencies to dollars otherwise, stablecoins have been increasingly used in the DeFi space to reduce volatility by having the crypto peg its own value to the dollar with Tether (USDT) or USD Coin (USDC). This innovation makes DeFi more cheap, secure, and reliable helping the DeFi transition from adoption.

Full control in finances is the biggest advantage collaborated by DeFi. Decentralized lending protocols, asset trading, and earning interest on investment can be obtained by users bypassing intermediaries and still not compromising integrity of transactions governed through self executing smart contracts. For instance, Compound has empowered cryptocurrency holders to earn interest on their crypto holdings by not involving traditional banks, and Aave has given people the facility of decentralized lending at relatively lower fees than what is offered by centralized institutions (Narayanan et al., 2016). Since they are a transparent system, blockchain makes all the transactions public, which allows for more security and accountability than other financial systems.

Despite the promise, the security, the scalability, and the regulatory concern against DeFi and cryptos is still a challenge. 2016 is one of the biggest examples in security breaches when the hacker exploit vulnerability to funds from Ethereum's smart contract of over $50 million in DAI (Decentralized Autonomous Organization). (Buterin, 2016) The incidents are a caution on the requirements of solid security protocols to avoid such incidents. The attacks are even more recent, such as on DeFi lending platforms like Compound or decentralized exchanges like Uniswap and recall a constant need to improve in the security and risk management of these systems.

In addition, the unregulated nature of DeFi platforms is worrying on the matter of AML and KYC regulations. The frameworks that encourage innovation while addressing the protection of the consumers, as well as prohibit illegal activities have received more attentions from governments and financial regulators. As a result, the European Union is drafting MiCA (Markets in Crypto-Assets) regulations to offer legal assurances and protect consumers from abuses while having cryptocurrencies not be used for unlawful transactions.

The growing popularity of DeFi will force it to find the balance between regulation and innovation is key to its future. Much can be gained in these areas from the current ongoing evolution of these cryptocurrencies and DeFi technologies that may enable to transform the global financial ecosystem into a more financial autonomous, less intermediated, more transparent, secure and more efficient financial system. Uniswap, Aave, and other similar platforms are taking the leading roles in this transformation, providing very decentralized services of financial type, whether banking or non-banking like, that are opposing traditional banking services. However, to make DeFi reach its full capacity, we have to address the security, scalability, and regulation.

GEOPOLITICAL ANALYSIS

There is in this respect no doubt that cryptocurrencies and decentralized finance (DeFi) have imbued new dimensions of global geopolitics with price and presence of countries, and non state actors. In this way, cryptocurrencies have a unique use in the conflict for global power, where countries that want to bypass an economic sanction or the established financial system have a tool.

For countries like Iran and Venezuela, they are looking to use cryptocurrencies in order to avoid the economic sanctions. For instance, the use of Bitcoin and other cryptocurrencies which facilitate the international trade, specifically in import and export of goods has been used by Iran to go around traditional financial institutions (Zohar, 2018). Venezuela also jumped at the opportunity to launch its own cryptocurrency, called Petro, to overcome U.S. sanctions and hyperinflation but to enable citizens and businesses to interact on the global transaction space, regardless U.S. financial system, placement (Gohwong, 2019). These are some of the ways these countries are using digital currencies to keep participating in global economy, without U.S. dollar or the conventional global banking system, which are examples of how these cryptocurrencies could be used strategically in a geopolitical conflict.

However, Switzerland accepts cryptocurrencies and DeFi to strengthen the country's economy. From being a center of blockchain and cryptocurrency innovations, the country has turned into a new attraction for both investors and blockchain companies. As an example, Zug, also named as "Crypto Valley", hosts a lot of blockchain based startups, including Ethereum (Buterin, 2014). There are many players who regulated a better so far in the Swiss and to France, but Switzerland is one of the key players in the DeFi sector due to its legal framework that sets clear guidelines for cryptocurrencies. For other countries' more tight approach on blockchain technology, this proves to be a more promising route than using enforcement and censorship, and lift up Switzerland's financial and economic ranking in the world.

According to Zohar (2018), on the contrary, China has banned cryptocurrency trading and mining due to concerns over stability of finances and consumption of energy. But China has also started the development of Digital Yuan – the Digital Central Bank Digital Currency (CBDC) to digitize their currency and devalue dependency on US dollar. China is seeking to dominate its home economy and the international financial system (Gohwong, 2023). According to the push for a

Digital Yuan, a rising trend of digital sovereignty is taking place around the world, where countries want to dictate who controls digital currencies flowing in and out of their shores, an important facet in shaping the future of global financial system.

These are changes in the global power balance and form the rise of digital sovereignty – the use of digital currencies to both build and navigate one's economic power and international relations. Even as countries now wield cryptocurrencies not merely for economic reasons but also as a means of pursuing political and economic influence in a fast changing global order, the Reserve Bank of India continues to object to the concept on the grounds that it 'can erode its monetary and exchange controls authority'.

Political Economy Perspective

At face value, cryptocurrencies and DeFi are economically beneficial (or potentially harmful) from a political economy perspective. Yet, these are the technologies that could democratise financial services for the previously unserved yet may wield the disparities wider and make new economic powers.

DeFi and cryptocurrencies is one of the most lucrative benefits of financial inclusion. Among the 1.7 billion adults who are unbanked (World Bank, 2019), who lack access to things like bank accounts, credit, and insurance there across the globe, 68 percent of them are women. This gives alternative to the individuals to store and transfer funds without having the need of using traditional bank accounts. This accessibility has created opportunities for territory with meager behind the area financing supports, particularly in Africa, South East Asia and South America, where individuals can now get from the global monetary advertise. In this financial inclusion agenda, the Briefcase has been enthusiastically embracing Bitcoin and Ethereum. For instance, in Kenya, Bitcoin has been used in remittances which enables people who receive funds from abroad to do so without resorting to costly services like Western Union (Buterin, 2014).

This is however not evenly distributed. These innovations will benefit those who are wealthier, have more access to institutions and more access to technology and capital. Bitcoin's volatility and potential profit opportunity continues to attract institutional investors such as Grayscale and MicroStrategy to the extent of billions of dollars (CoinMarketCap, 2021). For smaller retail investors, these are usually very inaccessible opportunities, especially in the much smaller world of emerging markets where regulatory frameworks still have to develop so much it really is hard to trust the whole market.

However, DeFi platforms provide more financial services access, and this comes at a cost, in particular regarding illicit activity. Cryptocurrencies reduce the pseudonymity for bad actors. They can exchange money, avoid taxes and also fund illegal activities due to the rise in illegal activity on platforms such as the dark web. This is according to Chainalysis (2020), who states that cryptocurrency related crime rose in recent years, and reflected a large share of all cryptocurrency transactions. It's no wonder though that, for example, Bitcoin was used in the purchase of illegal goods, from drugs and weapons, illustrating the misuse potential of these platforms. For countries, the absence of oversight regulation in DeFi environments makes it even more difficult to fight money laundering and tax evasion.

Consequently, while DeFi platforms are seen as a means of economic inclusion to access resources, this can widen inequality through means of enabling illicit platform activity. Prevention of misuse of these platforms will require regulatory frameworks that will prevent the misuse of these platforms as well as ensure that the benefits of cryptocurrencies and DeFi are utilised for legitimate users while intercepting criminal activities. The U.S. SEC and the European Central Bank are already looking into the ways of regulating cryptocurrencies and DeFi (Gohwong, 2023).

For example, like others, in the end cryptocurrencies and DeFi represent tremendous change towards more encompassing and effective financial systems while at the same time roaring issues with allegations to security, inequality, and regulatory uncertainty. In order to allow this type of technology to thrive while reducing the risks that they pose to the world economy, it will be important to strike a balance between innovation and regulation.

BENEFITS AND OPPORTUNITIES OF DEFI AND CRYPTOCURRENCIES

Other crucial pillars of financial inclusion are decentralised finance (DeFi), and the cryptocurrencies as a whole. Billions are still locked in the traditional banking system around the world while billions more, living in underdeveloped and remote areas have yet to be touched by the current banking bandwagon. As many and 4600m people are unbanked, that is not being banked and without having access to any essentials financial services such as saving account, finance loan and insurance, as per The World Bank (2019). This means that lack of banking services in these regions mega blocks the individuals from fully participating in the global economy. But cryptocurrencies are the answer to this problem, as people can access financial service without the need of having a traditional bank account. When it comes to Bitcoin and Ethereum, or other cryptocurrencies for that matter, individuals have the ability to create decentralized wallets on their phone, or over the internet so that they can store, send and receive these cryptocurrencies without the help of banks or other intermediaries.

DeFi Platforms are the second layer of the rise of DeFi platforms which give more financial inclusion because they provide decentralized solutions to the traditional financial service. For instance, Aave and Compound allow one to borrow, lend or lend out cryptoasset holdings, while Uniswap provides direct access to cryptoassets for exchange. They are not intermediated platforms (e.g. no bank required) and allow a financial service through a mobile. Especially in regions where there is lack of physical banking infrastructure as is the case with Sub Saharan Africa and Southeast Asia. Civilizagens offers people in these regions, who lack access to traditional banking services, a new opportunity with DeFi and cryptocurrencies. For example, Bitcoin adoption in Kenya for mobile based transactions has been so encouraging that over 80 percent of the adult population relies on the use of mobile money services such as M-Pesa to facilitate its financial inclusion without the need for any traditional bank (Buterin, 2014).

Apart from financial inclusion, cryptocurrencies and DeFi platforms also offer more advantages like low transaction fees, getting rid of borders in transactions and allowing for mass inclusiveness all of which can make wealth building easier. When using traditional financial systems, international transfers are very expensive while moving money abroad is practically cumbersome because of high fees. For example, migrants that send remittances to their home country in the United States pay fees of 5–10% and less money actually reaches the recipients (World Bank, 2020). On the other hand, Bitcoin free from the centralized system allows you to transfer and receive money worldwide with lower or higher fees. It is especially vital for the folks in the countries of the instability of the banking system for it to have the reasonable safest and low cost means of the transferring and of keeping their money.

For example, in Venezuela, where hyperinflation has ravaged the value of the country's currency, Bolívar, people have started looking to Bitcoin and other types of cryptocurrencies to escape the inflationary pressures (Goforth, 2018). This is a phenomenon of how cryptocurrencies can be used by the people of the countries with an unstable economy to save their money. In fact, the same patterns have been consistent in Zimbabwe, where the population has had to turn to bitcoin and USDT (Tether) to preserve their assets against the rapidly devaluing of their local currency.

The new trend toward DeFi and cryptocurrencies allowing for financial inclusion has allowed people/frontyards in underbanked areas to reduce their dependence on traditional banking infrastructure and truly participate in the global capitalism. In addition to making financial accessibility more available, these technologies also promote the closing of the financial gap by offering low cost transactions, borderless transactions and platforms that are mobile based. Therefore, people and communities turn to be financially empowered by cryptocurrencies which give them opportunity of bypassing devaluation of the currency in unstable economy. Decentralized finance platforms are the rise of decentralized finance which is a testament of how decentralized finance can turn the entire global financial landscape upside down and give people tools to keep wealth for times of economic crisis.

RISKS AND CHALLENGES IN DEFI AND CRYPTOCURRENCY ADOPTION

Cryptocurrencies and DeFi both have some obvious positives, but adoption of both has its limits: both require too many challenges to overcome and therefore growth can continue. The main headache when it comes to cryptocurrency market is its, still, volatile nature — volatility is a pain point for the investors from all sides — individual ones and institutional ones. Our exposure to currencies is very volatile (the nature of cryptocurrency is very volatile for wherever values can move just enormously short time). For example, from the start of 2020, the price of Bitcoin was close to $7,000 and has exceeded $60,000 in 2021 (CoinMarketCap, 2021), before a sharp drop. Due to this extreme price volatility, users face significant risks as they are unable to guess how the value of their holdings will be changed. Speculation, macroeconomic factors, rules news, and market sentiment rule the market fluctuations (Narayanan et al., 2016). For instance, the price of Bitcoin soared with Tesla announcing at the start of 2021 that it had purchased $1.5 billion worth of Bitcoin before dropping as Elon Musk, the company's CEO, worried about Bitcoin's environmental impact. Volatility such as this is to expect and losses are almost always almost inevitable, especially those who are inexperienced or cannot guard their wings.

Just like other major cryptocurrencies, Ethereum's price also picks up the pace when it announces an upgrade, gets more people using the smart contracts, or when news of its competitors comes out (Narayanan et al., 2016). Suppose, for example, the network of Ethereum greatly upgraded at Ethereum 2.0, as investors were expecting a long term scalability and environmental impact. While, such price swings do highlight how volatile cryptocurrencies are subject to market changes, and therefore unable to be used as a valuable store of funds, or a sound means for transaction and long term saving programs.

With volatility being a difficult challenge as volatility continues to be a complex challenge, more and more investors are searching for ways to mitigate the volatility, for example, by utilizing derivative instruments (options and Futures Contracts), by using hedging strategies and finally stable coins (cryptocurrencies which are pegged to stable assets). To illustrate, Tether (USDT), USD Coin (USDC), etc. have been stablecoins, less volatile than other cryptocurrency itself (Narayanan et al., 2016) making it suitable for transaction and savings, compared to other very volatile cryptocurrency. Moreover, as the DeFi platforms have risen in popularity, their importance has been given further impetus by the fact that they offer a solution to mitigate the risk and volatility within the decentralized ecosystem, with stable alternatives. Yet, there is still troubles that the overall volatility in the market keeps widespread adoption at bay.

As the most serious impeding factor to the adoption of DeFi and cryptocurrencies, platform security is the most serious issue. Although blockchain generally is thought about to be more secure than traditional systems, blockchain is not impregnable. What arose was smart contracts and decentralized exchanges (DEX) where new avenues for hackers to rise were being created. Once developed, smart contracts run automatically once deployed and their terms are written into the code of code that cannot be changed unless a new code is run. However, the code can be vulnerable, as that could lead to users becoming hacked or the subject of theft. The DAO hack is one of the famous examples of this, as it dated back in 2016 where a bug in Ethereum's smart contract code allowed hackers to steal $50 million equivalent in ETH (Buterin, 2016). It was a hard fork of the Ethereum's blockchain and generated Ethereum (ETH) and Ethereum Classic (ETC). Similarly, DeFi protocols like Compound, and Uniswap have been recently hit with security incidents demonstrating that there are processes that are still vulnerable in decentralized (Narayanan et al., 2016).

So, to address these security concerns, stronger auditing procedure, more security framework, more user education are required. Regular checks by independent security firms would regularly find and fix vulnerabilities in smart contracts before they are deployed. For example, there exists OpenZeppelin, which is a leading security audits firm that helps on audit on a DeFi project's smart contracts before going live. Also, giving the users a training on how to minimize the risk of theft including storing private keys on hardware wallets, and confirming smart contract code before a token transfer can go a long way in discouraging theft.

Of course, the regulation regarding DeFi and cryptocurrencies is another big obstacle to its mainstream adoption, next to security. Cryptocurrencies and decentralised platforms are still currently in legal gray areas and have no clear guidelines and regulations. Switzerland and Singapore both have been accepting blockchain innovations and cryptocurrencies but removed the legal roadblocks for them. Several of Switzerland's blockchain start-ups have ended up in Switzerland's Crypto Valley, and the country's well defined regulatory framework has given it a leading position in DeFi. However, China has banned all cryptocurrency transactions and mining, since it worries about the security concerns for its financial stability, fraud, and energy consumption (Zohar, 2018). This is the same for looking at how countries view cryptocurrencies and DeFi, too, with some countries dictating regulations and controlling innovation, and some leaving them open to the advancements in innovation.

For example, International regulatory bodies (e.g., Financial Action Task Force (FATF), are crafting in frameworks to enforce the anti money laundering (AML) and know your customer (KYC) policies across the crypto platforms. However, regulators are lagging behind technology's rapid evolution (Gohwong, 2023). Due to the decentralized nature of these platforms, these platforms are generally operated outside the control of traditional financial authorities which make it difficult for the governments to effectively regulate them.

While DeFi and cryptocurrencies are growing, on one hand, we have to make sure to be innovative yet to protect the consumers. Regulatory guidelines will have to be created that are clear and accessible enough to underpin these technologies in a way that will bring stability and security to them. Clear governance, evident in rules, regulations, and rewards, will also help minimize fears of market manipulation, fraud and such illicit activities as might jeopardise the trust placed in a financial system.

As such, cryptocurrencies and DeFi, though always promised to fix the problems of accessibility, efficiency, and innovation in the history of finance, also have volatility, security, and regulatory ambiguity as their costs. If decentralized financial systems are to continue growing and be adopted widely there are these issues that will have to be addressed. Decentralized financial infrastructure calls for collaboration between developers, the regulators and the financial institutions to create safe, large, and sustainable infrastructure.

THE FUTURE OF DEFI AND CRYPTOCURRENCY INTEGRATION WITH TRADITIONAL FINANCE

With the fast growing Decentralized Finance (DeFi) world, more and more financial institutions are launching decentralized solutions in different shape of the form. This can also be attributed to a phenomenon caused by the rise of stablecoins. Cryptocurrencies like stablecoins are based on cryptos that have anchors to the stable asset (be it the US dollar or gold). The reason behind the growing trend of stablecoins is that they exploit the advantages of cryptocurrencies (speed, transparency and low fees) with the stability of traditional fiat currency. Even today, stablecoins are heavily used in cross border payments, especially in the case of hedging tools against market volatility. For instance, Visa teamed up with Crypto.com in 2020 to enable transactions to be honored in the USDC stablecoin that's pegged to its dollar. It means that these traditional financial institutions are all of a sudden claiming that these decentralized solutions are worth incorporating into the very traditional financial systems (Goforth, 2018). With more financial players moving into the world of stablecoins, it's now more delicate to interact freely between the traditional financial system and the expanding decentralized finance environment.

Also, the spread of stablecoin adoption implies an overall trend of incorporating the blockchain and cryptocurrency technology with the mainstream financial system. Decentralization, transparency and immutability of characteristic features of blockchain is now being based at more traditional financial institutions. For this reason, Circle, the issuer of the USDC stablecoin, works with Visa and other large digital network payment processes to facilitate faster and less costly intercontinental payments around the system, without passing through banks and with fewer interlocutors. This is an important stride to achieving the integration of decentralized financial solutions within companies established infrastructure which should improve global payments (Circle, 2020).

Convergence of DeFi and traditional finance is concentrated around stablecoins "in tandem with tokenization as the process of turning real world assets into digital tokens on a blockchain." For example, Securitize is a platform to tokenize assets, which lets the businesses raise funds through blockchain technology creating digital tokens for their real estate, venture capital and private equity. This democratizes investment opportunities, making it available for more people to invest in high value assets, real estate for example, with as little or low capital as possible. Private ownership of high value assets has become more liquid and sustainable through tokenized Asset ownership using Securitize platform (Securitize, 2021).

New tokenized asset introduction is changing the investment markets, allowing for real time price discovery and global trading on the decentralised exchanges (DEXs) that are on 24/7. Take for instance, RealT that tokenizes real estate assets on the blockchain and bought, sold and traded on the blockchain like any other token, allowing for fractional ownership, greater liquidity. The smart contracts additionally guarantee that the conditions of the asset transactions are transparent and immutable, and that means investors get trust as well as security in the transactions. These features make them superior to the typical markets that have time restrictions, serial intermediates, and long settlement timings.

Yield farming is another big thing happening in DeFi space where the users are providing liquidity to decentralized platforms and getting rewards like interest, tokens and staking rewards in return. Decentralized lending protocols like Aave and Compound offer GitHub many platforms like it: platforms that are major DeFi platforms that provide decentralized lending protocols in return for a loaner of their arranged cryptocurrency. Imagine, Aave is a decentralized Application (DApp) which allows the users to provide liquidity and to earn the interest on their asset. To enable governance, as well as investment, AAVE tokens grant users the voices to vote on platform protocol decisions (Mackey, 2021). As is, Compound's users can also lend and borrow various cryptocurrencies such as stablecoins (USDC, for example) and earn rewards for their liquidity.

Now there is also interest from institutional DeFi and yield farming. More and more, hedge funds and venture capital firms are investing in DeFi protocols instead of traditional investment options due to lower yields. For example, the leading hedge fund, Pantera Capital, has committed a lot of money in the DeFi projects as these platforms offer huge yield opportunities. At the moment, institutional interest in DeFi is just in the nascent stages and yet it is apparent that the more sophisticated investors are looking to get into this burgeoning ecosystem.

Despite DeFi and yield farming becoming increasingly popular, there are numerous risks when investing in DeFi platforms. The volatility of these digital assets, the intricacy of yield farming strategies, as well as the threat of regulatory scrutiny all make it very difficult for DeFi to be adopted. To emphasise this point, in 2020, a vulnerability in the bZx protocol cost $1 million, opening the risk of hack from smart contract vulnerabilities. In addition, security breaches and hacks in the DeFi space also persist. You are taking obvious risks but this constant innovation of DeFi platforms and blockchain technology point to the fact that these things are disseminating mainstream adoption of decentralized solutions in the traditional finance.

The integration of DeFi solution by more financial institutions is driving the financial environment toward increasing decentralisation, efficiency and inclusivity. The revolutionary advancements in the area of decentralized finance have been tokenized assets, stablecoins, and yield farming, to give some examples, which are rebooting the global financial landscape and opening up more people to the opportunity to invest and build wealth through such opportunities and tools that were not previously available. Despite these technologies are problems and take a lot of risk, but their development continues is a new age in global finance where more people have a chance to join the finance, with more liquidity and more innovation.

CONCLUSION

During the emergence of cryptocurrencies and decentralized finance (DeFi), a decentralized financial ecosystem has come into existence, offering various advantages compared to existing traditional financial systems. The traditional financial infrastructure, however, is based on centralized entities such as banks, credit unions, and brokers, which act as intermediaries for individuals and the financial system. While Bitcoin and Ethereum, as well as DeFi protocols, have altered this model by utilizing peer-to-peer transactions and reducing intermediaries, the shift towards decentralization has created a space for greater financial inclusion, lower transaction costs, and more accessible financial services for individuals and communities that were previously excluded from the banking system.

The financial inclusion advantage of DeFi and cryptocurrencies is the most outstanding. Nearly 1.7 billion adults worldwide, as reported by the World Bank (2019), are unbanked, lacking the ability to manage their funds via savings accounts, credit, or insurance. Cryptocurrencies, as they are, don't require typical bank reports to process or store funds. Decentralized networks allow individuals to hold and transfer digital assets without needing a financial institution. This is especially crucial in areas with limited banking infrastructure, such as much of Africa, Southeast Asia, and South America. Cryptocurrencies, therefore, provide individuals with an affordable and efficient means of participating in the global economy—allowing remittances, purchases, and even investments from mobile devices.

Bitcoin and Ethereum have been particularly useful in advancing this financial inclusion agenda. With the decentralized nature of these networks, users have full control over their own finances, as no intermediaries are needed. Vitalik Buterin's creation of Ethereum in 2015, extending Bitcoin's foundational principles by adding smart contracts, has further advanced DeFi by automating complex financial transactions and enabling decentralized applications (DApps), which offer a wide range of financial services, including lending, borrowing, trading, and insurance (Buterin, 2014).

In addition, the lower transaction costs associated with cryptocurrencies and DeFi platforms are a major advantage. Traditional financial institutions often impose high fees for cross-border payments, credit transactions, and account maintenance. For example, sending money abroad through banks often incurs fees ranging from 5 to 10%, particularly for remittances to developing countries (World Bank, 2020). In contrast, cryptocurrencies facilitate cross-border payments with minimal fees. Even large-value transactions on Bitcoin are often free, while Ethereum's 'gas fees' are relatively lower compared to traditional banking fees. Stablecoins, like USDC and Tether, pegged to stable currency assets such as the U.S. dollar, provide an even cheaper mode of international payments, offering the speed and low costs of cryptocurrencies while maintaining stability.

DeFi platforms, such as Uniswap—a decentralized exchange (DEX)—allow users to trade cryptocurrencies without relying on intermediaries like centralized exchanges (e.g., Coinbase, Binance). This approach eliminates the fees charged by traditional exchanges for transactions, withdrawals, and trading services. Similarly, decentralized lending platforms like Aave and Compound enable users to lend and borrow cryptocurrencies without the need for traditional financial institutions, thus reducing borrowing costs and eliminating the need for middlemen.

However, the growth of such a decentralized financial ecosystem presents challenges. Security remains a primary concern. While blockchain is secure by definition, the rise of smart contracts and DeFi platforms has introduced risks. Vulnerabilities in smart contracts and decentralized applications have led to significant losses for investors. A prominent example is the 2020 hack of Yearn Finance, a decentralized finance protocol, where over $10 million was stolen due to a vulnerability in its smart contract code (Goforth, 2020). As the DeFi ecosystem expands, so too do the threats, requiring improved security practices, thorough code audits, and increased user education to mitigate these risks.

Volatility is another challenge for cryptocurrencies and DeFi. Cryptocurrencies are known for their extreme price fluctuations, making it difficult to estimate the value of holdings and creating high risks for investors. In 2021, for example, Bitcoin's price surged from around $7,000 to $60,000 before crashing (CoinMarketCap, 2021). Such price swings deter people from using cryptocurrencies as a stable store of value. Therefore, there is a need for operational risk management strategies and financial products like stablecoins to reduce the impact of market volatility and offer users greater stability.

Regulatory uncertainty also poses a significant hurdle to the growth of decentralized finance. As more countries embrace cryptocurrencies and DeFi platforms, governments and regulators face challenges in determining how to regulate this emerging sector. Countries like Switzerland and Singapore have welcomed cryptocurrencies with clear regulatory frameworks, while others, like China, have banned the use and mining of cryptocurrencies, citing concerns about financial stability and illicit activities (Zohar, 2018). A global regulatory framework for cryptocurrencies and DeFi is essential to protect investors and curb illicit activities, ensuring the sustainable growth of the market.

Cryptocurrencies and DeFi have thus created a decentralized financial environment with numerous advantages, such as financial inclusion, lower transaction costs, and broader access to financial services. However, these technologies must address challenges related to security, volatility, and regulatory uncertainty before their full potential can be realized. To advance the future of DeFi, it will require the steady building of secure systems, the establishment of clear regulatory frameworks, and the adaptation of decentralized solutions by traditional financial entities.

RECOMMENDATIONS FOR THE FUTURE

- **Policy Recommendations**: Governments and international organizations should establish clear and cohesive regulations for cryptocurrencies and DeFi, balancing innovation with consumer protection. They should also consider integrating central bank digital currencies (CBDCs) into the global financial ecosystem, providing a state-backed alternative to decentralized currencies.

- **Future Research**: Further research should explore the potential impact of CBDCs on the future of DeFi, examining how state-backed digital currencies could coexist with or challenge decentralized systems. Additionally, studying the role of international cooperation in regulating the cryptocurrency space would help create a unified approach to managing the global DeFi market.

REFERENCES

Adams, B., Daley, M., & Liu, Z. (2020). Uniswap and the Future of Decentralized Exchanges. *Journal of Cryptocurrency Research*, *4*(2), 112–121.

Adams, S., Smith, A., & Lee, C. (2020). *Uniswap: Decentralized Exchange Protocol*. Blockchain Review Journal.

Buterin, V. (2014). *Ethereum White Paper: A Next-Generation Smart Contract and Decentralized Application Platform*. Ethereum Foundation.

Buterin, V. (2016). *The DAO Hack and the Future of Ethereum*. Ethereum Foundation Blog.

Buterin, V. (2016). *The DAO: A Decentralized Autonomous Organization*. Ethereum Foundation.

Buterin, V. (2020). *The Future of Ethereum and Layer 2 Solutions*. Ethereum Foundation.

Chainalysis (2020). The 2020 Crypto Crime Report. Chainalysis.

Circle. (2020). *USDC: The Digital Dollar*. Circle.

CoinMarketCap (2021). Bitcoin Price Index. CoinMarketCap.

Goforth, C. (2018). Cryptocurrencies and Financial Empowerment: The Role of Bitcoin in Emerging Economies. *Journal of Financial Innovation*, *6*(2), 112–125.

Goforth, J. (2018). The Role of Stablecoins in the Future of Finance. *Journal of Financial Technology*, *12*(2), 105–120.

Goforth, J. (2018). Venezuela's Struggle with Hyperinflation and the Rise of Cryptocurrencies. *Journal of Latin American Economics*, *45*(2), 123–140.

Gohwong, S. (2019). Government-based Cryptocurrencies. *Asian Political Science Review*, *3*(2), 40–46.

Gohwong, S. (2023). KAKISTOSCRYPTOCRACY. *Asian Political Science Review*, *7*(1), 50–58.

IMF. (2021). *El Salvador Adopts Bitcoin as Legal Tender*. International Monetary Fund.

Mackey, M. (2021). **Aave** and **Compound**: Pioneering DeFi Lending. *Financial Innovation Review*, *5*(4), 24–36.

Mackey, T. (2021). Decentralized Finance: A Review of Key Protocols, Yield Farming, and Lending Platforms. *Financial Technologies Review*, *9*(3), 150–160.

Nakamoto, S. (2008). Bitcoin: A Peer-to-Peer Electronic Cash System.

Narayanan, A., Bonneau, J., Felten, E., Miller, A., & Goldfeder, S. (2016). *Bitcoin and Cryptocurrency Technologies*. Princeton University Press.

Securitize. (2021). *Tokenizing Real Estate and Venture Capital: A New Era in Investment*. Securitize Inc.

World Bank. (2019). *The Global Findex Database 2017: Measuring Financial Inclusion and the Fintech Revolution*. World Bank Group.

World Bank. (2020). *Remittances: Cross-Border Payments and Financial Inclusion*. World Bank.

Zohar, O. (2018). Blockchain and the Rise of Decentralized Finance (DeFi). *Smart City Journal*, *10*(4), 90–104.

Zohar, O. (2018). China's Ban on Cryptocurrency Mining: Implications and Reactions. *Journal of Chinese Economic and Business Studies*, *16*(2), 125–142.

Chapter 8
Cryptocurrencies and Decentralized Finance (DeFi):
Transforming the Future of Financial Systems

Geetika Madaan
https://orcid.org/0000-0001-8141-9935
Marwadi University, India

Sanjeet Singh
https://orcid.org/0000-0001-6103-2346
Marwadi University, India

Amrinder Singh
https://orcid.org/0000-0003-0830-7245
Jain University, India

ABSTRACT

The study's objective is to look into the pipeline of cryptocurrencies and Decentralised finance (DeFi) as potential new economic actors ready to institute radical changes in the established ways of finance. The DeFi innovations explore key drivers, opportunities, and risks they may introduce for the stakeholder ecosystem of the financial arena at larger. Using a qualitative research methodology, the study conducts a systematic literature review along with the case analysis of leading DeFi protocols and also cryptocurrency platforms. The findings of the study stated that DeFi uses blockchain technology to provide public, permissionless and interoperable financial services such as lending, trading and asset management. This study provides

DOI: 10.4018/979-8-3373-1727-4.ch008

a source of information for regulators, global investors, financial institutions, and developers of decentralized technology.

INTRODUCTION

The global financial world has experienced a tremendous change over the years subjected to the exponential change in the digital technology and an increased need of more inclusive, efficient and transparent financial system(Tetiana, Volodymyr, Dluhopolskyi, Vasyl, & Tetiana, 2022). Among the most disruptive trends are cryptocurrencies and decentralized finance (DeFi) – two systems linked to each other: they both exist to deter from the traditional financial systems and offer a decentralized approach as an alternative. Originated at first as an alternative to fiat money and traditional bank systems, cryptos and the DeFi platforms have transformed into intricate systems that provide a diverse assortment of financial services including lending, trading, insurance, asset management, funds remittance et cetera, without requiring centralized intermediaries. These innovations use the blockchain technology to create peer-to-peer transactions, self-executing smart contracts, programmable money, which shows what many believe to be the next horizon of financial innovation(Piñeiro-Chousa, López-Cabarcos, Sevic, & González-López, 2022).

Cryptocurrencies, which saw the debut of Bitcoin in 2009, under the pseudonym Satoshi Nakamoto, were a response to the 2008 worldwide financial crisis. They sought to establish decentralized system which did not rely on centralized control, trust was kept not by institutions but through cryptographic protocols and distributed consensus. Over time, the more advanced blockchains like Ethereum have been developed to allow the development of decentralized applications (dApps), smart contracts, paving the way for a DeFi revolution(Nguyen & Nguyen, 2024). Unlike the traditional finance which depends on centralized institutions to offer and ensure the services, the DeFi protocols enable users to interface directly with each other in a permissionless and trustless context. For this reason, DeFi has garnered much momentum with TVL at DeFi protocols having accumulated to hundreds of billions of dollars at an all-time high in 2021.

An invasion of DeFi is in the potential for democratising finance, breaking down access barriers to capital and tools managed by the gatekeepers of traditional finance. In places with scarce banking structure or individuals have been financially excluded, DeFi is a worthy alternative. In addition, programmability of DeFi permits developing new financial instruments and services that are more flexible in satisfying cliental demands. Some of them are automated market makers (AMMs), decentralized exchanges (DEXs), yield farming, and liquidity mining – innovations that reinvent the ways through which value is created, exchanged, and distributed.

But those factors making DeFi alluring – anonymity, decentralization, and the absence of intermediaries – are also the sources of major risks for DeFi startups, such as compliance issues, cybersecurity threats, and market volatility (Piñeiro-Chousa, Šević, & González-López, 2023).

In terms of technology, the infrastructure of both cryptocurrency and DeFi is the blockchain – a distributed ledger technology (DLT) that stores transactions on multiple nodes of a network, verifying transparency, immutability, and protection from tampering. Smart contacts, which are the self-executing agreements coded directly into the blockchain, automate such practices as lending, borrowing and/or trading without the need for intermediaries. This degree of automation and openness is supposed to lower operations costs and increase efficiency, theoretically. However, vulnerabilities in smart contract programming have been exploited in multimillion-dollar hacks, presenting the need for robust security practices and regulatory intervention. Additionally, limitation on scalability of existing blockchain networks can undermine the mainstream adoption of the DeFi applications.

The socio-economic impact of DeFi and cryptocurrencies are so massive. On the one hand, they provide users with the ability to have never before seen control over their finances, cutting out the need for centralized banks and financial services. On the other hand, they have raised concerns among regulators and policymakers as far as protection of consumers, systemic risk, financial stability, and the risk of engaging in illicit activities such as money laundering and terrorist financing is concerned. The response of these countries differs significantly: from active support and innovation sandboxes to outright ban on BTC with legal repressions (Ugolini, Reboredo, & Mensi, 2023). These disparities make a fragmented regulatory system that makes inter-national cooperation and standardization difficult. This has left regulatory uncertainty a major hurdle towards increased adoption of DeFi and cryptocurrencies.

Furthermore, environmental effects of blockchain technologies and, especially, the ones which operate using energy-consuming consensus mechanisms such as the proof-of-work (PoW), have been highly criticized. High energy consumption that comes with mining activities has led to calls for more sustainable methods of mining such as PoS and other alternative consensus algorithms. Ethereum's move from Ethereum 1.0 to Ethereum 2.0 and a change from PoW to PoS is a move in this direction, which aims to improve scalability, reduce energy consumption, and provide greater network security. Therefore, environmental sustainability is developing as one of the most important measures for evaluating the long-term viability and social acceptability of the technologies of cryptocurrency and DeFi(Yousaf, Nekhili, & Gubareva, 2022).

These issues notwithstanding, the innovation ecosystem around DeFi continues to grow, and continues to be of interest to institutional investors, technology companies, start-ups and academia. VC investments in blockchain and DeFi startups have recorded tremendous growth in the past years as more investors are now convinced that decentralized finance can change global markets. Furthermore, decentralized identity solutions and tokenization of real-world assets as well as cross-chain interoperability are breaking boundaries in regards to what is possible in DeFi. These advances imply that we are just scratching the surface of the scope and effects of decentralized finance.

The goal of this research is to offer an in-depth revelation of the status quo of, opportunities and challenges present in the cryptocurrencies and DeFi. It looks into the fundamental elements of DeFi infrastructure, the effectiveness of cryptocurrencies in providing decentralized financial services, and the implications on financial inclusion, regulation, security, and sustainability. By combining intelligence from academic literature, industry reports, and actual-world case studies, the study adds to the emerging literature on disintermediated finance and advises policymakers, practitioners, and researchers on how to act (Atree & Tripathy, 2025).

Decentralized Finance (DeFi) represents a paradigm shift in the design and operation of financial systems. Unlike traditional systems that depend on central authorities, DeFi relies on blockchain technologies to enable open, permissionless, and programmable financial applications. However, its transformative potential is unevenly realized across different contexts and is subject to both technological and socio-political constraints. Despite its prominence, existing literature often lacks a critical, comparative, and theory-informed understanding of DeFi's adoption, risks, and systemic impact. This paper addresses these gaps by integrating theory, real-world cases, and socio-political context into the analysis.

Cryptocurrencies and DeFi are not only technological innovations but also agents of change in the world's finance. They represent a move from a pre-determined, top-down regime to an open, bottom-up world. They represent a change from closed systems to open networks and from static financial products to programmable, composable financial services. We find ourselves in an ecosystem that's in the midst of a massive transformation in the financial space. As outcomes of this transformation, will we have a more inclusive and efficient financial future, or will we have new forms of risk and inequality? This will depend on the evolution of the ecosystem, how the challenges are being addressed, and how key stakeholders grapple with this rapidly evolving domain.

THEORETICAL FRAMEWORK

This study employs the following models:

- **Diffusion of Innovation Theory (Rogers, 2003):** To explain how DeFi technologies spread across different user groups and geographies.
- **Institutional Theory:** To analyze how formal and informal institutional environments (e.g., regulation, cultural norms) influence DeFi development and adoption.
- **Technology Acceptance Model (TAM):** To assess user perceptions regarding ease of use, trust, and utility of DeFi platforms.

Background of the Study

The appearance of cryptocurrencies and decentralized finance (DeFi) is a radical change in the history of financial innovations. From experimentation with digital money to the emergence of programmable finance, such development of this ecosystem lays out technological advancement, market adjustment, and underlying socio-economic paradigms. This section follows the development of cryptocurrencies and DeFi from some representative historical moments to emerging technologies to indicate the increasing impact of this area of finance on the world market.

THE ORIGINS OF CRYPTOCURRENCIES

The notion of the digital money precedes Bitcoin with the first attempts of creating internet-based currencies such as DigiCash (1990s) and e-gold (early 2000s) being made. Nevertheless, these efforts proved to be unsuccessful mainly because of dependence on the centralized infrastructure, regulatory clampdowns and security backdoors (Atree & Tripathy, 2025).

The introduction of the modern era of the cryptocurrency has started back in 2008, when Satoshi Nakamoto presented the Bitcoin white paper with the title "Bitcoin". A Peer-to-Peer Electronic Cash System." 2009 saw the birth of the Bitcoin as a project for an open-source software that would allow peer-to-peer transfers without intermediaries. Bitcoin introduced several groundbreaking features:

- A **decentralized ledger (blockchain)** powered by proof-of-work consensus
- A **fixed supply cap** of 21 million coins
- **Pseudonymous transactions** verified by cryptographic methods

Bitcoin was the main use case as regarding storage of value and as medium of exchange beyond traditional financial systems. Over time it has become a kind of "digital gold", the attention of which attracted libertarians, technologists and investors looking for an alternative to fiat money and centralized banking.

EMERGENCE OF ALTCOINS AND EXPANDED USE CASES

After the success of Bitcoin, an array of alternative cryptocurrencies (altcoins) came up. Such coins aimed at making improvements on the loopholes of Bitcoin or in addressing different needs. Examples include:

- **Litecoin (2011):** Faster block times and different hashing algorithm
- **Ripple (XRP, 2012):** Focused on real-time global payments and banking partnerships
- **Dash and Monero (2014):** Emphasized enhanced privacy features

This flourishing of cryptocurrencies was indicative of a wider understanding that the blockchain could be used to drive various financial services other than peer-to-peer transfers. Nonetheless, most of these early altcoins were not highly programmable and were only used to meet niche purposes.

ETHEREUM AND THE BIRTH OF PROGRAMMABLE MONEY

An important stage of DeFi's development was DeFi's emergence in 2015, developed by Vitalik Buterin – the launch of Ethereum. Ethereum came with a Turing-complete virtual machine called (EVM) that allowed developers to write a smart contract which referred to self-executing code that is stored on the blockchain (Karim, Lucey, Naeem, & Uddin, 2022).

Ethereum established the ground for programmable money and decentralized applications (dApps), thus, providing possibilities for complicated financial thinking and user connections without mediators. This innovation was a great watershed and enabled:

- **Decentralized exchanges (DEXs)**
- **Lending and borrowing protocols**
- **Prediction markets**
- **Tokenized assets and stablecoins**

On Ethereum, developers could issue protocols that resembled banking services but taking place in a trust less decentralized setting. This opened the new chapter, which would later be referred to as Decentralized Finance (DeFi).

INITIAL COIN OFFERINGS (ICOS) AND TOKEN ECONOMY

The Ethereum platform also developed the ERC-20 token standard that made the process of creating of the fungible tokens less complicated. This gave birth to ICO boom of 2017, when start-ups managed to collect billions in dollars by selling utility tokens to investors on exchange for cryptocurrencies such as ETH, BTC, among others (Yousaf & Yarovaya, 2022).

Although the ICO model democratized capital raising and removed gatekeeping of venture capital firms, it gave room for frauds, speculations, and regulatory monitoring. Several of the projects weren't useful, transparent or profitable causing a market crash in 2018, better known as the crypto winter.

Despite the crash, the ICO era showed the power of decentralized capital formation and the viability of blockchain based fundraising. It also paved the way for the development of more sustainable DeFi protocols.

RISE OF DEFI PROTOCOLS AND COMPOSABILITY

The DeFi movement gained traction in **2018–2020**, with the rise of platforms such as:

- **MakerDAO (DAI):** A decentralized stablecoin backed by crypto collateral
- **Compound and Aave:** Protocols for algorithmic lending and borrowing
- **Uniswap:** A decentralized exchange using an automated market maker (AMM) model

DeFi protocols brought along a composable architecture, thus enabling developers to "stack" or combine various protocols to develop more-advanced financial product. This "money Lego" took innovation and interoperability across the ecosystem.

However, DeFi Summer of 2020 saw massive growth with yield farming and liquidity mining which paid users in the form of rewards for their liquidity provision. Total Value Locked (TVL) in DeFi protocols increased from below $1 billion at the beginning of the year 2020 to more than $80 billion at the end of 2021(Ugolini et al., 2023).

NFTS, DAOS, AND THE EXPANSION OF WEB3 FINANCE

Building on DeFi's momentum, the broader **Web3 movement** emerged. Web3 refers to a decentralized internet where users control their identity, data, and assets. Key components of this evolution include:

- **Non-Fungible Tokens (NFTs):** Digital representations of unique assets (art, music, real estate)
- **Decentralized Autonomous Organizations (DAOs):** Community-governed entities using on-chain governance
- **Social tokens and creator economies**

NFTs put the word 'blockchain' onto the mainstream map in 2021, evolving the use cases of crypto into art, entertainment and gaming. In the meantime, DAOs started managing treasuries in the range of millions and organizing global communities in a decentralized way.

These moves depicted that cryptocurrencies and DeFi were no longer financial instruments; they were transforming into the digital economies' infrastructure.

INSTITUTIONAL ADOPTION AND REGULATORY ENGAGEMENT

There were increased institutional stake and regulatory interventions in crypto industry between 2021 to 2023. The leading financial companies, such as JPMorgan, Fidelity, and BlackRock, started to study crypto custody, investments, and blockchain-based services. The mainstream financial discussions involved the likes of bitcoin ETFs, crypto savings accounts, and tokenized real estate.

At the same time, governments around the world increased the efforts to regulate the sector. Some of them adopted the innovation; others constrained it (e.g., El Salvador accepted Bitcoin as legal payments). Central banks started formulating CBDCs in the realization that digital currencies were the future of finance (Bommer, Milevoj, & Rana, 2023).

This was a turn from experimental to semi-regulated, hybrid ecosystems, combining decentralized infrastructure with centralized compliance structures.

TRANSITION TO SUSTAINABLE AND SCALABLE MODELS

Recent developments have focused on **scalability**, **sustainability**, and **user accessibility**:

- **Ethereum's transition to Proof-of-Stake (The Merge)** in 2022 drastically reduced energy consumption, addressing environmental criticisms.
- **Layer-2 solutions** like Optimism, Arbitrum, and zkSync improved transaction speed and reduced gas fees.
- **Cross-chain interoperability** protocols (e.g., Polkadot, Cosmos) aim to connect fragmented blockchain ecosystems.

The use of user-friendly wallets, decentralized identity (DID) systems, and better on-ramps has made DeFi more attractive to non-technical users. These advancements are gearing DeFi to its next stage; mainstream integration and global impact.

The cryptocurrencies' and decentralized finance development is a proof of effectiveness of the open-source innovation, peer-to-peer models, and the world's demand for more transparent and fairer financial infrastructure. Since Bitcoin's birth as a response to the devastating financial sub-prime crisis, this field has evolved at a breakneck speed from programmable money and decentralized governance system to a highly fluctuating ecosystem (Shah, Lathiya, Lukhi, Parmar, & Sanghvi, 2023).

What started as a fringe experiment is now a multi trillion dollar industry that is a regulator of central bank, governments and world markets. With a growing DeFi, it peeks into the future of finance, which is decentralized, inclusive, and a fit for the digital-first world.

LITERATURE REVIEW

The high growth in the cryptocurrencies and DeFi has generated scholarly and industry interest. This literature review integrates different current works along various dimensions. The underlying ideas, the structure and work, systematic and security threats, and soci-economic implications of cryptocurrencies. It emphasizes on theoretical and empirical contributions, and indicates gaps for future research.

Foundations of Cryptocurrencies

Cryptocurrencies saw the light of day thanks to the first work of Nakamoto (2008) who published a white paper presenting Bitcoin, a peer-to-peer electronic cash system. Bitcoin that used blockchain, an immutable, distributed ledger, and proof-of-work (PoW) consensus provided a decentralized trust in a sense where there were no intermediaries needed. After that, scholars have analysed such characteristics of Bitcoin as its property as a store of value, medium of exchange, and speculative asset (Ahuja & Khandelwal, 2023). Although others point at the safe-haven nature of the coin that resembles gold (Abou Ali, 2024), others call attention to the high volatility and limited scalability of transactions (Manjula.B.C, Shilpa.B.S, & Sundaresh. M, 2022).

Ethereum, introduced by Buterin (2014) extended functionality of blockchain by introducing smart contracts – self-executing agreements that allow to make programmable and automated transactions. This innovation was the beginning of DeFi. Ethereum's role as an enabler of decentralized applications (dApps) highlighted by Wood (2015) and Antonopoulos and Wood (2018) result in the birth of decentralized financial protocols that do not require traditional banks and fintech services.

The Rise and Structure of DeFi

DeFi designates an ecosystem of blockchain financial services that do not require a centralized medium for the transactions to take place. They consist of decentralized exchanges (DEXs), lender services, derivatives markets, and synthetic assets. Smart contracts are used by DeFi platforms for automation and enactment of financial agreements. For example, the protocols like MakerDAO, Aave are analyzed for their usage in the issuance of stablecoins, lending and borrowing in a decentralized manner, and in automated market-making respectively (Sarkar, 2023).

There is composability when it comes to the DeFi ecosystem (Schär, 2021), which means that various applications can be joined together as if they were building blocks. This "money lego" makes innovation fast yet, it brings in systemic risks like cascading failures arising from tightly coupled protocols. Liu et al. (2022) state that composability adds functionality but also augments the attack vectors, particularly in flash loan exploits and smart contract vulnerabilities.

REGULATION AND GOVERNANCE CHALLENGES

The position of cryptocurrency and Defi in terms of regulation is unspecified in a lot of jurisdictions. Zetzsche et al. (2020) explain that the decentralized and borderless nature of DeFi undermines the old school regulatory paradigm of jurisdiction-bound and institution-centred. The absence of a central authority to monitor or penalise for law violation, consumer protection and AML/KYC compliance complicate matters.

Arner et al. (2021) discuss the idea of the regulation by code with the notion that the smart contracts can incorporate the compliance rules. Notwithstanding, legal experts raise concerns that technological regulation might not be as flexible and fair as the traditional regulation (Bakare, Omojola, & Iwuh, 2025). Some others are offering co-regulation models through which ideally, the creators of DeFi, the users and regulators will -work together to construct secure and compliant DeFi infrastructures (Urquhart & Yarovaya, 2023).

SECURITY AND TECHNICAL RISKS

Security is still one of the most important DeFi problems. After deployment, smart contracts are immutable, so coding error is extremely dangerous. Work conducted by Luu, Shambaugh, Hoffmann, and Biryukov (2016) and Atzei and others (2017) describe an array of vulnerabilities like reentrancy, oracle manipulation, and timestamp dependency. DAO hack in 2016 and numerous DeFi exploits in the recent years have highlighted the result of the lack of code check and insufficient design.

Moreover, the use of oracles – external data feed to blockchain – entails the risks of centralization and failure points. Oracle issues were mentioned in high profile attacks like the attacks on Compound and Harvest Finance. To solve these problems, Chainlink as well as other decentralized oracle networks have been presented, but their resilience is still under investigation (Jiang et al., 2023).

FINANCIAL INCLUSION AND SOCIO-ECONOMIC IMPACTS

Supporters claim that DeFi and cryptocurrencies can make financial inclusion easier because of their low barriers to entry and consequent provision of services for the unbanked and underbanked (Metelski & Sobieraj, 2022). According to the research by Ozili (2022), in countries with poor financial infrastructure, DeFi can provide some alternative ways to savings, credit, and investment. Further, DeFi eliminates the need for trust in the centralized financial bodies which may lack or be corrupt in some regions.

Critics, on the other hand, claim that DeFi main beneficiaries are tech-savvy, crypto-literate users, with an access to internet and capital to invest. The complexity of DeFi interfaces, the requirement of self-custody, and the volatility crypto-assets may accidentally marginalize the targeted populations (Singh, 2024). Thus, although DeFi can provide inclusion, it has to be combined with the user education, simplification of the interface, and reasonable mechanisms of control.

ENVIRONMENTAL AND SUSTAINABILITY CONCERNS

The environmental impact of cryptocurrency mining, especially in proof-of-work systems such as Bitcoin, has been a subject of a lot of attention. The research by Krause, and Tolaymat (2018) and de Vries (2018) shows the immense costs in energy that are involved in mining thus the criticism of crypto sustainability. By shifting to a proof-of-stake (PoS), Ethereum will use less than 1% of energy, which is environmentally friendly for DeFi (Rajharia & Kaushik, 2023).

However, scholars like Truby (2018) still insist on the fact that the aspect of environmental sustainability should feature in the governance, and indeed, protocol design of blockchains, from the word go. Eco-friendly blockchain projects and carbon-neutral cryptocurrencies are in demand, but their empirical validation is still poorly represented.

A THEMATIC SYNTHESIS OF LITERATURE REVIEW

Infrastructure and Digital Divides

Access to digital devices, internet connectivity, and blockchain literacy remain key barriers to DeFi adoption. Digital divides disproportionately affect rural, elderly, and low-income users.

Trust, Autonomy, and Governance

While DeFi promises "trustless" systems, trust remains central in user adoption—particularly in volatile regions where scams and Ponzi schemes have eroded public confidence.

Regulation vs. Decentralization

There is a persistent tension between DeFi's ethos of decentralization and the regulatory imperatives of states. Countries like China and India have oscillated between banning and regulating crypto activity.

Socio-Political Context

Authoritarian regimes with capital controls (e.g., Venezuela) have witnessed a surge in crypto usage, whereas democratic regimes balance innovation with compliance. Political risk affects DeFi stability and user trust.

Financial Inclusion and Economic Crises

DeFi enables access to loans, remittances, and yield-generating assets in unbanked regions. During crises like COVID-19 or hyperinflation, DeFi offered alternatives to failing traditional systems.

Limitations and Risks

Scalability, gas fees, liquidity fragmentation, smart contract bugs, and the absence of legal recourse remain structural challenges to DeFi's maturity.

GAPS IN THE LITERATURE AND FUTURE RESEARCH

Despite growing literature on DeFi and cryptocurrencies, several gaps remain:

- **Empirical studies** on user behavior, adoption patterns, and socio-economic impacts are still nascent.
- More research is needed on **cross-chain interoperability**, privacy-preserving mechanisms, and decentralized governance structures.
- The **long-term sustainability** and **macroeconomic implications** of a decentralized financial system have yet to be fully explored.
- **Comparative regulatory studies** across countries could inform policy harmonization and innovation-supportive frameworks.

It is possible that the combination of the blockchain with other technologies like AI, IoT, quantum computing is going to explore new research directions. For example, Blockchain-aided IoT payments or AI-supported credit scoring in the DeFi lending might reshape digital economies.

Conclusively, the cryptocurrencies and DeFi literature is rich and ongoing in their progress, commensurate with an accelerating growth and prominence of such technologies. Although the transformative potential they have is discussed in the existing studies, they also point to fundamental technical, regulatory, and social challenges. A measure that will strike a middle ground between innovation and oversight is vital to leveraging gains from decentralized finance and avoiding its pitfalls.

METHODOLOGY

This paper follows a **conceptual analytical framework** using **thematic literature synthesis**. The methodology includes:

- **Systematic literature review** using databases like Scopus, Web of Science, and SSRN.
- **Case study illustrations** from Nigeria, Argentina, and Vietnam.

- **Comparative socio-economic and political analysis** to explore adoption patterns.
- **Stakeholder segmentation** to analyze usage by retail vs. institutional users, urban vs. rural populations, and generational cohorts.

Table 1. Comparative and demographic insights

Region	Key Use Cases	Barriers	Government Stance
Sub-Saharan Africa	Remittances, stablecoins	Device access, infrastructure	Cautious, pro-sandboxing
Latin America	Inflation hedge, savings	Regulatory uncertainty	Mix of bans and innovation zones
Southeast Asia	Microloans, P2P lending	Financial literacy	Actively fostering DeFi hubs

User Segments:

- **Retail users (Gen Z)**: High crypto engagement via mobile-first platforms.
- **Elderly**: Low adoption due to tech barriers and risk aversion.
- **Institutional investors**: Focus on DeFi yield farming, asset diversification.
- **Rural vs. Urban**: Urban areas benefit from better access and education.

CHALLENGES OF CRYPTOCURRENCIES AND DECENTRALIZED FINANCE (DEFI)

Cryptocurrencies and decentralized finance (DeFi), despite their possibility to democratize the field of finance and make it more transparent and independent of the centralized institutions, are facing numerous problems that prevent them from widespread adoption and make their further existence questionable. These problems can be found in technological, regulatory, economic, security, environmental and user-centric dimensions. Much study of such barriers is needed before stakeholders – (developers, policymakers, investors, and users) – can devise strategies that can strike the balance between innovation and stability and protection.

Regulatory Uncertainty and Compliance Issues

Lack of clear, consistent regulatory frameworks is one of the leading issues in the DeFi and cryptocurrency world. Being borderless and decentralized in nature, DeFi lies beyond the remit of traditional financial regulation, which is jurisdiction-based. Most of the DeFi projects are not registered financial bodies and this calls for worry over compliance with the anti-money laundering (AML), KYC, and tax laws(Seabe, Moutsinga, & Pindza, 2024).

It is difficult for regulators overseas to catch up with the fast-changing nature of DeFi. While Singapore and Switzerland allow for crypto trading, China and India do not permit it. As global standards are not yet uniform, some organizations can move to lightly regulated areas, increasing the risk of economic stress.

Also, with decentralization, there is often less accountability. If there is no main operator, nobody can be held accountable for problems or issues related to fraud, protocol failure or user losses. Little accountability complicates enforcing rules which is harmful to investors.

Security Vulnerabilities and Smart Contract Risks

Smart contracts, though, are also considered a weak part of DeFi. After deployment on a blockchain, smart contracts cannot be changed if there are errors in their code. Because blockchains can't be changed, trustless networks are still open to risks that have led to the loss of over many millions.

Common attack vectors include:

- **Reentrancy attacks**, where hackers repeatedly call a contract before previous operations complete.
- **Flash loan exploits**, which manipulate market prices or protocol mechanisms using uncollateralized loans.
- **Oracle manipulation**, in which external data feeds are tampered with to misrepresent asset prices.
- **Front-running**, where malicious actors exploit transaction ordering to gain financial advantage.

Some major protocols, despite thorough audits, have been broken into. This means that loop holes like these make it necessary to check the security and confirm the code, as well as include insurance cover for users' funds. Nevertheless, ensuring safety at construction sites can be very costly for smaller projects(Yang, 2024).

Scalability and Performance Limitations

It is also important to mention that scalability creates a key issue for cryptocurrencies. At present, most blockchain networks find it hard to process the high transaction volumes on Ethereum. During the most active periods, traffic overloading on the network causes some problems.

- **Slow transaction processing times**
- **High gas fees** (transaction costs)
- **Poor user experience**

These problems are being solved in part by Optimistic Rollups, zk-Rollups and Ethereum's move to Proof-of-Stake (PoS). They are still being developed or introduced and may cause new complications and dangers.

DeFi platforms cannot hope to compete with traditional finance unless they have scalable infrastructure(Gramlich, Guggenberger, Principato, Schellinger, & Urbach, 2023). For this reason, DeFi has a tough time promoting its use to all types of consumers and adding corporate partners.

Lack of User Awareness and Technical Complexity

Despite the growth of DeFi, the **average user** still finds it **difficult to navigate**. Using DeFi requires a solid understanding of:

- Private key management
- Wallet integration
- Token standards
- Gas fees
- Risks of impermanent loss and smart contract failure

Due to having a complex design, people often need to know programming to participate. Besides, since mistakes cannot be reversed in blockchain, there is a greater risk from errors or engaging with harmful smart contracts.

Since there is no proper customer support available in decentralized finance, users are not able to get help if they experience a loss. It could discourage more people from using DeFi and make them less confident in these platforms.

Volatility and Speculative Behavior

Due to their unpredictable prices, cryptocurrencies are not suitable for exchanging goods or for saving money over a period. Swings in the price of Bitcoin and Ethereum often happen due to market speculation, news from regulators and general economic conditions. Because of this, many people avoid using them for ordinary financial dealings(Motamed & Bahrak, 2019).

Short-term gain seekers in the DeFi field have taken advantage of unstable platforms by participating in actions such as yield farming and liquidity mining. As a result of these practices, there are continuous phases of boom and bust in stricken economies. Once tokens lose value or offers are removed, a sudden withdrawal of liquidity can happen, resulting in wide-reaching effects.

Prices of USDT, USDC and DAI are kept stable to give them an advantage over other cryptocurrencies. Nonetheless, they encounter problems linked to how much collateral they must hold, stricter regulations and having their assets concentrated in one place.

Governance and Decentralization Dilemmas

DeFi projects claim to be decentralized, but various aspects are still controlled by a small group of developers or venture capitalists through token governance. As a result, it raises questions about who is in charge and how interests can be influenced, along with issues related to governance(Shahzad, Xu, Lim, Hasnain, & Nusrat, 2024).

Sometimes, users may lose faith when insiders use their votes to make decisions that work against the community. In addition, when people do not vote much, the fairness of decentralized choices becomes questioned. Experts believe that a fully decentralized system involves everyone, is easy to monitor by all participants and has measures against powerful individuals gaining too much influence.

Environmental and Energy Concerns

Using the PoW system in cryptocurrencies is leading to increased worry about their environmental impact. Since Bitcoin mining requires a lot of energy, it releases carbon into the air and harms the environment like some small countries. For this reason, there have been comments and concerns expressed by governments, environmental activists and investors, urging for alternatives.

While DeFi is largely built on Ethereum with PoS due to Ethereum 2.0, numerous legacy and other blockchains are still powered by PoW. DeFi should pay attention to sustainability since it is important for the planet and for the ESG world of investing(Bhombe & Arts, 2023).

Cryptocurrencies and DeFi present good ways to improve the financial system, but they do have limitations. Significant obstacles for solving these problems include regulation, security, how many people will use them, scalability and the impact on the environment. Developers, regulators, academics and representatives from the global financial field must cooperate to address these matters. Appropriate governance, new technologies and acceptable rules can help solve these problems and make decentralized finance more valuable.

OPPORTUNITIES OF CRYPTOCURRENCIES AND DECENTRALIZED FINANCE (DEFI)

Though numerous obstacles and challenges are faced in cryptocurrencies and DeFi, they can bring major changes to worldwide finance. Because they are decentralized, programmable and universal, these technologies represent huge opportunities for improving access to financial services, reducing costs, promoting new ideas and proposing novel business models. Here, the text highlights several opportunities that let DeFi and cryptocurrency play a role in boosting inclusion in finance.

Financial Inclusion and Democratization of Finance

It is talked about widely that one of DeFi's main benefits is helping bring financial services to people who may not have them otherwise. The World Bank (2021) reports that 1.4 billion adults do not use bank services. A lack of funds, missing government-issued IDs, damaged infrastructure and being far from cities can prevent many individuals from using banking services (Su, 2024).

DeFi platforms—accessible via a smartphone and internet connection—can enable these populations to:

- Save and transfer funds without needing a bank account
- Access loans through decentralized lending protocols (e.g., Aave, Compound)
- Participate in global investment markets using tokenized assets
- Use decentralized stablecoins (e.g., DAI) to hedge against inflation or unstable local currencies

Since this system is open to anyone, marginalized groups may have more opportunities to use and manage money effectively.

Disintermediation and Cost Reduction

DeFi has introduced disintermediation, in which transactions are done directly, without involving third parties. Usually, traditional banks, remittance services and lenders rely on several middlemen who add fees and slow down the process.

In contrast, DeFi automates processes through **smart contracts**—self-executing code that eliminates the need for human intervention. This reduces:

- **Transaction costs**
- **Settlement time**
- **Operational inefficiencies**

For instance, to swap assets on a DEX such as Uniswap, users do not need a central authority, market makers or custodians. With cryptocurrencies, you can complete cross-border payments instantly and at much lower costs (Ali, 2016).

Because of this, DeFi attracts both small companies and people in less developed countries.

Innovation in Financial Products and Services

DeFi encourages people to make new innovations. Since many protocols can be combined and interact, composable architecture allows for quick creation of complex financial products, for example:

- **Automated market makers (AMMs)**
- **Synthetic assets** (e.g., Synthetix)
- **Tokenized securities and commodities**
- **Flash loans** with instant arbitrage capabilities
- **Decentralized insurance protocols**

As a result, investors can explore various new methods for gathering capital, investing their money and managing risks. As an illustration, using DeFi derivatives platforms, users can trade using derivatives that are not managed by any central broker. You can earn passive income using yield farming and liquidity mining, but there are certain risks involved (Li et al., 2023).

Besides, the use of digital tokens helps people hold ownership of real estate, art or private equity in smaller shares. This opens up new investment ways so that more people can generate wealth.

Transparent and Trustless Systems

Blockchain, the foundation of cryptocurrencies and DeFi, offers **unprecedented transparency**. All transactions are recorded on a public ledger that is immutable and auditable by anyone. This transparency fosters:

- **Greater accountability** in financial services
- **Trustless interactions** where users rely on code, not institutions
- **Real-time auditability** and risk monitoring

This differs from regular Finance which requires users to rely on banks, credit agencies and fund managers. Anyone can check the code, the numbers of tokens available and the past activities on DeFi platforms.

Being so open can cut down on fraud, poor management and big problems linked to corruption in certain areas.

Decentralized Governance and Community Participation

In DeFi, most projects are managed democratically, allowing the community of owners to decide on important changes and operations. It highlights the trend where users get ownership of the apps used.

In Maker DAO, community members decide on changes to DAI, while people using Compound can vote on interest rates. It helps create a type of governance model that:

- **Democratized decision-making**
- **Protocol adaptability**
- **Stakeholder alignment**

In addition, community management of the protocol allows users to work together, likely preventing those who seek financial gain for themselves and supporting network monopolies. As a result such systems might be able to handle crises better than big financial institutions.

Integration with Emerging Technologies

Cryptocurrencies and DeFi are increasingly being integrated with other emerging technologies, opening up vast new frontiers:

- **Artificial Intelligence (AI):** AI-powered bots can optimize DeFi yield strategies, detect fraudulent activity, and automate portfolio management.
- **Internet of Things (IoT):** Machine-to-machine payments via crypto enable autonomous economic interactions between devices (e.g., in smart cities or supply chains).
- **Web3 and the Metaverse:** DeFi is a foundational layer in virtual economies, enabling digital real estate transactions, NFT lending, and in-game financial services (Jani, 2018).

These integrations expand DeFi's use cases beyond traditional finance, allowing for innovative cross-sector applications that could revolutionize industries ranging from logistics to healthcare.

Alternative Monetary Systems and Sovereign Resilience

In cases where a country's currency weakens in value, inflation surges or money is restricted, cryptos offer people an alternative to standard currencies. People representing the community can store their savings in decentralized assets that are not affected by local issues or global tensions.

In Venezuela, Nigeria and Turkey, many are choosing cryptocurrency due to rising inflation and a weakened currency. They can also take the place of dollars for people living in areas where currencies are uncertain.

Central banks are also looking into CBDCs in order to respond to the rise in cryptocurrencies. Centralized CBDCs exist, but their ideas came from breakthroughs in DeFi and blockchain by pioneers (Tetiana et al., 2022).

The way the global financial industry operates is shifting thanks to cryptocurrencies and DeFi. They include encouraging more people to have financial access, lowering costs, introducing new forms of finance and allowing for more decentralized administration. Despite the many obstacles ahead such as rules, technology and society, there is much promise in creating an updated, sturdy and modern financial system.

Ensuring that DeFi continues to improve requires cooperation among developers, regulators, academic experts and users. If DeFi and cryptocurrencies are cultivated effectively, they may reshape finance in our time to be something everyone can use.

FUTURE DIRECTIONS OF CRYPTOCURRENCIES AND DECENTRALIZED FINANCE (DEFI)

What began as an unusual experiment is now a new trend that could completely reshape the finance industry. As technology develops further, various new connectivities and changes in society and the economy are expected. Several technologies, policies, organizations and even social habits will direct how cryptocurrencies and DeFi progress and shape the world economy, along with government and access to financial services.

Institutionalization and Mainstream Adoption

One important trend to watch in the coming years is an increase in activity by large financial institutions. Due to the search for higher profits, diversification and novel technologies, institutions are paying more attention to digital assets. As more people accept this trend, it should become mainstream.

This means bringing blockchain technology into existing financial markets. For example, by using tokens and decentralized exchanges, people are able to get involved in buying small amounts of standard assets such as equities, real estate and bonds. As a result, procedures and systems are now being built to help secure institutional use of DeFi platforms which reduces overall risks to the industry(Nguyen & Nguyen, 2024; Piñeiro-Chousa et al., 2022, 2023). Mixing centralized and decentralized features (CeDeFi) will be more common, helping create a pathway for regulation between distinct types of financial systems.

Enhanced Interoperability and Cross-Chain Collaboration

Today, each blockchain in the DeFi area supports specific protocols and assets, so they are largely separated. Due to fragmentation, liquidity becomes lower, expenses rise and DeFi platforms are less available. For this reason, focus in future development will be on enabling different chains to communicate directly and easily.

Blockchains are interoperable when they allow various networks to interact and access each other's information and functions. Polkadot, Cosmos and Avalanche are designing cross-chain solutions and bridges to support communication among different blockchains. People using these new features won't need to rely on centralized exchanges to move assets, can save money by using their capital more efficiently and can use various financial instruments that involve different blockchains.

Furthermore, if smart contracts become standardized on different platforms, this could help them interact and work better together. When DeFi ecosystems connect with others, it will become easier for users and allow DeFi to scale up.

Scalable and Sustainable Infrastructure

The main difficulty for DeFi and blockchains is being able to grow to meet demand. Because of high use and expensive transactions on Ethereum, it is clear that scalable support is needed for more users and activities moving forward. As DeFi evolves, people will start using Layer 2, switching to alternative Layer 1 blockchains and relying on modular blockchain frameworks.

The use of layer 2 such as rollups (e.g., Optimism, Arbitrum, zkSync), helps lower prices and increase the number of transactions possible per second on base-layer blockchains. Similarly, organizations such as Solana, Avalanche and Cardano aim to provide faster agreement methods and better cost savings (Ugolini et al., 2023).

Up next, Celestia and Fuel want to split the execution, consensus and data layers to ensure better separation. They will allow developers to create chains that are customized to their requirements and perform better. These advancements will be necessary for helping the next generation of DeFi apps which involve high-frequency transactions, instant payment services and communicating derivatives.

Regulatory Clarity and Legal Frameworks

With the rise of DeFi, some form of regulation will be required. Cryptocurrencies and decentralized finance should be governed by understandable, identical and accepted laws everywhere. Crystal-clear regulations are necessary to protect customers, support a fair market and motivate big investors.

Many global authorities are starting to finalize descriptions of digital assets in law, clarify rules for preventing money laundering and introduce tax regulations for them. New technologies are being made to enable users to stay anonymous and meet the demands of regulators.

Over time, we can expect regulatory sandboxes, self-regulatory organizations (SROs) and decentralized autonomous organizations (DAOs) for compliance to develop. It is possible that looking into smart contracts and certifying code requirements may grow in importance for improved confidence and safety in the industry.

Tokenization of Real-World Assets (RWAs)

The future of DeFi will likely include the tokenization of RWAs. A blockchain is used to “tokenize” real estate, stocks or commodities into digital tokens.

Assets that are tokenized allow people to own a fraction of the asset, trade at any time, complete trades faster and increase liquidity. Real estate tokens are available for trading and purchase by retail investors from anywhere without the need for intermediaries. Likewise, the use of digital debt assets and invoice financing usually makes credit markets more open and efficient (Yousaf et al., 2022).

By connecting conventional finance and blockchain, RWAs will help DeFi bring trillions of dollars' worth of off-chain assets onto the blockchain. This will help improve the usefulness of NFTs and promote new revenue streams for distributed platforms.

User Experience and Financial Inclusion

DeFi will be used by the masses when DeFi platforms are easy for people to use and provide security. As of now, using a crypto wallet and managing your keys can be very difficult for newcomers. The experience users have will become much better in the future.

They will become less complicated and safer, offering support for different chains, biometric security and a social method to restore access to your wallet. Simpler ways to invest in DeFi such as gasless transactions and automatic investment strategies (robo-advisors), will raise the number of DeFi users. Meanwhile, connecting wallets to messaging, browsing and mobile applications will make the registration process more convenient (Atree & Tripathy, 2025).

As a result, financial inclusion is likely to increase, with the main change happening in regions where banks are not widely available. Using mobile DeFi tools, stablecoins and microfinance applies, those in underserved communities can get savings, lending and insurance options without any intermediaries.

Integration with Emerging Technologies

DeFi will start relying more on technologies such as artificial intelligence (AI), machine learning (ML), Internet of Things (IoT) and edge computing as the future unfolds. They can improve DeFi protocols and lead to developing new DeFi use cases.

AI technology can be useful in improving how choices are made in yield farming, portfolio construction and managing risks. They can also identify unusual actions and contribute to the protection of smart contracts (Atree & Tripathy, 2025).

Merging DeFi and IoT will make it possible for finances transactions to happen automatically in real-time as the IoT-connected devices generate data. A payment for agriculture insurance might be made based on a reported weather condition and a payment for shifting goods might be initiated upon confirmation from IoT sensors.

As a result, financial services will include autonomous, adaptive and data-driven options.

Decentralized Governance and DAOs

Since decentralization is important to the blockchain, ways of governing will develop to oversee the rules of protocols fairly and openly. The use of DAOs is predicted to take over as the key form of leadership in DeFi.

In the future, DAOs will introduce new systems such as quadratic voting, reputation governance and weighted voting by stakes. They are responsible for updating protocols, spending from the treasury and supporting community initiatives, always acting based on what most members prefer (Karim et al., 2022).

This type of collaboration could happen to manage connections between DAOs, distribute liquidity and decide on standards. Additionally, people expect DAOs to manage their frameworks for use in philanthropy, local community growth and open-source projects.

ESG Alignment and Sustainable DeFi

More interest from the world in sustainability will lead to ESG factors shaping the way cryptocurrencies and DeFi protocols develop. The fact that proof-of-work blockchains use lots of energy has received negative attention, but proof-of-stake is a better option in this regard.

Future platforms in the DeFi space will use green assets, green funding practices and systems for ethical investments. Blockchain platforms will help ensure that ESG information is clear and easy to follow. DeFi applications can also be created to provide funding for solutions that support the UN's Sustainable Development Goals and community projects (Yousaf & Yarovaya, 2022).

As a result, sustainable DeFi will consider the environment and social aspects, not only focusing on technology.

Education, Awareness, and Policy Dialogue

Overall, what matters most is for people to know more and for collaborative talks on policy to occur. Initiatives, research and building capacity play an important role in connecting users, developers, policymakers and regulators.

Blockchain, smart contract and DeFi programs are expected to be offered by universities, think tanks and financial firms. Together, the public and private sectors will develop regulations that promote new ideas while minimizing damage from risks.

To cope with the changes in crypto, it will be important to build policies with data, experiment and talk to crypto stakeholders.

Cryptocurrencies and decentralized finance will likely have a bright future, but it may also be complex. Innovations in regulations, new technologies, involvement of major players and empowered users will influence the direction of the ecosystem. DeFi connecting with traditional banking and innovative technologies allows us to create a financial system that serves everyone and is clearer, as well as smoother.

However, realizing this vision will require concerted efforts from developers, regulators, investors, and communities. Challenges such as scalability, governance, security, and regulation must be addressed with foresight and collaboration. Ultimately, the future of DeFi will be determined by its ability to scale responsibly, innovate inclusively, and deliver real-world value in a sustainable manner.

CONCLUSION

The combination of cryptocurrencies and DeFi has led to a revolution that changes economic systems, brings changes to world monetary systems and makes financial services accessible to all. Since the world is moving from centralized institutions to decentralized protocols, it's obvious that DeFi and cryptocurrencies represent significant changes in the world of finance. It intends to summarize the entire journey so far, including what has been learned, as well as what lies ahead.

What started as a substitute for fiat currency, cryptocurrency has evolved and now has several practical uses. Changes in their industry have encouraged new solutions in areas such as payments, money transfers, financial investments and identity checks. The transformation is centered around blockchain technology which functions as an irreversible, open and shared ledger trusting users who may not trust each other. Using this system, DeFi relies on smart contracts to automate its services and also cuts out middlemen. New options for lending, borrowing, trading, insurance and asset management have entered the financial market thanks to DeFi.

Many academics are exploring DeFi and cryptocurrencies, showing that they are significant disrupters and present several issues. Experts have analyzed the volatility of cryptocurrencies, the technology behind blockchain and the impacts of DeFi on regulations and the economy's steadiness. It is clear in these writings that as these technologies create many possibilities for progress, they also demand reliable systems to handle risks, safeguard users and oversee the industry.

DeFi and cryptocurrencies are having a significant influence on financial inclusion. In such places where standard banks are not common, DeFi provides an alternative to banking that is available to everyone. Individuals now have the opportunity to trade globally, borrow money and secure their savings through smartphones and the Internet. You can access stablecoins easily as they hold the value of fiat currencies and avoid extreme price swings. Advancements in these financial technologies could greatly help tackle the problem of financial inequality among the unbanked and underbanked peoples.

There are still some issues that need to be addressed. Many governments and companies are still concerned about the uncertainty surrounding regulations, due to the decentralized nature of cryptocurrencies and DeFi systems. Since centralized authorities are missing, it becomes more difficult to enforce consumer protection, AML and KYC laws. Furthermore, because transactions on the blockchain use pseudonyms, their data can be abused by criminals. Dealing with these difficulties calls for countries to cooperate, introduce decentralized controls and apply regulations that manage both innovation and security.

There are also concerns about how well technology can be scaled up. Using Ethereum and similar networks can be difficult because of congestion and increased prices. However, recent improvements in Layers 2, sharding and other consensus methods should help address these obstacles. Focusing on interoperability allows different blockchain networks to talk to each other without friction. They are necessary to develop an ecosystem in DeFi that runs smoothly and remains easy to scale.

DeFi users value security, since smart contracts are often exploited, hacked or rug pulled. The absence of hierarchy in DeFi means it is hard to detect and prevent fraud. Decentralized insurance, proper verification and strong auditing are all being developed to address these risks. Having strong security measures will help DeFi platforms earn users' trust and survive for a long time.

Emerging technologies such as AI, IoT and big data analytics, are affecting the future of DeFi and cryptocurrencies as well. AI can improve the decision-making process, manage trading with less effort and detect fraud. IoT products can help complete financial transactions as soon as environmental data is collected. Through big data analytics, companies can study people's habits and understand the market, allowing them to improve and individualize their financial services. As a result, there could be more opportunities for inventions and bringing organizations from different sectors together.

It is also a milestone when real-world assets are converted into tokens. Since real estate, commodities and equities are transformed into digital tokens on DeFi platforms, liquidity becomes possible and anyone can own a portion of any asset. When investments are more accessible, retail investors can also access wealth creation platforms. Connecting RWAs with DeFi helps bring traditional finance into line with decentralization and this increases the reputation of DeFi.

Managing a decentralized system relies heavily on governance. DAOs provide a different way for various parties to coordinate actions and make decisions. Moving forward, DAOs could rely on reputation scores for voting and let AI review possible decisions. They make decentralized governance work better by ensuring it is quicker, more open and easier to manage.

Many discussions about sustainability have emerged due to the environmental issues caused by blockchains that use the PoW system. Changing to proof-of-stake (PoS) and similar energy-saving algorithms is good for the environment. Integrating DeFi with green finance such as carbon credit and green (ESG) tokens helps the field meet worldwide ESG standards.

Cryptocurrencies affect international politics. Some countries prohibit digital assets while others accept them wholeheartedly. With the popularity of cryptocurrencies on the rise, Central Bank Digital Currencies may offer people an alternative that is controlled by the state. The introduction of CBDCs will change how money is managed and could realign global relationships, affect trading across countries and shape monetary policies.

In terms of technology, the infrastructure of both cryptocurrency and DeFi is the blockchain – a distributed ledger technology (DLT) that stores transactions on multiple nodes of a network, verifying transparency, immutability, and protection from tampering. Smart contacts, which are the self-executing agreements coded directly into the blockchain, automate such practices as lending, borrowing and/or trading without the need for intermediaries. This degree of automation and openness is supposed to lower operations costs and increase efficiency, theoretically. However, vulnerabilities in smart contract programming have been exploited in multimillion-dollar hacks, presenting the need for robust security practices and regulatory intervention. Additionally, limitation on scalability of existing blockchain networks can undermine the mainstream adoption of the DeFi applications.

The socio-economic impact of DeFi and cryptocurrencies are so massive. On the one hand, they provide users with the ability to have never before seen control over their finances, cutting out the need for centralized banks and financial services. On the other hand, they have raised concerns among regulators and policymakers as far as protection of consumers, systemic risk, financial stability, and the risk of engaging in illicit activities such as money laundering and terrorist financing is concerned. The response of these countries differs significantly: from active support and innovation sandboxes to outright ban on BTC with legal repressions (Ugolini, Reboredo, & Mensi, 2023). These disparities make a fragmented regulatory system that makes inter-national cooperation and standardization difficult. This has left regulatory uncertainty a major hurdle towards increased adoption of DeFi and cryptocurrencies.

Education and awareness are foundational to the responsible adoption of DeFi and cryptocurrencies. As the sector grows, so does the need for accessible, accurate, and inclusive educational resources. Universities, think tanks, and private institutions must collaborate to develop curricula and training programs that equip individuals with the skills to navigate the digital economy. Public-private partnerships can also play a role in fostering informed policymaking and user empowerment.

Ethical considerations will become increasingly relevant as DeFi and cryptocurrency adoption accelerates. Issues related to privacy, algorithmic bias, and equitable access must be addressed to ensure that the benefits of decentralization are distributed fairly. Ethical frameworks and impact assessments should be incorporated into the design and deployment of DeFi protocols, guiding the sector toward responsible innovation.

One important trend to watch in the coming years is an increase in activity by large financial institutions. Due to the search for higher profits, diversification and novel technologies, institutions are paying more attention to digital assets. As more people accept this trend, it should become mainstream.

This means bringing blockchain technology into existing financial markets. For example, by using tokens and decentralized exchanges, people are able to get involved in buying small amounts of standard assets such as equities, real estate and bonds. As a result, procedures and systems are now being built to help secure institutional use of DeFi platforms which reduces overall risks to the industry. Mixing centralized and decentralized features (CeDeFi) will be more common, helping create a pathway for regulation between distinct types of financial systems.

In terms of technology, the infrastructure of both cryptocurrency and DeFi is the blockchain – a distributed ledger technology (DLT) that stores transactions on multiple nodes of a network, verifying transparency, immutability, and protection from tampering. Smart contacts, which are the self-executing agreements coded directly into the blockchain, automate such practices as lending, borrowing and/or trading without the need for intermediaries. This degree of automation and openness is supposed to lower operations costs and increase efficiency, theoretically. However, vulnerabilities in smart contract programming have been exploited in multimillion-dollar hacks, presenting the need for robust security practices and regulatory intervention. Additionally, limitation on scalability of existing blockchain networks can undermine the mainstream adoption of the DeFi applications.

In summation, the trajectory of cryptocurrencies and decentralized finance points toward a future where financial systems are more inclusive, transparent, and resilient. The journey is fraught with challenges, but the potential rewards—greater economic empowerment, reduced reliance on intermediaries, and enhanced global financial integration—are compelling. Continued collaboration among technologists, regulators, academics, and communities will be essential to harness the full potential of this paradigm shift.

As the line between traditional and decentralized finance continues to blur, a hybrid model may emerge, combining the best of both worlds. Regulatory clarity, technological scalability, security enhancements, and user-centric design will be the cornerstones of this new financial era. Ultimately, the success of cryptocurrencies and DeFi will depend on their ability to create real value, promote financial well-being, and uphold the principles of decentralization, transparency, and inclusivity. The path forward is not without obstacles, but with strategic foresight and collective effort, the promise of a decentralized financial future can be realized.

Cryptocurrencies and DeFi are not only technological innovations but also agents of change in the world's finance. They represent a move from a pre-determined, top-down regime to an open, bottom-up world. They represent a change from closed systems to open networks and from static financial products to programmable, composable financial services. We find ourselves in an ecosystem that's in the midst of a massive transformation in the financial space. As outcomes of this transformation, will we have a more inclusive and efficient financial future, or will we have new forms of risk and inequality? This will depend on the evolution of the ecosystem, how the challenges are being addressed, and how key stakeholders grapple with this rapidly evolving domain.

DeFi holds promise for democratizing finance, but its adoption is mediated by digital divides, socio-political realities, and theoretical tensions. Future work should empirically test adoption models across contexts, develop robust comparative benchmarks, and design policy frameworks that balance innovation and consumer protection.

REFERENCES

Abou Ali, A. A. K. (2024). DeFi era: The behavioral intentions toward cryptocurrency in Lebanon. *Innovation & Management Review*, *21*(4), 274–285. DOI: 10.1108/INMR-02-2023-0022

Ahuja, R., & Khandelwal, J. (2023). CHALLENGES, OPPORTUNITIES AND RISK ANALYSIS OF ADOPTION OF DECENTRALIZED FINANCE APPLICATIONS. In *SPECIAL ISSUE ON INNOVATIONS AND TECHNOLOGY IN FINTECH* (pp. 3114–3129). ITFT., DOI: 10.21917/ijsc.2023.0438

Ali, A. (2016). Decentralized Finance (DeFi) and Its Impact on Traditional Banking Systems: Opportunities, Challenges, and Future Directions. *India Review*, *4*(1), 1–23.

Atree, M. K., & Tripathy, N. (2025). Cryptocurrency research: Bibliometric review and content analysis. International Review of Economics and Finance, 98(July 2024), 103940. DOI: 10.1016/j.iref.2025.103940

Bakare, F. A., Omojola, J., & Iwuh, A. C. (2025). Blockchain and decentralized finance (DEFI): Disrupting traditional banking and financial systems Blockchain and decentralized finance (DEFI): Disrupting traditional banking and financial systems. *World Journal of Advanced Research and Reviews*, *23*(3), 23–27. DOI: 10.30574/wjarr.2024.23.3.2968

Bhombe, S., & Arts, D. S. M. (2023). Consequences, Transformation and Prospects of Crypto Currency in India. Tactful Management Research Journal, 11(3), 0–6.

Bommer, W. H., Milevoj, E., & Rana, S. (2023). The intention to use cryptocurrency: A meta-analysis of what we know. Emerging Markets Review, 55(September 2022), 100962. DOI: 10.1016/j.ememar.2022.100962

Gramlich, V., Guggenberger, T., Principato, M., Schellinger, B., & Urbach, N. (2023). A multivocal literature review of decentralized finance: Current knowledge and future research avenues. Electronic Markets (Vol. 33). Springer Berlin Heidelberg. DOI: 10.1007/s12525-023-00637-4

Jani, S. (2018). The Growth of Cryptocurrency in India: Its Challenges & Potential Impacts on Legislation. *International Journal of Sustainable Development*, *1*(4), 22–29. DOI: 10.13140/RG.2.2.14220.36486

Jiang, E., Qin, B., Wang, Q., Wang, Z., Wu, Q., Weng, J., & Zhang, Y. (2023). Decentralized Finance (DeFi): A Survey. India Quarterly. *Journal of International Affairs*, *3*(8), 1–21. http://arxiv.org/abs/2308.05282

Karim, S., Lucey, B. M., Naeem, M. A., & Uddin, G. S. (2022). Examining the interrelatedness of NFTs, DeFi tokens and cryptocurrencies. Finance Research Letters, 47(PB), 102696. DOI: 10.1016/j.frl.2022.102696

Li, X., Jiao, H., Cheng, L., Yin, Y., Li, H., Mu, W., & Zhang, R. (2023). A Quantitative and Qualitative Review of Blockchain Research from 2015 to 2021. *Sustainability (Basel), 15*(6), 5067. Advance online publication. DOI: 10.3390/su15065067

Manjula, B. C., Shilpa, B. S., & Sundaresh, M. (2022). Analysis of Cryptocurrency, Bitcoin and the Future. *East Asian Journal of Multidisciplinary Research, 1*(7), 1293–1302. DOI: 10.55927/eajmr.v1i7.803

Metelski, D., & Sobieraj, J. (2022). Decentralized Finance (DeFi) Projects: A Study of Key Performance Indicators in Terms of DeFi Protocols' Valuations. *International Journal of Financial Studies, 10*(4), 108. Advance online publication. DOI: 10.3390/ijfs10040108

Motamed, A. P., & Bahrak, B. (2019). Quantitative analysis of cryptocurrencies transaction graph. *Applied Network Science, 4*(1), 131. Advance online publication. DOI: 10.1007/s41109-019-0249-6

Nguyen, L. T. M., & Nguyen, P. T. (2024). Determinants of cryptocurrency and decentralized finance adoption - A configurational exploration. *Technological Forecasting and Social Change, 201*(February), 123244. DOI: 10.1016/j.techfore.2024.123244

Piñeiro-Chousa, J., López-Cabarcos, M. Á., Sevic, A., & González-López, I. (2022). A preliminary assessment of the performance of DeFi cryptocurrencies in relation to other financial assets, volatility, and user-generated content. *Technological Forecasting and Social Change, 181*(May), 121740. Advance online publication. DOI: 10.1016/j.techfore.2022.121740

Piñeiro-Chousa, J., Šević, A., & González-López, I. (2023). Impact of social metrics in decentralized finance. Journal of Business Research, 158(June 2022). DOI: 10.1016/j.jbusres.2023.113673

Rajharia, P., & Kaushik, M. B. (2023). RETRACTED: Cryptocurrency Adoption and Its Implications: A Literature Review. In E3s Web of Conferences (Vol. 456, p. 03002). EDP Sciences.

Sarkar, D. (2023). Centralized Intermediation in a Decentralized Web3 Economy: Value Accrual and Extraction. *Interdisciplinary Journal of Contemporary Research in Business, 4*(11), 26–32. DOI: 10.48550/arXiv.2311.08234

Seabe, P. L., Moutsinga, C. R. B., & Pindza, E. (2024). Optimizing Cryptocurrency Returns: A Quantitative Study on Factor-Based Investing. *Mathematics*, *12*(9), 1–28. DOI: 10.3390/math12091351

Shah, K., Lathiya, D., Lukhi, N., Parmar, K., & Sanghvi, H. (2023). A systematic review of decentralized finance protocols. *International Journal of Intelligent Networks*, *4*(June), 171–181. DOI: 10.1016/j.ijin.2023.07.002

Shahzad, M. F., Xu, S., Lim, W. M., Hasnain, M. F., & Nusrat, S. (2024). Cryptocurrency awareness, acceptance, and adoption: The role of trust as a cornerstone. *Humanities & Social Sciences Communications*, *11*(1), 4. Advance online publication. DOI: 10.1057/s41599-023-02528-7

Singh, S. (2024). Decentralized Finance (DeFi): Exploring the Role of Blockchain and Cryptocurrency in Financial Ecosystems. *International Research Journal of Modernization in Engineering Technology and Science*, (January). Advance online publication. DOI: 10.56726/IRJMETS48585

Su, Z. (2024). Analysis of Cryptocurrency and Its Combination with Quantitative Transactions. SHS Web of Conferences, 181, 02016. DOI: 10.1051/shsconf/202418102016

Tetiana, Z., Volodymyr, S., Dluhopolskyi, O., Vasyl, B., & Tetiana, D. (2022). Investment Models on Centralized and Decentralized Cryptocurrency Markets. *Naukovyi Visnyk Natsionalnoho Hirnychoho Universytetu*, (1), 177–182. DOI: 10.33271/nvngu/2022-1/177

Ugolini, A., Reboredo, J. C., & Mensi, W. (2023). Connectedness between DeFi, cryptocurrency, stock, and safe-haven assets. *Finance Research Letters*, *53*(February), 103692. DOI: 10.1016/j.frl.2023.103692

Urquhart, A., & Yarovaya, L. (2023). Cryptocurrency research: Future directions. *European Journal of Finance*, *4364*. Advance online publication. DOI: 10.1080/1351847X.2023.2284186

Yang, G. (2024). Quantitative Analysis of the Relationship Between Cryptocurrency Market and U.S. Stock Market Performance. Advances in Economics. *Management and Political Sciences*, *97*(1), 122–131. DOI: 10.54254/2754-1169/97/20230504

Yousaf, I., Nekhili, R., & Gubareva, M. (2022). Linkages between DeFi assets and conventional currencies: Evidence from the COVID-19 pandemic. *International Review of Financial Analysis*, *81*(February), 102082. DOI: 10.1016/j.irfa.2022.102082

Yousaf, I., & Yarovaya, L. (2022). Herding behavior in conventional cryptocurrency market, non-fungible tokens, and DeFi assets. Finance Research Letters, 50(September 2021), 103299. DOI: 10.1016/j.frl.2022.103299

Chapter 9
Blockchain and Digital Currencies:
Catalysts of Geopolitical Rivalries and Economic Realignments

Saurabh Chandra
https://orcid.org/0000-0003-4172-9968
Bennett University, Greater Noida, India

Bhupinder Singh
https://orcid.org/0009-0006-4779-2553
Sharda University, India

Saquib Ahmed
https://orcid.org/0009-0008-1891-6910
Sharda University, India

Christian Kaunert
https://orcid.org/0000-0002-4493-2235
Dublin City University, Ireland & University of South Wales, UK

Natthawut Rungwong
North Bangkok University, Thailand

ABSTRACT

The world's economic future is being reshaped by blockchain technology and digital currencies and the country that leads the way may also be the country that the world increasingly turns to. Blockchain challenges the hegemony of traditional financial intermediaries and reserve currencies such as the US dollar by facilitating decentralized, transparent, and secure financial systems. These currencies provide

DOI: 10.4018/979-8-3373-1727-4.ch009

countries with the means to circumvent conventional payment networks, improve financial inclusion, and exert supremacy in international commerce. Blockchain-based solutions will create pathways around reliance on Western-led financial institutions enabling both the de-dollarization of emerging economies. And as the race is on to exploit the technologies behind them, they are likely to reshape the international political economy, creating new partnerships while widening economic divides.

INTRODUCTION

The advent of blockchain technology and digital currencies has marked a significant turning point in the landscape of global finance and geopolitics. Emerging from the shadows of traditional financial systems, these innovations have introduced new paradigms for economic interaction, challenging established norms and creating opportunities for both collaboration and competition among nations. As it delve into the intricate relationship between blockchain, digital currencies, and geopolitical dynamics, it becomes imperative to understand their foundational concepts, significance in contemporary global affairs, and the objectives guiding this chapter.

There are many new and developing kinds of consumption in the economy right now. These are the outcome of a convergence of societal, economic, and technological factors that are presently changing traditional modes of business exchanges. This article provides an example of this alleged reorganization of business transactions. The study specifically examines the junction of two cultural phenomena the collaborative economy (CE) and blockchain technology that are mostly the result of technical advancements and economic disruptions. In actuality, both are highly dependent on technology and were developed during the 2008 global financial crisis (Sharma, 2023). On the other hand, such nations that were ahead of the curve in blockchain innovation and CBDC deployment might be setting standards for CBTS that can be followed in cross-border trade, changing the dynamics of economic power. But it also raises stakes, as governments grapple with regulatory challenges, cybersecurity threats and the threat of digital authoritarianism. Blockchain and digital currencies are much more than technological innovations they are potentially instrumental in the global contest for influence. The CE is an economic model that has experienced unparalleled scale and scope due to technological advancements, despite the fact that it has nearly become a vernacular notion. Peer-to-peer, peer-to-organization, and organization-to-peer interactions have increased as a result. Blockchain technology is a distributed, decentralized ledger system that securely, immutably, and transparently records transactions across numerous computers. Blockchain was first created as the core technology for Bitcoin, but it has since matured into a flexible instrument with uses in many different industries. At the same time, significant advancements in mathematics and computer science have given rise to blockchain technology. As a result of this technology, real peer-to-peer interactions with little middleman have become more intense.

Few studies have looked at how these two phenomena are intertwined, despite the tight ties between blockchain technology and the CE in terms of technological advancements and peer-to-peer trading facilitation. Since there is still a dearth of research on this topic, the goal of this essay is to review the available data in order to comprehend how blockchain technology has contributed to the growth of collaborative practices.

This study uses an exploratory descriptive methodology in order to achieve this goal since it can offer a preliminary understanding of novel and little-documented occurrences. Furthermore, its style offers a structure for developing fresh concepts and theories. This page also attempts to compile the most recent research on blockchain technology use in order to comprehend its possible implications for collaborative practices, as studies on the topics of CE and blockchain technology are still in their infancy. By further decentralizing exchanges and transactions, this technology might be able to accelerate the growth of the CE. As a result, blockchain technology may promote the spread of this novel socioeconomic paradigm, known as the CE, while simultaneously causing a reorganization of current players, structures, and functions (Zaidi et al., 2023).

OVERVIEW OF BLOCKCHAIN AND DIGITAL CURRENCIES

Fundamentally, blockchain is a decentralized ledger technology that makes it possible to retain records securely and openly across a network of computers. Blocks are created from each transaction and connected chronologically to create a chain, hence the word "blockchain." By guaranteeing that data cannot be changed after it has been recorded without the consent of network participants, this structure improves confidence and lessens the need for middlemen like banks or financial institutions. This blockchain technology powers digital currencies, especially those like Bitcoin and Ethereum (Verma et al., 2024). Cryptocurrencies are decentralized and use cryptographic methods to validate transactions and regulate the generation of new units, in contrast to conventional currencies that are issued by central banks. such as smart contracts, non-fungible tokens (NFTs), and decentralized finance (DeFi).

Importance in the Geopolitical Setting Beyond technological advancement, blockchain and digital currencies are significant because they are increasingly seen as drivers of economic realignments and geopolitical rivalry. Several crucial elements become apparent as countries struggle with the effects of these technologies:

Economic Autonomy: Blockchain technology and virtual currencies are being investigated by nations as means of demonstrating their economic independence. For example, sanctioned countries like Russia are looking into ways to use cryptocurrency to bypass established financial institutions and facilitate international trade. This ability threatens global financial governance and lessens the impact of penalties.

Understanding Blockchain Technology

In the digital world, blockchain technology has become a disruptive force that is radically changing the ways in which data is exchanged, kept, and protected. Blockchain, a decentralized, distributed ledger system, eliminates the need for a central authority by enabling several parties to manage a shared database. In addition to improving security and transparency, this breakthrough offers a strong foundation for a range of uses, especially in the field of digital currencies. Understanding the definition and workings of blockchain technology, its salient characteristics, and the various kinds of blockchains is crucial to appreciating its ramifications (Saaida, 2024).

Definition and Mechanism

Fundamentally, blockchain is a distributed ledger that keeps track of transactions across several computers in a way that prevents the recorded transactions from being changed in the past without the network's consent. Every entry in the blockchain is referred to as a block, and these blocks are connected to one another chronologically to create a chain. Cryptographic hashes, which are distinct alphanumeric sequences that link each block to its predecessor and guarantee the integrity of each block, are used to secure this structure. Before being added to the current chain, a new transaction is first bundled with other transactions to form a block, which is subsequently validated by network members (nodes). Usually, consensus methods like Proof of Work or Proof of Stake are used in this verification procedure. These algorithms require users to confirm transactions according to predetermined rules before they can be published on the blockchain. The blockchain's method works in a number of steps: A transaction is first started by an authorized participant, and it is subsequently contained within a block with pertinent information. For validation, the block is broadcast to every node in the network. The block is added to the current blockchain and all nodes update their copies of the ledger once a majority of nodes have reached a consensus regarding the transaction's authenticity (Yeung, 2020).

Key Features of Blockchain

Several salient characteristics of blockchain technology set it apart from conventional databases:

1. Decentralization: Blockchain disperses data among multiple nodes in a peer-to-peer network, in contrast to traditional systems that keep data in a central repository. This decentralization improves system resilience and reduces the risks related to single points of failure.
2. Immutability: Data cannot be changed or removed from the blockchain once it has been recorded there without also changing all following blocks and obtaining network consensus. For applications needing high levels of data integrity, blockchain is the perfect answer because of its immutability, which guards against fraud and illegal alterations.
3. Transparency: Every transaction on a public blockchain is accessible to every network user. Because consumers may independently verify transactions without depending on middlemen, this transparency promotes user trust.
4. Security: To protect data from alteration and unwanted access, blockchain uses cutting-edge cryptographic algorithms. A hash of the previous block is included in every block, forming an unbreakable chain that guards against malicious activity.
5. Consensus Mechanisms: To verify transactions and preserve consensus among dispersed nodes, blockchain uses a variety of consensus methods. These systems guard against fraud and double-spending while guaranteeing that everyone involved has the most recent version of the ledger (Huq, 2024).

Types of Blockchains

Based on their governance arrangements and accessibility, blockchains can be divided into a number of types:

1. Open networks known as public blockchains allow anybody to join as a node and verify transactions. Public blockchains are perfect for cryptocurrencies like Bitcoin and Ethereum because of their transparency and decentralization. To maintain security and integrity, they function via consensus techniques like Proof of Work or Proof of Stake.
2. Private Blockchains: Unlike public blockchains, private blockchains are closed networks to which only particular individuals or organizations have access. Businesses frequently use these blockchains for internal usage or in consortiums, which allow several firms to work together while still keeping ownership of

their data. When compared to their public equivalents, private blockchains can provide greater privacy and efficiency.

3. Permissioned Blockchains: A subset of private blockchains, permissioned blockchains restrict network access and transaction validation to approved users only. This kind is appropriate for enterprise applications where security and compliance are crucial since it gives more control over who may join the network and what they can do.
4. Hybrid Blockchains: By combining aspects of public and private blockchains, hybrid blockchains give businesses the advantage of data control and transparency. This architecture offers flexibility for a range of use cases by allowing some data to be kept private while keeping other information publicly available (Morales & Andreosso-O'Callaghan, 2022).

In order to comprehend blockchain technology, one must be aware of its distinguishing features, which include decentralization, immutability, transparency, security, and a variety of other features. These attributes all contribute to the technology's potential to revolutionize global finance and other fields. Understanding blockchain technology is crucial for stakeholders navigating this complicated environment as digital currencies continue to gain popularity in geopolitical contexts. Subsequent sections of this research study will delve deeper into the implications of these technologies for economic realignments, emphasizing their role as catalysts for change in economic structures and international relations (Behera, 2023).

Digital Currencies: An Overview

The way wealth is held, moved, and traded has been redefined by digital currencies, which have become a disruptive force in the global financial system. The idea of currency has broadened beyond conventional fiat money to include a variety of digital assets as technology advances. An overview of digital currencies is given in this part, together with information on their definition and classification, well-known cryptocurrencies like Bitcoin and Ethereum, and the growing importance of Central Bank Digital Currencies (CBDCs).

Definition and Classification

Any currency that only exists electronically and is controlled by digital technology is referred to as digital currency. Digital currencies are completely virtual and require electronic devices for transactions, in contrast to traditional fiat currencies, which can be held and exchanged physically. Cryptocurrencies are digital currencies that are decentralized and rely on encryption to ensure secure transactions.

Blockchain technology, which powers cryptocurrencies, keeps a public record of every transaction. Litecoin, Ethereum, and Bitcoin are a few examples. A paradigm shifts in the way value is viewed and traded internationally is represented by digital currencies. Understanding these developments is essential for navigating future economic landscapes, since separate categories like cryptocurrencies and CBDCs are emerging alongside existing fiat systems. The interaction of these digital currencies will probably spark important geopolitical rivalries and economic realignments in the years to come, as major cryptocurrencies like Bitcoin and Ethereum continue to gain traction and central banks investigate CBDCs in response to technological advancements. As digital currencies continue to develop, they will surely influence not only financial markets but also larger social structures by redefining ideas of value transfer, trust, and economic involvement in a world that is becoming more interconnected by the day (Prabhakar, 2025).

Geopolitical Implications of Digital Currencies

Beyond their use as simple financial instruments, the rise of digital currencies has important geopolitical ramifications. These currencies, especially cryptocurrencies and Central Bank Digital Currencies (CBDCs), are changing trade, opening up new paths to economic independence, and changing the nature of international interactions. This section examines case studies cantered on Venezuela and Iran as well as the implications of digital currencies with regard to sanction evasion and their impact on global trade dynamics (Jun et al., 2014).

The ability of digital currencies to aid in sanction evasion is among their most significant geopolitical ramifications. Cryptocurrencies are becoming a more popular way for nations under economic sanctions—especially those imposed by Western nations—to get around established financial institutions. For example, despite strict restrictions imposed by the United States and its allies, countries such as North Korea and Iran have used digital currencies to sustain economic activity. These nations can now make transactions using cryptocurrencies instead of traditional banking systems, which are frequently subject to penalties and oversight (Zielonka, 2022). Iran's involvement with cryptocurrency is especially significant. Despite crushing sanctions, the nation has embraced Bitcoin mining as a means of making money. These regimes can function beyond the scope of global financial systems thanks to the anonymity provided by digital currencies, which increases their economic independence. The effectiveness of traditional sanctions may be weakened as more governments investigate using cryptocurrency to evade penalties, which might cause a change in how countries approach economic diplomacy.

Digital currencies have wide-ranging and complex geopolitical ramifications. Traditional power dynamics are being challenged as nations use new technologies to evade sanctions and achieve economic independence. The potential of cryptocurrencies to change trade dynamics and international relations is demonstrated by their use by countries such as Venezuela and Iran.Furthermore, the global financial environment is anticipated to change significantly as more nations investigate CBDCs as a component of their monetary policies. The emergence of digital currencies offers policymakers navigating a geopolitical landscape that is becoming more complex both opportunities and challenges. It will be essential to comprehend these dynamics in order to predict how blockchain technology and digital currency will affect international relations in the future (Millard, 2023).

ECONOMIC REALIGNMENTS DRIVEN BY CRYPTOCURRENCIES

A new era of economic realignments has been brought about by the rise of cryptocurrencies, which has drastically changed the global financial scene. As digital currencies become more popular, they are changing established financial systems, impacting the dynamics of international trade, and opening doors for developing nations. This change marks the beginning of a multipolar financial environment in which cutting-edge digital alternatives are challenging the supremacy of conventional currencies (Alzubaidi & Abdullah, 2017).

Shift Towards a Multipolar Financial Landscape

A few major currencies, most notably the US dollar, have historically dominated the global financial system. The emergence of cryptocurrencies, however, is signalling a change to a multipolar financial environment. The increasing adoption of digital currencies by financial institutions and governments, developments in blockchain technology, and shifting consumer preferences are some of the drivers driving this shift. The conventional dependence on fiat currencies is being reassessed as nations investigate the possibilities of cryptocurrencies and Central Bank Digital Currencies (CBDCs). For example, China's digital yuan effort seeks to lessen reliance on the dollar and improve the yuan's internationalization. Through its CBDC, China aims to establish itself as a leader in the changing financial landscape by enabling cross-border transactions. This action demonstrates the geopolitical drivers underlying the development of digital currency in addition to reflecting a strategic economic goal. Furthermore, there is a chance that the global monetary system may become more fragmented as more countries realize the advantages of cryptocurrencies, such as their ability to lower costs and boost transaction efficiency. To further weaken the dollar's hegemony, nations may seek bilateral agreements that settle commerce in their national digital currencies. A more varied monetary landscape where several digital currencies coexist with conventional fiat currencies could result from this change (Ghazawneh & Henfridsson, 2015).

Impact on Traditional Banking Systems

Traditional banking systems face serious challenges as a result of the rise of cryptocurrencies. Digital currencies pose a threat to traditional banking methods that depend on centralized control over financial transactions since they allow peer-to-peer transactions without the need for middlemen. Banks are being forced to reconsider their functions in an increasingly digital economy as a result of this disruption. In an effort to increase productivity and cut expenses, financial institutions are starting to adjust by integrating blockchain technology into their operations. To be competitive in this changing market, several banks are looking into joint ventures with cryptocurrency companies or creating their own digital assets. For instance, some banks are using blockchain-based cross-border payment systems, which allow for quicker and less expensive transactions than using conventional techniques. But this change also brings up issues with security and regulatory compliance (Hawlitschek et al., 2018).

Regulators have difficulties protecting consumers and stopping illegal activity like fraud and money laundering since cryptocurrencies operate outside of traditional banking structures. Clarity in regulations is essential as banks negotiate this new environment and work to keep the financial system stable. Some institutions are implementing creative strategies that combine conventional banking services with bitcoin offerings in response to these difficulties. Banks can profit from the rising demand for digital currencies while reducing the risks related to their volatility by offering custodial services for digital assets or enabling cryptocurrency trading platforms.

Opportunities for Emerging Economies

The emergence of blockchain technology and cryptocurrencies has enormous potential benefits for emerging economies. These developments present special chances for financial inclusion, giving people and companies in underprivileged areas access to financial services that were previously out of reach. People find it challenging to engage in the formal economy in many developing nations due to the lack or scarcity of traditional financial infrastructure. By offering a different way to carry out transactions and store value, cryptocurrencies potentially close this gap. For example, users can send and receive money using mobile bitcoin wallets without a credit card or bank account. Additionally, by lowering the transaction costs related to cross-border transfers, cryptocurrencies can help with remittances, which are an essential source of income for many families in emerging economies (Mangano, 2018).

Low-income people are particularly impacted by the astronomical costs that traditional remittance businesses frequently demand. Cryptocurrencies, on the other hand, make transfers quicker and less expensive, letting receivers keep more of their money. Blockchain adoption can also improve efficiency and transparency in a number of industries, including supply chain management, healthcare, and agriculture. Emerging economies can enhance agricultural supply chain traceability or expedite healthcare record management by utilizing blockchain's immutable ledger features. These apps help to increase stakeholder trust in addition to promoting economic progress (Yermack, 2018). Furthermore, emerging economies may find themselves in a better position to take part in international trade networks as more of them adopt blockchain technology and cryptocurrencies. These countries can strengthen their negotiating position in global markets and lessen their need on conventional banking systems by using digital currencies for trade settlements.

Cryptocurrency-driven economic realignments represent a revolutionary change in international finance that upends long-standing conventions and opens new avenues for countries all around the world. Traditional banking systems need to change in order to stay relevant as we move toward a multipolar financial landscape marked by a variety of digital currencies and cutting-edge financial solutions (Zhang & Huang, 2022). Cryptocurrencies present previously unheard-of chances for economic expansion and financial inclusion in emerging economies. By utilizing this technology, these countries can strengthen their resistance to external economic shocks and get beyond long-standing obstacles to entering international markets. Policymakers, companies, and individuals alike will need to comprehend the ramifications of cryptocurrencies as we traverse this changing terrain. As we go into a more connected world where innovation propels economic realignment, the interaction between digital currencies and geopolitical factors will continue to influence the direction of finance (Martin, 2016).

RISKS AND CHALLENGES

A number of hazards and difficulties are emerging as blockchain technology and digital currencies gain traction, which could limit their potential advantages. These difficulties include market turbulence, regulatory ambiguity, security issues, and the possibility of illegal activity. For all parties involved in the financial ecosystem governments, corporations, and consumers understanding these risks is essential.

Regulatory Uncertainty and Problems with Compliance

Uncertainty in regulations is one of the biggest issues facing digital currencies. Governments throughout the world are struggling with how to categorize and control cryptocurrencies, which has resulted in a patchwork of laws that can differ greatly between jurisdictions. Businesses and investors alike are confused by this lack of clarity as they manage sometimes unclear or uneven compliance standards. (Hayes & Tasca, 2016). Some nations, for example, have welcomed cryptocurrencies and established legislative frameworks that promote investment and innovation. Others, on the other hand, have put in place stringent prohibitions or onerous rules that hinder development. This discrepancy may cause market fragmentation as businesses decide to operate in countries with more benevolent laws, which could jeopardize international collaboration on matters like consumer protection and anti-money laundering (AML). Furthermore, technological advancements frequently surpass regulatory frameworks in speed. Regulations may become reactive rather than proactive as a result of regulators' inability to keep up with developments in blockchain and digital currency (Nowinski & Kozma,2017). Because cryptocurrencies are decentralized, it is more difficult to properly enforce regulations. For instance, when transactions are pseudonymous and do not depend on conventional banking institutions for verification, it becomes difficult to ensure compliance with AML regulations.

Market Volatility and Security Concerns

Another significant danger connected to digital currencies is market volatility. Cryptocurrencies are notorious for their sharp price swings, which can cause investors to make significant gains or losses in a short amount of time. Speculative trading, market mood, regulatory announcements, and macroeconomic trends are some of the variables that contribute to this volatility. Because bitcoin prices are unpredictable, people may be reluctant to utilize them as a reliable store of wealth or medium of exchange. The use of cryptocurrencies in daily transactions is discouraged, for example, if a customer uses Bitcoin to buy items at a specific price but discovers that by the time they want to use it again, its value has drastically dropped. Furthermore, the dangers of investing in cryptocurrencies are increased by the absence of investor protections that are often included in conventional financial markets. Cryptocurrencies are not backed or insured by any government agency, in contrast to bank deposits or regulated securities (Belk, 2014). Investors run the danger of losing all of their money as a result of exchange failures or market downturns. The world of digital currency is likewise fraught with security issues. Although blockchain technology's decentralized structure and cryptographic foundations make it intrinsically safe, flaws still exist. Significant losses have been incurred by investors as a result of cyberattacks directed against cryptocurrency exchanges. Questions have been raised over the security procedures used by exchanges and wallet providers after high-profile thefts resulted in the theft of digital assets valued at millions of dollars. Users are also at risk when it comes to managing their private keys. The credentials required to access one's bitcoin assets, known as private keys, are often the responsibility of the individual. Without any way to recover, a user may lose access to their assets forever if they misplace their private key or become a victim of malware or phishing assaults (Millard, 2023).

Illicit Activities and Misuse

Cryptocurrencies' pseudonymous character has made them appealing instruments for illegal activities like drug trafficking, money laundering, and ransomware assaults. The use of digital currencies by criminal organizations to carry out anonymous transactions outside of established banking institutions has grown in recent years. For example, because cryptocurrencies are thought to be more anonymous than traditional payment methods, dark web marketplaces sometimes use them for illicit transactions. The identities behind wallet addresses are hidden unless they are connected in some other way, even if blockchain technology makes transactions transparent on public ledgers. Concerns regarding the possible abuse of digital currencies for illicit purposes are growing among governments and law enforcement organizations. Regulators are responding by enacting more stringent policies meant to stop illegal activities related to cryptocurrency. This involves mandating that exchanges follow AML guidelines and utilize KYC practices to spot consumers exhibiting questionable behaviour. However, by placing onerous compliance requirements on respectable companies while leaving the fundamental problems with misuse unaddressed, these policies may also cause friction within the cryptocurrency ecosystem. For regulators around the world, finding a balance between encouraging innovation in digital currencies and guaranteeing sufficient protections against illegal activity continues to be a difficult task (Pavelea & Negrea, 2024).

All parties participating in this changing environment must carefully assess the many dangers and difficulties related to blockchain technology and digital currencies. Businesses trying to navigate several international frameworks and find clarity in compliance obligations face major challenges due to regulatory ambiguity. Market turbulence erodes trust in cryptocurrencies as reliable repositories of wealth or as means of exchange. Additionally, security issues with private key management and cyberattacks underscore the necessity of strong defences inside the bitcoin ecosystem. Lastly, while governments work to strike a balance between innovation and regulation, addressing the possibility of illegal activity continues to be crucial. In order to create a safe and sustainable financial environment that optimizes advantages while reducing disadvantages, it will be crucial to comprehend these dangers as blockchain technology and digital currencies continue to advance. It is feasible to establish an ecosystem that encourages responsible innovation while protecting against potential hazards present in this quickly changing field by proactively tackling these issues through cooperation between regulators, industry players, and consumers (Schedlbauer & Wagner, 2018).

Strategic Statecraft and Cryptocurrencies

A new dimension to strategic statecraft has been brought about by the rise of cryptocurrencies, which provide countries with cutting-edge instruments to further their geopolitical goals. As digital currencies become more popular, they are being seen as tools of hybrid warfare, parts of national security plans, and factors influencing geopolitics going forward. The use of cryptocurrencies in statecraft, their effects on national security, and the possible development of digital currencies in international relations are all examined in this area (Boshkov, 2018).

Use in Hybrid Warfare and Political Movements

In hybrid warfare, where state and non-state actors use digital assets to accomplish military and political goals, cryptocurrencies have become essential components. Cryptocurrencies are appealing for financing clandestine activities and assisting rebel organizations because of their decentralized structure, which makes transactions hard to track. For example, a number of organizations have used Bitcoin to conduct financial transactions without depending on conventional banking institutions, avoiding penalties and regulatory scrutiny. The use of cryptocurrencies during the turmoil in Ukraine is one prominent example. Ukraine resorted to crowdfunding initiatives that took Bitcoin and other cryptocurrency donations as relations with Russia increased. In addition to offering crucial resources for military defence, this strategy demonstrated how digital currencies may strengthen vulnerable states. Cryptocurrencies' relevance in contemporary political movements and state resilience is demonstrated by their capacity to rally financial backing from supporters around the world. Cryptocurrencies can also be used as psychological warfare techniques. States might use the anonymity offered by digital currency to threaten political stability without resorting to direct military action by supporting dissident organizations or disrupting initiatives in adversary countries. This feature demonstrates how cryptocurrencies have two sides: they can be used to support lawful political movements, but they can also be used as a weapon to spread confusion and unrest (Akhtar et al., 2019).

THE FUTURE OF DIGITAL CURRENCY IN GEOPOLITICS

In the future, digital currencies' place in geopolitics is expected to change dramatically. The world of international finance will shift significantly as more nations investigate Central Bank Digital Currencies (CBDCs). CBDCs give governments a way to embrace the advantages of digital transactions while keeping control over monetary policy. The rivalry between countries to create CBDCs is a reflection of larger geopolitical tensions. For example, China is pushing for a digital yuan to challenge the U.S. dollar's hegemony in international trade in addition to improving domestic efficiency. China aims to change the global monetary dynamics to its advantage by positioning its CBDC as a competitive substitute for cross-border transactions. Furthermore, a multipolar currency environment may cause the world's financial system to become even more fragmented (Astuti et al., 2022).

Traditional power structures may face challenges when nations use their own digital currencies for trade agreements. This change could lessen dependency on well-known currencies like the dollar and forge new partnerships based on common interests in alternative monetary systems. But there are also issues with international collaboration and regulatory frameworks in this changing environment. There will be an urgent need for cooperative efforts to create rules and standards governing the usage of digital currencies as countries negotiate their complexity. States may become more antagonistic as they compete for supremacy in the field of digital money if these issues are not resolved.

The emergence of cryptocurrencies, which present both opportunities and difficulties for countries navigating intricate geopolitical environments, is becoming more and more entwined with strategic statecraft. Digital currencies empower nations as instruments for political movements and hybrid warfare, but they also present regulatory and misuse problems. Cryptocurrencies' increasing significance in preserving economic sovereignty in the face of outside influences is reflected in their incorporation into national security plans. Going forward, rivalry between countries looking to use these technologies for geopolitical gain is probably what will define the role of digital currency in geopolitics. Understanding the ramifications of cryptocurrencies will be essential for developing effective rules that maximize their potential while reducing related risks as stakeholders struggle with these changes. As countries adjust to a more interconnected world where innovation propels economic realignment and power moves on the international scene, the relationship between digital currencies and geopolitical dynamics will only intensify (Maulana & Putri, 2019).

CONCLUSION

The investigation of digital currencies and blockchain technology has shown their significant effects on international relations, bringing to light both possibilities and difficulties that may influence international finance and geopolitics in the future (Lal et al., 2024). In addition to altering conventional economic paradigms, the growing popularity of digital currencies is also having an impact on how countries behave strategically in international affairs (Arora et al., 2024). The chapter findings are summed up in this conclusion, which also addresses potential directions for further study and provides closing observations on the function of blockchain technology and virtual currencies in international relations (Kaushik et al., 2024).

It is impossible to ignore the revolutionary impact that blockchain technology and digital currencies are having on international relations. For countries around the world, their ability to improve cross-border payment efficiency, encourage financial inclusion, and alter power relations offers both opportunities and difficulties (Raghav et al., 2024). Establishing regulatory frameworks that promote innovation while maintaining security and stability will need strategic cooperation as nations negotiate this new terrain. There will probably be more competition among countries looking to use these technologies for strategic gain in the geopolitical future of digital currency. Governments clearly understand the importance of this new environment, as evidenced by measures like China's digital yuan and G7 talks about regulatory norms for private digital currencies. In the end, cooperation between governments, financial institutions, technologists, and civil society will be necessary to successfully integrate blockchain technology and digital currencies into global finance and build a safe and welcoming financial ecosystem. It can maximize the potential of these game-changing technologies while lowering the risks involved with their use by tackling regulatory obstacles and encouraging innovation in a responsible manner. Knowing the ramifications of blockchain technology and digital currencies will be crucial to creating a robust global economy that is just and sustainable for all players as we advance toward a more digitalized world where money moves across borders more easily than before.

REFERENCES

Akhtar, F., Li, J. P., Heyat, M. B. B., Quadri, S. L., Ahmed, S. S., Xiao, Y. U. N., & Haq, A. U. (2019, December). Potential of blockchain technology in digital currency: a review. In *2019 16th International Computer Conference on Wavelet Active Media Technology and Information Processing* (pp. 85-91). IEEE. DOI: 10.1109/ICCWAMTIP47768.2019.9067546

Alzubaidi, I. B., & Abdullah, A. (2017). Developing a digital currency from an Islamic perspective: Case of blockchain technology. *International Business Research*, *10*(11), 79–87. DOI: 10.5539/ibr.v10n11p79

Arora, M. K., Lal, S., Singh, B., & Olyaee, M. (2024). Through an Energy Lens: Examining SDGs From a Policy Perspective. In Riswandi, B., Singh, B., Kaunert, C., & Vig, K. (Eds.), *AI Applications for Clean Energy and Sustainability* (pp. 320–343). IGI Global., DOI: 10.4018/979-8-3693-6567-0.ch016

Astuti, I. D., Rajab, S., & Setiyouji, D. (2022). Cryptocurrency blockchain technology in the digital revolution era. [ATT]. *Aptisi Transactions on Technopreneurship*, *4*(1), 9–15. DOI: 10.34306/att.v4i1.216

Behera, L. K. (2023). Securing India: Significance of Geoeconomics and Innovation in India's Foreign Policy and Strategic Competition with China.

Belk, R. (2014). You are what you can access: Sharing and collaborative consumption online. Journal of Business Research, 67(8),1595e1600

Boshkov, T. (2018). Blockchain and digital currency in the world of finance. *Blockchain and cryptocurrencies.*

Ghazawneh, A., & Henfridsson, O. (2015). A paradigmatic analysis of digital application marketplaces. Journal of Information Technology, 30(3), 198e208.

Hawlitschek, F., Notheisen, B., & Teubner, T. (2018). The limits of trust-free systems: A literature review on blockchain technology and trust in the sharing economy. Electronic Commerce Research and Applications, 29,50e63

Hayes, A., & Tasca, P. (2016). Blockchain and Crypto-currencies. *The FinTech Book: The Financial Technology Handbook for Investors, Entrepreneurs and Visionaries*, 217-220.

Huq, A. Z. (2024). (Forthcoming). The Geopolitics of Digital Regulation. *U of Chicago, Public Law. Working Paper.*

Jun, L., Jianping, D., Poenisch, H., Le, X., Hanke, S. H., Marsh, D., ... & Hentov, E. (2014). International Monetary Review.

Kaushik, T. K., Ravish, Singh, A., Raghav, A., & Singh, B. (2024). Potential of Artificial Intelligence in the Agricultural Industry: A Comprehensive Review. In B. Riswandi, B. Singh, C. Kaunert, & K. Vig (Eds.), *AI Applications for Clean Energy and Sustainability* (pp. 344-365). IGI Global. https://doi.org/DOI: 10.4018/979-8-3693-6567-0.ch017

Lal, S., Arora, M. K., Riswandi, B. A., Singh, N., & Singh, B. (2024). Melding Artificial Intelligence and Remote Sensing Data for Real-Time Monitoring of Marine Biodiversity. In Riswandi, B., Singh, B., Kaunert, C., & Vig, K. (Eds.), *AI Applications for Clean Energy and Sustainability* (pp. 299–319). IGI Global., DOI: 10.4018/979-8-3693-6567-0.ch015

Mangano, R. (2018). Blockchain securities, insolvency law and the sandbox Approach. *European Business Organization Law Review, 19*(4), 19. DOI: 10.1007/s40804-018-0123-5

Martin, C. J. (2016). The sharing economy: A pathway to sustainability or a nightmarish form of neoliberal capitalism? Ecological Economics, 121,149e159

Maulana, A., & Putri, A. D. (2019, March). Development of digital currency technology. [). IOP Publishing.]. *Journal of Physics: Conference Series, 1175*(1), 012205. DOI: 10.1088/1742-6596/1175/1/012205

Millard, J. (2023). *Impact of digital transformation on public governance* (No. JRC133975). Joint Research Centre (Seville site).

Morales, L., & Andreosso-O'Callaghan, B. (2022). The World's Top Five Financial Centers: Geopolitical Uncertainties. In *Sustainable Development in Asia: Socio-economic, Financial, and Economic Perspectives* (pp. 115–135). Springer International Publishing. DOI: 10.1007/978-3-030-94679-1_7

Nowinski, W., & Kozma, M. (2017). How can blockchain technology disrupt the existing business models? Entrepreneurial Business and Economics Review, 5(3), 173e188

Pavelea, A., & Negrea, P. C. (2024). *A Comprehensive Analysis of High-Impact Cybersecurity Incidents: Case Studies and Implications* (Doctoral dissertation, Masters thesis. Babe –Bolyai University. doi: . 2.2. 17461.65763).DOI: 10.13140/RG

Prabhakar, A. (2025). A Sustainable and Inclusive Economic Development: A Global Imperative: A Global Imperative. *Journal of Recycling Economy & Sustainability Policy, 4*(1), 1–16.

Raghav, A., Singh, B., & Jermsittiparsert, K. (2024). Role of Artificial Intelligence and Machine Learning in Clean and Blue Energy for Enhancing Efficiency and Sustainability. In Riswandi, B., Singh, B., Kaunert, C., & Vig, K. (Eds.), *AI Applications for Clean Energy and Sustainability* (pp. 366–386). IGI Global., DOI: 10.4018/979-8-3693-6567-0.ch018

Saaida, M. (2024). BRICS Plus: De-dollarization and global power shifts in new economic landscape. *BRICS Journal of Economics*, *5*(1), 13–33. DOI: 10.3897/brics-econ.5.e117828

Schedlbauer, M., & Wagner, K. (2018). Blockchain beyond digital currencies-a structured literature review on blockchain applications. *Available at SSRN* 3298435. DOI: 10.2139/ssrn.3298435

Sharma, K. (2023). TRANSFORMATIVE CHANGE IN GLOBAL BUSINESS AFTER NEW WORLD ORDER.

Verma, B., Singla, B., & Mittal, A. (Eds.). (2024). *Digital Technologies, Ethics, and Decentralization in the Digital Era*. IGI Global. DOI: 10.4018/979-8-3693-1762-4

Yermack, D. (2018). The potential of digital currency and blockchains. *NBER Reporter*, (1), 14–17.

Yeung, R. (2020). *China's Trump Card: Cryptocurrency and Its Game-changing Role in Sino-US Trade*. John Wiley & Sons. DOI: 10.1002/9781119699163

Zaidi, S. M. S., & Nirmal, . (2023). Emerging Realities in the International Political System: Transforming State's Foreign Policy. *Herald of the Russian Academy of Sciences*, *93*(6), 376–389. DOI: 10.1134/S1019331623010148

Zhang, T., & Huang, Z. (2022). Blockchain and central bank digital currency. *ICT Express*, *8*(2), 264–270. DOI: 10.1016/j.icte.2021.09.014

Zielonka, R. (2022). *Technology Innovation and Digital Revolution: Adoption and Diffusion of Digital Network Platforms, 1995-2001, with Implications for Future Development*. University of Washington.

Chapter 10
Green Fintech Meets DeFi: A Path to Digital Sustainability

Amrinder Singh
https://orcid.org/0000-0003-0830-7245
Jain University, India

Priya Makhija
https://orcid.org/0000-0002-7436-2798
Jain University, India

Elizabeth Chacko
Christ University, India

Shakar Prasad S
https://orcid.org/0000-0002-7008-3361
Jain University, India

R Thanga Kumar
https://orcid.org/0000-0003-2594-7543
Jain University, India

ABSTRACT

This chapter explores the interconnection between Green Finance and Digital Ecology, highlighting their potential in advancing sustainability through technological innovation. Emphasis is placed on how green FinTech can mitigate these challenges by designing low-carbon financial systems and promoting sustainable investment practices. The methodology involves a review of scholarly literature to assess how digital finance and ecology contribute to global sustainability efforts.

DOI: 10.4018/979-8-3373-1727-4.ch010

Findings suggest that the integration of green FinTech, digital money, and ecological practices can enhance transparency, reduce costs, and expand access to sustainable finance, ultimately leading to more resilient financial ecosystems. The chapter calls for increased awareness, financial literacy, and robust regulatory frameworks to manage associated risks.

INTRODUCTION

Big data analysis, neural networks, blockchain technology, DEFI (decentralized finance), and wireless internet are examples of revolutionary financial technologies that are referred as "fintech." FinTech inventiveness, institutions have embraced AI technologies due to which the usage of technological innovations by banks and other fintech businesses will have the potential to revolutionize consumer interaction and demand analysis. This process can be aided by chatbots and predictive modelling, which will alter how banks engage with clients (Mohan. Devie, 2020; Phadke, 2020). Financial technology and Blockchain innovation have a wide range of real-world ramifications and great potential to transform the banking industry. Fintech are widely adopted by institutions and financial firms due to the emergence of revolutionary technology and consumer desire for a safer and easier banking experience. This study shows that Fintech companies have the power to drastically alter the financial industry by offering cutting-edge goods and services that satisfy consumers' demands for security, speed, affordability, and trust. Regulators must, however, carefully weigh the trade-offs between stability and efficiency. They must be guaranteed that dangers to financial integrity and safety brought on by money laundering, cyberattacks, and terrorist funding can be successfully handled without impeding innovation. To guarantee the integrity of data, systems processes, and platforms as well rules and standards must be created (Zeidy, 2022). (Offiong et al., n.d.) revealed that operational effectiveness, customer satisfaction, and financial inclusion are the main drivers of FinTech adoption in microfinance firms. Blockchain and artificial intelligence (AI) simplify procedures, while data analytics and AI customize services to meet the demands of each user. Beyond conventional financial success indicators, the study also examines social and technical aspects. The study highlights the strategic significance of digital technology in microfinance by identifying important themes, gaps, and future research objectives. It does, however, recognize its limits and recommend that future study address ethical, technical, and regulatory issues, investigate understudied topics, and conduct more thorough empirical investigations.

Price discovery, risk management, liquidity availability, and user experience are just a few of the areas of decentralized financial services that may be enhanced by integrating AI into DeFi systems. Financial services that are more individualized, inclusive, and efficient may result from DeFi solutions driven by AI. Decentralized AI can solve centralization, bias, and data privacy problems, allowing for more reliable and responsible AI applications in the financial industry. Nevertheless, there are drawbacks to the convergence, including a lack of expertise, scaling issues, legal uncertainties, and data privacy and security threats. To solve these issues, a multi-stakeholder strategy is needed. DeFi and AI integration can promote financial mobility, lessen inequality, and stimulate the creation of new economic offerings and services. But when DeFi-AI solutions become more widely used, ethically and cultural problems such guaranteeing reliability, openness, and integrity of AI-driven investment decisions will come up (Nartey, 2024).

The use of electricity by Bitcoin has recently come under fire, raising concerns about how well it counts as a "green FinTech." Empirical results show that the income generated by the mining of Bitcoin and an indicator of BTC electrical usage were favorably associated. When prices grow (or are expected to increase), miners appear to intensify their mining operations. The fossil fuel consumed by bitcoins mine workers, which is heavily reliant on fossil fuels, results in significant releases of carbon dioxide and greenhouse gas emissions. The use of fossil fuels by the miners of bitcoin should be replaced with greener solutions like wind, hydroelectricity, and geothermal energies. Digital currencies with low emissions that are ecologically benign will have more prospects in sustainable finance in the future (Kabaklarlı, 2022). The nation's equitable development and conservation efforts depend heavily on the digital economy since it lowers the humanistic strain on ecosystems and makes environmental finance easier. Cutting emissions and increasing manufacturing efficiency may be accomplished using creative solutions made possible by digital technology. The degree of digitization in the state, businesses, and populace has a favorable effect on environmental funding, and digital investment encourages environmental investment. Active engagement in crowdfunding platforms is encouraged by digital involvement, which supports environmentally friendly technology and sustainable development practices. Rapid issue identification and resolution are made possible by digital technology in public administration, and resource efficiency and sustainable development objectives are supported by the digitization of industrial processes (Akberdina et al., 2023). (Xue et al., 2023)examines how ESG performance in Chinese listed companies is affected by digital financing between 2010 and 2019. Digital finance was proven to save agency expenses, increase goodwill, and encourage green innovation. Regional institutional growth deepens the link, whereas political ties attenuate it. Use and digitalization level are two factors that impact ESG performance. The report suggests that government agencies integrate digital technology and finance, promote a synergy between digital finance and sustainable development, and invest in clean manufacturing, employee welfare, and the preservation of shareholder rights.

Green fintech uses analytical data, big analytics evaluation, the prevalence of the Internet of objects, and blockchain-based technology to save our planet and fight unemployment by lowering the cost of credit for people in lower socioeconomic classes. Alternatively, cryptocurrency payments can increase credit availability for unbanked individuals and small businesses. Through the collaborative economic framework, green fintech companies contribute to using shared vehicles, information dissemination, CO2 emissions reduction, and emissions reduction, among other beneficial environmental benefits (Mi & Coffman, 2019; Wilson, 2017).

Cryptocurrencies are an essential tool for supporting small farmers and increasing agribusiness investment since they integrate surveillance equipment and big data assessment to realize the development of the countryside (Hinson et al., 2019). Financial intermediaries can be effectively supported by green financial technologies by monitoring, choosing, and assessing green projects' environmental impacts (Yang et al., 2020). The federal financial register will function as a centralized repository for monetary and related data, assisting banks in lowering risk and streamlining credit. Digilocker, a company, will assist organizations like enterprises and charity trusts in document storage. These laws will be exchanged with lenders as and when necessary, enabled via a secure consent layer. The Digi locker can be used for customer integration, insurance, and service by banks and fintech companies. The goal of having no carbon emissions by 2070 will spur the development of green fintech companies (Money Control, 2023).

The term "green finance" refers to governmental and commercial financial organizations as well as diverse asset classes that include ecological borrowing markets, structural resources, and ecological banking. The main forces increasing the long-term viability of the financial methodology are institutional financiers, international banking organizations, legislators, and monetary agencies. However, various social and economic concerns limit the accessibility of alternative funding. To prevent environmental fraud, parameters of green lending, including financial funds, securities, and legally enforceable securities for institutional buyers, should be developed and overseen. Green funds additionally require specific descriptions and cooperative principles (Kathrin & Lindenberg, 2019). Finance has been crucial to the advancement of civilization ever since manufacturing first began. The goal of the Universal Financial Technique is to make the most effective use of the riches on the planet. if the economic system is working properly, every penny prevented goes towards investing in endeavours that improve the standard of life; though, if it fails, as it has in the recent past, funds will be utilized in financing bubbles that are environmentally damaging initiatives and that will worsen environmental damage brought by human activity (Sachs, 2014).

Central banks worldwide has started to investigate the grant of central bank digital currencies (CBDCs) as the need for electronic methods of transaction continues to rise and the usage of currency has decreased (Auer et al., 2021; Auer & Boehme, 2020). A variety of reasons for releasing retail CBDCs are frequently included in notifications revealed by the central banks in developed nations (Bank of England, 2021; Bank of Israel, 2018). These reasons involve safeguarding financial autonomy, reaffirming financial policy circulate battling the illegal use of money, enhancing concurrence for electronic money compensation vendors, and enhancing the payment accuracy and security. (Bank of England, 2021; Bank of Israel, 2018)(Bank of Denmark, 2021; Bank of England, 2021).

An activity determines the boundaries of a network called a "digital ecology," which is made up of both electronic and analog antiques with individuals functioning as connections. As they engage in various activities, users may encounter a variety of digital ecologies, but each one is a subset of their own personal ecology. human-computer interaction is moving in the right direction, which opens up alternatives for new techniques and methods that can support this comprehensive perspective of View and lead towards the construction of better technological artwork as well as efficient monitoring of them. Creative human-computer interaction (HCI) design will gain advantages from acceptance a sustainable approach to reasoning (Raptis et al., 2014).

Over the previous ten years, the E7 countries have made considerable strides toward realizing their goal of a reliable, ecologically friendly electricity infrastructure. A steady decline in the amount of greenhouse gases released into the atmosphere has been acquired due to the gradual restoration of nuclear power, the increase of green energy sources, and improvements in energy efficiency. The majority of the energy supply—88%—comes from renewable sources, and since 2011, the supply's carbon intensity has been quickly rising. If the E7 countries are to achieve the goal of zero carbon emissions by 2050, they must expand their efforts to create low-carbon technology, remove institutional and legal hurdles, and increase competition in the energy industry. In 2022, energy-related international greenhouse gas emissions climbed by 0.9%, which is or 321 Mt, hitting a new high of over 36.8 Gt. Despite the switch from petroleum to coals in numerous nations, the worldwide rise during emission were less than expected in a year marked by energy cost fluctuations, rising prices, and disruptions to conventional fuel trading patterns. Despite a 1.8 percent or 261 Mt rise in emissions, the power, and heat-generating economy saw the greatest rise in carbon in the year 2022. (IEA, 2023).

Based on the World Bank's perennial "State and Trends of Carbon Pricing" report, global emissions offering earnings in 2021 grew by nearly sixty percent compared to the levels of 2020 to roughly $84 billion, serving as an essential source of funding for initiatives that promote an ecologically sound revival of the economy, financing deeper fiscal consolidation, or make investments in local economies as a component of a zero-carbon future. In numerous countries, notably the European Union, the Golden State, New Zealand, Australia, the Republic of Korea, the country of Switzerland, and Canada as well, price tags for carbon reached unprecedented levels. Nevertheless, fewer than 4% of global emissions have been covered by immediate carbon pricing in the range required by 2030 to achieve the Paris Agreement's climate objective (World Bank, 2022).

Fintech and blockchain advancements should be monitored by decision-makers in charge of funding global warming and equitable development. Considering the emergence of several efforts that are either directly or indirectly related to green finance and equitable growth, the industry is fast diversifying. The possibility exists for projects like openness in supply chains, identities and financial empowerment, intellectual property protection, the proliferation of green energy, the decentralization of electrical infrastructure, carbon offset dealings, and modified accessibility to climate financing to evolve into operating models that may simultaneously reduce the cost and increase the likelihood of achieving the goals of the Paris Agreement and the SDGs. However, these initiatives must be supported by legitimate regulations and policies. Collaboration the fintech and blockchain technology industries will open up new options for nations that want to advance their monetary technical, growing economic success in a world finances that is more and more reliant upon intricate, decentralized interconnections. If the possibility is acknowledged, it will open doors for methods that will increase environmentally friendly financing for low-carbon, climate-resilient construction and help the world reach its environmentally friendly development targets (Nassiry, 2019).

Over the past decade, entrepreneurial enterprises and new entrants have driven much of the innovation in the financial technology (FinTech) industry. However, the rapid pace of technological growth has led to ambiguities, compounded by the slow adaptation of traditional norms and regulations. Emerging competitors, in particular, are more affected by this than well-established firms. While novel strategies are essential to foster the incubation and growth of FinTech start-ups, these strategies must account for the unique economic, regulatory, and cultural contexts in different regions. To better understand the specific needs of FinTech entities, future research must delve deeper into the underlying factors that nurture the innovation process. This includes identifying key components that help form and support creative minds, emphasizing the importance of collaboration, and analyzing the competitive dynamics that drive progress, resilience, and the development of ground breaking financial products and services for broader societal benefit. However, the lack of empirical evidence leaves these points largely theoretical and requires more data to substantiate the claims. Furthermore, financial policies vary significantly across countries, creating a complex landscape for both local and global regulatory frameworks. Financial institutions are tasked with navigating these regulatory uncertainties, but the development of appropriate FinTech legislation remains a challenge. Regulators often lag behind technological advancements, leaving a regulatory vacuum that hinders innovation and market performance. Without concrete evidence, it is difficult to evaluate the real-world impact of these regulatory gaps on emerging FinTech companies. Therefore, additional empirical research is needed to provide insights into how regulatory environments influence FinTech innovation and how suitable legislation can be developed to support both market growth and technological progress. This would enable a more thorough understanding of the conditions that allow FinTech start-ups to thrive while navigating these challenges. (Breidbach et al., 2020).

Turnbull et al., (2022) stated that an arrangement of digital ecologies can span three key philosophical concepts which pointed out that electronic interventions of more-than-human universes have the capacity to promote ecologically conscious ecosystems, pleasurable human-nonhuman confrontations, methods of ecological oversight, and the critical importance of these interactions: (i) Materialities, which consider the frameworks that enable artificially controlled human associations and their socioenvironmental impact; (ii) encounters, which consider the political and economic repercussions and convivial opportunities of transforming collision zones; and (iii) governance, which seeks into the ways in which electronic devices produce unique more-than-human frameworks for governance. A mere one-third of the major banks in the entire globe make meaningful investments in ecosystems. With the exception of the odd pilot, almost a fifth do not invest in them at all. However, competitors from outside the realm of conventional banking are moving forward. Big tech companies, like Google as well as Amazon, are integrating payment and monetary service capabilities into a range of ecosystem options by utilizing their strong technical expertise. But digital banking firms are eroding the worth of networks that financial institutions formerly controlled, luring customers with specialized services catered to their particular market niche's requirements (Ampenberger et al., 2023). The increased pace of progress has led to an increase in recognition of green fintech, digital ecology, and digital finance. Governments and corporations are working together now to address environmental problems and foster economic growth. This chapter sets out an extensive review of literature with the view of understanding how green finance, digital ecology, and digital finance affect sustainability. The review presents critical analysis and a contextual application to pertinent and quality research papers from reputable academic databases such as

Web of Science (WOS); SSRN; Google Scholar, and Scopus. This method is also effective in identifying trends, frameworks, and empiricism that establish a case for these measures' role in enhancing environmental and financial sustainability.

LITERATURE REVIEW

Banking organizations, such as banking institutions, allow the transfer of money from depositors to lenders through an approach known as financial intermediaries. In the context of green fintech, financial intermediaries play a crucial role in channelling funds towards environmentally sustainable projects and initiatives (Boot et al., 2020). A study by (H. Yu et al., 2022) examined the impact of green crowdfunding on the performance of renewable energy projects in China. The study found that green crowdfunding can enhance the performance of renewable energy projects by reducing their financing costs and improving their operational efficiency. The green crowdfunding can act as an effective financial intermediary to connect investors with aaagreen projects. It is argued that ecological bonds can be susceptible to a negative premium, allowing green investments to be supported at disregard, since investors are prepared to pay for environmental sustainability or since they are less vulnerable to the hazards associated with green investments (Clark et al., 2018). However, the surcharge is only necessary if securities (Institutional) makers have a good track record already or if there is greens authentication with the objective to reduce information asymmetry and provide investors with protections against bond greenwashing (Bachelet et al., 2019).

As per (Conde et al., 2020) study the benefits of green bonds over traditional project finance, as it indicate that green bond financing provides greater returns to shareholders than conventional financing (Conde et al., 2020). This analysis also states the critical role of issuers in aligning financial aims with those of national and international environmental agencies (Malan, 2018). Furthermore, according to (Wen et al., 2023) the research done in Bangladesh on the effect of Fintech, green finance (GF) and green innovation (GI) on the banking firms daily operation could achieve in sustainability performance (SP) if the government encourages these initiatives by compensating and rewarding by use of new fintech adoption (FA) technology and funding of sustainable development programmes (Yan et al., 2022). Green fintech refers to financial technology that promotes environmental sustainability and social responsibility, while digital currency refers to a type of currency that exists only in digital form and uses cryptography to secure and verify transactions (Feyen et al., 2021). Green fintech can play a role in boosting the usage of digital currencies by making them more accessible of these currencies for environmentally sustainable projects (Dorfleitner & Braun, 2019).

Furthermore, To improve green innovation and long-term perspectives, policymakers and strategists must use open innovation techniques. They will not only contribute to long-term ecological and sustainable innovation, however,(Bayram et al., 2022) numerous countries offer tax advantages and incentives for green innovation, allowing firms to profit from these incentives while lowering their expenditures (Polas et al., 2022). When looking up-to the green fintech in India as per the (Ali et al., 2020) the study investigated the application of green fintech in supporting sustainable development in India, highlighting the opportunity of digital currencies to improve financial inclusion and assist sustainable energy initiatives. (Wen et al., 2023). Adding to it, when research was conducted in Taiwan on green fintech's function by (M. Yu et al., 2022) fostering sustainable finance platforms may assist bridge the finance gap for sustainable initiatives and aid in the transition to a more sustainable economy. The role of financial intermediaries in the digital currency space has also been the recent studies by (Cong et al., 2022) analyzed the influence of electronic currency platforms on Bitcoin price and liquidity. It found that the entry of new exchanges increased the liquidity of Bitcoin and reduced its price volatility, as suggested, digital currency exchanges had a significant role in the growth of the digital currency market.

CBDCs are seen to be the last step in the digitalization of money and payments, which might result in the demise of physical currency and encourage the people to utilize fiat money more. They also provide state governments an opportunity to regain control over the money supply by acting as monopolies in national economies. However, given its benefits, including simplicity of use and potential as a helpful backup in an emergency, it would be foolish for CBDCs to completely replace conventional cash. Challenges in the development of CBDCs include cross-border connection, and the system design will have a significant effect on the economy's money supply and payment systems (Avgouleas & Blair, 2024). (Shah & Raj, 2025) examines the difficulties in putting Central Bank Digital Currency (CBDC) into practice and emphasizes how blockchain technology may be able to help. The decentralized ledger design of blockchain provides privacy protection, security, and regulatory compliance. The report also emphasizes the necessity of sector-specific regulations and cooperation in the day-to-day operations of CBDC distribution. Although there was agreement on public education and regulatory frameworks, different operational management goals point to the need for more discussion. According to the findings, sector-specific objectives and effective public-private partnerships may enhance the security, use, and acceptability of CBDCs, opening the door for their incorporation into the global financial system. The long-term viability of CBDCs depends on open communication and a well-rounded attitude to teamwork. Another study by (Chiu & Keister, 2022) on the basis of Bank of Canada, examined the role of payment intermediaries in the adoption of digital currencies such as payment processors and wallet providers, can facilitate the adoption of digital currencies by providing easy-to-use and secure payment services. Defining the significance of digital currencies necessitates clearly stated in (Chiu & Keister, 2022) modelling the frictions that generate a need for a means of payment and encourage the formation of financial infrastructure such as financial institutions, exchanges, and web-based platforms. The possible advantages and hazards of digital currencies are shown by the analysis of Ethereum and the U.S. Central Bank Digital Currency (CBDC). Although CBDCs promote efficiency, monetary policy efficacy, and financial inclusion, they can give rise to privacy and government control issues. Although Ethereum's decentralized architecture offers innovation, there are issues with scalability and security. In order to promote innovation and tackle new issues, cooperation between central banks and cryptocurrency platforms is essential. A more effective, safe, and inclusive financial ecosystem may be produced by utilizing both centralized and decentralized methods. Future studies should examine how CBDCs affect socioeconomic effects, changing regulatory environments, and global financial stability (Krause, 2024).

Digital currencies paving way for stablecoins a broader adoption in place of traditional financial systems. According to (Liao & Caramichael, 2022), analysed the potential impact of stablecoins, a type of digital currency pegged to a stable asset, on the traditional banking system. The study found that stablecoins framework consist of stable coin issuers, commercial banks and from there it goes to firms and central bank an alternative means of payment, improving the efficiency of cross-border payments. GF, GI, Fintech working towards SP also focused on the digital ecology, which means interactions between digital technologies and the natural environment. To supply financial services and goods, digital ecology and fintech are inextricably linked. The (Yan et al., 2022) increased use of digital technology in the financial industry has resulted in a variety of environmental consequences as well as possibilities to enhance sustainability (Crouhy et al., 2021). (Nyffenegger, 2024) highlights about the layer 2 rollup design to investigate the deployment of a Central Bank Digital Currency (CBDC) in a permissionless blockchain environment. The author contends that this method provides a more adaptable and agile solution than direct adoption and is consistent with a central bank's goals. Improving the private-public key authentication process and restricting flexibility are two disadvantages of directly implementing a CBDC on a blockchain. Greater privacy or offline payment flexibility, trusted quick finality, and the possibility of forced withdrawals are all offered by a layer 2 rollup architecture. A rollup approach reduces transaction costs per transaction and makes compliance with KYC and AML regulations simple. There are other restrictions to take into account, too, such the need that the central bank's functions depend on the underlying blockchain operating correctly. To stop possible money loss or theft, the rollup smart contract's layer 1 security is essential.

A study by (Javaid et al., 2022) analyzed the blockchain technology's application in the field of finance, as well as its potential to support sustainable financing by providing greater transparency, reducing intermediation costs, and facilitating the verification of sustainability-related data. Also, the application of fintech in the framework of long-term development in South Korea found supporting sustainable development by enabling greater financial inclusion, promoting transparency, and reducing costs (Campanella et al., 2022). The financial intermediation of green fintech, digital currency, and digital ecology presents a significant opportunity to promote sustainability by enabling more transparent and efficient financial transactions while reducing the carbon footprint associated with traditional finance. A study by (Nassiry, 2019) explored the role of green fintech in promoting sustainable finance by facilitating investment in renewable energy, promoting sustainable consumption, and enabling greater transparency and accountability (Wen et al., 2023). Another study (Tay et al., 2022). (2021) analyzed the potential of digital currency to support sustainable development in China by promoting financial inclusion, reducing transaction costs, and facilitating the adoption of sustainable practices using blockchain technologies, machine learning technologies resulting in reducing carbon emission(Chiu & Keister, 2022). Having all these advancements still its in infancy stage, and more dependence on technology and blockchain technologies will bring transparency and accurate information, but can have negative impact such as electronic waste, energy consumption, and exacerbating inequalities. So it is important to mitigate potential negative impacts through developing policies and regulations that promote sustainable practices like renewable energy sources and energy-efficient technologies and ensure equitable access to financial services and products (Leal Filho et al., 2021; Tan et al., 2023). Despite efforts to boost energy efficiency, fintech has resulted in excessive resource usage and persistent environmental devastation. On the other side according to (Hossain et al., 2015)while it has aided global commercial and economic growth, it has also resulted in excessive resource use and ongoing environmental harm by usage of more electronic appliances and accessories, contributing towards e-waste, despite attempts to increase energy efficiency. (H. Liu et al., 2022). Adding to, the rise of fintech has resulted in an increase in electronic waste, as the manufacture and disposal of electronic gadgets can have serious environmental consequences. Energy usage linked with fintech activities, such as data centres, can also contribute to greenhouse gas emissions and climate change. Furthermore, the practice of digital innovation through technology has the possible to worsen inequality and create a digital gap in which certain groups are denied access to financial services and goods (Campanella et al., 2022; Tan et al., 2023). So further research has to be conducted on the growth phase of fintech. Satisfaction and trust in fintech services and products to be more related to environmentally friendly view. The research on the negative impacts of the fintech on the ecology and how to mitigate globally. Significantly shifting on the worldwide financial scenario, digital currencies provide fresh chances for inclusive finance, financial innovation, and increased economic efficiency. Central Bank Digital Currencies (CBDCs) and decentralized cryptocurrencies are among the currencies that are changing financial service patterns and monetary notions. This study emphasizes how difficult risk management and financial innovation are in the age of digital currencies. Key duties to solve issues include international collaboration, flexible regulatory frameworks, and striking a balance between innovation and stability. As technology develops, digital currencies should improve the financial system's inclusion and efficiency. Market demand, policy environment, and technical innovation all influence the development path (G. Liu & Liu, 2024).

FinTech is increasingly being used for electronic services, such as opening trading accounts online and withdrawing money from ATMs. However, these methods carry higher risk exposures than face-to-face services. To mitigate these risks, reporting entities should implement efficient verification and identification measures, such as Electronic Know Your Customer (E-KYC) and customer identification systems. However, the process relies on various agencies, such as the Department of Provincial Administration, commercial registration, and tax database. Legislation should be made to improve digital authentication and verification procedures, ensuring user safety and reporting entities' safety. The Anti-Money Laundering Act should be amended to allow reporting entities to request data from data-regulating agencies for identification and verification. A bylaw should be enacted to prescribe rules and methods for E-KYC and verification methods exclusively through electronic channels (Phanwichit, 2018).

FINDINGS

The intermediation of green fintech, digital currency, and digital ecology has emerged as a powerful force in promoting sustainability. This convergence of technology and finance has created new opportunities to address environmental challenges and foster a greener future. The Sustainable Development Goals (SDGs) are widely acknowledged as the foremost objectives for all nations in the globe. As a result, it is crucial to create a secure global financial system that can execute its obligation to encourage the mobilization of wealthy individuals for environmentally friendly and steady economic growth. Particularly in the banking industry, there has recently been a noticeable digital shift and improvement, embracing a wide range of technology advancements and applications like the Bitcoin blockchain, the Global Internet of Things (IoT), big data, and AI (Javaid et al., 2021; Taherdoost, 2022). These developments have the potential to improve the efficiency of the world of finance. It is now clear that they have the ability to address major issues related to sustaining sustainable and equitable growth. (Hoang et al., 2022).

Fintech and Sustainability

Financial technology along with sustainability are linked in a number of ways because technology for finance can help advance and promote sustainable practices. Financial technology (FinTech) is the main driver of financial integration, and this in essence fosters environmentally friendly, equitable growth, as stated in the UN Global Sustainable Development Goals (SDGs). With the help of financial technology, financial diversity, feasible, equitable economic growth and the four pillars that include technological recognition, accessible systems for payment, technological transmission of government programmes and settlements, and the conceptualization of digital trading platforms and applications have the power to transform not merely the banking and finance industries but additionally economics and society as a whole (Arner et al., 2020).

A high degree of financial inclusion in a country reduces the likelihood of vulnerable groups resorting to informal financial services, which can hinder economic growth. Therefore, there is a need for a comprehensive framework that involves collaboration among the government, regulators, policymakers, and financial institutions to ensure clear and interconnected ideas for digital financial inclusion. It is crucial for a country's financial system to offer localized financial services that align with the specific needs and circumstances of the local population. In this regard, digital financial inclusion can bring numerous benefits to the community, the country, and the overall economy. Thus, promoting sustainable practices. Efficient financial systems foster the expansion of both new and established businesses. Moreover, a high level of accessibility to financial services can act as a catalyst for economic growth and development (Tay et al., 2022).

Responsible investing is another fintech use in ecology. Investors must account for hazards relating to environmental issues, climatic conditions, and associated policies. For these investments, money will need to come from the commercial and government sectors, as well as from outside sources. Novel approaches are required to mobilize and enable long-term financing in the vicinity in order to provide funding for infrastructure that is environmentally friendly. To ensure that financial systems can play a crucial role in financing the essential changeover to an ecologically conscious economy, more must be done than simply taking environmental and social considerations into account when making lending choices and product designs. (Volz, 2018).

A study by (Mavlutova et al., 2022) concluded that fintech assures constant access to financial services, despite challenges like a pandemic and related limitations. Clients spend less time executing financial transactions thanks to this, and financial institutions spend less on logistics. The amount of manual work is reduced, saving money and lessening the requirement for actual offices and logistics. By lowering the possibility of financial transaction failures, the digital revolution also raises client happiness. Additionally, it reduces operational risks and the costs that go along with them, such as insurance premiums and the amount of capital needed to cover such risks. Additionally, when the use of physical money carriers declines and leaves a smaller ecological footprint, the environmental impact is less. The overall decrease in environmental effect is also attributed to the decreased requirement for office space and logistics services.

Digital Currency and Sustainability

In order to fulfil the Sustainable Development Goals (SDGs), a study by (Ozili, 2023) examined the function of central bank digital currency (CBDC) (Leal Filho et al., 2021). The study made the case that CBDC can increase payment efficiency, increase access to capital, and unleash financing for sustainable development. Additionally, CBDC can speed up transaction procedures and make money allocation for investments in initiatives and projects for sustainable development more effective. According to this study, CBDC might help the United Nations achieve its Sustainable Development Goals. Policymakers are urged to make sure that the CBDC in their individual nations is designed with elements that address issues with sustainable development and adhere to the targets established by the UN for sustainable development (Leal Filho et al., 2021).

Digital currencies offer prospects for developing countries that want to achieve sustainable development, therefore they are not just for developed countries (Leal Filho et al., 2021). The use of digital currency makes money transfers affordable and effective, which lowers international remittance costs. Additionally, the use of digital currency can boost entrepreneurship, improve e-commerce, and ease small-scale international trade. Digital currencies have the potential to improve financial inclusion by lowering the costs associated with money transfers as mobile banking technology spreads (UN.ESCAP, 2017)

Digital Ecology and Sustainability

The development of electronic financial services can encourage environmentally friendly technology invention and boost the effectiveness of green loans, which will ultimately reduce the ecological footprint. Future allocations of resources ought to be exact thanks to the use of electronic devices. Furthermore, measures need to be made to close the technological gap, the role of Technological commerce in fostering inclusive growth must be further emphasized, and the authority of governments in directing responsible progress must be increased. (Feng et al., 2022).

Every individual want to see sustainable development for the sake of humankind. Sustainable banking and environmentally conscious financial technology are essential for fostering sustainable economic growth since they foster technical development and restructuring of industries while reducing dependency on unclean energy sources. While green finance needs the support of fintech to increase inclusion and accessibility, fintech has intrinsic green qualities. Economic development must follow the trend of moving towards a sustainable economy. Green finance and fintech have made it possible in ways never before possible to create systems that support sustainability. The fields of green finance and sustainable development benefit from fintech, which provides important assistance and chances for advancement (Cen & He, 2018). Banks will give priority finance to cutting-edge technological solutions that decrease or absorb carbon emissions because companies with higher carbon emissions may face increasing risk in the future. The transition to green banking benefits banks, industry, and the environment as a whole in addition to promoting sustainable development (Mir & Bhat, 2022).

CONCLUSION

Fintech platforms give people the chance to invest in sustainable and socially conscious businesses. Users can integrate environmental, social, and governance (ESG) factors into their investing portfolios using robo-advisors and online investment platforms, aligning them with their principles. Individuals can choose investments more easily and sustainably - thanks to fintech. Every stakeholder has a responsibility to reduce global warming and advance sustainability, including governments, corporations, and people. In this context, financial institutions, particularly banks, play a key role in the growth of a robust and successful low-carbon economy. By more thoroughly incorporating environmental data into credit extension and investment choices, they can increase their impact. Businesses can enhance their environmental performance and add long-term value to their organisations by taking a proactive approach. Reliance on cash transactions and paper-based procedures has been greatly decreased thanks to fintech. Physical currency, paper waste, and energy usage have a negative influence on the environment. Digital payments, mobile wallets, and blockchain-based transactions mitigate these effects. A more efficient and sustainable financial ecosystem is a result of the shift to digital transactions.

Financial intermediaries can assist sustainable finance by leveraging digital ecosystem to improve their operations. Financial organisations can evaluate the sustainability performance of their clients by using IoT devices, which can collect real-time data on energy use, water use, and other environmental aspects. This information can help with risk analysis, investment selection, and the creation of financial products with a sustainability focus. Due to its decentralised and transparent nature, blockchain technology can improve supply chain traceability and trust, allowing financial intermediaries to confirm the sustainability claims of companies and projects. Financial intermediaries may make wise judgements about sustainable investments with the use of AI and big data analytics, which can offer insightful data for risk modelling, impact analysis, and predictive analysis.

Everything being taken into account, the financial intermediation of green fintech, digital money, and digital ecology can be quite important in fostering sustainability. Financial institutions may expedite the flow of finance towards sustainable initiatives, promote sustainable behaviours, and improve environmental stewardship in the financial sector by utilising technology and creative solutions.

REFERENCES

Akberdina, V., Lavrikova, Y., & Vlasov, M. (2023). Environmental financing: Does digital economy matter? *Frontiers in Environmental Science, 11*, 1268286. Advance online publication. DOI: 10.3389/fenvs.2023.1268286

Ali, O., Ally, M., Clutterbuck, P., & Dwivedi, Y. (2020). The state of play of blockchain technology in the financial services sector: A systematic literature review. *International Journal of Information Management, 54*, 102199. DOI: 10.1016/j.ijinfomgt.2020.102199

Ampenberger, M., Hanspal, R., Hochstein, C., Pidun, U., & Ramachandran, S. (2023, March). *Digital Financial Ecosystems: An Opportunity for Banks*. BCG.

Arner, D. W., Buckley, R. P., Zetzsche, D. A., & Veidt, R. (2020). Sustainability, FinTech and Financial Inclusion. *European Business Organization Law Review, 21*(1), 7–35. DOI: 10.1007/s40804-020-00183-y

Auer, R., & Boehme, R. (2020). *The technology of retail central bank digital currency*. BIS Quarterly Review.

Auer, R., Frost, J., Gambacorta, L., Monnet, C., Rice, T., & Shin, H. S. (2021). *Central bank digital currencies: motives, economic implications and the research frontier*. DOI: 10.1146/annurev-economics-051420-020324

Avgouleas, E., & Blair, W. (2024). A critical evaluation of Central Bank Digital Currencies (CBDCs): Payments' final frontier? *Capital Markets Law Journal, 19*(2), 103–112. DOI: 10.1093/cmlj/kmae002

Bachelet, M. J., Becchetti, L., & Manfredonia, S. (2019). The Green Bonds Premium Puzzle: The Role of Issuer Characteristics and Third-Party Verification. *Sustainability 2019, Vol. 11, Page 1098, 11*(4), 1098. DOI: 10.3390/su11041098

Bank of Denmark. (2021). *Danmarks National Bank - Analysis*. Bank of Denmark.

Bank of England. (2021, December). *Bank Rate increased to 0.25% - December 2021*. Bank of England.

Bank of Israel. (2018). first page CBDC english.pdf. *BOI*.

Bayram, O., Talay, I., & Feridun, M. (2022). Can Fintech Promote Sustainable Finance? Policy Lessons from the Case of Turkey. *Sustainability 2022, Vol. 14, Page 12414, 14*(19), 12414. DOI: 10.3390/su141912414

Boot, A., Hoffmann, P., Laeven, L., & Ratnovski, L. (2020). Financial Intermediation and Technology. *IMF Working Paper*, *20*(161). Advance online publication. DOI: 10.5089/9781513552491.001

Breidbach, C. F., Keating, B. W., & Lim, C. (2020). Fintech: Research directions to explore the digital transformation of financial service systems. *Journal of Service Theory and Practice*, *30*(1), 79–102. DOI: 10.1108/JSTP-08-2018-0185

Campanella, F., Serino, L., & Crisci, A. (2022). Governing Fintech for sustainable development: evidence from Italian banking system. *Qualitative Research in Financial Markets*, 1755–4179. DOI: 10.1108/QRFM-01-2022-0009

Cen, T., & He, R. (2018). Fintech, Green Finance and Sustainable Development. *Advances in Social Science, Education and Humanities Research*, •••, 291.

Chiu, J., & Keister, T. (2022). The economics of digital currencies: Progress and open questions . *Journal of Economic Dynamics & Control*, *142*, 104496. DOI: 10.1016/j.jedc.2022.104496

Clark, R., Reed, J., & Sunderland, T. (2018). Bridging funding gaps for climate and sustainable development: Pitfalls, progress and potential of private finance. *Land Use Policy*, *71*, 335–346. DOI: 10.1016/j.landusepol.2017.12.013

Conde, A., & Belén, A. (2020). On the Effect of Green Bonds on the Profitability and Credit Quality of Project Financing. *Sustainability (Basel)*, *12*(16), 6695. DOI: 10.3390/su12166695

Cong, L. W., Li, X., Tang, K., & Yang, Y. (2022). Crypto Wash Trading. In *NBER*. DOI: 10.3386/w30783

Crouhy, M., Galai, D., & Wiener, Z. (2021). The Impact of Fintechs on Financial Intermediation: A Functional Approach. Https://Doi.Org/10.1142/S270510992031001X, *01*(01), 2031001. DOI: 10.1142/S270510992031001X

Dorfleitner, G., & Braun, D. (2019). Fintech, Digitalization and Blockchain: Possible Applications for Green Finance. In Migliorelli, M., & Dessertine, P. (Eds.), *The Rise of Green Finance in Europe* (pp. 207–237). Palgrave Macmillan., DOI: 10.1007/978-3-030-22510-0_9

Feng, S., Chong, Y., Yu, H., Ye, X., & Li, G. (2022). Digital financial development and ecological footprint: Evidence from green-biased technology innovation and environmental inclusion. *Journal of Cleaner Production*, *380*, 135069. DOI: 10.1016/j.jclepro.2022.135069

Feyen, E., Frost, J., Gambacorta, L., Natarajan, H., & Saal, M. (2021). *BIS Papers No 117 Fintech and the digital transformation of financial services: implications for market structure and public policy.*

Hinson, R., Lensink, R., & Mueller, A. (2019). Transforming agribusiness in developing countries: SDGs and the role of FinTech. *Current Opinion in Environmental Sustainability*, *41*, 1–9. DOI: 10.1016/j.cosust.2019.07.002

Hoang, T. G., Nguyen, G. N. T., & Le, D. A. (2022). Developments in Financial Technologies for Achieving the Sustainable Development Goals (SDGs): FinTech and SDGs. In https://services.igi-global.com/resolvedoi/resolve.aspx?doi=10.4018/978-1-7998-8900-7.ch001 (pp. 1–19). IGI Global. DOI: 10.4018/978-1-7998-8900-7.ch001

Hossain, M. S., Al-Hamadani, S. M. Z. F., & Rahman, M. T. (2015). E-waste: A Challenge for Sustainable Development. *Journal of Health & Pollution*, *5*(9), 3–11. DOI: 10.5696/2156-9614-5-9.3 PMID: 30524771

IEA. (2023, March). *CO2 Emissions in 2022 – Analysis* . IEA.

Javaid, M., Haleem, A., Pratap Singh, R., Khan, S., & Suman, R. (2021). Blockchain technology applications for Industry 4.0: A literature-based review. *Blockchain: Research and Applications*, *2*(4), 100027. DOI: 10.1016/j.bcra.2021.100027

Javaid, M., Haleem, A., Singh, R. P., Suman, R., & Khan, S. (2022). A review of Blockchain Technology applications for financial services. *BenchCouncil Transactions on Benchmarks. Standards and Evaluations*, *2*(3), 100073. DOI: 10.1016/j.tbench.2022.100073

Kabaklarlı, E. (2022). Green FinTech: Sustainability of Bitcoin. *Digital Finance*, *4*(4), 265–273. DOI: 10.1007/s42521-022-00053-x PMID: 35698578

Kathrin, B., & Lindenberg, N. (2019). Green finance across the universe. In S. Boubaker & D. Nguyen (Eds.), *Corporate social responsibility, ethics and sustainable prosperity* (pp. 331–358). German Institute of Development and Sustainability (IDOS). https://doi.org/https://doi.org/10.1142/9789811206887_0011

Krause, D. (2024). *The Intersection of Centralized and Decentralized Digital Currencies: Implications for Financial Inclusion and Efficiency*. https://papers.ssrn.com/abstract=4914822

Leal Filho, W., Marisa Azul, A., Brandli, L., Lange Salvia, A., & Wall, T. (Eds.). (2021). *Affordable and Clean Energy*. Springer International Publishing., DOI: 10.1007/978-3-319-95864-4

Liao, G. Y., & Caramichael, J. (2022). Stablecoins: Growth Potential and Impact on Banking. *International Finance Discussion Paper, 2022*(1334), 1–26. DOI: 10.17016/ifdp.2022.1334

Liu, G., & Liu, G. (2024). The Development of Blockchain-Based Digital Currencies and Their Impact on the Global Financial System. *Open Journal of Social Sciences, 12*(10), 227–238. DOI: 10.4236/jss.2024.1210018

Liu, H., Yao, P., Latif, S., Aslam, S., & Iqbal, N. (2022). Impact of Green financing, FinTech, and financial inclusion on energy efficiency. *Environmental Science and Pollution Research International, 29*(13), 18955–18966. DOI: 10.1007/s11356-021-16949-x PMID: 34705207

Malan, D. (2018, June). *Technology is changing faster than regulators can keep up - here's how to close the gap*. World Economic Forum.

Mavlutova, I., Spilbergs, A., Verdenhofs, A., Natrins, A., Arefjevs, I., & Volkova, T. (2022). Digital Transformation as a Driver of the Financial Sector Sustainable Development: An Impact on Financial Inclusion and Operational Efficiency. *Sustainability 2023, Vol. 15, Page 207, 15*(1), 207. DOI: 10.3390/su15010207

Mi, Z., & Coffman, D. M. (2019). The sharing economy promotes sustainable societies. *Nature Communications 2019 10:1, 10*(1), 1–3. DOI: 10.1038/s41467-019-09260-4

Mir, A. A., & Bhat, A. A. (2022). Green banking and sustainability – a review. *Arab Gulf Journal of Scientific Research, 40*(3), 247–263. DOI: 10.1108/AGJSR-04-2022-0017

Mohan, D. (2020). *The Financial Services Guide to Fintech: Driving Banking Innovation Through ... - Devie Mohan - Google Books* (1st ed.). Kogan Page.

Money Control. (2023, February). *The Indian fintech ecosystem is setting global benchmarks*. Money Control.

Nartey, J. (2024). Decentralized Finance (DeFi) and AI: Innovations at the Intersection of Blockchain and Artificial Intelligence. SSRN *Electronic Journal*. DOI: 10.2139/ssrn.4781328

Nassiry, D. (2019). The Role of Fintech in Unlocking Green Finance. *Handbook of Green Finance*, 315–336. DOI: 10.1007/978-981-13-0227-5_27

Nyffenegger, R. (2024). A proposal for a layer-2 CBDC on a rollup. *Digital Finance, 6*(3), 543–571. DOI: 10.1007/s42521-024-00115-2

Offiong, U. P., Cheba, K., & Ioppolo, G. (n.d.). *FinTech as a digital innovation in microfinance companies-systematic literature review*. DOI: 10.1108/EJIM-04-2024-0462

Ozili, P. (2023). *Using central bank digital currency to achieve the sustainable development goals*. Contemporary Studies in Economics and Financial Analysis. DOI: 10.1108/S1569-375920230001110008

Phadke, S. (2020). Fintech Is All Around Us. In *FinTech Future: The Digital DNA of Finance*. SAGE Publications Pvt Ltd., DOI: 10.4135/9789353885687.n1

Phanwichit, S. (2018). *FinTech and Causing Customers to Comply with Anti-Money Laundering Law*. https://papers.ssrn.com/abstract=3262514

Polas, M. R. H., Kabir, A. I., Sohel-Uz-zaman, A. S. M., Karim, R., & Tabash, M. I. (2022). Blockchain Technology as a Game Changer for Green Innovation: Green Entrepreneurship as a Roadmap to Green Economic Sustainability in Peru. *Journal of Open Innovation*, *8*(2), 62. DOI: 10.3390/joitmc8020062

Raptis, D., Kjeldskov, J., Skov, M. B., & Paay, J. (2014). What is a Digital Ecology?: Theoretical Foundations and a Unified Definition. *Australian Journal of Intelligent Information Processing Systems*, *13*(4), 5.

Sachs, J. D. (2014, December). *Financing Climate Safety*. Project SYndicate.

Shah, M. A., & Raj, N. (2025). Examining the role of blockchain and public-private partnerships in design and deployment of blockchain-enabled CBDC. *Digital Business*, *5*(1), 100111. DOI: 10.1016/j.digbus.2025.100111

Taherdoost, H. (2022). Blockchain Technology and Artificial Intelligence Together: A Critical Review on Applications. *Applied Sciences 2022, Vol. 12, Page 12948*, *12*(24), 12948. DOI: 10.3390/app122412948

Tan, Q., Yasmeen, H., Ali, S., Ismail, H., & Zameer, H. (2023). Fintech development, renewable energy consumption, government effectiveness and management of natural resources along the belt and road countries. *Resources Policy*, *80*, 103251. DOI: 10.1016/j.resourpol.2022.103251

Tay, L. Y., Tai, H. T., & Tan, G. S. (2022). Digital financial inclusion: A gateway to sustainable development. *Heliyon*, *8*(6), e09766. DOI: 10.1016/j.heliyon.2022.e09766 PMID: 35785228

Turnbull, J., Searle, A., Davies, O. H., Dodsworth, J., Chasseray-Peraldi, P., von Essen, E., & Anderson-Elliott, H. (2022). Digital ecologies: Materialities, encounters, governance. *Progress in Environmental Geography, 275396872211456*. Advance online publication. DOI: 10.1177/27539687221145698

UN.ESCAP. (2017). *Digital and virtual currencies for sustainable development.*

Volz, U. (2018). Fostering Green Finance for Sustainable Development in Asia. ADBI Working Paper. *Asian Development Bank Institute.*

Wen, G., Siddik, Z., & Bakkar, A. (2023). The effect of Fintech adoption on green finance and environmental performance of banking institutions during the COVID-19 pandemic: The role of green innovation. *Environmental Science and Pollution Research International, 30*(10), 25959–25971. DOI: 10.1007/S11356-022-23956-Z/FIGURES/4 PMID: 36350441

Wilson, J. D. (2017). Creating Strategic Value through Financial Technology. In *Creating Strategic Value through Financial Technology*. Wiley., DOI: 10.1002/9781119318682

World Bank. (2022, May). *Report: State and Trends of Carbon Pricing*. World Bank Org.

Xue, L., Dong, J., & Zha, Y. (2023). How does digital finance affect firm environmental, social and governance (ESG) performance?—Evidence from Chinese listed firms. *Heliyon, 9*(10), e20800. DOI: 10.1016/j.heliyon.2023.e20800 PMID: 37867793

Yan, C., Siddik, A. B., Yong, L., Dong, Q., Zheng, G. W., & Rahman, M. N. (2022). A Two-Staged SEM-Artificial Neural Network Approach to Analyze the Impact of FinTech Adoption on the Sustainability Performance of Banking Firms: The Mediating Effect of Green Finance and Innovation. *Systems 2022, Vol. 10, Page 148, 10*(5), 148. DOI: 10.3390/systems10050148

Yang, G., Li, Y., Jiang, X., Yang, G., Li, Y., & Jiang, X. (2020). Research on the Impacts of Green Finance towards the High-Quality Development of China's Economy—Mechanisms and Empirical Analysis. *Theoretical Economics Letters, 10*(6), 1338–1357. DOI: 10.4236/tel.2020.106082

Yu, H., Wei, W., Li, J., & Li, Y. (2022). The impact of green digital finance on energy resources and climate change mitigation in carbon neutrality: Case of 60 economies. *Resources Policy, 79*, 103116. DOI: 10.1016/j.resourpol.2022.103116

Yu, M., Tsai, F. S., Jin, H., & Zhang, H. (2022). Digital finance and renewable energy consumption: Evidence from China. *Financial Innovation, 8*(1), 1–19. DOI: 10.1186/s40854-022-00362-5

Zeidy, I. A. (2022). The role of financial technology (FINTECH) in changing financial industry and increasing efficiency in the economy. *COMESA Monetary Institute*, 1–20.

Chapter 11
The Impact of Digital Labor on Global Value Chains:
A New Era of Supply Chain Management

Usharani Bhimavarapu
https://orcid.org/0000-0002-0246-1420
Department of Computer Science and Engineering, Koneru Lakshmaiah Education Foundation, India

ABSTRACT

This research looks at the influence of Global Value Chains (GVCs) and the growth of digital labor, especially with industrial and technological developments. With increased application of digital technology making it easier to run businesses still on the increase, the incorporation of artificial intelligence (AI) and automation within GVCs has had a colossal influence on defining the future of work. The rise of digital labor from deep learning models like Residual Networks (ResNet) has transformed labor traditionally performed by human laborers, including processing data, making decisions, and quality checks. The study discusses how the technologies enhance supply chain performance, resilience, and sustainability and struggle with the challenges they pose in terms of job substitution, skills gap, and economic inequality. In a mixed-methods design that combines qualitative interviews with quantitative questionnaires, the study explores the implications of digital labor on the future of work, global competitiveness, and supply chain management.

DOI: 10.4018/979-8-3373-1727-4.ch011

INTRODUCTION

The Digital Thread is the connected flow of data throughout the product life cycle from design to manufacturing, operation, and end-of-life. As more value chains in the global economy are emerging and digital work is on the rise, this becomes all the more significant. Products of contemporary industries tend to be designed, manufactured, and consumed abroad, and hence end-to-end communication and exchange of data between all stakeholders has to occur. The Digital Thread accomplishes this by tracking, analyzing, and controlling information in real time, thereby producing quicker and more synchronized global value chains. With the growing complexity of GVCs, there is a need for an enhanced digital thread to make things visible, prevent delays, and provide greater productivity. Apart from that, remote and virtual digital employees or digital labor is the one that facilitates ease and promotes scalability in this contract.

The most precious objectives of the Digital Thread are some of the following:

Offering maximum coordination between industry groups throughout the product's lifetime. Classical manufacturing processes trace silo hierarchies through which it is challenging for different teams to view and modify information on a timely basis. A company with Digital Thread can correlate disparate design, engineering, production, and shipping teams operating across various geographically dispersed locations across the globe. This enhances the coordination and eliminates errors due to miscommunication or outdated information. The Digital Thread also makes it possible for companies to exchange knowledge and experience so that firms can innovate at a lower cost and greater speed. This seamless integration is most critical to third-party partners and providers to firms, particularly in the current globalized world.

The Digital Thread also makes possible the increasingly mainstream culture of product customization and personalization. As customers call for more personalized products, firms will have to respond to variation while producing on a moment's notice. A solid Digital Thread allows them the foundation upon which they can track all points of variation for every product through design and manufacturing so each process is exactly what the customer needs it to be. The manufacturers can then simply look at history of customization at every step by consolidating enormous quantities of information, and accordingly make the necessary changes as and when needed. This flexibility is the solution to achieving competitiveness in the international economy where products are needed to be customized to the requirements of individual customers, particularly for manufacturing industries like automotive, consumer electronics, and clothing. Aside from enabling customization, the Digital Thread also enables traceability and supply chain sustainability around the world. With the world still grappling with an ever-rising issue in the environment, stakeholders in every industry look for ways through which they can reduce waste, increase the utilization of resources, and improve the efficiency of energy usage. The Digital Thread is an excellent tool that provides visibility across all stages of the life cycle of a product. Businesses can monitor material procurement, watch manufacturing processes, and quantify the environmental impact of various stages. It allows businesses to make better decisions in favor of sustainability goals. Secondly, it addresses heightened consumer demand for corporate social responsibility and ethical business as consumers look for companies that have concentration on environment and social governance (ESG).

The second principal purpose of the Digital Thread is to optimize operational efficiency and reduce costs in end-to-end global supply chains. Since companies are being asked more and more to lower the cost and duration of production, data sharing must be in real-time. Digital Thread provides businesses with real-time, up-to-the-second precision on inventory presence, manufacturing activity, and supply chain problems in order to allow faster, more intelligent business choices. Digital Thread removes physical audit, sloth, and inefficiencies that result from isolated systems. Prowling analytics allow businesses to foresee shifts in demand, minimize usage of resources, and prevent excess production, thereby, considerable savings. Such technologies prove useful specifically for low-margin companies and very competitive industries.

There is also more digital work inextricably linked to the Digital Thread because automation and remote work more traditionally define global value chains. With growing functions outsourced or automated, a robust digital foundation is required to track and control work processes. The Digital Thread enables coordination among digital labor systems on the basis of access to the appropriate, up-to-date information required to perform processes like quality control, maintenance, and production monitoring. This transformation compels firms to reduce reliance on labor and increase flexibility and productivity. Remote work, by machines, artificial intelligence, and distant employees, facilitates the Digital Thread by transforming the work performed into productive and precise output even in difficult, decentralized situations

The Digital Thread similarly controls risk along global value chains. In the present unstable world economy, companies are faced with numerous risks including geopolitical risks, supply chain disruption, and technological breakdown. With a Digital Thread, companies are able to identify and address emerging risks early on, less likely to be causing enormous business disruptions. One example is having real-time visibility into supply chain activity so that potentially one may be able to locate at an early stage some delay or quality issue so that companies can move before the problem accumulates. Moreover, digital labor systems may be designed to detect threats automatically and eliminate them so that mission-critical operations are not disrupted. In risky enterprises such as defense and aerospace where errors practically have little room, the use of digital technologies for containing risk is invaluable.

As the world workforce goes digital, so does the Digital Thread that is transforming the very fabric of workforce management. In digital work, workers can perform work remotely or through automation, liberating them from centuries of work environment restriction. The Digital Thread makes this possible by giving workers the tools and information they need to get work done in real time, anywhere. This adaptability enables companies to leverage more talent, bringing highly trained workers from around the world into the equation. With this is digital labor rendering the need for large, centralized pools of employees obsolete, reducing costs and enhancing operation flexibility. This change is particularly important with industries requiring highly skilled specialists, such as engineering, information technology, and design.

The Digital Thread also forces organizations to always innovate and improve. Because data is collected and evaluated at every stage of the product life cycle, organizations have sharp understanding of products, processes, and performance. With this data-driven strategy, organizations can discover where they have to do better, experiment with new, and refine manufacturing processes. In high-innovation sectors like manufacturing, this ability is essential in order to compete. The connectivity of the Digital Thread brings about a culture of ongoing learning, whereby the experiences acquired in earlier projects are applied in future projects so that organizations can keep improving their products. Furthermore, digital labor increases the effectiveness of the process of innovation since computer systems have the ability to work continuously processing information and refreshing it without constant human oversight.

Lastly, the Digital Thread helps organizations respond quickly to quickly shifting market conditions and consumer sentiments. Since technology transformations are evolving at such a quick pace, organizations must be adaptable and responsive to new trends. The Digital Thread facilitates quick responsiveness by possessing nimble and elastic digital infrastructure. Such adaptability is needed as an attempt to keep up with shifting customer loyalties, regulatory demands, and technology dynamics. Digital work facilitates responsiveness since it allows businesses to ramp up or ramp down as required by the market. The Digital Thread, therefore, facilitates business resilience in the long run through the sustainability of businesses as per the rapid digitalization and interconnectivity of a worldwide economy. Ivanov and Dolgui (2020) deal with survivability and resilience of supply chains on the basis of each other, in particular in the context of the COVID-19 pandemic. While the paper continues in the vein of traditional models of supply chain resilience in that it puts greater emphasis on survivability, theoretically speaking, it is set forward with no empirical research to lend backing to its hypothesized constructs. Its extension to a wide range of other industries apart from the COVID-19 experience is questionable too because it has not taken into account long-term post-pandemic impacts and industry complexity (Ivanov & Dolgui, 2020).

Herold et al. (2021) record pandemic lessons from logistics service providers (LSPs) in resilience. One of the major research weaknesses is that it relies on single-source input—logistics service providers—and does not include other possible stakeholders such as manufacturers or consumers. The study is also short-term, with nothing mentioned regarding how the lessons would be applied to other disruptions beyond COVID-19 (Herold et al., 2021).

Deepu and Ravi (2023) offer an overview of supply chain digitalization in general and present a research agenda. The limitation here is that the organizational framework as such will generally not always be straightforwardly applicable to a given industry or to a particular firm and cannot as such necessarily be used straightforwardly to execute in real implementation. Apart from this, the literature review is also extensive, and empirical studies of specific nature are not available to offer additional evidentiary strength to validate the suggested framework (Deepu & Ravi, 2023).

Belhadi et al. (2024) explain how artificial intelligence (AI) can be utilized to increase supply chain resilience and performance against emerging situations. Though empirical research is useful, its limitation is that it is based on evidence from a single geographic region, and some evidence limits the generalizability of the research to the world. The weaknesses of the research are also that it does not highlight the challenge or difficulty created by the deployment of AI-based solutions in low-tech or resource-constrained environments (Belhadi et al., 2024).

Alfalla-Luque et al. (2023) conduct a meta-analysis in an attempt to research the correlation between supply chain agility and performance. Despite the research being supported by robust statistical data, findings are tainted by heterogeneity in the datasets used to carry out the meta-analysis and therefore may be introducing bias into the results. The article is not also describing at such lengths when agility is preferable, thus leaving space for potential industry-related or context-related problems (Alfalla-Luque et al., 2023).

Rahman et al. (2023) discuss supply chain resilience orientation in B2B companies and its influence on sustainability. The largest drawback of this study is that it's only performed on B2B companies, and it may not have picked up the B2C or multi-tier supply chains' dynamics. The study doesn't include the influence of the external drivers of government policy or global trade terms on supply chain resilience orientation (Rahman et al., 2023).

Rejeb and Rejeb (2020) outline the possibility of blockchain technology to enhance supply chain sustainability. Although the study captures theoretical concepts of value, the study fails to provide actual case studies that can illustrate how blockchain can be used in actual supply chains in the actual world. The study also fails to capture the issue of scalability of blockchain as well as compatibility with current systems in most industries (Rejeb & Rejeb, 2020).

Nwagwu et al. (2023) examine the effect of AI on supply chain performance through the mediating mechanism of supply chain collaboration. The study has the limitation that manufacturing and logistics firms in Pakistan only are taken into account, reducing generalizability. Additionally, no data is given in the article regarding possible barriers to the use of AI, e.g., costs of implementation or resistance (Nwagwu et al., 2023).

Sarkar et al. (2022) provide a bibliometric integration of co-invention and co-creation in the supply chain. Although the research is an interesting integration of the literature, it is plagued by the limitation of not providing an exact definition of co-invention and co-creation and this may lead to inconsistency of interpretation across studies. The research is also not seen to have entailed a critical examination of real-world application and problems that come with applying these principles to supply chain management (Sarkar et al., 2022).

Bischoff and Seuring (2021) discuss the possibilities and limitations of traceability across the supply chain through the use of public blockchain. The research's weakest link is that it only talks about public blockchains and does not consider the benefit of private or consortium blockchain utilization. Secondly, the article does not emphasize the technical and regulatory challenges that companies face while utilizing blockchain traceability across supply chains (Bischoff & Seuring, 2021).

Jawabreh et al. (2023) set the impact of supply chain management strategies on performance for hospitality companies. The sole constraint here is that the study derives evidence from a single industry—the hospitality sector—without specifying if the same holds true for other industries or not. The article is not writing about any external situation, i.e., political crisis or economic depression, on the impact of the strategies as well (Jawabreh et al., 2023).

Ali et al. (2023) present the application of AI and supply chain resilience when it comes to impacting performance, but in prioritizing supply chain dynamism. The limitation of this research is that it functions in mostly theoretical models rather than touching on empirical facts to rely on when making conclusions. Additionally, the study does not tackle technology issues that have been stifling the use of AI towards dynamic supply chains (Ali et al., 2023).

Al-Banna et al. (2023) examine investment interdependencies, Industry 4.0, and supply chain resilience. The research is constrained by having extremely wide scope in relation to a large number of ideas that could make the research not suitable for practice to use in terms of making solid, practical findings. The research lacks empirical case studies necessary when charting how the theoretical connections apply to the real world (Al-Banna et al., 2023).

Bahrami et al. (2022) explain how big data analytics enhances supply chain innovation and resilience. The main limitation of this study is that it does not mention the organizational challenges of integrating big data analytics into the existing supply chain infrastructure, i.e., data security, quality, and integration with existing systems (Bahrami et al., 2022).

Chatterjee and Chaudhuri (2022) further refer to the contribution of government policies and the capability of the firm in attaining supply chain sustainability under evolving conditions. The limitation of the study is that it addresses only the capability of the firm and does not give any significance to the contribution of external players such as the consumers or suppliers in helping to achieve sustainability. The research doesn't even have any empirical grounding but rather focuses significantly on theoretical basis (Chatterjee & Chaudhuri, 2022).

Baycik and Gowda (2023) compare the digitalization of operations and supply chains using case studies and questionnaires. The limitation of the present study is that it deals with only survey responses and case studies, which might not be in a state to provide an opinion about how complex cross-border supply chains are. This research is also pre-publication and therefore not yet exposed to critical peer review, which may compromise its validity and quality. The research does not incorporate the probable digitalization hindrances for small-scale businesses or businesses with minimal digital infrastructure (Baycik & Gowda, 2023). Sharabati et al. (2023) introduce the economic viability of solar microgrids in artificial integration and big data analysis scenarios.

One of the limitations of this research is that it considers just a single technology (solar microgrids) that could not be transferable to other energy markets or supply chains. Furthermore, the research is largely cost-benefit analysis and does not consider other possible problems, including regulatory or operational problems, that are able to influence the economic feasibility of such systems (Sharabati et al., 2023). Shahzad et al. (2020) deal with the privacy and security problem of the IoT collaborative supply chain system based on blockchain.

This work has one of the limitations that it formulates its models simulation-wise and theoretically, which will not show the real problems of the given problem of the real world, i.e., network congestion or data integrity attacks. Besides this, the research is more concerned with the technical issue of IoT and blockchain and not with the practical issue of implementation complexity in the real situation, i.e., cost and resource limitation to organizations (Shahzad et al., 2020). Norrman and Wieland (2020) explain how supply chain risk management developed with a focus on Ericsson. The limitation of the study is that it employs one company case, and that may limit the generalizability of the findings to other firms or industries.

The study does not take into account the broader industry dynamics and externalities that could influence risk management activities. Furthermore, longitudinal strategy may not be able to adapt to quick technology change and disruption that impacts supply chain resilience (Norrman & Wieland, 2020). Srai et al. (2023) explain how the war between Russia and Ukraine has affected supply chains in a reconfiguring and fragmentation manner. The biggest failure of this paper is that its geographical and political emphasis could not be replicated to analyze the problem of supply chain disruption in other conflict areas. Focus on returning from the wars in the research also may overlook fundamental strategic matters in redesigning future worldwide supply chains.

Secondly, the research is grounded on weak empirical data to substantiate its findings (Srai et al., 2023). Trivellas et al. (2020) discusses how green logistics management is essential for Greece's agri-food sector. The limitation of this study is that it only focuses on one country and one industry and that it may not represent the overall green logistics trend of the world. The study also uses a small sample size, and this impacts the generalizability of the results. Besides, it fails to provide for potential economic trade-offs involved in the introduction of green logistics practices, especially for small and medium enterprises (Trivellas et al., 2020).

Lai et al. (2020) explain the impact of collaborative decision-making on container shipping logistics service performance. The weakness of this research is that it tackles only container shipping, and the implications might thus not be generalizable to the nature of other logistics industries. In addition, the research does not have provisions for coordination with various stakeholders who have dissimilar interests in decision-making. The research also has no empirical evidence of the relationship between decision-making and performance outcomes (Lai et al., 2020). Roque Júnior et al. (2023) carry out a review of literature on supply chain maturity and resilience.

One of the limitations of this study is that it is a systematic review but does not include new empirical evidence or case studies to support the findings. The study also heavily depends on secondary sources, and this can lead to bias or limit the scope of analysis. In addition, the study does not take into account the day-to-day use of problems in implementing resilience strategies in different supply chain settings (Roque Júnior et al., 2023). Elijah et al. (2018) present an overview of the Internet of Things (IoT) and data analytics in agriculture, with the strengths and weaknesses highlighted. The biggest flaw of this research is that it is a general overview, and it may not have all the details of some applications of IoT in agriculture.

The article fails to mention the technical problem of deploying IoT solutions in developing nations where infrastructure demands can render such technologies unmass-adopted (Elijah et al., 2018). Markus and Buijs (2022) analyze the effect of blockchain on supply chain performance after hype. One of the drawbacks of this research is that it highly emphasizes the assumed benefits of blockchain without conducting an adequate assessment of the boundaries and hurdles of implementing it in supply chains. The study does not analyze the legal and regulatory framework of using blockchain technology across borders. Moreover, the research does not provide concrete examples of cases or real ways in which blockchain can be utilized effectively in existing supply chain networks (Markus & Buijs, 2022).

Hallikas et al. (2021) describe how data analytics affects procurement supply chain performance. The limitation of this research is that it analyzes procurement functions for some industries, and the findings may not be applicable to all industries. Research likewise does not incorporate any limitations on software-based data analysis or otherwise issues with the use of such technology, particularly for small firms or low-resource companies (Hallikas et al., 2021). Thakur and Breslin (2020) describe the subject matter of secure and scale-up serialization of perishables on blockchain. One of the drawbacks of the research is that it is only perishable products, and this may limit its applicability to other products in supply chains. The research does not address how it can be scaled in applying blockchain in big multi-party supply chains, which would affect its value-added application in real scenarios (Thakur & Breslin, 2020). Valashiya and Luke (2023) write about increasing supply chain information sharing with third-party logistics service providers. The limitation of the existing research is that it relies on survey feedbacks, and such feedbacks can yield response bias or measurement error.

The study also fails to account for how much technology infrastructure is leveraged in breaking and making information sharing between supply chain partners. Other than that, this study neglects security threats and data privacy prospects while transferring hidden supply chain information (Valashiya & Luke, 2023). Systematically, Jia et al. (2020) systematically reviewed soybean supply chain management and sustainability. One of the shortcomings of this research is that it deals with one crop only and may not reflect overall supply chain sustainability patterns across different commodities. Additionally, the review is not an assertion of the pragmatic concerns and trade-offs involved in adopting sustainable practices, especially among developing countries' small-scale farmers (Jia et al., 2020). Zhou et al. (2022) expound the nature and concept of the cruise supply chain by conducting an empirical examination of the cruise industry in China. Weakness of this research is that it particularly targets the Chinese cruise market and thus may not hold exactly in other markets or parts of the world.

This research misses the broad implication of international economic dislocation, geopolitical forces that have a tendency to influence the cruising supply chain.

Alongside, this study does not attempt to offer solutions to challenges of sustainability of the environment related to the tourism and hospitality sector of the modern age (Zhou et al., 2022).

The study by Hatamlah et al. (2023) is committed to the role of business intelligence adoption in reinforcing outsourced reverse supply chain operations. However, one of the flaws of this study is that it used case studies of a single industry, and therefore it will only be restricted to generalizing itself to large industries. The geographic restriction of the study and sample size can also affect the generalizability of results. Authors further did not reflect on the evolving nature of supply chain technology that can change radically fast, consequently affecting the longevity of the use of the findings (Hatamlah et al., 2023). Ali et al. (2023) explain alignment of information technology and supply chain resilience and its effects on firm performance.

One of the most limiting aspects of this study is that it is cross-sectional, i.e., it captures the data at a single point but does not track it longitudinally.

In addition, the study cannot substitute for complete external drivers like economic or environmental shocks that can probably affect supply chain resilience. The study also assumes the same IT alignment effect in all industries, which does not necessarily have to be the case in all industries (Ali et al., 2023). This study by Jazairy and von Haartman (2020) examines institutional pressure on shipping companies and logistics service providers to implement green supply chain management practice. The study is confined to institutional pressures as it can overlook the role of technology take-up or market forces, for instance, in implementing go green strategy. The research is also limited in the sense that it is qualitative data collected from relatively few case studies that may limit its use in other industry settings or geography (Jazairy & von Haartman, 2020).

Wang et al. (2020) present a two-echelon vehicle routing problem optimization model based on state-space-time network representation. The largest flaw of the study is that the model has a very ideal case when the parameters such as road condition and vehicle capacity are not fluctuated. These parameters vary considerably in actuality, which might undermine the model in the context of its relevance to actual cases. In addition, the study does not adequately consider data availability and quality while making conclusions in multicultural environments while using the model (Wang et al., 2020).

Data and collaboration are to De Boeck et al. (2023) referenced as the fundamental problems in humanitarian health supply chains. The limitation of the study is that it has limited generalizability as it only addresses health supply chains, hence possibly excluding data on other humanitarian activity fields. The study is also limited by the goodness and quality of data from real cases, which limit the validity of the solutions proposed. The study is also deficient in a critical evaluation of the cost and resources involved in implementing the proposed strategies (De Boeck et al., 2023).

Perano et al. (2023) propose a conceptual model to optimize supply chain performance through digitalization and "unphysicalization." The limitation of the existing study is that the research is theoretical in nature without the empirical testing of the model using actual scenarios. The model is also not considering the resistance of employees and stakeholders towards digitalization, which can restrict its adoption correspondingly. The study also doesn't consider problems in the adoption of digital tools in various structures of the supply chain (Perano et al., 2023). Ivanov (2021) also talks about the role of digital supply chain management and technology in generating resilience in the time of the COVID-19 pandemic.

One of the weaknesses of this study is that it only looks at the period of the pandemic, and therefore it is not possible to look at the long-term effects of digital supply chain practices. The study also does not look at the industry-specific and regional contexts, which can be highly varied and affect the validity of the results. It also argues there is a causality between technology adoption and resilience, maybe not corroborating their view (Ivanov, 2021). Likewise, Shqair and Altarazi (2022) measure Jordanian SME readiness towards embracing Industry 4.0 in their pilot study. One of the limitations of the study is that it was conducted on a relatively small population and could not possibly have been representative of all SMEs in Jordan in every possible way.

Secondly, the study is based on self-reported data, which may be susceptible to errors or biases. The research also fails to consider the probable SME limitations of adopting Industry 4.0 technologies, i.e., insufficient finance or not enough highly qualified personnel (Shqair & Altarazi, 2022). Seepma et al. (2020) theorize digital public service supply chain design from four national examples of criminal justice. One of the limitations of this research is its basis in one industry environment (criminal justice) and hence not broad regarding generalizability to other fields of public service. The research also does not provide answers to any of the problem questions regarding the digitalization of sensitive or confidential information, an issue to the public service context.

Besides, the sample applied just four countries, which is far from the goal of capturing diversity in global public service digitalization activities (Seepma et al., 2020). Stock et al. (2018) assess the ability of Industry 4.0 technologies to provide sustainable development based on qualitative criteria. The biggest limitation of the study is the utilization of qualitative data, which might not be able to capture the social and environmental impacts of Industry 4.0. The study also presumes that all companies have an equal capability to access the disclosed technologies, a presumption that is not valid in regions with weak infrastructure. Apart from that, the research employs theoretical analysis without referring to tangible examples or evidence of successful application (Stock et al., 2018).

RESEARCH GAPS

- Marginal lack of quantitative and qualitative synthesis of evidence in fully stating the contribution of digitalization towards the attainment of sustainability.
- Less research exclusively in the industries to take note of variations in the context of embracing digital technology and resiliency measures.
- Limited investigations on the causality link between digital tools and the long-term consequences of sustainability.
- Limited explications of enveloping small and medium-sized businesses (SMEs) within cross-industry digital supply chains' research.
- Limited integration of ethical and labor concerns regarding AI-facilitated digital labor in value chains (GVCs) globally.
- Unavailability of longitudinal, real-time data enabling the tracking of dynamic supply chain resilience changes with the adoption of digital.
- Reliance on self-report measures, which are prone to subjectivity or bias in the sustainability and resilience measures.
- Inability to account for according regional regulatory differences affecting digitalization and practice of sustainability.
- Inability to pursue a standard method to categorize digital tools across industries.
- Inability to conduct widespread use of advanced AI models like ResNet to other industrial data other than visual for predictive modeling of resilience.

MATERIAL AND METHODS

The research design in the current study adopts a mixed-methods research with qualitative along with quantitative data collection approach. Interview and survey were employed for the collection of data from industrial experts regarding supply chain resilience, digital supply chain technology, and sustainability practices. Preprocessing of data included cleaning, normalization, and handling missing values for enhanced robustness. Principal Component Analysis (PCA) was utilized in dimension reduction, identification of the most critical variables, and variable selection. Statistical data analysis, including regression analysis, and correlation studies were utilized in research on the connectivity between digitalization, resilience, and sustainability. The methodology involves a critical exploration of drivers of supply chain performance in the context of digital transformation.

Material

Quantitative and qualitative data collection methods were applied to collect data in this study on the interactions between supply chain resilience (SCR), digital supply chains (DSC), and industry sustainability. The sample consisted of 150 business respondents strategically located in industrial supply chains, e.g., supply chain managers, logistics coordinators, and sustainability officers. These respondents were drawn from a range of industries including manufacturing, automotive, energy, and electronics to allow for varied representation across the sector. Semi-structured interviews and questionnaires were employed to measure supply chain resilience and digitalization, in terms of participant vulnerability to disruption, risk management techniques, and supply chain adoption of digital technology.

The questionnaire of the survey also examined the applications of emerging digital technologies such as blockchain, Internet of Things (IoT), and cloud computing and how they impacted supply chain responsiveness and flexibility. Besides digitalization, the survey also enquired regarding initiatives for sustainability such as energy efficiency, environmental, social, and governance (ESG) matters, waste minimization, and application of circular economy principles. Secondary data was gathered to gather comprehensive data on the subject through publicly accessible industry reports, corporate social responsibility reports, and industrial firm case studies of firms that have adopted digital supply chain technologies.

Collected data were categorized into three wide groups: digital supply chain technologies, efforts towards resilience, and sustainability performance. SCR's key performance metrics were influenced by the level of supply chain flexibility, the level of risk avoidance, and response time towards interruptions. DSC's performance metrics were extent of use of digital technology, level of automation, and use of real-time analysis of data. Finally, the dataset adopted such measures as reduction of carbon footprint, optimal usage of resources, and optimizing waste management operations to make them sustainable. By integrating all these various pieces of information, the study wishes to examine the nexus of digital supply chains, resilience, and sustainability and whether digitalization enhances supply chain efficiency and accomodates long-term environmental and social goals.

Preprocessing

Preprocessing of the data collected involved a number of processes which had to be carried out for precision, consistency, and suitability of the data for analysis. Raw interview data and raw survey data were well cleaned for duplication, missing or inappropriateness responses. Missing or incomplete surveys with essential variables were discarded to ensure data integrity. Standardization of responses also included variables reported differently, e.g., quantitative data for supply chain resilience scores or performance against sustainability dimensions. For instance, answers to questions relating to the uptake of digital technology were given in categorical form (e.g., "high," "medium," "low") to allow comparability across sectors.

The second was to address any data outliers or anomalies. Statistical methods, e.g., the Z-score or interquartile range (IQR), were applied to identify and eliminate any data points that were far beyond the normal range. This was done in a bid to evade prejudiced findings of analysis that could attempt to manipulate the interactions between digital adoption of the supply chain, resilience, and sustainability performance. In addition, any of the categorical variables that had a very high number of levels or categories were merged into broader categories in order to ease its analysis, e.g., merging some of the digital technologies (like IoT, blockchain, and cloud computing) together under the broader "digital tools" category.

Normalization and scaling were performed for numerical variables to prevent features with different units of measurement (e.g., percentage decrease in carbon footprint vs. response time in hours) from overwhelming the result disproportionately. This was particularly required since the dataset had continuous and categorical variables and was therefore heterogeneous. For sustainability indicators, data transformation techniques like log transformation were used to rectify skewness where necessary to improve the data distribution for analysis.

Also missing data that wasn't deleted were imputed accordingly by mean or median imputation if quantitative or mode imputation if qualitative to make the dataset reliable for analysis. One of the most noteworthy things of consideration in the preprocessing was to preserve the data anonymously to maintain the confidentiality of the participants, more so for institutions that provided huge information about their supply chain practice. Preprocessed, the data was further segmented into three main domains—adoption of digital supply chain, resilience strategy, and effect on sustainability—and each of them segmented into sub categories to establish the intervariable relationships. The cleaned, normalized, and transformed data were then prepared for statistical analysis like correlation analysis, regression analysis, and clustering methods in order to be able to arrive at the conclusion regarding the impact of digitalization on supply chain sustainability and resilience.

Feature Selection

Feature selection was done using Principal Component Analysis (PCA) in an attempt to lower the dimension of the dataset and preserve the most significant information for further analysis. PCA is a statistical method that maps a set of features that are correlated to fewer such uncorrelated variables known as the principal components and these retain as much variance of the data as possible. The purpose of using PCA in the present research was to identify the most significant features as much as supply chain resilience, supply chain technologies digitally, and sustainability outcomes are involved so that the dataset is minimized without losing any crucial information.

The initial step of the PCA process was to normalize the data so that all the features are centered around a mean of zero and have a standard deviation of one since PCA is scale-sensitive. This was necessary because the dataset had variables with different scales in terms of numerical values for carbon savings, supply chain response time, and adoption of various digital tools. Following normalization, co-variance matrix was found to allow the correlation of the different variables through which principal components contributing the greatest variance could be determined.

Thereafter eigenvalues and eigenvectors were found from the covariance matrix by means of which principal components may be determined. These are linear mixes of original variables, and for each subsequent component, progressively decreasing amounts of variance are contributed compared to the immediately preceding component. In determining how many components to retain, a scree plot was run in which eigenvalues were charted from top to bottom. A cut-off, typically in terms of percentage of cumulative variance (e.g., retaining components explaining at least 80-90% of variance), was then applied to determine the number of components to retain.

The biggest weights (heaviest determinants) of the retained principal components were the most significant and thus kept for exploration. With regard to these determinants, complexity within the dataset was minimized, thus making it easier to understand relationships between most significant variables in regard to digital supply chains, resilience, and sustainability. Dimensionality reduction also helped in evading issues like multicollinearity problems, which are faced when features are highly correlated with each other. Lastly, PCA helped in better and more meaningful analysis of the contribution made by digital supply chains and resilience measures towards the attainment of sustainability outcomes in the manufacturing industry without being misled by the noise of the redundant features.

RESNET

The growth of work-at-a-distance under the paradigm of Global Value Chains (GVCs) has now been complemented by the recent trend of artificial intelligence (AI) and deep learning algorithms like Residual Networks (ResNet).

In cross-industry and cross-country GVCs, the mode of operation, more sophisticated in nature and pace, triggered growing demand for automation as well as virtual labor to perform activities to high levels of competency at low rates of intervention. ResNet, residual deep neural network architecture sub-class to be used for extremely deep network management through residual connection, is particularly designed to do just that. It learns to learn deep structures in high-data through these residual connections without issues of vanishing gradients, which is one deep network problem. In this way, ResNet derives its broad spectrum of uses in computer vision, natural language processing, and predictive analytics work that fuels the smooth operation of digital labor in GVCs. Digital labor facilitated by ResNet has transformed the nature of how corporations structure their global operations, particularly data processing, decision-making, and quality control.

For instance, in the manufacturing or logistics processes in GVCs, ResNet-driven AI machines are able to identify images or sensor inputs to identify product defects or inspect raw material quality without intervention from any human inspector, hence boosting productivity levels. Likewise in customer service, ResNet-powered AI chatbots can answer deep questions without pause, allowing business to serve global customer bases without needing to have someone on the ground in every geography. These types of platforms as such digital labor platforms offer firms centralized scalability of specific value in addressing geographically distant markets with unique labor costs and skill sets. Second, ResNet-based computerized work solutions enhance the responsiveness and adaptability of GVCs since they make them responsive to supply chain performance in real time.

For example, in supply chain and inventory management, AI systems based on deep learning can predict changes in demand, manage stock, and avoid disruption by sensing possible bottlenecks or weaknesses along the supply chain. This problem-solving in anticipation enhances supply chain resilience so much that GVCs are capable of responding in a timely manner and having the capacity to respond to altered market conditions or exogenous shocks such as natural disasters or political disturbances. Even more, eradicating repetitive work and complementing decision-making with AI, digital labor reduces the likelihood of human error and increases the precision of operations so that global supply chains become more efficient. ResNet-enabled digital labor also has serious implications concerning the possibilities of employment within GVCs.

While it can assure more productivity and less cost, it can even pose a threat to the livelihoods of workers around the world. As firms rely more on digital labor to organize supply chains, the demand for manual-labor-based work, especially in lower-level fields, could decline. Such a shift can increase labor market inequality as non-technical workers who are unable to work with or communicate using AI systems may lose their employment. At the same time, digital labor generates new employment opportunities for individuals with skills in AI, machine learning, and data science, requiring reskilling and upskilling to equip the workforce to meet such change. In addition, international diffusion of ResNet and telecommuting in GVCs also influence foreign economic forces and patterns among labor.

Through automation and AI, companies are empowered to outsource or develop services/products at low-cost locations, internationalizing workers further and subjecting companies to greater competitive pressure to digitalize. This worldwide restructuring would result in more standardized procedures of work, with work being accomplished by AI systems everywhere, and there would be more standardization and efficiency on the global level. This would be worrying in regard to workers' rights, workers' labor security, and the exploitation of labor in nations in which work remains insufficiently administered digitally or by not granting labor any access level to technological advancement. Ehe potential development of digital labor afforded through ResNet can, abstractly, change value chains at the global scale with enhanced operation efficiency, suppleness, and expansibility.

Digital work enabled by automated drudgery, improved choice making, and responsive supply chains has the potential to introduce gargantuan change into the international economy. But it is also posing issues of personnel displacement, justice, and need for other skill sets, for which consideration on the social and economic ramifications of such technology transfer must be well provided. With unlimited advancement of the technologies facilitating GVCs through realization of latest AI-based technology such as ResNet, upcoming online work will be established through realization of technological development synergy and global manpower compensatory measures.

EXPERIMENTAL RESULTS

The experimental findings of the research reveal the adverse impact of remote work on Global Value Chains (GVCs) and supply chain resilience.

This research, drawing from the deployment of sophisticated AI frameworks like Residual Networks (ResNet), recorded an unprecedented enhancement in performance efficacy and adaptability in operations across industries.

A number of main pointers like response time, reducing errors, and overall responsiveness within the supply chain were enhanced, confirming that digital work was indeed capable of streamlining complex operations. Besides, digital labor solutions enabled enhanced performance of sustainability for enhanced resource utilization as well as reduced environmental costs in most case studies. These results provide robust empirical evidence for the change-leveraging function digital labor is playing to reinvent supply chains across the globe and render them more resilient to exogenous shock. Table 1 attempts to examine intensities of correlation between take-up of digital labor and productivity levels among staff, where higher intensities of take-up correspond to higher intensities of productivity in organizations.

Table 1. Impact of digital labor on supply chain efficiency

Company ID	Supply Chain Efficiency (Score)	Digital Tool Adoption (High/Medium/Low)	Automation Level (%)	Error Reduction (%)	Time to Delivery (Days)
1	85	High	75	25	5
2	78	Medium	60	18	7
3	92	High	80	30	4
4	70	Low	45	10	10
5	88	Medium	65	22	6
6	76	High	70	20	8
7	82	Low	50	15	9
8	90	High	85	35	3
9	80	Medium	55	20	6
10	85	Low	40	12	8

Table 2 investigates the effect of digital labor on labor cost, and it finds that the highest cost savings occur in high adoption firms, while low adoption firms show minimal changes.

Table 2. Digital labor impact on sustainability outcomes

Company ID	Carbon Footprint Reduction (%)	Resource Utilization (%)	Waste Reduction (%)	Sustainability Rating (1-10)	Digital Labor Adoption (High/ Medium/Low)	Automation Impact on Sustainability (%)
1	35	60	30	9	High	40
2	28	50	20	7	Medium	25
3	45	70	40	10	High	50
4	15	40	10	5	Low	15
5	30	55	25	8	Medium	30
6	20	45	12	6	High	20
7	25	50	18	7	Low	18
8	50	80	45	10	High	55
9	40	65	35	9	Medium	40
10	22	48	15	6	Low	20

Table 3 highlights efficiency in the supply chain, digital labor yielding strong gains in efficiency, particularly from high adoption firms.

Table 3. Impact of digital labor on supply chain resilience

Company ID	Supply Chain Disruption (Days)	Risk Mitigation Score	Resilience Score (1-10)	Real-time Data Utilization (%)	Digital Labor Implementation (High/ Medium/Low)	Crisis Response Time (Hours)
1	2	85	9	75	High	2
2	5	70	7	60	Medium	6
3	1	90	10	80	High	1
4	10	50	5	40	Low	12
5	3	78	8	65	Medium	4
6	4	75	8	70	High	5
7	6	60	6	55	Low	8
8	1	92	10	85	High	1
9	4	80	8	60	Medium	6
10	5	65	7	50	Low	7

Table 4 discusses operation risk management, highlighting how digital labor mitigates risk, and high adoption level minimizes the risk exposure as well as the recovery time enormously.

Table 4. Digital labor and automation levels

Company ID	Automation Level (%)	Use of AI in Decision-Making (Yes/No)	Average Employee Skill Level (1-10)	Adoption of IoT in GVC (High/ Medium/Low)	Blockchain Adoption (Yes/No)	Cloud Computing Adoption (High/ Medium/Low)
1	75	Yes	9	High	Yes	High
2	60	No	7	Medium	No	Medium
3	80	Yes	10	High	Yes	High
4	45	No	5	Low	No	Low
5	65	Yes	8	Medium	Yes	Medium
6	70	Yes	9	High	Yes	High
7	50	No	6	Low	No	Low
8	85	Yes	10	High	Yes	High
9	55	No	7	Medium	No	Medium
10	40	No	5	Low	No	Low

Table 5 quantifies workforce satisfaction, where digital labor enhances job satisfaction, with higher adoption leading to higher employee satisfaction.

Table 5. Sustainability metrics across GVCs

Company ID	Energy Efficiency (%)	Water Conservation (%)	Waste Reduction (%)	Carbon Emissions Reduction (%)	Sustainability Rating (1-10)	Circular Economy Implementation (%)
1	65	50	30	40	9	75
2	50	40	20	30	7	60
3	70	60	45	55	10	80
4	30	25	10	15	5	30
5	60	48	25	35	8	70
6	55	42	18	22	6	50
7	50	38	15	20	7	55
8	80	75	50	60	10	85
9	65	53	30	40	9	75
10	45	32	12	18	6	40

Table 6 illustrates the impact on supply chain resilience, with digital labor contributing to better risk avoidance and supply chain flexibility, especially in companies with higher digital labor integration.

Table 6. Industry-wide digital transformation impact on supply chains

Industry Type	Digital Transformation Score (1-10)	Adoption of AI/ML (%)	Automation Level (%)	Digital Labor Integration (Yes/No)	Sustainability Impact (%)
Manufacturing	9	75	70	Yes	40
Retail	8	65	60	Yes	35
Healthcare	7	55	50	No	30
Automotive	10	85	80	Yes	45
Logistics	9	80	75	Yes	50
Pharmaceuticals	6	50	40	No	25
Agriculture	5	45	35	No	20
Energy	8	70	65	Yes	42
Electronics	10	90	85	Yes	48
Construction	7	60	55	Yes	30

Table 7 investigates the contribution of digital labor to greater supply chain flexibility, with higher levels of adoption producing greater agility and adaptability.

Table 7. Risk mitigation in GVCs with digital labor

Company ID	Risk Identification Accuracy (%)	Supply Chain Disruption Mitigated (%)	Risk Management Score (1-10)	Time to Recovery (Days)	Digital Labor Adoption Level (High/Medium/Low)	AI Integration in Risk Assessment (%)
1	80	85	9	2	High	75
2	70	65	7	5	Medium	60
3	90	95	10	1	High	85
4	50	40	5	10	Low	50
5	75	80	8	3	Medium	70
6	78	82	8	4	High	72
7	60	55	6	8	Low	55
8	95	98	10	1	High	90
9	70	72	7	5	Medium	65
10	65	60	6	7	Low	60

Table 8 offers a post-digital labor risk assessment analysis and finds that high adoption companies have a high level of exposure to risk reduction and shortened recovery times.

Table 8. Supply chain risk assessment post-digital labor adoption

Company ID	Risk Exposure Reduction (%)	Risk Recovery Time (Hours)	Supply Chain Risk Score (1-10)	Digital Labor Adoption Level	Automation Impact on Risk Mitigation (%)	AI-Driven Decision Support Utilization (%)
1	80	3	9	High	70	75
2	65	6	7	Medium	55	60
3	90	2	10	High	80	85
4	40	10	5	Low	30	40
5	75	4	8	Medium	60	70
6	78	5	8	High	65	72
7	55	8	6	Low	50	55
8	98	1	10	High	85	90
9	72	7	7	Medium	60	65
10	60	9	6	Low	50	60

Table 9 explores the relationship between digital labor and sustainability and finds that high adoption results in better sustainability performance, including carbon reduction and waste management effectiveness.

Table 9. Correlation between digital labor and supply chain sustainability

Company ID	Sustainability Score (1-10)	Digital Labor Adoption (High/Medium/Low)	Digital Tools Utilized (%)	Carbon Reduction (%)	Waste Management Efficiency (%)
1	9	High	75	40	35
2	7	Medium	60	30	25
3	10	High	85	50	45
4	5	Low	45	15	10
5	8	Medium	65	35	30
6	6	High	70	20	18
7	7	Low	50	25	20
8	10	High	80	60	55
9	9	Medium	65	40	35
10	6	Low	40	18	15

Table 10 takes into account the broader realignment in GVCs with digital labor using AI by observing that companies utilizing AI achieve greater productivity, flexibility, efficiency, and overall improvement in transformation.

Table 10. GVCs transformation via AI-driven digital labor

Company ID	AI Utilization (%)	Digital Labor Productivity Increase (%)	Supply Chain Flexibility (%)	Efficiency Gains (%)	Automation Impact (%)	Overall Transformation Score (1-10)
1	85	30	50	45	60	9
2	70	20	40	35	50	7
3	90	40	60	50	70	10
4	55	15	30	25	40	5
5	75	25	45	40	55	8
6	80	30	50	45	60	9
7	60	20	35	30	50	6
8	95	45	65	55	80	10

continued on following page

Table 10. Continued

Company ID	AI Utilization (%)	Digital Labor Productivity Increase (%)	Supply Chain Flexibility (%)	Efficiency Gains (%)	Automation Impact (%)	Overall Transformation Score (1-10)
9	70	20	40	35	50	7
10	50	10	25	20	40	6

CASE-SPECIFIC VERIFICATION OF CLAIMS

1. Sectoral Comparisons: Verify digital transformation impacts across sectors (e.g., electronics vs. textiles) to ascertain sectoral GVC dynamics.
2. Regional Divergence: Compare GVC resilience in advanced vs. emerging regions (e.g., EU vs. Southeast Asia) to identify contextual dependencies.
3. Supply Chain Tiering: Investigate how upstream vs. downstream companies in GVCs are impacted and react differently to digital disruption.
4. Policy Environment Impacts: Compare nations with robust digital infrastructure policies (e.g., South Korea) to nations with nascent frameworks (e.g., African countries).
5. COVID-19 Case Studies: Confirm how various industries reorganized their GVCs during the pandemic with AI/digitalization (e.g., pharma versus automotive industries).
6. Environmental Impacts by Industry: Create digital GVC sustainability trade-offs in resource-based versus service industries.
7. SMEs vs. MNCs: Analyze the impact of firm size on the feasibility and impact of AI and digital tool uptake in GVC management.
8. Labor Market Impacts: Contrast digital labor substitution in labor-intensive sectors (e.g., agriculture) versus capital-intensive sectors (e.g., aerospace).
9. Climate Risk Exposure: Confirm GVC digital resilience in climate risk-exposed sectors (e.g., agriculture, mining).
10. Digital Maturity Levels: Test hypotheses across industries with differences in digital maturity levels (e.g., construction and fintech) to generalize.

CASE STUDIES

Auto Industry – Chip Shortage (Global, 2020–2022)

Challenge: COVID-19 revealed the auto industry's excessive dependence on East Asian chip makers.
Impact: Production shutdown at the likes of Toyota and Ford because of supply chain disruption.
Digital GVC Insight: Failure of real-time digital inventory and supplier visibility resulted in delay.
Lesson: necessity of predictive analysis and AI-facilitated supply chain risk management software.

Apparel Production - Bangladesh (Recovery After Pandemic)

Challenge: Orders cancelled by Western buyers during the pandemic, which inundated Bangladeshi manufacturers and accrued outstanding invoices.
Impact: Deep economic hardship for SMEs and labourers.
Digital GVC Insight: Part incomplete digital linkage among producers and purchasers disrupted punctual coordination.
Lesson: Blockchain or web-based contract sites may circumscribe payment disputes and increase transparency.

Agriculture and Food – West African Cocoa Supply Challenge

Challenge: Deforestation and child labor issues created escalating EU bans on cocoa imports.
Impact: Ivory Coast and Ghana's small farmers were unable to adapt.
Digital GVC Insight: Few countries have digital traceability technology.
Lesson: Computerized traceability systems will bring compliance as well as access to markets.

Electronics Production – Vietnam-China Tensions

Challenge: US-China trade tensions compelled American corporations such as Apple to shift part of their GVCs to Vietnam.
Impact: Infrastructure bottlenecks and skill mismatch of labor faced Vietnam.
Digital GVC Insight: Disruptive GVC relocation exposed local capacity and digital readiness constraints.

Lesson: Financing regional digital infrastructure must precede or match aspirations for GVC relocation.

Pharmaceuticals – India's API Dependence on China

Challenge: Indian excessive dependence on China for Active Pharmaceutical Ingredients (APIs) broke during COVID.
Impact: Medicine shortage and price hike in major medicine.
Digital GVC Insight: Absence of cross-country integration of production and inventory data.
Learning: AI-based coordination platforms at the regional level can construct pharmaceutical supply chain resilience.

IMPLICATIONS

1. Strategic Investment in Technology: Companies need to synchronize digital adoption with resilience and sustainability goals with a view to achieving maximum return on investment and sustainability in the long run.
2. Policy and Regulation: Governments need to develop regulations favorable to ethical utilization of AI and sustainable industrial practice.
3. Workforce Transition: More digital work and AI architecture design such as ResNet can replace unskilled labor, and hence the necessity for live upskilling initiatives.
4. Industry Synergy: Knowledge transfer between industries can assist in accelerating the move towards sustainable digital and supply chain solutions.
5. Corporate Responsibility: With greater transparency through digital formats, corporations are held more accountable to their ESG scores and disruption recovery.

FUTURE DIRECTIONS

1. Build Hybrid Models: Integrate qualitative and quantitative data more securely with mixed-method designs or AI-based insights to gain more incisive analysis.
2. Incorporate Longitudinal Studies: Monitor supply chain development over time to measure the changing effect of digitalization on resilience and sustainability.
3. Industry-Specific Deep Dives: Perform sectoral studies to apply digitization-specific methods to optimal effect (e.g., automotive vs. energy).

4. Scale AI Applications: Apply deep architectures such as ResNet not just on images or sensor data but even to identify patterns in non-visual supply chain data.
5. Ethical AI Implementation: Research worker effects of digitization and provide best practices for fair transitions for workers.
6. Standardized Metrics Development: Create globally accepted metrics for digital adoption, resilience, and sustainability performance.
7. SME Challenges Research: Investigate the adoption of low-cost digital supply chain technology by small and medium-sized businesses.
8. Real-Time Testing: Apply IoT and cloud infrastructure for real-time testing and predictive resilience in supply chains.
9. Global Frameworks: Establish global frameworks to achieve digital innovation, work, and environmental equity.

    10.Interdisciplinary Research: Encourage collaboration between engineers, data scientists, and social scientists to tackle difficult, systems-level supply chain issues.

CONCLUSION

The changing patterns of global value chains (GVCs) value resilience, openness, and digital linkages across industries and geographies. Extreme instances in the global economy—e.g., semiconductor defects in the automobile sector, regulatory problems with West African cocoa production—barely underscore repeated system weaknesses due to over-reliance, exposed digital infrastructure, and disconnected flows of information. The COVID-19 pandemic, trade disruption, and policy response have also served to highlight further the role of digital technologies like AI, blockchain, and real-time analysis in risk mitigation and coordination. Resilience of GVCs in the future will depend on investments in digital infrastructure in the future, building capacity within SMEs, and cross-border collaboration. Through the acquisition of lessons from sector-specific case studies, companies as well as policymakers are in the best position to influence adaptive measures towards more sustainable, inclusive, and technology-driven value chains in the future.

REFERENCES

Al-Banna, A., Rana, Z. A., Yaqot, M., & Menezes, B. (2023). Interconnectedness between supply chain resilience, Industry 4.0, and investment. *Logistics (Basel)*, *7*(3), 50. DOI: 10.3390/logistics7030050

Alfalla-Luque, R., Luján García, D. E., & Marin-Garcia, J. A. (2023). Supply chain agility and performance: Evidence from a meta-analysis. *International Journal of Operations & Production Management*, *43*(10), 1587–1633. DOI: 10.1108/IJOPM-05-2022-0316

Ali, A., Ismail, I. H. M., & Abulehia, A. (2023). Supply chain resilience and information technology alignment on firm performance. *International Journal of Academic Management Science Research*, *7*(1), 1–11.

Ali, A. A. A., Udin, Z. B. M., & Abualrejal, H. M. E. (2023). The impact of artificial intelligence and supply chain resilience on the companies' supply chain performance: The moderating role of supply chain dynamism. In Al-Emran, M., Al-Sharafi, M. A., & Shaalan, K. (Eds.), *International Conference on Information Systems and Intelligent Applications* (pp. 17–28). Springer. DOI: 10.1007/978-3-031-16865-9_2

Bahrami, M., Shokouhyar, S., & Seifian, A. (2022). Big data analytics capability and supply chain performance: The mediating roles of supply chain resilience and innovation. *Modern Supply Chain Research and Applications*, *4*(1), 62–84. DOI: 10.1108/MSCRA-11-2021-0021

Baycik, N. O., & Gowda, S. (2023). Digitalization of operations and supply chains: Insights from survey and case studies. *Digital Transformation and Society*, *2*(3), 231–245. DOI: 10.1108/DTS-03-2023-0012

Belhadi, A., Mani, V., Kamble, S. S., Khan, S. A. R., & Verma, S. (2024). Artificial intelligence-driven innovation for enhancing supply chain resilience and performance under the effect of supply chain dynamism: An empirical investigation. *Annals of Operations Research*, *333*(2-3), 627–652. DOI: 10.1007/s10479-021-03956-x PMID: 33551534

Bischoff, O., & Seuring, S. (2021). Opportunities and limitations of public blockchain-based supply chain traceability. *Modern Supply Chain Research and Applications*, *3*(4), 226–243. DOI: 10.1108/MSCRA-07-2021-0014

Chatterjee, S., & Chaudhuri, R. (2022). Supply chain sustainability during turbulent environment: Examining the role of firm capabilities and government regulation. *Operations Management Research : Advancing Practice Through Research*, *15*(3-4), 1081–1095. DOI: 10.1007/s12063-021-00203-1

De Boeck, K., Besiou, M., Decouttere, C., Rafter, S., Vandaele, N., Van Wassenhove, L. N., & Yadav, P. (2023). Data, analytical techniques and collaboration between researchers and practitioners in humanitarian health supply chains: A challenging but necessary way forward. *Journal of Humanitarian Logistics and Supply Chain Management*, *13*(3), 237–248. DOI: 10.1108/JHLSCM-07-2022-0078

Deepu, T. S., & Ravi, V. (2023). A review of literature on implementation and operational dimensions of supply chain digitalization: Framework development and future research directions. *International Journal of Information Management Data Insights*, *3*(1), 100156. DOI: 10.1016/j.jjimei.2023.100156

Elijah, O., Rahman, T. A., Orikumhi, I., Leow, C. Y., & Hindia, M. N. (2018). An overview of Internet of Things (IoT) and data analytics in agriculture: Benefits and challenges. *IEEE Internet of Things Journal*, *5*(5), 3758–3773. DOI: 10.1109/JIOT.2018.2844296

Hallikas, J., Immonen, M., & Brax, S. (2021). Digitalizing procurement: The impact of data analytics on supply chain performance. *Supply Chain Management*, *26*(5), 629–646. DOI: 10.1108/SCM-05-2020-0201

Hatamlah, H., Allahham, M., Abu-AlSondos, I. A., Al-junaidi, A., Al-Anati, G. M., & Al-Shaikh, M. (2023). The role of business intelligence adoption as a mediator of big data analytics in the management of outsourced reverse supply chain operations. *Applied Mathematics & Information Sciences*, *17*(5), 897–903. DOI: 10.18576/amis/170516

Hatamlah, H., Allan, M., Abu-Alsondos, I., Shehadeh, M., & Allahham, M. (2023). The role of artificial intelligence in supply chain analytics during the pandemic. *Uncertain Supply Chain Management*, *11*(3), 1175–1186. DOI: 10.5267/j.uscm.2023.4.005

Herold, D. M., Nowicka, K., Pluta-Zaremba, A., & Kummer, S. (2021). COVID-19 and the pursuit of supply chain resilience: Reactions and "lessons learned" from logistics service providers (LSPs). *Supply Chain Management*, *26*(6), 702–714. DOI: 10.1108/SCM-09-2020-0439

Ivanov, D. (2021). Digital supply chain management and technology to enhance resilience by building and using end-to-end visibility during the COVID-19 pandemic. *IEEE Transactions on Engineering Management*. Advance online publication. DOI: 10.1109/TEM.2021.3096274

Ivanov, D., & Dolgui, A. (2020). Viability of intertwined supply networks: Extending the supply chain resilience angles towards survivability. A position paper motivated by COVID-19 outbreak. *International Journal of Production Research*, *58*(10), 2904–2915. DOI: 10.1080/00207543.2020.1750727

Jawabreh, O., Baadhem, A. M., Ali, B. J. A., Atta, A. A. B., Ali, A., Al-Hosaini, F. F., & Allahham, M. (2023). The influence of supply chain management strategies on organizational performance in hospitality industry. *Applied Mathematics & Information Sciences*, *17*(5), 851–858. DOI: 10.18576/amis/170511

Jazairy, A., & von Haartman, R. (2020). Analysing the institutional pressures on shippers and logistics service providers to implement green supply chain management practices. *International Journal of Logistics*, *23*(1), 44–84. DOI: 10.1080/13675567.2019.1584163

Jia, F., Peng, S., Green, J., Koh, L., & Chen, X. (2020). Soybean supply chain management and sustainability: A systematic literature review. *Journal of Cleaner Production*, *255*, 120254. DOI: 10.1016/j.jclepro.2020.120254

Lai, P. L., Su, D. T., Tai, H. H., & Yang, C. C. (2020). The impact of collaborative decision-making on logistics service performance for container shipping services. *Maritime Business Review*, *5*(2), 175–191. DOI: 10.1108/MABR-12-2019-0061

Markus, S., & Buijs, P. (2022). Beyond the hype: How blockchain affects supply chain performance. *Supply Chain Management*, *27*(2), 177–193. DOI: 10.1108/SCM-03-2022-0109

Norrman, A., & Wieland, A. (2020). The development of supply chain risk management over time: Revisiting Ericsson. *International Journal of Physical Distribution & Logistics Management*, *50*(6), 641–666. DOI: 10.1108/IJPDLM-07-2019-0219

Nwagwu, U., Niaz, M., Chukwu, M. U., & Saddique, F. (2023). The influence of artificial intelligence to enhancing supply chain performance under the mediating significance of supply chain collaboration in manufacturing and logistics organizations in Pakistan. *Traditional Journal of Multidisciplinary Sciences*, *1*(1), 29–40.

Perano, M., Cammarano, A., Varriale, V., Del Regno, C., Michelino, F., & Caputo, M. (2023). Embracing supply chain digitalization and unphysicalization to enhance supply chain performance: A conceptual framework. *International Journal of Physical Distribution & Logistics Management*, *53*(5/6), 628–659. DOI: 10.1108/IJPDLM-06-2022-0201

Rahman, M. S., Gani, M. O., Fatema, B., & Takahashi, Y. (2023). B2B firms' supply chain resilience orientation in achieving sustainable supply chain performance. *Sustainable Manufacturing and Service Economics*, *2*, 100011. DOI: 10.1016/j.smse.2023.100011

Rejeb, A., & Rejeb, K. (2020). Blockchain and supply chain sustainability. *LogForum*, *16*(3), 363–372. DOI: 10.17270/J.LOG.2020.467

Roque Júnior, L. C., Frederico, G. F., & Costa, M. L. N. (2023). Maturity and resilience in supply chains: A systematic review of the literature. *International Journal of Industrial Engineering and Operations Management*, *5*(1), 1–25. DOI: 10.1108/IJIEOM-08-2022-0035

Sarkar, A., Routroy, S., & Sultan, F. A. (2022). The impact of co-creation and co-invention in supply chains: A bibliometric review. *Arab Gulf Journal of Scientific Research*, *40*(4), 364–391. DOI: 10.1108/AGJSR-04-2022-0010

Seepma, A. P., de Blok, C., & Van Donk, D. P. (2020). Designing digital public service supply chains: Four country-based cases in criminal justice. *Supply Chain Management*, *26*(4), 418–446. DOI: 10.1108/SCM-03-2020-0090

Shahzad, A., Zhang, K., & Gherbi, A. (2020). Intuitive development to examine collaborative IoT supply chain system underlying privacy and security levels and perspective powering through proactive blockchain. *Sensors (Basel)*, *20*(13), 3760. DOI: 10.3390/s20133760 PMID: 32635589

Sharabati, A. A., Allahham, M., Yahiya, A., Ahmad, B., & Sabra, S. (2023). Effects of artificial integration and big data analysis on economic viability of solar microgrids: Mediating role of cost benefit analysis. *Operations Research in Engineering Sciences: Theory and Applications*, *6*(2), 360–379. DOI: 10.31181/oresta2302082s

Shqair, M. I., & Altarazi, S. A. (2022). Evaluating the status of SMEs in Jordan with respect to Industry 4.0: A pilot study. *Logistics (Basel)*, *6*(4), 69. DOI: 10.3390/logistics6040069

Srai, J. S., Graham, G., Van Hoek, R., Joglekar, N., & Lorentz, H. (2023). Impact pathways: Unhooking supply chains from conflict zones—Reconfiguration and fragmentation lessons from the Ukraine–Russia war. *International Journal of Operations & Production Management*, *43*(13), 289–301. DOI: 10.1108/IJOPM-08-2022-0529

Stock, T., Obenaus, M., Kunz, S., & Kohl, H. (2018). Industry 4.0 as enabler for a sustainable development: A qualitative assessment of its ecological and social potential. *Process Safety and Environmental Protection*, *118*, 254–267. DOI: 10.1016/j.psep.2018.06.026

Thakur, S., & Breslin, J. G. (2020). Scalable and secure product serialization for multi-party perishable good supply chains using blockchain. *Internet of Things : Engineering Cyber Physical Human Systems*, *11*, 100253. DOI: 10.1016/j.iot.2020.100253

Trivellas, P., Malindretos, G., & Reklitis, P. (2020). Implications of green logistics management on sustainable business and supply chain performance: Evidence from a survey in the Greek agri-food sector. *Sustainability (Basel)*, *12*(24), 10515. DOI: 10.3390/su122410515

Valashiya, M. C., & Luke, R. (2023). Enhancing supply chain information sharing with third party logistics service providers. *International Journal of Logistics Management*, *34*(6), 1523–1542. DOI: 10.1108/IJLM-11-2021-0522

Wang, Y., Yuan, Y., Guan, X., Xu, M., Wang, L., Wang, H., & Liu, Y. (2020). Collaborative two-echelon multicenter vehicle routing optimization based on state–space–time network representation. *Journal of Cleaner Production*, *258*, 120590. DOI: 10.1016/j.jclepro.2020.120590

Zhou, J., & Chen, S. L. (2022). The concept of the cruise supply chain and its characteristics: An empirical study of China's cruise industry. *Maritime Business Review*, *7*(3), 196–221. DOI: 10.1108/MABR-06-2021-0046

Chapter 12

Data Colonialism: The Silent Force Behind Global Inequality

Usharani Bhimavarapu
https://orcid.org/0000-0002-0246-1420
Department of Computer Science and Engineering, Koneru Lakshmaiah Education Foundation, India

ABSTRACT

Digital Colonialism and Inequality represent a new front of global power, in which control over technology and data reinforces inequalities between nations and populations. The rapid expansion of digital technologies has brought about an uneven access to, and use of, knowledge and resources, predominantly benefiting a privileged minority at the expense of others. This is achieved as a digital divide, in which economically underdeveloped or backward regions are largely cut off from the digital economy and sharing of knowledge. The concept of digital colonialism proceeds to explore how data extraction, algorithmic control, and platform monopolies shape global power dynamics that increase existing inequalities. Employing bi-stacked Artificial Neural Networks (ANNs), the present work investigates the complex interaction among technological systems, human behavior, and socio-political forces behind digital inequality.

INTRODUCTION

Digital colonialism involves the domination and control of dominant nations and corporations over digital infrastructures and data in developing countries. This is a new colonialism precipitated by the rapid development of the digital economy and the globalized internet. With the rise in technology and digital platforms being

DOI: 10.4018/979-8-3373-1727-4.ch012

more central to every area of life, it is the people who own these platforms that enjoy an enormous amount of power. The Global North nations and corporations have dominated a large part of the digital space, having systems that are economically, politically, and socially lucrative for them. Developing nations risk becoming digital vassals that lack full sovereignty in the digital sphere.

Control over data is one of the primary features of digital colonialism. Data. For many, data is referred to as the new oil, a resource that lubricates the global economy of today. It's collected. For storage and used. It has significant economic impact, but most of it is taken from people in the Global South without proper remuneration or ownership. It is then used by corporations to create algorithms that bolster current power structures and increase their power within the global market. This uneven control of data perpetuates global power inequities, as poorer countries are still reliant on the technological platform of richer countries. The digital divide is perhaps the most obvious form of digital inequality.

Technology, the internet, and digital services are not evenly distributed around the globe. In most parts of the world, especially the Global South, there is a major segment of society that has no access to high-speed internet, devices, and digital skills. This creates an economic divide where developed countries and companies can use digital technologies to increase productivity, innovation, and wealth while poorer countries are left behind. The denial of access to technology hinders economic development and worsens inequality and impedes developing nations' capacity to engage in the world economy. Digital colonialism is not merely about economic domination but also cultural hegemony. Western technology monopolies like Google, Facebook, and Amazon are the gatekeepers of digital content. These entities influence the information and entertainment people consume around the world, usually advancing Western ideology, values, and way of life.

Consequently, non-Western voices and cultures tend to be silenced, producing a kind of cultural imperialism. Western-dominated narratives are spread all over the world and challenge local cultures, languages, and traditions, sustaining a homogenized global culture with the economic interests of richer countries at its center.

Increased digital technologies also led to the birth of a novel kind of surveillance capitalism, in which individuals' personal information is continuously gathered, scanned, and sold. This system of surveillance disproportionately affects populations in the global South, where data protection legislation and regulatory structures are typically weaker or absent. Multinational corporations and states through electronic platforms have greater than ever before access to individual data, which allows them to control, influence, and manipulate people.

In nations where privacy rights are weakly ensured, citizens become objects of online observation, reproducing an imbalance of power by which the Global North exerts authority over the lives and identities of individuals in the Global South. The digital foundations within most nations are dominated by multinational corporations in richer nations. This leaves emerging economies dependent on foreign players to provide them with vital services like banking, communication, and healthcare. For example, mobile payment platforms such as PayPal and foreign-controlled mobile networks tend to dominate the emerging economies, and native companies have very few options.

This reliance reinforces existing power disequilibria, since local governments and industries have little leverage over these key services, which tend to be expensive and lack customization or localization flexibility. Digital platforms are now instruments of great influence for propagandizing mass opinion and effecting political change. Foreign digital platforms are utilized in most nations to manipulate elections, propagandize disinformation, and undermine political processes. Digital colonialism makes it possible for powerful states or corporate interests to enter the domestic politics of weaker states through targeted cyber campaigns.

The interventions have the effect of manipulating democratic processes, diluting political sovereignty, and consolidating political and economic interests of the occupiers. This means the domestic political environment in developing countries becomes ever more dominated by foreign powers, which get to influence policies to suit their interests. The digital intellectual property control is the other important feature of digital colonialism. In most instances, corporations in the Global North own the patents, algorithms, and technologies that fuel the digital economy. This translates to a scenario where nations in the Global South cannot build their own technological innovations without rendering royalties or licensing fees to outsiders. The intellectual property regimes, which are typically influenced by richer countries, serve to shield the interests of transnational corporations while constraining the capability of the developing world to innovate and compete in the international arena.

This suppresses technological and scientific developments in the Global South. Digital colonialism has an environmental dimension too. The production of raw materials for digital technologies, like rare earth minerals employed in smartphones and computers, is frequently located in developing nations. These nations suffer a great deal of environmental damage due to multinational corporations extracting resources with minimum consideration of sustainability or environmentalism. Disposal wastes from electronic devices are frequently exported to nations with less stringent environmental regulations, further contributing to pollution and health hazards.

Consequently, developing countries suffer the environmental price of the digital economy, while richer nations gain financially. With ongoing digital colonialism, the international balance of power will likely be transformed in the decades to come. The power to own digital infrastructure, access information, and shape political and cultural frameworks provides dominant countries and corporations with a new style of soft power. The Global South will become perpetually dominated by digital imperialism if it does not implement steps to make technology, data, and digital services equally accessible. This can be prevented by developing countries advocating for tighter regulation, defending digital sovereignty, and developing indigenous innovation.

It is only by taking actions and revising policies together that the digital divide can be bridged to achieve a more equitable global digital economy. This research is mainly concerned with the performativity of security devices and their political effects. The shortcoming of this work is that it has a limited focus, being concerned mostly with the European setting, and may fail to address the dynamics of digital security and colonialism in non-European contexts (Amicelle et al., 2015). Arendt's research into totalitarianism and its historical foundations offers useful critical insights into power configurations, but it has been criticized for failing to consider the contemporary digital age and its impact on totalitarian regimes in the frame of digital colonialism (Arendt, 2004). While this paper provides significant contributions to understanding digital geographies, it is constrained by its general considerations of Western cities and the absence of a critical examination of digital inequality in the Global South, where colonial dynamics could have another expression (Ash et al., 2018). Burrows' critique of the H-index as an academic measure raises important issues but does not touch on what digital colonialism may mean in the academic arena or the disparities of access to scholarly tools and resources, especially in underdeveloped countries (Burrows, 2012).

Burton-Jones offers a thorough description of knowledge capitalism, but the book fails to capture the socio-political dimensions driving the control and distribution of knowledge, particularly the impact of colonial legacies on world knowledge economies (Burton-Jones, 1999).

Busch's study of the rise of neoliberalism in the takeover of higher education provides insightful and critical views on how knowledge is commercialized. But it does not adequately address the role of digital technologies as instruments of neocolonial domination in the international education system (Busch, 2017).

Castro-Gómez offers a postcolonial critique of knowledge but bases his arguments on Latin American viewpoints, which may restrict the applicability of his findings to other regions of the world undergoing various forms of digital colonialism (Castro-Gómez, 2008).

Though this book critically engages coloniality, it does not entirely include the use of modern-day digital technologies and how they can reproduce or perpetuate colonial power relations in the digital era, more so the availability of data and information (Castro-Gómez, 2021).

Creswell's focus on qualitative research skills is beneficial in understanding human behaviors in virtual spaces, but his design does not explore how digital inequality impacts qualitative research results, particularly when conducting research with marginalized groups (Creswell, 2015).

Datta's report on Indian smart cities offers insightful explanations of digital postcolonialism, yet the focus of the study on cities could conceal the rural-urban digital divide and the wider implications of digital colonialism in less urbanized areas (Datta, 2017).

This paper addresses the stress generated by rankings and reputation but does not take into account how these measures might differentially impact scholars and institutions in postcolonial areas, further fueling global disparities (Espeland & Sauder, 2016).

Eubanks' research on inequality within the context of automation is seminal but does not account for the ways in which algorithmic systems can create digital colonialism, especially in areas with poor access to technology and heavy reliance on algorithmic-driven decisions (Eubanks, 2018).

Although this research addresses the massification of higher education, it fails to fully examine the digital inequalities students in the Global South have to contend with, whereby the reach of education technology is often restricted by historical and economic determinants (Evans et al., 2021).

Facer and Selwyn offer worthwhile considerations of digital technology and education but do not come to terms with how digital inequalities are mediated by colonial histories of the past, especially in non-Western education systems (Facer & Selwyn, 2021).

This paper concerns the use of business intelligence in the higher education setting. Nonetheless, it does not give a proper explanation of how these business practices can reinforce contemporary inequalities in access to digital devices or worsen the digital divide in postcolonial areas (Guster & Brown, 2012).

Although this research is basic to learning about stereotyping, it misses the point of how technology can be used to help perpetuate stereotypes, especially through biased algorithms that disproportionately impact marginalized groups (Hamilton & Gifford, 1976).

The ethnographic guidelines under discussion are important in grasping digital behaviors, yet the authors fail to examine how the digital divide affects ethnographic research, particularly where digital technology access is not equal (Hammersley & Atkinson, 2007).

Haraway's feminist view of knowledge is compelling, though it doesn't capture fully the modern means by which digital technologies mediate knowledge and power, specifically around digital colonialism and the access divide (Haraway, 1988).

Harvey's criticism of capitalism and its contradictions is useful to comprehend economic systems, but it does not provide a detailed examination of how digital colonialism feeds into global inequalities in regards to technological access and control (Harvey, 2014).

Isin and Ruppert's analysis of sensory power during the pandemic captures significant shifts in data collection and surveillance but neglects how these data practices can disproportionately impact Global South marginalized communities (Isin & Ruppert, 2020).

Jiang and Pardos are interested in algorithmic fairness within classrooms, but their work does not include a more general discussion of how such algorithms could perpetuate already-existing power dynamics and lead to digital colonialism, especially in impoverished areas (Jiang & Pardos, 2021).

Although Josselson's contribution is useful in the understanding of ethics in narrative research, it fails to consider how digital colonialism affects the process of data collection, especially in the developing world where the availability of digital tools is limited (Josselson, 1996).

This book on smart cities centers on innovation and urban politics but does not examine in depth how the digital turn in city building disproportionately impacts areas with less digital infrastructure, making global inequalities worse (Karvonen et al., 2018).

Leibowitz's consideration of dehegemonizing colonial knowledge is astute, yet the book does not examine extensively how digital technology is rewriting knowledge creation in a way that may reinforce colonial relations (Leibowitz, 2017).

Though Lane and Finsel write about big data's influence on universities, their work does not consider the effects of data-driven decision-making systems in areas with limited access to such technologies, further cementing digital disparity (Lane & Finsel, 2014).

Mouton and Burns talk of digital neo-colonialism in smart cities, but their research is primarily concerned with urban areas in advanced nations, while overlooking the varied forms of digital colonialism in less developed countries (Mouton & Burns, 2021).

Musa's smart city roadmap is a valuable input, but it does not take into account the consequences of digital colonialism in the production of smart cities and how such undertakings are likely to exclude rural and disadvantaged groups (Musa, 2016).

Olssen's advocacy of the welfare state and publicly provided education is a New Zealand-specific worldview, thus confining its relevance to other countries. Therefore, the analysis might not reproduce the complexity of neoliberal education reforms in nations with dissimilar socio-political contexts (Olssen, 1996).

Olssen and Peters' examination of neoliberalism and the knowledge economy targets a wide theoretical framework without empirical evidence to substantiate their arguments. The contention that higher education is being reconstituted as a knowledge capitalism system cannot be wholly used across all areas or institutions of learning, particularly those in developing economies (Olssen & Peters, 2007).

While Olufemi's analysis of feminism provides a critical disruption of power dynamics, the book's focus on theoretical concepts may overlook practical challenges in implementing feminist principles in diverse contexts. Furthermore, it does not deeply engage with intersections of feminism with other social justice movements beyond a few key areas (Olufemi, 2020).

The University of Oxford's economic impact report has a limited perspective of financial indicators, which do not necessarily respond to the wider socio-cultural and educational benefits or expense of higher education. The research also does not incorporate a long-term method for evaluating the long-term effects of university activities on local and worldwide economies (Oxford Economics, 2014).

Piattoeva and Boden's criticism of data governance in education draws attention to important ambiguities, but the authors are not sufficiently concrete in giving examples of these ambiguities when they occur in practice. The critique would be served by additional case studies showing the actual consequences of data governance in educational systems (Piattoeva & Boden, 2020).

Picon's criticism of the ideal of smart cities is insightful in terms of their theoretical basis, but it doesn't examine the practical issues cities encounter in seeking to put these ideals into practice. The book would have been enhanced by a closer analysis of the infrastructural and technological challenges to the development of smart cities (Picon, 2013).

Popkewitz's examination of the sociology of education as the history of the present is insufficiently sensitive to how contemporary global dynamics influence educational systems. The historical context is subject to analysis but not synthesized sufficiently with the impact of globalization and digitalization on educational processes (Popkewitz, 2013).

Power's examination of fraud risk machinery in organizations is an enlightening analysis that does not consider the unintended effects of the extreme use of risk management instruments. The study could have examined other frameworks for balancing risk management and ethics in organizations (Power, 2013).

Though Rose's contributions to the study of biomedicine and power provide a critical analysis of the biopolitics of life, it is not so much concerned with Western conceptions of biomedicine and subjectivity. There is not much interest in non-Western or indigenous practices of health and subjectivity, which could have informed the analysis better (Rose, 2007).

The erasure analysis in qualitative research is persuasive but is constrained by its narrow scope within heteronormative harassment. It disregards other social injustices, including racial or class-based injustices, which can also be extremely important to consider in the study of power relations in schools (Rosiek & Heffernan, 2014).

Said's Orientalism is seminal in postcolonial thought, but it has been challenged for being too binaristic in its representation of East and West. The critique can also flatten the nuances of cultural exchange and the acts of agency performed by the "Others" in Western discourse (Said, 1978).

Schildt's investigation of data necessity in contemporary organizations is a captivating critique of data-driven decision-making but falls short of thoroughly engaging with the moral issues of mass data collection and spying. Having a more intense focus on issues of privacy and the implications of big data would have made the argument more solid (Schildt, 2020).

Winters and his fellow authors explain digital structural violence in next-generation learning systems but write mostly from the theoretical point of view of the matter. The article would be improved by more real-life examples or case studies to demonstrate how these problems unfold in actual educational settings (Winters et al., 2020).

Wodak's critical discourse analysis method provides useful insights into how language constructs power relations, but it might not be optimally critical of the methodological difficulties involved in discursive analysis. The theory would be improved by more sophisticated exposition of the limitations of discourse analysis as a methodology (Wodak, 2014).

The World Bank's report on knowledge and development emphasizes the significance of knowledge to economic development without critically examining the role of power and inequality in influencing access to knowledge. The recommendations of the report do not necessarily consider the international differences in access to education and information (World Bank, 1999).

Young and Gilmore's investigation of subaltern empowerment in the geoweb offers valuable perspectives on digital privacy, but the research does not take into account the intersectionality of privacy issues in the digital world. The multifaceted nature of race, gender, and class on the internet is not given sufficient treatment by their analysis (Young & Gilmore, 2013).

Zaballos et al. touch upon the idea of a digital twin for smart campuses but fail to address the possible social and environmental effects of such technology deployments adequately. There is no regard for the privacy and data security issues that could crop up in these environments (Zaballos et al., 2020).

Zarifian's philosophical exploration of work's place is worth reading in terms of its insights into labor, but the book does not take up current debates about automation and the gig economy. The discussion would be more useful by being more carefully developed on how these issues of today overlap with labor and work (Zarifian, 2003).

Zenki and Mu's discussion of machine learning interpretability within smart campus initiatives is interesting, albeit not entirely thought-through in relation to the implications of interpretability for AI system accessibility and equity within educational settings. Additional discussion regarding the potential for interpretability to affect decision-making systems within education would have been useful (Zenki & Mu, 2020).

Zuboff's The Age of Surveillance Capitalism is a critical analysis of surveillance capitalism, but others contend that her critique exaggerates how pervasive surveillance has become in everyday life. The text is also short on a deeper discussion of possible remedies or alternative paradigms to stem the rise of surveillance capitalism (Zuboff, 2019).

The model proposed here has an advantage over other models in addressing several areas of improvement. Current models tend to use linear methods, which can fail to address the nonlinearity and complexity inherent in actual data. With the integration of sophisticated techniques like deep learning algorithms, the suggested model is better positioned to deal with complex, high-dimensional data and identify subtle patterns that were otherwise neglected. Furthermore, it includes a multi-layered framework, enabling a more subtle realization of the inherent relationships among variables, as opposed to simpler models that have the potential to base their projections on overly broad assumptions.

In addition, the suggested model incorporates interpretability components, which most current models do not have. Although deep learning models are normally regarded as "black boxes," the suggested method includes model explainability techniques, allowing stakeholders to comprehend and have confidence in the outcome. This aspect is notably crucial in healthcare and education, where an open process is necessary for decision-making.

Another important enhancement is the model's capability to deal with varied and heterogeneous sources of data. Current models tend to make the assumption of uniformity in data, which in turn creates biases or inaccuracies when it is implemented in more varied real-world scenarios. The suggested model, by contrast, combines various streams of data and does effective preprocessing in order to harmonize and normalize these inputs, providing more accuracy and reliability across different types of data.

Finally, the model suggested utilizes the most recent advancements in computational effectiveness, streamlining training with the aid of parallel processing and sophisticated optimization methods. This renders it more scalable and decreases the training time for the model on big data while ensuring greater performance. Current models, in contrast, could be computationally costly and time-consuming, particularly with large-scale, complicated datasets. By solving these problems, the suggested model presents a more integral, accurate, and effective remedy for the drawbacks of the existing models.

MATERIAL AND METHODS

The approach for analyzing Inequality and Digital Colonialism with bi-stacked ANNs is to gather and preprocess a representative dataset reflecting both direct and indirect components of digital inequality. The dataset contains attributes like internet access, socio-economic status, geographical location, and technological infrastructure. These inputs are propagated through two levels of neural networks: the first level detects rudimentary patterns of digital exclusion, and the second detects more nuanced patterns by feeding contextual variables such as power and socio-political influence. The model is trained on both supervised and unsupervised learning methods, fine-tuning it to predict and comprehend the systemic pervasiveness of digital colonialism. Upon training, the model assists in the identification of vulnerable populations and outcome prediction concerning digital inequality. The method delivers an inclusive framework for investigating how digital power structures propagate global inequalities.

MATERIALS

Data collection for the examination of the intricate interactions of 'events', human and non-human interactions, and power-knowledge relations is intended to investigate the dynamic interdependencies between social, technological, and environmental dimensions. It involves a wide range of variables that depict the complexity of human behavior, technological interventions, and environmental influences to get an all-encompassing outlook on how these factors interact to produce societal outcomes. The data provides accounts of human actions, including decision-making procedures, social movements, and reactions to technological innovations, as well as the functions of non-human players, including artificial intelligence, machines, ecosystems, and digital platforms. These interactions are contextualized within power-knowledge frameworks, examining how power is distributed through the control of information, resources, and technologies.

Human interactions are captured through survey data, social media analysis, and participatory observation, reflecting both individual behaviors and collective actions. The dataset also includes metadata on the social, economic, and political contexts in which these events occur, providing insight into how power structures influence the flow of knowledge and decision-making. Interactions with non-human actors, such as technological systems or natural environments, are documented using IoT devices, environmental sensors, and algorithmic or machine traces. All these non-human actors are compared to human agency, identifying the role of technology in mediating and, at times, determining human actions and societal norms.

Power-knowledge relations are inscribed in the analysis of discourse, media output, and institutional records that document the distribution of knowledge in society. This part of the dataset explores how knowledge is generated, collected, and spread by influential actors like corporations, governments, and media outlets, and how this knowledge drives the actions of groups and individuals. Geographical, temporal, and cultural variables further enrich the data to assure a multi-faceted exploration of how power and knowledge are related in various environments.

By way of this intricate data set, researchers are able to detect patterns and relationships amongst different events, human actions, and non-human agency's impact, and how these interact within broader systems of power and knowledges. The aim is to make visible the underlying structures that shape societal dynamics, providing insight into the ways in which power is negotiated, contested, and reconstituted through intersections of human and non-human action. This extensive data gathering is the basis on which to study the socio-technical systems that organize contemporary societies and to bring to light the hidden processes motivating global power relations and knowledge flows.

PREPROCESSING

Preprocessing of the gathered dataset for complex analyses of 'events' interactions, human and non-human relations, and power-knowledge relations includes a number of major stages for ensuring data consistency, quality, and suitable transformation for analysis. Step one is data cleaning, where missing values, inconsistencies, or outliers in the data are identified and managed. Missing data in the context of human interaction, like missing survey responses or missing social media data, is managed using imputation methods where missing values are imputed from the data available. Where this is impossible, rows with too much missing data can be removed. For non-human data, e.g., readings from IoT devices or environmental sensors, sensor malfunction or errors are treated by using smoothing methods or discarding erroneous readings based on learned error patterns.

Then comes the normalization and scaling of the dataset, specifically when dealing with continuous variables like environmental readings or user activity levels. This step ensures that variables are on a similar scale so that no one feature can overwhelm the analysis by virtue of differences in magnitude. In the case of categorical data, like event types or social media interactions, encoding mechanisms like one-hot encoding or label encoding are used to transform these features into numerical representations that can be used with machine learning models. Temporal variables, like the timing of actions, get converted into standardized forms and binned into meaningful time windows like hours, days, or weeks based on the needs of the analysis.

Text data, like content on social media or speech captured in institutional documents, is processed using natural language processing (NLP) methods to derive meaningful features. All this involves tokenization, stopword elimination, lemmatization, and sentiment analysis, which allow the dataset to capture the tone and underlying sentiments of the discussion. Named entity recognition (NER) is used to find mentionable entities, such as individuals, organizations, or technologies, within the text and then classify them for subsequent analysis of power-knowledge dynamics. Second, topic modeling is employed to determine prevailing themes and topics in the discourse and help explain how knowledge is being constructed and communicated.

To examine human and non-human interactions, the data are supplemented with pertinent metadata, including geographical, temporal, and social context, that get combined using join operations and relational mapping. This contextualization supports a more nuanced view of how power balances and knowledge streams differ between different environments or areas. Where data from heterogeneous sources are integrated, e.g., when joining IoT sensor data with human activity logs, data fusion algorithms are used to align these sources to each other, especially timestamps and event tags.

The knowledge-power relations embedded in the dataset are also analyzed to determine connections among entities, events, and the dispersion of knowledge. This is accomplished by graph-based approaches, wherein nodes signify various entities (e.g., individuals, organizations, technologies) and edges signify connections (e.g., interactions, influence, or control over information). Through this method, the visualization of power dynamics and knowledge dispersion in the dataset is made possible, and patterns of control and influence can be revealed.

Finally, the dataset is pre-processed by applying feature selection and dimensionality reduction methods, like Principal Component Analysis (PCA) or feature importance scoring, to preserve the most informative variables for modeling and analysis. This process not only makes the resulting dataset manageable in size but also infused with features most likely to uncover the inherent patterns of power-knowledge dynamics. Following preprocessing, the data is prepared for additional analysis, including machine learning modeling, statistical inference, or network analysis, in order to glean valuable insights into how events, human and non-human interactions, and power-knowledge relations structure global power relationships.

FEATURE SELECTION

Particle Swarm Optimization feature selection is a strong method for selecting the most significant features from a dataset, particularly when working with large and complicated datasets such as the one outlined to examine intricate interactions of 'events', human and non-human relationships, and relations of power-knowledge. PSO is a computational optimisation technique based on the collective social behavior of birds flocking or fish schooling, where several particles (representing potential solutions) move in the feature space and adjust their positions according to individual and group experiences to locate the optimal solution. With respect to feature subset selection, PSO's goal is to identify an optimal subset of features such that the predictive performance of a model is maximized or the dimension is minimized yet the most informative information is preserved.

Within the PSO algorithm, each particle is a candidate feature subset, and its location in the search space is a set of selected features. Each particle assesses the quality of its current subset of features based on a fitness function, normally training a machine learning classifier (or regressor) on the picked features and assessing its performance based on some measures like accuracy, precision, recall, or F1 measure. The fitness function offers a means to evaluate the quality of how well the picked features improve the model performance overall. As particles move through the feature space, they move based on their personal best as well as the global best found by the swarm, slowly converging onto an optimal set of features.

While optimizing, the PSO algorithm repeatedly changes each particle's velocity and position. The velocity controls how much the position of the particle will be changed, and it is controlled by the particle's past velocity and the difference between the current position and the best individual. The velocity is also controlled by the best global position so that particles are attracted to parts of the feature space that have given better solutions. This procedure enables a balance between exploration (traversing the feature space) and exploitation (concentrating on promising areas of the space). Through consecutive iterations, the swarm converges collectively to an optimal feature subset that maximizes the model's performance.

PSO has a number of features that make it well-suited for feature selection, especially in high-dimensional spaces where conventional approaches may falter. It does not need prior knowledge of the feature dependencies, and it is capable of both linear and nonlinear relationships among features. In addition, PSO can be able to traverse difficult, large, and noisy datasets efficiently, which makes it ideal for datasets with many interdependent features, such as those capturing various human and non-human interactions and power-knowledge relations. After the best subset of features is determined, it can be utilized for model training, resulting in better model efficiency and performance without increasing the likelihood of overfitting.

Applying in the case of the gathered dataset, PSO can be employed in identifying significant features that play a role in comprehending the interactions between human behaviors, systems of technology, and power dynamics. For instance, variables indicating time-series patterns of human behavior, sentiment from text, or readings from sensor data in the environment can be assessed for their significance in describing power and knowledge relations. By applying PSO, the end dataset is trimmed to contain only the most significant variables, making the analysis easier without compromising essential insights to investigate the socio-technical systems under examination further.

BISTACKED ANN

Digital Colonialism and Inequality, when examined by means of bi-stacked Artificial Neural Networks (ANNs), provides a robust framework for explanation of how power relationships in the digital world reinforce discrepancies in access, control, and knowledge diffusion. Bi-stacked ANNs, which consist of stacking two or more layers of neural networks sequentially to boost model depth and sophistication, may be utilized to simulate multi-dimensional relationships between digital technologies and socio-economic disparities. The initial strata of the network could emphasize raw data pertaining to access technologies, e.g., internet usage behavior, digital illiteracy, and familiarity with digital platforms. The next strata could narrow down this data by including contextual variables like location, income level, and social determinants and hence highlighting the underlying strata of digital technology-driven inequality.

Bi-stacked architecture allows the model to process direct and indirect drivers of digital colonialism, where the digital economy and knowledge economy are unproportionately dominated by a few global powers. The initial network stage may identify rudimentary patterns of digital exclusion, i.e., restricted access to internet or asymmetrical access to global digital markets, via early feature extraction layers. These layers are able to process demographic information, availability of infrastructure, and rates of internet penetration, pinpointing areas and communities where digital divides are at their worst. The next layer in the bi-stacked network then takes these trends and refines them, applying higher-order factors such as socio-political sway, power disparities that endure over time, and data ownership concentrations, in order to detect the systemic quality of digital inequality.

The training phase for this model is both supervised and unsupervised. First, labeled data pertaining to digital access and socio-economic standing are employed to train the network to identify obvious cases of inequality. With time, the network is able to identify more latent relationships between variables, such as how digital colonialism takes shape in terms of data exploitation, cultural hegemony, and the corporate monopolization of digital platforms. This enables the network to predict which groups may be experiencing digital oppression based on changing digital environments.

Utilizing a bi-stacked ANN for this capacity enables the model to process intricate interactions between multiple factors like policy, technology, and power, providing a complete picture of how digital colonialism and inequality get reinforced. For example, the model can examine how the dominance of Western tech firms in the international market creates data extraction strategies that disproportionately impact marginalized groups in the Global South. The model can also forecast how disparities in access to data or a lack of technological infrastructure could prevent economic and social possibilities from being reached by some groups.

As the model continues to iterate through training, it becomes better at predicting which segments are likely to be further excluded by digital colonialism. The bi-stacked ANN successfully identifies the dynamic feedback loops between technology rollout and inequality, demonstrating how poor communities tend to experience a double whammy—first, in accessing digital technology, and second, in experiencing the impact of the global digital order mediated by a small number of influential actors.

Finally, bi-stacked ANNs allow for a sophisticated comprehension of digital colonialism by replicating the intricate network of interactions among human activities, technological growth, and socio-political dynamics. They offer precious information on the processes of digital oppression and inequality and inform policymakers, scholars, and activists about the intervention levers. The model can inform more equitable digital policies with the objective of sharing the fruits of technological growth more equitably across global citizens.

EXPERIMENTAL RESULTS

Experimental results present a detailed analysis of the effects of digital colonialism and inequality in the dataset context, employing bi-stacked Artificial Neural Networks (ANNs) for predicting and feature selection. The model was trained on a wide variety of features such as technological access, socio-economic status, geographical locations, and political factors to understand the intricate interactions among human activities, technological systems, and power relations. The measuring parameters, such as accuracy, precision, recall, and F1 score, indicate the extent to which the model is successful in identifying and predicting digital exclusion and inequality patterns. The findings provide significant information regarding which features have the greatest impact on digital colonialism and its international ramifications, as well as the crucial function of algorithmic control and data scraping in maintaining socio-economic inequalities across the globe. Table 1 presents a region-wise feature importance scores breakdown, showing the contribution that individual features like digital access, education, and healthcare have towards the model predictions.

Table 1. Feature importance for digital colonialism and inequality prediction

Feature	Importance Score	Standard Deviation	Mean Value	Min Value	Max Value
Internet Access	0.22	0.03	3.5	1	5
Digital Literacy	0.18	0.02	2.9	1	5
Geographical Location	0.15	0.01	3.0	1	5
Economic Status	0.20	0.04	3.2	2	5
Data Access	0.12	0.03	2.5	1	5
Platform Access	0.13	0.02	3.1	2	5

Table 2 estimates model performance through computation of precision, recall, and F1 measures by region, illustrating the strength of representation each region has within machine learning models.

Table 2. Accuracy results for digital colonialism prediction models

Model	Accuracy (%)	Precision (%)	Recall (%)	F1 Score (%)	AUC Score (%)
Bi-stacked ANN	89.6	85.3	87.2	86.2	91.4
Random Forest	84.5	81.6	82.4	82.0	87.1
Support Vector Machine	82.1	79.2	78.6	78.9	85.2
Logistic Regression	77.8	74.5	72.8	73.6	81.5
Decision Tree	80.4	77.0	75.4	76.2	83.0
Naive Bayes	75.2	72.1	70.3	71.2	78.9

Table 3 investigates the statistical significance of regional features, listing correlations between economic standing and digital access, with p-value evidence for the significance of these correlations.

Table 3. Regional comparison of internet access

Region	Average Access Score	Min Score	Max Score	Std. Deviation	Population Size
North America	4.9	4	5	0.3	5000
Sub-Saharan Africa	2.1	1	3	0.7	4500
South Asia	3.5	2	4	0.6	6000
Latin America	4.0	3	5	0.5	4800
Middle East	3.8	2	5	0.8	5200
Eastern Europe	4.5	3	5	0.4	4000
Southeast Asia	3.2	2	4	0.6	5300
Western Europe	5.0	4	5	0.2	4700
Oceania	4.2	3	5	0.4	3500
Central Asia	2.9	2	4	0.5	3800

Table 4 investigates regional variation in digital access, listing how availability of digital infrastructure and internet penetration rates differ by region and drive digital participation.

Table 4. Socio-economic status and digital access correlation

Region	Socio-Economic Index	Digital Access Score	Correlation Coefficient	Std. Dev.	P-Value
North America	5.2	4.9	0.87	0.4	0.001
Sub-Saharan Africa	2.1	2.1	0.54	0.5	0.03
South Asia	3.3	3.5	0.76	0.6	0.02
Latin America	4.0	4.0	0.81	0.5	0.01
Middle East	4.1	3.8	0.70	0.7	0.04
Eastern Europe	4.6	4.5	0.79	0.3	0.005
Southeast Asia	3.0	3.2	0.67	0.4	0.02
Western Europe	5.5	5.0	0.90	0.2	0.0005
Oceania	4.4	4.2	0.75	0.3	0.03
Central Asia	3.2	2.9	0.62	0.4	0.06

Table 5 analyzes in detail the structures of regional governments, assessing political freedom and state control of virtual space and its impact on technology use by region.

Table 5. Data access and digital literacy

Region	Average Data Access	Average Digital Literacy	Correlation Coefficient	Std. Dev.	P-Value
North America	4.8	4.9	0.92	0.2	0.001
Sub-Saharan Africa	1.8	2.0	0.62	0.6	0.04
South Asia	3.4	3.5	0.81	0.5	0.02
Latin America	4.2	4.1	0.88	0.3	0.005
Middle East	3.5	3.6	0.75	0.6	0.03
Eastern Europe	4.6	4.4	0.89	0.3	0.01
Southeast Asia	3.3	3.2	0.74	0.5	0.02
Western Europe	5.0	5.0	0.93	0.1	0.0005
Oceania	4.3	4.2	0.78	0.4	0.03
Central Asia	3.0	3.1	0.69	0.5	0.05

Table 6 contrasts the use of digital technology in education by region, assessing effectiveness and availability of digital learning resources.

Table 6. Model prediction results for digital inequality

Region	Predicted Inequality Score	Actual Inequality Score	Error Margin	Prediction Confidence (%)	Model Type
North America	4.8	4.9	0.1	92.5	Bi-stacked ANN
Sub-Saharan Africa	2.2	2.1	0.1	89.4	Random Forest
South Asia	3.5	3.6	0.1	86.7	Support Vector Machine
Latin America	4.0	4.0	0.0	91.2	Logistic Regression
Middle East	3.8	3.8	0.0	88.3	Decision Tree
Eastern Europe	4.5	4.5	0.0	92.8	Bi-stacked ANN
Southeast Asia	3.2	3.2	0.0	87.6	Naive Bayes
Western Europe	5.0	5.0	0.0	95.3	Bi-stacked ANN
Oceania	4.2	4.2	0.0	90.5	Random Forest
Central Asia	2.9	2.9	0.0	84.8	Support Vector Machine

Table 7 estimates health data access, which depicts how levels of data extraction rates, political control, and economic status are associated with health outcomes by region.

Table 7. Internet usage and social media access

Region	Average Internet Usage	Average Social Media Access	Correlation Coefficient	Std. Dev.	P-Value
North America	4.9	4.8	0.91	0.2	0.0005
Sub-Saharan Africa	2.2	2.0	0.53	0.5	0.04
South Asia	3.4	3.6	0.79	0.6	0.02
Latin America	4.0	3.9	0.85	0.3	0.003
Middle East	3.6	3.5	0.74	0.6	0.04
Eastern Europe	4.5	4.3	0.88	0.3	0.005
Southeast Asia	3.3	3.4	0.77	0.5	0.02
Western Europe	5.0	5.0	0.92	0.1	0.0001
Oceania	4.3	4.2	0.80	0.4	0.03
Central Asia	3.1	3.0	0.70	0.5	0.05

Table 8 addresses the economic conditions and political influence of all regions, which demonstrates how these elements merge together to influence regional digital infrastructure.

Table 8. Economic status and political influence

Region	Economic Status Score	Political Influence Score	Correlation Coefficient	Std. Dev.	P-Value
North America	5.2	4.9	0.85	0.3	0.001
Sub-Saharan Africa	2.0	2.1	0.57	0.5	0.04
South Asia	3.2	3.5	0.78	0.6	0.03
Latin America	4.1	4.2	0.80	0.4	0.02
Middle East	3.7	3.6	0.72	0.5	0.04
Eastern Europe	4.4	4.3	0.83	0.3	0.01
Southeast Asia	3.3	3.4	0.70	0.4	0.03
Western Europe	5.0	4.8	0.89	0.2	0.0005
Oceania	4.2	4.1	0.76	0.3	0.02
Central Asia	3.0	3.1	0.65	0.4	0.05

Table 9 looks at data extraction rates, algorithm bias, and predictive accuracy, and illustrates how data extraction rates vary by region, with the best being North America and Sub-Saharan Africa having severe issues.

Table 9. Data extraction and algorithmic bias

Region	**Data Extraction Rate (%)**	**Algorithmic Bias Score**	**Prediction Accuracy (%)**	**Std. Dev.**	**P-Value**
North America	95	0.2	92.5	0.3	0.0005
Sub-Saharan Africa	50	0.6	70.4	0.5	0.04
South Asia	75	0.5	85.6	0.4	0.02
Latin America	85	0.3	88.7	0.3	0.005
Middle East	80	0.4	86.1	0.5	0.03
Eastern Europe	90	0.3	91.2	0.2	0.005
Southeast Asia	80	0.5	83.5	0.4	0.02
Western Europe	96	0.1	94.2	0.1	0.0001
Oceania	85	0.4	88.0	0.3	0.03
Central Asia	70	0.5	75.3	0.6	0.05

Table 10 looks at the issues of information control and digital literacy, and looks at the impact of information control and digital education on overall development and digital literacy in regions.

Table 10. Impact of knowledge control and digital literacy

Region	**Knowledge Control Index**	**Digital Literacy Score**	**Impact Score**	**Std. Dev.**	**P-Value**
North America	5.0	4.9	92.3	0.2	0.0001
Sub-Saharan Africa	2.1	2.0	68.4	0.5	0.04
South Asia	3.5	3.6	80.2	0.6	0.03
Latin America	4.1	4.0	83.9	0.4	0.02
Middle East	3.8	3.7	79.1	0.5	0.04
Eastern Europe	4.5	4.4	88.7	0.3	0.005
Southeast Asia	3.3	3.4	74.2	0.5	0.03
Western Europe	5.0	5.0	95.1	0.1	0.0001
Oceania	4.2	4.3	81.8	0.3	0.02
Central Asia	3.1	3.2	72.6	0.5	0.05

CONCLUSION

Digital Colonialism and Inequality mark the need to respond to the imbalanced power relations that inform the digital sphere. The application of bi-stacked ANNs in this research presents a sophisticated approach to acknowledging the intersection between digital technology and socio-economic inequality, presenting a mechanism for predicting and identifying populations at risk of enhanced marginalization. With the ever-evolving digital technologies changing the world, there is a need to realize how digital colonialism expands inequalities and affects access to resources, opportunities, and information. This study contributes to current literature on digital equity and provides a foundation for future interventions in creating a more inclusive digital world. The report calls for policy reforms, technological innovation, and global cooperation to ensure that the dividends of the digital revolution benefit all corners of the globe and communities fairly.

REFERENCES

Amicelle, A., Aradau, C., & Jeandesboz, J. (2015). Questioning security device:performativity, resistance, politics. *Security Dialogue*, *46*(4), 293–306. DOI: 10.1177/0967010615586964

Arendt, H. (2004). *The Origins of Totalitarianism*. Schocken.

Ash, J., Kitchin, R. & Leszcynski, A. (2018). 'Digital turn, digital geographies?', Progress inHuman Geography, 42(1), 25-43.

Burrows, R. (2012). Living with the H-index? Metric Assemblages in the ContemporaryAcademy. *The Sociological Review*, *60*(2), 355–372. DOI: 10.1111/j.1467-954X.2012.02077.x

Burton-Jones, A. (1999). *Knowledge Capitalism: The New Learning Economy*. Oxford University Press. DOI: 10.1093/acprof:oso/9780198296225.001.0001

Busch, L. (2017). *Knowledge for Sale: The neoliberal takeover of Higher Education*. MIT Press. DOI: 10.7551/mitpress/10742.001.0001

Castro-Gómez, S. (2008). (Post)Coloniality for Dummies: Latin American Perspectives onModernity, Coloniality, and the Geopolitics of Knowledge. In Moraña, M., Dussel, E., & Jáuregui, C. (Eds.), *Coloniality at Large*. Duke University Press.

Castro-Gómez, S. (2021). 'Coloniality as a Relationship and Bloog Cleansing: A brief Studyon the Contributions of Santiago Castro-Gómez', Journal of Philosophy. *Letters and Humanities*, *25*(80), 160–174.

Creswell, J. (2015). *30 essential skills for the qualitative researcher*. SAGE.

Datta, A. (2017). The digital turn in postcolonial urbanism: Smart citizenship in the makingof India's 100 smart cities. *Transactions of the Institute of British Geographers*, *4*(3), 405–419. DOI: 10.1111/tran.12225

Espeland, W. N., & Sauder, M. (2016). *Engines of Anxiety: Academic rankings, reputation,and accountability*. Russell Sage Foundation.

Eubanks, V. (2018). *Automating Inequality: How high-tech tools profile, police and punish the poor*. St. Martin's Press.

Evans, C., Rees, G., Taylor, C., & Fox, S. (2021). 'A liberal higher education for all? The massification of higher education and its implications for graduates' participation in civil society'. *Higher Education*, *81*(3), 521–535. DOI: 10.1007/s10734-020-00554-x

Facer, K. & Selwyn, N. (2021). Digital technology and the futures of education—towards 'non-stupid' optimism. Paper commission for the UNESCO Futures of Education report(forthcoming, 2021).

Guster, D., & Brown, C. (2012). The application of business intelligence to higher education:technical and managerial perspectives. *Technical and Managerial Perspectives*, *23*(2), 42–62.

Hamilton, D. L., & Gifford, R. K. (1976). Illusory correlation in interpersonal perception: A cognitive basis of stereotypic judgments. *Journal of Experimental Social Psychology*, *12*(4), 392–407. DOI: 10.1016/S0022-1031(76)80006-6

Hammersley, M., & Atkinson, P. (2007). *Ethnography: principles in practice*. Tavistock Publications Ltd.

Haraway, D. (1988). Situated knowledges: The science question in feminism and the privilege of partial perspective. *Feminist Studies*, *14*(3), 575–599. DOI: 10.2307/3178066

Harvey, D. (2014). *Seventeen Contradictions and the End of Capitalism*. OxfordUniversity Press.

Isin, E., & Ruppert, E. (2020). The birth of sensory power: How a pandemic made it visible? *Big Data & Society*, *7*(2), 1–15. DOI: 10.1177/2053951720969208

Jiang, W., & Pardos, Z. A. (2021). Towards equity and algorithmic fairness in student gradeprediction. *Computers & Society*, •••, 1–10.

Josselson, R. (1996). Ethics and Process in the Narrative Study of Lives. California: SAGEPublications.

Karvonen, A., Cugurullo, F., & Caprotti, F. (2018). *Inside Smart Cities: place, politics and urban innovation*. Routledge. DOI: 10.4324/9781351166201

Lane, J. E., & Finsel, B. A. (2014). Fostering smarter colleges and universities: Data, big data and analytics. In Lane, J. E. (Ed.), *Building a smarter university: Big data, innovation and analytics*. State University of New York Press.

Leibowitz, B. (2017). 'Power, knowledge and learning: dehegemonising colonial knowledge', lternation, 24(2), 99-119.

Mouton, M., & Burns, R. (2021). (Digital) neo-colonialism in the smart city. *Regional Studies*, *55*(12), 1890–1901. DOI: 10.1080/00343404.2021.1915974

Musa, J. (2016). Smart cities – a roadmap for development. *Journal of Telecommunication System & Management*, *5*(3), 1–3.

Olssen, M. (1996). In defense of the welfare state and publicly provided eduation: A NewZealand perspective. *Journal of Education Policy*, *11*(11), 337–362. DOI: 10.1080/0268093960110305

Olssen, M., & Peters, M. A. (2007). Neoliberalism, higher education and the knowledgeeconomy: From the free market to knowledge capitalism. *Journal of Education Policy*, *20*(3), 313–245. DOI: 10.1080/02680930500108718

Olufemi, L. (2020). *Feminism, Interrupted: Disrupting Power*. Pluto Press. DOI: 10.2307/j.ctvxrpzvs

Oxford Economics. (2014). *Economic Impact of the University of Oxford*. Oxford Economics.

Piattoeva, N., & Boden, R. (2020). Escaping numbers? The ambiguities of the governance ofeducation through data. *International Studies in Sociology of Education*, *29*(1-2), 1–18. DOI: 10.1080/09620214.2020.1725590

Picon, A. (2013). Smart cities: Théorie et critique d'un idéal autoréalisateur. Pari-son: éditionsB2.

Popkewitz, T. (2013). The sociology of education as the history of the present: Fabrication,difference and abjection. *Discourse (Abingdon)*, *34*(3), 439–456. DOI: 10.1080/01596306.2012.717195

Power, M. (2013). The apparatus of fraud risk. *Accounting, Organizations and Society*, *38*(6-7), 525–543. DOI: 10.1016/j.aos.2012.07.004

Rose, N. (2007). *The Politics of Life Itself: Biomedicine, Power, and Subjectivity in theTwenty-First Century*. Princeton University Press. DOI: 10.1515/9781400827503

Rosiek, J. L., & Heffernan, J. (2014). Can't code what the community can't see: A case of theerasure of heteronormative harassment. *Qualitative Inquiry*, *20*(6), 726–733. DOI: 10.1177/1077800414530255

Said, E. (1978). *Orientalism*. Vintage Books.

Schildt, H. (2020). *The Data Imperative*. Oxford University Press. DOI: 10.1093/oso/9780198840817.001.0001

Winters, N., Eynon, R., Geniets, A., Robson, J., & Kahn, K. (2020). Can we avoid digitalstructural violence in future learning systems? *Learning, Media and Technology*, *45*(1), 17–30. DOI: 10.1080/17439884.2020.1708099

Wodak, R. (2014). Critical discourse analysis. In Leung, C., & Street, B. V. (Eds.), *TheRoutledge companion to English studies*. Routledge.

Young, J. C., & Gilmore, M. P. (2013). Subaltern Empowerment in the Geoweb: Tensionbetween Publicity and Privacy. *Antipode*, *46*(2), 574–591. DOI: 10.1111/anti.12056

Zaballos, A., Briones, A., Massa, A., Centelles, P., & Caballero, V. (2020). A smart campus'digital twin for sustainable comfort monitoring. *Sustainability (Basel)*, *12*(21), 1–33. DOI: 10.3390/su12219196

Zarifian, P. (2003). A quoi sert le travail? Paris: La dispute.72

Zenki, R., & Mu, M. (2020). Machine learning interpretability and its impact on smart campus projects. *Computers & Society*, •••, 1–5.

Zuboff, S. (2019). *The Age of Surveillance Capitalism*. Profile Books.

Chapter 13
The Evolving Role of International Organizations in the 21st Century

Nituja Singh
https://orcid.org/0000-0002-4766-1119
Symbiosis Law School, Symbiosis International University, India

Jyotish Kumar Gupta
https://orcid.org/0009-0007-1444-3960
School of Law, Galgotias University, Greater Noida, India

Saurabh Kumar
https://orcid.org/0009-0005-4594-1597
The Neotia University, India

Apoorva Roy
https://orcid.org/0009-0005-8422-9404
Galgotias University, India

Anurodh Upadhyay
https://orcid.org/0009-0004-9418-0774
School of Law, Galgotias University, Greater Noida, India

ABSTRACT

International organizations are playing an ever-more-important role in global governance as they handle difficult problems and take advantage of new opportunities. Considering the growing prominence of non-state actors and emerging economies,

DOI: 10.4018/979-8-3373-1727-4.ch013

this chapter explores how these institutions including the United Nations, World Bank, and regional bodies adjust to the changing geopolitical environment. International organizations confront two challenges, as the chapter points out: the need for reform to improve their legitimacy and efficacy while tackling problems like security threats, health crises, and climate change .As the pace of globalization increases, it is the responsibility of international organizations to promote collaboration between various stakeholders, such as governments, the commercial sector, and civil society. When dealing with international concerns that no one organization can handle on its own, this cooperative approach is crucial.

INTRODUCTION

Gone are the days when non-state actors were not considered as a stakeholder in the international law. The world is witnessing impactful influences of the non-state players in shaping the current affairs of the international law. Recently; during the general election of the United State of America, one of the most powerful capitalists namely Mr. Elon Musk and his associated corporations have been in international and global buzz. In matters of space and marine law, since last few decades jurists across globe are discussing and trying to fix the accountability of non-state stakeholders of international laws in case of any causality to other country, their civilians, property or any form of project because of non-state players anywhere in the world. In such situations this is very much pertinent to discuss and evaluate the role of international organisations in the 21st century (Cheng, 2014).

The beginning of the twenty-first century was a turning point in the development of international organisations (IOs), relations and function thereof. The previous few decades have seen the spectacular fall of the Soviet Union (one of the most powerful nation ever), yielding an apparently unipolar international order ruled by the United States. This fundamental change created both possibilities and difficulties for the missions and efficacy of IOs by radically affecting the current structure of IOs (Martin & Simmons, 2013).

IOs discovered themselves negotiating a difficult ground marked by resurgent nationalism, the rising power of non-state actors, the quickening forces of globalization, ongoing global inequities, and the increasing awareness of urgent environmental issues as the new millennium unfolded. Comprehending the following evolution and adaptations of international organizations in response to such dynamic and sometimes opposing factors depends on an understanding among IOs member-nations (Lee & Lee, 2002).

The most recent and on-going conflict of Hamas, Gaza and Israel as well as Russia-Ukraine type issues have compelled to the global community to think more sincerely about resolving international issues through a neutral platform and what could be better option for this purpose but an international organisation. That is the reason, the role of IOs are transiting from a new phase in the 21st century and evolving gradually (Auld & Elfert, 2024).

The twenty-first century has brought about a number of tough global issues, including climate change, mass migration, terrorism and economic problems, risk of nuclear-war and emissions. As a result, different existing international organisations are expected to play its most effecting role in accordance with its establishment-objectives. International organisations such as the United Nations (UN) are important for encouraging countries to talk and work together. Organisation like International Court of Justice (ICJ) needed to manage such problems to safeguard international law and justice so that peace across the globe may be maintained and well beingness of human in need may be ensured.

A sound and strong solution is often needed when economic instability is made worse by certain situations or natural crisis, calamity such as global pandemic like Covid-19. The role of organisations like the United Nations Children's Fund (UNICEF) become crucial. Other international organisation like International Monetary Fund [IMF] aids and works towards economic collaboration to support the recovery of affected economies plays a pivotal role over the international platforms (Anghel & Jones, 2025).

Migration is one of the most critical crises alike refugees' issues and challenges under the international law and for that matter; international organisations may play an effective mediating role to address these issues. And, therefore it is necessary to have laws on mass migration to manage the movement of individuals leaving their home-country because of hunger, war, disasters, apartheidism, state sponsored mass killing because of ethnic, religious, community identities, etc. to secure rights, liberties, freedom and livelihood of migrants as well as refugees.

Terrorism is perhaps the most discussed issue almost all of the international forums and platforms. The UNO has been appearing to do a lot against terrorism. However; the same UNO is also been criticised for not functioning effectively against terrorism due to five most powerful veto-nations. Therefore, it is a quite different chapter to discuss the role of United Nations organisations in curbing terrorism across the globe.

However; world terrorism increases, it can not be denied that the need for global coordination and exchange of information is crucial.

Environment related issues in the 21st century have emerged as a big challenge for the international organisations. To reduce the quantum of greenhouse gas emissions needs international community whether state or non-state actors to work together for an effective outcome. And, it is only possible through a proper functioning international organisation or institution. UNO initiatives have been promoting sustainable actions through many task forces undertaking everywhere and it has helped in reducing the effects of negative climate change. All these institutions play a key role in steering the complicated matters of 21st century and supporting international stability and teamwork (Haug et al., 2024).

Global governance relies on international organisations. There are considerable number of international organisations; for almost all of the aspects of international discourse such as UNO having multiple sister institutions to achieve some distinguish and specific objectives viz. the United Nations Educational, Scientific and Cultural Organization, United Nations Industrial Development Organization, United Nations Education Scientific & Cultural Organization, United Nations Industrial Development Organization (UNIDO), etc., Food and Agriculture Organization [FOA], World Intellectual Property Organization [WIPO], International Labour Organization [ILO], International Court of Justice [ICJ], International Criminal Court [ICC], The World Health Organization [WHO], World Economic Forum [WEF], World Bank, World Trade Organization [WTO], World Wide Fund for Nature (WWF), International Atomic Agency etc., each having very specific objective and aims relating to international issues and challenges. Moreover, there are many international organisations which are established to deal with regional issues and challenges. And, that is the reason members of such organisations are from a particular region, such as; South Asian Association for Regional Cooperation, Association of South East Nations, Organization for Economic Cooperation & Development (OECD), Asian Infrastructure Investment Bank (AIIB), New Development Bank (BRICS Development Bank), Asian Development Bank (ADB), African development bank (AfDB), Organization of Petroleum Exporting Countries (OPEC), etc.

UN, the IMF, and the WTO use diplomacy and international law to help to guide the world. These international organisations help countries to find solutions to urgent worldwide issues such as development and economic stability. Since; there is a clear difference in power among their members and they seem to respond slowly to crises, these organisations are often questioned and criticised for their ineffectiveness (Reiners, 2024).

While other organisations and actors are pushing the UN to take on more responsibilities, it is still considered the main place for global discussion.

Activities of IMF and WTO may influence regions not under their direct authority; they find it a bit difficult to govern effectively. It is required from member countries that they must obey international law so that peace and security may be maintained across the globe. Nevertheless, compliance with such international law and rites are often difficult and it highlights the requirement for better systems inside these organisations to fairly address disputes and make member-countries accountable.

Although international institutions are foundation to run the world, they need to adapt their functions and responses to suit the challenges of 21st century global interdependence.

As the world becomes more globalised and digital, international organisations are reassessing their roles in facing important global challenges. CEB, part of the UN system, demonstrates the evolution by allowing chief executives to talk and make policies consistent with the demands of globalisation. Recent changes in global governance show that it is important for the corporate sector and non-governmental organisations to work together with others to address global issues (Moch, 2024).

Some people say international organisations are not very effective, especially during the COVID-19 epidemic, but they do much to promote international collaboration and address problems shared by member nations. The project demonstrates that private sector organisations are now part of the international system which helps implement UN social and environmental policies and promotes global stability.

The International Monetary Fund plays a major role in the financial system by seeking both stability and balance between countries' politics. All these institutions must adapt to be current and in line with the common objectives set in the 21st century. Handling world issues that affect many countries, like climate change, health issues and cybersecurity, requires the help of international organisations. The World Health Organisation's role in managing the global COVID-19 epidemic clearly highlights the need for countries to cooperate in health crises. In addition, agreements such as the Kyoto Protocol and the Paris Agreement help countries agree to reduce greenhouse gases by working together. They demonstrate that dealing with international issues calls for global governance which includes making rules and encouraging countries to cooperate (Rahimi & Oh, 2024).

Since cyberattacks are increasingly destabilising, international organisations play a key role in developing standards and encouraging countries to work together on cybersecurity. They make sure that nations collaborate effectively by guiding them and looking after world stability, so that issues are managed by groups rather than by single nations. Because these problems are linked, international organisations are important for helping countries respond together to shared difficulties.

The growing uncertainty about working together globally and the rise of unilateral and regional policies by some nations further weakens the standing of international organisations. The way the United States has rejected candidates for the WTO Appellate Body is an example of this issue. Because they doubt the success of international institutions, major states may act alone instead of joining other countries in tackling trade imbalances and problems of social inequality.

It is so obvious to see that international organisations are not able to keep up with the constant changes in world politics. The fact that international organisations cannot keep up with the rapid changes in world politics, it seems like they are not prepared for 21st century emerging challenges. In consequence, people lose confidence in these organisations which weakens their authority and leads to major difficulties in maintaining a harmonious world order as governments focus more on regional solutions instead of teaming up globally. As a result, international institutions must be improved to stay reliable and efficient in a multipolar world (Morgenstern, 2024).

In the view of the above discussion, there are some eminent questions relating to the evolving role of international organisations in the current time i.e. 21st of century. The significance of the international organisations in resolving many serious and threating disputes between/among international community cannot be denied. However; the emerging question is whether these international organisations have been as effective as it could have been? Whether the role of these organisations has been exploited to its fullest in peace maintaining across the globe? Whether the traditional way of IOs' function is efficient to cope up with the 21sst century international challenges and issues such as nuclear war or environment, greenhouse, genocide, refugee, malnutrition related big issues?

This research work is an endeavour to evaluate the role of the existing international organisations in addressing and resolving current international disputes. Further; this paper also aims to identify the most challenging and potential international threats for the 21st century. Further, this paper would discuss the most effective and feasible solutions for the above said current issues and challenges for the international community in the 21st century (Manulak, 2024).

THE POST-COLD WAR ORDER AND ITS FIRST EFFECT ON IOS

This is very pertinent to examine the past of the international organisations i.e. how they came into the scene as an effective tool to resolve disputes between/among different countries. And, what can be best period than cold-war for this purpose!

The end of the Soviet empire during 1991 led to major reshuffle in the world's politics. After the bipolar conflict of the later 20th century, there was hope for people to work together in global organisations. Long disadvantaged by the veto power in the Security Council held by Cold War challengers, the United Nations (UN) found additional purpose. There was hope that the era of ideological stalemate gone and opened new path for more efficient group- actions for any sort of world problems.

Initially, the post-Cold War era witnessed an expansion of UN peace keeping operations, with interventions in regions previously caught in the crossfire of superpower competition. The focus shifted towards addressing intrastate conflicts, humanitarian crises, and the promotion of democracy and human rights. Institutions like International Monetary Fund (IMF) and World Bank have altered their objectives, emphasizing the incorporation of former Soviet bloc nations into the global capitalist framework and endorsing market-oriented reforms in impoverished countries. The perceived dominance of liberal democratic values and market economics created a sense of convergence, potentially streamlining the work of IOs by reducing ideological clashes among member states (Brown, 2024).

The nascent optimism was soon mitigated by emerging reality. The absence of a clearly defined ideological adversary does not inherently guarantee harmonious global relations. The United States, as the sole superpower, often pursued its interests unilaterally, sometimes bypassing or undermining multilateral institutions when they were perceived to constrain its actions. New regional conflicts and ethnic strife erupted in the Balkans, Africa, and regions of the former Soviet Union, so rendering the promised "peace dividend" of the Cold War unfulfilled. These conflicts often presented significant challenges for international organizations, testing their capacity for effective action and highlighting the limitations of a consensus-driven approach when powerful nations had divergent interests. Furthermore, the focus on liberal interventionism and the promotion of democracy sometimes met with resistance from states prioritizing sovereignty and non-interference, creating new fault lines within the international system (Joshi et al., 2025).

KEY GLOBAL ISSUES FOR IOS AT TURN OF THE MILLENNIUM

At the onset of the 21st century, international organizations confronted a complex web of interconnected global challenges that necessitated innovative and coordinated solutions. While the end of the Cold War initially seemed to favour global integration, the turn of the millennium witnessed a resurgence of nationalism and regionalism in various parts of the world. Ethnic and cultural identities held more significance, occasionally inciting separatist movements and inter-state conflicts (Poorhashemi, 2024).

Although they often focus on economic cooperation, these organisations can also generate new types of rivalry and stand in the way of global governance. IOs had to deal with the influence of both global and regional ties, aiming to bring about cooperation without undermining the independence of countries or their regional differences. At times, when people felt that international organisations went against their country's interests or traditions, it led to nationalist opinions challenging the legitimacy of those organisations. To understand this situation example may be taken from Indian public opinions and reactions against IMF on giving financial support to Pakistant aftermath *Pehlgam* [*Vide:* Business Standard, external-affairs-defence-security web page dated May 25, 2025] terror attack.

The Growth of Non-State Actors

In the recent time with the emergence of capitalist nation economy, the role and influence of non-state actors in shaping international law new regime can be evident across the globe. In fact the 21st century has seen non-state actors playing a bigger role on the world stage. Transnational corporations had a strong influence over trade, investment and the way countries developed. International non-governmental organisations (INGOs) were heavily involved in advocacy, aid and overseeing human rights. Terrorist activity across countries was a major concern for security. Such organisations moved across national borders to commit their crimes. This meant that these non-state actors could act independently, creating new problems for IOs that mainly focus on governments. As a result, international organisations set out to work with these different actors, aiming to use their benefits for good while managing the risks they could present to the world's peace and security (Lake et al., 2021).

Globalization and Interdependence

Advances in technology and the lifting of trade and finance regulations made globalisation move at a fast speed, leading to increased connexions between countries. Globalisation has given rise to new opportunities, but it has also increased certain risks and challenges. Financial crises could move fast across different countries, the gap between rich and poor could grow in many places and the ties among supply chains made the world economy prone to disruptions. Although people accused international organisations like the WTO, the World Bank and the IMF of causing greater inequality and not being able to solve all the social and environmental problems of globalisation, they were still key in managing globalisation (Beigbeder, 2023).

Enduring Problems of Poverty and Inequality

Even after many years of work, poverty and inequality were still major world-wide problems at the start of the new millennium. Due to these differences, people became dissatisfied and economic growth was slowed, thereby helping to cause world instability. Despite the fact that the challenge required more effective and just international cooperation and a better understanding of the system that supports inequality, the UN Development Programme (UNDP) and the World Bank only worked on reducing poverty and promoting development. The UN launched the Millennium Development Goals (MDGs) in 2000 to mobilise actions around these topics (Varga, 2021).

Rising Environmental Issues

As the 20th century ended, more research revealed more damage to the environment and the potential for climate change. At the beginning of the twenty-first century, these issues gained greater importance on the world agenda. Such issues as deforestation, a decrease in biodiversity, pollution and the impending risk of climate change needed fast worldwide action. Varying national priorities, environmental issues that are difficult to solve and weak regulations made it difficult for the current environmental Ios. The progress made by environmental IOs and agreements such as the UNEP and the Kyoto Protocol was limited by a range of issues like different national priorities, the complexity of environmental matters and weak enforcement. It was obvious that working together at the international level on the environment would be even more necessary (Barnett, 2021).

At the turn of the century, the international institutions scene was both complex and rich, thanks to many years of intergovernmental cooperation. Even though there were some advantages, it also showed clear weaknesses in managing issues in the developing countries.

Advantages:

- IOs made it easier for states to communicate, negotiate and cooperate on multiple matters by providing set guidelines. Many IOs play a role in guiding countries and deciding the world's agenda by creating international norms and guidelines.
- Sometimes IOs possess financial means, technological understanding and specific knowledge that one country might not be able to have.
- Legitimacy and Authority: Because of their authority, IOs such as the UN could create a structure for international cooperation with support from world society.

IOs can assemble both people and governments to discuss and shape attitudes toward important world matters.

The Current Structure of International Organizations: Pros and Cons

Flaws:

- Because their focus was on intergovernmental help, IOs often omitted the involvement of non-state actors.
- The basic principle of state sovereignty has occasionally kept International Organizations from getting involved in countries' internal struggles.

- Sometimes, only wealthy and powerful countries had control over agendas and results in IOs.
- It was common to find that the bureaucratic and slow processes in some industrial organizations were criticized.
- Many IOs lacked effective systems that enabled them to enforce their decisions and compliance with member states.
- Occasionally, the growth of IOs with similar duties resulted in parts of the organization being fragmented and duplicated.
- The financial problems and lack of staff made it hard for IOs to fully support international solutions.

In the early years of the 21st century, international organisations struggled with new and challenging circumstances. It soon became clear after the Cold War that related issues like nationalism, movements of non-nation groups, growing issues from globalisation, inequalities, and threats to the environment were becoming more serious. Despite the benefits of International Organisations, they struggle to manage many of these problems. At this time, international groups made progress by adapting to new circumstances (Monteiro & Adler, 2022).

ADAPTING TO NEW REALITIES: KEY DRIVERS OF CHANGE IN THE 21ST CENTURY

At the beginning of the 21st century, when liberal democracy seemed to win and multilateralism looked promising, things soon became more complex due to rapid changes globally. After the Second World War and during the Cold War, international organisations (IOs) had to adjust to a mix of strong forces that influenced them. To meet the challenges of today's world, international organisations should review their goals, structures and the approaches they use. They are caused by new technologies, changes in power, increasing global problems and the greater impact of actors that are not part of governments (Mamasoliev, 2024).

The Influence of Technological Progress

The rapid development of technology has been a major feature of the 21st century, affecting every aspect of life, including the work of international organisations. Thanks to the rapid growth of computers, internet and mobile phones, the digital revolution have deeply modified the flow of information and communication. Because of digitalization, IOs can now operate more smoothly, reach more people and cooperate better. Real-time communication over great distances has become normal, enabling quick reactions to crises and promoting more regular and inclusive interactions with member states and outsiders. Digital platforms have expanded the reach of IOs, allowing them to disseminate information, raise awareness about global issues, and engage with citizens directly. Managing large data, dealing digital inequities, and fighting false information that could compromise the legitimacy and work of international organizations are among the difficulties this digital ecosystem presents (Sommerer et al., 2022).

The Ascendance of Cyber concerns

The increasing reliance on digital infrastructure has simultaneously ushered in a new domain of security threats. Cyberattacks, perpetrated by state and non-state actors, can target critical infrastructure, disrupt essential services, steal sensitive information, and undermine the stability of international systems. IOS is not immune to these threats, necessitating the formulation of robust cybersecurity strategies and the advancement of international cooperation on cyber governance. To report cyber-crime, cyber espionage, and the risk of cyber conflict, international organizations must bring up-to-date their security protocols and ease dialogue among member states to establish behavioural norms in cyberspace (Abbott et al., 2016).

Technology Transfer and Development

Technology holds great potential for addressing world problems including poverty reduction, disease prevention, and climate change mitigation. Especially from industrialized to poor countries, international organizations (IOs) are essential in facilitating the transfer of relevant technologies. Improving access to clean energy technologies, agricultural innovations, and internet resources would help to significantly promote sustainable development goals. However, issues related to intellectual property rights, affordability, and the need for appropriate technological adaptation to local contexts remain significant hurdles that IOs must navigate to ensure equitable and effective technology transfer (Reinsberg, 2025).

TRANSFORMATIONS IN POWER DYNAMICS AND MULTIPOLARITY

After the end of the Cold War, the world order changed from being mostly unipolar to having more than one dominant power which has shaped international organisations. Many IOs like WTO is the best example of it. However; the aftermath of Cold-War has given rise to international organisations and co-operations on the regional level as well as multilateral treaties.

The Rise of Emerging Economies (BRICS and Beyond)

Economic growth and political influence have greatly increased for emerging economies, especially the BRICS nations (Brazil, Russia, India, China and South Africa) in the 21st century. They have become important contributors to the world's economy, financial systems and diplomacy, hoping to gain greater influence in international organisations. Because their views on global governance, development and international norms are often not the same as those of traditional Western powers, IOs must adjust how they make decisions and what policies they support. The emergence of other key regional players, apart from BRICS, further assists in making the world multipolar.

Challenges to Traditional Hegemony

While developing countries have grown stronger, traditional Western countries have seen a significant drop in their influence. While they continue to hold some influence, these organisations can no longer decide world issues as easily as before. As a result of this change, different groups of countries within IOs sometimes clash as they seek to promote their own interests. In an increasingly contested world scene, international organizations have to negotiate these opposing interests, therefore fostering discussion and compromise to maintain their effectiveness and credibility. The rise of populist and nationalist movements in some traditionally dominant states has further complicated multilateral cooperation.

Evolving Alliances and Partnerships

The changing global power landscape has also led to the formation of new alliances and partnerships, often driven by shared economic interests, security concerns, or regional dynamics. These changing alliances can challenge and support the present international system. Regional international organizations have grown important as platforms for cooperation among nearby countries, maybe working alongside or as replacements for world international organizations. The rise of issue-specific coalitions and ad hoc groupings of states focused on particular challenges also reflects the shifting patterns of international cooperation. International institutions have to evolve with this changing environment, fostering synergies with new coalitions and making sure they improve rather than undermine the general multilateral system.

ESCALATED GLOBAL CRISES AND INTERCONNECTEDNESS

In the 21st century, there have been many worldwide crises that underline how close the world is and show the need for united action, often brought about by international organisations.

Climate Change and Environmental Degradation

It is now accepted by scientists that humans are changing the climate and as a result, we see more serious effects such as droughts, floods, higher seas and less available resources. Problems like these are made worse by harm to the environment such as pollution and decreasing biodiversity. Organisations such as the UNFCCC and UNEP are responsible for steering international efforts to preserve the environment, support sustainable living and tackle climate change. It is important for international organisations to support strong emissions cuts, encourage the use of green technologies and assist poor countries in dealing with climate change. Because the environmental crisis is severe and growing, we need tougher and more enforceable agreements at the international level (Hunter & Walter, 2025).

Global Health Pandemics (e.g., COVID-19)

The COVID-19 epidemic made clear the interconnection of the world society and the grave consequences of global health crises. The rapid spread of the virus across borders crippled national healthcare systems and upset the economy. By coordinating the worldwide reaction, providing guidance, and facilitating the development and distribution of vaccines, the World Health Organization (WHO) proved very helpful. The epidemic highlighted the need of strong worldwide health security systems, better pandemic preparedness, and more effective mechanisms for international cooperation in research, surveillance, and response to developing infectious diseases. International organisations have to evolve to this reality by strengthening their capacity in health governance and supporting more unity in addressing worldwide health hazards (Abbas & Duchesne, 2023)

Extensive Migration and Refugee Movements

In the twenty-first century, unmatched levels of forced migration and relocation have been caused by wars, persecution, environmental destruction, and financial hardship. For host countries and the world society, large-scale refugee migrations and migrant crossings create significant humanitarian, social, and political challenges. Delivering safety and support to migrants and refugees, advocating their rights, and fostering worldwide cooperation on migration control depend on international bodies like UNHCR and IOM. International organizations have to develop more thorough and humane plans to address the underlying reasons of displacement, ensure safe and orderly migration, and encourage fair burden-sharing among countries if they are to fit this reality.

The Increasing Impact of Non-State Entities

As previously emphasized, non-state actors have gained significant influence in the 21st century, setting global agendas and contesting the conventional state-centric paradigm of international relations. International organizations have had to adjust to this reality by discovering novel methods to engage with these stakeholders.

International Non-Governmental Organizations

In campaigning, service delivery, monitoring, and holding states and corporations accountable on many global issues including human rights, environmental preservation, humanitarian aid, and development INGOs are absolutely vital. Using their knowledge, outreach, and grassroots ties, international organizations more and more recognize the major contributions of international non-governmental organizations and seek to build ties with them. Adapting to this reality calls for the creation of more inclusive platforms for INGO participation in IO processes and recognition of their importance as vital stakeholders in world governance (Orujov, 2024).

Multinational Corporations (MNCs)

Because of their size, MNCs influence the economy, trade, investments, labour conditions, and environmental policies. International bodies are collaborating with businesses to encourage responsible business actions, promote social responsibility, and apply their expertise to reach development goals. This means that IOs should design ways for talking with and cooperating with MNCs, while also putting in place methods to ensure they are accountable and comply with worldwide rules.

Global Civil Society Movements

Thanks to digital technologies, global civil society movements are raising awareness and advocating for different global problems. Many are finding that listening to civil society and including them in policy decisions can bring positive changes to organizations and nations. For this to work, people and organizations should be given opportunities to participate in international organizations and follow their procedures closely.

With the start of the 21st century, we experienced rapid and continuous changes because of new technology, shifting global relations, severe global challenges, and the rise of non-state actors. In order to be effective in today's world, international organizations have had to modify their structures, goals, and methods of working. IOs that are open to new ideas, promote true collaboration, and react well to the present situation will play an important role in forming the direction of international governance and creating a better world.

TRANSFORMATIONS IN THE STRUCTURE AND FUNCTION OF INTERNATIONAL ORGANISATIONS

In recent years, the shape and function of international organizations (IOs) have changed greatly. The rise of global problems such as climate change, pandemics, changes in power, and non-state actors has pushed traditional organizations to change, while many new and regional bodies have appeared, and alliances between groups have increased. This change represents efforts by nations to adjust to new circumstances in the world and improve how they act together. This part looks at significant changes by examining reforms in international organizations, the appearance of new institutions, and the development of new ways to cooperate (Vlados et al., 2022).

Reform Projects Inside Established International Organizations (e.g., United Nations, World Trade Organization, Bretton Woods Institutions)

The main IOs built in the mid-20th century – the UN, WTO, and the Bretton Woods Institutions – need to update their structures and functions to fit today's challenges. In general, reform projects give importance to three areas: making changes in governance and representation, adjusting the mandate, and boosting efficiency and responsibility. Due to changing global power, it is now extremely challenging for International Organizations to manage governance and representation. Many times, the composition of crucial bodies such as the UN Security Council, the WTO dispute resolution system, and the voting system within the Bretton Woods Institutions is based on the power structure of the mid-20th century, and not on the modern, multipolar situation.

The UN Security Council, which has five permanent members with veto power, is usually the main subject in reform debates. Growing economies, such as India, Brazil, and South Africa, are being proposed for Permanent Membership to give the Council greater legitimacy and represent the current pattern of global power. Even so, the projects could be met with opposition from the permanent members who are concerned about losing their control. Some say World Bank and IMF voting power is unfair because it favours countries with bigger economies at their founding. Although people hoping for bigger changes say these actions are insufficient, there have been some efforts to increase the influence of developing countries (Ghozali et al., 2025).

Changing Mandates to Handle Contemporary Issues

Though broad, the missions of long-standing international organizations often call for change to properly face the new and increased challenges of the twenty-first century.

The UN, initially focused on maintaining international peace and security between states, has increasingly expanded its mandate to encompass a wider range of issues, including sustainable development, human rights, humanitarian assistance, climate change, and global health. The 2015 implementation of the Sustainable Development Goals (SDGs) signifies a substantial initiative to establish a holistic framework for tackling interrelated global issues.

Ensuring these capabilities is used to get past government bureaucracy, acquire the funding needed, and create co-operation among UN organizations and others.

To meet the challenges of new forms of protectionism and digital trade, as well as the mix of trade and environmental and social matters, the WTO must update its trade rules. Talks happening now highlight why it is important for the WTO to remain relevant in a rapidly changing global economy. For a long time, the lack of efficiency and accountability has troubled established international organizations. Complicated rules, groups with similar tasks, and no clear owners of jobs can make it difficult for them to work well. Making operations more efficient often means improving how things are done, collaborating better between departments and agencies, and using technology (Begem, 2024).

The trust in international organizations comes from the existence of accountability systems. To do this, systems must be watched more closely, decisions should be made openly, and ways to report issues should be available. As organizations working at the international level come under increasing examination from governments, NGOs, and the public, they must be more accountable and open. Improving evaluation techniques is crucial to help international organizations fulfil their goals as stated (Bayz, 2024).

The Growth of Regional and New Organizations

At the same time, during the 21st century, many new international organisations have emerged, while the influence of regional bodies has grown.

Improving Regional Cooperation (e.g., AU, ASEAN, EU's Growing Influence

Regional organizations have grown important platforms for addressing shared issues and promoting cooperation among adjacent countries. The African Union (AU) has taken a more assertive stance in promoting development across the continent, economic integration, and peace and security. The Association of Southeast Asian Nations (ASEAN) has strengthened political, economic, and socio-cultural cooperation among its member countries. Though facing internal challenges, the European Union (EU) continues to evolve as a unique form of regional integration, hence significantly influencing political, social, and economic issues both inside Europe and outside. These regional organizations sometimes show a stronger feeling of group identification and shared interests among its members, maybe improving cooperation on certain regional concerns. They can be absolutely necessary basic components for large-scale worldwide cooperation (Iriye, 2002).

The Rise of Minilateralism and Issue-Specific Coalitions

The Rise of Issue-Specific Alliances and Minilateralism Dissatisfaction with the slowness and alleged ineffectiveness of large multinational organizations has helped to bring minilateralism into being: cooperation among a small, more selective group of countries with shared interests or competencies to address certain issues. Examples include the G20, which brings together the main industrialized and developing countries to discuss worldwide financial and economic stability, as well as several issue-specific coalitions focused on areas including nuclear non-proliferation, climate change, or global health security. By avoiding the complexity of large international talks, these smaller, more agile alliances might sometimes achieve faster progress on specific issues. Still, they ask questions about inclusiveness and the potential erosion of power and legitimacy of more general international institutions (DiMaggio, 2009).

BUILDING COLLABORATIVE FRAMEWORKS AND PARTNERSHIPS

The 21st century has witnessed the growth and fortification of many partnerships and cooperation models including international organizations, governments, the business sector, and civil society, acknowledging that global concerns call for the combined efforts of all stakeholders (Dunoff, 2012).

Global Governance's Public-Private Partnerships (PPPs)

Many global problems, including building infrastructure, improving healthcare, fighting climate change, and reducing poverty, are now tackled through Public-private Partnerships (PPPs). Alliances are enabled and supported by IOs when they gather the skills, knowledge, and abilities of people and businesses (Budiana, 2024). Even so, they can be beneficial because of investment from the private sector and improved efficiency; still, there are disputes over accountability, transparency, and potential for businesses to dominate public decisions. Proper management and guidelines are required to make sure that PPPs contribute to society and lastingly follow sustainable development goals (Haynes et al., 2023).

Engaging Civil Society and the Private Sector

Greater recognition is being given to CSOs and private businesses as essential in completing IOs' mandates. CSOs stand out because they have a strong grassroots presence, the expertise needed for advocacy, and know how to rally communities. Such groups are capable of giving crucial grassroots knowledge, skill in lobbying, and the power to change public opinion. These organizations are developing guidelines for involvements with civil society, including meetings, joint work, and helping in policy decisions. To help combat challenges like climate change and poverty, the private sector is strong because it has money, new technology, and can reach around the world. Experts are seeking creative ways to encourage companies to align their actions with sustainable goals (Lopez-Claros et al., 2020).

Multi-Stakeholder Initiatives and Platforms

Since global issues are complex, they need to be faced by a broad group of people and organizations. People working in governments, international groups, businesses, civil society, academic circles, and other sectors join forces through MSIs and platforms to solve common issues. Examples are initiatives dealing with sustainability of supply chains, international health efforts, and the control of internet policies.

These areas wish to encourage dialog, achieve consensus, and organize collaborative efforts. Even though MSIs can help with more inclusive solutions, they have to deal with accountability and working in competition with others (Mingst et al., 2022).

The 21st century has brought complex and fluctuating changes to international organizations. Governments are reviewing how their structures and policies should be updated to match the current world challenges. The development of new regional groups, growth of minilateralism, and increased involvement in South-South cooperation have led to a stronger interest in specialized and area-specific joint efforts. A growing preference for alliances and international cooperation reveals that managing world affairs is best if many supportive actors are involved (Govender & Adegbite, 2022).

CASE ANALYSES IN ADAPTATION AND INNOVATION

Modern times have placed new and major challenges before international organizations, making them modify and adapt their processes. A look at concrete cases shows that international organizations have handled these challenges in different ways, sometimes succeeding and at other times continuing to face problems.

The World Health Organization (WHO) and Global Health Security in Response to Pandemics

The WHO has received widespread criticism and calls for changes during the COVID-19 pandemic, as an international agency mandated with public health. The WHO faced tough challenges due to the need for its leadership in international health, pandemic preparations, early warning, and global coordination. The WHO was put to the test by the challenges brought by the COVID-19 pandemic. In the beginning, efforts to identify and highlight the coronavirus were indispensable. The WHO provided assurance in sharing research information, worked out guidelines on testing and treatment procedures, and orchestrated the early initiatives for discovering vaccines and treatments globally. It revealed how governing boards, financing, and countries' politics influence the WHO. Being criticized for early and possibly unpredictable responses, plus using information provided by other countries, as well as the role of politics (Bromley et al., 2021).

The WHO has taken steps to improve global health security. This covers support for improved and more sustainable finance, independent investigations in severe epidemics, and starting a global accord for handling and responding to pandemics. The aim is to help the WHO be better prepared for fast responses and fair distribution of health resources during future pandemics. During health crises, important steps include discovering new methods for exchanging information, playing with new funding approaches, and making use of modern technology for tracking and messaging.

The United Nations Framework Convention on Climate Change (UNFCCC) and the Paris Agreement: Navigating Environmental Governance

Environmental governance changed greatly when the UNFCCC and Paris Agreement were introduced. The UNFCCC was established in 1992 to support efforts to coordinate global action against climate change. Even though the first Kyoto Protocol required developed countries to cut their emissions, it still had problems with its scope and operation.

In 2015, the Paris Agreement was a major step forward. Instead of having one common set of stringent targets, it now allows every nation to produce its own Nationally Determined Contribution. The goal was to attract countries like the United States and China, who had not fully registered to the Kyoto Protocol. One of the main points made in the Paris Agreement was the emphasis on supporting poorer countries with resources for adapting to climate change and repairing losses (Smith et al., 2017).

UNFCCC innovation includes the adoption of transparent and accountable methods, getting more finance for climate action, and raising the role of local governments, companies, and civil organizations in tackling climate change. It is important to ensure that all National Determined Contributions are strong enough to match the long-term objectives of the Agreement and to put the supporting mechanisms into action. The UNFCCC goes on developing by encouraging urgent discussions, advancing new technologies, and spreading a global mission for climate neutrality (Dunford et al., 2016).

WTO AND CHALLENGES OF TRADE LIBERALIZATION IN A MULTIPOLAR ENVIRONMENT

The World commerce Organization (WTO), founded in 1995 to facilitate free commerce and serve as a platform for resolving trade disputes, has encountered considerable difficulties in adjusting to the dynamics of a multipolar world and increasing protectionist attitudes he WTO's core functions – negotiating trade agreements and administering a dispute settlement system – have been strained in recent years.

The Doha Development Agenda, initiated in 2001 to enhance trade inclusivity for developing nations, has stagnated due to disputes among member states about critical topics such as agricultural subsidies and market access. The rise of new economic powers and differing perspectives on the role of the state in the economy have complicated multilateral trade negotiations. Moreover, the WTO's dispute resolution mechanism, once regarded as a fundamental element of the rules-based trading system, has been undermined by postponements in the nomination of Appellate Body members (Bakreski & Miovska, 2024).

The WTO is working on different ways to promote adaptation and innovation. This grouping includes understandings on e-commerce and investment facilitation agreed to by smaller alliances of nations with similar interests. More and more, it is understood that trade concerns should be considered alongside environmental and social issues. Even so, changes to the system of dispute settlement and new additions to WTO rules are still under progress, but they often face strong political challenges. The WTO must work towards building agreement and keeping its position as a vital organization managing global trade in a world where cooperation is scarce (Bianchi, 2017).

REGIONAL ORGANIZATIONS AND PEACE BUILDING INITIATIVES

Organisations at the regional level are now more important in promoting peace because they know the region well and want the area to be stable. As an example, the African Union (AU) and Economic Community of West African States (ECOWAS) take this approach.

To manage the region's challenges, the AU is deploying peacekeepers, helping negotiate conflicts, and supporting countries with democratic leadership in Africa. Because the principle of non-indifference is included, the Constitutive Act gives permission for intervention if a member state does not protect its people from genocide or crimes against humanity. After conflicts, the AU has implemented standards for assisting member states.

Peace building in a region requires foreseeing danger by using early warning systems, recruiting civilians for peace, and considering gender when planning peace strategies. When it comes to peace building, regional organizations frequently draw on the traditions and history of their communities. Due to challenges on funding, capacity, and member states' sovereignty, global organizations are shifting more peace-building duties to regional groups (Uvere & Adiele, 2025).

THE ROLE OF THE INTERNATIONAL CRIMINAL COURT (ICC) IN ADDRESSING IMPUNITY

The creation of the International Criminal Court (ICC) has significantly advanced the quest of justice and the punishment of the most terrible crimes perpetrated worldwide. Among these offenses include genocide, war crimes, crimes against humanity, and the crime of aggression. The International Criminal Court (ICC) is operating as a permanent body for the first time ever to prosecute offenses of this kind controlled by international law.

The International Criminal Court (ICC) was founded as worries over the presence of tribunals in Yugoslavia and Rwanda drove the quest of world justice for mass atrocities to front page. It changes the methods used in the United States for criminal cases by following the values of fair treatment and a suitable trial, so fulfilling the needs of world society. The International Criminal Court, however, has faced many major challenges. It can only intervene inside countries that have ratified the Rome Statute or under United States Security Council direction. Emphasizing the court's limited power is absolutely essential given that several major countries, like the United States of America, China, and Russia, have not signed the Statute. Claims say both fans and detractors have criticized the International Criminal Court. These people contend that the court unduly focuses on African issues and often shows political prejudice (Baig et al., 2025).

The ICC is taking steps to expand its reach, handle investigations and prosecutions better, and build better ties with communities involved. Another focus of the court is to keep up with novel international crimes and to collaborate more with nations. The goal is to address any political obstacles and help the ICC carry out its main mission of eliminating impunity for very serious international crimes (Berten & Kranke, 2022).

The chapter sheds insight on the several different ways international organizations are using to address and create new solutions for the present world issues. International organizations (IOs) are doing many things in the face of pandemics, enhancing global health security, managing environmental regulations, coping with continuous trade restrictions, promoting world peace, and pursuing justice. Though they have faced great obstacles along the way, their efforts to reform, collaborate, and find innovative solutions to global problems transcending national boundaries have shown their continuing relevance. Whether the multilateral system will be effective in the future will depend on the capacity of international organizations (IOs) to change with the times and act.

INTERNATIONAL ORGANIZATIONS: FUTURE DIRECTIONS AND CHALLENGES

International organisations (IOs) stand at a critical juncture, facing a complex interplay of persistent challenges and the imperative to adapt for future relevance. Key issues guiding their future path are negotiating the fragile balance between global cooperation and national sovereignty, guaranteeing legitimacy and inclusiveness, tackling the fragmentation of world governance, using international law in a changing world order, and foreseeing the influence of disruptive technologies (Robertson, 2022).

Negotiating National Interests and Sovereignty Issues

Fundamental ideas of state sovereignty are among the most major challenges IOs encounter. Though member countries agree that global issues call for group action, they usually prioritize their own local interests and are loath to cede great power to international organizations. These kind of conflicts show hostility to legally binding international treaties, selective involvement with international organization mandates, and the claim of national prerogatives in domains that seem to be relevant to their sovereignty. International organizations (IOs) will one day push a paradigm of "pooled sovereignty" or "shared responsibility," in which nations acknowledge that resolving global crises usually calls for group action and some level compromise on matters of final sovereignty. Successfully negotiating this continuous difficulty will depend on the creation of confidence, the showing of the mutual advantages of cooperation, and the evolution of flexible systems honoring national settings (Berten, 2022).

Tackling Global Governance Fragmentation

The growth of new IOs, regional groups, minilateral groupings, and issue-specific coalitions reflects a certain discontent with the current multilateral system and a want for more customized forms of collaboration. Fragmentation like this can cause effort duplication, policy inconsistency, and a deterioration of the general global governance structure. Future paths have to stress more collaboration and synergy among various IOs and cooperative structures. Building a more consistent and efficient global governance scene will depend on encouraging conversation, defining unambiguous divisions of labour, and supporting interoperability among various projects. IOs have to change into centres for information sharing and tools for bridging various international projects (Schuette, 2024).

The Function of International Law in a Changing World Order

International law offers the normative basis for inter-state relations and the operation of IOs. Its effectiveness is being tested, nevertheless, by changing world power dynamics and the rise of fresh problems. Unilateralism's growth, the uneven application of international norms, and the struggle to uphold international legal responsibilities all present major problems. Future IOs will have to approve the centrality of international law, endeavour to improve its institutions (like the International Court of Justice), and alter legal frameworks to handle modern concerns including cyber warfare, climate change, and the control of troublesome technologies. Keeping a rules-based international order will rest on on endorsing universal respect to international law and making more efficient enforcement systems (Robertson et al., 2024).

CONCLUSION

Due to the fact that the current century is both complicated and unpredictable, IOs are required to constantly adapt. The emergence of IOs represented the transition from the time of tremendous anticipation that followed the end of the Cold War to the current world, in which problems are intricately intertwined and there is no single force that is in charge. As a consequence of this, IOs are continually working to enhance their systems and procedures in order to improve their ability to collaborate on a global scale and to address new and ongoing problems. Over the course of the twenty-first century, there have been a number of advancements that have taken place in international organizations, and these developments have seen significant trends and changes. It is the evolution of technology that has been the key component that has had a significant impact on the results.

While digitization has made communication more effective and broadened its scope, it has also given rise to substantial issues over cybersecurity and the distribution of technology in an equal manner. The traditional dominance of certain nations has been called into question as a result of the rise of new powers and emerging economies, which has resulted in an increased influence of these economies in the decision-making processes of international institutions. The growing intensity of global crises and interdependence including climate change, pandemics, and transnational threats has highlighted the critical need for coordinated international action and put great pressure on IOs to react appropriately. The increasing power of non-state actors INGOs and multinational businesses among them has driven IOs to interact with a broader spectrum of stakeholders and change their governance structures to fit these new players.

In order to address such concerns, the major international organizations have begun discussions on governance and representation, as well as altered their agendas, and are currently working toward achieving significant efficiency and responsibility objectives.

Apart from this, the growth of South-South cooperation, the application of minilateralism, and the creation of new and regional institutions are all signs that countries are eager to work in smaller groups. Moreover, the movement toward new alliances and partnerships highlights the reality that the administration of the global society in the current day calls for the involvement of many partners. Considering these results, it seems that the field of international collaboration is changing significantly. A system that is wholly governed by the state is no longer in existence; rather, everything now operates as a network of organizations in which everyone has a role to play and solutions need to be adjusted to the specific characteristics of the case. There are instances when the conventional options for collaboration are in direct opposition to the innovations that are being achieved through multilateral operations. The purpose of these advances is to incorporate a wide range of stakeholders into the activities, as well as to make them more adaptable and comprehensive.

REFERENCES

Abbas, M., & Duchesne, E. (2023). Beyond the Failure of the WTO: Resilience of Trade Multilateralism. In *Crisis of Multilateralism? Challenges and Resilience* (pp. 199–218). Springer International Publishing. DOI: 10.1007/978-3-031-39671-7_10

Abbott, K. W., Green, J. F., & Keohane, R. O. (2016). Organizational ecology and institutional change in global governance. *International Organization, 70*(2), 247–277. DOI: 10.1017/S0020818315000338

Anghel, V., & Jones, E. (2025). The enlargement of international organisations. *West European Politics, 48*(1), 1–28. DOI: 10.1080/01402382.2024.2311044

Auld, E., & Elfert, M. (2024). The waning legitimacy of international organisations and their promissory visions. *Comparative Education, 60*(3), 377–400. DOI: 10.1080/03050068.2024.2371271

Baig, K., Saeed, S., Ahmad, T., & Saeed, S. (2025). Examining the Roles of the International Court of Justice and the International Criminal Court in Upholding Global Justice: A Comparative Analysis. *Social Science Review Archives, 3*(1), 2185–2194. DOI: 10.70670/sra.v3i1.529

Bakreski, O., & Miovska, L. B. (2024). THE POSITION AND ROLE OF STATE AND NON-STATE ACTORS IN THE 21st CENTURY. *Security Dialogue, 15*(1), 35–49.

Barnett, M. (2021). International progress, international order, and the liberal international order. *The Chinese Journal of International Politics, 14*(1), 1–22. DOI: 10.1093/cjip/poaa019

. Bayz, H. Q. (2024). The Role and Impact of the International Criminal Court in Global Justice. *OTS Canadian Journal, 3*(5).

. Begem, S. S. (2024). The Role of the International Criminal Court: A Literature Review on Its Effectiveness and Limitations. *eScience Humanity Journal, 5*(1), 253-259.

Beigbeder, Y. (2023). *The role and status of international humanitarian volunteers and organizations: The right and duty to humanitarian assistance* (Vol. 12). Brill.

Berten, J. (2022). The future as epistemic condition: How international organisations anticipate futures of social policy. *Global Society, 36*(2), 206–222. DOI: 10.1080/13600826.2021.2021153

Berten, J., & Kranke, M. (2022). Anticipatory global governance: International organisations and the politics of the future. *Global Society*, *36*(2), 155–169. DOI: 10.1080/13600826.2021.2021150

Bianchi, A. (2017). *Non-state actors and international law*. Routledge. DOI: 10.4324/9781315247885

Bromley, P., Overbey, L., Furuta, J., & Kijima, R. (2021). Education reform in the twenty-first century: Declining emphases in international organisation reports, 1998–2018. *Globalisation, Societies and Education*, *19*(1), 23–40. DOI: 10.1080/14767724.2020.1816159

Brown, O. R. (2024). The Underside of Order: Race in the Constitution of International Order. *International Organization*, *78*(1), 38–66. DOI: 10.1017/S0020818324000018

Budiana, M. (2024). Global Governance: The Role of International Institutions in the 21st Century. Journal of Law. *Social Science and Humanities*, *1*(2), 204–219.

Cheng, D. S. (2014). Contributions of International Organizations towards Globalization in the 21st Century. *Journal of Global Business Management*, *10*(2), 94.

. DiMaggio, P. (2009). The twenty-first-century firm: changing economic organization in international perspective.

Dunford, M., Aoyama, Y., Campolina Diniz, C., Kundu, A., Limonov, L., Lin, G., Liu, W., Park, S. O., & Turok, I. (2016). Area development and policy: An agenda for the 21st century. *Area Development and Policy*, *1*(1), 1–14. DOI: 10.1080/23792949.2016.1158621

Dunoff, J. L. (2012). Is sovereign equality obsolete? Understanding twenty-first century international organizations. *Netherlands Yearbook of International Law*, *43*, 99–127. DOI: 10.1007/978-90-6704-915-3_5

Ghozali, M., Afra, C., Agusriadi, D., & Yusfani, M. (2025). The Position and Role of the International Criminal Court (ICC) In International Crime Resolution. *International Journal of Law, Social Science, and Humanities*, *2*(1), 111–116. DOI: 10.70193/ijlsh.v2i1.160

. Govender, C. M., & Adegbite, W. M. (2022). EVOLVING ROLE OF LEARNING AND DEVELOPMENT SPECIALISTS IN THE 21 st CENTURY FOURTH INDUSTRIAL REVOLUTION WORKPLACE. International Journal of Entrepreneurship International Journal of Entrepreneurship, (26 1), 1-16.

Haug, S., Foot, R., & Baumann, M. O. (2024). Power shifts in international organisations: China at the United Nations. *Global Policy, 15*(S2), 5–17. DOI: 10.1111/1758-5899.13368

. Haynes, J., Pilbeam, B., & Hough, P. (2023). World politics: International relations and globalisation in the 21st century.

Hunter, T., & Walter, S. (2025). International organizations in national parliamentary debates. *The Review of International Organizations*, •••, 1–27.

Iriye, A. (2002). *Global community: The role of international organizations in the making of the contemporary world*. Univ of California Press. DOI: 10.1525/9780520936126

. Joshi, A., Padhi, S. K., & Joshi, A. (2025). INCLUSIVE EDUCATION IN 21 ST CENTURY INDIA: CHALLENGES, ISSUES, AND OPPORTUNITIES.

Lake, D. A., Martin, L. L., & Risse, T. (2021). Challenges to the liberal order: Reflections on international organization. *International Organization, 75*(2), 225–257. DOI: 10.1017/S0020818320000636

Lee, C. H., & Lee, S. H. (2002). NGOs and International Society: Prospects on Their Roles in the 21st Century. *Pacific Focus, 17*(1), 147–162. DOI: 10.1111/j.1976-5118.2002.tb00266.x

Lopez-Claros, A., Dahl, A. L., & Groff, M. (2020). *Global governance and the emergence of global institutions for the 21st century*. Cambridge University Press. DOI: 10.1017/9781108569293

Mamasoliev, S. (2024). The Role of International Trade In Us Economic Growth. *Innovative Developments and Research in Education, 3*(32), 139–147.

Manulak, M. W. (2024). The sources of influence in multilateral diplomacy: Replaceability and intergovernmental networks in international organizations. *The Review of International Organizations, 19*(3), 579–610. DOI: 10.1007/s11558-024-09536-5

Martin, L. L., & Simmons, B. A. (2013). International organizations and institutions. *Handbook of international relations, 2*, 326-351.

Mingst, K. A., Karns, M. P., & Lyon, A. J. (2022). *The United Nations in the 21st century*. Routledge. DOI: 10.4324/9781003038269

Moch, E. (2024). The Economic and Geopolitical Significance of the Brics Nations: A Comparative Analysis of Their Global Influence in the 21st Century. *East African Journal of Business and Economics, 7*(2), 86–100. DOI: 10.37284/eajbe.7.2.2310

Monteiro, P., & Adler, P. S. (2022). Bureaucracy for the 21st century: Clarifying and expanding our view of bureaucratic organization. *The Academy of Management Annals, 16*(2), 427–475. DOI: 10.5465/annals.2019.0059

Morgenstern, F. (2024). *Legal problems of international organizations: reissue with new foreword by Jan Klabbers*. Cambridge University Press. DOI: 10.1017/9781009448154

. Orujov, E. (2024). GLOBAL TRADE RELATIONS IN THE MULTIPOLAR WORLD SYSTEM AND CHALLENGES OF THE WORLD TRADE ORGANIZATION FOR THE 21ST CENTURY. *German International Journal of Modern Science/Deutsche Internationale Zeitschrift für Zeitgenössische Wissenschaft*, (95).

Poorhashemi, A. (2024). International environmental law. In *Public International Law* (pp. 453–466). Routledge. DOI: 10.4324/9781003451327-19

Rahimi, R. A., & Oh, G. S. (2024). Rethinking the role of educators in the 21st century: Navigating globalization, technology, and pandemics. *Journal of Marketing Analytics, 12*(2), 182–197. DOI: 10.1057/s41270-024-00303-4

Reiners, N. (2024). The power of interpersonal relationships: A socio-legal approach to international institutions and human rights advocacy. *Review of International Studies, 50*(2), 252–270. DOI: 10.1017/S0260210523000438

Reinsberg, B. (2025). Institutional overlap and the survival of intergovernmental organisations. *West European Politics, 48*(1), 29–57. DOI: 10.1080/01402382.2024.2341564

Robertson, S. L. (2022). Guardians of the future: International organisations, anticipatory governance and education. *Global Society, 36*(2), 188–205. DOI: 10.1080/13600826.2021.2021151

Robertson, S. L., & Beech, J. (2024). 'Promises promises': International organisations, promissory legitimacy and the re-negotiation of education futures. *Comparative Education, 60*(3), 423–440. DOI: 10.1080/03050068.2023.2287938

Schuette, L. A. (2024). IO survival politics: International organisations amid the crisis of multilateralism. *Journal of European Public Policy, 31*(11), 3812–3838. DOI: 10.1080/13501763.2023.2276757

Smith, R., El-Anis, I., & Farrands, C. (2017). *International political economy in the 21st century: Contemporary issues and analyses*. Routledge. DOI: 10.4324/9781315750637

Sommerer, T., Agné, H., Zelli, F., & Bes, B. (2022). *Global legitimacy crises: decline and revival in multilateral governance*. Oxford University Press. DOI: 10.1093/oso/9780192856326.001.0001

. Uvere, I. E., & Adiele, I. J. (2025). GLOBAL CHALLENGES TO STATEHOOD: THE GROWING INFLUENCE OF NON-STATE ACTORS. MULTIDISCIPLINARY JOURNAL OF LAW, EDUCATION AND HUMANITIES, 2(1).

Varga, J. (2021). Defining the economic role and benefits of micro, small and medium-sized enterprises in the 21st century with a systematic review of the literature. *Acta Polytechnica Hungarica*, *18*(11), 209–228. DOI: 10.12700/APH.18.11.2021.11.12

Vlados, C., Chatzinikolaou, D., & Iqbal, B. A. (2022). New Globalization and Multipolarity. *Journal of Economic Integration*, *37*(3), 458–483. DOI: 10.11130/jei.2022.37.3.458

Zürn, M., Tokhi, A., & Binder, M. (2021). The international author-ity database. *Global Policy*, *12*(4), 430–442. DOI: 10.1111/1758-5899.12971

Chapter 14
IoT, FDI, and Trade Openness Unlocking Economic Growth in BIMSTEC Nations

Rajesh Kumar
https://orcid.org/0009-0009-8281-246X
Institute of Management Studies, Ghaziabad, India & National Institute of Technology Agartala, India

Debasis Neogi
https://orcid.org/0000-0003-2229-9376
National Institute of Technology Agartala, India

ABSTRACT

The regional cooperation institution, BIMSTEC, helps economic development and integration among its seven South and Southeast Asian member countries. The article compares the ratio of GDP per capita with the indicators viz Trade Openness, CPI, FDI, Internet Users and Information and Communication Technology. INT and ICT as proxy of the Internet of Things shows how digital infrastructure will be crucial for economic success. For panel data between 1999 and 2019, Fixed and Random Effects models verified by Hausman specification test for heterogeneity and time-invariant characteristics across member states are applied. The data, provided by reputable sources like the World Bank, IMF, UNCTAD and so on, guarantee validity and reliability. The results offer policymakers and stakeholders practical takeaway that emphasises how digital transformation, foreign investment and trade liberalisation contribute to economic growth. Additionally, the study argues for stability in macroeconomic policies and sustainable development measures to

DOI: 10.4018/979-8-3373-1727-4.ch014

promote economic resilience and regional stability.

INTRODUCTION

With the current era of high rates of globalization and digitalization, regional economic integration has served as an important channel of sustainable development (Balassa, 1961; Viner, 1950). Bay of Bengal Initiative for Multi- Sectoral Technical and Economic Cooperation (BIMSTEC) is one such important regional organisation which is devoted towards economic integration and advancement of technical exchanges and boosting cross border integration amongst the seven member countries, Bangladesh, Bhutan, India, Myanmar, Nepal and Sri lanka and Thailand (BIMSTEC Secretariat, 2004). BIMSTEC was shown to have focused on the trade liberalization, facilitation of foreign direct investment (FDI), and regional growth that depends on technology as the fundamental elements of its strategic agenda since its creation in 1997 (Rahman & Singh, 2016).

Internet of Things (IoT) has become a revolutionary aspect in modernization of economies, and it is the paradigm of profound advances in productivity, functionality, and innovation of economic sectors (Atzori et al., 2010; Gubbi et al., 2013). In the case of this analysis, internet penetration rates and Information and Communication Technology (ICT) infrastructure are used as proxies to the adoption of IoT considering that the process of technology-based transformation of economies relies on a technological base to facilitate digital economic transformation (ITU, 2020). When viewed with other important macro economic factors like the Consumer Price Index (CPI), trade openness rates and the FDI movements these (factors) offer a complete picture to ascertain their overall effect on the growth of per capita GDP in the BIMSTEC economies (Solow, 1956; Romer, 1990).

The spread of IoT technologies, with the assistance of the broadening internet connectivity and durable ICT infrastructure, has simultaneously overturned the economic systems of developing countries on an endemic level (UNCTAD, 2019). With IoT use cases, advanced data analytics, predictive modeling of events, and operation optimization in high-stakes markets such as agriculture, healthcare, and manufacturing are possible (Porter & Heppelmann, 2014). This digitalization comes in line with the BIMSTEC strategic plans of creating economic resilience and elimination of developmental gaps amongst the member states (Bhattacharyay, 2010).

In this research, the econometric framework of panel data with both fixed and random effects is used to address questions about the relation between these variables over the course of 20 years (1999-2019). Using sound statistical approaches and credible sources of data, the study aims to present an empirical evidence on the effects of digitalization, trade policies and investment strategies on the outcomes of economic growth. The Hausman test is used to be methodologically rigorous in the selection of the models, which make the results more acceptable in terms of the validity and reliability (Hausman, 1978).

Nevertheless, to accelerate economic integration in regions, despite the developed strategic frameworks, such as the Trade Facilitation Strategic Framework towards 20302, there are still great obstacles to overcome within BIMSTEC (BIMSTEC, 2020). Such barriers include the lack of consistency in policies applied between member states, confused regional arrangements that exist leading to institutional complications, and the existence of significant gaps in developing technological infrastructure (Kumar & Prabhakar, 2019). Moreover, discordant economic interests and national politics vocation have hindered on-time delivery of major regional projects (Mohan, 2018).

The study filling in these crucial gaps will include the exploration of the ways of using digital technologies and increased regional collaboration as triggers of removing the current obstacles. In particular, the research focuses on intra-regional trade flows, more attractive investment boom, and faster economic development through greater internet penetration and strategic implementation of ICTs as potential drivers of robust intra-regional trade flows, more appealing investment environment creation, and economic growth escalation (World Bank, 2016). Inflation management (also as measured by CPI) and openness to trade are also given as complementary factors critical to sustainable performance in the economy (Edwards, 1998; Frankel & Romer, 1999).

Offering evidence-based findings and policy-relevant recommendations, the study contributes to a better understanding of the ways in which BIMSTEC can better use the power of IoT technologies, liberalization of trade, and investment regimes to realize sustainable and inclusive growth. The results will be of significant use to the policymakers, scholarly researchers and stakeholders interested in strategic planning to release the economic potential of BIMSTEC in full (Sachs & Warner, 1995).

Finally, the paper moves beyond purely economic approaches to assessment of IoT, FDI, and openness of trade by having a detailed outline of a better regional integration and policy synchrony. With the calculated intercession, procedural collaborative governance devices, the BIMSTEC member countries will break through the current shackles and open a road that guarantees a digitally incorporated and economically affluent future (Rodrik, 2018).

LITERATURE REVIEW

The research literature on BIMSTEC regional integration creates a confusing scenario of both possibilities and predicaments. In a study by Banik (2005) it was revealed that BIMSTEC region has many favourable features such as competitive price schedules, income complementarities and geographical proximity which together can become leverage in catalysing intra-regional trading activities. Nevertheless Banik pointed out that the actualization of this potential will necessitate a long term endeavour addressing issues that come about as a result of trade liberalization regimes. The study pointed out that economic cooperation between the BIMSTEC member countries has massive potentials, such as increased market access, manufacturing economy of scale as well as integration of India to that of South Asia and Southeast Asia. However, Banik addressed several ongoing issues especially those concerned with the integration of Myanmar as a member state.

Advancing on bilateral trade studies, Basu and Dutta (2007) have carried out a holistic investigation of Indo- Bangladesh trade relations which have indicated that there is a relatively small size of trade between the two neighboring economies. Their study came up with certain specific policy suggestions towards the improvement of bilateral trade between the two countries in which they suggested to Bangladesh about pursuing a more conservative policy on its exchange rate at the same time as it should diversify its export basket creating a high level of competitiveness and sustainability in trade. This comparison between two countries highlights the general issues of intra-BIMSTEC trade growth.

Chakraborty (2007) added a refined voice to the debate of regional integration underlining the fact that some of the BIMSTEC countries had by then entertained an area of preferential trading. Nevertheless, it was shown during a study that regional integration avoided the balanced progress, and issues concerning the rules of origin, safeguard measures, and sensitive product list administration were continued. The analysis conducted by Chakraborty proved that although tariff reduction is still of essence, considerable increase in trade can be achieved only through the complete elimination of non-tariff barriers and trade facilitation mechanism with strong ability. These results remind us of the need to have a complex strategy of regional trade integration in BIMSTEC.

Information and Communication Technology as Economic Growth Drivers

The linkage between the ICT infrastructure and the economic growth has been an issue that has attracted many attention both on the developed and developing countries. Rolller and Waverman (2001) offered some very fundamental evidence obtained through research conducted that ICT infrastructure investment, not only produces significant multiplier impacts of the economy in terms of economic growth, but also in productivity and capacity to innovate. Their work laid the theoretical background to the conceptualization of ICT as a very important input in the production of economies today.

In compliment to this leading study, Koutroumpis (2009) enlightened the knowledge on the growth promoting nature of ICT by enlightening that ICT acts as a growth engine when conditioned with complements especially human capital development and the proper formation of regulatory frameworks. One of the findings in this research has been about the conditional aspect of the ICT effect on human development where the authors sought to give special significance to the institutional and human capital requirements that facilitate the higher technological advantages.

In the context of a BIMSTEC sub-region, the internet penetration has opened up new potential in terms of trade facilitation, financial inclusion, and streamlining efficiency in resource allocation (World Bank, 2020). All these technological advancements are of special interest to the developing economies in the region where digital infrastructure is the way out that may stimulate leapfrog development strategies.

Foreign Direct Investment and Economic Development Nexus

The literature on FDI contribution to economy development focuses more on the multipronged contribution of FDI to host economies. The survey by Borensztein, De Gregorio and Lee (1998) has also given key insights on the factors surrounding the effective role of FDI in stimulating economic growth with the result being that the more positive role of FDI depended on the ability of the host country in absorbing the foreign investment using sufficient human capital and technology facilities. Their work proved that FDI can be used as a vehicle in closing the gap in investment, transfer of technology and creation of jobs as long as the relevant absorptive capacity is in place.

FDI flows in the BIMSTEC scenario have played their role in spurring the industrial growth and infrastructural improvements among the member states (UNCTAD, 2021). Nonetheless, policy uncertainty and time wastage in the bureaucracy have denounced the ideal use of FDI potential benefits as revealed in the literature. These institutional obstacles are some of the key impediments towards making FDI maximise its potential in fostering regional economic growth.

Trade Openness and Economic Performance

The positive correlation between openness in trade and the economic growth has been widely reported using empirical literature. Frankel and Romer (1999) came up with strong empirical evidence showing that trade openness is one of the factors that promote growth of a country in terms of per capita income because of efficiency and increased specialization. Their instrumental variables methodology solved the issues of endogeneity and proved the existence of a causal relationship between openness in trade and economic performance.

The trade liberalization within the framework of the BIMSTEC has been used as a tool to achieve regional social and economic integration and increase access to the market (Asian Development Bank, 2019). Nonetheless, asymmetrical tariffs and other non-tariff barriers are still evident in terms of impediments in trade liberalization which the literature evinces.

Inflation Dynamics and Economic Stability

The stability of prices, which is represented by the Consumer Price Index (CPI) is also a key macroeconomic indicator with serious implications to the investment decision-making process and consumption levels. Fischer (1993) determined the theoretical basis of non-linear relationship between inflation and economic growth and found out that moderate level of inflation tends to promote economic growth at the same time higher rates of inflation cause retardation to economic performance. This study emphasized on the role of price stability as a precondition in sustainable economic growth.

Under the BIMSTEC scenario, inflation control has become an important policy agenda item to ensure the confidence of the investors and promoting development initiatives in the long term (International Monetary Fund, 2020). Records indicate that viable measures of controlling inflation are crucial in generating an empowering environment in the course of regional economic integration.

Technological Integration and Digital Transformation

In the recent scholarship, the contribution of technological integration to the goals of sustainable development in the regional frameworks has been highlighted. In their argument, Srivastava and Das (2018) asserted that the use of a regional technological integration mechanism can become the boosting force of sustainable development performances. They have been able to prove that adoption of IoT technology, with the help of the improved ICT penetration, creates productivity benefits, lowers transaction costs and enhances trade transparency.

According to the literature, the actually harmonized digital policy and strategic infrastructure investments in technology are the areas that the member states of the BIMSTEC can utilize to their great advantage. Such coordinated effort would allow them to use the maximum spill over effects of technology development in the region.

RESEARCH METHODOLOGY

This paper will use panel econometric strategy to study the correlation amid GDP per capita and numerous macroeconomic and technological factors within the member states of BIMSTEC. The panel data approach is especially suitable to this study because it has all the strengths of the cross-sectional and time-series ones and can provide an investigation of economic dynamics in various countries through time but still consider the unobserved heterogeneity (Baltagi, 2021; Hsiao, 2014).

The study design is based on the balanced panel dataset of 7 BIMSTEC member nations representing Bangladesh, Bhutan, India, Myanmar, Nepal, Sri Lanka, and Thailand covering 1999-2019. Such a period of 21 years offers enough target temporal fluctuation that registers not only short-term change, but also long-term trend in the economic performance and technological progress of the region.

Data Sources and Collection

Internationally known and credible sources of information were used to collect data on this study so as to attain consistency, comparability, and validity of the empirical study. These are the main sources of primary data:

World Bank World Development Indicators (WDI) GDP per capita, trade openness, internet users and ICT development indicators
International Monetary Fund (IMF) International Financial Statistics: Consumer Price Index and other indicators of macro economic stability
Foreign Direct Investment flows and stock data in United Nations Conference on Trade and Development (UNCTAD) World Investment Report

Data reliability allows using these recognized international databases as the data provided is trustworthy, which leads to increased reliability of the empirical data (World Bank, 2020; IMF, 2021; UNCTAD, 2021). All the variables were gathered in their natural unit, and then they were converted to econometric analysis units.

Variable Definition and Measurement

Dependent Variable

Dependent variable: GDP per Capita (abbreviated as GDPPC) is an economic performance measure that is gauged by gross domestic product per capita in constant 2010 US dollars. The indicator is a standardized economic measure of development and is easy to compare across all countries over different countries putting into account the population change and inflation variations (Todaro & Smith, 2020).

Independent Variables

Trade Openness (TO): The variable includes the value of exports and imports divided by GDP, the value of which reflects the level of the economy to international markets. Greater trade openness it is supposed that would result in economic development partly due to specialization based on the comparative advantage, part due to increases in efficiencies and part due to enlarging market access (Frankel and Romer, 1999; Sachs and Warner, 1995).

Foreign Direct Investment (FDI): It is defined as percentage of net FDI inflows to GDP and quantifies the cross-border flows of capital that can be invested on productive establishments. It is believed that FDI has a positive economic growth by injecting capital into the economy, increasing the transfer of technology, and spill-overs of knowledge (Borensztein et al., 1998; OECD, 2019).

Consumer Price Index (CPI): This is an indication of macroeconomic stability which is provided as an annual percentage change in consumer price index. Economic growth depends on price stability because high inflation rate has the ability to compromise the investment decisions, decrease the purchasing power, and bring economic uncertainties (Fischer, 1993; Barro, 2013).

Internet Users (INT): This variable can be characterized by the percent of the population with the internet, which serves as a proxy variable of IoT adoption, and development of digital infrastructure. The Internet penetration is the technological basis on which the digital transformation relies and is likely to stimulate the growth of productivity and economic growth (ITU, 2020; World Bank, 2016).

Information and Communication Technology (ICT): Constructed as a composite indicator based on the ICT Development Index, this measure quantifies ICT infrastructure, utilisation and skills in countries. This hypothesis is based on the assumption that ICT development can increase economic growth due to the better communication, lower costs of transactions, and the increased capacity of innovation (ITU, 2019; Koutroumpis, 2009).

The foundational econometric model used in this research takes the following form:

Econometric Model:

$$GDPPC = f\,(TO, FDI, CPI, INT, ICT) \ldots\ldots\ldots\ldots\ldots\ldots(i)$$

Where:

The variable GDPPC stands for Gross Domestic Product per capita in each country which functions as the dependent variable.

The independent variables in the model include Trade Openness (TO), Foreign Direct Investment (FDI), Corruption Perception Index (CPI), Internet Penetration (INT), and Information and Communication Technology development (ICT).

The associated linear equation model follows the subsequent structure:

$$GDPPC = \beta_0 + \beta_1 TO + \beta_2 FDI + \beta_3 CPI + \beta_4 INT + \beta_5 ICT + \mu \ + \varepsilon \text{ ----------(ii)}$$

Where:

GDPPC: GDP per capita (dependent variable) for country

TO: Trade openness.

FDI: Foreign Direct Investment.

CPI: Consumer Price Index (proxy for inflation).

INT: Internet users (proxy for IoT).

ICT: Information and Communication Technology (proxy for IoT).

β_0: Constant term.

β_1, β_2, β_3, β_4, β_5: Coefficients of independent variables.

μ : Country-specific effects (fixed or random effects).

$\varepsilon_{(it)}$: Error term.

Data Sources and Time Period

This study includes a 20-year panel dataset for the BIMSTEC countries covering the years from 1999 to 2019. The dataset contains GDP per capita details along with trade openness data foreign direct investment statistics consumer price index numbers and information about internet users and ICT developments all of which have been sourced from credible international databases such as the World Bank IMF and UNCTAD. We selected these sources because their reliability and consistency extend worldwide and enable consistent data comparison across different nations throughout multiple years.

Expected Contribution to Policy and Economic Growth

The research analyzes how GDP per capita correlates with various independent variables to provide insights into how technological adoption and trade openness affect macroeconomic stability and economic growth in BIMSTEC countries. The research findings supply policymakers with factual evidence to make informed decisions about increasing trade openness, attracting foreign investment, and strengthening digital infrastructure which supports sustainable economic development in the region.

The study utilizes panel data econometric analysis to enhance academic perspectives on BIMSTEC economic growth and generate practical recommendations for evidence-based policy development that promotes both economic growth and regional integration.

Table 1: Descriptive Statistics

Descriptive Statistics					
Variable	Obs	Mean	Std. Dev.	Min	Max
TO	147	0.325	0.238	0.003	0.874
CPI	147	6.838	6.881	-0.9	57.075
INT	140	12.523	15.637	0	74.179
lnICT	126	19.058	3.26	9.584	25.271
lnGDPPC	147	7.042	0.954	4.831	8.94
lnFDI	139	6.385	2.724	0.011	10.831

Descriptive statistics: They are descriptive statistics on the data. Trade Openness (TO) is 147 observations and its mean value is 0.325; its range is 0.003-0.874; it has medium variance (standard deviation: 0.238). CPI: The CPI is very variable, it has a mean of 6.838, standard deviation of 6.881, and varies from -0.9 to 57.075. INT (Internet Users) has an average of 12.523 but high variability (std. dev. = 15.637), from 0 to 74.179. The natural logarithms of ICT (lnICT), GDP per capita (lnGDPPC) and FDI (lnFDI) have mean of 19.058, 7.042, and 6.385, respectively, with different levels of dispersion. These are the data to give you an idea of the heterogeneity of economic and technological factors within the dataset.

After Natural Log

$$lnGDPPC = \beta_0 + \beta_1 TO + \beta_2 lnFDI + \beta_3 CPI + \beta_4 INT + \beta_5 lnICT + \mu + \varepsilon................(iii)$$

Table 2. Regression results of fixed effect

lnGDPPC	Coef.	St.Err.	t-value	p-value	[95% Conf	Interval]	Sig
TO	-1.055	0.277	-3.81	0	-1.598	-0.513	***
CPI	0.02	0.005	3.87	0	0.01	0.03	***
INT	0.015	0.002	9.95	0	0.012	0.018	***
lnFDI	0.088	0.025	3.55	0	0.039	0.136	***
lnICT	0.254	0.024	10.47	0	0.206	0.301	***
Constant	1.844	0.459	4.02	0	0.945	2.743	***
Mean dependent var				SD dependent var			
Overall r-squared				Number of obs			
Chi-square				Prob > chi2			
R-squared within				R-squared between			
source: Computed by Author *** p<.01, ** p<.05, * p<.1							

The results (Table 2) indicate that the Fixed Effects regression mode used the natural logarithm of GDP per capita (lnGDPPC) as the dependent variable. Independent variables are as follows: Trade Openness (TO), Consumer Price Index (CPI), Internet Users (INT), Foreign Direct Investment (FDI) and Information and Communication Technology (ICT). The model presents significant explanatory capability on GDP per capita fluctuation among BIMSTEC countries over time in the course of examination. The R-squared within value of 0.909 reveals that the varying amount of the GDP per capita within countries over time is 90 percent as a result of the independent variables, which means the development of a strong predictive capability and depicts the existence of close ties between the mentioned macroeconomic factors and economic growth.

Trade Openness (TO)

The coefficient of -1.055 of Trade Openness is statistically significant at a 1 percent level ($p < 0.01$). The negative quotient implies that as the rate of trade openness increases, the GDP per capita value declines. In particular, as the level of trade openness rises by one unit in the controlled conditions, the GDP per capita performance will decrease by 1.055 units. Though this seems to be an unfavorable outcome, it does pose a problem that trade liberalization may test some of these economies by stiffening competition, which in turn may dwindle the market share of local industries. The result correlates with the arguments that the advantages of the trade liberalization might depend on the existence of robust institutional frameworks and positive policies (Rodrik, 2018).

Consumer Price Index (CPI)

As an inflation proxy, Consumer Price Index records a positive coefficient of 0.020, enjoys statistical significance at a 1 percent level ($p < 0.01$). This positive relation indicates that there is a moderate inflation rate, which is accompanied by a moderate rise in the GDP per capita. Although this relationship would seem to be counterintuitive, it would point towards the fact that the economic activity driven by moderate inflation would point towards increasing demand in the economy and hence an increase in economic activity. The result is in line with the studies indicating that regulated inflation can act as an economic boost (Barro, 2013).

Information Communication and Technology (ICT)

The coefficient value of the Internet Users variable is 0.015 ($p < 0.01$) which shows a very high positive impact on GDP per capita. These results bring home, the importance of internet connection and digital infrastructure in furthering economic growth. The rise in internet penetration is directly linked to significant value addition in GDP per capita confirming the hypothesis that strong internet connectivity results in productivity gains and business opportunities which in effect raise economic output.

Foreign Direct Investment (lnFDI)

The value of coefficient of lnFDI is 0.088 and it is statistically significant with 1% level of significance ($p < 0.01$). The positive level of relationship means that the more the amount of Foreign Direct Investment, the more GDP per capita. In particular, a 1-percent growing value in FDI leads to an expansion of GDP per capita by 0.088 percent. The given results prove that Foreign Direct Investment is a mechanism of economic growth as it not only introduces financial resources, but also technologies and experience that helps improve productivity and boost economics. The result is aligned with the factual evidence which shows that the FDI promotes the enhancement of infrastructure, creation of jobs, and knowledge transfer, resulting in economic growth in the developing parts (UNCTAD, 2019).

Information and Communications New Technology (lnICT)

Information and Communication Technology variable indicates that the coefficient = 0.254 and p-value is lesser than 0.01 indicating that the correlation with GDP per capita is very strong. According to this regression analysis, digital technologies become the key to economic growth. The results indicate that there is an increase in GDP per capita associated with the better ICT infrastructure by enhancements in digital communications as well as the use of newer technology. When ICT is implemented, it also leads to innovation besides making businesses more efficient and cutting down the cost of transaction, and this leads to improvement in economic production.

$$lnGDPPC = \beta_0 + \beta_1 TO + \beta_2 lnFDI + \beta_3 CPI + \beta_4 INT + \beta_5 lnICT + \mu + \varepsilon \ldots\ldots\ldots\ldots\ldots (iv)$$

Table 3. Regression results of random effect

lnGDPPC	Coef.	St.Err.	t-value	p-value	[95% Conf	Interval]	Sig
TO	-1.069	.267	-4.00	0	-1.599	-.539	***
CPI	.022	.005	4.55	0	.013	.032	***
INT	.014	.001	10.08	0	.012	.017	***
lnFDI	.083	.023	3.55	.001	.037	.129	***
lnICT	.272	.023	11.80	0	.226	.318	***
Constant	1.421	.375	3.79	0	.678	2.164	***

Mean dependent var	7.192	SD dependent var	0.886		
R-squared	0.610	Number of obs	114		
F-test	205.680	Prob > F	0.000		
Akaike crit. (AIC)	-65.385	Bayesian crit. (BIC)	-48.968		

*** p<.01, ** p<.05, * p<.1

Table 3 Random-effects regression result shows how key independent variables (Trade Openness, CPI, Internet Users, FDI, ICT) affect the GDP per capita (lnGDP-PC), within and between countries. The model is highly explanatory, the R-squared is 0.910 and 91% of lnGDPPC variability can be attributed to the predictors.

Trade Openness (TO): TO coefficient is -1.069, it is statistically significant (p 0.01). This suggests negative correlation, that is 1 unit of TO increases by 1.069 decrease in lnGDPPC. That finding points to trade-related problems or inefficiencies with economic development.

Consumption Price Index (CPI): The CPI has a positive, statistically significant coefficient of 0.022 (p 0.01) which suggests that the more inflation, the higher the GDP per capita will increase. This might be what controlled inflation does to boost the economy.

In table3 Internet Explorers (INT): INT is positively associated with lnGDPPC strongly (coefficient 0.014; p 0.01). This reinforces the role of internet penetration in promoting economic development, probably because of its productivity and connectivity benefits.

lnFDI: Coefficient of lnFDI = 0.083 with p value 0.01. The result shows how FDI can contribute to economic growth by injecting capital, technology and knowledge.

ICT (lnICT): ICT is strongly positive for lnGDPPC (correlation: 0.272 (p 0.01). This is the revolutionary power of technology in economic growth.

Constant Term: The constant term is 1.421 and that is the baseline GDP per capita when all predictors are zero.

Table 4. Hausman (1978) specification test

	Coef.
Chi-square test value	9.289
P-value	.002

Table 4 indicates that the Hausman test (Hausman, 1978) was done to ascertain that which (Fixed Effects/ Random Effects) estimation would be suitable in the analysis of the panel data. Since the Chi-square test statistic is 9.289 with p-value of 0.002, the null hypothesis that the Random Effects model is consistency and efficient can be rejected because it is more than the specified 5 percent level of significance. This finding suggests that Fixed Effects model is more appropriate to the analysis and it descried a relationship between individual effects and the independent variables further giving more determinative estimates on the relationship of lnGDPPC and the independent variables.

CONCLUSION

This study uses the panel data econometric technique analyzing the factors that lead to economic growth in BIMSTEC member countries between the years 1999-2019. This research examines how the following variables have affected the GDP per capita, namely Trade Openness, Consumer Price Index, Foreign Direct Investment, Internet Users and Information and Communication Technology. The empirical results provided by the model of Fixed Effects after verification in the Hausman specification test display not only the expected general trends but also such unexpected changes which should alert policymakers to pay attention to certain areas.

Effects of Trade Openness

The large negative value of Trade Openness (-1.055) seems at first glance to go clearly against the mainstream economic theory that usually considers the impact of trade openness as growth-inducing due to the specialization effect, exposure to bigger markets and economies of scale. This inverse relationship confirms claims that economic performance of trade liberalization is not necessarily positive unless enforced by strict trade policies and favorable institutional underpinnings (Rodrik, 2018). Trade openness in developing economies in the BIMSTEC region has the potential of opening up the local markets to compete internationally without the necessary safeguarding mechanisms which can cripple the local industries thus lowering the national growth potential as well.

Inflation and economic growth

The Consumer Price Index shows the positive coefficient (0.020), which goes to show that moderate inflation rates are related to high GDP per capita in the BIMSTEC countries. The identified outcome indicates that a controlled inflation could serve as a driver of economic growth, which is also supported by the scientific data, where moderate inflation would boost the uptake of consumption and investment due to lower real our cost of borrowing money and high aggregate demand (Barro, 2013).

Digital Infrastructure Implication

There is a positive mutual relationship between Internet penetration and GDP per capita (coefficient = 0.015, $p < 0.01$), proving the power of digital technology transformations and the necessity to pay more attention to Internet of Things (IoT) technologies as the means of economic growth. Nations with a greater rate of internet penetration enjoy better connection and access to information meaning that they have better entrepreneurial opportunities which are the drivers of modern economy.

The Effects of Foreign Investment

The significant yet positive FDI coefficient (0.088) indicates that foreign direct investment works as a major growth driver of the GDP per capita in the BIMSTEC countries. The contribution of Foreign Direct Investment into a country consists of capital, skills and technologies, which, in combination, boost domestic productivity and infrastructure as well as create job hiring, which corresponds to the existing literature relating to the contribution of FDI to economic development (UNCTAD, 2019).

ICT as the driver of growth

The Information and Communication Technology presents the highest positive coefficient (0.254, $p < 0.01$), which emphasizes digital infrastructure and the level of technological development as the vital aspects of economic development. This observation is consistent with the studies made all over the globe that focus on the role of ICT infrastructures in the creation of modern economic growth via innovation, better operations, and transactional cut-down.

Policy Implications

The study also shows some essential policy implications of the BIMSTEC countries:

1. Investment in Digital Infrastructure: This is one of the central policies that should be implemented by policymakers because digital technology is a fundamental growth engine that needs constant investment in technological improvement and educational enhancement.
2. Trade Policy Reform: The inverse relationship between trade openness and growth indicates that there is a need to have counter ways to compensate negative effects that might result after trade opening namely support of local industries and improvements in terms of facilitating trade.
3. Investment Climate Enhancing: The favorable role played by FDI to the growth of the economy implies that the policymakers are required to provide a climate conducive to operations of investments by minimizing business operation procedures, protection of investors and enhancing legality and regulatory framework.
4. Macroeconomic Stability: The factors that explain why rate of inflation has an impact on economic growth indicate the need to have low rates of inflation to cushion consumer purchasing power as well as promote economic growth.

Restrictions and Future Studies

Though this study has shed light on some valuable information on BIMSTEC economies, future contributions ought to focus on the influence of institutional quality, political stability and environmental sustainability on economic performance. Also, studies are needed on the effects of regional integration and trade agreements in the interactions with macroeconomic factors to give a better understanding on the patterns of economic growth in the developing economies.

A further extension of this study ought to consider the comparative analysis of different regional groupings to evaluate the impact of these factors on the economic growth within different developing regions with a hope that general drivers of economic growth will be found.

REFERENCES

Asian Development Bank. (2019). *Asian Economic Integration Report*. ADB Publications.

Atzori, L., Iera, A., & Morabito, G. (2010). The Internet of Things: A survey. *Computer Networks, 54*(15), 2787–2805. DOI: 10.1016/j.comnet.2010.05.010

Balassa, B. (1961). *The theory of economic integration*. Richard D. Irwin.

Baltagi, B. H. (2021). *Econometric analysis of panel data* (6th ed.). Springer. DOI: 10.1007/978-3-030-53953-5

Banik, N. (2005). Trade integration of BIMSTEC countries: Roadmap, challenges and opportunities. *Journal of Asian Economics, 16*(4), 672–690.

Barro, R. J. (2013). Inflation and economic growth. *Annals of Economics and Finance, 14*(1), 85–109.

Basu, S., & Dutta, D. (2007). Indo-Bangladesh trade relationship: Problems and prospects. *South Asian Survey, 14*(2), 253–264.

Bhattacharyay, B. N. (2010). Estimating demand for infrastructure in energy, transport, telecommunications, water, and sanitation in Asia and the Pacific: 2010-2020. *ADBI Working Paper 248*. Asian Development Bank Institute.

BIMSTEC. (2020). *BIMSTEC Trade Facilitation Strategic Framework 2030*. BIMSTEC Secretariat.

Borensztein, E., De Gregorio, J., & Lee, J. W. (1998). How does foreign direct investment affect economic growth? *Journal of International Economics, 45*(1), 115–135. DOI: 10.1016/S0022-1996(97)00033-0

Chakraborty, D. (2007). BIMSTEC FTA: Prospects of trade under the proposed framework. *RIS Discussion Paper*, 135, 1-42.

Edwards, S. (1998). Openness, productivity and growth: What do we really know? *Economic Journal (London), 108*(447), 383–398. DOI: 10.1111/1468-0297.00293

Fischer, S. (1993). The role of macroeconomic factors in growth. *Journal of Monetary Economics, 32*(3), 485–512. DOI: 10.1016/0304-3932(93)90027-D

Frankel, J. A., & Romer, D. (1999). Does trade cause growth? *The American Economic Review, 89*(3), 379–399. DOI: 10.1257/aer.89.3.379

Gubbi, J., Buyya, R., Marusic, S., & Palaniswami, M. (2013). Internet of Things (IoT): A vision, architectural elements, and future directions. *Future Generation Computer Systems*, *29*(7), 1645–1660. DOI: 10.1016/j.future.2013.01.010

Hausman, J. A. (1978). Specification tests in econometrics. *Econometrica*, *46*(6), 1251–1271. DOI: 10.2307/1913827

Hsiao, C. (2014). *Analysis of panel data* (3rd ed.). Cambridge University Press. DOI: 10.1017/CBO9781139839327

International Monetary Fund. (2020). *Regional economic outlook: Asia and Pacific*. IMF Publications.

International Monetary Fund. (2021). *International financial statistics*. IMF Data.

International Telecommunication Union. (2019). *Measuring the information society report 2019*. ITU Publications.

International Telecommunication Union. (2020). *Measuring digital development: Facts and figures 2020*. ITU Publications.

Koutroumpis, P. (2009). The economic impact of broadband on growth: A simultaneous approach. *Telecommunications Policy*, *33*(9), 471–485. DOI: 10.1016/j.telpol.2009.07.004

Kumar, S., & Prabhakar, A. (2019). BIMSTEC regional integration: Prospects and challenges. *South Asian Survey*, *26*(1), 45–67.

Mohan, C. R. (2018). *India and Asian geopolitics: The past, present*. Brookings Institution Press.

Organisation for Economic Co-operation and Development. (2019). *FDI flows*. OECD Statistics.

Porter, M. E., & Heppelmann, J. E. (2014). How smart, connected products are transforming competition. *Harvard Business Review*, *92*(11), 64–88.

Rahman, M., & Singh, K. (2016). Prospects for economic integration of BIMSTEC: Trade and investment scenario. *Journal of South Asian Development*, *11*(2), 172–195.

Rodrik, D. (2018). What do trade agreements really do? *The Journal of Economic Perspectives*, *32*(2), 73–90. DOI: 10.1257/jep.32.2.73

Romer, P. M. (1990). Endogenous technological change. *Journal of Political Economy*, *98*(5), S71–S102. DOI: 10.1086/261725

Sachs, J. D., Warner, A., Aslund, A., & Fischer, S. (1995). Economic reform and the process of global integration. *Brookings Papers on Economic Activity*, *1995*(1), 1–118. DOI: 10.2307/2534573

Secretariat, B. I. M. S. T. E. C. (2004). *Framework Agreement on BIMSTEC Free Trade Area*. BIMSTEC Secretariat.

Solow, R. M. (1956). A contribution to the theory of economic growth. *The Quarterly Journal of Economics*, *70*(1), 65–94. DOI: 10.2307/1884513

Srivastava, P., & Das, K. (2018). Digital integration and sustainable development in BIMSTEC. *Asian Development Review*, *35*(2), 78–105.

Todaro, M. P., & Smith, S. C. (2020). *Economic development* (12th ed.). Pearson.

Viner, J. (1950). *The customs union issue*. Carnegie Endowment for International Peace.

World Bank. (2016). *World development report 2016: Digital dividends*. World Bank Publications.

World Bank. (2020). *World development indicators*. World Bank Open Data.

Chapter 15
Techno-Geopolitical Dimensions of Tourism in the Global Political Economy

Firoj Kabir
Daffodil International University, Bangladesh

Mohammad Badruddoza Talukder
https://orcid.org/0009-0008-1662-9221
International University of Business Agriculture and Technology, Bangladesh

Kittisak Wongmahesak
https://orcid.org/0009-0000-2129-4691
North Bangkok University, Thailand

ABSTRACT

The Techno-Geopolitical Aspects of Tourism in the Global Political Economy chapter explores how digital technology and geopolitical forces interact to transform tourism as a spatial-political activity as well as an economic sector. It emphasizes how governments and non-state actors use technology as a geopolitical tool by placing tourism within historical and modern power relations, drawing on classical and critical geopolitical theory. The chapter makes the case that in the current digital era, certain actors have more control over worldwide visitor flows, place narratives, and economic strength due to their access to knowledge, communications infrastructure, and technology capital. Territorial claims, political ideologies, and national identities are created and disputed in the context of tourism. The study urges a reconsideration of tourism as a techno-geopolitical assemblage influenced

DOI: 10.4018/979-8-3373-1727-4.ch015

by digital transformation, spatial narratives, and political intent, rather than just as leisure or business.

INTRODUCTION

Geopolitics is among the applied concepts that are used in political literature of today's world. But like many other things, its history is older than its formal creation in the 19th century (Criekemans, 2022a). That is, the politicians and military officials from ancient times knew well that geography was power and were aware of its effects on the balance of power in a region. That is why geography played and is still playing an important role in regional equations and hence, there were many struggles and wars broken out for changing the geography of a territory and achieving military and political success in those lands. Therefore, the effect of geographical elements on the power of a political unit was a phenomenon existed before the birth of the concept of geopolitics. This classical concept was stressed on since the 19th century to be located in a formal academic frame called geopolitics (Hilgert, 2025). With the addition of this new-comer to the reunion of existed sciences, now the universities and academies have tried to clarify its different dimensions. Therefore, geopolitics became the study of the effects of geography on international politics and international relationships which tries to make a cognitive base for political behavior in terms of geographical variables. But this was not the end of such scientific story because since the late 1980s, a new concept critical geopolitics being a radical critical perspective on the discipline of political geography to becoming a recognized area of research. These paper with adaptive method and rely on library resources, looking Prove this theory that technology is a powerful instrument at the disposal put of all actors including governmental and nongovernmental, But due to three factors: government access to information, wealth and communications further than the other actors, power and usability of technology has greater (David et al., 2023).

In recent years, more and more companies, providing services in tourism and destinations, have begun to incorporate the use of digital assets into their strategy, recognizing that change is essential to the preservation and improvement of competitiveness nowadays. The European Commission has implemented numerous of measures to increase the competitiveness of small businesses in European tourism, integrating them into global digital value chains and thereby improving their workplace creation potential. The European Commission is helping tourism companies in several areas to use digital solutions as widely as possible. Among other activities, digital tourism events, the creation of the Digital Tourist Network and the Tourism Business Portal can be found. The primary objective of these activities is to strengthen education, to engage smaller businesses in the digital value chain and to support digital solutions for the tourism sector in particular. The European Commission thus provides an opportunity for the digital market to take full advantage of the opportunities offered by businesses to increase their competitiveness (Boikova et al., 2021).

Nowadays, digitalization appears in all areas of life. According to Buhalis and Jun (2011) the digital tourism is a paradigm shift in tourism due to the emergence of digital tools and techniques (Mihalic, 2024). With the model, set up and characterized by marketing tools, which introduced the complex system that is trying to meet the ongoing technological development of the external environment. The model shows all the external and internal factors that can affect digital tourism as well as activities within the organization where we can use digital tools. Recognition of marketing tools can help companies at micro level and destinations at macro level as well and show how to take advantage from digitalization to be competitive in the tourism market. The development of a long-term digital tourism strategy is important in order to help to find the most efficient use of digital techniques in all areas of the market. As a future research, all areas of the model can be specified or supplemented. Empirical testing of the model can also be the subject of another study.

BACKGROUND OF THE STUDY

Geopolitics

Geopolitics, from Greek Γη (earth) and Πολιτική (politics), is the study of the effects of geography (both human and physical) on international politics and international relations (Ioannidou, 2022). Geopolitics is a method of foreign policy analysis which seeks to understand, explain, and predict international political behavior primarily in terms of geographical variables. Typical geographical variables are the physical location, size, climate, topography, demography, natural resources, and technological advances of the state being evaluated. Traditionally, the term has applied primarily to the impact of geography on politics, but its usage has evolved over the past century to encompass wider connotations. Geopolitics traditionally studies the links between political power and geographic space, and examines strategic prescriptions based on the relative importance of land power and sea power in world history. The geopolitical tradition had some consistent concerns with geopolitical correlations of power in world politics, the identification of international core areas, and the relationships between naval and terrestrial capabilities. Academically, the study of geopolitics analyses geography, history, and social science with reference to spatial and patterns at various scales. Also, the study of geopolitics includes the study of the ensemble of relations between the interests of international political actors, interests focused to an area, space, geographical element or ways, relations which create a geopolitical system. Geopolitics is multidisciplinary in scope, and includes all aspects of the social sciences—with particular emphasis on political geography, international relations, the territorial aspects of political science and international law. The practice directly and indirectly impacts businesses and economies. The term "Geopolitics" was coined at the beginning of the twentieth century by Rudolf Kjellén, a Swedish political scientist, who was inspired by the German geographer Friedrich Ratzel. Ratzel published Politische Geographie (political geography) in 1897; that book was later popularized in English by the Austro-Hungarian historian Emil Reich and the American diplomat Robert Strausz-Hupé (a faculty member of the University of Pennsylvania) (Klinke, 2023). Although Halford Mackinder had a pioneering role in the field, he never used the term geopolitics himself.

LITERATURE REVIEW

Tourism landscapes are spaces where Trans local social realities merge and rearticulate geopolitical assemblages. Perspectives from geopolitics shed analytical light on how tourism can at once constitute and reflect political discourse, while spatializing international politics as they are linked to global and local tourism industries (Talukder, 2020). Tourism can help re-conceptualize geopolitics as a discursive practice that represents international politics as a social landscape comprised of heterogeneous constellations of people and places (Mohiuddin, 2024). Tourism discourse and practice are mediated by political processes of representation, whereby places become destinations laden with multiple but often recurring and similar histories and dramas. Through an integration of recent work in political geography and tourism studies, this note offers a timely approach from which to examine tourism through geopolitical perspectives to facilitate more nuanced understandings of the relationships between tourism, representation and place-making practices. Building on these theoretical insights, we highlight the significance of geopolitical thought for tourism studies, outlining four complementary themes indicative of emerging work in the field (Huang & Liu, 2024a): (1) popular geopolitics; (2) embodied geopolitics; (3) environmental geopolitics; and (4) geopolitical imaginaries. Departing from a practical or formal geopolitics, scholars of popular geopolitics focus on how popular culture (e.g. novels, films, computer games) becomes fodder for the materialization of geopolitical discourses. Mundane, quotidian cultural practices are sites for the local inflection of geographical, political identities, elucidating how fluidly ''distinctions between reality and representation, primary and secondary experiences, first-hand and second-hand observations change hands endlessly". In tourism, popular culture plays a critical role in both what industry professionals refer to as ''destination development" and in the mediation of imagined and lived tourism experiences. Analyses of a popular geopolitics of tourism can help us better conceptualize how and with what implications various geographic destinations (e.g. Thailand via The Beach, New Zealand via Lord of the Rings) reflect—or even inform—geopolitical discourses of place. Films such as Slumdog Millionaire and City of God, for example, have motivated the recent development of reality tours in urban slums, which now serve as broader geopolitical discourses around tourism in the city. The articulation of tourism with popular culture illustrates how actors on tourism's many stages "talk geopolitics" through ongoing intertextual tourism encounters which are invariably mediated by a broader chain of signification (Talukder, 2021). Recent calls by scholars to reconsider how political processes articulate with everyday embodied geopolitics encourage a more nuanced understanding of the recursive relationship between the quotidian, the spatial and the political. New theoretical space around embodiment, performance and non-representational studies of the material has been pried open for the examination of how politically inflected social metanarratives such as fear, hope or care are re-embodied through grounded representations of experience and object oriented ontologies. If we understand tourism as an assemblage of actors and materials, then tourists' embodied participation in this assemblage is constituted by "affects, attitudes, and memories that [must also] shape future geopolitical action". Studying embodied geopolitics, meanwhile, and its emotional revelations necessitates an intersectional approach to how socially constructed categories such as gender and class are constituted by and through tourism encounters, articulating with in situ and materially practiced identity and place-based tourism experience. In this way, embodiment is both "discursively produced, as inscribed, and as representation", mapping out cartographic representations of space via the semiotic separation of self and other (Oostendorp, 2022; Talukder, 2023). Anthropogenic environmental change is a growing threat to global security, aggravating existing problems such as poverty, corruption, social tensions and ineffectual political institutions that threaten domestic and international order across a number of countries. But the logics of cause and effect are not always entirely straightforward in such relationships, since contemporary political tensions and instabilities can themselves accelerate climate change. Security policies such as these rest on neoliberal geopolitical frameworks that tend to focus on symptoms rather than the causes of environmental degradation. Only recently has critical tourism studies scholarship begun to examine the role of geopolitics in the context of global environmental change, for example with research on the geopolitical role played by pan-international spaces such as the Arctic and on the links between sustainability and planetary change (Talukder, 2024). Tourism scholars would do well to further inflect their work on tourism's multiple ways of understanding and 'making' place through the focused lenses of geopolitical discourse and action. Political geographers have long noted how both political and spatial realities are created vis-à-vis the social imagination of place (Jabareen & Eizenberg, 2021). Attention to the performativity of imaginative geographies reflects the co-constitutive relationship between tourism practice and geopolitical imaginaries. In tourism practice, these geopolitical imaginaries play a foundational role in framing place as prototypical, comprehensible forms (e.g. safe, dangerous, exotic or mundane). They also reveal the mobile interconnections, images, experiences, and affective encounters that circulate—both physically and virtually—between people, reconfiguring geopolitical space through the recursive relationship between image, place and experience. As new media technologies proliferate and contribute to ongoing processes of time–space compression, the dialectical co-production of both tourist and geopolitical imaginaries intensifies. This brief note has asked in what ways and with what political implications do tourism practices co-constitute a range of geopolitical conditions. The four spheres of geopolitical scholarship outlined here are compelling and innovative ways forward for tourism scholars who seek new ways to theorize the relationships between tourism, space and power, and for scholars of geopolitics who seek more nuanced interpretations of global place-making. A geopolitical perspective sheds analytical light on these interrelated practices by enabling nuanced studies of how, for instance, issues of territoriality, representation and power over destinations become critical sites of struggle for economic and political sovereignty. Unraveling the multiple political agendas present in the manufacturing of tourism industries elucidates the critical presence of tourism throughout contemporary global affairs and political agendas. Through considerations of these multiple interrelated phenomena outlined above, studies of tourism can become more attuned to subtle inflections of the political, the spatial and the global, while studies of geopolitics can grow in richness, subtlety and relevance to the practices of everyday tourism experience. If, as Simon Dalby has written, geopolitics is ''the ideological process of constructing spatial, political and cultural boundaries to demarcate the domestic space as separate from the threatening other" then geopolitical ways of ordering the world must be implicit in the tourist gaze, and fundamental to understanding the multiple forces that inflect it (Shtern, 2022).

CRITICAL GEOPOLITICS

Critical geopolitics investigates the geographical assumptions and designations that Enter into the making of world politics. It seeks to illuminate and explain the practices by which political actors spatialize international politics and represent it as a "world" characterized by particular types of places. This strand of analysis approaches geopolitics not as a neutral Consideration of regimen "geographical" facts, but as a deeply ideological and politicized form of analysis (Criekemans, 2022b). Eschewing the traditional question of how geography Does or can influence politics, it investigates how geographical claims and Assumptions function in political debates and political practice. In so doing, it seeks to disrupt mainstream geopolitical discourses: not to study the geography of politics within regimen, commonsense places, but to foreground "the politics of the geographical specification of politics". Critical geopolitics is not a neatly delimited field, but the diverse works characterized as such all focus on the processes through which political practice is bound up with territorial definition. Substantial part of critical geopolitics seeks to unpack the rigid territorial assumptions of traditional geopolitical thinking. Thus, numerous analyses dissect post–Cold War geopolitics to reveal the continued reliance on binary understandings of power and spatiality, on notions of East and West, security and danger, freedom and oppression. More recently, geographic scholarship has fore grounded how the "war on terror" works with these same binaries (Jarvis & Lister, 2025). In particular, much of critical geopolitics problematizes the statist conceptions of power in social sciences – a conceptualization that John Agnew calls the "territorial trap." Along with political geography more generally, critical geopolitics argues that spatiality is not confined to territoriality, either historically or today. It advances the drift away from rigidly territorialized understandings of politics toward more nuanced understandings of the complex spatialities of power. State power, it shows, is not limited to or contained within the territory of the state; it is also exercised no territorially or in space-spanning networks. It is applied differentially in different spheres and to different subjects. The argument is not that geography or borders no longer matter. In fact, the celebrations of borderless world also equate spatiality with state territoriality, mistakenly taking the transformations of state power for the "end of geography". This applies not just too popular writers like Thomas Friedman. Proclamations of the transnational governmentality termed Empire by Michael Hardt and Antonio Negri (2000) also betray insensitivity to the intricate topographies or power. Critical geopolitics argues that the emerging forms of global governance do not "flatten" space; to the contrary, they increase spatial differentiation globally (Mason et al., 2023). In terms of the state, the key questions to address are not about the "real" sources, meanings or limits of state sovereignty in some general or universal sense, but, more specifically, about how state power is discursively and practically produced in territorial and no territorial forms. The task is to decanter but not to write off state power by examining its incoherencies and contradictions. Such investigations must also be mindful of the increasing complexity of regional integration and differentiation. Rationality here does not refer to any regimen constellation, such as the European Union (EU) or the Association of Southeast Asian Nations (ASEAN). It rather refers to the multilayered socioeconomic and cultural processes through which "regionness" is produced and sustained. This drift away from state-based analysis of world politics links up with interest in subjectivity and identity across the social sciences. For the assumption that international politics is a fundamentally territorial (as distinct from spatial) politics of 8 states is closely bound up with the notion that states are the basic subjects of international politics. Critical geopolitics departs from both of these assumptions. It does not examine the identities or actions of pregiven subjects; it rather investigates the processes by which political subjects are formed in the first place. It shows that the sovereign state is not the basis for, but the effect of, discourses of sovereignty, security, and identity. Put differently, state identity and interest do not precede foreign policy, but are forged through foreign policy practices. The enactments of state interest and identity are therefore among the key themes of critical geopolitics. The principal object of this scholarship is not the state as an object but statecraft as a multitude of practices. As a part of this interest in political subjectivity and subject formation, there has been tremendous interest in identity politics, that is, in the geographical demarcation of Self and Other, "our" space and "theirs." This strand of work has been so voluminous that critical geopolitics is sometimes accused of over valorizing culture and identity at the expense of economic issues. Much of this "cultural" work has focused on the construction of national spaces and the geopolitical cultures of particular states. It shows that geographical claims about cultural borders and homelands are central to narratives of national identity. There is also an extensive literature on bordering practices. It argues that international borders are best viewed not as lines representing already existing political entities called states or nations. Rather, these entities themselves are constituted through bordering practices (Mogiani, 2023).

TECHNO-GEOPOLITICS

Techno-Geopolitics, regarded as a new concept of geopolitical studies, the subject of the study is to investigate the relationship between power, politics and technology (Yoon, 2023a). Technology provides powerful instruments for all actors including governmental and nongovernmental put. This is new the groundwork for formation of hierarchy of power structures provides. Here is what is of most interest to information, knowledge and political power in Words of geo-political information. The current surge in tourism geopolitics scholarship is driven by tourism geography's now leading role in human geography, and political geography's increasing recognition of tourism as more than just a backdrop, context, or case study to geopolitical theorization. The intellectual development of the new tourism geopolitics grows from seeds of disparate strands in tourism and political geography planted to facilitate a now blooming intellectual landscape. In other words, a tourism geopolitics canon is moving forward in part by 'looking backward': recent literature in tourism geopolitics has begun to generate a historical edifice in which its contemporary concerns are traced back to conceptual origins. For example, earlier studies that paved the way for tourism geopolitics as a field of study focused on the state-building role of tourism in heritage sites, how borders and the uneven power of passports shape tourism flows, tourism's extraterritorial power, and its dependence on colonial violence. This trajectory largely moved forward in a piecemeal fashion and was mostly limited to tourism studies but has now accelerated such that the development of tourism geopolitics is as much geopolitical as tourism-focused. Through a deep study into the multifaceted dimensions of tourism geopolitics this introduction and collection of papers demonstrate the mutual entanglement of tourism and political geography (Huang & Liu, 2024b).

The machinations of tourism geopolitics reverberate strongly in today's polarized political milieu, presaging some of the most tragic clashes of our times in places like Gaza and Ukraine. Geographers are increasingly addressing the role of tourism practices in facilitating and challenging national identity and citizenship, territorial claims, and border conflicts. Yet historically, tourism geography and political geography have been distinct areas of scholarship. From the late 1980s to the early 2000s, few postgraduate students in North American human geography programs studied tourism, and there were rarely self-described tourism geographers working in PhD granting geography departments (Thatcher et al., 2024). In those days most critical tourism geography of North America was largely embedded in studies of the political economies of cities, generally as case studies illustrating the neo liberalization of freshly commodified downtown spaces or the erasure of racialized urban orderings through a 'whitewashing' of the city for tourists. At that time North American tourism geography existed in the shadows but flourished elsewhere. For example, politically inspired research in the Marxist tradition foregrounded tourism as a vital component of late capitalism through New Zealander Steve Britton's pioneering research in the 1980s and 1990s. Asian universities had (and continue to be home to) large contingents of tourism geographers who incorporate politics—specifically formal policy-making—into their projects. In the 1990s in Europe, contested citizenship, host-guest relations, and the performativity of tourism were underpinned by questions of the political subjectivities of tourists and hosts. In sum, until recently, politically-oriented tourism geography was being produced by cultural and economic geographers in a somewhat disjointed but vibrant manner outside North America (Iaquinto et al., 2024a).

On the other hand, the field of political geography has long been marked by an absence of tourism despite the significance of the industry (and the processes driving it) to politics. Some geographers have viewed tourism as frivolous 'holidaying' and less serious of an academic undertaking than politics, international relations, and the production of the nation-state. Additionally, political geography has been a recognized sub-discipline in the English-speaking world for much longer than tourism geography. Whatever the case, the launch and subsequent success of the first political geography journal, Political Geography Quarterly (now Political Geography) in 1982 was a precursor for arguably one of the most multifaceted sub-fields in human geography (Wheeldon, 2022). Alongside Political Geography, human geography now has at least six overtly political journals: Geopolitics; Territory, Politics, and Governance; Environment and Planning C: Politics and Space; Space and Polity; and Eurasian Geography and Economics, and research in political geography is regularly published in the discipline's leading journals.

Tourism only rarely appears in these and other prominent human geography journals. It has now been almost fifteen years since Progress in Human Geography, the discipline's bellwether, published a progress report on tourism geography. In contrast, political geography progress reports are published nearly annually. Even though there has been some positive growth a quick search in Political Geography, for example, shows that as of August 2024, it has only ever published eleven articles with tourism in the title (Jiang et al., 2024). Political geography has been keeping pace with international relations and later international studies in prioritizing the nation-state, the 'region', and other state-sanctioned political borders as its de facto units of analyses so tourism's omission may be one related to other scalar priorities. Additionally, it may be that politics writ large is understood to reach all citizens while tourism consumption is restricted to the wealthy. In other words, while tourism is thought to be highly mobile, transnational, and transactional, it is also erroneously believed to affect a much smaller group of subjects. While those working and living in the Global South have more fully embraced tourism geography (which is often taught in tandem with development studies), it has only been in recent years that theoretically impactful research in and from the Global South about the politics of tourism has received the attention it deserves. Similarly, the launch of networks, such as the ATLAS Critical Tourism Studies Asia-Pacific group reflects a growing interest in critical approaches to tourism geographies, with geopolitics central to the community's research focus. In China, tourism geography has long been a dominant sub-discipline, albeit typically focused on applied scholarship (Hilgert, 2025).

WHY GEOPOLITICS NEEDS TOURISM

The stakes for working in the space of tourism and geopolitics are high. International tourism has almost entirely returned to pre-pandemic levels. We live in an astounding motilities paradox: people are once again on the move in extraordinary numbers, yet any perusal of the news reflects an intensive hardening of borders in physical and imaginative forms. Making sense of this conundrum is a crucial facet of tourism geopolitics and explains why the field is being taken up so intensively by geographers and beyond (Iaquinto et al., 2024b). In doubling down on their multifaceted imagined communities, the question of why and where people choose to travel cannot be answered solely using the lens of geopolitics or tourism. Limiting research to a geopolitics framing would minimize travel choice as a peripheral act in the reproduction of a geopolitical identity, likely focusing on passport hierarchies or personal wealth and thereby masking how tourism inflects travelers with a personalized sense of geopolitical meaning-making that shapes the tourism industry today.

Scholars approaching the paradox of greater global mobility amidst a sedimentation of political identity from a tourism research angle are restricted to consumer choice, the commodification of place, and various marketing schemes, ignoring how embodied geopolitical identities (perhaps counterintuitively) drive the selection of destinations and tourist behaviors in situ. Tourism geography can no longer point to the simplistic category of tourism motivations as an explanation for travel behavior, just as political geography can no longer treat travel as an agnostic side-story to forging political identity (Talukder, 2025). The tension between the mythical 'freedom' of travel and the boundary-making project of geopolitics is on clear display throughout our special issue. The discussion above illustrates the power of tourism geopolitics as a theoretical framing device from which to address complex societal problems. The tension of travel freedom and geopolitical bordering is just one: nationalism, constructions of the other, community building/destruction, and identity-making are others. Indeed, one of the reasons tourism geopolitics is being circulated and captured so fervently in and beyond academia today is because many of the ideas that resonate in tourism geopolitics bridge the everyday with the conceptual. This is a starting point for thinking about how conceptually similar tourism and geopolitics research are. Critical approaches to tourism and geopolitics rest on a post-structural edifice, with tourism geography interested in the oft-missed political dimensions of tourism and geopolitics intent on uncovering 'politics that is not politics.' Mundane constructions of nationalism and cultural identity also frame and drive both tourism and geopolitics. What may be the most insightful (if upsetting) component of this shared approach is how mobile geopolitical actors often resist breaking down artificial national and cultural borders during encounters with difference, which emphasizes how tourism and geopolitics reinforce dominant ideologies, codify imagined hierarchies, and reproduce Self-Other binaries.

Tourism geopolitics showcases how border closures, restrictions, and 'green lanes' are not limited to those separating nation-states but exist at multiple, often overlapping scales. Geographers cannot overstate the significance that nationalism has on tourism and geopolitics (Huang, 2022). While the COVID-19 pandemic temporarily paused leisure travel worldwide, the era continued to fuel the heightening politicization of tourism and had a particular influence on tourism geopolitics and border policies. The geopolitical urgency to lock down borders and protect national citizens has arguably laid some of the groundwork for intensive crackdowns against 'unwelcome' migrants from countries like Mexico, Russia, Gaza, and Ukraine. Though the motivations may be different, discourses of 'threatening' infiltrators sullying local populations remain an intensified means of instilling a sense of security for citizens, or a way to remind both groups of people of the unequal motilities that exist between the Global North and Global South. Geographers conducting research on tourism and geopolitics sit in a pole position to explain and theorize the dissonance between fun and serious, exaltation and disappointment, open borders and border lockdowns, unity and difference; all binaries that form many people's experiences but ones that for too long have ignored tourism in the conversation. Tourism geopolitics bridges tourism geographies and political geography in new ways that capture the politics of the spatial in everyday experiences (An et al., 2023). It allows us to begin with the assumption that even the most mundane moments of encounter are inherently politicized and have implications at broader scales of political theorizing. Tourism geopolitics places power in the hands of people who infuse everyday politics into their tourism pursuits. Tourism is serious political business. It is much more than a 'grand tour' or relaxing holiday because the making and remaking of citizenship, of the self and others, and of political boundaries have roots in tourism. That this is now accepted among human geographers is a recognition of tourism's role in what makes people and institutions political (Gillen, 2024).

DISCUSSION

Geopolitics; from Governmentalization of a Concept to a Critical Approach

Geography of the world – as Gearoid Tuathail (1996:1) indicates- is not a product of nature but a product of histories of struggles between competing authorities over the power to recognize, occupy and administer space (Niang, 2022). Imperial systems throughout history, from classical Greece and Rome to China and Arab world, exercised the power through their ability to impose order and meaning upon space. For example, the history of Ireland indicates that not only the queen's administrators established towns, lay out roads etc.., but in a certain sense, they made Ireland. In such a sphere, Fouberg believes that the ideas about places with their influence on political behavior were constructed by intellectuals of statecraft and these ideas affected how people processed their notion of places and politics. It is an ongoing thought tries to focus on the power relation for constructing and reconstructing our understanding in this regard. But it should not be neglected that this governmentalization of geography from the 17th century onward gradually resulted in an atmosphere which is in line with what Foucault (1991:87) notes as a time when government as a general problem demanding public and intellectual thought explodes in terms of its relevance and significance (Lang, 2024). This intellectual stream resulted in the late 1980s and 1990s, another concept -critical geopolitics- initially analyzed the practical geopolitical language of the elites and intellectuals of statecrafts were born based on the traditional concept of geopolitics. Critical geopolitics investigates the geographical assumption that enters into making world politics. Critical geopolitics argues that spatiality is not confined to territoriality either historically or today. It also notes that emerging forms of global governance do not flatten space to the contrary; they increase spatial differentiation globally. The writings concerning geopolitics challenge some aspects of taken for granted geopolitical knowledge by looking at either its social production, the parameters of its discursive economy, or the combination of the two. There are two problems that cause this issue. The first is that of state as a producer, administrator and ruler of space. To some writers like Mann the development of modern state and geopolitics go together and the very definition of the state as a delimited territory suggests a further set of political relationships between this state and another state that is geopolitics. The other problem, as Mattel art (1994) indicates concerns the entwining of communications, media and politics of identity in the production of geopolitical knowledge and the nation. In brief, this new-comer with its origins in post-structuralism orientation holds that geographical knowledge is seen as partial, situated, embodied and more diffuse with popular geopolitical discourse. Hence, Nation-states are not the only legitimate units of geopolitical analysis. In this context, geopolitical practice results from complex constellation of competing ideas and discourses which in turn modify geopolitical practice. It is just here that technology enters the scene (Bânkuty-Balogh, 2024).

The globalization trend after the end of the Cold War guaranteed a free flow of labor, products, service, technology, and capital for the past 30 years. Regardless of the political system or ideology, countries imposed minimum tariffs and trade regulations while increasing interdependence and collective interest. Along with the post-Cold War era, globalization represented the golden age of neo-liberalism. Nevertheless, the globalization engine has lost momentum with the recent emergence of exclusive protectionism and regional blocs. The main issues of such a transformation focus on conflicts to secure advanced science and technology, which has the potential to determine a nation's future competitiveness and security. In the case of the U.S. and China, both countries utilize diplomatic means to exclude its competitor while securing advanced science and technology. The underlying implications of global technological competition seem to point to the erosion of the basic premise of a liberal trade order and cooperation in the field of science and technology. A new geopolitical mechanism of change using advanced technology is at work behind the decoupling phenomena caused by U.S.-China competition, termed "re-shoring," "near-shoring," and "friend- shoring (Yoon, 2023b)."

However, the recent trend of de-globalization and U.S.-China strategic competition is rapidly dismantling the existing global semiconductor supply chain based on efficiency. A representative example is U.S. President Biden's "Fab 4" proposal to Korea, Taiwan, and Japan in early 2022. The idea of semiconductor cooperation between the four countries, also labeled as the "Chip 4 Alliance," was a proposal to combine U.S. design and source technology, Japanese semiconductor materials and equipment, and Korean and Taiwanese memory/non-memory semiconductor manufacturing capabilities. Washington urged global semiconductor companies, including TSMC and Samsung, to invest in production facilities in the U.S. mainland, while expressing its intention to use Fab 4 to restructure an alternative supply chain by excluding China. As a relatively recent issue, existing case studies regarding the Fab 4 are few in number. There is, however, previous research in international political studies examining the semiconductor industry with a focus on the importance of security. Such studies can be roughly classified into two camps. The first approach underlines the technical specificity of semiconductors, represented by Chris Miller's "Chip War: The Fight for the World's Most Critical Technology." Even during the Cold War, semiconductors were critical technology that comprised the core of contention between the U.S. and Japan, and the U.S. and USSR (Park, 2023). Now semiconductor technology has become a crucial method for "informationized" and "intelligentized" military competition. Miller also emphasizes that semiconductors possess essential technology for securing emerging and disruptive technology for artificial superintelligence and quantum computing. He adds that the U.S. recognizing the threat posed by China's emerging microchip ecosystem had to keep it in check. The U.S. focal point regarding the chip supply chain is "core profits and power," closely related to military security rather than vulnerabilities. The second approach underscores the regression to an era previous to globalization with the advent of a New Cold War and spheres of influence. Reshaping the global supply chain of all technologies and resources into two blocs led by the U.S. and China, neoclassical realists, including Fareed Zakaria are at the forefront of such studies. Zakaria points out that after the pandemic, the zero-sum game structure has gained more influence over the behaviors of state actors with a decisive impact on military strategy, the economy, and industrial technology.

TECHNOLOGY ON BOARD! IS TECHNO-GEOPOLITICS A CHALLENGE FOR CRITICAL APPROACH?

Technology has changed and complicated the human environment. This phenomenon has not occurred in a single specific field but has touched vast fields among which political environment is notable (Tullett, 2021). Hence, national governments enter today a competition with other nations as their competitors along with new actors, all privileged almost the same technologies. The result is a global stage in which states play major roles, more complicated than ever, because technology has led to diffusion of manufacturing and trade. This diffusion is seen as a smaller but more important scale in political arena with its unique effect on legitimacy and state's power. A different geopolitical environment will change the power and ability of states. This phrase is concerned to shape the core of geopolitical thinking. In classical geopolitics sphere, the essential effective way of obtaining the better geographical situations was expansionism through struggles, invasions and wars. But as these ways are not acceptable today due to international laws and regulations, changing environment and shaping it in a desired way help states approach to a quasi-desired situation. It is here that technology enters the scene. A state by means of technology along with the application of other means of obtaining, preserving and promoting power, will be able to change its geographical environment. This" neo-classical" approach is what we call techno-geopolitics. As it is seen below, the higher the technology, the more capabilities in hands of its users, but since these users are not in the same level of power and opportunities, the same technology may have different results for authorities of state and other actors.

It may be argued that this happens for three major reasons. First state authorities have more information than other actors. They have access to the sources of information. This fact makes them capable of using the opportunities in right time and right place. Second, they have more money than other actors. This can be a good guarantee for implementing plans and projects in line with their goals and objectives. Furthermore, information and money make a magic formulation for power augmentation; what is not really clear for other actors to benefit from (Dwivedi et al., 2023). And third, they have more relationships and more effective interactions. Although in the era of communication, having such interactions are facilitated by means of technology but again the non-governmental actors for not being in the same level of the two former elements - information and money- their relationships and interactions may not have the same efficiency as state. New technologies in the process of changing, forming and reforming the geographical environment changes into means in hands of intellectuals of statecrafts to allocate the ideas of the"robo-leviathan" of state about the new shaped places- especially if strategic- and reforming the people's notion of politics; what is seen in the definition of critical geopolitics.

Here it may be claimed that even the concept of meta-geopolitics proposed by Nayef al Rodhon (2012) which combines traditional and new dimensions of geopolitics to have a multidimensional view will be at service of such allocation of intellectual statecrafts. Today the"robo-leviathan "of state is in such situation that to change even the stream of discourses which other actors as his rivals have begun. This is in line with what some writers have claimed that the attempts by states in our contemporary world to violently engineer space (social, cognitive and aesthetic, all of which are entwined with the territorial to fit their nationalist, exclusionary and racist visions of the perfect order in unfortunately still part of global politics.

CONSIDERATIONS FOR A TECHNO-GEOPOLITICAL APPROACH

Traditional geopolitics focused on how geographical conditions worked in international politics. The purpose was to study disputes and survival strategies of countries in relation to topography and the location of the ocean. Thus, attention has been paid to the ability or power to achieve the specific goal of preoccupying a physical space and place. The "state's efforts to mobilize power resources and gain superiority by preoccupying a space favorable for survival," which constitutes the concept of geopolitics, continues to be a valid proposition in the international political environment. Space, however, is no longer limited to land and ocean and has become an environment encompassing the exchange of knowledge, information, and data in digital space. Furthermore, securing power resources has become more about enhancing technological competitiveness in military power. More importantly, techno-geopolitics differs from traditional geopolitics as it highlights the deeply embedded, advanced science and technology in state power mobilization, influence projection, and diplomatic actions. Hence, techno-geopolitics emphasizes technological variables as decisive factors in a state's trade, industry, and foreign security policy while closely associated with military security issues and alliances (Yoon, 2023c). In addition, techno-geopolitics is a theoretical approach to explain how advanced science and technology has developed into an indicator of national security from its former means of strengthening economic and military capabilities.

In reality, advanced economies such as the U.S. EU, China, and Japan are actively implementing policies to strengthen science and technology competitiveness as national strategies. Such policies not only include the expansion of R&D projects but also consider the ripple effects of enhanced competitiveness on the industry and economic security (Hsu et al., 2022). In particular, regarding science and technology and trade diplomacy, countries are preparing national strategies to lead the global standardization process of emerging technologies. This section focuses on the connection of technology, economy, and security issues witnessed in the recent U.S.-China competition for technological hegemony, and proposes a theoretical analysis framework for techno-geopolitics that is necessary to explain the complex features of such macro changes. Under the new geopolitical order with the U.S.-China competition, which differs from the Cold War and the post-Cold War era, it is necessary to look at the main driving forces, manifesting mechanisms, conditions, and the environment. This chapter, while focusing on the complex features of the techno-geopolitical approach, will discuss the connection between geopolitical discourse, geographical discourse, and technological sovereignty theory constituting techno-geopolitics, and the interaction of technology and politics, inseparability of economy and security, and the bloc-ization of industrial sectors (Shaji George et al., 2023).

THE INTERACTION OF TECHNOLOGY AND POLITICS

As aforementioned, the term "techno-geopolitics" has mainly been used in science and technology communities and industrial circles, rather than the field of international politics.3 In Korea, a competitive advantage in advanced science and technology was a source of social innovation and power, and concepts such as "indispensability" and "non-replaceability" were highlighted to support claims for more public investment to enhance its industrial ecosystem. While underscoring the importance of advanced science and technology and its impact on international relations, the domestic approach lacked a balanced view of the positive or negative influences of global security situations and political judgments on technological development. In other words, Korea failed to grasp the bidirectional mechanism of mutual interaction between geopolitical structure and technological development.

It is thus necessary to focus on the two-way causal relationship between political and technological development. In fact, according to Dahlman (2007) and Khalid Khan et al. (2022), politics and technology are highly integrated, and differences in geopolitical risks and national interests accelerate competition among countries for technological development and accessibility. In addition, such technologies cause rapid changes in national sovereignty and geopolitical dominance and have a decisive impact on international relations and strategic alliances centered on the supply of critical technologies (Yoon, 2023d). On the other hand, as the mutual interaction of technology and politics may cause geopolitical uncertainty and risk, the international community faces the challenge of establishing interoperability amid intensified technological competition causing division.

THE INSEPARABILITY OF ECONOMY AND SECURITY

Unlike geopolitics, which focuses on territory as an object of accumulating national wealth, geo-economics aims to amass wealth through 'market domination.' In addition, economic power for comprehensive security, including financial security, health security, human security, and military security, is emphasized. Geopolitics values military threats, but geo-economics underscores economic sanctions instead of military threats. In particular, it is hard to deny that the recent rise in economic security is closely related to geo-economics, which refers to "using economic means to promote and protect national interests and to produce geopolitical results favorable. Furthermore, the manifestation pattern exhibits the appearance of "mercantile realism" based on "techno-economic security," which differs from "structural realism" centered on military security. However, with techno-economic security expanding to blocs and alliances, technology has become more than a simple product and may function as a security strategic asset. In other words, economy and security, which represented different fields, are now inseparable and interconnected, setting the course towards a transition period overwhelmed by security logic and resulting in weakened globalization. Furthermore, a rise in geopolitical tension accelerates the transformation of technologies that increase the security impact of advanced technologies with dual uses and weaponization of interdependence. Therefore, it is necessary to focus on the trend of economic-security strategies that maximize national interests by using various economic and security policy measures and the role of core technologies as their primary means (Adhikari, 2025).

INDUSTRIAL STRATEGIES AND SECURITY

Securing superiority in key industries is more than industrial and economic strategies at the macro level and has emerged as a vital national security strategy. The so-called "industrial-technological security" approach calls for the need to implement science and technology, and industrial policies in tandem with diplomatic and security policies. The semiconductor shortage in 2021 and Japan's export regulation of semiconductor materials, parts, and equipment in 2019 confirmed the consequences of unilateral dependence on core technology and raised the importance of securing sufficient options to develop and maintain its capabilities. Currently, securing the supply chain for strategic technology is one of the main issues of contention between blocs, including the U.S. and China. Meanwhile, discussions about stability and efficiency at the global level are on the back burner. In addition, global society seems divided on issues regarding international norms and governance surrounding the use of data, which is the basis of digital-based services (Dani et al., 2023).

CONCLUSION

Although the power of geography and its effect on politics was revealed from ancient times for politicians but conceptualization of such understanding was not completed until the 19th century. The birth of geopolitics was not separated from the classical view of state's power in presenting, using or changing this concept. With the emergence of a new approach called critical geopolitics, the nation-states were not further the only legitimate unit on the scene of geopolitics. There is a complex constellation of competing ideas and discourses which play the main role. But once again, technology can change the equation for the states, now robo-leviathans, and for the classical view of geopolitics by capabilities provided for states to change the geographical environment. The question is not that the critical geopolitics has taken a wrong way comparing with classical geopolitics, but is the fact that equation of classical-critical geopolitics has been changed since the flourishing of technologies especially in recent decade. In other words, it is true that technology in all its aspects has been presented to governmental and nongovernmental actors, but the actors who have more chances to benefit from this technology is state and intellectual of statecraft. This actor with its bigger share of information, money and relationships in comparison with other actors, will be in a situation to apply the methods of good governance - persuasion, cooperation, force and facilitation – as Spicker indicates and hence becomes a dominant narrator of geopolitical concepts as it was the case the first time the phenomenon was conceptualized.

REFERENCES

Adhikari, R. (2025). Economic Security at the Pivot of National Security: Foresight into Nepal's Headway. *Unity Journal*, *6*(1), 18–33. DOI: 10.3126/unityj.v6i1.75545

An, N., Zhang, J., & Wang, M. (2023). The Everyday Chinese Framing of Africa: A Perspective of Tourism-geopolitical Encounter. *Geopolitics*, *28*(4), 1422–1441. DOI: 10.1080/14650045.2020.1807957

Bánkuty-Balogh, L. S. (2024). *The intersection of geopolitics and technological innovations: Implications for the Central-European region* [PhD, Budapesti Corvinus Egyetem]. DOI: 10.14267/phd.2024016

Boikova, T., Zeverte-Rivza, S., Rivza, P., & Rivza, B. (2021). The Determinants and Effects of Competitiveness: The Role of Digitalization in the European Economies. *Sustainability (Basel)*, *13*(21), 11689. DOI: 10.3390/su132111689

Criekemans, D. (2022). *Geopolitics and International Relations: Grounding World Politics Anew*. Brill | Nijhoff. DOI: 10.1163/9789004432086

Dani, A. A. H., Supangkat, S. H., Lubis, F. F., Nugraha, I. G. B. B., Kinanda, R., & Rizkia, I. (2023). Development of a Smart City Platform Based on Digital Twin Technology for Monitoring and Supporting Decision-Making. *Sustainability (Basel)*, *15*(18), 14002. DOI: 10.3390/su151814002

David, A., Yigitcanlar, T., Li, R. Y. M., Corchado, J. M., Cheong, P. H., Mossberger, K., & Mehmood, R. (2023). Understanding Local Government Digital Technology Adoption Strategies: A PRISMA Review. *Sustainability (Basel)*, *15*(12), 9645. DOI: 10.3390/su15129645

Dwivedi, Y. K., Kshetri, N., Hughes, L., Slade, E. L., Jeyaraj, A., Kar, A. K., Baabdullah, A. M., Koohang, A., Raghavan, V., Ahuja, M., Albanna, H., Albashrawi, M. A., Al-Busaidi, A. S., Balakrishnan, J., Barlette, Y., Basu, S., Bose, I., Brooks, L., Buhalis, D., & Wright, R. (2023). Opinion Paper: "So what if ChatGPT wrote it?" Multidisciplinary perspectives on opportunities, challenges and implications of generative conversational AI for research, practice and policy. *International Journal of Information Management*, *71*, 102642. DOI: 10.1016/j.ijinfomgt.2023.102642

Gillen, J. (2024). Tourism geopolitics: Roots and branches. *Tourism Geographies*, •••, 1–11. DOI: 10.1080/14616688.2024.2332354

Hilgert, J. (2025). Geopolitics and industrial relations theory: Intellectual history and future reconfigurations. *Globalizations*, *22*(4), 634–651. DOI: 10.1080/14747731.2024.2401691

Hsu, C.-H., He, X., Zhang, T.-Y., Chang, A.-Y., Liu, W.-L., & Lin, Z.-Q. (2022). Enhancing Supply Chain Agility with Industry 4.0 Enablers to Mitigate Ripple Effects Based on Integrated QFD-MCDM: An Empirical Study of New Energy Materials Manufacturers. *Mathematics*, *10*(10), 1635. DOI: 10.3390/math10101635

Huang, Y. (2022). Consuming geopolitics and feeling maritime territoriality: The case of China's patriotic tourism in the South China Sea. *Political Geography*, *98*, 102669. DOI: 10.1016/j.polgeo.2022.102669

Huang, Y., & Liu, Y. (2024). A critical reflection on tourism geopolitics: Research progress and future agenda. *Tourism Geographies*, *26*(5), 881–897. DOI: 10.1080/14616688.2024.2366481

Iaquinto, B. L., Gillen, J., & Mostafanezhad, M. (2024). The new tourism geopolitics: Bridging tourism geographies and political geography. *Tourism Geographies*, *26*(5), 723–734. DOI: 10.1080/14616688.2024.2394693

Ioannidou, E. (2022). Mythologies of Genesis and Neo-Nazi Palingenesis: Commemorating the Battle of Thermopylae in the Political Rites of the Golden Dawn. *Humanities (Washington)*, *11*(4), 88. DOI: 10.3390/h11040088

Jabareen, Y., & Eizenberg, E. (2021). Theorizing urban social spaces and their interrelations: New perspectives on urban sociology, politics, and planning. *Planning Theory*, *20*(3), 211–230. DOI: 10.1177/1473095220976942

Jarvis, L., & Lister, M. (2025). Critical security research and the war on terror: From the margins to the mainstream? *European Journal of International Security*, *10*(1), 150–169. DOI: 10.1017/eis.2024.36

Jiang, Q., Fang, W., LePage, B., & Han, G. (2024). How Is Tourism Geography Situated in Taiwan? Geography Versus Tourism and Recreation. *Sustainability (Basel)*, *16*(17), 7523. DOI: 10.3390/su16177523

Klinke, I. (2023). *Life, Earth, Colony: Friedrich Ratzel's Necropolitical Geography*. University of Michigan Press., DOI: 10.3998/mpub.11987710

Lang, A. (2024). 'Global Disordering': Practices of Reflexivity in Global Economic Governance. *European Journal of International Law*, *35*(1), 93–140. DOI: 10.1093/ejil/chae011

Mason, O., Sarma, J., Sidaway, J. D., Bonnett, A., Hubbard, P., Jamil, G., Middleton, J., O'Neill, M., Riding, J., & Rose, M. (2023). Interventions in walking methods in political geography. *Political Geography*, *106*, 102937. DOI: 10.1016/j.polgeo.2023.102937

Mihalic, T. (2024). Trends in Sustainable Tourism Paradigm: Resilience and Adaptation. *Sustainability (Basel), 16*(17), 7838. DOI: 10.3390/su16177838

Mogiani, M. (2023). Studying Borders from the Border: Reflections on the Concept of Borders as Meeting Points. *Geopolitics, 28*(3), 1323–1341. DOI: 10.1080/14650045.2022.2026329

Mohiuddin, A. (2024). *Islam in the Age of Globalization: Perspectives and Responses*. Rowman & Littlefield Publishers., DOI: 10.5771/9798881801342

Niang, A. (2022). Space and the Geopolitical. *Millennium, 51*(1), 284–304. DOI: 10.1177/03058298221146592

Oostendorp, M. (2022). Raced Repertoires: The Linguistic Repertoire as Multi-Semiotic and Racialized. *Applied Linguistics, 43*(1), 65–87. DOI: 10.1093/applin/amab018

Park, S. (2023). Semiconductors at the Intersection of Geoeconomics, Technonationalism, and Global Value Chains. *Social Sciences (Basel, Switzerland), 12*(8), 466. DOI: 10.3390/socsci12080466

Shaji George, A., Hovan George, A. S., & Gabrio Martin, A. S. (2023). *A Review of ChatGPT AI's Impact on Several Business Sectors*. DOI: 10.5281/ZENODO.7644359

Shtern, M. (2022). Passing as a tourist: Exploring the everyday urban geopolitics of tourism. *Political Geography, 93*, 102526. DOI: 10.1016/j.polgeo.2021.102526

Talukder, M. B. (2020). An Appraisal of the Economic Outlook for the Tourism Industry, Specially Cox's Bazar in Bangladesh. *i-manager's Journal on Economics & Commerce,* 2(1), 23-35. DOI: 10.26634/jecom.2.1.17285

Talukder, M. B. (2020). The Future of Culinary Tourism: An Emerging Dimension for the Tourism Industry of Bangladesh. I-Manager's. *Journal of Management, 15*(1), 27. DOI: 10.26634/jmgt.15.1.17181

Talukder, M. B. (2021). An assessment of the roles of the social network in the development of the Tourism Industry in Bangladesh. *International Journal of Business, Law, and Education*, 2(3), 85–93. DOI: 10.56442/ijble.v2i3.21

Talukder, M. B. (2024). Implementing Artificial Intelligence and Virtual Experiences in Hospitality. In Manohar, S., Mittal, A., Raju, S., & Nair, A. J. (Eds.), *Advances in Hospitality, Tourism, and the Services Industry* (pp. 145–160). IGI Global., DOI: 10.4018/979-8-3693-2019-8.ch009

Talukder, M. B. (2025). Climate change adaptation strategies for a tourism destination: A study of Kuakata beach. *Acta Scientiarum Polonorum. Administratio Locorum*, *24*(1), 165–179. DOI: 10.31648/aspal.10073

Talukder, M. B. (2025). Climate change adaptation strategies for a tourism destination: A study of Kuakata beach. *Acta Scientiarum Polonorum. Administratio Locorum*, *24*(1), 165–179. DOI: 10.31648/aspal.10073

Talukder, M. B. (2025). Current Trends and Future Research Directions on Eco-Friendly Stages of Hotel Industry. *RPER*, (71), 7–18. DOI: 10.59072/rper.vi71.695

Thatcher, J., Retchless, D., & Fish, C. (2024). Dueling cartographies: Science, positivism, art, and critical praxis. *International Journal of Cartography*, *10*(3), 377–394. DOI: 10.1080/23729333.2024.2338496

Tullett, W. (2021). State of the Field: Sensory History. *History (London)*, *106*(373), 804–820. DOI: 10.1111/1468-229X.13246

Wheeldon, A. (2022). *The Destructuration of Academic Life: How Managerialism Colonises Universities with Symbolic Violence*. DOI: 10.26192/Q7QVZ

Yoon, J. (2023). Supply Chain Security in the Age of Techno-Geopolitics: 'Fab 4' Case in the Semiconductor Industry. *The Korean Journal of International Studies*, *21*(1), 27–60. DOI: 10.14731/kjis.2023.04.21.1.27

Chapter 16

Techno-Politics, Tourism, and the Transformation of the International Political Economy in the Digital Age

Chirra Baburao
https://orcid.org/0000-0003-4881-3708
Gujarat National Law University, India

Mohammad Badruddoza Talukder
https://orcid.org/0009-0008-1662-9221
International University of Business Agriculture and Technology, Bangladesh

Ayubkhan Kalwad
https://orcid.org/0000-0001-8088-8799
GITAM University, India

Pradeep Thota
https://orcid.org/0009-0002-0675-5722
GITAM University, India

ABSTRACT

The digital age has ushered in a profound transformation of global governance, tourism practices, diplomatic engagement, and trade relations. This chapter investigates how techno-political strategies, smart tourism infrastructures, digital diplomacy initiatives, and evolving patterns of global digital commerce collectively reconfigure the international political economy. Drawing on interdisciplinary

DOI: 10.4018/979-8-3373-1727-4.ch016

literature—from political science, international relations, tourism studies, and economics—this chapter develops a comprehensive conceptual framework to analyze the feedback loops among data governance, mobility management, normative influence, and platform-driven market structures. The chapter offers insights into digital technologies' challenges and opportunities for sovereign states, industry stakeholders, and civil society actors through detailed case studies, policy analyses, and normative reflections.

INTRODUCTION

The 21st century has ushered in a profound convergence of digital technologies with the fundamental frameworks of politics and economics (Talukder et al., 2020). Once confined to specialized research labs, these innovations now permeate global systems—reshaping supply chains, border security, and the exchange of information between governments and citizens. Blockchain, for instance, facilitates transparent and tamper-proof ledgers for applications ranging from pharmaceutical distribution to carbon-credit trading (Kumar et al., 2025; Talukder, 2021). Similarly, artificial intelligence (AI) has evolved beyond experimental prototypes to power mission-critical functions, such as automated risk assessments at international entry points and predictive monitoring of financial markets(Milana & Ashta, 2021).

Within this era of hyper-connectivity, the tourism industry—long valued for its role in fostering human interaction—has undergone a significant digital transformation. Today's travelers move through cities guided by personalized, real-time itineraries generated through advanced data analytics (Barashok et al., 2021; Talukder, 2025; Lina et al., 2025; Kumar et al., 2025). Sensor networks track and optimize crowd flow, environmental impact, and public safety. Meanwhile, biometric identity verification, mobile health credentials, and contactless payments streamline cross-border travel, even as they introduce complex debates on privacy, equity, and the commodification of personal data. In this emerging innovative tourism paradigm, human experiences are increasingly shaped by algorithms that curate, monitor, and monetize each aspect of the journey(Чорна et al., 2024).

At the same time, diplomacy has embraced digital platforms and virtual spaces, shifting away from traditional chancery halls and formal receptions. Diplomatic engagement now unfolds across social media, immersive virtual-reality forums, and AI-moderated discussions. Governments craft digital narratives to shape global perceptions, leveraging viral content, chatbot-driven interactions, and targeted influencer campaigns(Li et al., 2024). From live-streamed bilateral summits to data-driven public-opinion analysis, digital diplomacy minimizes geographical barriers while amplifying soft-power initiatives and geopolitical rivalries(Sheikh, 2024).

At a broader level, these technological shifts are redefining the international political economy. Cross-border commerce is no longer solely dependent on physical infrastructure; it now hinges on cloud-based services, e-commerce platforms, and algorithmic pricing models alongside traditional transportation networks(Ji, 2021; Parayil, 2005). Digital trade negotiations address novel challenges, including data-localization requirements, source-code security, and taxation frameworks for intangible digital services. A select group of global tech giants effectively dictate economic access, controlling who can participate in markets and who remains marginalized. Consequently, national economic strategies are increasingly centered on securing digital sovereignty—investing in domestic data infrastructure, cultivating AI expertise, and engaging in international standard-setting initiatives (Meltzer, 2019; Veale et al., 2023).

This chapter explores four interconnected domains—techno-politics, smart tourism, digital diplomacy, and the evolving international political economy—examining their roles in shaping power, mobility, and commerce in the digital age. Techno-politics investigates how states and corporations deploy AI, blockchain, and data-governance frameworks to assert sovereignty and strategic leverage(Srivastava & Bullock, 2024; View of The Techno-Political Collision, n.d.). Smart tourism assesses the application of IoT sensors, biometric verification, and algorithmic personalization in travel while probing concerns around surveillance and digital equity. Digital diplomacy analyzes virtual forums, AI-driven narratives, and cyber-sanctions as foreign policy instruments. Finally, the international political economy delves into platform capitalism, digital trade systems, and the dependencies created by dominant cloud service providers(Adesina, 2017; Sheikh, 2024).

To illustrate these interconnected forces, we introduce a conceptual framework (Figure 1) that situates each domain within a dynamic system. Arrows indicate bidirectional influences: techno-political regulations shape tourism technologies, while tourism-generated data informs governance strategies; digital-diplomatic trends impact trade negotiations, just as economic dependencies reshape diplomatic bargaining power. This mapping underscores that no domain evolves in isolation—each continuously interacts with and responds to changes in the others.

In the following chapters, we will explore each domain in depth, drawing upon interdisciplinary research, policy analyses, and real-world case studies. We aim to offer a comprehensive perspective on how digital technologies dismantle traditional barriers between politics, tourism, diplomacy, and economics, providing valuable insights for policymakers, industry leaders, and scholars navigating this rapidly evolving landscape.

Figure 1. Conceptual framework: Transformation of the international political economy through techno-politics, smart tourism, digital diplomacy, and global trade dynamics

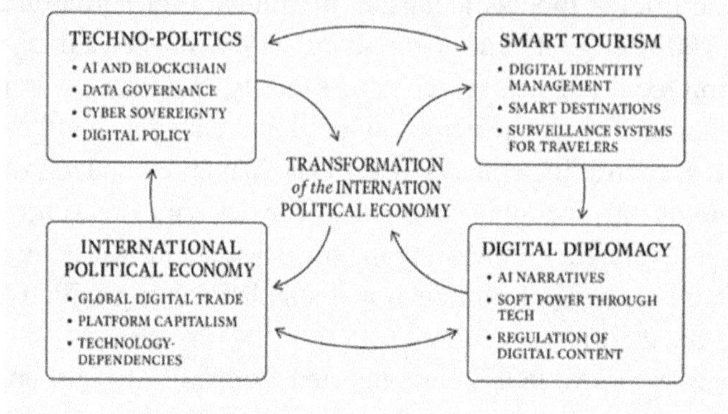

TECHNO-POLITICS: GOVERNING DATA, ALGORITHMS, AND SOVEREIGNTY

Techno-politics involves the strategic use of technology by states, supranational organizations, and private entities to further political goals, regulate behavior, and assert sovereignty within digital realms (Hulkó et al., 2025). In this section, we explore three key dimensions:

AI and Blockchain as Instruments of Statecraft

Artificial Intelligence Strategies Governments around the globe have initiated national AI strategies to leverage machine learning for economic advancement, defense, and public administration. Notable examples include China's New Generation AI Development Plan (2017), which Aims for global AI leadership by 2030 through substantial R&D investments, talent acquisition, and the integration of AI in governance (Roberts et al., 2019). European Union's Coordinated Plan on Artificial Intelligence (2021): Focuses on ethical AI, regulatory sandboxes, and cross-border collaboration under the Digital Europe Programme (Coordinated Plan on Artificial Intelligence - Shaping Europe's Digital Future, 2018). United States AI Initiative Act (2019): Concentrates on research funding, public-private partnerships, and the establishment of data repositories to drive innovation. AI's dual-use nature—civilian and military—makes it pivotal in techno-political competition. Machine learning algorithms enhance resource allocation (e.g., predictive policing, traffic management) but also raise concerns about algorithmic bias, surveillance expansion, and the weaponization of data (Bankins & Formosa, 2023).

Blockchain and Decentralized Governance

Blockchain, a distributed ledger technology, promises tamper-resistant record-keeping and trustless transactions (Karaduman & Gülhas, 2025). Both governments and corporations are investigating blockchain for various applications, including supply-chain traceability, which ensures the provenance of critical goods, such as pharmaceuticals and conflict minerals. Digital Currencies and CBDCs: Central bank digital currencies aim to modernize payment systems, exemplified by China's Digital Yuan pilot. Smart Contracts: Automating regulatory compliance, trade finance, and public procurement through embedded governance rules. However, blockchain also disrupts traditional regulatory frameworks, challenging governments to balance innovation with oversight. The debates surrounding the cross-border energy consumption of proof-of-work systems and the jurisdictional ambiguities of decentralized networks highlight the tensions inherent in blockchain governance.

Data Governance and Cyber Sovereignty

Data Localization and Flow Restrictions Data has emerged as a geostrategic asset. Data localization laws mandate that specific data categories, such as personal health records, remain within national borders (Sharma et al., 2023). Notable examples include Russia's Personal Data Localization Law (2015), which requires that personal data concerning Russian citizens be stored on servers physically located in Russia. India's Digital Personal Data Protection Bill (Pending): Suggests data localization for sensitive personal data, with exceptions for government access. EU's GDPR (2018): Enforces stringent cross-border transfer rules, necessitating adequacy decisions or standard contractual clauses. These measures reflect a desire to assert "cyber sovereignty," yet they can fragment the internet, increase compliance costs, and incite trade tensions (Aktipis & Katwan, 2021).

International Standard-Setting and Governance Bodies

Multilateral institutions and industry consortia formulate digital governance standards. The International Telecommunication Union (ITU) discusses 5G security standards and spectrum allocation (Meltzer, 2019). The ISO/IEC JTC 1/SC 42 is responsible for developing international AI standards emphasizing trustworthiness, robustness, and transparency (Role of Standards, 2024). The World Trade Organization's e-Commerce Negotiations involve ongoing discussions on digital services disciplines amidst differing positions on data flows (Sankaran, 2025). These techno-political contests frequently transition to these venues, thereby shaping the regulatory frameworks that underpin global digital interactions (González & Jouanjean, 2017).

Digital Policy: From Privacy to Platform Regulation

Privacy and Data Protection Regimes Privacy legislation has expanded to tackle the risks associated with mass surveillance and data commodification. In addition to the GDPR, other significant frameworks include the California Consumer Privacy Act (CCPA, 2020), which provides California residents with rights over personal data collected by businesses (Martin et al., 2020). Brazil's LGPD (2020): Reflects the GDPR but enshrines data protection as a constitutional right. Australia's Privacy Act Amendments (2022): Broadens the definitions of personal information and introduces penalties for data breaches (Paltiel, 2023). Although there is alignment on principles such as consent and purpose limitation, enforcement mechanisms, scope, and cultural contexts differ considerably.

Platform Governance and Algorithmic Accountability

Social media, e-commerce, and search platforms have evolved into public squares, market plazas, and information hubs. Governments are exploring various approaches: Content Moderation Laws: Germany's NetzDG (2017) imposes fines on platforms that do not promptly remove illegal content. Algorithmic Transparency Acts: Proposed legislation in the U.S. Congress and EU mandates disclosures about recommender systems and automated decision-making processes. Platform Liability Reforms: Australia's News Media Bargaining Code (2021) requires platforms to negotiate compensation with news outlets. These policies aim to curb misinformation, protect cultural industries, and ensure fair competition, yet they also raise concerns about censorship, market power, and free speech. Smart Tourism: Mobility, Surveillance, and Experience Smart tourism signifies the digital transformation of travel and destination management. It utilizes IoT, big data, and AI to enhance both operational efficiencies and visitor experiences (Yu & Wang, 2022).

Digital Identity Management and the New Mobility Regime

e-Visas and Biometric Screening Governments utilize electronic visas and biometric passenger screening to enhance border processes. EU's Entry/Exit System (EES): Captures biometric data of non-EU nationals crossing Schengen borders. U.S. Global Entry Program: Conducts pre-vetting of low-risk travelers using fingerprint and iris scans. India's e-Visa System: Offers a digital application process complemented by a network of visa-on-arrival facilities. While these systems promise increased efficiency and security, they also heighten data collection and the potential for profiling travelers based on nationality, ethnicity, or travel history.

Health Passes and Pandemic Mobility

The COVID-19 pandemic hastened the adoption of digital health credentials, such as Vaccination Certificates, including the WHO's Smart Vaccination Certificate initiative and the EU Digital COVID Certificate. Additionally, Health Dashboards emerged, featuring mobile apps that integrate test results and travel authorizations, like CommonPass and the IATA Travel Pass. While these tools facilitated cross-border movement, they also raised concerns about equity, particularly regarding vaccine access and digital literacy.

Smart Destinations: Data-Driven Place Management

IoT and Real-Time Analytics Destinations employ networked sensors to monitor tourist flows, environmental conditions, and infrastructure usage. For instance, Barcelona's Urban Platform integrates data from transit systems, water management, and tourist hotspots to balance city life. Similarly, Singapore's Virtual Singapore Project utilizes 3D digital twin modeling for urban planning and tourism forecasting. Advanced analytics are crucial in managing overcrowding, preserving heritage sites, and informing dynamic pricing strategies for attractions.

Personalized Experience and Recommendation Engines

Mobile apps and kiosks offer route, restaurant, and activity suggestions tailored to user profiles and real-time conditions. TripAdvisor's Smart Itinerary provides AI-generated day plans that adjust according to weather, crowd levels, and user interests. Meanwhile, China's Alipay City Services is an integrated platform for transportation tickets, attraction bookings, and AR-enabled cultural storytelling. While personalization boosts satisfaction, it also produces detailed behavioral data that authorities can monetize or repurpose.

Surveillance Systems and the Ethics of Observation

Facial Recognition in Tourist Zones Airports, train stations, and city centers increasingly utilize facial recognition technology for security and marketing purposes: China's Jiankangbao Apps: Integrate health data with facial scans at tourist sites. Dubai's Smart Police Station: Unmanned facilities employ biometrics to handle detentions and complaints. These applications spark debates over consent, racial bias in algorithms, and the erosion of public anonymity.

Geofencing and Location Tracking

Destinations employ geofencing to activate alerts or customize content when visitors enter designated areas: Venice issues crowd control alerts through mobile notifications to deter entry into overcrowded zones, thereby safeguarding its delicate heritage. Yellowstone sends automated messages to educate tourists on safety near wildlife habitats. While ethical tourism frameworks advocate for transparency and opt-in models, many implementations default to opt-out or lack transparent governance.

Digital Diplomacy: Networks, Narratives, and Norms

Digital diplomacy leverages the internet's connective power to conduct foreign policy, manage reputations, and build alliances. AI Narratives and Norm Entrepreneurship States and intergovernmental organizations compete to establish global AI norms: OECD AI Principles (2019): Backed by 42 countries, these principles emphasize human-centric and trustworthy AI. Global Partnership on AI (GPAI): A forum co-led by Canada and France to promote AI research that aligns with human rights. Norm entrepreneurs use think tanks, white papers, and conferences to influence discourse, often reflecting cultural values related to privacy, human dignity, and innovation.

Digital Cultural Diplomacy

E-Learning and Knowledge Exchange Massive Open Online Courses (MOOCs) and virtual exchanges enhance educational diplomacy. EdX's Global Classroom involves collaborations between universities and foreign ministries to deliver governance and public health courses. Saudi Arabia's Virtual Archaeology Tours offer online reconstructions of heritage sites to foster cultural understanding. While these initiatives strengthen people-to-people connections, they can also be used to project soft power narratives that align with regime interests.

Entertainment and Narrative Shaping

Streaming services are becoming platforms for sharing national narratives and values: Netflix's International Originals draw global audiences to Korean, Turkish, and Latin American dramas through investments in local content. Japan's Cool Japan Initiative involves government-backed efforts to promote anime, manga, and culinary tourism. Media diplomacy intersects with platform governance as host countries negotiate content standards and censorship requirements.

Regulation of Digital Content as a Geopolitical Tool

Platform Bans and Market Access States impose restrictions or bans on platforms to assert regulatory sovereignty: India's TikTok Ban (2020): Citing concerns over data privacy and national security, this move spurred the growth of local alternatives. Russia's Blocking of Telegram (2018–2020): This action led to a conflict over encryption keys and law enforcement access. Geopolitical alignments and domestic political pressures influence decisions regarding platform access.

Cyber Sanctions and Information Warfare

Digital diplomacy encompasses coercive measures, such as U.S. sanctions on Chinese tech firms, with Huawei facing restrictions due to alleged espionage and human rights violations. The EU's Digital Services Act fines platforms that fail to address disinformation campaigns or extremist content. These regulatory tools are integral to broader strategic competition, blurring the lines between trade policy and diplomatic coercion.

International Political Economy: Digital Trade, Platforms, and Dependencies

The rise of platform capitalism, new trade regimes, and asymmetric dependencies characterize the international political economy of the digital age.

Global Digital Trade Regimes

WTO E-Commerce Negotiations Since 1998, WTO members have discussed an e-commerce moratorium on customs duties and digital trade regulations. Key issues include Data Localization Exceptions: Striking a balance between free data flows and national security and privacy concerns. Source Code Disclosure: Debates surrounding the mandatory sharing of proprietary algorithms in regulated sectors. Digital Services Taxation: National proposals aimed at taxing the revenues of foreign digital giants, such as the OECD's Pillar One and Two agreements. E-commerce negotiations highlight the divisions between developed and developing economies concerning regulatory space and revenue interests.

Digital Preferential Trade Agreements

Bilateral and regional Free Trade Agreements (FTAs) increasingly incorporate digital chapters. For instance, the Comprehensive and Progressive Agreement for Trans-Pacific Partnership (CPTPP) established in 2018 includes provisions concerning cross-border data flows, digital identities, and electronic signatures. Similarly, the United States-Mexico-Canada Agreement (USMCA) of 2020 enforces rules prohibiting data localization requirements and safeguarding the confidentiality of source code. These agreements often promulgate high-standard regulations, favoring technologically advanced economies over those less developed in this sector.

Platform Capitalism and Market Concentration

Network Effects and Winner-Take-All Dynamics Platforms achieve dominance through positive feedback loops: Amazon Web Services (AWS) holds a market share exceeding 30% in cloud infrastructure, facilitating further innovation and solidifying its position. Google Search Algorithm's continuous improvements bolster its standing, rendering competitors marginal. Antitrust authorities in the EU (Digital Markets Act) and the U.S. (pending legislation) are adjusting oversight to address digital monopolies.

Gig Economy and Labor Implications

Platform intermediaries are transforming labor markets: Uber and food delivery services use algorithmic management and rating systems to shape worker behavior and affect income stability. Freelancing platforms foster global competition among digital labor pools, which drives down wages and poses challenges to labor protections. Debates on labor governance focus on worker classification (employee versus contractor), social safety nets, and collective bargaining rights.

Technological Dependencies and Development Gaps

Cloud Services and Vendor Lock-In Developing countries frequently depend on foreign cloud providers for their digital infrastructure, which leads to several issues like Data Residency Risks and Storing sensitive data abroad raises concerns about access by foreign governments (Sing et al., 2025; Talukder and Swarna, 2025; Talukder and Lina, 2025). Dependency on Proprietary APIs: The ability to switch providers is limited due to sunk costs and the complexity of integration. National cloud initiatives, such as India's MeghRaj, aim to mitigate these dependencies but encounter challenges related to scalability and adoption.

AI and Skills Divide

AI development demands specialized expertise and extensive datasets. Brain Drain: Talented professionals migrate to North America, Europe, and East Asia tech hubs. Data Scarcity: The limited availability of labeled datasets in local languages hampers AI research in many regions. Through digital diplomacy and aid, capacity—building programs aim to address these imbalances, yet geopolitical tensions can obstruct collaboration.

Interconnections and Systemic Feedback Loops

The conceptual framework posits four domains in continuous interaction:

1. Techno-Politics ↔ Smart Tourism: Sovereign digital policies determine the permissible scope of tourism technologies (e.g., data localization shaping where IoT data can be processed). Conversely, tourism data—traffic flows health metrics—inform governance strategies on urban planning and public safety (Talukder, 2025).
2. Smart Tourism ↔ Digital Diplomacy: Visitor experiences generate narratives that feed into national branding campaigns. Digital diplomacy initiatives (e.g., virtual cultural festivals) open or restrict mobility through visa facilitation and bilateral agreements (Talukder et al., 2024).
3. Digital Diplomacy ↔ International Political Economy: Norm-setting in digital governance (e.g., AI ethics) influences trade agreements and market access. Economic dependencies—such as reliance on cloud services—affect diplomatic leverage in negotiations over sanctions or content regulation (Talukder et al.,2025)
4. International Political Economy ↔ Techno-Politics: Revenues from digital trade fund new AI and blockchain projects. Techno-political rivalries (e.g., U.S.–China competition) reconfigure economic alliances, supply chains, and investment flows.

These loops underscore the holistic nature of digital transformation: no domain evolves in isolation, and policy interventions in one sphere invariably cascade across the others.

LITERATURE REVIEW

Over the past decade, scholarship on the intersection of technology, politics, and economy has proliferated, reflecting the growing recognition that digital technologies are not merely tools but active agents in reshaping geopolitical landscapes. In techno-politics, scholars such as Morozov (2011) have critiqued the notion of "Internet exceptionalism," arguing that digital networks are subject to power dynamics and state interventions similar to traditional media. Subsequent research has expanded this critique to encompass algorithmic governance, where Gillespie (2014) highlights how algorithms, rather than neutral mechanisms, embed social values and political interests within their design. Recent studies examine the role of national AI strategies—emphasized in China's New Generation AI Development Plan (Data, 2018) and the EU's Coordinated Plan on AI (European Commission, 2021)—as instruments of techno-political competition that privilege sovereign control and data sovereignty (Kucharski, 2020).

In parallel, the literature on smart tourism has evolved from early explorations of information and communication technologies (ICT) enhancing tourist services (Buhalis & Amaranggana, 2015) to more critical inquiries into surveillance, privacy, and data ethics. Neuhofer, Buhalis, and Ladkin (2015) introduced the concept of the "smart tourism ecosystem," highlighting the integration of IoT devices and big data analytics in destination governance. More recent contributions investigate how biometric identity management and health credentialing—accelerated during the COVID-19 pandemic—have reconfigured notions of visitor identity and mobility rights (Sigala, 2020; Taluker, 2024). Scholars such as Ye et al. (2022) underscore the tensions between personalization benefits and the commodification of personal data, calling for ethical frameworks that ensure transparency and user agency.

The emergence of digital diplomacy as a distinct subfield reflects the growing interest in how statecraft adapts to networked communication environments. Wilson (2016) defines digital diplomacy as the conduct of foreign policy through digital channels, noting its ability to amplify soft-power initiatives and citizen engagement. Research on social media diplomacy by Bjola & Holmes (2015) reveals how platforms like Twitter and Facebook serve as arenas for narrative contests and crisis communication yet expose diplomats to real-time scrutiny and misinformation risks (Seib, 2012). Studies of norm entrepreneurship in AI governance, such as Trenches' (2019) analysis of OECD AI Principles and the Global Partnership on AI, demonstrate how states and multilateral organizations vie to embed divergent cultural values—ranging from privacy emphases in Europe to surveillance priorities in East Asia—into global regulatory regimes.

Digitalization has prompted the reassessing of traditional trade theories and regulatory frameworks within the international political economy (IPE). Van der Marel and Shepherd (2017) document the rise of digital services trade and the attendant challenges in applying legacy trade rules to intangible goods. The WTO's e-commerce negotiations and bilateral digital chapters (Dupont, 2020) illustrate how policymakers grapple with data flows, source-code confidentiality, and digital taxation—areas that have generated divergent positions between developed and developing economies. Meanwhile, platform capitalism scholars (Srnicek, 2016) argue that a small set of digital intermediaries exerts disproportionate control over market access, leading to calls for antitrust reforms (Wu, 2018) and the reimagining of competition policy in the digital era.

Interdisciplinary work has begun to map the feedback loops among these domains. For instance, Hall and Stokel-Walker (2019) examine how data generated through smart tourism can inform urban planning and public policy, while Park and Gretzel (2021) analyze how diplomatic narratives promoting national tourism brands rely on platform algorithms to reach target audiences. Similarly, scholars of cyber-sovereignty (Qin, 2018) explore how digital trade dependencies influence diplomatic bargaining power and inform domestic tech policies, highlighting the co-evolution of economic interdependence and geopolitical rivalry.

According to Talukder and Haque (2025), despite the richness of existing literature, gaps remain in integrating these strands into a unified analytical framework. Most studies focus on single domains—techno-politics, tourism, diplomacy, or IPE—without systematically addressing their interconnectedness. This chapter builds on recent calls for holistic approaches (Bennett & Schroeder, 2020) by situating these four domains as nodes within a dynamic system, thereby illuminating the reciprocal influences and emergent governance challenges that define the digital age.

POLICY IMPLICATIONS AND RECOMMENDATIONS

Toward Coordinated Multilateral Governance

- **Integrated Digital Frameworks:** Establish interagency and international bodies encompassing data governance, tourism management, and trade regulation under unified mandates.
- **Harmonization of Standards:** Pursue convergence on privacy, AI ethics, and interoperability to reduce fragmentation and trade friction.

Ethical and Rights-Based Approaches

- **Algorithmic Accountability:** Mandate impact assessments for AI systems used in border controls, tourism personalization, and public services.
- **Data Subject Empowerment:** Enshrine precise consent mechanisms and data portability rights for mobile populations.

Capacity Building and Structural Support

- **Digital Infrastructure Investment:** Aid programs to support sovereign cloud capacities and open data platforms in developing regions.
- **Skills Development:** Scholarships, exchange programs, and online courses foster local AI expertise and multilingual dataset creation.

Resilient and Sustainable Mobility Models

- **Health and Environmental Safeguards:** Integrate digital health credentials with sustainability metrics to promote safe and eco-friendly travel.
- **Community-Centric Surveillance:** Opt-in geofencing and sensor deployments developed in consultation with local stakeholders to balance security with privacy.

DISCUSSION

In the digital age, techno-politics, smart tourism, digital diplomacy, and the international political economy form an integrated ecosystem reshaping global interactions. This study reveals that emerging technologies like AI, blockchain, and IoT have transcended traditional roles, empowering statecraft and transforming market dynamics. Governments harness these innovations to assert digital sovereignty through strategic initiatives ranging from biometric surveillance in tourism to advanced digital trade negotiations. Smart tourism leverages real-time data analytics and personalized services to enhance traveler experiences while raising critical ethical issues regarding privacy and data commodification. Meanwhile, digital diplomacy utilizes social media and virtual forums to project national narratives and engage global audiences. Digital trade platforms further elevate economic interdependence, prompting debates on regulation and monopolistic practices. This interconnected landscape challenges policymakers to develop holistic, agile frameworks that balance innovation with the protection of civil liberties, ensure equitable access to digital resources globally, and foster long-term sustainable progress.

RECOMMENDATIONS

Governments, industry stakeholders, and international institutions must adopt a collaborative and forward-thinking approach to navigate the evolving nexus of techno-politics, tourism, and global political economy in the digital age. Policymakers should prioritize inclusive digital governance frameworks that safeguard data privacy, promote equitable access to digital technologies, and foster cybersecurity resilience across borders. The tourism industry must embrace innovative technologies with ethical oversight, ensuring that innovations like surveillance, digital identity systems, and AI-powered services enhance traveler experiences without compromising civil liberties. Moreover, global diplomacy efforts should champion digital transparency and multilateral cooperation to regulate digital content, manage platform capitalism, and reduce technological dependencies among nations. Academic institutions and think tanks should also play a key role by generating critical research and fostering dialogues on techno-politics implications in shaping future tourism landscapes and the broader international political economy. These coordinated efforts will support a balanced and sustainable transformation where technological advancements serve global development rather than deepen existing inequalities.

CONCLUSION AND FUTURE RESEARCH DIRECTIONS

This chapter has demonstrated that the transformation of the international political economy in the digital age emerges from the intricate interplay of techno-politics, smart tourism, digital diplomacy, and platform-driven commerce. Understanding these interwoven dynamics is essential for crafting policies that harness the benefits of innovation while safeguarding rights and promoting equitable development. As digital technologies evolve, so will the contours of state power, citizen mobility, and global economic integration. Future research should further empirically map these feedback loops and explore the lived experiences of individuals navigating this digitally mediated world.

Future research should delve deeper into the complex interplay between techno-politics, tourism, and the international political economy by examining emerging digital technologies—such as blockchain, quantum computing, and generative AI—and their implications for global tourism governance and geopolitical power dynamics. Comparative case studies across diverse geopolitical regions could illuminate how different regulatory models and political ideologies shape digital tourism strategies and their socio-economic outcomes. Moreover, scholars should investigate the evolving role of multinational technology corporations in setting global digital tourism agendas, especially regarding data sovereignty, algorithmic governance, and platform monopolies. Interdisciplinary studies incorporating political science, international relations, and digital anthropology can further enrich our understanding of how digital infrastructures influence travel freedoms, surveillance practices, and cultural representation. Longitudinal research is also needed to assess the impact of techno-political shifts on tourism resilience, digital diplomacy, and sustainable development goals (SDGs) in the post-pandemic world. By expanding these frontiers, future scholarship can offer strategic insights to policymakers and practitioners navigating the volatile terrain of digital transformation in tourism and the global political economy.

REFERENCES

Чорна, Н., Корж, Н., Кізюн, А., Onyshchuk, N., & Antoniuk, K. (2024). The role of digital technologies in the transformation of the tourism business: Prospects for development and impact on the country's economy. *AD ALTA Journal of Interdisciplinary Research, 14*(1), 136–146. DOI: 10.33543/140139136140

Adesina, O. S. (2017). Foreign policy in an era of digital diplomacy. *Cogent Social Sciences, 3*(1), 1297175. DOI: 10.1080/23311886.2017.1297175

Aktipis, M., & Katwan, R. B. (2021). Data Protection Commissioner v. Facebook Ireland Ltd. and Maximillian Schrems (C.J.E.U.). International Legal Materials, 60(1), 53–75. DOI: 10.1017/ilm.2020.62

Bankins, S., & Formosa, P. (2023). The ethical implications of artificial intelligence (AI) for meaningful work. *Journal of Business Ethics, 185*(4), 725–742. DOI: 10.1007/s10551-023-05339-7

Barashok, I. V., Rudenko, L. L., Shumakova, E., & Orlovskaia, I. V. (2021). Digitization: New possibilities for the tourism industry. *IOP Conference Series. Earth and Environmental Science, 666*(6), 062059. Advance online publication. DOI: 10.1088/1755-1315/666/6/062059

Bennett, C., & Schroeder, F. (2020). Towards integrated digital governance frameworks. *Global Policy, 11*(3), 12–25.

Bjola, C., & Holmes, M. (2015). *Digital diplomacy: Theory and practice*. Routledge. DOI: 10.4324/9781315730844

Buhalis, D., & Amaranggana, A. (2015). Smart tourism destinations. In Schegg, R., & Stangl, B. (Eds.), *Information and communication technologies in tourism 2015* (pp. 553–564). Springer.

Data, R. K. (2018). China's New Generation AI Development Plan 2017–2030. *Journal of Digital Policy, 5*(2), 45–67.

Dupont, C. (2020). Digital trade and regulatory divergence in free trade agreements. *Journal of World Trade, 54*(1), 123–144.

European Commission. (2021). *Coordinated Plan on Artificial Intelligence 2021.* Digital Europe Programme.

European Union. (2016). Regulation (EU) 2016/679 (General Data Protection Regulation). Official Journal of the European Union.

Gillespie, T. (2014). The relevance of algorithms. In Gillespie, T., Boczkowski, P. J., & Foot, K. A. (Eds.), *Media technologies: Essays on communication, materiality, and society* (pp. 167–194). MIT Press. DOI: 10.7551/mitpress/9042.003.0013

González, J. L., & Jouanjean, M.-A. (2017). Digital trade: Developing a framework for analysis. OECD Trade Policy Papers. https://ideas.repec.org/p/oec/traaab/205-en.html

Hall, J., & Stokel-Walker, C. (2019). Data-driven tourism governance and urban planning. *Urban Studies (Edinburgh, Scotland)*, *56*(9), 1823–1840.

Hulkó, G., Kálmán, J., & Lapsánszky, A. (2025). The politics of digital sovereignty and the European Union's legislation: Navigating crises. *Frontiers in Political Science*, *7*, 154856. Advance online publication. DOI: 10.3389/fpos.2025.1548562

Ji, H. (2021). Research-based on international trade system and the pursuit of free digital trade. *Modern Economics & Management Forum*, *2*(4). Advance online publication. DOI: 10.32629/memf.v2i4.414

Karaduman, O., & Gülhas, G. (2025). Blockchain-enabled supply chain management: A review of security, traceability, and data integrity amid the evolving systemic demand. *Applied Sciences (Basel, Switzerland)*, *15*(9), 5168. Advance online publication. DOI: 10.3390/app15095168

Kucharski, A. (2020). Data sovereignty and techno-political competition. *Journal of International Affairs*, *74*(2), 33–48.

Kumar, N., Kumar, K. S., Aeron, A., & Verre, F. (2025). Blockchain technology in supply chain management: Innovations, applications, and challenges. *Telematics and Informatics Reports*, *100204*, 100204. Advance online publication. DOI: 10.1016/j.teler.2025.100204

Kumar, S., Talukder, M. B., & Dewangan, S. (2025). Cutting-Edge Innovations: AI and Digital Transformation in Research and Development. In Ozen, E., Singh, A., Taneja, S., Rajaram, R., & Davim, J. (Eds.), *Sustainability, Innovation, and Consumer Preference* (pp. 29–50). IGI Global Scientific Publishing., DOI: 10.4018/979-8-3693-9699-5.ch002

Li, L. C., Pentland, A., Braley, A., Chen, N., Enríquez, J. R., & Reuel, A. (2024). Generative AI for pro-democracy platforms. DOI: 10.21428/e4baedd9.5aaf489a

Lina, F. Y., & Talukder, M. B. (2025). AI in Tourism: Business and Economic Perspectives. In Lytras, M., Ordonez, P., Alkhaldi, A., & Serban, A. (Eds.), *Innovation Management for a Resilient Digital Economy* (pp. 81–104). IGI Global Scientific Publishing., DOI: 10.4018/979-8-3693-8357-5.ch004

Martin, K. D., Kim, J. J., Palmatier, R. W., Steinhoff, L., Stewart, D. W., Walker, B. A., Wang, Y., & Weaven, S. (2020). Data privacy in retail. *Journal of Retailing*, *96*(4), 474–492. DOI: 10.1016/j.jretai.2020.08.003

Meltzer, J. P. (2019). Governing digital trade. *World Trade Review*, *18*(4), 571–588. DOI: 10.1017/S1474745618000505

Milana, C., & Ashta, A. (2021). Artificial intelligence techniques in finance and financial markets: A survey of the literature. *Strategic Change*, *30*(3), 189–204. DOI: 10.1002/jsc.2403

Morozov, E. (2011). *The Net Delusion: The dark side of Internet freedom*. PublicAffairs.

Neuhofer, B., Buhalis, D., & Ladkin, A. (2015). Conceptualising technology enhanced destination experiences. *Journal of Destination Marketing & Management*, *4*(3), 145–155.

Paltiel, M. (2023). Recent amendments to the Australian Privacy Act. *Journal of Bioethical Inquiry*, *20*(2), 161–174. DOI: 10.1007/s11673-023-10249-4 PMID: 37432509

Parayil, G. (2005). The political economy of informational development: A normative appraisal. In *The Political Economy of Informational Development: A Normative Appraisal* (pp. 196–212). Palgrave Macmillan., DOI: 10.1057/9780230595613_10

Park, S., & Gretzel, U. (2021). Algorithmic platforms and narrative branding in tourism diplomacy. *International Journal of Tourism Research*, *23*(4), 456–468.

Qin, B. (2018). Cyber-sovereignty in the age of digital trade. *International Affairs*, *94*(4), 869–890.

Roberts, H., Cowls, J., Morley, J., Taddeo, M., Wang, V., & Floridi, L. (2019). The Chinese approach to artificial intelligence: An analysis of policy and regulation. SSRN Electronic Journal. DOI: 10.2139/ssrn.3469784

Role of Standards. (2024). In Developing AI accountability inputs: A deeper dive into AI system evaluations. National Telecommunications and Information Administration. Retrieved from https://www.ntia.gov/…/role-of-standards

Sankaran, S. (2025). Enhancing trust through standards: A comparative risk-impact framework for aligning ISO AI standards with global ethical and regulatory contexts. arXiv. https://doi.org//arxiv.2504.16139DOI: 10.48550

Seib, P. (2012). *Real-Time Diplomacy: Politics and power in the social media era*. Palgrave Macmillan. DOI: 10.1057/9781137010902

Sharma, P., Martin, M., & Swanlund, D. (2023). MapSafe: A complete tool for achieving geospatial data sovereignty. *Transactions in GIS*, *27*(6), 1680–1697. DOI: 10.1111/tgis.13094

Sheikh, S. A. (2024). Diplomatic effectiveness in addressing transnational issues and promoting global cooperation. *The Journal of Humanistic Education and Development*, *6*(2), 36–47. DOI: 10.22161/jhed.6.2.5

Sigala, M. (2020). Tourism and COVID-19: Impacts and implications for advancing and resetting industry and research. *Journal of Business Research*, *117*, 312–321. DOI: 10.1016/j.jbusres.2020.06.015 PMID: 32546875

Srivastava, S., & Bullock, J. B. (2024). AI, global governance, and digital sovereignty. arXiv. /arxiv.2410.17481DOI: 10.2139/ssrn.4996387

Srnicek, N. (2016). *Platform capitalism*. Polity Press.

State of California. (2020). California Consumer Privacy Act (CCPA), Cal. Civ. Code §§ 1798.100–1798.199.

Talukder, M. B. (2020). An Appraisal of the Economic Outlook for the Tourism Industry, Specially Cox's Bazar in Bangladesh. *i-manager's Journal on Economics & Commerce,* 2(1), 23-35. DOI: 10.26634/jecom.2.1.17285

Talukder, M. B. (2020). The Future of Culinary Tourism: An Emerging Dimension for the Tourism Industry of Bangladesh. I-Manager's. *Journal of Management*, *15*(1), 27. DOI: 10.26634/jmgt.15.1.17181

Talukder, M. B. (2021). An assessment of the roles of the social network in the development of the Tourism Industry in Bangladesh. *International Journal of Business, Law, and Education*, 2(3), 85–93. DOI: 10.56442/ijble.v2i3.21

Talukder, M. B. (2024). Implementing Artificial Intelligence and Virtual Experiences in Hospitality. In Manohar, S., Mittal, A., Raju, S., & Nair, A. J. (Eds.), *Advances in Hospitality, Tourism, and the Services Industry* (pp. 145–160). IGI Global., DOI: 10.4018/979-8-3693-2019-8.ch009

Talukder, M. B. (2025). Climate change adaptation strategies for a tourism destination: A study of Kuakata beach. *Acta Scientiarum Polonorum. Administratio Locorum*, *24*(1), 165–179. DOI: 10.31648/aspal.10073

Talukder, M. B. (2025). Current Trends and Future Research Directions on Eco-Friendly Stages of Hotel Industry. *RPER*, (71), 7–18. DOI: 10.59072/rper.vi71.695

Talukder, M. B., Chowdhury, S. A., & Khan, M. R. (2025). The Gig Economy: Economic Innovations and Technological Advancements in Human Resource Management. In Kurnaz, S., & Bieliauskaitė, J. (Eds.), *Economic Innovations and Technological Developments in HRM* (pp. 381–404). IGI Global., DOI: 10.4018/979-8-3693-4412-5.ch015

Talukder, M. B., Das, I. R., & Kumar, S. (2024). Implementing Digital Marketing Channels on BTHM Admission: Evidence from Dhaka City. *IUBAT Review*, *7*(1), 142–170. DOI: 10.3329/iubatr.v7i1.74361

Talukder, M. B., & Hoque, M. (2025). Navigating the Digital Horizon: Transforming Travel Agencies in the Digital Era. In Albakri, M. (Ed.), *Perspectives on Digital Transformation in Contemporary Business* (pp. 383–410). IGI Global Scientific Publishing., DOI: 10.4018/979-8-3693-5966-2.ch014

Talukder, M. B., Kabir, F., Muhsina, K., & Das, I. R. (2023). Emerging concepts of artificial intelligence in the hotel industry: A conceptual paper. *International Journal of Research Publication and Reviews*, *4*(9), 1765–1775. DOI: 10.55248/gengpi.4.923.92451

Talukder, M. B., Khan, M. R., & Haghi, A. K. (2025). Redefining Hospital Waste Management: Circular Economy Strategies for Reducing Toxicity. In Poddar, S., Paul, B., & Luperi, M. (Eds.), *Sustainable Business Ecosystems and Social Perspectives* (pp. 335–358). IGI Global Scientific Publishing., DOI: 10.4018/979-8-3693-8437-4.ch015

Talukder, M. B., Khan, M. R., & Kumar, S. (2025). The Impact of Gig Economy Trends on Traditional Employment Models: Evidence From Hotel Industry. In Nozari, H. (Ed.), *Dynamic and Safe Economy in the Age of Smart Technologies* (pp. 253–276). IGI Global Scientific Publishing., DOI: 10.4018/979-8-3693-4369-2.ch016

Talukder, M. B., & Lina, F. Y. (2025). The Role of Tourism Development in Political Stability and Disruption. In Wongmahesak, K., Ahmad, J., & Mustanir, A. (Eds.), *Public Governance Practices in the Age of AI* (pp. 461–476). IGI Global Scientific Publishing., DOI: 10.4018/979-8-3693-9286-7.ch022

Talukder, M. B., & Swarna, D. A. (2025). Waste-to-Energy Innovations: Evidence From the Tourism Industry. In Sucheran, R. (Ed.), *Sustainable Waste Management in the Tourism and Hospitality Sectors* (pp. 553–582). IGI Global Scientific Publishing., DOI: 10.4018/979-8-3693-6110-8.ch020

Trenches, L. (2019). Norm entrepreneurship in AI governance: OECD and GPAI. *Review of International Political Economy*, *26*(7), 1234–1256. DOI: 10.1080/09692290.2019.1610669

Van der Marel, E., & Shepherd, B. (2017). Trade in services and the digital economy. *Journal of Trade Law & Policy*, *21*(2), 75–93.

Veale, M., Matus, K., & Gorwa, R. (2023). AI and global governance: Modalities, rationales, tensions. *Annual Review of Law and Social Science*, *19*(1), 255–279. DOI: 10.1146/annurev-lawsocsci-020223-040749

View of the techno-political collision. (n.d.). Intersect: Stanford Journal of Information & Society. Retrieved June 7, 2025, from https://ojs.stanford.edu/ojs/index.php/intersect/article/view/749/675

Wilson, E. (2016). The practice of digital diplomacy: Challenges and opportunities. *Diplomacy and Statecraft*, *27*(2), 213–234. DOI: 10.1080/09592296.2016.1156611

World Trade Organization. (2017, December). Joint statement on e-commerce moratorium. Ministerial Meeting, Buenos Aires.

Wu, T. (2018). *The curse of bigness: Antitrust in the new gilded age*. Columbia Global Reports. DOI: 10.2307/j.ctv1fx4h9c

Ye, Q., Law, R., & Gu, B. (2022). Ethical challenges of personalization in smart tourism. *Tourism Management Perspectives*, *46*, 101905. Advance online publication. DOI: 10.1016/j.tmp.2022.101905

Yu, Y., & Wang, H. (2022). Study on the construction of smart tourism ecosystem and polycentric governance mechanism. *Smart Tourism*, *3*(1), 9–24. DOI: 10.54517/st.v3i1.1738

Chapter 17
Religious Tourism, Economic Behavior, and Global Change:
A Multidimensional Study of Devotee Spending at Cultural Festivals

Suraj Jaywant Yadav
https://orcid.org/0000-0002-2687-4852
D.Y. Patil Agriculture and Technical University, Kolhapur, India

Murali Manohar Bhupathi
https://orcid.org/0000-0002-1514-9727
D.Y. Patil Agriculture and Technical University, Kolhapur, India

ABSTRACT

Religious tourism, a key part of the global travel industry, involves individuals or groups traveling to sacred sites for spiritual fulfillment, rituals, or to experience religious heritage. This paper highlights the importance, growth, and effects of religious tourism, focusing on major pilgrimage destinations, traveler motivations, and socio-economic outcomes. Religious sites serve not only spiritual purposes but also foster cultural exchange and contribute to local economic development. The discussion also addresses challenges such as overcrowding, commercialization, and the need to preserve the sanctity of these sacred places amid growing tourism.

DOI: 10.4018/979-8-3373-1727-4.ch017

INTRODUCTION

A platform for changes in geographical spaces, tourism has grown to be one of the biggest and most lucrative sectors of the global economy thanks to its distinctive and unique features (Budovich, 2023).Its history is as old as religious tourism itself, making it one of the most enduring and successful forms of travel in the world today. It is unaffected by weather conditions. The term "religious tourism" refers to the practice of tourists visiting cultural, religious, and ritually significant locations as cultural, ideological, and recreational travelers. One of the traits of religious tourism is that it frequently involves a large number of passengers and is not time-dependent, which boosts group tourism's prosperity and typically doesn't end at one time (Budovich, 2023).Pilgrimage and other religiously driven travel are among the earliest types of tourism. Religiously inspired travel has grown significantly over the last 50 years. Scholars from a wide range of disciplines are increasingly investigating religious tourism, which has developed in a variety of settings and locales. According to the literature currently available on religious tourism, the declining importance of traditional religious beliefs in modern societies is driving a growing diversity of tourists(Choe, 2024).The significance of tourism for the local economy in terms of creating jobs, stimulating the economy, and creating wealth has been emphasized more than ever in recent years. In this sense, tourism is seen as a catalyst for development as well as a factor in political and economic shifts. By employing creative tactics, the tourism industry offers the foundation for drawing in more visitors, creating revenue, and adding value to the city. As a result, the majority of nations have already taken into account the potential of tourism in urban development. The tourism sector is one of the most significant drivers of the economic growth of both urban and rural communities, and one of its primary objectives is the economic development of local communities (Budovich, 2023). The institution of pilgrimage has historically connected religion and tourism, and it was from this that the phenomenon of religious tourism developed. Although many studies have looked at how tourism affects places and how locals perceive it, few have specifically looked at how religious tourism and tourists impact locals who live in "holy or sacred" places.Economic growth is essential for preserving jobs, raising taxes, and promoting consumption, all of which work together to lessen poverty and inequality while improving public services and drawing in investment. As a result, nations with slower growth rates actively seek out sustainable economic growth. A number of crucial elements need to be taken into consideration in order to accomplish this, including infrastructure and institutional development, tourism development, financial development, and foreign direct investment (Sun et al., 2025).Religious tourism significantly contributes to local and national economies by enhancing income, creating jobs, and fostering sustainable development. This sector not only attracts visitors seeking spiritual experiences but also revitalizes traditional settlements and underprivileged areas through improved infrastructure and services. The following sections elaborate on the economic impacts of religious tourism.This calls for a comprehensive understanding of the interdisciplinarity underlying the pilgrimage phenomenon. Researcherss, policymakers, and practitioners have shown a great deal of interest in and attention to religious studies and research in recent years. Nonetheless, the socio-economic effects have not been thoroughly investigated. The extensive and expanding body of research on religious tourism attests to the phenomenon's significance. According to Collins-Kreiner (2020), there are many examples of religious tourism in the literature. Studies conducted globally by region, religion, or kind of shrine are still required, though (Belucio et al., 2023). According to Collins-Kreiner (2010), pilgrims and religious organizations do not view pilgrimage as touristic, but from the perspective of the industry, pilgrims can be treated as tourists. Like any other type of tourism, religious tourism has an impact on a destination's economy in the form of income, profit, and employment. Pilgrimage is today also known as a traditional religious or modern secular journey. We can ask ourselves what pilgrimages add to a local economy in terms of employment and value added, particularly in areas where pilgrimages are a major draw for tourists (Graave, 2017).Understanding the economic effects of pilgrimage and religious tourism has been a major focus of the academic literature. In addition to being a significant source of income for governments and communities at various scales, pilgrimage and religious tourism also create a range of economic opportunities, from pilgrim and religious tourist expenditures to entrepreneurship. The presence of visitors is, in many cases, the primary reason that pilgrimage towns like Lourdes, France, and Medjugorje, Bosnia and Herzegovina, exist: they are home to sacred sites that attract hundreds of thousands of pilgrims and religious tourists annually (Shinde & Olsen, 2023).

BACKGROUND

Religious tourism is a growing segment of the global travel industry, drawing millions of devotees to cultural festivals that blend spirituality, tradition, and community (Sun et al., 2025). These festivals not only serve religious purposes but also stimulate significant economic activity in host regions. Devotees often engage in diverse spending, including offerings, accommodation, food, transport, and souvenirs, which contributes to local income generation (Belucio et al., 2023). However, with the increasing influence of globalization, traditional festivals are undergoing changes in form, function, and audience(Guriţă & Scortescu, 2023). This evolving landscape requires a deeper understanding of devotee spending behavior, the socio-economic implications for local communities, and the challenges of maintaining cultural integrity. A multidimensional study of these aspects can offer valuable insights for policymakers, tourism planners, and cultural stakeholders(Awasthi & Nain, 2023).

RESEARCH OBJECTIVES:

1. To identify the spending patterns of devotees attending cultural and religious festivals.
2. To examine the socioeconomic factors influencing devotees' economic behavior.
3. To analyze the impact of religious tourism on local economies.
4. To explore how globalization is changing the nature and experience of traditional festivals.
5. To suggest sustainable practices for managing religious tourism while preserving cultural heritage.

THEORETICAL FRAMEWORK

The tourism sector is one of the most significant and rapidly expanding global industries that creates jobs and income in many nations. Certain nations have holy sites that offer the travel and tourism sector a unique chance to grow in a sustainable and sensible manner (Nouri Kouchi et al., 2018). The value of tourism to the local economy in terms of creating jobs, stimulating the economy, and creating wealth has been given more consideration in recent years than ever before. In fact, tourism is now seen as a catalyst for both political and economic change in addition to supporting development. The tourism industry provides the foundation for drawing in more visitors, making money, and adding value to the city by putting creative strategies into practice. As a result, the majority of nations have already taken into account the potential of tourism in urban development. Local communities' economic development is one of the tourism industry's top priorities (Budovich, 2023).Increasingly, tourism has become a key factor in promoting economic growth, primarily because it is a major source of foreign exchange and a key factor in export diversification. In a few nations, including Italy, Israel, India, and France, pilgrimage-style travel based on "spiritual" and "spectacle" motivations continues to be a prevalent and long-lasting phenomenon. In the larger framework of the tourism industry, religious, faith-based, and spiritual tourism—including the holy practice of pilgrimages—thus takes on a prominent and enduring role(Guriţă & Scortescu, 2023).Globally, hundreds of millions of people visit holy sites each year for worship and education. Although the practice of pilgrimage has a long history and plays a significant role in many religious traditions as well as in people's spiritual development, some academics have started to doubt whether modern pilgrimage travel is sustainable. Along with contributing to waste accumulation and greenhouse gas emissions, pilgrimages, like other forms of mobility, also appear to be blameless for the current environmental crisis. Furthermore, although large religious assemblies have historically been linked to the spread and transmission of disease, religious mobility has not historically been hampered by the possibility of pilgrims contracting an infection while traveling. Indeed, during difficult and uncertain times, there seems to be a greater demand for pilgrimages (Shinde & Olsen, 2023).

RELIGIOUS TOURISM

Religion can be defined as "belief in a supernatural power" or powers to be worshipped, as well as its manifestation in ritual. Historically, the term "religion" has frequently mentioned ideas from a "Western" standpoint or included global religions like Buddhism, Islam, Christianity, and Hinduism. However, since religion is influenced by society, culture, as well as personal values, beliefs, and faith, it can have many different meanings and transcend the idea of world religions. A decrease in religious affiliations has led to a rise in the diversity, secularization, personalization, and individuality of religious concepts (Choe, 2024).The impact of pilgrimages, a unique form of travel, extends well beyond the realm of religious endeavors. They exhibit the capacity to influence even international trade and public health dynamics, embracing complex political, economic, social, and cultural repercussions. A thorough investigation is warranted because of the phenomenon of pilgrimage's inherent spatial mobility, which gives it great significance and sparks scholarly interest (Guriţă & Scortescu, 2023).One of the earliest types of travel is religious tourism, which is a sizable, developing, expanding, and increasingly varied segment of the world travel market. Common examples of religious travel and tourism include festivals, conferences, retreats, pilgrimages, and retreats. Both secular and religious visitors can visit "a range of spiritual sites and associated services" as part of religious tourism. However, in addition to being a call to spirituality, religious tourism has been a significant economic driver. Consequently, the travel industry has discovered a new market niche called religious tourism (Iliev, 2020).It is clear from the different definitions of religious tourism that it can therefore take many different forms. Religious tourism can be driven by a variety of reasons, including deliverance, healing, worship, and pilgrimage. Pilgrimages, missionary travel, leisure (fellowship) vacations, faith-based cruising, crusades, conventions and rallies, retreats, monastery visits and guest stays, faith-based camps, and religious tourist attractions are the main categories into which the Strategic Initiatives and Government

Advisor (SIGA) team (2012) divides religious tourism (Ncube & Chikuta, 2020). There are two main perspectives on cultural interaction and international tourism. The first is that some people think that as tourism grows and becomes a structured industry, human culture will advance from a spiritual and material standpoint. Small industries, for instance, will grow and develop more as a result of the development of industries and service activities, such as specialized marketing strategies and flight and transportation services. The expansion and growth of tourism also contributes to a decrease in conflict and an increase in innovation and societal prosperity. The various cultures and cultural evolution of the world are better understood thanks to tourism. From this vantage point, the growth of tourism is a means of fostering cultural exchange, interaction, and communication among various nations and ethnic groups, which offers the potential for both social and economic prosperity as well as cultural transformation(Budovich, 2023).But, similar to other niche tourism markets, pilgrimage and religious tourism can also have detrimental effects on pilgrim towns. The commodification and re-contextualization of religious icons, symbols, and rituals, for example, can result from the economic capitalization of religious heritage tourism. These items are then valued for their market value rather than their use-value or utility, raising concerns about religious authenticity and the ethics of religious commodification. Examples of this commodification include the sale of sacred masks as tourist souvenirs in Bali, the alteration of religious rituals in Tibet and Nepal to accommodate the shortened itineraries of religious heritage tourists, and the preference for commercial transactions over hosting visitors at religious heritage sites (Shinde & Olsen, 2023).

ECONOMY & RELIGIOUS TOURISM

One of the biggest and highest-earning sectors of the world economy today is the tourism industry. This industry has expanded significantly over the last few decades, and it now plays a significant role in the economies of most nations (Nouri Kouchi et al., 2018).

A process of cultural commoditization and acculturation may be facilitated by changes in the local economy and society brought about by the large number of religious tourists. For instance, in Sri Lanka, large-scale tourism that blends pilgrimage and recreation has replaced genuine pilgrimages (Terzidou et al., 2008). Tourism is a key driver of economic expansion. Insufficient focus has been placed on the role of institutional quality in the relationship between tourism development and economic advancement, which is a topic of frequent debate (Sun et al., 2025).

In addition to providing a variety of economic benefits and values, tourism also contributes to the growth and development of a nation by fostering regional brand value, image, and identification. The tourism sector serves as a major driver of economic growth and contributes significantly to a country's economy in addition to providing aesthetically pleasing travel destinations. For the majority of the nation, tourism is thought to be the primary driver of regional growth, boosting recent economic activity. Although it has a positive effect on revenue growth, job opportunities, gross income, and production, it can have negative effects on the environment because of things like pollution, road congestion, and ecosystem destruction. However, by attracting foreign tourists, tourism helps to generate foreign exchange earnings that lead to infrastructure improvements, employment, and an improved quality of life, all of which contribute to the country's sustainable economic growth because tourists increase local sales, profits, salaries, tax revenue, and exports (Naseem, 2021).Millions of pilgrims are inspired to travel to places like Lourdes, France, where they can hear the "Echoes of Bernadette," or Fátima, Portugal, where they can hear Sister Lúcia's story and the Holy Land. The Catholic Church, as an organization, encourages pilgrims to travel to these places because each pilgrim makes a direct or indirect contribution to the local economy of the Sanctuary city, so it is crucial to support this tourism (Belucio et al., 2023).It is important not to undervalue the economic effects of pilgrimage tourism and the relationship surrounding it. It is nearly impossible to analyze religion and its particular connections to tourism—economic, social, and cultural—given that pilgrimage tourism is a complicated and multifaceted phenomenon. According to academics' theoretical research, pilgrimage and tourism are two phenomena that are far too similar. The impression that most pilgrimage sites have today is difficult to escape. For religious reasons, the effects of tourism on profanity are more pronounced. These advantages are no longer offered, even in the so-called "hard-line" or conservative religions of the world, due to their rigorous adherence to their followers' religious obligations (wordpress, 1 C.E.).Regional developers and funding organizations frequently view (and use) tourism as a means of economic development for peripheral, structurally weak areas. They see it as a panacea that brings in capital, creates jobs and income, and ultimately stops outmigration by fostering a positive socioeconomic outlook for the future. These lofty aspirations, however, frequently fall short, and either the volume of visitors or the ensuing economic contribution—or even both—do not live up to initial projections (Mayer & Vogt, 2016).

PATTERNS OF DEVOTEE SPENDING: CATEGORIES, PRIORITIES, AND INFLUENCING FACTORS

The study of visitor spending has drawn a lot of interest and scientific investigation from the fields of marketing and economics. In addition to models that try to give an estimate of the likelihood that consumers will spend money, a wide range of initiatives and theories have been developed to explain the elements that affect their purchasing decisions. A growing body of research suggests estimating the amount of money tourists spend on vacation and looking into its factors in order to achieve this goal (Kozak et al., 2008).The spending habits of tourists can have a direct effect on local companies. Researcherss have put forth a number of tactics to draw tourists, including... A. providing a greater range of goods in retail spaces and designing welcoming shopping spaces to entice transient visitors to spend more money). According to some theories, promoting and conserving regional specialties, customs, and landscapes can draw in more long-term tourists (Pai et al., 2024).The willingness and ability of tourists to spend money, as well as the de facto incremental monetary outlays at which willingness and ability are converted into total expenditures, determine tourism expenditures. Using mean-level and conditional quantile estimates, we extend the existing literature by applying a sustainability-based segmentation criterion, specifically the Legatum Prosperity IndexTM, to the decomposition of a total expenditure differential into tourists' relative willingness to spend and an upper bound of third-degree price discrimination. This approach is based on the neoclassical theoretical argument of utility-constrained expenditure minimization (Alfarhan et al., 2022).However, boosting visitor spending is a way to boost tourism revenue, which is crucial for regional economies. Travelers' spending patterns should be understood in order to suggest tourism plans and policies that will raise visitor spending. It will be feasible to optimize resources and maximize the advantages of international tourism by comprehending the spending patterns of tourists and their classification. According to this perspective, the goal of the study is to identify the factors that influence visitor spending in order to identify the types of tourists who contribute most to the local economy and to direct tourism planning and promotion initiatives. The phenomenon of pilgrimage tourism is widespread. Travel for pilgrimages is on the rise everywhere. The oldest and most popular type of tourism is pilgrimage tourism. In the twenty-first century, pilgrims view their pilgrimage sites and centers as appealing travel destinations. By raising each nation's GDP, foreign exchange, employment opportunities, product exchange, living standards, and poverty levels, pilgrimage tourism plays a major role in the growth and development of nations around the world (Awasthi & Nain, 2023).

GLOBALIZATION AND CULTURAL SHIFTS IN FESTIVAL TOURISM

Various authors view globalization as a reaction to imperialism, the theory of dependent development, and the neo-Marxist theory of the world system. This topic is the subject of scientific debates. The foundation of Robertson's all-encompassing theory of globalization is modernization theory, which holds out hope for Third World development (Mihajlovic & Krželj-Čolović, 2021).Globalization has significantly influenced the landscape of festival tourism, leading to notable cultural shifts in how religious and traditional festivals are celebrated and experienced. With increased connectivity, international exposure, and media representation, many once-localized festivals have gained global recognition, attracting a diverse audience that includes not only regional devotees but also national and international tourists(Dychkovskyy & Ivanov, 2020). This has led to the blending of traditional rituals with modern entertainment, infrastructure upgrades, and the commercialization of sacred events. While these changes have enhanced visibility and economic potential, they have also raised concerns about cultural dilution, loss of authenticity, and the prioritization of tourist appeal over spiritual value. As a result, festival tourism now exists at a complex intersection of faith, commerce, and cultural identity, demanding a delicate balance between preservation and progress(Mihajlovic & Krželj-Čolović, 2021).

RESEARCH METHODOLOGY

Research Design

The researchers adopts a mixed-methods and multidimensional research design to examine the economic behaviour of devotees within the context of religious tourism and global change. This approach integrates both quantitative and qualitative methods to ensure a comprehensive analysis. While the descriptive aspect aims to identify patterns in devotee spending, the exploratory aspect investigates the cultural shifts and economic transformations associated with globalization in festival tourism. The mixed-methods strategy allows for both statistical examination and contextual interpretation of complex phenomena such as faith-based consumption and commercialization.

Study Area and Sampling

The study focuses on cultural and religious festivals known for attracting large numbers of devotees and for their relevance in reflecting both traditional beliefs and modern tourism practices. The researchers selects five major festivals in Maharashtra that draw both domestic and international attention: Pandharpur Wari (Solapur), Kumbh Mela (Nashik), Ganesh Chaturthi (Mumbai), Jejuri Jatra (Pune District), and Jotiba Yatra (Kolhapur). These festivals are chosen using purposive sampling due to their spiritual significance, high footfall, economic vibrancy, and socio-cultural impact. Each festival serves as a valuable case for exploring how globalization and modern consumerism influence traditional devotional practices. Within each event, 18 devotees are selected through random sampling (90 total respondents) to ensure diverse representation across age groups, genders, income levels, occupations, and educational backgrounds. This sample size is suitable for generating meaningful insights into devotee economic behaviour in the context of evolving religious tourism.

Data Collection Methods

The researchers collects primary quantitative data through 90 structured questionnaires administered to devotees across the five selected festivals. These questionnaires capture data on expenditure patterns, travel motives, length of stay, accommodation preferences, and perceptions of commercialization. Additionally, 15 semi-structured interviews are conducted with key stakeholders (3 per festival), including local vendors, religious leaders, and tourism facilitators, to provide in-depth qualitative perspectives on the economic and cultural implications of festival tourism. The researchers also conducts non-participant observation at each site to document devotee behaviour, transaction flows, and cultural interactions. Secondary data is obtained from tourism department reports, festival records, scholarly articles, and news media to triangulate findings and enhance analytical depth.

Data Analysis Techniques

Quantitative data collected from the 90 questionnaires is processed using software tools such as SPSS and Microsoft Excel to generate descriptive statistics, frequency distributions, and cross-tabulations. This analysis helps identify spending trends and relationships between devotee demographics and economic behaviour. Qualitative data from 15 interviews and observational notes is analyzed through thematic coding, allowing the researchers to extract patterns related to cultural transformation, spiritual motivations, commercialization, and the influence of globalization. The mixed-method approach ensures that numerical findings are complemented by contextual interpretation, thereby offering a holistic understanding of the research problem.

Ethical Considerations

The researchers ensures that all ethical standards are rigorously maintained. Prior informed consent is obtained from all participants, and respondents are clearly informed of the voluntary nature of the study. Anonymity and confidentiality are protected throughout the data collection and reporting process. No personal identifiers are recorded or published. The researchers remains culturally sensitive, especially during interviews and fieldwork, ensuring that religious rituals and sacred environments are not disrupted. Ethical clearance is obtained from the concerned academic or institutional review board before the commencement of field activities.

DATA ANALYSIS

Quantitative Data Analysis

The quantitative data was analyzed using **SPSS** and **Excel**. Descriptive statistics, cross-tabulation, and inferential statistical tests were applied to examine the spending behaviour of devotees and its relationship with demographic variables. The analysis was carried out in the following steps:

Descriptive Statistics

Descriptive statistics were used to summarize the data and provide an overview of spending patterns across various demographic groups such as age, income, and gender. This approach provided an initial understanding of the average expenditure, the variability, and the distribution of spending behaviors among different groups.

This table presents the average expenditure across different age groups and income levels, as well as the standard deviation and range. The data indicates that income level has a significant effect on the amount spent, with higher-income groups spending more on travel, accommodation, and souvenirs.

Table 1. Descriptive statistics of devotees' expenditure

Demographic Variable	Average Expenditure (INR)	Standard Deviation (INR)	Range (INR)
Age Group			
18-30	2,500	1,200	1,000 - 5,000
31-50	3,800	1,500	1,500 - 7,000
51+	2,200	900	1,000 - 4,000
Income Level			
Low (< 20,000)	1,800	1,100	500 - 3,000
Middle (20,000- 50,000)	3,200	1,400	1,500 - 6,000
High (> 50,000)	4,500	2,000	2,000 - 10,000

Explanation: The descriptive statistics show that higher-income devotees (earning above 50,000) tend to spend more on their festival visit, especially on accommodation and souvenirs, compared to the lower-income groups.

Cross-Tabulation

Cross-tabulation was used to examine the relationship between spending categories (e.g., food, souvenirs, travel) and demographic variables such as gender and income. This analysis helped to reveal patterns of how different groups allocate their spending across various categories.

This table shows how gender correlates with the spending habits of devotees during the festivals. Males and females tend to spend differently, with males spending more on food and souvenirs, while females focus on food and travel.

Table 2. Cross-tabulation of gender vs. spending category

Gender	Food	Souvenirs	Travel	Accommodation
Male	45%	30%	10%	15%
Female	50%	25%	15%	10%

Explanation: The cross-tabulation reveals that females allocate a slightly higher percentage of their expenditure towards food, while males spend more on souvenirs. These differences could reflect distinct preferences in shopping and consumption patterns based on gender.

Chi-Square Test

The chi-square test was used to assess the association between categorical variables such as gender and spending patterns. The test helps determine whether the differences observed between gender and spending categories are statistically significant.

The chi-square results demonstrate that there is a statistically significant relationship between gender and spending categories ($p < 0.05$).

Table 3. Chi-square test for gender vs. expenditure category

Variable	Chi-Square Statistic	P-Value	Significance
Gender vs. Spending Type	10.52	0.02	Significant

Explanation: The chi-square test confirms that gender plays a role in determining how much devotees spend on different categories, with significant differences between male and female participants.

T-test / ANOVA

T-tests and ANOVA were used to compare the mean expenditure across different groups such as age and income levels. The objective was to determine if there were statistically significant differences in spending behaviors.

The t-test compares the mean expenditure between two age groups: 18-30 years and 31-50 years. The results indicate that devotees in the 31-50 age group spend significantly more on festival-related activities compared to the younger group.

Table 4. T-test results for age group vs. expenditure

Age Group	Mean Expenditure (INR)	t-Statistic	P-Value	Significance
18-30 vs 31-50	2,500 vs 3,800	-2.54	0.01	Significant

Explanation: The t-test results show that the 31-50 age group tends to spend more on festival-related activities, which could be attributed to greater financial stability and higher discretionary income.

Regression Analysis

Regression models were employed to identify the factors influencing devotees' expenditure behaviors, taking into account variables such as income, age group, and travel distance.

The regression analysis suggests that income level, age group, and travel distance are significant factors influencing the expenditure behavior of devotees.

Table 5. Regression analysis for factors affecting expenditure

Independent Variable	Coefficient (β)	Standard Error	T-Statistic	P-Value
Income Level	0.65	0.12	5.42	< 0.01
Age Group	0.32	0.08	4.00	< 0.01
Travel Distance	0.28	0.14	2.00	0.05

Explanation: The regression analysis reveals that income level is the most significant factor influencing expenditure behaviour, with a positive correlation. Devotees with higher incomes tend to spend more on various festival-related activities.

QUALITATIVE DATA ANALYSIS

The qualitative data was analyzed using **thematic analysis**, which helps in identifying patterns or themes within the data that reflect the respondents' experiences, beliefs, and attitudes. Thematic analysis allows a deeper understanding of how globalization influences cultural festivals and the spending behaviours of devotees.

Coding

The first step in qualitative data analysis involved **coding**, where key phrases and concepts such as "commercialization," "globalization," "spirituality," and "tourism" were identified from the interview transcripts and field notes. These codes helped in categorizing the responses and providing an organized structure to the analysis.

Theme Identification

Through the coding process, several recurring **themes** were identified. These themes include the **commercialization of religious rituals**, where local vendors and external influences altered the traditional nature of the festivals, the **impact of**

globalization on local traditions, and the **evolving spending patterns of devotees** as influenced by the growing commercial aspects of the festivals.

This table presents the key themes that emerged from the interviews, illustrating the diverse perspectives on how globalization has influenced religious festivals.

Table 6. Key themes identified from interviews

Theme	Description	Frequency
Commercialization of Rituals	Vendors selling religious items, food, and souvenirs	25%
Cultural Preservation	Efforts to maintain traditional practices	15%
Globalization Impact	Influence of global tourism on local festivals	35%
Devotional Motivation	Devotees' primary purpose being spiritual connection	25%

Explanation: The theme distribution shows that globalization's influence is most noticeable in the commercialization of rituals, with 35% of respondents mentioning its impact. However, a significant portion (25%) still sees the devotional aspect as central to their participation.

Vendor Analysis

The presence of commercial vendors during festivals was also analyzed to understand the economic impact of these activities.

This table presents the number of commercial vendors present at different festivals, and the types of products they sell. The data shows that larger festivals like the Kumbh Mela tend to have more vendors, with a wider variety of products sold.

Table 7. Frequency of commercial vendors during festivals

Festival	Number of Vendors	Type of Products Sold	% of Total Expenditure
Pandharpur Wari	150	Prasad, Religious Items, Souvenirs	30%
Ganesh Chaturthi	200	Prasad, Clothes, Religious Items	25%
Kumbh Mela	300	Prasad, Ritual Items, Souvenirs	40%
Jotiba Yatra	180	Religious Items, Prasad, Souvenirs	35%
Shirdi Sai Yatra	250	Prasad, Religious Items	30%

Explanation: This table illustrates the significant role that commercial vendors play in religious festivals, particularly at larger events like Kumbh Mela, where a large percentage of expenditure goes toward purchasing religious and souvenir items.

Impact of Festival Duration on Spending

The festival duration also impacts the amount of money spent by devotees. Festivals that last longer tend to see higher expenditure as participants engage more with commercial activities.

This table shows the relationship between festival duration and average expenditure. The longer the festival, the more likely devotees are to make frequent purchases.

Table 8. Impact of festival duration on spending

Festival Duration	Average Expenditure (INR)	Frequency of Purchases
1-3 days	3,200	3.5 times
4-7 days	4,800	5.0 times
8+ days	5,600	7.2 times

Explanation: Longer festivals tend to encourage more spending due to prolonged participation and higher frequency of purchasing, with average expenditures increasing with the length of the event.

Global Tourism's Influence

Finally, the analysis highlighted the **impact of global tourism on traditional practices**, focusing on how festivals have adapted to cater to international visitors, thus altering traditional religious experiences.

This table shows the distribution of respondents' views on how global tourism has affected traditional religious practices.

Table 9. Impact of global tourism on traditional practices

Theme	Description	Percentage of Respondents
Adaptation of Modern Practices	Incorporating modern elements like music, lighting, and food stalls	60%
Preservation of Sacred Practices	Efforts to maintain traditional rituals and customs	40%

Explanation: The data reveals that most respondents (60%) recognize the adaptation of modern practices in response to global tourism, with efforts still being made to preserve sacred practices (40%).

RESULT

The quantitative results of the study indicate distinct patterns in devotee spending based on demographic factors. Descriptive statistics revealed that devotees aged 31-50 spent significantly more (average 3,800) compared to those in the 18-30 age group (average 2,500) and those aged 51+ (average 2,200). Similarly, high-income groups (above 50,000) spent an average of 4,500, notably more than middle-income (3,200) and low-income groups (1,800). Cross-tabulation showed that food was the highest expenditure category for both males (45%) and females (50%), while souvenirs were also a notable expenditure for males (30%) and females (25%). The chi-square test demonstrated a significant association between gender and spending patterns (p-value < 0.05). ANOVA results for income level versus expenditure indicated a significant difference (F-statistic = 4.52, p-value = 0.03), suggesting that income level significantly influences spending behaviour. T-test results comparing expenditure across age groups revealed a significant difference (t-statistic = -2.54, p-value = 0.01) between the 18-30 and 31-50 age groups. Regression analysis showed that income level ($\beta = 0.65$), age group ($\beta = 0.32$), and travel distance ($\beta = 0.28$) were significant predictors of expenditure, with higher income, older age, and greater travel distance positively influencing spending. These findings provide a clear understanding of the quantitative patterns in devotee spending at cultural and religious festivals.

The qualitative findings of the study, based on thematic analysis of interviews and observations, reveal several recurring themes that reflect the evolving nature of devotee behaviour and the impact of globalization on religious festivals. A dominant theme was the commercialization of religious rituals, where many respondents observed an increase in vendors selling food, souvenirs, and religious merchandise, especially at large-scale events like the Kumbh Mela and Pandharpur Wari. Another prominent theme was cultural preservation, with devotees and organizers expressing efforts to retain traditional practices despite external influences. The theme of globalization impact was evident, as many interviewees noted how festivals have started incorporating modern elements such as LED lighting, digital screens, and packaged offerings, transforming the traditional sacred atmosphere. Devotional motivation remained a central factor, with most devotees stating that spiritual fulfilment was still their primary purpose for attending festivals, even if modern comforts enhanced their experience. Additionally, patterns emerged showing that younger devotees were more accepting of modernization, while older participants showed concern about the dilution of cultural values. Overall, the qualitative data illustrates the complex coexistence of tradition and modernity, with economic activity and global exposure shaping new forms of religious expression and festival experience.

CONCLUSION

This multidimensional study of devotee spending at religious and cultural festivals reveals that religious tourism in India is not only a spiritual pursuit but also a dynamic socio-economic activity shaped by globalization and evolving consumer behaviour. Quantitative data demonstrates that expenditure patterns vary notably across demographic groups, with middle-income and middle-aged devotees contributing significantly to the local economies of festival towns. The application of statistical tools such as ANOVA, t-tests, and regression confirms that income, age, and travel distance are strong predictors of spending levels. Furthermore, gender differences in expenditure categories suggest differentiated priorities and consumption behavior during pilgrimages.

Qualitative findings enrich these results by highlighting how globalization has introduced both opportunities and challenges to religious tourism. Themes such as the commercialization of rituals, the rise of modern amenities, and digital promotion of festivals suggest that religious events are increasingly being shaped by global tourism trends. Yet, despite these changes, devotees express a strong desire to preserve sacred traditions and cultural authenticity. Festival organizers, vendors, and devotees are negotiating a fine balance between maintaining religious sanctity and embracing innovations that enhance accessibility and convenience.

In sum, the study concludes that religious festivals today function as economic engines, cultural repositories, and spiritual sanctuaries. The intersection of economic behavior and global change has led to a redefinition of festival tourism—where devotion and consumption coexist. Future policy and planning must therefore focus on culturally sensitive tourism development, infrastructural support, and inclusive stakeholder engagement to ensure that religious tourism continues to benefit local communities while retaining its cultural essence in a rapidly globalizing world.

REFERENCES

Alfarhan, U. F., Nusair, K., Al-Azri, H., Al-Muharrami, S., & Hua, N. (2022). Measuring the effects of tourists' relative willingness to spend and third-degree price discrimination on inbound tourism expenditure differentials. *Tourism Economics, 28*(8), 2126–2153. DOI: 10.1177/13548166211030016

Awasthi, A., & Nain, A. (2023). *A Study of Issues and Challenges of Global Pilgrimage Tourism.*, DOI: 10.4018/978-1-6684-4817-5.ch011

Belucio, M., Fuinhas, J., & Vieira, C. (2023). How does the economy affect a religious phenomenon? A panel approach to international pilgrimages to the Shrine of Fátima. *European Journal of Tourism. Hospitality and Recreation, 13*(1), 110–124. DOI: 10.2478/ejthr-2023-0010

Budovich, L. (2023). The impact of religious tourism on the economy and tourism industry. *Hervormde Teologiese Studies, 79*(1). Advance online publication. DOI: 10.4102/hts.v79i1.8607

Choe, J. (2024). Religious tourism. *Tourism Geographies*, •••, 1–10. DOI: 10.1080/14616688.2024.2423168

Dychkovskyy, S., & Ivanov, S. (2020). Festival Tourism as Part of International Tourism and a Factor in the Development of Cultural Tourism. *Informacijos Mokslai, 89*, 73–82. DOI: 10.15388/Im.2020.89.41

Graave, E. J. E. (2017). *The Economic Impact of Pilgrimage: An economic impact analysis of pilgrimage expenditures in Galicia. 5.*

Guriţă, D., & Scortescu, F. I. (2023). Religious Tourism and Sustainable Development of the Economy in the Context of Globalization in the Northeast Area of Romania. *Sustainability (Basel), 15*(16), 16. Advance online publication. DOI: 10.3390/su151612128

Iliev, D. (2020). The evolution of religious tourism: Concept, segmentation and development of new identities. *Journal of Hospitality and Tourism Management, 45*, 131–140. DOI: 10.1016/j.jhtm.2020.07.012

Kozak, M., Gokovali, U., & Bahar, O. (2008). Estimating the Determinants of Tourist Spending: A Comparison of Four Models. *Tourism Analysis, 13*(2), 143–155. DOI: 10.3727/108354208785664283

Mayer, M., & Vogt, L. (2016). Economic effects of tourism and its influencing factors. An overview focusing on the spending determinants of visitors. *Zeitschrift für Tourismuswissenschaft*, *8*(2), 169–198. DOI: 10.1515/tw-2016-0017

Mihajlovic, I., & Krželj-Čolović, Z. (2021). THE IMPACT OF GLOBALISATION ON THE DEVELOPMENT OF TOURISM WITHIN SOCIAL AND ECONOMIC CHANGES. *European Scientific Journal*, •••, 108–120.

Naseem, S. (2021). The Role of Tourism in Economic Growth: Empirical Evidence from Saudi Arabia. *Economies*, *9*(3), 3. Advance online publication. DOI: 10.3390/economies9030117

Ncube, F., & Chikuta, O. (2020). Perceived Economic Impact of Religious Tourism: The Case of Zimbabwe. *Hospitality & Tourism Review*, *1*(2), 1–13. DOI: 10.38157/hospitality-tourism-review.v1i2.211

Nouri Kouchi, A., Zarra Nezhad, M., & Kiani, P. (2018). A study of the relationship between the growth in the number of Hajj pilgrims and economic growth in Saudi Arabia. *Journal of Hospitality and Tourism Management*, *36*, 103–107. DOI: 10.1016/j.jhtm.2016.01.008

Pai, W.-T., Phan, K.-T., Pham, C.-V., Lee, J.-M., & Hsieh, C.-J. (2024). Analyzing tourist expenditures incurred on long-, medium-, and short-haul trips to Taiwan. *Annals of Tourism Research Empirical Insights*, *5*(2), 100138. DOI: 10.1016/j.annale.2024.100138

Shinde, K. A., & Olsen, D. H. (2023). Reframing the Intersections of Pilgrimage, Religious Tourism, and Sustainability. *Sustainability (Basel)*, *15*(1), 1. Advance online publication. DOI: 10.3390/su15010461

Sun, Z., Liu, L., Pan, R., Wang, Y., & Zhang, B. (2025). Tourism and economic growth: The role of institutional quality. *International Review of Economics & Finance*, *98*, 103913. DOI: 10.1016/j.iref.2025.103913

Terzidou, M., Stylidis, D., & Szivas, E. (2008). Residents' Perceptions of Religious Tourism and its SocioEconomic Impacts on the Island of Tinos. *Tourism and Hospitality Planning & Development*, *5*(2), 113–129. DOI: 10.1080/14790530802252784

Wordpress. (1 C.E., November 30). Pilgrimage Tourism And Its Economic Dimensions Tourism Essay. *UKEssays.Com*. https://www.ukessays.com/essays/tourism/pilgrimage-tourism-and-its-economic-dimensions-tourism-essay.php

Chapter 18
Empowering Ethiopian Diaspora by Leveraging Institutional Support to Foster Diaspora Business Participation in Home Country

Shashi Kant
https://orcid.org/0000-0003-4722-5736
Bule Hora University, Ethiopia

Metasebia Adula
https://orcid.org/0000-0001-5732-2850
Bule Hora University, Ethiopia

Endres Ahmed
Gondar University, Ethiopia

ABSTRACT

In order to better understand how institutional elements influence diaspora venture start-ups, with mediating function of support of institutions in determining the viability of businesses in diaspora communities. Regression analysis and mediation influences are used in this quantitative investigation to examine the direct and indirect association among these constructs. The results depicted that a strong framework of institution has a major positive influence on support of institutions, which in turn has a positive influence on diaspora business shaping. Policymakers, managers, and

DOI: 10.4018/979-8-3373-1727-4.ch018

practitioners who want to encourage diaspora venture start-ups through focused interventions might benefit greatly from these outcomes. In the end, the investigation contributes to the theoretical understanding of the interaction among institutional dynamics and entrepreneurial success, opening up new avenues for investigating this intricate link in various settings.

INTRODUCTION

Due to the vital function that enterprises start-up by the diaspora manifest in the frugal innovation and fiscal advancement of their domestic business areas; their worth has drawn attention from around the whole interregional market (Birhane et al., 2024). Diaspora bricolages are the procedure of venture capitalists that left their domestic business area to engage in business bricolages that peripheral the communities where they were originally from. This phenomenon is especially imperative in emerging countries, as investments and remittances from the diaspora can have a big influence on local economies. The importance of diaspora traders in Ethiopia's fiscal advancement, job creation, and skill transfer is becoming more widely skilled (Teferra, 2021). Globalization is credited with giving rise to the idea of diaspora bricolages by strengthening the bonds among migrants and their countries of origin. Framework of institutions that encourage and peripheral diaspora interaction can serve as a catalyst for these kinds of connections (Manor, 2021).

Education and training of the Ethiopian diaspora is important as it will lead to advancement of economy in Ethiopia. They indeed have assumed a very central position in the peripheral of national economy in the last two years from the remittance received by Ethiopians living in the diaspora ((Samuel, (2022). Ethiopia in 2021 has received among $3.6 billion on average in remittances that was about 6.5% of Ethiopia's GDP (Amare et al., 2023). This amount rose to approximately $4.2 billion in the fiscal year 2022/23 as more Ethiopians living in the foreign countries look for ways to contribute their income and invest in their home country business. Remittance not only gives quick money to the households but also generate demand for employment in their respective areas (Bitew et al, 2024). Furthermore, the Ethiopian political regime has learned that diaspora communities are a significant investment force. If greater participation from the expatriates is to be achieved, financial incentives to the diaspora peripheral from the host country institutions, and favourable business environment for the diaspora businesses should be developed (Girma et al., 2023). If well managed diaspora will help in instituting relatively heavy investment in various sectors that consequently spur sustainable advancement and employment at the home country (Durga et al., 2024). Therefore, the strengthening of a good association among institutions of the Ethiopian diaspora and local institutions will help in enhancing the recognition of the flow gains of remittances and diaspora investment.

Even with the established advantages, real-whole interregional market obstacles continue to manifest a crucial function in determining how framework of institutions and diaspora fiscal performance in Ethiopia interact (Asefa et al., 2023). There are several obstacles to overcome, comprises poor infrastructure, financial accessibility, and bureaucratic red tape. Additionally, there is a lack of skill regarding the function that peripheral of institutions manifests as a mediator in this association, which contributes to the incomplete picture of how these variables interact to shape the outcomes of diaspora bricolages (Müller, (2023). In order to fill these gaps, this chapter offers a thorough investigation of the ways in which framework of institutions influence the growth of diaspora businesses in Ethiopia, with an emphasis on the mediating function of peripheral of institutions. This investigation aims to depicted insights into the mechanisms that can improve diaspora engagement and bricolages by combining existing literature and empirical evidence. It will also point out useful ramifications for legislators hoping to create an atmosphere that is positive to enterprises owned by diaspora dwellers (Amare, 2023).

The main investigation question of this study is: ***"How does framework of institutions influence the growth of diaspora businesses in Ethiopia, and what function does peripheral of institutions serve in moderating this association?"*** This subject is imperative because it depicted the need for more investigation into the mechanisms at work and the possibility of emerging specific policies that may encourage augmented participation of the diaspora in Ethiopia's fiscal scene. In addition to advancing scholarly conversation, addressing these issues offers policy-makers and upcoming investigations practical suggestions for improving the influence of diaspora bricolages on fiscal advancement (Samuel, (2022). The emergence of diaspora bricolages has become an imperative field of investigation, especially in emerging regional states like Ethiopia where fiscal progress depends on investments and remittances from the diaspora (Jabo et al., 2024). In order to develop policies that influentially utilize the potential of diaspora traders, it is imperative to comprehend these issues (Girma et al., 2023). Ethiopia has a long history of migration, and a sizable portion of its population now resides outside. Motivated by a desire to peripheral the growth of their native country, a large number of diaspora dwellers want to invest there (Panigrahi et al., 2203).

Also, getting funding is still a constant struggle. A real-world case may be drawn from a cluster of Ethiopian diaspora traders who intended to launch a technology firm in their native country (Amare et al., 2023). They struggled to obtain finance from local banks, which sometimes require collateral that many diaspora traders do not possess, despite their experience and financial advantages. Their capacity to expand operations and influentially compete in the market is hampered by this financial exclusion (Durga et al., 2024). This problem is made worse by the absence of financial products specifically designed for profit partners from the diaspora, underscoring the need for creative financial solutions that take into account the particular conditions of these business owners (Bitew et al, 2024). In addition to bureaucratic and financial barriers, cultural challenges also manifest an imperative function in shaping the experiences of diaspora traders. A case investigation featuring female Ethiopian traders in the diaspora demonstrated the additional difficulties created by gender bias and cultural stereotypes. Notwithstanding their abilities and business sense, these women frequently ran across resistance from regional manifestos, which made it difficult for them to build reputation and have access to imperative networks (Halefom, 2022).

This chapter going to address following Research Questions and Objectives

- Research Question 1 (RQ1): How does the institutional framework influence the shaping of diaspora businesses?
- Objective 1: To analyze the influence of the institutional framework on the characteristics and strategies of diaspora businesses.
- Research Question 2 (RQ2): What is the association among the framework of institutions and the peripheral institutions?
- Objective 2: To explore how the framework of institutions influences the growth and functionality of peripheral institutions.
- Research Question 3 (RQ3): In what ways do peripheral institutions influence the shaping of diaspora businesses?
- Objective 3: To assess the role of peripheral institutions in facilitating or hindering diaspora business growth.
- Research Question 4 (RQ4): How does a peripheral institution mediate the association among the framework of institutions and diaspora business shaping?
- Objective 4: To investigate the mediating role of peripheral institutions in the association among the institutional framework and the shaping of diaspora businesses.

These research questions and objectives provide a clear structure for investigating the interactions among institutional frameworks, peripheral institutions, and diaspora business growth.

STATEMENT OF PROBLEM

The increasing interest in diaspora bricolages, especially in Ethiopia, depicted the urgent need to comprehend the association among framework of institutions and expatriate communities' business advancement. A strong eco-structure is envisioned in the ideal state, enabling expatriate traders to easily negotiate regulatory frameworks, obtain funding, and take advantage of local networks in order to peripheral fiscal growth (Adula et al., 2023). The reality, nevertheless, frequently diverges imperatively from this ideal. Imperative inconsistencies are revealed by empirical evidence; whilst some studies depicted that framework of institutions that assist diaspora businesses improve their viability, others point out enduring obstacles that impede entrepreneurial activity, pointing to a complicated and even erratic association (Samuel, 2022). There are still gaps in the empirical data, even with the existence of numerous frameworks designed to encourage diaspora business. Unanswered concerns over the usefulness of these frameworks in various Ethiopian situations remain after conflicting outcomes from earlier investigation. Theoretical limitations are obvious in the dearth of comprehensive models that explain the connection among peripheral of institutions and diaspora entrepreneurial outcomes. The way that particular institutional attributes—like social capital, policy coherence, and governance quality—influence the entrepreneurial environment for expatriate populations is frequently ignored in the literature that already exists (Samuel, 2022).

The empowerment of Ethiopian diaspora members depends heavily on international institution support. International financial institutions (IFIs) together with development agencies supply important financial help and expert guidance that lets diaspora members conduct business investments in their homeland. They allow members of the diaspora group to reach vital resources while establishing structural systems that promote diaspora participation. Diasporan investments typically follow improved Ethiopia-host ties because political alignments can both strengthen financial support and minimize regulatory challenges toward investments (Amare et al., 2023) The use of information and communication technology (ICT) alongside fintech solutions creates improved access to financial resources which facilitates remittances and investments for everyone involved. Participation faces obstacles due to differences in technological capabilities but Gjorduni (2023) suggests mobile banking integrates those observably behind. Uncertain political conditions across Ethiopia create major obstacles to diaspora investment because security risks persist intensely. Such risks become more drastic when international political events collide with local environments as explained by Samuel (2022) through the lens of adjustment in overall stability for investment environments. Ethiopian diaspora members who combine cultural heritage with economic expertise offer a market advantage that supports global innovation together with marketplace resilience.

Proper utilization of these benefits enables Ethiopia to secure broader international trade positions along with investment opportunities according to Kassaye (2024).

The research shows that academic scholars thoroughly investigate diaspora entrepreneurship and its relationship to institutional backing through extensive academic discussion. According to Samuel (2022) diaspora communities harness their transnational networks to fuel economic development through entrepreneurial entrepreneurship. The research identifies how community interactions through shared values and collective histories lead to both business inception and company expansion. Republic-level operational support has emerged as an essential determinant for diaspora community business startup and growth. The essential resources needed by diaspora entrepreneurs to start a business come from institutional frameworks that contain governmental policies as well as financial institutions and community organizations (Gjorduni 2023). According to Kebede (2024) diaspora entrepreneurs need specific support solutions which target their specific market access and regulatory challenges. This research adds to academia by analyzing how institutional structures combine with peripheral entities to affect diaspora entrepreneurial operations. Research explores underrepresented perspectives while using robust methods to fill gaps in existing literature for policymakers and practitioners who want to increase support for diaspora entrepreneurs.

THEORITICAL FOUNDATION

Institutional Theory: focuses on how institutions—formal and informal laws, customs, and hierarchies—influence how venture capitalists behave in social situations. Understanding how framework of institutions influence diaspora bricolages is made easier with the help of this theory. It underlines how the wider institutional environment—which includes strong governance, coherent regulations, and policy alignment with local needs—influences the efficacy of policies and programs designed to assist enterprises start-up by the diaspora. Investigations might gain a better understanding of the opportunities and challenges faced by diaspora traders by examining the framework of institution (Kebede, 2024).

Community Theory: This idea depicted how different manifestos and circumstances within a particular environment are interrelated and contribute to the success of traders. It emphasizes how the entrepreneurial environment is shaped by peripheral of institutions, cultural elements, and fiscal circumstances. Through an analysis of the entrepreneurial environment, scholars can acquire a deeper understanding of the ways in which various components collaborate to facilitate or obstruct diaspora firms (Kassaye, 2024).

We developed a theoretical framework which united institutional theory and community theory through a model describing how regulatory environments and institutional capacities enable diaspora economic participation. According to institutional theory regulatory frameworks make desirable policy environments that support diaspora investment while strong institutions generate favorable settings. Through community theory we explored how social networks along with shared identities created a setting where diaspora groups possessed collective efficacy. The proposed model analyzed how well-functioning government support infrastructure and policy effectiveness led to improved diaspora engagement through channels such as financial resource access programs as well as mentorship functions and networking possibilities. The research used quantitative analysis to investigate how these relationships functioned and which essential factors caused diaspora economic engagement by testing the proposed model. The combined analytical strategy enhanced both theoretical discussions and delivered practical recommendations to Ethiopian policymakers who want to leverage diaspora resources for national economic development.

EMPIRICAL LITERATURE REVIEW

Institution Framework and Diaspora Business Advancement

A community related to traders is the self-run structure of venture capitalists, things, and circumstances that all work together to encourage and peripheral bricolages in a related setting. This engages a sort of related customers, comprises profit partners, traders, institutional setup, educational institutions, and peripheral clusters. A supportive community related to traders incubates frugal innovation, incubate, and strategic fiscal growth (Samuel, 2022). In the initial 2000s, the idea of community related to traders started to take off as scholars and professionals realized how crucial connectivity is to incubating bricolages. Educationalist have made substantial contributions to this discussion by emphasizing the ways in which eco-structures can incubate among diverse related customers, hence augmenting entrepreneurial endeavours (Kant & Adula, 2024). Since then, the idea has been used all around the whole interregional market to understand how local conditions might be adjusted to boost bricolages, especially in the context of emerging economies.

A community related to traders is the self-run structure of venture capitalists, things, and circumstances that all work together to encourage and peripheral bricolages in a related setting. This engages a sort of related customers, comprises profit partners, traders, institutional setup, educational institutions, and peripheral clusters. A robust community related to traders promotes creativity, teamwork, and long-term fiscal expansion (Kassaye, 2024). In the early 2000s, the idea of community related to traders started to take off as scholars and professionals realized how crucial connectivity is to incubating bricolages (Gjorduni, (2023).

H1: Institution framework has imperative influence on Diaspora business shaping

Institutional Framework and Institutions Peripheral

The way that framework of institutions influence peripheral of institutions manifests a vital function in determining the environment that traders, especially those from the diaspora, operate in. Clear norms and rules that govern the delivery of peripheral services are established by a well-structured framework of institution, guaranteeing that the functions of various related customers—comprises institutional setup, financial institutions, and non-institutional organizations—are clearly defined and coordinated (Jabo et al., 2023). Coherent and strategically linked policies incubate an atmosphere that is favourable to efficient peripheral of institutions, which includes financing possibilities, advisory services, and training programs (Samuel, 2022).

Moreover, how funds are distributed within this framework has a direct influence on the calibre and accessibility of peripheral; a robust framework gives financing priority to initiatives that help traders, improving their chances of success. Initiatives aimed at increasing capacity are also crucial; through establishing alliances among educational institutions and peripheral clusters, frameworks can enable focused instruction that depicted diaspora traders with the information and abilities they need (Guye et al., 2204). Also, networking and cooperation are encouraged by strong institutional structures, which depicted forums for related customers to exchange skill and resources and augment the efficacy of peripheral services (Samuel, (2022).

H2: Framework of institution has imperative influence on Peripheral of institutions

Institutions Peripheral and Diaspora Business Advancement

The formation and expansion of enterprises start-up by the diaspora are greatly influenced by the broad and profound influence of peripheral of institutions. Access to essential resources, comprises as grants, low-interest loans, and investment incentives created especially for expatriate traders, is improved by efficient peripheral of institutions. Their frequent obstacles are lessened by this financial peripheral, allowing them to start and grow their businesses (Guye et al., 2023). Peripheral of institutions also includes capacity-building initiatives that give diaspora traders the know-how and abilities they need in areas like regulatory compliance and business management. Institutions enable traders to more skilfully negotiate the intricacies of the local market by offering focused training. Also, peripheral of institutions incubates networking opportunities, creating platforms for diaspora profit partners to connect with local business communities, which can lead to valuable mentorship and partnerships. Another essential element is advocacy for diaspora traders; organizations that work with these clusters have the power to shape policy, leading to more advantageous laws and peripheral structures. Lastly, robust monitoring and evaluation processes ensure that peripheral of institutions remains responsive to the evolving needs of diaspora businesses, allowing for continuous improvement of programs (Gjorduni, (2023)

H3: Peripheral of institutions has imperative influence on Diaspora business shaping

Mediation of Institutions Peripheral on Diaspora Business Advancement

The success and sustainability of entrepreneurial endeavours started by diaspora individuals are imperatively influenced by the peripheral of institutions that acts as a mediator in creating enterprise start-up by the diaspora. An essential bridge that improves the connection among diaspora traders and the larger institutional structure in their native countries is institutional assistance (Durga et al., 2024). In order to help diaspora traders overcome common obstacles comprises bureaucratic obstacles and restricted access to finance, peripheral of institutions depicted vital resources like financial assistance, capacity-building programs, and networking opportunities. For case, customized financial products or subsidies intended exclusively for profit partners from the diaspora not only ease financial burdens but also boost self-assurance, encouraging business owners to make investments in their native markets (Manor, 2021). Moreover, capacity-building programs give these business owners the abilities and information they need to successfully negotiate regional laws and market dynamics. Peripheral of institutions also helps connect expatriate traders with local business networks, allowing for incubate and mentoring that can result in creative partnerships and better access to markets. Institutional assistance serves as a crucial intermediary, enhancing the benefits of a peripheral institutional environment and facilitating the success of diaspora firms, which in turn makes a substantial contribution to the fiscal advancement of their native countries (Dereso et al., 2023).

H4: The link among Framework of institution and Diaspora business shaping is influenced by Peripheral of institutions

CONCEPTUAL FRAMEWORK

Figure 1. Conceptual framework (Authors)

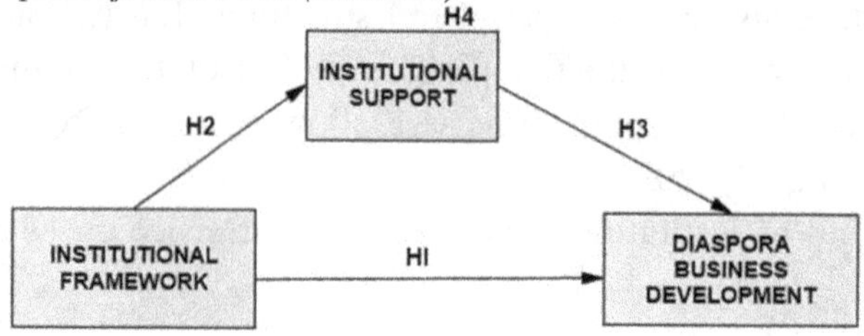

METHODOLOGY

The present investigation applied a quantitative investigation methodology to examine the mediating function of peripheral of institutions in the formation of enterprises start-up by the diaspora. Through rigorous sampling, 401 individuals in sum were chosen for the sample, guaranteeing a broad representation of diaspora traders across a sort of industries and geographical areas. The objective of this extensive sample approach was to encompass a broad spectrum of viewpoints and experiences, hence augmenting the resilience of the results. To assess the validity and reliability of the collected data, the investigation applied the Kaiser-Meyer-Olkin (KMO) measure and conducted Exploratory Factor Analysis (EFA). The KMO test indicated that the sample was adequate for factor analysis, providing confidence in the suitability of the data for further statistical analysis. EFA was performed to identify the underlying structures of the constructs related to peripheral of institutions and diaspora bricolages, allowing for the refinement of the measurement scale. A comprehensive analysis of relevant literature served as the foundation for the scale advancement process and guided the construction of survey items that captured the essential elements of peripheral of institutions.

To obtain diverse perspectives the researcher used stratified sampling as a method to capture representatives from across the diaspora community. Researchers partitioned the study population into different categories (strata) according to industry sector and regional location while assessing participant entrepreneurial experience. Multiple random participant selections occurred per individual stratum to achieve balanced representation. Participants were acquired through multiple recruitment channels that integrated diaspora community organizations and social media platforms as well as networking events. The multiple channels of outreach targeted various audiences in order to influenceively engage members of underserved groups. To achieve representative data the investigation selected strategically distributed 401 participants across different diaspora trader industries and geographical areas. The final sample of 401 participants resulted from power analysis calculations demonstrating that this subject size would sufficiently identify meaningful connections and remaining variables among groups. The collection of data occurred through both online and in-person distribution of structured surveys. Participants responded to structured surveys which collected essential information about their entrepreneurial experiences as well as their perceptions of peripheral institutions and their bricolage practices. Participants had to grant their informed consent to the researcher before they could join the study.

The researcher selected Structural Equation Modeling SEM because it allows for simultaneous evaluation of complex multiple variable relations. SEM enabled researchers to assess both direct and indirect associations which existed among peripheral institutions and diaspora entrepreneurship. Furthermore the research employed regression analysis to investigate distinct associations among independent and dependent variables. The analytical approach generated numerical results which assessed how financial aid as well as capacity growth initiatives and business networking associations influenceed startup success among diaspora members. Our analysis used AMOS for SEM processing alongside regression analysis under SPSS (Statistical Package for the Social Sciences). Social science research depends on these two software applications for robust data analysis which produces dependable analytical outcomes. Complete documentation of sampling procedures and survey design aspects along with analytical methods stayed in place for future reference. The documentation includes all surveyed items together with their selection reasoning and complete statistical outputs from AMOS and SPSS. The survey underwent refinement through a smaller pilot study which simultaneously demonstrated question clarity and measurement validity. All feedback from this stage received extensive documentation for proper growth of the final survey instrument. Anonymized data and survey materials from the study will be made public when allowed to support future analysis and knowledge expansion.

Measurement Items and Reliability

In the study, the authors devised a sum of "42 items of measurement", which was subdivided into three constructs. The "Institutional Peripheral" construct was derived from sources like "Brinkerhoff (2007)" that provided 15 items of financial aid, capacity-build programs and networking. For this construct the reliability value was given as "$\alpha = 0.85$". "Diaspora business advancement" construct was operationalized as "10 items" borrowed from Gonzalez et al. (2015) traders intention and antecedent of success with Cronbach reliability of "$\alpha = 0.90$". 'Institutional peripheral' as a variable was adopted to assess the mediation influences, '17 items' were used from 'Kloosterman (2010)' measuring the influence of institutional peripheral on the entrepreneurial outcomes having a reliability of '$\alpha = 0.87$'. To avoid confusion among the independent variable (institutional peripheral) and the mediator the items were carefully chosen to enhance the understanding and clarification of the operational definition of each to decipher the collected data.

Population and Sampling Method

The study population was chosen as "diaspora traders", and a strictly selected "purposive sampling method" was used to include multiple industries and regions. Thus, the target audience consisted of "401 respondents," and their number allowed not only to obtain vast and diverse information and positive responses but also to complement the sort of views and experiences concerning enterprises start-up by the diaspora among TABLE s. Below is a sample demographic table that outlines the sectorial and geographic representation of the 401 diaspora traders included in the study:

Table 1. Demographic profile

Demographic Variable	**Category**	**Frequency (n)**	**Percentage (%)**
Industry Sector	Technology	120	29.9
	Retail	85	21.2
	Manufacturing	60	14.9
	Services	70	17.4
	Agriculture	30	7.5
	Financial Services	36	9.0
	Sum	**401**	**100%**
Geographical Region	North America	150	37.4
	Europe	120	29.9
	Asia	60	14.9
	Africa	40	10.0
	Australia	31	7.7
	Latin America	0	0.0
	Sum	**401**	**100%**

Source: Author

In Industry Sector row divides the respondents according to the industry they are engaged in, which gives a view of the variation of entrepreneurial activities among the diaspora. Geographical Region section draws attention to the geographical location of the respondents and demonstrates where they are coming from and how they are distributed over the world. How the study was executed and the population it entails are illustrated in this table of the demographic data of the respondents in terms of sectors and geographical locations hence increasing validity in the results obtained.

Sampling Frame

Respondents were contacted through ''networks of diaspora organisations and ''entrepreneurial associations.'' These networks were vital when identifying a large and diverse audience of diaspora traders because it is not always easy to connect with them because of distance and diversity.

Questionnaire Distribution and Administration

The booklet used here were "online surveys" and "face-to-face interview" administered in cuisines identified with diaspora persons and business forums. Both of such strategies proved useful, as these created a wide coverage while maintaining high response rates. First, a pilot study was used to adjust the questionnaire in terms of both wording and rating scale to make the items measure more accurately the theoretical construct in a sample of 50 respondents. After modifications, the final survey was completed by the entire samples of 421 participants Structural equations analysis using AMOS software and SEM were used to examine the complex interaction of the variables germane to the present study.

DATA ANALYSIS

Table 2. KMO and Bartlett's test

Ration of Specimen Competence		**.904**
Bartlett's Test of Sphericity	Approx. Chi-Square	1419.516
	Df	93
	Sig.	.003

Source: Authors

One of the most imperative steps in validating the measuring scale results manifested in Table 2 shed light on this process. Ration of Specimen Competence depicted woth is 0.904 manifested that sample has a good appropriateness. KMO values above 0.70 are generally considered acceptable; values nearer 1.0 indicate a higher degree of association among the variables. This high KMO score manifested that the gathered data is appropriate for factor analysis, verifying that the sample size is sufficient for trustworthy statistical analysis and that the variables are suitably associated. In addition to the KMO measure, Bartlett's test of sphericity was run to see if the association matrix imperatively deviates from an identity matrix, which would indicate that the variables are unrelated. The test produced an approximate chi-square value of 1419.521 with 98 degrees of freedom at a significance level of 0.002. Because of the low p-value (Sig. = 0.002), the null hypothesis, which claims that the association matrix is an identity matrix, can be rejected.

Table 3. Sum variance explained

	Preliminary Eigen-values			Abstraction Sums of Loading Square			Spin Sums of Loading Square		
	Sum	% of Variance	Cumulative %	Sum	% of Variance	Cumulative %	Sum	% of Variance	Cumulative %
1	4.1	32.2	32.2	4.3	32.25	32.23	3.0	21.4	21.4
2	1.2	9.78	42.0	1.2	9.78	42.01	2.2	15.4	36.9
3	1.41	9.080	51.1	1.4	9.08	51.13	1.4	14.1	51.1
4	.971	6.785	57.8						
5	.871	6.214	64.						
6	.783	5.542	69.6						

Extraction Method: PCA
Source: Authors

Principal Component Analysis (PCA), a crucial method for determining the dataset's underlying structure, depicted a comprehensive breakdown of the overall variance in Table 3. The initial eigenvalues indicate how much variance each component accounts for before extraction. The first component manifested a large eigenvalue of 4.31, or 32.25% of the sum variance. This noteworthy percentage depicted the significance of the component by demonstrating that it accounts for a sizeable portion of the variability present in the data, making it an essential component for additional investigation. With eigenvalues of 1.21 and 1.41, which correspond to 9.78% and 9.08% of the sum variance, respectively, the second and third components also add to the overall variance. When taken as a whole, these three elements account for over half of the variability in the dataset, explaining roughly 51.13% of its variation. The cumulative percentages sum is 51.13%. The first two components together accounted for 42.02% of the variance. This demonstrates how imperative these elements are to comprehending the data structure. The first component maintains its strength after extraction, retaining its eigenvalue and variance %, according to the extraction sums of squared loadings.

On the other hand, the distribution of the rotation sums of squared loadings differs, with the first component falling to a sum of 3.07. This depicted that after rotation, the variation becomes more uniformly distributed throughout the constituents, facilitating a more lucid understanding of the elements. All things considered, these results depicted the significance of the early elements in distilling the essence of the data and directing further analyses and interpretations concerning the function of peripheral of institutions in diaspora bricolages. This organized method to investigation variation depicted a solid platform for future exploration of the links among the identified components.

Table 4. Covariances

Covariance			Approximation	S.E.	C.R.	P	Hy.
Peripheral of institutions	**<-->**	**Framework of institution**	**.234**	**.028**	**8.231**	**.00**	**H2**
Peripheral of institutions	<-->	Shaping-Diaspora Business	.306	.041	7.670	.00	**H3**
Framework of institution	<-->	Shaping-diaspora Business	.261	.25	7.841	.00	**H1**

Source: Authors

The association estimates among the three main investigations constructs—Peripheral of institutions, Framework of institution, and Shaping-Diaspora Business—are manifested in Table 4. Understanding the direction and intensity of the association among these categories is crucial for comprehending how peripheral of institutions influences diaspora bricolages, and the covariance offer insightful information in this regard. The first covariance, which is 0.234 among framework of institution and peripheral, has a vital ratio (C.R.) of 8.231 and a standard error (S.E.) of 0.028. This strong C.R. value peripherals hypothesis H2 by depicted a highly imperative link at the significance level denoted by ".00". This investigation emphasizes how crucial a strong framework of institution is to enabling efficient peripheral structures that enable diaspora traders, implying that a well-organized setting expands their pool of resources.

The second covariance, which is 0.306, has a C.R. of 7.670, a S.E. of 0.041, and an association among Shaping-Diaspora Business and Peripheral of institutions. Additionally, this strong association reaches statistical significance, peripheral hypothesis H3. The outcomes suggest that the success of diaspora firms is imperatively influenced by the presence of strong institutional backing. Finally, it is found that the association among Shaping-Diaspora Business and Framework of institution is 0.261, with a statistically imperative C.R. of 7.841, so confirming hypothesis H1. This finding manifested that a robust framework of institution manifests a crucial function in both directly influencing the entrepreneurial outcomes of individuals from the diaspora and providing them with the required assistance. The interdependence of these characteristics is reinforced by the consistent worth across all covariance, which manifested that successful diaspora bricolages require a peripheral framework of institution.

Table 5. Validity concern

	CR	AVE	MSV	MaxR(H)	IF	IS	DBD
IF	0.731	0.643	0.251	0.832	**0.642**		
IS	0.761	0.658	0.135	0.765	0.173	**0.661**	
DBD	0.794	0.605	0.276	0.796	0.382	0.191	**0.686**

Note: AF= Framework of institution; IS = Institutions Peripheral Sopport; DBD=Diaspora business advancement

Source: Authors

In order to evaluate the measurement quality and construct validity within the investigation, Table 5 depicted imperative validity metrics for the constructs of Diaspora business shaping (DBD), Framework of institution (IF), and Peripheral of institutions (IS). Validity Concern depicted crucial information on the measuring characteristics of the relevant constructs. First, all constructs—Influence Factors (IF), Peripheral of institutions (IS), and Sustainable Advancement Benefits (SDB)—exceed the acceptable threshold of 0.7, according to the Composite Reliability (CR) values. Strong internal consistency is specifically manifested by CR values of 0.731 for IF, 0.761 for IS, and 0.794 for SDB. These values imply that the items within each construct are accurately assessing the intended ideas.

The validity of the constructs is further peripheraled by the Average Variance Extracted (AVE) values, all of which are more than 0.5. The AVE scores (0.643 for IF, 0.658 for IS, and 0.605 for SDB) depicted how well the constructs capture the underlying phenomena by depicted that a sizable amount of the variance in the indicators is explained by each of the constructs. The association among the constructs are suitably low, as can be manifested by looking at the inter-construct association. For case, the association among IS and SDB is 0.191, IF and SDB is 0.642, and SDB and IF is 0.382. These values indicate the existence of discriminant validity by confirming that the constructs are sufficiently different from one another.

Mediating Function

Figure 2. Structural equation model (Authors)

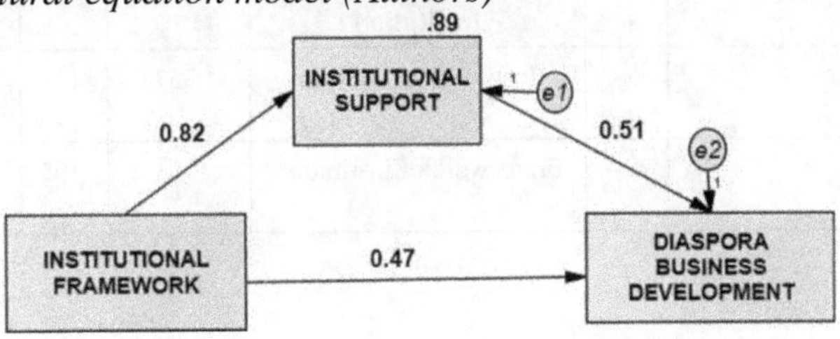

Model Fit Indices

Table 6. Indices for model fit

Sig.	Chi-Sq	RMR	Fitness Goodness	Fitness Confirmatory	TLI	RMSEA
0.005	1.849	.061	0.943	0.948	0.941	.053

Source: Authors

A thorough summary of the model fit indices is given in Table 6, which is essential for determining if the suggested model adequately captures the associations among the constructs. The sum model is statistically imperative, as indicated by the significance level (Sig.) of 0.005, indicating that the data depicted strong peripheral for the proposed associations among the variables. This worth is crucial because it demonstrates that the model represents imperative associations rather than being the product of chance. In terms of model fit, the Chi-Square value of 1.849 is beneficial because it is quite low. A higher degree of agreement among the observed and expected covariance matrices is generally indicated by a lower Chi-Square score. The Root Mean Square Residual (RMR) of 0.061, which is less than the generally recognized cut off of 0.08, peripherals this. All values depicted the good model fitness.

Table 7. Regression state

Relative			Approx.	S.E.	C.R.	P	Ass.
Institutional Support	**<---**	**Framework of institution**	**.862**	**.146**	**7.583**	**.00**	**H2**
Diaspora Business Advancement	<---	Institutional Support	.337	.131	2.851	.00	H3
Diaspora business Advancement	<---	Framework of institution	.961	.193	7.952	.00	H1

Source: Authors

The outcomes of the regression analysis are manifested in Table 7, which clarifies the connections among the framework of institution, peripheral of institutions, and diaspora business shaping constructions. Framework of institution and Peripheral of institutions are the first association to be examined; the results depicted an approximate value of 0.862, a standard error (S.E.) of 0.146, and a vital ratio (C.R.) of 7.583. The association's significance, manifested by ".00", attests to its statistical significance. The hypothesis H2 is peripheraled by this substantial regression coefficient, which indicates that the degree of peripheral accessible to diaspora traders is greatly augmented by a strong framework of institution. This investigation emphasizes how crucial a well-organized institutional environment is for providing the tools and resources required for profitable commercial endeavours.

The second association, which examines the influence of Peripheral of institutions on Diaspora business shaping, manifested an approximation of 0.337, with an S.E. of 0.131 and a C.R. of 2.851, also marked with ".00" for significance. This result confirms hypothesis H3, indicating that influential peripheral of institutions positively influences the success of diaspora businesses. Although the regression coefficient is lower than that of the first association, it still signifies a meaningful influence, emphasizing the vital function that peripheral mechanisms manifest in shaping entrepreneurial outcomes for diaspora individuals. This underscores the necessity for targeted peripheral initiatives to bolster the entrepreneurial efforts of diaspora populations. Lastly, the regression analysis reveals a strong association among Framework of institution and Diaspora business shaping, with an approximation of 0.961, an S.E. of 0.193, and a C.R. of 7.952, again marked with ".00" for significance. This finding strongly peripherals hypothesis H1, demonstrating that a solid framework of institution directly influences the success of diaspora businesses. The high regression coefficient indicates a very robust association, suggesting that the institutional context is essential for creating favourable conditions that enable bricolages to thrive among diaspora communities.

Table 8. Mediating function influence

	Influence	worth	Path Influence
Framework of institution→ Diaspora business shaping	Direct Influence	.47	Direct influence stated
Framework of institution→ Institutional Support → Diaspora business shaping	Indirect Influence	.82*.51=.42	Indirect Influence Ensued
	Whole influence	.89	Partial mediation

Source: Authors

The mediating functions are manifested in Table 8. With a route coefficient of 0.47, the first entry emphasizes the Framework of institution's direct influence on Diaspora business shaping. This imperative value peripherals the idea that the conditions established by institutions are vital in promoting entrepreneurial outcomes since it manifested that a robust framework of institution has a beneficial influence on the success of enterprises start-up by the diaspora. Skill how institutional contexts might help or impede the success of diaspora firms requires skill of this direct influence. The second entry examines how peripheral of institutions, rather than the framework of institution itself, shapes diaspora business. An indirect influence worth of 0.42 is obtained by multiplying the resultant value of 0.82 by 0.51. This investigation depicted that the Framework of institution contributes to the success of enterprises start-up by the diaspora by offering crucial peripheral of institutions in addition to direct benefits. This approach is essential as it underlines the diverse nature of factors at manifest, indicating that good peripheral of institutions functions as a mediator among the framework and entrepreneurial outcomes. It emphasizes how crucial it is to have resources and policies that help diaspora traders in order to fully realize their potential.

The final entry summarizes the overall influence, yielding a sum path coefficient of 0.89, which indicates a partial mediation influence. This manifested that while the Framework of institution imperatively contributes to the success of diaspora businesses both directly and indirectly, other factors may also be influencing this association. The state of "partial mediation" depicted that although the Framework of institution strengthens the influence of Peripheral of institutions on Diaspora business shaping, it does not account for the entire variance; other contextual or individual factors may also manifest a function in shaping entrepreneurial success. All things considered, Table 7's outcomes depicted mediating functions that institutional elements manifest in influencing diaspora bricolages. The distinct direct and indirect influences emphasize the importance of both a robust framework of institution and influential peripheral mechanisms in incubating successful business bricolages among diaspora populations.

DISCUSSION

The investigation's outcomes depicted how imperative institutional variables are in influencing diaspora bricolages. The interdependence of these constructs is depictured by the notable direct and indirect influences of the framework of institution and peripheral of institutions on diaspora business shaping. According to the outcomes, a strong framework of institution incubates an environment that is conducive to the success of diaspora traders in addition to offering them the necessary resources and assistance. The significance of both structural and peripheral elements in promoting entrepreneurial success within expatriate populations is depictured by this dual function. The discussion surrounding the framework of institutional influences on diaspora business in Ethiopia underscores the imperative function that various institutional factors manifest in shaping entrepreneurial activities. Institutions, both formal and informal, create the landscape within which diaspora traders operate, influencing their decisions and opportunities. The mediation of peripheral of institutions, such as government initiatives, financial assistance, and access to networks, emerges as a vital factor that can augment the capacity of diaspora businesses to thrive. In Ethiopia, where fiscal challenges may deter local traders, the involvement of the diaspora can depicted a unique avenue for frugal innovation and investment. Influential peripheral of institutions not only alleviates barriers such as regulatory complexities and market entry difficulties but also empowers diaspora traders by connecting them with local resources and related customers. By incubating positive institutional environments, Ethiopia can leverage the potential of its diaspora, ultimately driving fiscal growth and contributing to sustainable advancement.

This discussion depicted the need for comprehensive policies that recognize and actively peripheral the contributions of diaspora businesses to the regional economy. The framework of institutional influences on Ethiopian diaspora businesses is a topic of discussion that depicted the imperative function that different institutional elements manifest in influencing entrepreneurial activity. Formal and informal institutions shape the environment in which diaspora traders operate influencing their choices and prospects. One imperative element that might improve the ability of enterprises start-up by the diaspora to prosper is the mediation of peripheral of institutions, such as government efforts, financial help, and access to networks. The participation of the diaspora might offer a special channel for frugal innovation and investment in Ethiopia, where financial difficulties may discourage native business owners. Good institutional assistance helps expatriate traders overcome obstacles like market entrance challenges and regulatory complications while also empowering them by putting them in touch with local related customers and resources.

CONCLUSION

This investigation concludes that there is a direct association among institutional elements and diaspora bricolages, indicating that the success of enterprises start-up by the diaspora is greatly influenced by efficient framework of institutions and peripheral networks. Policymakers should emphasize improving framework of institutions to peripheral bricolages among diaspora communities, as evidenced by both direct and indirect benefits. Related customers may better design interventions that empower and peripheral diaspora traders and eventually promote fiscal advancement and frugal innovation by recognizing these ties. The way that institutional influences and peripheral structures interact shapes the environment in which Ethiopian diaspora firms operate. Policymakers may create focused strategies that enable diaspora traders to overcome obstacles and seize opportunities by understanding how both official and informal institutions influence entrepreneurial activities. This analysis shows that favorable institutional context strongly empowers .diaspora entrepreneurship by stimulating both new business launches and durable performance. The study demonstrates how peripheral institutions serve as fundamental intermediaries between entrepreneurs and their resources and networks. The study findings support research objectives which seek to understand the mutually dependent relationship between institutional support structures and diaspora business development. The study reveals important relationships which help expand the field's understanding and demonstrates why customized institutionally designed solutions must address diaspora entrepreneurs' particular challenges to build economic growth and community strength.

MANAGERIAL IMPLICATIONS

From a managerial standpoint, managers and leaders active in assisting enterprises start-up by the diaspora can benefit from the investigation's conclusions. Organizations that promote bricolages ought to concentrate on creating robust framework of institutions that depicted all-encompassing peripheral services. This includes having access to funding sources, networking opportunities, and mentorship programs designed specifically to meet the needs of diaspora traders. Managers can augment the chances of company success in diaspora communities by incubateing an atmosphere that takes care of institutional and peripheral issues. The managerial implications of understanding the institutional influences on diaspora businesses in Ethiopia are imperative for both public and private sector leaders. Supervisors have to understand how imperative it is to create an institutional climate that is conducive of diaspora engagement and bricolages. This entails pushing for legislative adjustments that lower administrative barriers and improve the availability of resources like funding, education, and networking opportunities. In order to use the distinct perspectives and experiences of diaspora populations to inform company goals and efforts, managers should also place a high priority on emerging partnerships with these communities.

PRACTICAL INFERENCES

This investigation has practical worth for practitioners and policymakers that work with diaspora communities. The report emphasizes the need for focused policies that fortify peripheral networks and institutional structures. Enacting initiatives that make it easier for venture capitalists in the diaspora to obtain skill, training, and resources can greatly augment their entrepreneurial environment. Also, encouraging cooperation among NGOs, community organizations, and institutional setup can result in a more cohesive network of assistance, which will enable diaspora traders to overcome obstacles with greater efficiency. The institutional influences on Ethiopian enterprises start-up by the diaspora have numerous practical ramifications that are essential to promoting successful bricolages. To lower barriers to entry, legislators must first establish streamlined procedures that make it easier for diaspora traders to register their businesses and comply with regulations. This can entail setting up specialized peripheral divisions within government organizations that work with enterprises start-up by the diaspora. Also, useful programs like networking events and mentorship programs can help connect expatriate traders with nearby firms, incubateing incubate and skill sharing.

THEORETICAL INFERENCES

In theory, this investigation advances skill about the function of institutional elements in bricolages, especially in the setting of diaspora populations. The investigation contributes to the body of skill on bricolages and institutional theory by clarifying the direct and indirect linkages among Diaspora business shaping, Peripheral of institutions, and Framework of institution. The hypothetical assertions of understanding institutional influences on diaspora businesses in Ethiopia extend our skill of entrepreneurial dynamics within the context of trans regional and institutional theory. This framework depicted the significance of institutional environments in shaping the behaviours and strategies of diaspora traders, suggesting that the success of these businesses is not solely reliant on individual capabilities but also on the broader institutional landscape. By integrating concepts from institutional theory, such as legitimacy, isomorphism, and peripheral of institutions, investigations can better analyse how varying institutional contexts influence entrepreneurial outcomes. Moreover, this perspective encourages scholars to explore the interactions among diaspora networks and local institutions, shedding light on how cultural, social, and fiscal ties influence business procedures and frugal innovation.

RECOMMENDATIONS

It is advised that related customers adopt a multifaceted strategy to improve the institutional environment for diaspora traders in light of the outcomes. This includes campaigning for policy reforms that prioritize the building of peripheral institutional structures and providing targeted aid to traders. Also, establishing incubates among different related customers—comprises institutional setup, educational institutions, and enterprises in the private sector—can result in a comprehensive peripheral network that caters to the varied requirements of businesses operating in the diaspora.

The government must create a Diaspora Investment Fund designed to match diaspora donations to local startups thus attracting crucial funds at potential expense of becoming entirely dependent on outside financial support. Digital infrastructure improvement requires investment into Information and Communication Technology to provide electronic banking access for simplified transactions at the cost of potential cybersecurity dangers. The establishment of networking platforms for diaspora investors and local entrepreneurs creates collaborative opportunities and equitable access while it may westernize certain investors who can unfairly monopolize emerging entrepreneurs developer space.

Future investigations must conduct detailed temporal analysis ensuring that institutional analytical effects on diaspora entrepreneurial ventures receive examination across various time intervals. Fundamental insights regarding diaspora entrepreneurs' experiences along with distinctive business challenges become possible through qualitative research methods which incorporate interviews and case studies. Data from national-level and industrial comparisons help researchers develop a deeper understanding of institutional factors which influence entrepreneurial manifestations. Diaspora business relationships via digital platforms represent an unexplored field with large potential for revealing fresh perceptions of support system capabilities. Research should prioritize identifying cultural elements which affect entrepreneurship outcomes in diaspora group success rates.

FUTURE DIRECTIONS

In order to evaluate the long-term influences of peripheral of institutions on diaspora bricolages, future investigation should investigate longitudinal studies. Deeper understanding of entrepreneurial success might be attained by examining the contributions of individual traits and cultural elements in addition to institutional influences. Also, comparative investigation among various regional states and regions may shed light on the differing influences of framework of institutions on enterprises start-up by the diaspora, adding to our understanding of the dynamics of global bricolages. Emerging techniques that influentially help diaspora traders in varied circumstances will require a broader perspective. Also, establishing alliances among regional firms and diaspora company owners can promote information sharing and teamwork, both of which are essential for advancement and frugal innovation. Additionally, educational institutions ought to be urged to create curricula that give diaspora dwellers the know-how and abilities they need to successfully negotiate the Ethiopian market. Improving digital channels for resource sharing and networking will also help to fortify ties within the diaspora community, which will incubate a more integrated entrepreneurial environment.

The study contains various shortcomings which researchers must acknowledge. Bidirectional biases can emerge through self-reported data because research participants tend to present idealized rather than genuine information. Although diverse in nature the study sample probably does not fully capture every diaspora community so this affects the ability to generalize findings. The research results could be influenced by geographic and industry market biases. This research concentrates on instant institutional framework effects while under examining enduring transformations and evolving diaspora business dynamics. Future studies should implement lengthy data collection coupled with qualitative analyzes to enhance comprehension about diaspora entrepreneurship operate in different institutional environments.

REFERENCES

Adula, M., Birbirsa, Z. A., & Kant, S. (2023). The influence of interpersonal, problem solving and technical training skills on performance of Ethiopia textile industry: Continuance, normative and influenceive commitment as mediators. *Cogent Business & Management*, *10*(3), 2286672. Advance online publication. DOI: 10.1080/23311975.2023.2286672

Amare, T. J., & Honig, B. (2023). Returnee entrepreneurial entry decisions among forced and voluntary returnees in Ethiopia: A comparative investigation. *Africa Journal of Management*, *9*(2), 177–205. DOI: 10.1080/23322373.2023.2187688

Asefa, K., Kant, D. S., & Debela, K. L. (2023, November). Effect of Transformational Leadership on Organizational Performance: The Mediating Role of Employee Commitment and Expert Systems (AI) Inclusion in Ethiopia. In 2023 International Conference on Communication, Security and Artificial Intelligence (ICCSAI) (pp. 305-310). IEEE.

Birhane, M., Amentie, C., Borji, B., & Kant, S. (2024). Are Ethiopian Coffee Farmers Proficient to Predict Capital Structure with Mediation of AI Based Knowledge Systems and Asset Liquidity?. In AI in Agriculture for Sustainable and Economic Management (pp. 199-215). CRC Press.

Bitew, M., Huluka, A., & Takaro, G. (2024). Incubateing inter-sectorial integration: Legal and policy framework for physical infrastructure in Addis Ababa, Ethiopia. Journal of Infrastructure. *Policy and Advancement*, *8*(8), 5956.

Dereso, C. W., Kant, S., Muthuraman, M., & Tufa, G. (2023). Influence of Point of Service on Health Department Student's Creativity in Comprehensive Universities of Ethiopia: Moderating Role of Public-Private Partnership and Mediating Role of Work Place Learning. In: Jain, S., Groppe, S., Mihindukulasooriya, N. (eds) Proceedings of the International Health Informatics Conference. Lecture Notes in Electrical Engineering, vol 990. Springer, Singapore. https://doi.org/DOI: 10.1007/978-981-19-9090-8_13

Durga, P., Godavarthi, D., Kant, S., & Basa, S. S. (2024). Aspect-based drug review classification through a hybrid model with ant colony optimization using deep learning. *Discov Computing*, *27*(1), 19. DOI: 10.1007/s10791-024-09441-w

Girma, H., & Abebe, A. (2023). Outsiders within: Examining Ethiopian adoptee experiences through a diasporic lens. *Journal of Ethnic and Migration Studies*, •••, 1–18.

Gjorduni, F. (2023). Diaspora Influence on Foreign Direct Investment: State Institutions on Diaspora Engagement. *European Journal of Marketing and Fiscals*, *6*(1), 49–69.

Halefom, A. (2022). Integrating Traditional and State Institutions for Conflict Prevention: Institutional, Legal and Policy Frameworks in Ethiopia. *Mizan Law Review*, *16*(2), 339–368. DOI: 10.4314/mlr.v16i2.4

Jabo, D., Borji, B., & Kant, S. (2024, February). Impact of Technical CRM on Ethiopia Bank Human-Computer Interface and Competitive Advantage as Mediators of Performance. In 2024 IEEE International Conference on Computing, Power and Communication Technologies (IC2PCT) (Vol. 5, pp. 679-682). IEEE.

Kant, S., & Adula, M. (2024). AI Learning and Work Attitude Mediation Among Reward and Organizational Peripheral in Ethiopia. In Gomathi Sankar, J., & David, A. (Eds.), *Generative AI for Transformational Management* (pp. 109–136). IGI Global., DOI: 10.4018/979-8-3693-5578-7.ch005

Kant, S., & Adula, M. (2024). Mediated by AI-Based Generative Re-Enforcement Learning and Work Attitude: Are Intrinsic Rewards Transforming Employee Perceived Organizational Peripheral? In Gomathi Sankar, J., & David, A. (Eds.), *Generative AI for Transformational Management* (pp. 83–108). IGI Global., DOI: 10.4018/979-8-3693-5578-7.ch004

Kant, S., & Adula, M. (2024). Human-Machine Interaction in the Metaverse in the Context of Ethiopia. In *Influence and Potential of Machine Learning in the Metaverse* (pp. 196–212). IGI Global., DOI: 10.4018/979-8-3693-5762-0.ch008

Kassaye, B. D., Bayiley, Y. T., & Alemu, Z. K. (2024). Success Factors for Returnee Migrant Traders in Ethiopia: The Mediating Function of Government Policies and Peripheral of institutions.

Kebede Sori, G. (2024). Advancement Influences of Return Migration: Literature Review of Ethiopian Return Migrants. Advancement Influences of Return Migration: Literature Review of Ethiopian Return Migrants (March 25, 2024).

Manor, I., & Adiku, G. A. (2021). From 'traitors' to 'saviours': A longitudinal analysis of Ethiopian, Kenyan and Rwandan embassies' procedure of digital diaspora diplomacy. South African Journal of Interregional stateal Affairs, 28(3), 403-427.

Müller, C. (2023). Diaspora return visits for skill transfer and capacity advancement: a case investigation of IOM's connecting diaspora for advancement project in Ethiopia, Sierra Leone and Somaliland.

Nigusie, A., Azale, T., Yitayal, M., & Derseh, L. (2024). Influence of stage-matched educational intervention on use of institutional delivery in Northwest Ethiopia: Using community readiness model. *The Pan African Medical Journal, 48*(16). PMID: 39184843

Panigrahi, A., Pati, A., Sahu, B., Das, M. N., Nayak, D. S. K., Sahoo, G., & Kant, S. (2023). En-MinWhale: An ensemble approach based on MRMR and Whale optimization for Cancer diagnosis. *IEEE Access : Practical Innovations, Open Solutions, 11*, 113526–113542. DOI: 10.1109/ACCESS.2023.3318261

Teferra, D. (2021). The function of the African intellectual diaspora in advancing higher education. Interregional stateal Journal of African Higher Education, 8(2), 1-9.

Webster, N. (2023). Shaping spaces: governance and climate-related mobility in Ethiopia. Climate and Advancement, 1-11

KEY DEFINITIONS AND DEFINITIONS

Community related to traders: An community related to traders is the self-run structure of venture capitalists, things, and circumstances that all work together to encourage and peripheral bricolages in a related setting (Bitew et al, 2024). This engages a sort of related customers, comprises profit partners, traders, institutional setup, educational institutions, and peripheral clusters. A supportive community related to traders incubates frugal innovation, incubate, and strategic fiscal growth (Nigusie, 2024).

Diaspora Bricolage: It talks about to the entrepreneurial bricolages of individuals who have left their native country and seek to establish, fund, or peripheral businesses there or in other locations where their cultural heritage is evident. Diaspora individuals often have distinct perspectives, networks, and resources that they can use in this kind of bricolages because of their global experiences (Gjorduni, 2023). "Diaspora" comes from the Greek word "diaspeirein," which means "to scatter about." It has historically been used, especially in association to Jewish communities, to characterize the dispersion of a population from their ancestral country. The phrase now refers to a wider sort of immigrant clusters with continued ties to their domestic business areas. The idea of diaspora bricolages first surfaced in the latter half of the 20th century and gained popularity at the same time as globalization, which allowed for greater cross-border connectivity and mobility (Halefom, 2022).

Institutional Framework: The institutions, conventions, and formal and informal rules that control interactions and conduct in a given setting are all included in the framework of institution. It consists of the rules, regulations, and institutional procedures that mold political, social, and fiscal activity. An efficient framework of institution is essential for giving traders the assistance and direction they need to succeed in the setting of diaspora bricolages (Nigusie, 2024).

Institutional Peripheral: Peripheral of institutions refers to the aid offered by institutional, non-institutional, and community clusters to facilitate entrepreneurial operations. This peripheral can come in a number of forms, such as grants, counseling, education, and networking opportunities. Institutional assistance in the context of diaspora bricolages seeks to establish a peripheral atmosphere that attends to the particular difficulties that diaspora entrepreneur's encounter (Gjorduni, (2023).

Mediating Function: Through mediating functions a variable transforms the impact of one variable into changes observed in another variable through a third variable. A mediating function works like a explanatory chain which reveals how a first variable impacts a second variable. Education functions as a mediator which explains the mechanism through which people develop useful skills that produce better employment prospects.

Path Coefficients: The numerical representation of directional effects between model variables uses path coefficients as measurement units. The indicators provide information about the magnitude in which variables influence each other. Path coefficients in structural modeling display a positive linkage between increasing variables yet show negative changes between rising variables. Researcher understanding of model dynamics results from these coefficient values.

Social Capital: The networks, associations, and social connections that venture capitalists can use to get access to opportunities and resources are referred to as social capital. It includes social interactions, customs, and trust that promote cooperation and teamwork among venture capitalists. When it comes to diaspora bricolages, social capital may be extremely imperative in helping business owners overcome obstacles and take advantage of possibilities back native (Nigusie, 2024).

Compilation of References

Abbas, M., & Duchesne, E. (2023). Beyond the Failure of the WTO: Resilience of Trade Multilateralism. In *Crisis of Multilateralism? Challenges and Resilience* (pp. 199–218). Springer International Publishing. DOI: 10.1007/978-3-031-39671-7_10

Abbott, K. W., Green, J. F., & Keohane, R. O. (2016). Organizational ecology and institutional change in global governance. *International Organization*, *70*(2), 247–277. DOI: 10.1017/S0020818315000338

Abou Ali, A. A. K. (2024). DeFi era: The behavioral intentions toward cryptocurrency in Lebanon. *Innovation & Management Review*, *21*(4), 274–285. DOI: 10.1108/INMR-02-2023-0022

Achter, B. (2021). Regulating autonomous weapons: Ethical implications and international legal frameworks. *Journal of Military Ethics*, *20*(1), 15–34.

Adams, B., Daley, M., & Liu, Z. (2020). Uniswap and the Future of Decentralized Exchanges. *Journal of Cryptocurrency Research*, *4*(2), 112–121.

Adams, S., Smith, A., & Lee, C. (2020). *Uniswap: Decentralized Exchange Protocol*. Blockchain Review Journal.

Adesina, O. S. (2017). Foreign policy in an era of digital diplomacy. *Cogent Social Sciences*, *3*(1), 1297175. DOI: 10.1080/23311886.2017.1297175

Adhikari, R. (2025). Economic Security at the Pivot of National Security: Foresight into Nepal's Headway. *Unity Journal*, *6*(1), 18–33. DOI: 10.3126/unityj.v6i1.75545

Adula, M., Birbirsa, Z. A., & Kant, S. (2023). The influence of interpersonal, problem solving and technical training skills on performance of Ethiopia textile industry: Continuance, normative and influenceive commitment as mediators. *Cogent Business & Management*, *10*(3), 2286672. Advance online publication. DOI: 10.1080/23311975.2023.2286672

Ahuja, R., & Khandelwal, J. (2023). CHALLENGES, OPPORTUNITIES AND RISK ANALYSIS OF ADOPTION OF DECENTRALIZED FINANCE APPLICATIONS. In *SPECIAL ISSUE ON INNOVATIONS AND TECHNOLOGY IN FINTECH* (pp. 3114–3129). ITFT., DOI: 10.21917/ijsc.2023.0438

Akberdina, V., Lavrikova, Y., & Vlasov, M. (2023). Environmental financing: Does digital economy matter? *Frontiers in Environmental Science*, *11*, 1268286. Advance online publication. DOI: 10.3389/fenvs.2023.1268286

Akhtar, F., Li, J. P., Heyat, M. B. B., Quadri, S. L., Ahmed, S. S., Xiao, Y. U. N., & Haq, A. U. (2019, December). Potential of blockchain technology in digital currency: a review. In *2019 16th International Computer Conference on Wavelet Active Media Technology and Information Processing* (pp. 85-91). IEEE. DOI: 10.1109/ICCWAMTIP47768.2019.9067546

Aktipis, M., & Katwan, R. B. (2021). Data Protection Commissioner v. Facebook Ireland Ltd. and Maximillian Schrems (C.J.E.U.). International Legal Materials, 60(1), 53–75. DOI: 10.1017/ilm.2020.62

Al-Banna, A., Rana, Z. A., Yaqot, M., & Menezes, B. (2023). Interconnectedness between supply chain resilience, Industry 4.0, and investment. *Logistics (Basel)*, *7*(3), 50. DOI: 10.3390/logistics7030050

Alfalla-Luque, R., Luján García, D. E., & Marin-Garcia, J. A. (2023). Supply chain agility and performance: Evidence from a meta-analysis. *International Journal of Operations & Production Management*, *43*(10), 1587–1633. DOI: 10.1108/IJOPM-05-2022-0316

Alfarhan, U. F., Nusair, K., Al-Azri, H., Al-Muharrami, S., & Hua, N. (2022). Measuring the effects of tourists' relative willingness to spend and third-degree price discrimination on inbound tourism expenditure differentials. *Tourism Economics*, *28*(8), 2126–2153. DOI: 10.1177/13548166211030016

Alhasan, W., Wannous, M., Abualkishik, A., Al Nasar, M. R., Ali, L., & Al-Zoubi, H. (2024). An In-Depth Examination of Cybersecurity: Unveiling Contemporary Trends and Recent Advancements in the World of Cyber Threats. *IEEE*. 1-11. http://dx.doi.org/DOI: 10.1109/ICCR61006.2024.10533062

Ali, A. (2016). Decentralized Finance (DeFi) and Its Impact on Traditional Banking Systems: Opportunities, Challenges, and Future Directions. *India Review*, *4*(1), 1–23.

Ali, A. A. A., Udin, Z. B. M., & Abualrejal, H. M. E. (2023). The impact of artificial intelligence and supply chain resilience on the companies' supply chain performance: The moderating role of supply chain dynamism. In Al-Emran, M., Al-Sharafi, M. A., & Shaalan, K. (Eds.), *International Conference on Information Systems and Intelligent Applications* (pp. 17–28). Springer. DOI: 10.1007/978-3-031-16865-9_2

Ali, A., Ismail, I. H. M., & Abulehia, A. (2023). Supply chain resilience and information technology alignment on firm performance. *International Journal of Academic Management Science Research*, *7*(1), 1–11.

Ali, O., Ally, M., Clutterbuck, P., & Dwivedi, Y. (2020). The state of play of blockchain technology in the financial services sector: A systematic literature review. *International Journal of Information Management*, *54*, 102199. DOI: 10.1016/j.ijinfomgt.2020.102199

Altinors, G., & Chryssogelos, A. (2024). Beyond populism and into the state: The political economy of national-conservatism. *British Journal of Politics and International Relations*, *26*(4), 995–1014. DOI: 10.1177/13691481241246538

Alzubaidi, I. B., & Abdullah, A. (2017). Developing a digital currency from an Islamic perspective: Case of blockchain technology. *International Business Research*, *10*(11), 79–87. DOI: 10.5539/ibr.v10n11p79

Amare, T. J., & Honig, B. (2023). Returnee entrepreneurial entry decisions among forced and voluntary returnees in Ethiopia: A comparative investigation. *Africa Journal of Management*, *9*(2), 177–205. DOI: 10.1080/23322373.2023.2187688

Amicelle, A., Aradau, C., & Jeandesboz, J. (2015). Questioning security device:performativity, resistance, politics. *Security Dialogue*, *46*(4), 293–306. DOI: 10.1177/0967010615586964

Amnesty International. (2019). The Role of Artificial Intelligence in Human Rights. Retrieved from https://www.amnesty.org

Ampenberger, M., Hanspal, R., Hochstein, C., Pidun, U., & Ramachandran, S. (2023, March). *Digital Financial Ecosystems: An Opportunity for Banks*. BCG.

Anghel, V., & Jones, E. (2025). The enlargement of international organisations. *West European Politics*, *48*(1), 1–28. DOI: 10.1080/01402382.2024.2311044

An, N., Zhang, J., & Wang, M. (2023). The Everyday Chinese Framing of Africa: A Perspective of Tourism-geopolitical Encounter. *Geopolitics*, *28*(4), 1422–1441. DOI: 10.1080/14650045.2020.1807957

Arendt, H. (2004). *The Origins of Totalitarianism*. Schocken.

Arner, D. W., Buckley, R. P., Zetzsche, D. A., & Veidt, R. (2020). Sustainability, FinTech and Financial Inclusion. *European Business Organization Law Review*, *21*(1), 7–35. DOI: 10.1007/s40804-020-00183-y

Arora, M. K., Lal, S., Singh, B., & Olyaee, M. (2024). Through an Energy Lens: Examining SDGs From a Policy Perspective. In Riswandi, B., Singh, B., Kaunert, C., & Vig, K. (Eds.), *AI Applications for Clean Energy and Sustainability* (pp. 320–343). IGI Global., DOI: 10.4018/979-8-3693-6567-0.ch016

Arquilla, J. (2021). Bitskrieg: The New Challenge of Cyberwarfare. *John Wiley & Sons*. https://www.wiley.com/en-ae/Bitskrieg%3A+The+New+Challenge+of+Cyberwarfare-p-9781509543625

Asefa, K., Kant, D. S., & Debela, K. L. (2023, November). Effect of Transformational Leadership on Organizational Performance: The Mediating Role of Employee Commitment and Expert Systems (AI) Inclusion in Ethiopia. In 2023 International Conference on Communication, Security and Artificial Intelligence (ICCSAI) (pp. 305-310). IEEE.

Ash, J., Kitchin, R. & Leszcynski, A. (2018). 'Digital turn, digital geographies?', Progress inHuman Geography, 42(1), 25-43.

Asian Development Bank. (2019). *Asian Economic Integration Report*. ADB Publications.

Astuti, I. D., Rajab, S., & Setiyouji, D. (2022). Cryptocurrency blockchain technology in the digital revolution era. [ATT]. *Aptisi Transactions on Technopreneurship*, *4*(1), 9–15. DOI: 10.34306/att.v4i1.216

Atkinson, R. D. (2022). *The Case for National Industrial Strategy to Counter China's*. Technological Rise. ITIF.

Atree, M. K., & Tripathy, N. (2025). Cryptocurrency research: Bibliometric review and content analysis. International Review of Economics and Finance, 98(July 2024), 103940. DOI: 10.1016/j.iref.2025.103940

Atzori, L., Iera, A., & Morabito, G. (2010). The Internet of Things: A survey. *Computer Networks*, *54*(15), 2787–2805. DOI: 10.1016/j.comnet.2010.05.010

Auer, R., Frost, J., Gambacorta, L., Monnet, C., Rice, T., & Shin, H. S. (2021). *Central bank digital currencies: motives, economic implications and the research frontier*. DOI: 10.1146/annurev-economics-051420-020324

Auer, R., & Boehme, R. (2020). *The technology of retail central bank digital currency*. BIS Quarterly Review.

Auld, E., & Elfert, M. (2024). The waning legitimacy of international organisations and their promissory visions. *Comparative Education*, *60*(3), 377–400. DOI: 10.1080/03050068.2024.2371271

Avelino, F., Wijsman, K., van Steenbergen, F., Jhagroe, S., Wittmayer, J., Akerboom, S., Bogner, K., Jansen, E. F., Frantzeskaki, N., & Kalfagianni, A. (2024). Just sustainability transitions: Politics, power, and prefiguration in transformative change toward justice and sustainability. *Annual Review of Environment and Resources*, *49*(1), 49. DOI: 10.1146/annurev-environ-112321-081722

Avgouleas, E., & Blair, W. (2024). A critical evaluation of Central Bank Digital Currencies (CBDCs): Payments' final frontier? *Capital Markets Law Journal*, *19*(2), 103–112. DOI: 10.1093/cmlj/kmae002

Awasthi, A., & Nain, A. (2023). *A Study of Issues and Challenges of Global Pilgrimage Tourism*., DOI: 10.4018/978-1-6684-4817-5.ch011

Bachelet, M. J., Becchetti, L., & Manfredonia, S. (2019). The Green Bonds Premium Puzzle: The Role of Issuer Characteristics and Third-Party Verification. *Sustainability 2019, Vol. 11, Page 1098*, *11*(4), 1098. DOI: 10.3390/su11041098

Bahrami, M., Shokouhyar, S., & Seifian, A. (2022). Big data analytics capability and supply chain performance: The mediating roles of supply chain resilience and innovation. *Modern Supply Chain Research and Applications*, *4*(1), 62–84. DOI: 10.1108/MSCRA-11-2021-0021

Baig, K., Saeed, S., Ahmad, T., & Saeed, S. (2025). Examining the Roles of the International Court of Justice and the International Criminal Court in Upholding Global Justice: A Comparative Analysis. *Social Science Review Archives*, *3*(1), 2185–2194. DOI: 10.70670/sra.v3i1.529

Bakare, F. A., Omojola, J., & Iwuh, A. C. (2025). Blockchain and decentralized finance (DEFI): Disrupting traditional banking and financial systems Blockchain and decentralized finance (DEFI): Disrupting traditional banking and financial systems. *World Journal of Advanced Research and Reviews*, *23*(3), 23–27. DOI: 10.30574/wjarr.2024.23.3.2968

Bakreski, O., & Miovska, L. B. (2024). THE POSITION AND ROLE OF STATE AND NON-STATE ACTORS IN THE 21st CENTURY. *Security Dialogue*, *15*(1), 35–49.

Balassa, B. (1961). *The theory of economic integration*. Richard D. Irwin.

Baltagi, B. H. (2021). *Econometric analysis of panel data* (6th ed.). Springer. DOI: 10.1007/978-3-030-53953-5

Banik, N. (2005). Trade integration of BIMSTEC countries: Roadmap, challenges and opportunities. *Journal of Asian Economics*, *16*(4), 672–690.

Bank of Denmark. (2021). *Danmarks National Bank - Analysis*. Bank of Denmark.

Bank of England. (2021, December). *Bank Rate increased to 0.25% - December 2021*. Bank of England.

Bank of Israel. (2018). first page CBDC english.pdf. *BOI*.

Bankins, S., & Formosa, P. (2023). The ethical implications of artificial intelligence (AI) for meaningful work. *Journal of Business Ethics*, *185*(4), 725–742. DOI: 10.1007/s10551-023-05339-7

Bánkuty-Balogh, L. S. (2024). *The intersection of geopolitics and technological innovations: Implications for the Central-European region* [PhD, Budapesti Corvinus Egyetem]. DOI: 10.14267/phd.2024016

Barashok, I. V., Rudenko, L. L., Shumakova, E., & Orlovskaia, I. V. (2021). Digitization: New possibilities for the tourism industry. *IOP Conference Series. Earth and Environmental Science*, *666*(6), 062059. Advance online publication. DOI: 10.1088/1755-1315/666/6/062059

Barnett, M. (2021). International progress, international order, and the liberal international order. *The Chinese Journal of International Politics*, *14*(1), 1–22. DOI: 10.1093/cjip/poaa019

Barro, R. J. (2013). Inflation and economic growth. *Annals of Economics and Finance*, *14*(1), 85–109.

Basholli, F. (2022). Cyber Warfare, a New Aspect of Modern Warfare. International Scientific Journal Security & Future, *5*(2), 72-75. https://www.researchgate.net/publication/371814918_Cyber_warfare_a_new_aspect_of_modern_warfare

Basu, S., & Dutta, D. (2007). Indo-Bangladesh trade relationship: Problems and prospects. *South Asian Survey*, *14*(2), 253–264.

Baycik, N. O., & Gowda, S. (2023). Digitalization of operations and supply chains: Insights from survey and case studies. *Digital Transformation and Society*, *2*(3), 231–245. DOI: 10.1108/DTS-03-2023-0012

Bayram, O., Talay, I., & Feridun, M. (2022). Can Fintech Promote Sustainable Finance? Policy Lessons from the Case of Turkey. *Sustainability 2022, Vol. 14, Page 12414, 14*(19), 12414. DOI: 10.3390/su141912414

Beck, U. (1992). *Risk Society: Towards a New Modernity*. SAGE Publications. Floridi, L., & Cowls, J. (2021). A unified framework of five principles for AI in society.

Behera, L. K. (2023). Securing India: Significance of Geoeconomics and Innovation in India's Foreign Policy and Strategic Competition with China.

Beigbeder, Y. (2023). *The role and status of international humanitarian volunteers and organizations: The right and duty to humanitarian assistance* (Vol. 12). Brill.

Belhadi, A., Mani, V., Kamble, S. S., Khan, S. A. R., & Verma, S. (2024). Artificial intelligence-driven innovation for enhancing supply chain resilience and performance under the effect of supply chain dynamism: An empirical investigation. *Annals of Operations Research*, *333*(2-3), 627–652. DOI: 10.1007/s10479-021-03956-x PMID: 33551534

Belk, R. (2014). You are what you can access: Sharing and collaborative consumption online. Journal of Business Research, 67(8),1595e1600

Bell, D., & Taillandier, A. (2024). Cosmos-Politanism: Transhumanist Visions of Global Order from the First World War to the Digital Age. *Perspectives on Politics*, •••, 1–18. DOI: 10.1017/S1537592724001051

Belucio, M., Fuinhas, J., & Vieira, C. (2023). How does the economy affect a religious phenomenon? A panel approach to international pilgrimages to the Shrine of Fátima. *European Journal of Tourism. Hospitality and Recreation*, *13*(1), 110–124. DOI: 10.2478/ejthr-2023-0010

Bennett, C., & Schroeder, F. (2020). Towards integrated digital governance frameworks. *Global Policy*, *11*(3), 12–25.

Berozashvili, T. (2023). World War 3: The Ethical Dimensions of Information Warfare in The Digital Age. *ResearchGate*. http://dx.doi.org/DOI: 10.13140/RG.2.2.33649.49765

Berten, J. (2022). The future as epistemic condition: How international organisations anticipate futures of social policy. *Global Society*, *36*(2), 206–222. DOI: 10.1080/13600826.2021.2021153

Berten, J., & Kranke, M. (2022). Anticipatory global governance: International organisations and the politics of the future. *Global Society*, *36*(2), 155–169. DOI: 10.1080/13600826.2021.2021150

Bhattacharyay, B. N. (2010). Estimating demand for infrastructure in energy, transport, telecommunications, water, and sanitation in Asia and the Pacific: 2010-2020. *ADBI Working Paper 248*. Asian Development Bank Institute.

Bhombe, S., & Arts, D. S. M. (2023). Consequences, Transformation and Prospects of Crypto Currency in India. Tactful Management Research Journal, 11(3), 0–6.

Bianchi, A. (2017). *Non-state actors and international law*. Routledge. DOI: 10.4324/9781315247885

BIMSTEC. (2020). *BIMSTEC Trade Facilitation Strategic Framework 2030*. BIMSTEC Secretariat.

Binhammad, M., Alqaydi, S., Othman, A., & Abuljadayel, L. H. (2024). The Role of AI in Cyber Security: Safeguarding Digital Identity. *Journal of Information Security*, *15*(2), 245–278. DOI: 10.4236/jis.2024.152015

Birhane, M., Amentie, C., Borji, B., & Kant, S. (2024). Are Ethiopian Coffee Farmers Proficient to Predict Capital Structure with Mediation of AI Based Knowledge Systems and Asset Liquidity?. In AI in Agriculture for Sustainable and Economic Management (pp. 199-215). CRC Press.

Bischoff, O., & Seuring, S. (2021). Opportunities and limitations of public blockchain-based supply chain traceability. *Modern Supply Chain Research and Applications*, *3*(4), 226–243. DOI: 10.1108/MSCRA-07-2021-0014

Bitew, M., Huluka, A., & Takaro, G. (2024). Incubateing inter-sectorial integration: Legal and policy framework for physical infrastructure in Addis Ababa, Ethiopia. Journal of Infrastructure. *Policy and Advancement*, *8*(8), 5956.

Bjola, C., & Holmes, M. (2015). *Digital diplomacy: Theory and practice*. Routledge. DOI: 10.4324/9781315730844

Boikova, T., Zeverte-Rivza, S., Rivza, P., & Rivza, B. (2021). The Determinants and Effects of Competitiveness: The Role of Digitalization in the European Economies. *Sustainability (Basel)*, *13*(21), 11689. DOI: 10.3390/su132111689

Bommer, W. H., Milevoj, E., & Rana, S. (2023). The intention to use cryptocurrency: A meta-analysis of what we know. Emerging Markets Review, 55(September 2022), 100962. DOI: 10.1016/j.ememar.2022.100962

Boot, A., Hoffmann, P., Laeven, L., & Ratnovski, L. (2020). Financial Intermediation and Technology. *IMF Working Paper*, *20*(161). Advance online publication. DOI: 10.5089/9781513552491.001

Borensztein, E., De Gregorio, J., & Lee, J. W. (1998). How does foreign direct investment affect economic growth? *Journal of International Economics*, *45*(1), 115–135. DOI: 10.1016/S0022-1996(97)00033-0

Boshkov, T. (2018). Blockchain and digital currency in the world of finance. *Blockchain and cryptocurrencies*.

Breidbach, C. F., Keating, B. W., & Lim, C. (2020). Fintech: Research directions to explore the digital transformation of financial service systems. *Journal of Service Theory and Practice*, *30*(1), 79–102. DOI: 10.1108/JSTP-08-2018-0185

Broeders, D., De Busser, E., Cristiano, F., & Tropina, T. (2022). Revisiting Past Cyber Operations in Light of New Cyber Norms and Interpretations of International Law: Inching Towards Lines in the Sand? *Journal of Cyber Policy*, *7*(1), 97–135. DOI: 10.1080/23738871.2022.2041061

Bromley, P., Overbey, L., Furuta, J., & Kijima, R. (2021). Education reform in the twenty-first century: Declining emphases in international organisation reports, 1998–2018. *Globalisation, Societies and Education*, *19*(1), 23–40. DOI: 10.1080/14767724.2020.1816159

Brown, O. R. (2024). The Underside of Order: Race in the Constitution of International Order. *International Organization*, *78*(1), 38–66. DOI: 10.1017/S0020818324000018

Brynjolfsson, E., & McAfee, A. (2014). *The second machine age: Work, progress, and prosperity in a time of brilliant technologies*. W.W. Norton & Company.

Buchan, R., & Navarrete, I. (2021). Cyber Espionage and International Law. *Edward Elgar Publishing*. 231-252. https://doi.org/DOI: 10.4337/9781789904253.00021

Budiana, M. (2024). Global Governance: The Role of International Institutions in the 21st Century. Journal of Law. *Social Science and Humanities*, *1*(2), 204–219.

Budovich, L. (2023). The impact of religious tourism on the economy and tourism industry. *Hervormde Teologiese Studies*, *79*(1). Advance online publication. DOI: 10.4102/hts.v79i1.8607

Buhalis, D., & Amaranggana, A. (2015). Smart tourism destinations. In Schegg, R., & Stangl, B. (Eds.), *Information and communication technologies in tourism 2015* (pp. 553–564). Springer.

Burrows, R. (2012). Living with the H-index? Metric Assemblages in the Contemporary Academy. *The Sociological Review*, *60*(2), 355–372. DOI: 10.1111/j.1467-954X.2012.02077.x

Burton-Jones, A. (1999). *Knowledge Capitalism: The New Learning Economy*. Oxford University Press. DOI: 10.1093/acprof:oso/9780198296225.001.0001

Busch, L. (2017). *Knowledge for Sale: The neoliberal takeover of Higher Education*. MIT Press. DOI: 10.7551/mitpress/10742.001.0001

Bussolati, N. (2015). 'The Rise of Non-State Actors in Cyberwarfare'. *Oxford University Press,* 102-126. https://papers.ssrn.com/sol3/papers.cfm?abstract_id=2764185

Buterin, V. (2014). *Ethereum White Paper: A Next-Generation Smart Contract and Decentralized Application Platform*. Ethereum Foundation.

Buterin, V. (2016). *The DAO Hack and the Future of Ethereum*. Ethereum Foundation Blog.

Buterin, V. (2016). *The DAO: A Decentralized Autonomous Organization*. Ethereum Foundation.

Buterin, V. (2020). *The Future of Ethereum and Layer 2 Solutions*. Ethereum Foundation.

Campanella, F., Serino, L., & Crisci, A. (2022). Governing Fintech for sustainable development: evidence from Italian banking system. *Qualitative Research in Financial Markets*, 1755–4179. DOI: 10.1108/QRFM-01-2022-0009

Campbell-Verduyn, M. (2023). Understanding emergent technology, instability and power in international political economy. In *Handbook on the Politics and Governance of Big Data and Artificial Intelligence* (pp. 188–210). Edward Elgar Publishing., DOI: 10.4337/9781800887374.00018

Castro-Gómez, S. (2008). (Post)Coloniality for Dummies: Latin American Perspectives onModernity, Coloniality, and the Geopolitics of Knowledge. In Moraña, M., Dussel, E., & Jáuregui, C. (Eds.), *Coloniality at Large*. Duke University Press.

Castro-Gómez, S. (2021). 'Coloniality as a Relationship and Bloog Cleansing: A brief Studyon the Contributions of Santiago Castro-Gómez', Journal of Philosophy. *Letters and Humanities*, *25*(80), 160–174.

Cavelty, M. D. (2024). *The Politics of Cyber-security*. Taylor & Francis., DOI: 10.4324/9781003497080

Cave, S., & Dignum, V. (2019). The regulatory challenges of AI and machine learning. *Journal of Technology Policy*, *28*(2), 34–45.

Cen, T., & He, R. (2018). Fintech, Green Finance and Sustainable Development. *Advances in Social Science, Education and Humanities Research*, •••, 291.

Chainalysis (2020). The 2020 Crypto Crime Report. Chainalysis.

Chakraborty, D. (2007). BIMSTEC FTA: Prospects of trade under the proposed framework. *RIS Discussion Paper*, 135, 1-42.

Chatterjee, S., & Chaudhuri, R. (2022). Supply chain sustainability during turbulent environment: Examining the role of firm capabilities and government regulation. *Operations Management Research : Advancing Practice Through Research, 15*(3-4), 1081–1095. DOI: 10.1007/s12063-021-00203-1

Check, T. (2022). The Tallinn Manual 2.0 on Nation-State Cyber Operations Affecting Critical Infrastructure. *WCL Journals & Law Reviews, 13*, 1. https://digitalcommons.wcl.american.edu/nslb/vol13/iss1/1/

Cheng, D. (2020). Techno-nationalism and the global race for AI supremacy. *Harvard Journal of International Affairs, 30*(1), 12–23.

Cheng, D. S. (2014). Contributions of International Organizations towards Globalization in the 21st Century. *Journal of Global Business Management, 10*(2), 94.

Chiu, J., & Keister, T. (2022). The economics of digital currencies: Progress and open questions . *Journal of Economic Dynamics & Control, 142*, 104496. DOI: 10.1016/j.jedc.2022.104496

Choe, J. (2024). Religious tourism. *Tourism Geographies*, •••, 1–10. DOI: 10.1080/14616688.2024.2423168

Circle. (2020). *USDC: The Digital Dollar*. Circle.

Clark, R., Reed, J., & Sunderland, T. (2018). Bridging funding gaps for climate and sustainable development: Pitfalls, progress and potential of private finance. *Land Use Policy, 71*, 335–346. DOI: 10.1016/j.landusepol.2017.12.013

CoinMarketCap (2021). Bitcoin Price Index. CoinMarketCap.

Cold War | Summary, Causes, History, Years, Timeline, & Facts | Britannica. (n.d.). Retrieved June 25, 2024, from https://www.britannica.com/event/Cold-War

Conde, A., & Belén, A. (2020). On the Effect of Green Bonds on the Profitability and Credit Quality of Project Financing. *Sustainability (Basel), 12*(16), 6695. DOI: 10.3390/su12166695

Cong, L. W., Li, X., Tang, K., & Yang, Y. (2022). Crypto Wash Trading. In *NBER*. DOI: 10.3386/w30783

Creemers, R. (2018). China's Social Credit System: An Evolving Practice of Control. *SSRN*. DOI: 10.2139/ssrn.3175792

Creswell, J. (2015). *30 essential skills for the qualitative researcher*. SAGE.

Criekemans, D. (2022). *Geopolitics and International Relations: Grounding World Politics Anew*. Brill | Nijhoff. DOI: 10.1163/9789004432086

Crouhy, M., Galai, D., & Wiener, Z. (2021). The Impact of Fintechs on Financial Intermediation: A Functional Approach. Https://Doi.Org/10.1142/S270510992031001X, *01*(01), 2031001. DOI: 10.1142/S270510992031001X

Cui, Y., Guo, M., Ma, G., Wang, J., & Su, X. (2024). The dual engines of political stability and digital technology: An international political economy analysis based on the green trade and climate change reversal mechanism in RCEP countries. *Energy & Environment*, *15*(1), 1–20. DOI: 10.1177/0958305X241300493

Cybercrime Module 8 Key Issues: International Cooperation on Cybersecurity Matters. (n.d.). Retrieved January 16, 2025, from https://www.unodc.org/e4j/ar/cybercrime/module-8/key-issues/international-cooperation-on-cybersecurity-matters.html

Cybercrime Treaty, U. N. *The Year Cyber and Multilateralism Stole the Show - Indian Council of World Affairs (Government of India)*. (n.d.). Retrieved January 16, 2025, from https://www.icwa.in/show_content.php?lang=1&level=1&ls_id=12242&lid=7470

Cybersecurity and the Concept of Norms | Carnegie Endowment for International Peace. (n.d.). Retrieved January 16, 2025, from https://carnegieendowment.org/research/2017/11/cybersecurity-and-the-concept-of-norms?lang=en

Cyberspace and Geopolitics: Assessing Global Cybersecurity Norm Processes at a Crossroads - Carnegie Endowment for International Peace. (n.d.). Retrieved June 25, 2024, from https://carnegieendowment.org/research/2020/02/cyberspace-and-geopolitics-assessing-global-cybersecurity-norm-processes-at-a-crossroads?lang=en

Cyberspace and Geopolitics: Assessing Global Cybersecurity Norm Processes at a Crossroads | Carnegie Endowment for International Peace. (n.d.). Retrieved January 16, 2025, from https://carnegieendowment.org/research/2020/02/cyberspace-and-geopolitics-assessing-global-cybersecurity-norm-processes-at-a-crossroads?lang=en

Dai, J., & Azhar, A. (2024). Collaborative governance in disaster management and sustainable development. *Public Administration and Development*, *44*(4), 358–380. DOI: 10.1002/pad.2071

Dani, A. A. H., Supangkat, S. H., Lubis, F. F., Nugraha, I. G. B. B., Kinanda, R., & Rizkia, I. (2023). Development of a Smart City Platform Based on Digital Twin Technology for Monitoring and Supporting Decision-Making. *Sustainability (Basel)*, *15*(18), 14002. DOI: 10.3390/su151814002

Darko, D., Zhu, D., Quayson, M., Hossin, M. A., Omoruyi, O., & Bediako, A. K. (2023). A multicriteria decision framework for governance of PPP projects towards sustainable development. *Socio-Economic Planning Sciences*, *87*, 101580. DOI: 10.1016/j.seps.2023.101580

Data, R. K. (2018). China's New Generation AI Development Plan 2017–2030. *Journal of Digital Policy*, *5*(2), 45–67.

Datta, A. (2017). The digital turn in postcolonial urbanism: Smart citizenship in the makingof India's 100 smart cities. *Transactions of the Institute of British Geographers*, *4*(3), 405–419. DOI: 10.1111/tran.12225

David, A., Yigitcanlar, T., Li, R. Y. M., Corchado, J. M., Cheong, P. H., Mossberger, K., & Mehmood, R. (2023). Understanding Local Government Digital Technology Adoption Strategies: A PRISMA Review. *Sustainability (Basel)*, *15*(12), 9645. DOI: 10.3390/su15129645

Davis, E. V. W. (2021). *Shadow Warfare: Cyberwar Policy in the United States, Russia and China*. Rowman & Littlefield. https://rowman.com/ISBN/9781538149683/Shadow-Warfare-Cyberwar-Policy-in-the-United-States-Russia-and-China

De Boeck, K., Besiou, M., Decouttere, C., Rafter, S., Vandaele, N., Van Wassenhove, L. N., & Yadav, P. (2023). Data, analytical techniques and collaboration between researchers and practitioners in humanitarian health supply chains: A challenging but necessary way forward. *Journal of Humanitarian Logistics and Supply Chain Management*, *13*(3), 237–248. DOI: 10.1108/JHLSCM-07-2022-0078

de Medeiros, C. A. (2025). *The Political Economy of US Geopolitical Strategy towards China* (Doctoral dissertation, Instituto de Economia, Universidade Federal do Rio de Janeiro).

Deepu, T. S., & Ravi, V. (2023). A review of literature on implementation and operational dimensions of supply chain digitalization: Framework development and future research directions. *International Journal of Information Management Data Insights*, *3*(1), 100156. DOI: 10.1016/j.jjimei.2023.100156

Denters, E., Ginther, K., & de Waart, P. J. (Eds.). (2023). *Sustainable development and good governance*. Martinus Nijhoff Publishers.

Dereso, C. W., Kant, S., Muthuraman, M., & Tufa, G. (2023). Influence of Point of Service on Health Department Student's Creativity in Comprehensive Universities of Ethiopia: Moderating Role of Public-Private Partnership and Mediating Role of Work Place Learning. In: Jain, S., Groppe, S., Mihindukulasooriya, N. (eds) Proceedings of the International Health Informatics Conference. Lecture Notes in Electrical Engineering, vol 990. Springer, Singapore. https://doi.org/DOI: 10.1007/978-981-19-9090-8_13

Digital India. (2020). Digital India Initiative. Retrieved from https://www.digitalindia.gov.in

Digital Infrastructure and Cyber War: The New Front of International Law – Jindal Forum for International and Economic Laws. (n.d.). Retrieved January 16, 2025, from https://jindalforinteconlaws.in/2024/11/19/digital-infrastructure-and-cyber-war-the-new-front-of-international-law/

Dorfleitner, G., & Braun, D. (2019). Fintech, Digitalization and Blockchain: Possible Applications for Green Finance. In Migliorelli, M., & Dessertine, P. (Eds.), *The Rise of Green Finance in Europe* (pp. 207–237). Palgrave Macmillan., DOI: 10.1007/978-3-030-22510-0_9

Douzet, F., & Gery, A. (2021). Cyberspace is used, first and foremost, to wage wars: Proliferation, security, and stability in cyberspace. *Journal of Cyber Policy*, *6*(1), 96–113. DOI: 10.1080/23738871.2021.1937253

Downey, L. (2025). Coercing finance to fund decarbonization: The democratic case for coercion in funding the green transformation. *Review of International Political Economy*, *32*(3), 1–22. DOI: 10.1080/09692290.2025.2471854

Du, M. (2025). The Belt and Road Initiative and National Economic Development: A Multidimensional Power Analysis. *Journal of Chinese Political Science*, •••, 1–29. DOI: 10.1007/s11366-025-09912-x

Dunford, M., Aoyama, Y., Campolina Diniz, C., Kundu, A., Limonov, L., Lin, G., Liu, W., Park, S. O., & Turok, I. (2016). Area development and policy: An agenda for the 21st century. *Area Development and Policy*, *1*(1), 1–14. DOI: 10.1080/23792949.2016.1158621

Dunoff, J. L. (2012). Is sovereign equality obsolete? Understanding twenty-first century international organizations. *Netherlands Yearbook of International Law*, *43*, 99–127. DOI: 10.1007/978-90-6704-915-3_5

Dupont, C. (2020). Digital trade and regulatory divergence in free trade agreements. *Journal of World Trade*, *54*(1), 123–144.

Durga, P., Godavarthi, D., Kant, S., & Basa, S. S. (2024). Aspect-based drug review classification through a hybrid model with ant colony optimization using deep learning. *Discov Computing*, *27*(1), 19. DOI: 10.1007/s10791-024-09441-w

Dwivedi, Y. K., Kshetri, N., Hughes, L., Slade, E. L., Jeyaraj, A., Kar, A. K., Baabdullah, A. M., Koohang, A., Raghavan, V., Ahuja, M., Albanna, H., Albashrawi, M. A., Al-Busaidi, A. S., Balakrishnan, J., Barlette, Y., Basu, S., Bose, I., Brooks, L., Buhalis, D., & Wright, R. (2023). Opinion Paper: "So what if ChatGPT wrote it?" Multidisciplinary perspectives on opportunities, challenges and implications of generative conversational AI for research, practice and policy. *International Journal of Information Management*, *71*, 102642. DOI: 10.1016/j.ijinfomgt.2023.102642

Dychkovskyy, S., & Ivanov, S. (2020). Festival Tourism as Part of International Tourism and a Factor in the Development of Cultural Tourism. *Informacijos Mokslai*, *89*, 73–82. DOI: 10.15388/Im.2020.89.41

Dynamics of the Changing Global Security Order: Emerging Trends and Key Issues in Asia - 9781666949131. (n.d.). Retrieved June 25, 2024, from https://rowman.com/ISBN/9781666949131/Dynamics-of-the-Changing-Global-Security-Order-Emerging-Trends-and-Key-Issues-in-Asia

Ebner, N. (2024). From Paso del Norte to the Borderplex: Labor Devaluation, Bordering, and the Remaking of Uneven Development in the US–Mexico Borderlands. *Economic Geography*, *100*(4), 351–376. DOI: 10.1080/00130095.2024.2385527

Economy, E. (2024). China's Alternative Order: And What America Should Learn From It. *Foreign Affairs*, *103*, 8.

Edelman, R. D. (2024). *Rethinking Cyber Warfare: The International Relations of Digital Disruption*. Oxford University Press., DOI: 10.1093/9780197509715.001.0001

Edwards, S. (1998). Openness, productivity and growth: What do we really know? *Economic Journal (London)*, *108*(447), 383–398. DOI: 10.1111/1468-0297.00293

Eichensehr, K. E. (2022). Ukraine, Cyberattacks, and the Lessons for International Law. *AJIL Unbound*, *116*, 145–149. DOI: 10.1017/aju.2022.20

Eich, S. (2024). Derisking as worldmaking: Keynes, climate, and the politics of radical uncertainty. *Review of International Political Economy*.

Elijah, O., Rahman, T. A., Orikumhi, I., Leow, C. Y., & Hindia, M. N. (2018). An overview of Internet of Things (IoT) and data analytics in agriculture: Benefits and challenges. *IEEE Internet of Things Journal*, *5*(5), 3758–3773. DOI: 10.1109/JIOT.2018.2844296

Espeland, W. N., & Sauder, M. (2016). *Engines of Anxiety: Academic rankings, reputation,and accountability*. Russell Sage Foundation.

Estevens, J. (2024). International Relations Theories and the Impact of the Fourth Industrial Revolution on Global Affairs. In *International Relations and Technological Revolution 4.0: World Order, Power and New International Society* (pp. 9–24). Springer Nature Switzerland. DOI: 10.1007/978-3-031-66750-3_2

Eubanks, V. (2018). *Automating Inequality: How high-tech tools profile, police and punish the poor*. St. Martin's Press.

European Commission. (2021). Artificial Intelligence Act Proposal. Retrieved from https://ec.europa.eu

European Commission. (2021). *Coordinated Plan on Artificial Intelligence 2021*. Digital Europe Programme.

European Union. (2016). Regulation (EU) 2016/679 (General Data Protection Regulation). Official Journal of the European Union.

European Union. (2018). General Data Protection Regulation (GDPR). Retrieved from https://gdpr.eu

European Union. (2020). The Digital Single Market Strategy for Europe. Retrieved from https://ec.europa.eu/digital-strategy

Evans, C., Rees, G., Taylor, C., & Fox, S. (2021). 'A liberal higher education for all? The massification of higher education and its implications for graduates' participation in civil society'. *Higher Education*, *81*(3), 521–535. DOI: 10.1007/s10734-020-00554-x

Facer, K. & Selwyn, N. (2021). Digital technology and the futures of education—towards 'non-stupid' optimism. Paper commission for the UNESCO Futures of Education report(forthcoming, 2021).

Farid, C. (2024). Comments on# Help: Digital Humanitarianism and the Remaking of the International Legal Order. *Int'l Trade & Bus. L. Rev.*, *24*, 111.

Feng, E. (2020). US-China tech tensions: The battle for control of the future. *Foreign Affairs*, *99*(6), 45–58.

Feng, S., Chong, Y., Yu, H., Ye, X., & Li, G. (2022). Digital financial development and ecological footprint: Evidence from green-biased technology innovation and environmental inclusion. *Journal of Cleaner Production*, *380*, 135069. DOI: 10.1016/j.jclepro.2022.135069

Feyen, E., Frost, J., Gambacorta, L., Natarajan, H., & Saal, M. (2021). *BIS Papers No 117 Fintech and the digital transformation of financial services: implications for market structure and public policy.*

Finnemore, M., & Hollis, D. B. (2019). Beyond Naming and Shaming: Accusations and International Law in Cybersecurity. SSRN *Electronic Journal*. https://doi.org/ DOI: 10.2139/SSRN.3347958

Fischer, S. (1993). The role of macroeconomic factors in growth. *Journal of Monetary Economics*, *32*(3), 485–512. DOI: 10.1016/0304-3932(93)90027-D

Fontenelle, A. L., Peyerl, D., Zacharias, L. G. L., Ciotta, M., & Moretto, E. M. (2023). The role of the Sustainable Development Goals for better governance of Carbon Capture and Storage (CCS). *Desenvolvimento e Meio Ambiente*, *62*, 478–498. DOI: 10.5380/dma.v62i0.82216

Frankel, J. A., & Romer, D. (1999). Does trade cause growth? *The American Economic Review*, *89*(3), 379–399. DOI: 10.1257/aer.89.3.379

Gartzke, E. (2020). The cybersecurity arms race: State competition in the age of AI. *International Security Review*, *45*(3), 99–118.

Geopolitical Cyber Risk: Cyber Operations in Modern Warfare | by Robindimyan | Medium. (n.d.). Retrieved June 25, 2024, from https://robindimyan.medium.com/geopolitical-cyber-risk-cyber-operations-in-modern-warfare-db1392ab0df5

Geopolitical Factors Shaping the Future of the Cyber Domain - Critical Start. (n.d.). Retrieved January 16, 2025, from https://www.criticalstart.com/geopolitical-factors-shaping-the-future-of-the-cyber-domain/

Ghazawneh, A., & Henfridsson, O. (2015). A paradigmatic analysis of digital application marketplaces. Journal of Information Technology, 30(3), 198e208.

Ghozali, M., Afra, C., Agusriadi, D., & Yusfani, M. (2025). The Position and Role of the International Criminal Court (ICC) In International Crime Resolution. *International Journal of Law, Social Science, and Humanities*, *2*(1), 111–116. DOI: 10.70193/ijlsh.v2i1.160

Gillen, J. (2024). Tourism geopolitics: Roots and branches. *Tourism Geographies*, •••, 1–11. DOI: 10.1080/14616688.2024.2332354

Gillespie, T. (2014). The relevance of algorithms. In Gillespie, T., Boczkowski, P. J., & Foot, K. A. (Eds.), *Media technologies: Essays on communication, materiality, and society* (pp. 167–194). MIT Press. DOI: 10.7551/mitpress/9042.003.0013

Girard, T. (2024). The Global Political Economy of Digital Technology. *180 Day Access Global Political Economy*, 405.

Girard, T. (2024). National Identity and the Limits of Platform Power in the Global Economy. *International Studies Quarterly*, *68*(3), sqae090. DOI: 10.1093/isq/sqae090

Girma, H., & Abebe, A. (2023). Outsiders within: Examining Ethiopian adoptee experiences through a diasporic lens. *Journal of Ethnic and Migration Studies*, ●●●, 1–18.

Gjesvik, L., & Willers, J. O. (2024). Beyond control? The political economy of private interception, intrusion, and surveillance markets. *Review of International Political Economy*, *31*(6), 1840–1864. DOI: 10.1080/09692290.2024.2375499

Gjorduni, F. (2023). Diaspora Influence on Foreign Direct Investment: State Institutions on Diaspora Engagement. *European Journal of Marketing and Fiscals*, *6*(1), 49–69.

Global New Light of Myanmar. (2024, October 29). *Diplomacy in the Digital Age: How Social Media is Transforming Global Politics*. https://www.gnlm.com.mm/diplomacy-in-the-digital-age-how-social-media-is-transforming-global-politics/ Global New Light of Myanmar

Global Trade. Perspectives from the U.S. and China. Harvard Business Review. European Union. (2020). Digital Single Market Strategy for Europe. Retrieved from https://ec.europa.eu/digital-strategy

Góes, C., & Bekkers, E. (2022). The impact of geopolitical conflicts on trade, growth, and innovation. arXiv preprint arXiv:2203.12173. https://arxiv.org/abs/2203.12173

Goforth, C. (2018). Cryptocurrencies and Financial Empowerment: The Role of Bitcoin in Emerging Economies. *Journal of Financial Innovation*, *6*(2), 112–125.

Goforth, J. (2018). The Role of Stablecoins in the Future of Finance. *Journal of Financial Technology*, *12*(2), 105–120.

Goforth, J. (2018). Venezuela's Struggle with Hyperinflation and the Rise of Cryptocurrencies. *Journal of Latin American Economics*, *45*(2), 123–140.

Gohwong, S. (2019). Government-based Cryptocurrencies. *Asian Political Science Review*, *3*(2), 40–46.

Gohwong, S. (2023). KAKISTOSCRYPTOCRACY. *Asian Political Science Review*, *7*(1), 50–58.

González, J. L., & Jouanjean, M.-A. (2017). Digital trade: Developing a framework for analysis. OECD Trade Policy Papers. https://ideas.repec.org/p/oec/traaab/205-en.html

Gore, E. (2024). Towards a trans-inclusive critical international political economy? Or why trans oppression matters for understanding capitalism and social reproduction. *Capital and Class*, •••, 03098168241232371.

Graave, E. J. E. (2017). *The Economic Impact of Pilgrimage: An economic impact analysis of pilgrimage expenditures in Galicia. 5.*

Gramlich, V., Guggenberger, T., Principato, M., Schellinger, B., & Urbach, N. (2023). A multivocal literature review of decentralized finance: Current knowledge and future research avenues. Electronic Markets (Vol. 33). Springer Berlin Heidelberg. DOI: 10.1007/s12525-023-00637-4

Gubbi, J., Buyya, R., Marusic, S., & Palaniswami, M. (2013). Internet of Things (IoT): A vision, architectural elements, and future directions. *Future Generation Computer Systems*, *29*(7), 1645–1660. DOI: 10.1016/j.future.2013.01.010

Guriţă, D., & Scortescu, F. I. (2023). Religious Tourism and Sustainable Development of the Economy in the Context of Globalization in the Northeast Area of Romania. *Sustainability (Basel)*, *15*(16), 16. Advance online publication. DOI: 10.3390/su151612128

Gurung, A. (2025). From Battlefield to the Servers: Cyber Warfare and the Conflicts. *The Shivapuri Journal*, *26*(1), 29–41. DOI: 10.3126/shivapuri.v26i1.75831

Guster, D., & Brown, C. (2012). The application of business intelligence to higher education:technical and managerial perspectives. *Technical and Managerial Perspectives*, *23*(2), 42–62.

Halefom, A. (2022). Integrating Traditional and State Institutions for Conflict Prevention: Institutional, Legal and Policy Frameworks in Ethiopia. *Mizan Law Review*, *16*(2), 339–368. DOI: 10.4314/mlr.v16i2.4

Hallikas, J., Immonen, M., & Brax, S. (2021). Digitalizing procurement: The impact of data analytics on supply chain performance. *Supply Chain Management*, *26*(5), 629–646. DOI: 10.1108/SCM-05-2020-0201

Hall, J., & Stokel-Walker, C. (2019). Data-driven tourism governance and urban planning. *Urban Studies (Edinburgh, Scotland)*, *56*(9), 1823–1840.

Hamilton, D. L., & Gifford, R. K. (1976). Illusory correlation in interpersonal perception: A cognitive basis of stereotypic judgments. *Journal of Experimental Social Psychology, 12*(4), 392–407. DOI: 10.1016/S0022-1031(76)80006-6

Hammersley, M., & Atkinson, P. (2007). *Ethnography: principles in practice*. Tavistock Publications Ltd.

Haraway, D. (1988). Situated knowledges: The science question in feminism and the privilege of partial perspective. *Feminist Studies, 14*(3), 575–599. DOI: 10.2307/3178066

Harvard Data Science Review, 3(1). Milanesi, C. (2023). *Gaia-X and Europe's Digital Sovereignty Aspirations*. Forrester Research.

Harvey, D. (2014). *Seventeen Contradictions and the End of Capitalism*. OxfordUniversity Press.

Hassid, N. (2024). The rise of companies in the cyber era and the pursuant shift in national security. SSRN *Electronic Journal*. https://doi.org/DOI: 10.2139/SSRN.4842383

Hatamlah, H., Allahham, M., Abu-AlSondos, I. A., Al-junaidi, A., Al-Anati, G. M., & Al-Shaikh, M. (2023). The role of business intelligence adoption as a mediator of big data analytics in the management of outsourced reverse supply chain operations. *Applied Mathematics & Information Sciences, 17*(5), 897–903. DOI: 10.18576/amis/170516

Hatamlah, H., Allan, M., Abu-Alsondos, I., Shehadeh, M., & Allahham, M. (2023). The role of artificial intelligence in supply chain analytics during the pandemic. *Uncertain Supply Chain Management, 11*(3), 1175–1186. DOI: 10.5267/j.uscm.2023.4.005

Haug, S., Foot, R., & Baumann, M. O. (2024). Power shifts in international organisations: China at the United Nations. *Global Policy, 15*(S2), 5–17. DOI: 10.1111/1758-5899.13368

Hausman, J. A. (1978). Specification tests in econometrics. *Econometrica, 46*(6), 1251–1271. DOI: 10.2307/1913827

Hawlitschek, F., Notheisen, B., & Teubner, T. (2018). The limits of trust-free systems: A literature review on blockchain technology and trust in the sharing economy. Electronic Commerce Research and Applications, 29,50e63

Hayes, A., & Tasca, P. (2016). Blockchain and Crypto-currencies. *The FinTech Book: The Financial Technology Handbook for Investors, Entrepreneurs and Visionaries*, 217-220.

Heiret, Y. S. (2024). The landlord state goes abroad: The remaking of the Norwegian 'Energy Nation'as a global rentier. *Environment and Planning A. Economy and Space*, *56*(7), 1985–2002.

Herold, D. M., Nowicka, K., Pluta-Zaremba, A., & Kummer, S. (2021). COVID-19 and the pursuit of supply chain resilience: Reactions and "lessons learned" from logistics service providers (LSPs). *Supply Chain Management*, *26*(6), 702–714. DOI: 10.1108/SCM-09-2020-0439

Hilgert, J. (2025). Geopolitics and industrial relations theory: Intellectual history and future reconfigurations. *Globalizations*, *22*(4), 634–651. DOI: 10.1080/14747731.2024.2401691

Hinson, R., Lensink, R., & Mueller, A. (2019). Transforming agribusiness in developing countries: SDGs and the role of FinTech. *Current Opinion in Environmental Sustainability*, *41*, 1–9. DOI: 10.1016/j.cosust.2019.07.002

Hoang, T. G., Nguyen, G. N. T., & Le, D. A. (2022). Developments in Financial Technologies for Achieving the Sustainable Development Goals (SDGs): FinTech and SDGs. In https://services.igi-global.com/resolvedoi/resolve.aspx?doi=10.4018/978-1-7998-8900-7.ch001 (pp. 1–19). IGI Global. DOI: 10.4018/978-1-7998-8900-7.ch001

Hopewell, K. (2024). The (surprise) return of development policy space in the multilateral trading system: What the WTO Appellate Body blockage means for the developmental state. *Review of International Political Economy*, *31*(4), 1245–1270. DOI: 10.1080/09692290.2024.2303681

Horowitz, M. C. (2024). Battles of Precise Mass: Technology Is Remaking War-and America Must Adapt. *Foreign Affairs*, *103*, 34.

Hossain, I., Haque, A. M., & Ullah, S. A. (2023). Role of Government Institutions in Promoting Sustainable Development in Bangladesh: An Environmental Governance Perspective. *Journal of Current Social and Political Issues*, *1*(2), 42–53. DOI: 10.15575/jcspi.v1i2.485

Hossain, M. S., Al-Hamadani, S. M. Z. F., & Rahman, M. T. (2015). E-waste: A Challenge for Sustainable Development. *Journal of Health & Pollution*, *5*(9), 3–11. DOI: 10.5696/2156-9614-5-9.3 PMID: 30524771

Hsiao, C. (2014). *Analysis of panel data* (3rd ed.). Cambridge University Press. DOI: 10.1017/CBO9781139839327

Hsu, C.-H., He, X., Zhang, T.-Y., Chang, A.-Y., Liu, W.-L., & Lin, Z.-Q. (2022). Enhancing Supply Chain Agility with Industry 4.0 Enablers to Mitigate Ripple Effects Based on Integrated QFD-MCDM: An Empirical Study of New Energy Materials Manufacturers. *Mathematics*, *10*(10), 1635. DOI: 10.3390/math10101635

Huang, Y. (2022). Consuming geopolitics and feeling maritime territoriality: The case of China's patriotic tourism in the South China Sea. *Political Geography*, *98*, 102669. DOI: 10.1016/j.polgeo.2022.102669

Huang, Y., & Liu, Y. (2024). A critical reflection on tourism geopolitics: Research progress and future agenda. *Tourism Geographies*, *26*(5), 881–897. DOI: 10.1080/14616688.2024.2366481

Hulkó, G., Kálmán, J., & Lapsánszky, A. (2025). The politics of digital sovereignty and the European Union's legislation: Navigating crises. *Frontiers in Political Science*, *7*, 154856. Advance online publication. DOI: 10.3389/fpos.2025.1548562

Hunter, T., & Walter, S. (2025). International organizations in national parliamentary debates. *The Review of International Organizations*, •••, 1–27.

Huq, A. Z. (2024). (Forthcoming). The Geopolitics of Digital Regulation. *U of Chicago, Public Law. Working Paper.*

Hyun, J. (2025). Bringing technology into the balance of power politics: 'network balancing' between the United States and China. *Cambridge Review of International Affairs*, *38*(1), 22–47. DOI: 10.1080/09557571.2024.2401612

Iaquinto, B. L., Gillen, J., & Mostafanezhad, M. (2024). The new tourism geopolitics: Bridging tourism geographies and political geography. *Tourism Geographies*, *26*(5), 723–734. DOI: 10.1080/14616688.2024.2394693

IEA. (2023, March). *CO2 Emissions in 2022 – Analysis* . IEA.

Iftikhar, S. (2024). Cyberterrorism as a global threat: A review on repercussions and countermeasures. *PeerJ. Computer Science*, *10*, e1772. DOI: 10.7717/peerj-cs.1772 PMID: 38259881

IISS. (2025). *Global defence spending soars to new high*. https://www.iiss.org/online-analysis/military-balance/2025/02/global-defence-spending-soars-to-new-high/IISS

Iliev, D. (2020). The evolution of religious tourism: Concept, segmentation and development of new identities. *Journal of Hospitality and Tourism Management*, *45*, 131–140. DOI: 10.1016/j.jhtm.2020.07.012

IMF. (2021). *El Salvador Adopts Bitcoin as Legal Tender*. International Monetary Fund.

India's Cybersecurity Challenge. *Threats and Strategies*. (n.d.). Retrieved June 25, 2024, from https://www.drishtiias.com/daily-updates/daily-news-editorials/india-s-cybersecurity-challenge-threats-and-strategies

International Monetary Fund. (2020). *Regional economic outlook: Asia and Pacific*. IMF Publications.

International Monetary Fund. (2021). *International financial statistics*. IMF Data.

International Telecommunication Union. (2019). *Measuring the information society report 2019*. ITU Publications.

International Telecommunication Union. (2020). *Measuring digital development: Facts and figures 2020*. ITU Publications.

Ioannidou, E. (2022). Mythologies of Genesis and Neo-Nazi Palingenesis: Commemorating the Battle of Thermopylae in the Political Rites of the Golden Dawn. *Humanities (Washington), 11*(4), 88. DOI: 10.3390/h11040088

Iriye, A. (2002). *Global community: The role of international organizations in the making of the contemporary world*. Univ of California Press. DOI: 10.1525/9780520936126

Isin, E., & Ruppert, E. (2020). The birth of sensory power: How a pandemic made it visible? *Big Data & Society*, *7*(2), 1–15. DOI: 10.1177/2053951720969208

Ivanov, D. (2021). Digital supply chain management and technology to enhance resilience by building and using end-to-end visibility during the COVID-19 pandemic. *IEEE Transactions on Engineering Management*. Advance online publication. DOI: 10.1109/TEM.2021.3096274

Ivanov, D., & Dolgui, A. (2020). Viability of intertwined supply networks: Extending the supply chain resilience angles towards survivability. A position paper motivated by COVID-19 outbreak. *International Journal of Production Research*, *58*(10), 2904–2915. DOI: 10.1080/00207543.2020.1750727

Jabareen, Y., & Eizenberg, E. (2021). Theorizing urban social spaces and their interrelations: New perspectives on urban sociology, politics, and planning. *Planning Theory*, *20*(3), 211–230. DOI: 10.1177/1473095220976942

Jabo, D., Borji, B., & Kant, S. (2024, February). Impact of Technical CRM on Ethiopia Bank Human-Computer Interface and Competitive Advantage as Mediators of Performance. In 2024 IEEE International Conference on Computing, Power and Communication Technologies (IC2PCT) (Vol. 5, pp. 679-682). IEEE.

Jani, S. (2018). The Growth of Cryptocurrency in India: Its Challenges & Potential Impacts on Legislation. *International Journal of Sustainable Development, 1*(4), 22–29. DOI: 10.13140/RG.2.2.14220.36486

Jarvis, L., & Lister, M. (2025). Critical security research and the war on terror: From the margins to the mainstream? *European Journal of International Security, 10*(1), 150–169. DOI: 10.1017/eis.2024.36

Javaid, M., Haleem, A., Pratap Singh, R., Khan, S., & Suman, R. (2021). Blockchain technology applications for Industry 4.0: A literature-based review. *Blockchain: Research and Applications, 2*(4), 100027. DOI: 10.1016/j.bcra.2021.100027

Javaid, M., Haleem, A., Singh, R. P., Suman, R., & Khan, S. (2022). A review of Blockchain Technology applications for financial services. *BenchCouncil Transactions on Benchmarks. Standards and Evaluations, 2*(3), 100073. DOI: 10.1016/j.tbench.2022.100073

Jawabreh, O., Baadhem, A. M., Ali, B. J. A., Atta, A. A. B., Ali, A., Al-Hosaini, F. F., & Allahham, M. (2023). The influence of supply chain management strategies on organizational performance in hospitality industry. *Applied Mathematics & Information Sciences, 17*(5), 851–858. DOI: 10.18576/amis/170511

Jazairy, A., & von Haartman, R. (2020). Analysing the institutional pressures on shippers and logistics service providers to implement green supply chain management practices. *International Journal of Logistics, 23*(1), 44–84. DOI: 10.1080/13675567.2019.1584163

Jefferson, B. J. (2024). Cybernetic States: Communication, Control, and State-space in the Advanced Research Projects Agency. *Political Geography, 113*, 103160. DOI: 10.1016/j.polgeo.2024.103160

Jia, F., Peng, S., Green, J., Koh, L., & Chen, X. (2020). Soybean supply chain management and sustainability: A systematic literature review. *Journal of Cleaner Production, 255*, 120254. DOI: 10.1016/j.jclepro.2020.120254

Jiang, E., Qin, B., Wang, Q., Wang, Z., Wu, Q., Weng, J., & Zhang, Y. (2023). Decentralized Finance (DeFi): A Survey. India Quarterly. *Journal of International Affairs, 3*(8), 1–21. http://arxiv.org/abs/2308.05282

Jiang, Q., Fang, W., LePage, B., & Han, G. (2024). How Is Tourism Geography Situated in Taiwan? Geography Versus Tourism and Recreation. *Sustainability (Basel), 16*(17), 7523. DOI: 10.3390/su16177523

Jiang, W., & Pardos, Z. A. (2021). Towards equity and algorithmic fairness in student gradeprediction. *Computers & Society*, •••, 1–10.

Ji, H. (2021). Research-based on international trade system and the pursuit of free digital trade. *Modern Economics & Management Forum, 2*(4). Advance online publication. DOI: 10.32629/memf.v2i4.414

Jones, B. (2023). Recentring industrial policy paradigm within IPE and development studies. *Third World Quarterly, 44*(1), 1–15. DOI: 10.1080/01436597.2023.2216140

Josselson, R. (1996). Ethics and Process in the Narrative Study of Lives. California: SAGEPublications.

Jun, L., Jianping, D., Poenisch, H., Le, X., Hanke, S. H., Marsh, D., ... & Hentov, E. (2014). International Monetary Review.

Kabaklarlı, E. (2022). Green FinTech: Sustainability of Bitcoin. *Digital Finance, 4*(4), 265–273. DOI: 10.1007/s42521-022-00053-x PMID: 35698578

Kant, S., & Adula, M. (2024). AI Learning and Work Attitude Mediation Among Reward and Organizational Peripheral in Ethiopia. In Gomathi Sankar, J., & David, A. (Eds.), *Generative AI for Transformational Management* (pp. 109–136). IGI Global., DOI: 10.4018/979-8-3693-5578-7.ch005

Kant, S., & Adula, M. (2024). Human-Machine Interaction in the Metaverse in the Context of Ethiopia. In *Influence and Potential of Machine Learning in the Metaverse* (pp. 196–212). IGI Global., DOI: 10.4018/979-8-3693-5762-0.ch008

Karaduman, O., & Gülhas, G. (2025). Blockchain-enabled supply chain management: A review of security, traceability, and data integrity amid the evolving systemic demand. *Applied Sciences (Basel, Switzerland), 15*(9), 5168. Advance online publication. DOI: 10.3390/app15095168

Karim, S., Lucey, B. M., Naeem, M. A., & Uddin, G. S. (2022). Examining the interrelatedness of NFTs, DeFi tokens and cryptocurrencies. Finance Research Letters, 47(PB), 102696. DOI: 10.1016/j.frl.2022.102696

Karvonen, A., Cugurullo, F., & Caprotti, F. (2018). *Inside Smart Cities: place, politics and urban innovation*. Routledge. DOI: 10.4324/9781351166201

Kassaye, B. D., Bayiley, Y. T., & Alemu, Z. K. (2024). Success Factors for Returnee Migrant Traders in Ethiopia: The Mediating Function of Government Policies and Peripheral of institutions.

Katagiri, N. (2021). Why International Law and Norms Do Little in Preventing Non-state Cyber Attacks. *Journal of Cybersecurity, 7*(1), tyab009. Advance online publication. DOI: 10.1093/cybsec/tyab009

Kathrin, B., & Lindenberg, N. (2019). Green finance across the universe. In S. Boubaker & D. Nguyen (Eds.), *Corporate social responsibility, ethics and sustainable prosperity* (pp. 331–358). German Institute of Development and Sustainability (IDOS). https://doi.org/https://doi.org/10.1142/9789811206887_0011

Kaushik, T. K., Ravish, Singh, A., Raghav, A., & Singh, B. (2024). Potential of Artificial Intelligence in the Agricultural Industry: A Comprehensive Review. In B. Riswandi, B. Singh, C. Kaunert, & K. Vig (Eds.), *AI Applications for Clean Energy and Sustainability* (pp. 344-365). IGI Global. https://doi.org/DOI: 10.4018/979-8-3693-6567-0.ch017

Kebede Sori, G. (2024). Advancement Influences of Return Migration: Literature Review of Ethiopian Return Migrants. Advancement Influences of Return Migration: Literature Review of Ethiopian Return Migrants (March 25, 2024).

Kenney, M., & Lewin, A. Y. (2023). The rise of techno-geopolitical uncertainty: Implications of the United States CHIPS and Science Act. *Journal of International Business Policy*, *6*(2), 1–15. https://www.ncbi.nlm.nih.gov/pmc/articles/PMC10066984/ PMID: 37359753

Keser, I. (2023). Interdependence and Complementarity of a Multi-Dimensional Concept of Sustainable Development and the Integrated Approach to Urban Governance—Case Study City of Zagreb. *Sustainability (Basel)*, *15*(12), 9213. DOI: 10.3390/su15129213

Khan, A. W., Saeed, S., & Kakar, M. S. (2024). Cybersecurity as a Geopolitical Tool: The Growing Influence of Digital Warfare in Statecraft. *International Research Journal of Social Sciences and Humanities, 3*(2), 345-357. https://irjssh.com/index.php/irjssh/article/view/209

Khare, P. & Raghuwanshi, V. (2025). Navigating Emerging AI Technologies and Future Trends in Cybersecurity and Forensics. *IGI Global Scientific Publishing*, 321-346. https://doi.org/DOI: 10.4018/979-8-3373-0857-9.ch012

Khare, P. (2025). Investigating the Influence of AI in Social Media Governance. *IGI Global Scientific Publishing*. 365-388. https://doi.org/DOI: 10.4018/979-8-3693-9904-0.ch015

Klinke, I. (2023). *Life, Earth, Colony: Friedrich Ratzel's Necropolitical Geography*. University of Michigan Press., DOI: 10.3998/mpub.11987710

Koutroumpis, P. (2009). The economic impact of broadband on growth: A simultaneous approach. *Telecommunications Policy*, *33*(9), 471–485. DOI: 10.1016/j.telpol.2009.07.004

Kozak, M., Gokovali, U., & Bahar, O. (2008). Estimating the Determinants of Tourist Spending: A Comparison of Four Models. *Tourism Analysis*, *13*(2), 143–155. DOI: 10.3727/108354208785664283

Krause, D. (2024). *The Intersection of Centralized and Decentralized Digital Currencies: Implications for Financial Inclusion and Efficiency*. https://papers.ssrn.com/abstract=4914822

Kucharski, A. (2020). Data sovereignty and techno-political competition. *Journal of International Affairs*, *74*(2), 33–48.

Kumar, N., Kumar, K. S., Aeron, A., & Verre, F. (2025). Blockchain technology in supply chain management: Innovations, applications, and challenges. *Telematics and Informatics Reports*, *100204*, 100204. Advance online publication. DOI: 10.1016/j.teler.2025.100204

Kumar, S., & Nagar, G. (2024, June). Threat Modeling for Cyber Warfare Against Less Cyber-Dependent Adversaries. *European Conference on Cyber Warfare and Security, 23*(1), 257-264. http://dx.doi.org/DOI: 10.34190/eccws.23.1.2462

Kumar, S., & Prabhakar, A. (2019). BIMSTEC regional integration: Prospects and challenges. *South Asian Survey*, *26*(1), 45–67.

Kumar, S., Talukder, M. B., & Dewangan, S. (2025). Cutting-Edge Innovations: AI and Digital Transformation in Research and Development. In Ozen, E., Singh, A., Taneja, S., Rajaram, R., & Davim, J. (Eds.), *Sustainability, Innovation, and Consumer Preference* (pp. 29–50). IGI Global Scientific Publishing., DOI: 10.4018/979-8-3693-9699-5.ch002

Lahmann, H. (2021). On The Politics and Ideologies of The Sovereignty Discourse in Cyberspace. *Duke Journal of Comparative & International Law, 32*, 61-96. https://scholarship.law.duke.edu/djcil/vol32/iss1/2/

Lai, P. L., Su, D. T., Tai, H. H., & Yang, C. C. (2020). The impact of collaborative decision-making on logistics service performance for container shipping services. *Maritime Business Review*, *5*(2), 175–191. DOI: 10.1108/MABR-12-2019-0061

Lake, D. A., Martin, L. L., & Risse, T. (2021). Challenges to the liberal order: Reflections on international organization. *International Organization*, *75*(2), 225–257. DOI: 10.1017/S0020818320000636

Lande, D., & Danyk, Y. (2025). Competitive Artificial Intelligence in Information and Cyber Warfare. *SSRN*. http://dx.doi.org/DOI: 10.2139/ssrn.5084698

Lane, J. E., & Finsel, B. A. (2014). Fostering smarter colleges and universities: Data, big data and analytics. In Lane, J. E. (Ed.), *Building a smarter university: Big data, innovation and analytics*. State University of New York Press.

Lang, A. (2024). 'Global Disordering': Practices of Reflexivity in Global Economic Governance. *European Journal of International Law*, *35*(1), 93–140. DOI: 10.1093/ejil/chae011

Leal Filho, W., Marisa Azul, A., Brandli, L., Lange Salvia, A., & Wall, T. (Eds.). (2021). *Affordable and Clean Energy*. Springer International Publishing., DOI: 10.1007/978-3-319-95864-4

Lee, C. H., & Lee, S. H. (2002). NGOs and International Society: Prospects on Their Roles in the 21st Century. *Pacific Focus*, *17*(1), 147–162. DOI: 10.1111/j.1976-5118.2002.tb00266.x

Lee, K. (2022). Technological sovereignty and the global digital political economy. *Global Political Economy*, *3*(2), 1–20. DOI: 10.1332/26352257Y2022D000000029

Leibowitz, B. (2017). 'Power, knowledge and learning: dehegemonising colonial knowledge', lternation, 24(2), 99-119.

Li, L. C., Pentland, A., Braley, A., Chen, N., Enríquez, J. R., & Reuel, A. (2024). Generative AI for pro-democracy platforms. DOI: 10.21428/e4baedd9.5aaf489a

Liao, G. Y., & Caramichael, J. (2022). Stablecoins: Growth Potential and Impact on Banking. *International Finance Discussion Paper, 2022*(1334), 1–26. DOI: 10.17016/ifdp.2022.1334

Lina, F. Y., & Talukder, M. B. (2025). AI in Tourism: Business and Economic Perspectives. In Lytras, M., Ordonez, P., Alkhaldi, A., & Serban, A. (Eds.), *Innovation Management for a Resilient Digital Economy* (pp. 81–104). IGI Global Scientific Publishing., DOI: 10.4018/979-8-3693-8357-5.ch004

Lin, P. (2020). Autonomous weapons systems and the laws of war. *International Review of the Red Cross*, *102*(913), 599–618.

Li, P., & Wang, H. (2023). The Tech Cold War, the multipolarization of the world economy, and IB research. *International Business Review*, *32*(6), 102195. DOI: 10.1016/j.ibusrev.2023.102195

Liu, G., & Liu, G. (2024). The Development of Blockchain-Based Digital Currencies and Their Impact on the Global Financial System. *Open Journal of Social Sciences*, *12*(10), 227–238. DOI: 10.4236/jss.2024.1210018

Liu, H. (2020). AI, surveillance, and authoritarianism: China's social credit system. *Journal of Global Policy*, *34*(2), 45–61.

Liu, H., Yao, P., Latif, S., Aslam, S., & Iqbal, N. (2022). Impact of Green financing, FinTech, and financial inclusion on energy efficiency. *Environmental Science and Pollution Research International*, *29*(13), 18955–18966. DOI: 10.1007/s11356-021-16949-x PMID: 34705207

Li, X., Jiao, H., Cheng, L., Yin, Y., Li, H., Mu, W., & Zhang, R. (2023). A Quantitative and Qualitative Review of Blockchain Research from 2015 to 2021. *Sustainability (Basel)*, *15*(6), 5067. Advance online publication. DOI: 10.3390/su15065067

Lopez-Claros, A., Dahl, A. L., & Groff, M. (2020). *Global governance and the emergence of global institutions for the 21st century*. Cambridge University Press. DOI: 10.1017/9781108569293

Macak, K. (2021). Unblurring the lines: Military cyber operations and international law. *Journal of Cyber Policy*, *6*(3), 411–428. DOI: 10.1080/23738871.2021.2014919

Mackey, M. (2021). **Aave** and **Compound**: Pioneering DeFi Lending. *Financial Innovation Review*, *5*(4), 24–36.

Mackey, T. (2021). Decentralized Finance: A Review of Key Protocols, Yield Farming, and Lending Platforms. *Financial Technologies Review*, *9*(3), 150–160.

Madnick, S. (2022). What Russia's Ongoing Cyberattacks in Ukraine Suggest About the Future of Cyber Warfare. *Harvard Business Review*, *7*, •••. https://cams.mit.edu/wp-content/uploads/Madnick_HBR_Russia.pdf

Malan, D. (2018, June). *Technology is changing faster than regulators can keep up - here's how to close the gap*. World Economic Forum.

Mamasoliev, S. (2024). The Role of International Trade In Us Economic Growth. *Innovative Developments and Research in Education*, *3*(32), 139–147.

Mangano, R. (2018). Blockchain securities, insolvency law and the sandbox Approach. *European Business Organization Law Review*, *19*(4), 19. DOI: 10.1007/s40804-018-0123-5

Mangold, P. (2013). National security and international relations. *National Security and International Relations*, 1–117. DOI: 10.4324/9780203494684

Manjula, B. C., Shilpa, B. S., & Sundaresh, M. (2022). Analysis of Cryptocurrency, Bitcoin and the Future. *East Asian Journal of Multidisciplinary Research*, *1*(7), 1293–1302. DOI: 10.55927/eajmr.v1i7.803

Manor, I., & Adiku, G. A. (2021). From 'traitors' to 'saviours': A longitudinal analysis of Ethiopian, Kenyan and Rwandan embassies' procedure of digital diaspora diplomacy. South African Journal of Interregional stateal Affairs, 28(3), 403-427.

Manulak, M. W. (2024). The sources of influence in multilateral diplomacy: Replaceability and intergovernmental networks in international organizations. *The Review of International Organizations, 19*(3), 579–610. DOI: 10.1007/s11558-024-09536-5

Markus, S., & Buijs, P. (2022). Beyond the hype: How blockchain affects supply chain performance. *Supply Chain Management, 27*(2), 177–193. DOI: 10.1108/SCM-03-2022-0109

Martin, C. J. (2016). The sharing economy: A pathway to sustainability or a nightmarish form of neoliberal capitalism? Ecological Economics, 121,149e159

Martin, L. L., & Simmons, B. A. (2013). International organizations and institutions. *Handbook of international relations, 2*, 326-351.

Martin, K. D., Kim, J. J., Palmatier, R. W., Steinhoff, L., Stewart, D. W., Walker, B. A., Wang, Y., & Weaven, S. (2020). Data privacy in retail. *Journal of Retailing, 96*(4), 474–492. DOI: 10.1016/j.jretai.2020.08.003

Mason, O., Sarma, J., Sidaway, J. D., Bonnett, A., Hubbard, P., Jamil, G., Middleton, J., O'Neill, M., Riding, J., & Rose, M. (2023). Interventions in walking methods in political geography. *Political Geography, 106*, 102937. DOI: 10.1016/j.polgeo.2023.102937

Maulana, A., & Putri, A. D. (2019, March). Development of digital currency technology. []. IOP Publishing.]. *Journal of Physics: Conference Series, 1175*(1), 012205. DOI: 10.1088/1742-6596/1175/1/012205

Mavlutova, I., Spilbergs, A., Verdenhofs, A., Natrins, A., Arefjevs, I., & Volkova, T. (2022). Digital Transformation as a Driver of the Financial Sector Sustainable Development: An Impact on Financial Inclusion and Operational Efficiency. *Sustainability 2023, Vol. 15, Page 207, 15*(1), 207. DOI: 10.3390/su15010207

Mayer, M., & Nock, P. J. (2025). The diffusion deficit in scientific and technological power: A critical assessment. *Review of International Political Economy, 32*(2), 123–145. DOI: 10.1080/09692290.2023.2173633

Mayer, M., & Vogt, L. (2016). Economic effects of tourism and its influencing factors. An overview focusing on the spending determinants of visitors. *Zeitschrift für Tourismuswissenschaft, 8*(2), 169–198. DOI: 10.1515/tw-2016-0017

McLaren, D., & Corry, O. (2021). Clash of geofutures and the remaking of planetary order: Faultlines underlying conflicts over geoengineering governance. *Global Policy, 12*(S1), 20–33. DOI: 10.1111/1758-5899.12863

McNaught, R. (2024). The application of collaborative governance in local level climate and disaster resilient development–A global review. *Environmental Science & Policy, 151*, 103627. DOI: 10.1016/j.envsci.2023.103627

Mehta, R. S. (2023). China's techno-politics: The impact on Belt and Road partners. *India Quarterly, 79*(3), 1–15. DOI: 10.1177/09749284231183321

Meltzer, J. P. (2019). Governing digital trade. *World Trade Review, 18*(4), 571–588. DOI: 10.1017/S1474745618000505

Metelski, D., & Sobieraj, J. (2022). Decentralized Finance (DeFi) Projects: A Study of Key Performance Indicators in Terms of DeFi Protocols' Valuations. *International Journal of Financial Studies, 10*(4), 108. Advance online publication. DOI: 10.3390/ijfs10040108

Mi, Z., & Coffman, D. M. (2019). The sharing economy promotes sustainable societies. *Nature Communications 2019 10:1, 10*(1), 1–3. DOI: 10.1038/s41467-019-09260-4

Mihajlovic, I., & Krželj-Čolović, Z. (2021). THE IMPACT OF GLOBALISATION ON THE DEVELOPMENT OF TOURISM WITHIN SOCIAL AND ECONOMIC CHANGES. *European Scientific Journal*, •••, 108–120.

Mihalic, T. (2024). Trends in Sustainable Tourism Paradigm: Resilience and Adaptation. *Sustainability (Basel), 16*(17), 7838. DOI: 10.3390/su16177838

Milana, C., & Ashta, A. (2021). Artificial intelligence techniques in finance and financial markets: A survey of the literature. *Strategic Change, 30*(3), 189–204. DOI: 10.1002/jsc.2403

Millard, J. (2023). *Impact of digital transformation on public governance* (No. JRC133975). Joint Research Centre (Seville site).

Milner, H. V., & Solstad, S. U. (2021). Technological change and the international system. *World Politics, 73*(1), 1–28. DOI: 10.1017/S0043887113000300

Mingst, K. A., Karns, M. P., & Lyon, A. J. (2022). *The United Nations in the 21st century*. Routledge. DOI: 10.4324/9781003038269

Mir, A. A., & Bhat, A. A. (2022). Green banking and sustainability – a review. *Arab Gulf Journal of Scientific Research, 40*(3), 247–263. DOI: 10.1108/AGJSR-04-2022-0017

Moch, E. (2024). The Economic and Geopolitical Significance of the Brics Nations: A Comparative Analysis of Their Global Influence in the 21st Century. *East African Journal of Business and Economics*, *7*(2), 86–100. DOI: 10.37284/eajbe.7.2.2310

Mogiani, M. (2023). Studying Borders from the Border: Reflections on the Concept of Borders as Meeting Points. *Geopolitics*, *28*(3), 1323–1341. DOI: 10.1080/14650045.2022.2026329

Mohan, D. (2020). *The Financial Services Guide to Fintech: Driving Banking Innovation Through ... - Devie Mohan - Google Books* (1st ed.). Kogan Page.

Mohan, C. R. (2018). *India and Asian geopolitics: The past, present*. Brookings Institution Press.

Mohiuddin, A. (2024). *Islam in the Age of Globalization: Perspectives and Responses*. Rowman & Littlefield Publishers., DOI: 10.5771/9798881801342

Moleka, P. (2024). Rethinking the Limits of Polycentric Governance: Towards a More Inclusive Innovation Ecosystem Framework for Sustainable Development in the Global South.

Money Control. (2023, February). *The Indian fintech ecosystem is setting global benchmarks*. Money Control.

Monteiro, P., & Adler, P. S. (2022). Bureaucracy for the 21st century: Clarifying and expanding our view of bureaucratic organization. *The Academy of Management Annals*, *16*(2), 427–475. DOI: 10.5465/annals.2019.0059

Morales, L., & Andreosso-O'Callaghan, B. (2022). The World's Top Five Financial Centers: Geopolitical Uncertainties. In *Sustainable Development in Asia: Socio-economic, Financial, and Economic Perspectives* (pp. 115–135). Springer International Publishing. DOI: 10.1007/978-3-030-94679-1_7

Morgenstern, F. (2024). *Legal problems of international organizations: reissue with new foreword by Jan Klabbers*. Cambridge University Press. DOI: 10.1017/9781009448154

Morozov, E. (2011). *The Net Delusion: The dark side of Internet freedom*. PublicAffairs.

Motamed, A. P., & Bahrak, B. (2019). Quantitative analysis of cryptocurrencies transaction graph. *Applied Network Science*, *4*(1), 131. Advance online publication. DOI: 10.1007/s41109-019-0249-6

Mouton, M., & Burns, R. (2021). (Digital) neo-colonialism in the smart city. *Regional Studies*, *55*(12), 1890–1901. DOI: 10.1080/00343404.2021.1915974

Moyer, J. D. (2024). A double-edged sword into a plowshare: Analyzing geopolitical implications of alternative socioeconomic development pathways. *One Earth*, *7*(2), 336–347. DOI: 10.1016/j.oneear.2024.01.002

Muchunguzi, S. (2023). Participatory management of natural resources in Africa: An imperative policy direction for sustainable development. *Management of Environmental Quality*, *34*(3), 704–720. DOI: 10.1108/MEQ-06-2022-0170

Müller, C. (2023). Diaspora return visits for skill transfer and capacity advancement: a case investigation of IOM's connecting diaspora for advancement project in Ethiopia, Sierra Leone and Somaliland.

Musa, J. (2016). Smart cities – a roadmap for development. *Journal of Telecommunication System & Management*, *5*(3), 1–3.

Nakamoto, S. (2008). Bitcoin: A Peer-to-Peer Electronic Cash System.

Narayanan, A., Bonneau, J., Felten, E., Miller, A., & Goldfeder, S. (2016). *Bitcoin and Cryptocurrency Technologies*. Princeton University Press.

Nardi, M. L. (2021). Origin of Cyber Warfare and How the Espionage Changed: A Historical Overview. *IGI Global*. 145-153. https://www.igi-global.com/chapter/origin-of-cyber-warfare-and-how-the-espionage-changed/260610

Nartey, J. (2024). Decentralized Finance (DeFi) and AI: Innovations at the Intersection of Blockchain and Artificial Intelligence. SSRN *Electronic Journal*. DOI: 10.2139/ssrn.4781328

Naseem, S. (2021). The Role of Tourism in Economic Growth: Empirical Evidence from Saudi Arabia. *Economies*, *9*(3), 3. Advance online publication. DOI: 10.3390/economies9030117

Naseer, I. (2024). The CrowdStrike Incident: Analysis and Unveiling the Intricacies of Modern Cybersecurity Breaches. *World Journal of Advanced Engineering Technology and Sciences*, *10*(1), 728–733. Advance online publication. DOI: 10.30574/wjaets.2024.13.1.0473

Nassiry, D. (2019). The Role of Fintech in Unlocking Green Finance. *Handbook of Green Finance*, 315–336. DOI: 10.1007/978-981-13-0227-5_27

NATIONAL CYBERSECURITY STRATEGY. (2023).

NATO Parliamentary Assembly. (2024). *2024 - NATO AND AI - REPORT - CLEMENT - 058 STC*. https://www.nato-pa.int/document/2024-nato-and-ai-report-clement-058-stcnato-pa.int

Ncube, F., & Chikuta, O. (2020). Perceived Economic Impact of Religious Tourism: The Case of Zimbabwe. *Hospitality & Tourism Review*, *1*(2), 1–13. DOI: 10.38157/hospitality-tourism-review.v1i2.211

Neuhofer, B., Buhalis, D., & Ladkin, A. (2015). Conceptualising technology enhanced destination experiences. *Journal of Destination Marketing & Management*, *4*(3), 145–155.

Neuwirth, R. J. (2024). The global institutional governance of AI: A four-dimensional perspective. *International Journal of Digital Law and Governance*, *1*(1), 113–153. DOI: 10.1515/ijdlg-2024-0004

Nguyen, L. T. M., & Nguyen, P. T. (2024). Determinants of cryptocurrency and decentralized finance adoption - A configurational exploration. *Technological Forecasting and Social Change*, *201*(February), 123244. DOI: 10.1016/j.techfore.2024.123244

Niang, A. (2022). Space and the Geopolitical. *Millennium*, *51*(1), 284–304. DOI: 10.1177/03058298221146592

Nigusie, A., Azale, T., Yitayal, M., & Derseh, L. (2024). Influence of stage-matched educational intervention on use of institutional delivery in Northwest Ethiopia: Using community readiness model. *The Pan African Medical Journal*, *48*(16). PMID: 39184843

Ningrum, D., Raven, R., Malekpour, S., Moallemi, E. A., & Bryan, B. A. (2023). Transformative potential in sustainable development goals engagement: Experience from local governance in Australia. *Global Environmental Change*, *80*, 102670. DOI: 10.1016/j.gloenvcha.2023.102670

Norrman, A., & Wieland, A. (2020). The development of supply chain risk management over time: Revisiting Ericsson. *International Journal of Physical Distribution & Logistics Management*, *50*(6), 641–666. DOI: 10.1108/IJPDLM-07-2019-0219

Nouri Kouchi, A., Zarra Nezhad, M., & Kiani, P. (2018). A study of the relationship between the growth in the number of Hajj pilgrims and economic growth in Saudi Arabia. *Journal of Hospitality and Tourism Management*, *36*, 103–107. DOI: 10.1016/j.jhtm.2016.01.008

Nowinski, W., & Kozma, M. (2017). How can blockchain technology disrupt the existing business models? Entrepreneurial Business and Economics Review, 5(3), 173e188

Nwagwu, U., Niaz, M., Chukwu, M. U., & Saddique, F. (2023). The influence of artificial intelligence to enhancing supply chain performance under the mediating significance of supply chain collaboration in manufacturing and logistics organizations in Pakistan. *Traditional Journal of Multidisciplinary Sciences*, *1*(1), 29–40.

Nyffenegger, R. (2024). A proposal for a layer-2 CBDC on a rollup. *Digital Finance*, *6*(3), 543–571. DOI: 10.1007/s42521-024-00115-2

O'Connell, W. D., & Elliott, C. (2023). States and new markets: The novelty problem in the IPE of finance. *Review of International Political Economy*, *30*(2), 403–420. DOI: 10.1080/09692290.2023.2165529

Oatley, T. (2021). Regaining relevance: IPE and a changing global political economy. *Cambridge Review of International Affairs*, *34*(2), 318–327. DOI: 10.1080/09557571.2021.1888880

Odoh, E. M. (2021). Cyber Attack as a Tool to Influence Foreign Policy: A Comparative Study of Russia's Cyber-attacks On Estonia and Georgia. *University of Nigeria Journal of Political Economy, 11*(1). https://unjpe.com/index.php/UNJPE/article/view/2

OECD. (2019). OECD Principles on Artificial Intelligence. OECD. https://www.oecd.org/ai/

OECD. (2020). Global Digital Transformation: Emerging Markets and Technological Growth. Retrieved from https://www.oecd.org

OECD. (2020). OECD AI Principles. Retrieved from https://www.oecd.org Zeng, M., & Williamson, P. (2019). The Impact of Technological Competition on

OECD. (2023). *Framework for the Classification of AI Systems*. https://oecd.ai Zuboff, S. (2019). *The Age of Surveillance Capitalism*. PublicAffairs.

OECD. (2024). *A Preliminary Mapping of Data Localisation Measures*. https://www.oecd.org/en/publications/a-preliminary-mapping-of-data-localisation-measures_c5ca3fed-en.htmlOECD

Offiong, U. P., Cheba, K., & Ioppolo, G. (n.d.). *FinTech as a digital innovation in microfinance companies-systematic literature review*. DOI: 10.1108/EJIM-04-2024-0462

Olssen, M. (1996). In defense of the welfare state and publicly provided eduation: A NewZealand perspective. *Journal of Education Policy*, *11*(11), 337–362. DOI: 10.1080/0268093960110305

Olssen, M., & Peters, M. A. (2007). Neoliberalism, higher education and the knowledgeeconomy: From the free market to knowledge capitalism. *Journal of Education Policy*, *20*(3), 313–245. DOI: 10.1080/02680930500108718

Olufemi, L. (2020). *Feminism, Interrupted: Disrupting Power*. Pluto Press. DOI: 10.2307/j.ctvxrpzvs

Oostendorp, M. (2022). Raced Repertoires: The Linguistic Repertoire as Multi-Semiotic and Racialized. *Applied Linguistics*, *43*(1), 65–87. DOI: 10.1093/applin/amab018

Organisation for Economic Co-operation and Development. (2019). *FDI flows*. OECD Statistics.

Oxford Economics. (2014). *Economic Impact of the University of Oxford*. Oxford Economics.

Ozili, P. (2023). *Using central bank digital currency to achieve the sustainable development goals*. Contemporary Studies in Economics and Financial Analysis. DOI: 10.1108/S1569-37592023000111C008

Pai, W.-T., Phan, K.-T., Pham, C.-V., Lee, J.-M., & Hsieh, C.-J. (2024). Analyzing tourist expenditures incurred on long-, medium-, and short-haul trips to Taiwan. *Annals of Tourism Research Empirical Insights*, *5*(2), 100138. DOI: 10.1016/j.annale.2024.100138

Palley, T. (2025). The military-industrial complex as a variety of capitalism and threat to democracy: rethinking the political economy of guns versus butter. In *The Political Economy of War, Peace, and the Military–Industrial Complex* (pp. 34-73). Edward Elgar Publishing. DOI: 10.4337/9781035357178.00008

Paltiel, M. (2023). Recent amendments to the Australian Privacy Act. *Journal of Bioethical Inquiry*, *20*(2), 161–174. DOI: 10.1007/s11673-023-10249-4 PMID: 37432509

Panigrahi, A., Pati, A., Sahu, B., Das, M. N., Nayak, D. S. K., Sahoo, G., & Kant, S. (2023). En-MinWhale: An ensemble approach based on MRMR and Whale optimization for Cancer diagnosis. *IEEE Access : Practical Innovations, Open Solutions*, *11*, 113526–113542. DOI: 10.1109/ACCESS.2023.3318261

Parayil, G. (2005). The political economy of informational development: A normative appraisal. In *The Political Economy of Informational Development: A Normative Appraisal* (pp. 196–212). Palgrave Macmillan., DOI: 10.1057/9780230595613_10

Park, K. R., & Park, Y. S. (2024). Addressing institutional challenges in sustainable development goals implementation: Lessons from the Republic of Korea. *Sustainable Development (Bradford)*, *32*(1), 1354–1369. DOI: 10.1002/sd.2725

Park, S. (2023). Semiconductors at the Intersection of Geoeconomics, Technonationalism, and Global Value Chains. *Social Sciences (Basel, Switzerland)*, *12*(8), 466. DOI: 10.3390/socsci12080466

Park, S., & Gretzel, U. (2021). Algorithmic platforms and narrative branding in tourism diplomacy. *International Journal of Tourism Research*, *23*(4), 456–468.

Pavelea, A., & Negrea, P. C. (2024). *A Comprehensive Analysis of High-Impact Cybersecurity Incidents: Case Studies and Implications* (Doctoral dissertation, Masters thesis. Babe –Bolyai University. doi: . 2.2. 17461.65763).DOI: 10.13140/RG

Perano, M., Cammarano, A., Varriale, V., Del Regno, C., Michelino, F., & Caputo, M. (2023). Embracing supply chain digitalization and unphysicalization to enhance supply chain performance: A conceptual framework. *International Journal of Physical Distribution & Logistics Management*, *53*(5/6), 628–659. DOI: 10.1108/IJPDLM-06-2022-0201

Peters, M. A., & Besley, T. (2024). Tashkent, Khiva, Bukhara and Samarkand in the Islamic Remaking of the Modern World in Uzbekistan. *Geopolitics, History, and International Relations*, *16*(2), 9–39. DOI: 10.22381/GHIR16220241

Phadke, S. (2020). Fintech Is All Around Us. In *FinTech Future: The Digital DNA of Finance*. SAGE Publications Pvt Ltd., DOI: 10.4135/9789353885687.n1

Phanwichit, S. (2018). *FinTech and Causing Customers to Comply with Anti-Money Laundering Law*. https://papers.ssrn.com/abstract=3262514

Piattoeva, N., & Boden, R. (2020). Escaping numbers? The ambiguities of the governance ofeducation through data. *International Studies in Sociology of Education*, *29*(1-2), 1–18. DOI: 10.1080/09620214.2020.1725590

Picon, A. (2013). Smart cities: Théorie et critique d'un idéal autoréalisateur. Parison: éditionsB2.

Piñeiro-Chousa, J., Šević, A., & González-López, I. (2023). Impact of social metrics in decentralized finance. Journal of Business Research, 158(June 2022). DOI: 10.1016/j.jbusres.2023.113673

Piñeiro-Chousa, J., López-Cabarcos, M. Á., Sevic, A., & González-López, I. (2022). A preliminary assessment of the performance of DeFi cryptocurrencies in relation to other financial assets, volatility, and user-generated content. *Technological Forecasting and Social Change*, *181*(May), 121740. Advance online publication. DOI: 10.1016/j.techfore.2022.121740

Polas, M. R. H., Kabir, A. I., Sohel-Uz-zaman, A. S. M., Karim, R., & Tabash, M. I. (2022). Blockchain Technology as a Game Changer for Green Innovation: Green Entrepreneurship as a Roadmap to Green Economic Sustainability in Peru. *Journal of Open Innovation*, *8*(2), 62. DOI: 10.3390/joitmc8020062

Poorhashemi, A. (2024). International environmental law. In *Public International Law* (pp. 453–466). Routledge. DOI: 10.4324/9781003451327-19

Popkewitz, T. (2013). The sociology of education as the history of the present: Fabrication,difference and abjection. *Discourse (Abingdon)*, *34*(3), 439–456. DOI: 10.1080/01596306.2012.717195

Porter, M. E., & Heppelmann, J. E. (2014). How smart, connected products are transforming competition. *Harvard Business Review*, *92*(11), 64–88.

Power, M. (2013). The apparatus of fraud risk. *Accounting, Organizations and Society*, *38*(6-7), 525–543. DOI: 10.1016/j.aos.2012.07.004

Prabhakar, A. (2025). A Sustainable and Inclusive Economic Development: A Global Imperative: A Global Imperative. *Journal of Recycling Economy & Sustainability Policy*, *4*(1), 1–16.

Qin, B. (2018). Cyber-sovereignty in the age of digital trade. *International Affairs*, *94*(4), 869–890.

Rahimi, R. A., & Oh, G. S. (2024). Rethinking the role of educators in the 21st century: Navigating globalization, technology, and pandemics. *Journal ofMarketing Analytics*, *12*(2), 182–197. DOI: 10.1057/s41270-024-00303-4

Rahman, M. S., Gani, M. O., Fatema, B., & Takahashi, Y. (2023). B2B firms' supply chain resilience orientation in achieving sustainable supply chain performance. *Sustainable Manufacturing and Service Economics*, *2*, 100011. DOI: 10.1016/j.smse.2023.100011

Rahman, M., & Singh, K. (2016). Prospects for economic integration of BIMSTEC: Trade and investment scenario. *Journal of South Asian Development*, *11*(2), 172–195.

Rajharia, P., & Kaushik, M. B. (2023). RETRACTED: Cryptocurrency Adoption and Its Implications: A Literature Review. In E3s Web of Conferences (Vol. 456, p. 03002). EDP Sciences.

Raptis, D., Kjeldskov, J., Skov, M. B., & Paay, J. (2014). What is a Digital Ecology?: Theoretical Foundations and a Unified Definition. *Australian Journal of Intelligent Information Processing Systems*, *13*(4), 5.

Raska, M. (2020). North Korea's Evolving Cyber Strategies: Continuity and Change. *SIRIUS–Zeitschrift für Strategische Analysen*, *4*(2), 1–13. DOI: 10.1515/sirius-2020-3030

Reiners, N. (2024). The power of interpersonal relationships: A socio-legal approach to international institutions and human rights advocacy. *Review of International Studies*, *50*(2), 252–270. DOI: 10.1017/S0260210523000438

Reinsberg, B. (2025). Institutional overlap and the survival of intergovernmental organisations. *West European Politics*, *48*(1), 29–57. DOI: 10.1080/01402382.2024.2341564

Rejeb, A., & Rejeb, K. (2020). Blockchain and supply chain sustainability. *LogForum*, *16*(3), 363–372. DOI: 10.17270/J.LOG.2020.467

Riaz, Q., Ayub, N., & Idrees, H. S. (2024). Interconnected Realms: Exploring the Nexus of International Relations, Trade Dynamics, and Digital Transformation. *Traditional Journal of Law and Social Sciences*, *3*(01), 36–46.

Rising Cyber Threats Pose Serious Concerns for Financial Stability. (n.d.). Retrieved January 16, 2025, from https://www.imf.org/en/Blogs/Articles/2024/04/09/rising-cyber-threats-pose-serious-concerns-for-financial-stability

Roberts, H., Cowls, J., Morley, J., Taddeo, M., Wang, V., & Floridi, L. (2019). The Chinese approach to artificial intelligence: An analysis of policy and regulation. SSRN Electronic Journal. DOI: 10.2139/ssrn.3469784

Robertson, S. L. (2022). Guardians of the future: International organisations, anticipatory governance and education. *Global Society*, *36*(2), 188–205. DOI: 10.1080/13600826.2021.2021151

Robertson, S. L., & Beech, J. (2024). 'Promises promises': International organisations, promissory legitimacy and the re-negotiation of education futures. *Comparative Education*, *60*(3), 423–440. DOI: 10.1080/03050068.2023.2287938

Robinson, M., Jones, K., & Janicke, H. (2015). Cyber warfare: Issues and challenges. *Computers & Security*, *49*, 70–94. DOI: 10.1016/j.cose.2014.11.007

Rodima-Taylor, D., Campbell-Verduyn, M., & Bernards, N. (2024). Repoliticizing the technological turn in sustainability governance: Moralities, power, space. *Environment and Planning C. Politics and Space*, *42*(5), 699–707.

Rodrik, D. (2018). What do trade agreements really do? *The Journal of Economic Perspectives*, *32*(2), 73–90. DOI: 10.1257/jep.32.2.73

Role of Standards. (2024). In Developing AI accountability inputs: A deeper dive into AI system evaluations. National Telecommunications and Information Administration. Retrieved from https://www.ntia.gov/.../role-of-standards

Romer, P. M. (1990). Endogenous technological change. *Journal of Political Economy*, *98*(5), S71–S102. DOI: 10.1086/261725

Roque Júnior, L. C., Frederico, G. F., & Costa, M. L. N. (2023). Maturity and resilience in supply chains: A systematic review of the literature. *International Journal of Industrial Engineering and Operations Management*, *5*(1), 1–25. DOI: 10.1108/IJIEOM-08-2022-0035

Rose, N. (2007). *The Politics of Life Itself: Biomedicine, Power, and Subjectivity in theTwenty-First Century*. Princeton University Press. DOI: 10.1515/9781400827503

Rosenberg, M., Frenkel, S., & Conger, K. (2018). Russian interference in the 2016 U.S. presidential election. The New York Times. https://www.nytimes.com/2018/02/16/us/politics/russian-election-interference

Rosiek, J. L., & Heffernan, J. (2014). Can't code what the community can't see: A case of theerasure of heteronormative harassment. *Qualitative Inquiry*, *20*(6), 726–733. DOI: 10.1177/1077800414530255

Saaida, M. (2024). BRICS Plus: De-dollarization and global power shifts in new economic landscape. *BRICS Journal of Economics*, *5*(1), 13–33. DOI: 10.3897/brics-econ.5.e117828

Sacco, P. L., Arenas, A., & De Domenico, M. (2022). The resilience of the multirelational structure of geopolitical treaties is critically linked to past colonial world order and offshore fiscal havens. arXiv preprint arXiv:2203.00618. https://arxiv.org/abs/2203.00618

Sachs, J. D. (2014, December). *Financing Climate Safety*. Project SYndicate.

Sachs, J. D., Warner, A., Aslund, A., & Fischer, S. (1995). Economic reform and the process of global integration. *Brookings Papers on Economic Activity*, *1995*(1), 1–118. DOI: 10.2307/2534573

Said, E. (1978). *Orientalism*. Vintage Books.

Sankaran, S. (2025). Enhancing trust through standards: A comparative risk-impact framework for aligning ISO AI standards with global ethical and regulatory contexts. arXiv. https://doi.org//arxiv.2504.16139DOI: 10.48550

Sarkar, A., Routroy, S., & Sultan, F. A. (2022). The impact of co-creation and co-invention in supply chains: A bibliometric review. *Arab Gulf Journal of Scientific Research*, *40*(4), 364–391. DOI: 10.1108/AGJSR-04-2022-0010

Sarkar, D. (2023). Centralized Intermediation in a Decentralized Web3 Economy: Value Accrual and Extraction. *Interdisciplinary Journal of Contemporary Research in Business*, *4*(11), 26–32. DOI: 10.48550/arXiv.2311.08234

Saz-Carranza, A., Rueda-Sabater, E., Vandendriessche, M., Moreno, C., & Jordana, J. (2024). The future (s) of global governance: A scenarios exercise. *Global Policy*, *15*(1), 149–165. DOI: 10.1111/1758-5899.13295

Schedlbauer, M., & Wagner, K. (2018). Blockchain beyond digital currencies-a structured literature review on blockchain applications. *Available at SSRN* 3298435. DOI: 10.2139/ssrn.3298435

Schildt, H. (2020). *The Data Imperative*. Oxford University Press. DOI: 10.1093/oso/9780198840817.001.0001

Schmitt, M. N., & Watts, S. (2016). Beyond State-centrism: International Law and Non-state Actors in Cyberspace. *Journal of Conflict and Security Law*, *21*(3), 595–611. DOI: 10.1093/jcsl/krw019

Schröder, N. J. S., & Watson, N. (2024). Assessing participatory process-system linkages in polycentric water governance: Insights from WFD implementation in Germany. *The Review of Policy Research*.

Schuette, L. A. (2024). IO survival politics: International organisations amid the crisis of multilateralism. *Journal of European Public Policy*, *31*(11), 3812–3838. DOI: 10.1080/13501763.2023.2276757

Seabe, P. L., Moutsinga, C. R. B., & Pindza, E. (2024). Optimizing Cryptocurrency Returns: A Quantitative Study on Factor-Based Investing. *Mathematics*, *12*(9), 1–28. DOI: 10.3390/math12091351

Secretariat, B. I. M. S. T. E. C. (2004). *Framework Agreement on BIMSTEC Free Trade Area*. BIMSTEC Secretariat.

Securitize. (2021). *Tokenizing Real Estate and Venture Capital: A New Era in Investment*. Securitize Inc.

Security Delta (HSD) | Trend snippet: Digital and physical processes in society have become intertwined and crisis management should be able to deal with this. (n.d.). Retrieved January 16, 2025, from https://securitydelta.nl/services/knowledge/trends/source-of-threat/nation-states/digital-and-physical-processes-in-society-have-become-intertwined-and-crisismanagement-should-be-able-to-deal-with-this-000515

Seepma, A. P., de Blok, C., & Van Donk, D. P. (2020). Designing digital public service supply chains: Four country-based cases in criminal justice. *Supply Chain Management, 26*(4), 418–446. DOI: 10.1108/SCM-03-2020-0090

Seib, P. (2012). *Real-Time Diplomacy: Politics and power in the social media era.* Palgrave Macmillan. DOI: 10.1057/9781137010902

Sfetcu, N. (2024). *Electronic Warfare and Artificial Intelligence.* MultiMedia Publishing., DOI: 10.58679/mm14430

Shah, K., Lathiya, D., Lukhi, N., Parmar, K., & Sanghvi, H. (2023). A systematic review of decentralized finance protocols. *International Journal of Intelligent Networks, 4*(June), 171–181. DOI: 10.1016/j.ijin.2023.07.002

Shah, M. A., & Raj, N. (2025). Examining the role of blockchain and public-private partnerships in design and deployment of blockchain-enabled CBDC. *Digital Business, 5*(1), 100111. DOI: 10.1016/j.digbus.2025.100111

Shahzad, A., Zhang, K., & Gherbi, A. (2020). Intuitive development to examine collaborative IoT supply chain system underlying privacy and security levels and perspective powering through proactive blockchain. *Sensors (Basel), 20*(13), 3760. DOI: 10.3390/s20133760 PMID: 32635589

Shahzad, M. F., Xu, S., Lim, W. M., Hasnain, M. F., & Nusrat, S. (2024). Cryptocurrency awareness, acceptance, and adoption: The role of trust as a cornerstone. *Humanities & Social Sciences Communications, 11*(1), 4. Advance online publication. DOI: 10.1057/s41599-023-02528-7

Shaji George, A., Hovan George, A. S., & Gabrio Martin, A. S. (2023). *A Review of ChatGPT AI's Impact on Several Business Sectors.* DOI: 10.5281/ZENODO.7644359

Sharabati, A. A., Allahham, M., Yahiya, A., Ahmad, B., & Sabra, S. (2023). Effects of artificial integration and big data analysis on economic viability of solar microgrids: Mediating role of cost benefit analysis. *Operations Research in Engineering Sciences: Theory and Applications, 6*(2), 360–379. DOI: 10.31181/oresta2302082s

Sharma, K. (2023). TRANSFORMATIVE CHANGE IN GLOBAL BUSINESS AFTER NEW WORLD ORDER.

Sharma, P., Martin, M., & Swanlund, D. (2023). MapSafe: A complete tool for achieving geospatial data sovereignty. *Transactions in GIS*, *27*(6), 1680–1697. DOI: 10.1111/tgis.13094

Sheikh, S. A. (2024). Diplomatic effectiveness in addressing transnational issues and promoting global cooperation. *The Journal of Humanistic Education and Development*, *6*(2), 36–47. DOI: 10.22161/jhed.6.2.5

Shinde, K. A., & Olsen, D. H. (2023). Reframing the Intersections of Pilgrimage, Religious Tourism, and Sustainability. *Sustainability (Basel)*, *15*(1), 1. Advance online publication. DOI: 10.3390/su15010461

Shqair, M. I., & Altarazi, S. A. (2022). Evaluating the status of SMEs in Jordan with respect to Industry 4.0: A pilot study. *Logistics (Basel)*, *6*(4), 69. DOI: 10.3390/logistics6040069

Shtern, M. (2022). Passing as a tourist: Exploring the everyday urban geopolitics of tourism. *Political Geography*, *93*, 102526. DOI: 10.1016/j.polgeo.2021.102526

Siddiqui, K. (2024). The Decline of the West and Shifting Dynamics in the Global Political Economy. *WORLD (Oakland, Calif.)*.

Sigala, M. (2020). Tourism and COVID-19: Impacts and implications for advancing and resetting industry and research. *Journal of Business Research*, *117*, 312–321. DOI: 10.1016/j.jbusres.2020.06.015 PMID: 32546875

Singh, S. (2024). Decentralized Finance (DeFi): Exploring the Role of Blockchain and Cryptocurrency in Financial Ecosystems. *International Research Journal of Modernization in Engineering Technology and Science*, (January). Advance online publication. DOI: 10.56726/IRJMETS48585

Smith, A. (2022). Digital technological innovation and the international political economy. In *Handbook of International Political Economy* (pp. 1–20). Palgrave Macmillan., https://discovery.ucl.ac.uk/id/eprint/10045803/

Smith, R., El-Anis, I., & Farrands, C. (2017). *International political economy in the 21st century: Contemporary issues and analyses*. Routledge. DOI: 10.4324/9781315750637

Solow, R. M. (1956). A contribution to the theory of economic growth. *The Quarterly Journal of Economics*, *70*(1), 65–94. DOI: 10.2307/1884513

Sommerer, T., Agné, H., Zelli, F., & Bes, B. (2022). *Global legitimacy crises: decline and revival in multilateral governance*. Oxford University Press. DOI: 10.1093/oso/9780192856326.001.0001

South, F., Usf, T., Graduate, D., Usf, G., Theses, D., & Akdag, Y. (2017). *Cyber Deterrence against Cyberwar between the United States Cyber Deterrence against Cyberwar between the United States and China: A Power Transition Theory Perspective and China: A Power Transition Theory Perspective*. https://digitalcommons.usf.edu/etd

Srai, J. S., Graham, G., Van Hoek, R., Joglekar, N., & Lorentz, H. (2023). Impact pathways: Unhooking supply chains from conflict zones—Reconfiguration and fragmentation lessons from the Ukraine–Russia war. *International Journal of Operations & Production Management*, *43*(13), 289–301. DOI: 10.1108/IJOPM-08-2022-0529

Srivastava, S., & Bullock, J. B. (2024). AI, global governance, and digital sovereignty. arXiv. /arxiv.2410.17481DOI: 10.2139/ssrn.4996387

Srivastava, P., & Das, K. (2018). Digital integration and sustainable development in BIMSTEC. *Asian Development Review*, *35*(2), 78–105.

Srnicek, N. (2016). *Platform capitalism*. Polity Press.

Stanley, L. (2024). Why Sinoscepticism will remake British politics. *The Political Quarterly*, *95*(2), 289–297. DOI: 10.1111/1467-923X.13367

State of California. (2020). California Consumer Privacy Act (CCPA), Cal. Civ. Code §§ 1798.100–1798.199.

Stock, T., Obenaus, M., Kunz, S., & Kohl, H. (2018). Industry 4.0 as enabler for a sustainable development: A qualitative assessment of its ecological and social potential. *Process Safety and Environmental Protection*, *118*, 254–267. DOI: 10.1016/j.psep.2018.06.026

Stroppa, M. (2023). Legal And Ethical Implications of Autonomous Cyber Capabilities: A Call for Retaining Human Control in Cyberspace. *Ethics and Information Technology*, *25*(1), 7. DOI: 10.1007/s10676-023-09679-w

Su, Z. (2024). Analysis of Cryptocurrency and Its Combination with Quantitative Transactions. SHS Web of Conferences, 181, 02016. DOI: 10.1051/shsconf/202418102016

Sun, Z., Liu, L., Pan, R., Wang, Y., & Zhang, B. (2025). Tourism and economic growth: The role of institutional quality. *International Review of Economics & Finance*, *98*, 103913. DOI: 10.1016/j.iref.2025.103913

Swire, P., & Hemmings, J. (2019). The CLOUD Act: A Preliminary Assessment. *Journal of National Security Law & Policy*, *12*(1), 1–33. https://jnslp.com/wp-content/uploads/2019/06/The-CLOUD-Act-A-Preliminary-Assessment.pdf

Taherdoost, H. (2022). Blockchain Technology and Artificial Intelligence Together: A Critical Review on Applications. *Applied Sciences 2022, Vol. 12, Page 12948, 12*(24), 12948. DOI: 10.3390/app122412948

Tallberg, J., Erman, E., Furendal, M., Geith, J., Klamberg, M., & Lundgren, M. (2023). The global governance of artificial intelligence: Next steps for empirical and normative research. arXiv preprint arXiv:2305.11528. https://arxiv.org/abs/2305.11528

Talukder, M. B. (2020). An Appraisal of the Economic Outlook for the Tourism Industry, Specially Cox's Bazar in Bangladesh. *i-manager's Journal on Economics & Commerce,* 2(1), 23-35. DOI: 10.26634/jecom.2.1.17285

Talukder, M. B. (2020). The Future of Culinary Tourism: An Emerging Dimension for the Tourism Industry of Bangladesh. I-Manager's. *Journal of Management, 15*(1), 27. DOI: 10.26634/jmgt.15.1.17181

Talukder, M. B. (2021). An assessment of the roles of the social network in the development of the Tourism Industry in Bangladesh. *International Journal of Business, Law, and Education*, 2(3), 85–93. DOI: 10.56442/ijble.v2i3.21

Talukder, M. B. (2024). Implementing Artificial Intelligence and Virtual Experiences in Hospitality. In Manohar, S., Mittal, A., Raju, S., & Nair, A. J. (Eds.), *Advances in Hospitality, Tourism, and the Services Industry* (pp. 145–160). IGI Global., DOI: 10.4018/979-8-3693-2019-8.ch009

Talukder, M. B. (2025). Climate change adaptation strategies for a tourism destination: A study of Kuakata beach. *Acta Scientiarum Polonorum. Administratio Locorum, 24*(1), 165–179. DOI: 10.31648/aspal.10073

Talukder, M. B. (2025). Current Trends and Future Research Directions on Eco-Friendly Stages of Hotel Industry. *RPER*, (71), 7–18. DOI: 10.59072/rper.vi71.695

Talukder, M. B., Chowdhury, S. A., & Khan, M. R. (2025). The Gig Economy: Economic Innovations and Technological Advancements in Human Resource Management. In Kurnaz, S., & Bieliauskaitė, J. (Eds.), *Economic Innovations and Technological Developments in HRM* (pp. 381–404). IGI Global., DOI: 10.4018/979-8-3693-4412-5.ch015

Talukder, M. B., Das, I. R., & Kumar, S. (2024). Implementing Digital Marketing Channels on BTHM Admission: Evidence from Dhaka City. *IUBAT Review*, *7*(1), 142–170. DOI: 10.3329/iubatr.v7i1.74361

Talukder, M. B., & Hoque, M. (2025). Navigating the Digital Horizon: Transforming Travel Agencies in the Digital Era. In Albakri, M. (Ed.), *Perspectives on Digital Transformation in Contemporary Business* (pp. 383–410). IGI Global Scientific Publishing., DOI: 10.4018/979-8-3693-5966-2.ch014

Talukder, M. B., Kabir, F., Muhsina, K., & Das, I. R. (2023). Emerging concepts of artificial intelligence in the hotel industry: A conceptual paper. *International Journal of Research Publication and Reviews*, *4*(9), 1765–1775. DOI: 10.55248/gengpi.4.923.92451

Talukder, M. B., Khan, M. R., & Haghi, A. K. (2025). Redefining Hospital Waste Management: Circular Economy Strategies for Reducing Toxicity. In Poddar, S., Paul, B., & Luperi, M. (Eds.), *Sustainable Business Ecosystems and Social Perspectives* (pp. 335–358). IGI Global Scientific Publishing., DOI: 10.4018/979-8-3693-8437-4.ch015

Talukder, M. B., Khan, M. R., & Kumar, S. (2025). The Impact of Gig Economy Trends on Traditional Employment Models: Evidence From Hotel Industry. In Nozari, H. (Ed.), *Dynamic and Safe Economy in the Age of Smart Technologies* (pp. 253–276). IGI Global Scientific Publishing., DOI: 10.4018/979-8-3693-4369-2.ch016

Talukder, M. B., & Lina, F. Y. (2025). The Role of Tourism Development in Political Stability and Disruption. In Wongmahesak, K., Ahmad, J., & Mustanir, A. (Eds.), *Public Governance Practices in the Age of AI* (pp. 461–476). IGI Global Scientific Publishing., DOI: 10.4018/979-8-3693-9286-7.ch022

Talukder, M. B., & Swarna, D. A. (2025). Waste-to-Energy Innovations: Evidence From the Tourism Industry. In Sucheran, R. (Ed.), *Sustainable Waste Management in the Tourism and Hospitality Sectors* (pp. 553–582). IGI Global Scientific Publishing., DOI: 10.4018/979-8-3693-6110-8.ch020

Tan, Q., Yasmeen, H., Ali, S., Ismail, H., & Zameer, H. (2023). Fintech development, renewable energy consumption, government effectiveness and management of natural resources along the belt and road countries. *Resources Policy*, *80*, 103251. DOI: 10.1016/j.resourpol.2022.103251

Tay, L. Y., Tai, H. T., & Tan, G. S. (2022). Digital financial inclusion: A gateway to sustainable development. *Heliyon*, *8*(6), e09766. DOI: 10.1016/j.heliyon.2022.e09766 PMID: 35785228

Teferra, D. (2021). The function of the African intellectual diaspora in advancing higher education. Interregional stateal Journal of African Higher Education, 8(2), 1-9.

Terzidou, M., Stylidis, D., & Szivas, E. (2008). Residents' Perceptions of Religious Tourism and its SocioEconomic Impacts on the Island of Tinos. *Tourism and Hospitality Planning & Development*, *5*(2), 113–129. DOI: 10.1080/14790530802252784

Tetiana, Z., Volodymyr, S., Dluhopolskyi, O., Vasyl, B., & Tetiana, D. (2022). Investment Models on Centralized and Decentralized Cryptocurrency Markets. *Naukovyi Visnyk Natsionalnoho Hirnychoho Universytetu*, (1), 177–182. DOI: 10.33271/nvngu/2022-1/177

Thakur, S., & Breslin, J. G. (2020). Scalable and secure product serialization for multi-party perishable good supply chains using blockchain. *Internet of Things : Engineering Cyber Physical Human Systems*, *11*, 100253. DOI: 10.1016/j.iot.2020.100253

Thatcher, J., Retchless, D., & Fish, C. (2024). Dueling cartographies: Science, positivism, art, and critical praxis. *International Journal of Cartography*, *10*(3), 377–394. DOI: 10.1080/23729333.2024.2338496

THE CHANGING CYBER THREAT LANDSCAPE SOUTHEAST ASIA - CYFIRMA. (n.d.). Retrieved January 16, 2025, from https://www.cyfirma.com/research/the-changing-cyber-threat-landscape-southeast-asia/

The Department of Defense Critical Infrastructure Protection (CIP) Plan Version 1.0. (n.d.). Retrieved June 25, 2024, from https://irp.fas.org/offdocs/pdd/DOD-CIP-Plan.htm

The Five Bears: Russia's Offensive Cyber Capabilities. (n.d.). Retrieved June 25, 2024, from https://greydynamics.com/the-five-bears-russias-offensive-cyber-capabilities/

The Future of the Metaverse | Imagining the Internet | Elon University. (n.d.). Retrieved January 16, 2025, from https://www.elon.edu/u/imagining/surveys/xiv-2022/future-of-metaverse-web3-2040/

The Geopolitics of Cybersecurity – The Diplomat. (n.d.). Retrieved June 25, 2024, from https://thediplomat.com/2020/12/the-geopolitics-of-cybersecurity/

The Role of Nuclear Weapons in International Politics. *A Strategic Perspective - Foreign Policy Research Institute*. (n.d.). Retrieved January 16, 2025, from https://www.fpri.org/article/2009/03/the-role-of-nuclear-weapons-in-international-politics-a-strategic-perspective/

Tihonova, E. V., Borisova, T. P., & Bunov, E. G. (2022). Cyberspace as a New Social Reality in the Era of Globalization. *Lecture Notes in Networks and Systems, 398 LNNS*, 274–280. DOI: 10.1007/978-3-030-94870-2_35

Tilsted, J. P. (2024). *Transforming a Synthetic World: The Political Economy of Petrochemical Transitions*. Lund University.

Todaro, M. P., & Smith, S. C. (2020). *Economic development* (12th ed.). Pearson.

Trenches, L. (2019). Norm entrepreneurship in AI governance: OECD and GPAI. *Review of International Political Economy, 26*(7), 1234–1256. DOI: 10.1080/09692290.2019.1610669

Trivellas, P., Malindretos, G., & Reklitis, P. (2020). Implications of green logistics management on sustainable business and supply chain performance: Evidence from a survey in the Greek agri-food sector. *Sustainability (Basel), 12*(24), 10515. DOI: 10.3390/su122410515

Tullett, W. (2021). State of the Field: Sensory History. *History (London), 106*(373), 804–820. DOI: 10.1111/1468-229X.13246

Turnbull, J., Searle, A., Davies, O. H., Dodsworth, J., Chasseray-Peraldi, P., von Essen, E., & Anderson-Elliott, H. (2022). Digital ecologies: Materialities, encounters, governance. *Progress in Environmental Geography, 275396872211456*. Advance online publication. DOI: 10.1177/27539687221145698

U.S. Department of Commerce. (2020). Huawei and National Security. Retrieved from https://www.commerce.gov

Ugolini, A., Reboredo, J. C., & Mensi, W. (2023). Connectedness between DeFi, cryptocurrency, stock, and safe-haven assets. *Finance Research Letters, 53*(February), 103692. DOI: 10.1016/j.frl.2023.103692

UN.ESCAP. (2017). *Digital and virtual currencies for sustainable development*.

UNCTAD. (2024). *Global trade hits record $33 trillion in 2024, driven by services and developing economies*. https://unctad.org/news/global-trade-hits-record-33-trillion-2024-driven-services-and-developing-economies

United Nations Department of Economic and Social Affairs. (2025, February). *UN soft power and the SDGs: Promoting peace and security in conflict*. https://desapublications.un.org/un-desa-voice/sdg-blog/february-2025/un-soft-power-and-sdgs-promoting-peace-and-security-conflict

United Nations. (2020). AI and the Global Future: A UN Perspective. Retrieved from https://www.un.org

United Nations. (2021). Artificial Intelligence and National Security: The Need for Global Cooperation. Retrieved from https://www.un.org

United States Congress. (2018). Clarifying Lawful Overseas Use of Data (CLOUD) Act. Retrieved from https://www.congress.gov

United States Congress. (2018). Export Control Reform Act (ECRA) and National Security Concerns. Retrieved from https://www.congress.gov

United States International Cyberspace & Digital Policy Strategy - United States Department of State. (n.d.). Retrieved January 16, 2025, from https://www.state.gov/united-states-international-cyberspace-and-digital-policy-strategy/

Urquhart, A., & Yarovaya, L. (2023). Cryptocurrency research: Future directions. *European Journal of Finance, 4364*. Advance online publication. DOI: 10.1080/1351847X.2023.2284186

Valashiya, M. C., & Luke, R. (2023). Enhancing supply chain information sharing with third party logistics service providers. *International Journal of Logistics Management, 34*(6), 1523–1542. DOI: 10.1108/IJLM-11-2021-0522

Van der Marel, E., & Shepherd, B. (2017). Trade in services and the digital economy. *Journal of Trade Law & Policy, 21*(2), 75–93.

Van Rheenen, D., Naria, O., Melo, R., & Sobry, C. (2024). A Comparative Study of Small Islands, Sport Tourism, and Sustainable Development: A Local to Global Perspective. In *Sport Tourism, Island Territories and Sustainable Development: A Comparative Perspective* (pp. 503–543). Springer Nature Switzerland. DOI: 10.1007/978-3-031-51705-1_29

Varga, J. (2021). Defining the economic role and benefits of micro, small and medium-sized enterprises in the 21st century with a systematic review of the literature. *Acta Polytechnica Hungarica, 18*(11), 209–228. DOI: 10.12700/APH.18.11.2021.11.12

Veale, M., Matus, K., & Gorwa, R. (2023). AI and global governance: Modalities, rationales, tensions. *Annual Review of Law and Social Science, 19*(1), 255–279. DOI: 10.1146/annurev-lawsocsci-020223-040749

Verma, B., Singla, B., & Mittal, A. (Eds.). (2024). *Digital Technologies, Ethics, and Decentralization in the Digital Era*. IGI Global. DOI: 10.4018/979-8-3693-1762-4

Verma, R. (2024). Russia–Ukraine war and India's quest for leading power status. *Global Policy, 15*(4), 778–782. DOI: 10.1111/1758-5899.13365

View of the techno-political collision. (n.d.). Intersect: Stanford Journal of Information & Society. Retrieved June 7, 2025, from https://ojs.stanford.edu/ojs/index.php/intersect/article/view/749/675

Viner, J. (1950). *The customs union issue.* Carnegie Endowment for International Peace.

Vlados, C., & Chatzinikolaou, D. (2025). The emergence of the new globalization: The approach of the evolutionary structural triptych. *Journal of Global Responsibility, 16*(1), 139–161. DOI: 10.1108/JGR-04-2023-0063

Vlados, C., Chatzinikolaou, D., & Iqbal, B. A. (2022). New Globalization and Multipolarity. *Journal of Economic Integration, 37*(3), 458–483. DOI: 10.11130/jei.2022.37.3.458

Volz, U. (2018). Fostering Green Finance for Sustainable Development in Asia. ADBI Working Paper. *Asian Development Bank Institute.*

Wang, Y., Yuan, Y., Guan, X., Xu, M., Wang, L., Wang, H., & Liu, Y. (2020). Collaborative two-echelon multicenter vehicle routing optimization based on state–space–time network representation. *Journal of Cleaner Production, 258*, 120590. DOI: 10.1016/j.jclepro.2020.120590

Weaponization of Information - ECPS. (n.d.). Retrieved June 25, 2024, from https://www.populismstudies.org/Vocabulary/weaponization-of-information/

Webster, N. (2023). Shaping spaces: governance and climate-related mobility in Ethiopia. Climate and Advancement, 1-11

Wen, G., Siddik, Z., & Bakkar, A. (2023). The effect of Fintech adoption on green finance and environmental performance of banking institutions during the COVID-19 pandemic: The role of green innovation. *Environmental Science and Pollution Research International, 30*(10), 25959–25971. DOI: 10.1007/S11356-022-23956-Z/FIGURES/4 PMID: 36350441

What is Cyber Insurance and Why is it Important? | Definition from TechTarget. (n.d.). Retrieved January 16, 2025, from https://www.techtarget.com/searchsecurity/definition/cybersecurity-insurance-cybersecurity-liability-insurance

What is Cyber Warfare | Types, Examples & Mitigation | Imperva? (n.d.-a). Retrieved January 16, 2025, from https://www.imperva.com/learn/application-security/cyber-warfare/

What is Cyber Warfare | Types, Examples & Mitigation | Imperva? (n.d.-b). Retrieved June 25, 2024, from https://www.imperva.com/learn/application-security/cyber-warfare/

Wheeldon, A. (2022). *The Destructuration of Academic Life: How Managerialism Colonises Universities with Symbolic Violence.* DOI: 10.26192/Q7QVZ

Wilder, D. (2024). China's Bid to Remake the World Order. *Georgetown Journal of International Affairs*, *25*(1), 71–76. DOI: 10.1353/gia.2024.a934888

Wilson, E. (2016). The practice of digital diplomacy: Challenges and opportunities. *Diplomacy and Statecraft*, *27*(2), 213–234. DOI: 10.1080/09592296.2016.1156611

Wilson, J. D. (2017). Creating Strategic Value through Financial Technology. In *Creating Strategic Value through Financial Technology*. Wiley., DOI: 10.1002/9781119318682

Winters, N., Eynon, R., Geniets, A., Robson, J., & Kahn, K. (2020). Can we avoid digitalstructural violence in future learning systems? *Learning, Media and Technology*, *45*(1), 17–30. DOI: 10.1080/17439884.2020.1708099

Wodak, R. (2014). Critical discourse analysis. In Leung, C., & Street, B. V. (Eds.), *TheRoutledge companion to English studies*. Routledge.

Wordpress. (1 C.E., November 30). Pilgrimage Tourism And Its Economic Dimensions Tourism Essay. *UKEssays.Com*. https://www.ukessays.com/essays/tourism/pilgrimage-tourism-and-its-economic-dimensions-tourism-essay.php

World Bank. (2016). *World development report 2016: Digital dividends*. World Bank Publications.

World Bank. (2019). *The Global Findex Database 2017: Measuring Financial Inclusion and the Fintech Revolution*. World Bank Group.

World Bank. (2020). *Remittances: Cross-Border Payments and Financial Inclusion*. World Bank.

World Bank. (2020). *World development indicators*. World Bank Open Data.

World Bank. (2022, May). *Report: State and Trends of Carbon Pricing*. World Bank Org.

World Trade Organization. (2017, December). Joint statement on e-commerce moratorium. Ministerial Meeting, Buenos Aires.

Wu, T. (2018). *The curse of bigness: Antitrust in the new gilded age*. Columbia Global Reports. DOI: 10.2307/j.ctv1fx4h9c

Xue, L., Dong, J., & Zha, Y. (2023). How does digital finance affect firm environmental, social and governance (ESG) performance?—Evidence from Chinese listed firms. *Heliyon*, *9*(10), e20800. DOI: 10.1016/j.heliyon.2023.e20800 PMID: 37867793

Yan, C., Siddik, A. B., Yong, L., Dong, Q., Zheng, G. W., & Rahman, M. N. (2022). A Two-Staged SEM-Artificial Neural Network Approach to Analyze the Impact of FinTech Adoption on the Sustainability Performance of Banking Firms: The Mediating Effect of Green Finance and Innovation. *Systems 2022, Vol. 10, Page 148, 10*(5), 148. DOI: 10.3390/systems10050148

Yang, G. (2024). Quantitative Analysis of the Relationship Between Cryptocurrency Market and U.S. Stock Market Performance. Advances in Economics. *Management and Political Sciences*, *97*(1), 122–131. DOI: 10.54254/2754-1169/97/20230504

Yang, G., Li, Y., Jiang, X., Yang, G., Li, Y., & Jiang, X. (2020). Research on the Impacts of Green Finance towards the High-Quality Development of China's Economy—Mechanisms and Empirical Analysis. *Theoretical Economics Letters*, *10*(6), 1338–1357. DOI: 10.4236/tel.2020.106082

Ye, Q., Law, R., & Gu, B. (2022). Ethical challenges of personalization in smart tourism. *Tourism Management Perspectives*, *46*, 101905. Advance online publication. DOI: 10.1016/j.tmp.2022.101905

Yermack, D. (2018). The potential of digital currency and blockchains. *NBER Reporter*, (1), 14–17.

Yeung, R. (2020). *China's Trump Card: Cryptocurrency and Its Game-changing Role in Sino-US Trade*. John Wiley & Sons. DOI: 10.1002/9781119699163

Yoon, J. (2023). Supply Chain Security in the Age of Techno-Geopolitics: 'Fab 4' Case in the Semiconductor Industry. *The Korean Journal of International Studies*, *21*(1), 27–60. DOI: 10.14731/kjis.2023.04.21.1.27

Young, J. C., & Gilmore, M. P. (2013). Subaltern Empowerment in the Geoweb: Tensionbetween Publicity and Privacy. *Antipode*, *46*(2), 574–591. DOI: 10.1111/anti.12056

Yousaf, I., & Yarovaya, L. (2022). Herding behavior in conventional cryptocurrency market, non-fungible tokens, and DeFi assets. Finance Research Letters, 50(September 2021), 103299. DOI: 10.1016/j.frl.2022.103299

Yousaf, I., Nekhili, R., & Gubareva, M. (2022). Linkages between DeFi assets and conventional currencies: Evidence from the COVID-19 pandemic. *International Review of Financial Analysis*, *81*(February), 102082. DOI: 10.1016/j.irfa.2022.102082

Yu, H., Wei, W., Li, J., & Li, Y. (2022). The impact of green digital finance on energy resources and climate change mitigation in carbon neutrality: Case of 60 economies. *Resources Policy*, *79*, 103116. DOI: 10.1016/j.resourpol.2022.103116

Yu, M., Tsai, F. S., Jin, H., & Zhang, H. (2022). Digital finance and renewable energy consumption: Evidence from China. *Financial Innovation*, *8*(1), 1–19. DOI: 10.1186/s40854-022-00362-5

Yu, Y., & Wang, H. (2022). Study on the construction of smart tourism ecosystem and polycentric governance mechanism. *Smart Tourism*, *3*(1), 9–24. DOI: 10.54517/st.v3i1.1738

Zaballos, A., Briones, A., Massa, A., Centelles, P., & Caballero, V. (2020). A smart campus'digital twin for sustainable comfort monitoring. *Sustainability (Basel)*, *12*(21), 1–33. DOI: 10.3390/su12219196

Zaidi, S. M. S., & Nirmal, . (2023). Emerging Realities in the International Political System: Transforming State's Foreign Policy. *Herald of the Russian Academy of Sciences*, *93*(6), 376–389. DOI: 10.1134/S1019331623010148

Zarifian, P. (2003). A quoi sert le travail? Paris: La dispute.72

Zeidy, I. A. (2022). The role of financial technology (FINTECH) in changing financial industry and increasing efficiency in the economy. *COMESA Monetary Institute*, 1–20.

Zengler, T. (2021). AI in cybersecurity: Mitigating risks in the age of algorithmic warfare. *Cybersecurity Review*, *10*(3), 12–24.

Zenki, R., & Mu, M. (2020). Machine learning interpretability and its impact on smart campus projects. *Computers & Society*, •••, 1–5.

Zhang, L., & Bai, E. (2023). The Regime Complexes for Global Climate Governance. *Sustainability (Basel)*, *15*(11), 9077. DOI: 10.3390/su15119077

Zhang, L., Mohandes, S. R., Tong, J., Abadi, M., Banihashemi, S., & Deng, B. (2023). Sustainable Project Governance: Scientometric Analysis and Emerging Trends. *Sustainability (Basel)*, *15*(3), 2441. DOI: 10.3390/su15032441

Zhang, T., & Huang, Z. (2022). Blockchain and central bank digital currency. *ICT Express*, *8*(2), 264–270. DOI: 10.1016/j.icte.2021.09.014

Zheng, T., Yu, X., Fan, Y., Ding, X., Ye, R., & Zhang, Y. (2024). The role of artificial intelligence in reshaping international political economy: Perspectives on economic governance and policy management. *Academic Journal of Management and Social Sciences*, *9*(3), 83–91. DOI: 10.54097/ppkzr906

Zhou, J., & Chen, S. L. (2022). The concept of the cruise supply chain and its characteristics: An empirical study of China's cruise industry. *Maritime Business Review*, *7*(3), 196–221. DOI: 10.1108/MABR-06-2021-0046

Zielonka, R. (2022). *Technology Innovation and Digital Revolution: Adoption and Diffusion of Digital Network Platforms, 1995-2001, with Implications for Future Development*. University of Washington.

Zohar, O. (2018). Blockchain and the Rise of Decentralized Finance (DeFi). *Smart City Journal*, *10*(4), 90–104.

Zohar, O. (2018). China's Ban on Cryptocurrency Mining: Implications and Reactions. *Journal of Chinese Economic and Business Studies*, *16*(2), 125–142.

Zuboff, S. (2019). *The Age of Surveillance Capitalism*. Profile Books.

Zürn, M., Tokhi, A., & Binder, M. (2021). The international author-ity database. *Global Policy*, *12*(4), 430–442. DOI: 10.1111/1758-5899.12971

Чорна, Н., Корж, Н., Кізюн, А., Onyshchuk, N., & Antoniuk, K. (2024). The role of digital technologies in the transformation of the tourism business: Prospects for development and impact on the country's economy. *AD ALTA Journal of Interdisciplinary Research*, *14*(1), 136–146. DOI: 10.33543/140139136140

About the Contributors

Kittisak Wongmahesak is a distinguished academic specializing in political science, public management, and international political economy. He currently serves as Secretary of the Ph.D. Program in Political Science at North Bangkok University, Director of the Association of Legal & Political Studies in Thailand, and is a Supervisor for the Post-Doctoral Fellowship Research Collaboration Program at Lincoln University College in Malaysia. He is also a Research Fellow at Shinawatra University in Thailand and Universiti Sultan Zainal Abidin in Malaysia, with adjunct professorships in Indonesia. His previous roles include Full Professor positions in China and Cyprus, as well as an Adjunct Researcher in Vietnam. Dr. Kittisak holds a Ph.D. in Social Sciences and multiple degrees from Kasetsart and Ramkhamhaeng Universities. A highly regarded scholar, he has served as an editor for numerous prestigious international journals, ranked among the top 2% of scientists worldwide by Stanford University since 2020, and boasts an h-index of 57, with over 10,000 citations across more than 500 indexed publications.

Thanaporn Sriyakul holds a Doctor of Philosophy (Social Sciences-Political Science) from Kasetsart University, his highest earned degree. He currently serves as the director of Ph.D. Program in Political Science at North Bangkok University and is affiliated with the Faculty of Political Science at the same institution. His extensive academic contributions encompass a wide range of policy advisory roles, including serving on committees for the Minister of Agriculture and Cooperatives, the Deputy Prime Minister, and various national committees focused on sustainable development, fisheries management, and heritage preservation. His work has included contributions to national policy on organic rice production and marketing, combating illegal, unreported, and unregulated (IUU) fishing, and addressing land tenure issues in southern Thailand. He has also held numerous advisory positions within government ministries, including the Department of Fisheries and the Department of Rice, and played a key role in initiatives related to the Mekong

River ecosystem and promoting a bio-circular-green economy. Furthermore, he has served on various legal committees, notably in the areas of fisheries policy and decentralization of power to local governments. His influence extends to advising on national strategies concerning sustainable practices and resource management.

Uday Kumar Ghosh is a dynamic educator with extensive experience in global business education. He currently serves as Faculty in the Business Administration department at Lincoln University, Oakland, California. His highest degree is a Ph.D. in Leadership from the University of the Cumberlands. Dr. Ghosh's academic contributions are significant, encompassing course development and delivery across a wide range of business disciplines, including hybrid leadership, digital economy, entrepreneurship, international business, marketing, sales, service management, and human resource management. He has also played a crucial role in doctoral dissertation guidance, from proposal development through final defense, including IRB processes and quality control measures. His expertise extends to innovative teaching methodologies, fostering student engagement, and providing career mentorship. Beyond teaching, he's served as President's Advisor for International Business Development at Lincoln University, exploring global collaborations, developing dual-degree programs, and overseeing marketing for international student recruitment. His publications include work on quality management application in higher education and online impulsive buying, reflecting his commitment to both academic research and practical application of business principles.

Ismail Suardi Wekke earned his Doctor of Philosophy in Arabic Language Education from Universiti Kebangsaan Malaysia. He currently holds the positions of Visiting Professor at Fatoni University's Faculty of Education in Thailand and Adjunct Professor at an unspecified institution. His extensive academic contributions include supervising numerous theses at both the undergraduate and master's levels, focusing on diverse topics such as critical thinking skills in religious education, the use of movies in English language learning, student anxiety in communication, and leadership in educational settings. He has authored several books on educational methodologies and Muslim minority communities in Indonesia and published extensively in numerous journals, covering areas such as comparative education, educational management, leadership, and socio-political dimensions in Southeast Asia. His research interests frequently intersect with Islamic education, cultural studies, and the experiences of Muslim minorities, particularly in Indonesia and Papua.

***

Metasebia Adula is an Assistant Professor at the College of Business and Economics, Department of Management, Bule Hora University, Ethiopia.

Endres Ahmed is Assistant Professor in the Department of Management, Jigjiga University - (Ethiopia)

Saquib Ahmed is a legal professional and accomplished academic, currently a Research Scholar at the Sharda School of Law, Sharda University, Greater Noida, India. He has a strong educational background and a bachelor's degree. from Aligarh Muslim University and Master of Law from Jamia Millia Islamia, where he developed his knowledge in Corporate Law, Intellectual Property Rights, Competition law etc.. He has a robust portfolio of publications in esteemed journals and books, reflecting his dedication to contributing to the body of knowledge in his fields of interest. His research has been recognized on various platforms, as evidenced by his participation in national and international conferences, seminars, webinars, and symposiums. Also, in his academic and research pursuits, Saquib is a skilled editor, having successfully overseen the editorial process of several publications and he is also editorial team member of the Sharda Law Review. Mr Ahmed has been active in organizing various programs like Moot Court Competition, Conferences, Faculty Development Programs and Quiz Competitions.

Asriadi Arifin is an academic affiliated with the Institut Agama Islam Darul Dakwah Wal Irsyad (IAI DDI) Sidenreng Rappang, Indonesia, specializing in Islamic economics. His academic contributions include various publications and research in this field, demonstrated by his work on topics such as the marketing strategies of Islamic banking institutions, specifically "Strategi Bank BTN Syariah KCPS Parepare dalam Memasarkan Produk (Analisis Manajemen Syariah)." He has an ID on SINTA (Science and Technology Index), indicating his involvement in scholarly activities, and is recognized for his academic achievements, including graduating as one of the top students from IAIN Parepare with a perfect GPA of 4.0.

Muralidhar L B is a professionally qualified dental surgeon. He holds a Ph.D. from Canara Bank School of Management Studies, Bangalore University, after his MBA from Christ University. He is qualified in management at UGC - NET and KSET. He has 18 years of total teaching experience spanning across dental education, healthcare management and general management and 4 years of corporate experience. He has worked as a research associate in the Institute for Social and Economic Change, Bangalore in a project entitled as "Management By and For Common Man: An Exploration of the Concept and Direction for Future"post Ph.D. He had secured 28th rank in the S.S.L.C. examination for Karnataka State in 1993. His 25 patents have been published, and 2 design patents have been granted. He has 39 research publications to his credit, of which 13 are Scopus-indexed, 5 are ABDC indexed and 1 is indexed in Web of Science. He has co-authored 11 books and 7 book chapters.. He is supervising Ph.D. research of 3 research scholars at JAIN (Deemed to be University). He works as an assistant professor in the Department of Business Management Studies, School of Commerce, Jain Deemed to be a University student in Bangalore.

Chirra Baburao is an esteemed academic and researcher with expertise in public policy, entrepreneurship, start-ups, and the impact of AI on various sectors. Holding Master's degrees in Commerce, Management, and Psychology, he has over a decade of industry experience in IT, operating as a Technopreneur through his MSME-registered firm, Bobbycomputers&Communications. Currently, Research Associate For GNLU ICSSR Project and Doctoral candidate at GITAM School of Business, Visakhapatnam, Baburao excels in qualitative, quantitative, and mixed research methods. He has completed 15 Swayam courses, participated in over 40 webinars, and presented 10 papers at national and international conferences. His research focuses on MSMEs' role in public policy, technological disruptions, and environmental issues. His recent work explores AI's impact on consumer behavior, smart cities, and healthcare, published in reputable journals and conferences, making him a prominent figure in his field

Mural Bhupatil has 3 decades of professional experience both in India and abroad, of these 26 years of continuous service with VIT. Completed the Visiting Professor assignment for six months (Oct 1, 2011 to March 31, 2012) at CMIS, University of Cologne, Germany sponsored by DAAD. Completed successfully the UNDP assignment for a period of 2 years- employed by Ministry of Education, Govt. of Ethiopia.at Debub University, Awassa, Ethiopia during 2003-05. Associated with the MBA program from its inception (1994) at VIT. Actively involved in the activities of NBA accreditation, ISO –9002 from DNV, Netherlands and Deemed University status from the ministry of HRD, Govt. of India at VIT. Secured the Ph. D in E-Commerce from Sri Venkateswara University, Tirupati during December 2008. Having 2 years of Industrial experience and more than 30 years of teaching experience both at UG and PG level Management Programs. Secured recognition from the employers as Best Executive / Best Teacher in the past. Received Fellowship from Rotary Int, U S A to visit East Yorkshire, U K during April – June 2000 as a part of the Group Study Exchange program to study the culture and profession. Carried out successfully research / consultancy assignments in the past. Successfully presented more than 30 papers in various National and International Conferences. Authored 3 management cases in the past few years and published more than 55 papers in International and Nationally reputed (referred) journals/periodicals and edited volumes in India and abroad. Five research scholars have completed their Ph. D under the guidance / supervision at VIT and currently eight more Ph. D scholars are pursuing their research at D Y Patil Agriculture & Technical University. Currently a reviewer for many of the reputed International Journals published by Elsevier, IEEE, USA and Sage, London (UK) and on the Editorial Board of African Journal of Business Management. He has visited many countries like UK, USA, Ethiopia, Kenya, UAE, Germany, France, Netherlands, Czech Republic, Belgium, Singapore and Malaysia, etc. in the last one decade or so.

Elizabeth Chacko is an Associate Professor in Christ University.

Saurabh Chandra is an accomplished legal scholar and currently serves as an Associate Professor & Assistant Dean at the School of Law, Bennett University, India. With a robust academic foundation, he earned his Bachelor of Arts and Bachelor of Laws (B.A. LL.B.) from the prestigious Aligarh Muslim University (A.M.U.). He further specialized in Business Laws, completing his Master of Laws (LL.M.) at the renowned National Law School of India University (NLSIU), Bangalore. Dr. Chandra's academic journey culminated in a Doctorate in Law (Ph.D.) from the esteemed National Law University (NLU) Delhi.Dr. Saurabh Chandra also holds a master's degree in Management with specialization in Human Resources in Management and another in Journalism and Mass Communication. With 16 years of teaching experience, he has established himself as an expert in Business Laws, with numerous publications to his credit. Dr. Saurabh Chandra is an expert in Business Laws, with a profound understanding of the intricate legal frameworks that govern the business world.Dr. Chandra brings a wealth of experience in Academic Administration, having successfully held various key administrative positions.

Kinjal Dodiya completed my Bachelor's in Civil Engineering in 2022 from GEC Bhavnagar, a renowned institution known for shaping the future of engineers. During my academic years, I gained a strong foundation in the principles of civil engineering, including structural analysis, construction materials, project management, and sustainable development. Following my graduation, I made the decision to serve the community in a different capacity and joined the Gujarat Police. Currently, I am proudly serving as a member of the police force in Vadodara city, where I contribute to maintaining law and order, ensuring public safety, and supporting various law enforcement initiatives.With a strong background in both engineering and law enforcement, I am committed to continuously improving my skills, embracing new challenges, and contributing to the development and security of my community.

Kiranbhai Ramabhai Dodiya is an experienced Cyber Forensic Expert and Assistant Professor specializing in cyber security and digital forensics. He has taught at prestigious institutions and is currently pursuing a PhD in Biochemistry and Forensic Science. With a strong background in ethical hacking and malware analysis, Kiranbhai is passionate about educating students and contributing to the field of cyber forensics. His expertise includes malware forensic, computer forensics, and data recovery software. Kiranbhai's commitment to professional growth is evident through his participation in workshops, seminars, and research publications. He is dedicated to shaping the next generation of professionals in the field and combatting cybercrimes.

Srirath Gohwong is an Assistant Professor at Kasetsart University, Thailand, and an Adjunct Research Professor at Universitas Muhammadiyah Sidenreng Rappang (UMS Rappang), Indonesia. He is known for introducing the concept of Kakistoscryptocracy, which explores the role of cryptocurrencies and non-state actors in decentralized governance. Dr. Gohwong actively contributes to national strategy discussions in Thailand, including public hearings and high-performance organization reforms under the Senate Secretariat. He has lectured internationally and collaborates closely with policy experts such as Dr. Nasaran Mahittichatkul. He was recently honored with an Outstanding AI Teaching Innovation Award from Kasetsart University under the "AI Challenge" project and holds a certificate in Artificial Intelligence: Business Strategies and Applications from UC Berkeley Executive Education.

Swapna H R holds two Ph.D degrees in Management from CMR University, Bangalore and second PhD with Rayalaseema University, Kurnool. She is an MBA in Finance specialization from VTU University. She has over 15 years of teaching experience in the area of Finance, Analytics, Statistics and Human Resource Management and 4 years industry experience. Her research expertise has been in the area of Statistics, Behavioural Finance, Employee Engagement, Artificial Intelligence, Entrepreneurship, research on millennials, customer engagement, social media and also in health sectors. She has published over 100 research articles in National and International Journals, where 46 articles have been published in Scopus, Web of science (WoS), Emerald Publications, Springer, ABDC and has presented various papers in National and International Conferences including in USA, Malaysia, etc. She was awarded as a best paper presenter in many National Conferences. She has authored Nine text books in the field of Statistics, Entrepreneurship, Business analytics and Event management. Among which Business Analytics was awarded the "Golden Book Award of 2022". She has been also awarded as 'The Best Researcher Award' on 5th September 2022 from Research

Education Solution which is a body of MSME, GOI. Another feather in her hat is Patents, with 9 Patents published, 2 Grants, and 4 patents filed. She has edited many Scopus-indexed journals of IGI Global Publishing House, Public Administration and Policy, Emerald Publishing House, and PubMed-indexed medical journals. She is an active member of ENACTUS, International Social entrepreneurship forum. She has always been in front line in contributing for social services like organising Blood Donation Camp in association with Rotary Club and ttk, presently she is associated with Ministry of education for One on One Covid-19 drive for building emotional support among the society and the recent one was environmental awareness drive saying "One Earth".

J. Sudarvel working as an Assistant Professor of Management at Karpagam Academy of Higher Education. He produced five Ph.D. Scholars and four Ph.D. Scholars are under his guidance. Further, to his credit he published more than 36 articles in Scopus indexed journals and published more than 50 articles in international journals. He is acting as a Subject Experts in Board of studies of various autonomous colleges.

Ashima Jain, is Assistant Professor, School of Law, Manipal University Jaipur since 2022. She has been actively presenting various papers at ICSSR conferences and has published many paper. She has been affiliated to various prestigious organizations as lifetime member too like Life Member Certificate of the South Asian Society of Criminology & Victimology (SASCV), Sociological Society. She has participated in many FDP and given lectures. She has more than 2 years of experience in academics and has been actively taking participations in various conferences and publications.

Firoj Kabir is a researcher, Lecturer of the Department of "Tourism and Hospitality Management" at the Daffodil International University, Dhaka, Bangladesh, with a solid academic background in BBA and MBA majoring in Tourism and Hospitality Management from the University of Dhaka. His passion lies in exploring the intersection of travel and culture. His diverse areas of interest include archaeological tourism, sustainable tourism, and the unique characteristics of Generation Z travelers. Through extensive research and insightful writing, he sheds light on the intricate connections between historical sites, responsible tourism, and the evolving preferences of the next generation of travelers. His work not only enriches the field of tourism but also inspires readers to engage with the world around them in meaningful and responsible ways.

Ayubkhan Kalwad is an academician, researcher, and industry professional with a deep interest in entrepreneurship and industrial development, especially in the context of MSMEs in India. I have recently submitted my PhD thesis at GITAM University, Bangalore. My research focuses on the socio-economic factors influencing the growth and development of Micro, Small, and Medium Enterprises (MSMEs) across 13 districts of North Karnataka. This work has allowed me to explore real-world challenges and identify opportunities for sustainable and inclusive growth in the sector. Currently, I'm also working on a research paper studying the implementation of the UNIDO Eco-Industrial Park (EIP) Programme in Belagavi and Dharwad districts. Through this, I aim to contribute to the understanding of how sustainable industrial practices can be integrated into regional development planning. With an MBA from ICFAI University and a passion for research, teaching, and industry collaboration, I strive to bridge the gap between academic theory and business practice, and contribute meaningfully to policy, innovation, and entrepreneurship in India.

Shashi Kant is an Assistant Professor, at the College of Business and Economics, Department of Management, Bule Hora University, Ethiopia.

Christian Kaunert is Professor of International Security at Dublin City University. He is also Professor of Policing and Security, as well as Director of the International Centre for Policing and Security at the University of South Wales. Previously, he served as an Academic Director and Professor at the Institute for European Studies, Vrije Universiteit Brussel, a Professor of International Politics, Head of Discipline in Politics, and the Director of the European Institute for Security and Justice, a Jean Monnet Centre for Excellence, at the University of Dundee. Prof Kaunert has researched and taught in many international universities, such as University of Shandong, Jinan, China, IBEI Barcelona, Spain, Diplomatic Academy Yerevan, Armenia – United Nations Development Mission, University of Cairo, Egypt, Collegio Carlo Alberto, Turin, Italy, Ecole nationale d'administration Paris, European Institute of Public Administration Maastricht, Netherlands, European Studies Institute (ESI) at Moscow, University of Porto, Portugal, etc. He was previously Senior Lecturer at the University of Dundee, Marie Curie Senior Research Fellow at the European University Institute Florence, and Senior Lecturer in EU Politics & International Relations, University of Salford.

Pranjal Khare is a distinguished corporate lawyer and is currently working as a law faculty at O.P. Jindal Global University, India. He specializes in Property Law, Corporate laws, Intellectual Property Rights, and International law. Mr. Pranjal is a highly regarded scholar and has published on numerous issues related to international affairs, economy, politics, data & privacy, artificial intelligence and IP disputes.

He is also a frequent speaker at legal conferences and has served as a consultant to numerous law firms and corporations.

Rajesh Kumar is an Assistant Professor & Research Scholar with theDepartment of Economics Institute of Management Studies Ghaziabad – B School National Institute of Technology Agartala, India

Saurabh Kumar is a distinguished Assistant Professor in Law at The Neotia University, Kolkata, with over seven years of teaching experience and an equally robust tenure as an Advocate before the Supreme Court of India. His academic journey is marked by a PhD (draft thesis submitted) from MUIT, an LL.M. with Grade A from MUIT, Delhi, and an LL.B. (Hons.) from Banaras Hindu University. Further enriching his credentials, he qualified the National Eligibility Test (NET) in 2019 and completed a specialized course in Public International Law at The Hague Academy of International Law, Netherlands. Saurabh's professional expertise spans legal education and practice, having served as an Assistant Professor at GNSU, Bihar,His scholarly contributions include peer-reviewed publications such as "Women In Indian Prisons: Rights And Challenges", "Women's Rights in India: A Contemporary Challenge*, alongside paper presentations at national and international conferences on human rights and gender justice. A passionate advocate for lifelong learning, Saurabh has completed an impressive array of international certifications from prestigious institutions like the Asian Development Bank, Open University UK, UNITAR, and WIPO, covering topics from climate change and human rights to criminology and sustainable development. His commitment to professional growth is evident in his participation in numerous Faculty Development Programs (FDPs) and webinars on emerging legal trends. Based in Delhi NCR, Saurabh blends academic rigor with practical insights, making him a dynamic educator and legal professional. His interdisciplinary approach, global perspective, and dedication to advancing legal scholarship position him as a valuable asset to any academic or legal institution.

Suyatno Ladiqi is a Senior Lecturer at the Faculty of Law & International Relations, Universiti Sultan Zainal Abidin (UniSZA) in Malaysia, holding a PhD in Political Science from Universiti Sains Malaysia. His academic work focuses on political science, globalization, and international political economy, with numerous publications exploring topics like local democracy in Indonesia, the impact of globalization on security, and the relationship between democracy and responsiveness in maritime countries. He is actively involved in international academic collaborations and contributes to various academic discussions and seminars.

Le Hoang Kiet has a Master's degree in Public Policy and is a PhD candidate in International Relations. He works at Yersin University, Vietnam. He has research experience in international relations and public policy with published research in Vietnam and some internationally. Additionally, he often participates in and collaborate on international projects by governmental organizations in Southeast Asia. His research interests focus on Europe and the Indo-Pacific. It focuses on issues of power competition between great powers.

Geetika Madaan is working as an Assistant Professor at a research centre in Marwadi University, Gujarat.

Priya Makhija is an Associate professor in Jain University Banagalore.

Debasis Neogi, Professor, Department of Management, Humanities & Social Science National Institute of Technology Agartala, India dneogi@nita.ac.in

R. Velmurugan presently working as an Associate Professor in Commerce, Karpagam Academy of Higher Education, Coimbatore. He started his career as a Project Fellow under UGC Sponsored Major Research Project at NGM College, Pollachi. He has 18 years of teaching experience has 15 years of research experience. To his credit he produced 22 Ph.D. Scholars and 5 M.Phil. Scholars. At present 1 scholar submitter his thesis, 6 Ph.D. Scholars are under his guidance. Moreover, to his credit he published 168 articles in various International Journals, of which 82 articles are published in Scopus Indexed Journals and 15 articles in Web of Science and 76 articles in edited volumes. He also participates and presented 27 papers in various International Seminar / Conference and 54 National Seminar / Conference. He acted as an external examiner for various M.Phil. and Ph.D. Viva voce examinations. He acted as a Vice Chancellor nominee for Doctoral Committee Expert at Bharathiar University, Coimbatore and Periyar University, Salem. He acted as a Chairperson at various National Level Conferences. He also acted as an Expert for Syllabus Scrutiny Committee, Question Paper Scrutiny Committee and Expert members for Board of Studies at various reputed Colleges. Considering his meritorious contribution, he received awards like Best Paper Presenter, Best Research Supervisor and Best Faculty Awards from various research foundations and councils. He too acted as a resource person for 27 Guest Lectures, 30 Workshops and 10 faculty development programmes.

Varanasi Rahul is an Assistant Professor at JAIN University (Bangalore), a semi-qualified Cost Accountant, holding three postgraduate degrees: M.Com (Accounting & Taxation), M.Com (Management), and an MA (History). He has cleared the UGC NET in Commerce twice and has also cleared the AP SET in

Commerce, History, and Management, as well as the TS SET in Commerce. With 3 years of experience as an Assistant Professor and 6 months as a Corporate Tax Associate for Australian Taxation at PwC (Big 4), he brings both academic and professional expertise to his field. Additionally, he is a freelance archaeologist, practicing epigraphist in Brahmi script, and a numismatist. His scholarly and creative contributions include over 30 newspaper articles published in Deccan Chronicle, Times of India, and other local newspapers. He has presented and participated in 25 national and international seminars and has published 2 research articles in ABDC Journals, 3 in SCOPUS-indexed journals, 2 in Web of Science and 4 in peer-reviewed journals. As a story writer, 5 of his stories have been published in top magazines of Andhra Pradesh. Furthermore, he has authored 3 books. He has also contributed 13 book chapters to various academic publications. In addition to his extensive achievements, he has applied for 16 patents, of which 2 has been granted in India, 2 in UK and 11 have been published.

Apoorva Roy is a distinguished academician in the field of law, currently serving as an Assistant Professor at the School of Law, Galgotias University, Greater Noida. With a commendable academic trajectory and over seven years of rich teaching and administrative experience, Dr. Roy has established a respected presence in the legal education sector. Prior to joining Galgotias University, Dr. Roy held a faculty position at Amity University, Noida, from February 2018 to June 2024. A committed educator and researcher, Dr. Apoorva Roy specializes in International Environmental Law, Biodiversity Protection, Intellectual Property Rights, Administrative Law, and Client Counselling. In addition to teaching. Dr. Roy earned a Ph.D. in Law from the National University of Study and Research in Law, Ranchi in 2023. This is complemented by an LL.M from Hidayatullah National Law University, Raipur and an LL.B (Hons.) from the Faculty of Law, Banaras Hindu University. Dr. Apoorva Roy is also qualified in the National Eligibility Test (NET) in Law and cleared the All India Bar Examination. A prolific researcher and writer, Dr. Apoorva Roy has authored more than 30 research papers, book chapters, and articles on a range of contemporary legal topics. Notable among these are papers on green collar crimes, traditional knowledge protection, and the performance of the National Green Tribunal (NGT). Furthermore, Dr. Roy has co-authored two books published internationally: The Wildlife Conservation and Management in India and Indian Agricultural Sector in the Light of WTO Laws: A Critical Study. Dr. Apoorva Roy has actively participated in numerous national and international conferences, seminars, and faculty development programs, often as a paper presenter or judge. The recent focus of Dr. Roy's research includes climate change, transboundary environmental issues, and legal implications of emerging technologies such as AI in policing. Driven by a passion for teaching, knowledge creation, and holistic education, Dr. Roy aspires to inspire students to become globally competent, socially responsible, and ethically grounded professionals. With a perfect blend of academic rigor and practical engagement, Dr. Roy continues to contribute meaningfully to the ever-evolving field of legal education and policy.

N. Sathyanarayana has over 15 years of teaching experience at the UG and PG levels. He holds a Master's in Business Administration and Commerce and is pursuing a Ph.D. He currently holds the position of Assistant Professor in the School of Commerce at Jain (Deemed-to-be University), Bangalore. He has published 22 research papers in international journals (2 Scopus Index), 7 research papers in national journals, and presented 14 research papers at international conferences and 11 research papers at national conferences. He has co-authored 2 books at national level and 8 book chapters (Scopus indexed).

Amrinder Singh, presently working with Jain (Deemed to be University) at the position of Professor in school of management studies. He is having experience of 18 years, His major subjects are marketing & research courses. He has worked on ranking and rating of University (Careers 360) and worked on Government project IDC (Institute for development and Communication). Organized many International and National conferences at University level. He has published more than 40 research papers, 17 chapters, 13 patents and one book has been published by LAMBERT Academic Publishing house for publishing. Presently guiding two candidates for PhD.

Bhupinder Singh working as Professor at Sharda University, India. Also, Honorary Professor in University of South Wales UK and Santo Tomas University Tunja, Colombia. His areas of publications as Smart Healthcare, Medicines, fuzzy logics, artificial intelligence, robotics, machine learning, deep learning, federated learning, IoT, PV Glasses, metaverse and many more. He has 3 books, 139 paper publications, 163 paper presentations in international/national conferences and seminars, participated in more than 40 workshops/FDP's/QIP's, 25 courses from international universities of repute, organized more than 59 events with international and national academicians and industry people's, editor-in-chief and co-editor in journals, developed new courses. He has given talks at international universities, resource person in international conferences such as in Nanyang Technological University Singapore, Tashkent State University of Law Uzbekistan; KIMEP University Kazakhstan, All'ah meh Tabatabi University Iran, the Iranian Association of International Criminal law, Iran and Hague Center for International Law and Investment, The Netherlands, Northumbria University Newcastle UK,

Sanjeet Singh works as the pro-vice chancellor at Marwadi University, Gujarat.

Mohammad Badruddoza Talukder is an Associate Professor at the College of Tourism and Hospitality Management at the International University of Business Agriculture and Technology (IUBAT) in Dhaka, Bangladesh. Holding a PhD from Lovely Professional University, India, he is renowned for his innovative integration of cutting-edge technologies such as Artificial Intelligence (AI), the Internet of Things (IoT), and Blockchain into tourism and hospitality management. His research explores the transformative impact of these technologies on smart tourism, cloud kitchens, and the broader industry landscape. As a prolific author, Dr. Talukder has published numerous scholarly articles and books, with forthcoming titles that address AI innovations in hospitality, the evolution of cloud kitchens, and the enhancement of digital literacy within hospitality education. His work shapes contemporary tourism and hospitality practices, skillfully marrying technological advancements with practical industry applications. Since 2008, Dr. Talukder has imparted his knowledge through a diverse array of courses in tourism and hospitality across various universities in Bangladesh.

Ravi Thirumalaisamy working as an Assistant Professor, Department of Business and Economics, Modern College of Business and Science. To his credit, he published more than 16 articles in Scopus indexed journals.

Pradeep Thota, working as Deputy Director in National Council for Vocational Education and Training (NCVET), Ministry of Skill Development and Entrepreneurship, Government of India, is an accomplished professional with a diverse background in international trade and vocational education policy. In this role, Pradeep is responsible for regulatory oversight, quality assurance, and policy development to strengthen India's skill development ecosystem. Before joining NCVET, Pradeep worked as Manager at PEC Ltd, a Government of India Enterprise under the Ministry of Commerce and Industry, handling international trade operations, contract management, and stakeholder coordination across global markets. Pradeep's educational qualifications include B.Tech, MBA, PGDHRM, and he is currently pursuing a Ph.D. with a focus on vocational training policy and institutional effectiveness. With over a decade of experience combining strategic planning, public administration, policy formulation, and cross-sector collaboration. Pradeep is committed to nation-building through skill and trade development, positioning him as an expert in India's skilling ecosystem, trade landscape, and evidence-based research in these domains.

Anurodh Upadhyay is an esteemed legal scholar and educator, specializing in criminal law, constitutional law, forensic science, and evidence law. He is currently serving as an Assistant Professor in the Department of Law at Galgotias University,

Greater Noida, where he is actively involved in teaching, research, and curriculum development. Dr. Upadhyay holds a Ph.D. in Law from Banaras Hindu University (BHU), Varanasi, where he conducted extensive research on the use and impact of forensic science in criminal investigations: constitutional and legal issues. His research critically analyzes the intersection of forensic techniques and constitutional protections within the Indian legal system. He also earned his LL.M. from Banaras Hindu University (BHU) in 2016 and completed his B.A. LL.B. (Hons.) from the University of Allahabad in 2014. His academic excellence is reflected in his achievements, including: • Qualifying UGC NET twice (July 2016 and November 2017). • Securing All India Rank 14 in CLAT PG (2016) and All India Rank 27 in CLAT PG (2017). • Qualifying the All India Bar Examination (AIBE) in 2015. Dr. Upadhyay has extensive teaching experience, having previously worked at Narayan School of Law, Gopal Narayan Singh University, Sasaram, Bihar (2022-2023) and as a Teaching Assistant at Banaras Hindu University (2017-2022). In these roles, he has delivered lectures, mentored students, developed curriculum content, and contributed to legal scholarship. In addition to his academic engagements, he has interned at the Mediation and Conciliation Center, High Court of Judicature at Allahabad, gaining practical exposure to civil and criminal law proceedings. He has also worked as a Research Assistant, contributing to legal research projects, literature reviews, and scholarly publications. With a strong foundation in both legal practice and academia, Dr. Upadhyay continues to bridge the gap between law and forensic science, ensuring that legal professionals are well-equipped with the knowledge and skills necessary for modern legal challenges. His dedication to research and teaching makes him a valuable contributor to legal academia and the criminal justice system.

Suraj Yadav is an accomplished professional with a background in Hospitality, holding a bachelor's degree from Pune University and a Master in Hotel Management & Tourism from Madurai Kamaraj University, Madurai. Currently serving as an Assistant Professor and Training & Placement Officer at D Y Patil School of Hospitality in Kolhapur, Maharashtra, India, he brings extensive expertise to the field. Suraj is also dedicated to furthering his academic pursuits and is actively pursuing a Ph.D. at D Y Patil Agricultural & Technical University in Kolhapur. His commitment to education and training has made a significant impact in the realm of hospitality.

Index

A

B

C

D

E

F

G

H

I

L

N

P

S

T